MW01698240

CLYMER®

POLARIS

SPORTSMAN 400 • 2001-2003, SPORTSMAN 500 • 1996-2003 & XPLORER 500 • 1997

The world's finest publisher of mechanical how-to manuals

PRIMEDIA
Information Data Products
P.O. Box 12901, Overland Park, Kansas 66282-2901

FIRST EDITION
First Printing April, 2001
Second Printing March, 2003

SECOND EDITION
First Printing January, 2004
Second Printing August, 2005

Printed in U.S.A.

CLYMER and colophon are registered trademarks of PRIMEDIA Business Magazines & Media Inc.

ISBN: 0-89287-893-2

Library of Congress: 2003116556

MEMBER MOTORCYCLE INDUSTRY COUNCIL, INC.

AUTHOR: Ed Scott.

TECHNICAL PHOTOGRAPHY: Ed Scott and Ron Wright.

TECHNICAL AND PHOTOGRAPHIC ASSISTANCE: Jordan Engineering, Oceanside, California. Special thanks to Ed Rubel at Roetan Industries, Victor, New York, for providing the Victor Specialty Tools used during the disassembly and photography of the Sportsman 500.

TECHNICAL ILLUSTRATIONS: Mitzi and Errol McCarthy.

WIRING DIAGRAMS: Bob Meyer.

PRODUCTION: Dennis Conrow.

EDITOR: James Grooms.

TOOLS AND EQUIPMENT: K & L Supply Co. at www.klsupply.com.

COVER: Photographed by Mark Clifford Photography at www.markclifford.com.

PRIMEDIA
Business Magazines & Media

P.O. Box 12901, Overland Park, KS 66282-2901 • 800-262-1954 • 913-967-1719

The following books and guides are published by PRIMEDIA Information Data Products.

CLYMER® — CLYMER® PROSERIES — AC-U-KWIK® — I&T SHOP SERVICE — PRIMEDIA PRICE DIGESTS Your Valuation & Specification Authority — EC&M Books

More information available at *primediabooks.com*

CONTENTS

QUICK REFERENCE DATA

ATV INFORMATION

MODEL:______________________________ YEAR:____________

VIN NUMBER:______________________________________

ENGINE SERIAL NUMBER:______________________________

CARBURETOR SERIAL NUMBER OR I.D. MARK:______________________

TIRE INFLATION PRESSURE (COLD)*

Model	kPa	PSI
Front wheels	34.5	5
Rear wheels	34.5	5

*Tire pressure for original equipment tires. Aftermarket tires may require different inflation pressure.

RECOMMENDED LUBRICANTS, FLUIDS AND CAPACITIES

Item	Lubricant or fluid type
Engine oil	Polaris Premium 4 Synthetic 10W/40 or 10W/40 motor oil
Transmission oil	Polaris synthetic gear case oil (part No. 2871478)
Front gear case	Polaris front gearcase lube (part No. 2871653), or API GL5 80-90 gear lube
Front hubs	Polaris demand drive hub fluid (part No. 2871654), or ATF Type F.
Brake fluid	DOT 3 brake fluid
Coolant	50:50 mixture ethylene glycol-based coolant compounded for aluminum radiators and engines
Grease	Polaris all season grease, or equivalent

RECOMMENDED CAPACITIES

Item	Quantity
Engine oil	1.89 L (2 U.S. qts.)
Transmission oil	946.3 cc (32 U.S. oz.)
Front gear case (all years)	96 cc (3.25 U.S. oz.)
Front hubs	75 cc (2.5 U.S. oz.)
Coolant	Approx. 2.16 L (2.25 U.S. qts.)

MAINTENANCE AND TUNE-UP TORQUE SPECIFICATIONS

Item	N•m	in.-lb.	ft.-lb.
Crankcase oil drain plug	19	–	14
Cylinder head cover screws	8.2	72	–
Front gear case drain plug	9.4	83	–
Handlebar upper holder bolts	13-17	115-150	–
Oil tank drain plug	19	–	14
Oil tank screen and fitting	20	–	15
Valve adjuster locknuts	6-7	53-62	–
Wheel lug nuts			
Front	21	–	15
Rear	21	–	15

MAINTENANCE AND TUNE-UP SPECIFICATIONS

Item	Specification
Disc brake pad thickness wear limit	
2003 Sportsman 500 & 500 H.O.	
Rear brake	4.6 mm (0.180 in.)
All other models and years	
Front and rear brakes	3.81 mm (0.150 in.)
Valve clearance (cold)	
Intake and exhaust	0.15 mm (0.006 in.)
Spark plug	
400 cc	
Heat range	NGK BKR5E
Gap	0.9 mm (0.036 in.)
500 cc	
Heat range	
1996-1997	NGK BKR5ES
1998-2001	NGK BKR5E
2002-on	NGK BKR6E
Gap	
1996-1998	0.6-0.7 mm (0.024-0.028 in.
1999-2000	0.7 mm (0.028 in.)
2001-on	0.9 mm (0.036 in.)
Idle speed	
1996-1988, 2001-on	1100-1300 rpm
1997-2000	1000-1400 rpm
Carburetor pilot air screw (34 mm)	
1996	1 1/2 turns out
1997-1998	2 turns out
1999-2000	2 5/8 turns out
2001-on (400 cc)	2 3/4 turns out
Carburetor pilot air screw (40 mm)	
2001	2 1/2 turns out
2002-on	2 turns out

REPLACEMENT BULBS

Item	Specification
Headlights	12 volt, 60/60 watt Halogen
Grill mounted lights	
1996	12 volt, 37.5 watt (2)
1997	12 volt, 35 watt (2)
1998-on	12 volt, 27 watt
Taillight	12 volt, 8.26 watt
Brake light	12 volt, 6.9 watt
Indicator lights	
1996	12 volt, 1.25 watt
1997-on	12 volt, 1.0 watt

NOTE: Refer to the Supplement at the back of this manual for information unique to 2001-on models, including the Sportsman 400.

CHAPTER ONE

GENERAL INFORMATION

This detailed, comprehensive manual covers the Polaris Sportsman 400, 500 and Xplorer 500 4 × 4 from 1996-on.

Keep this book handy in the toolbox. Reading and using it will help to better understand how the vehicle runs, lower repair costs and generally improve personal satisfaction with the vehicle.

The following tables are included at the end of this chapter:

Table 1 lists model year and number.

Table 2 lists general dimensions.

Table 3 lists vehicle weight (dry).

Table 4 lists decimal and metric equivalents.

Table 5 lists general torque specifications.

Table 6 lists conversion tables.

Table 7 lists technical abbreviations.

Table 8 lists metric tap and drill sizes.

Tables 1-8 are at the end of this chapter.

MANUAL ORGANIZATION

All dimensions and capacities are expressed in English units familiar to U.S. mechanics, as well as in metric units.

This chapter provides general information and discusses equipment and tools useful both for preventive maintenance and troubleshooting.

Chapter Two provides methods and suggestions for the quick and accurate diagnosis and repair of problems. Troubleshooting procedures discuss typical symptoms and logical methods to pinpoint the trouble.

Chapter Three explains all periodic lubrication and routine maintenance necessary to keep the vehicle running well. Chapter Three also includes recommended tune-up procedures, eliminating the need to constantly consult chapters on the various assemblies.

Subsequent chapters describe specific systems such as the engine, clutch/drive belt system, transmission, exhaust, cooling, suspension and brakes. Each chapter provides disassembly, repair and assembly procedures in a simple step-by-step form.

If a repair is impractical for a home mechanic, it is so indicated. It is usually faster and less expensive to take such repairs to a dealer or competent repair shop. Specifications concerning a particular system are included at the end of the appropriate chapter.

Some of the procedures in this manual specify special tools. In most cases, the tool is illustrated either in actual use or alone. Well-equipped mechanics may find they can substitute similar tools already on hand or can fabricate their own.

NOTES, CAUTIONS AND WARNINGS

The terms NOTE, CAUTION and WARNING have specific meanings in this manual. A NOTE provides additional information to make a step or procedure easier or clearer. Disregarding a NOTE could cause inconvenience, but would not cause equipment damage or personal injury.

A CAUTION emphasizes areas where equipment damage could result. Disregarding a CAUTION could cause permanent mechanical damage; however, personal injury is unlikely.

A WARNING emphasizes areas where personal injury or even death could result from negligence. Mechanical damage may also occur. WARNINGS *are to be taken seriously.* In some cases, serious injury or death has resulted from disregarding similar warnings.

SAFETY FIRST

Professional mechanics can work for years and never sustain a serious injury. If a few rules of common sense and safety are observed, many safe hours can be enjoyed servicing the ATV. Ignoring these rules can injure someone working on the vehicle, or damage the ATV.

1. *Never* use gasoline or any type of low flash point solvent to clean parts. See *Cleaning Parts* and *Handling Gasoline Safely* in this chapter for additional information on parts cleaning, gasoline use and safety.

NOTE

The flash point is the lowest temperature at which the vapors from a combustible liquid will ignite when in open air. A low flash point solvent will ignite at a lower temperature than a high flash point solvent.

2. *Never* smoke or use a torch in the vicinity of flammable liquids in open containers, such as gasoline or cleaning solvent.
3. If welding or brazing is required on the vehicle, remove the fuel tank, carburetor, and front and rear shocks to a safe distance at least 50 feet (15 m) away.
4. Use the proper sized wrenches to avoid damage to fasteners.
5. When loosening a tight or stuck nut, be guided by what would happen if the wrench slips.
6. When replacing a fastener, make sure to use one with the same measurements and strength as the old one. Incorrect or mismatched fasteners can result in damage to the vehicle and possible personal injury. Beware of fastener kits that are filled with cheap and poorly made nuts, bolts, washers and cotter pins. Refer to *Fasteners* in this chapter for additional information.
7. Keep all hand and power tools in good condition. Wipe greasy and oily tools after using them. Dirty tools are difficult to hold and can cause injury. Replace or repair worn or damaged tools.
8. Keep the work area clean and uncluttered.
9. Wear safety goggles during all operations involving drilling, grinding, the use of a cold chisel, using chemicals, cleaning parts, when using compressed air or *anytime* the safety of eyes is involved.
10. Make sure to wear the correct type of clothes for the job. Long hair should be tied up or covered with a cap so that it cannot be caught by a piece of moving equipment or tool.

11. Keep an approved fire extinguisher nearby. Be sure it is rated for gasoline (Class B) and electrical (Class C) fires.

12. When drying bearings or other rotating parts with compressed air, never allow the air jet to rotate the bearing or part. The air jet is capable of rotating them at speeds far in excess of those for which they were designed. The bearing or rotating part is very likely to disintegrate and cause serious injury and damage. To prevent bearing damage when using compressed air, hold the inner bearing race by hand.

WARNING

The improper use of compressed air is very dangerous. Using compressed air to dust off clothes, the ATV or workbench can cause flying particles to be blown into eyes or skin. ***Never*** *direct or blow compressed air into skin or through any body opening (including cuts) as this can cause severe injury or death. Compressed air must be used carefully; never allow children to use or play with any compressed air equipment or hoses.*

13. Never work on the upper part of the vehicle while someone is working underneath it.

14. When putting the vehicle on a stand, make sure the vehicle is secure before walking away from it.

15. Never carry sharp tools in clothing pockets.

16. There is always a right and wrong way to use tools. Learn to use them the right way.

17. Do not start and run the ATV in an enclosed area. The exhaust gases contain carbon monoxide, a colorless, odorless, poisonous gas. Carbon monoxide levels build quickly in a small closed area and can cause unconsciousness and death in a short time. When it is necessary to start and run the vehicle during a service procedure, always do so outside, or in a service area equipped with a ventilating system.

CLEANING PARTS

Cleaning parts is one of the more tedious and difficult service jobs performed in the home garage. While there are a number of chemical cleaners and solvents available for home and shop use, most are poisonous and extremely flammable. To prevent chemical overexposure, vapor buildup, fire and serious injury, observe all manufacturer's directions and warnings while noting the following.

1. Read the entire product label before using the chemical. Observe the precautions and warnings on the label. Always know what type of chemical is being used.

2. If the chemical product must be mixed, measure the proper amount according to the directions.

3. Always provide sufficient ventilation when working with solvents or other chemicals. If a chemical can be smelled, there is some vapor in the air. The stronger the smell, the stronger the vapor concentration.

4. If a product is listed as combustible, flammable or an extremely flammable liquid, the danger of fire increases as the vapor collects and builds up in the shop.

5. If a product is listed as a poison, the vapor is poisonous as well as the liquid.

6. To prevent skin exposure, wear protective gloves when cleaning parts. Select a pair of chemical-resistant gloves suitable for the type of chemicals that will be used. Replace the gloves when they become thin, damaged, change color, or swell.

7. Wear safety goggles when using chemicals and cleaning parts.

8. Do not use more than one type of cleaning solvent at a time.

9. If a part must be heated to remove a bearing, clean it thoroughly to remove all oil, grease and cleaner residue. Then wash with soapy water and rinse with clear water.

10. Wear a respirator if the instruction label says to do so.

11. Keep chemical products out of reach of children and pets.

12. To prevent sparks, use a nylon bristle brush when cleaning parts.

13. When using a commercial parts washer, read and follow the manufacturer's instructions for selecting the type of solvent to use. Parts washers must be equipped with a fusible link designed to melt and drop the cover in the event of fire.

14. Wash both hands and arms thoroughly after cleaning parts.

HANDLING GASOLINE SAFELY

Gasoline, a volatile flammable liquid, is one of the most dangerous items in the shop. However, because gasoline is used so often, many people forget that it is a dangerous product. Gasoline should be used only as fuel for internal-combustion engines. Never use gasoline to clean parts, tools or to wash hands. When working on an ATV, motorcycle or any other type of gasoline engine, gasoline will always be present in the fuel tank, fuel line and carburetor. To avoid a disastrous accident when working around gasoline or on the fuel system, carefully observe the following precautions:

1. *Never* use gasoline to clean parts. See *Cleaning Parts* in this chapter for additional information on parts cleaning and safety.
2. When working on the fuel system, work outside or in a well-ventilated area.
3. Do not add fuel to the fuel tank or service the fuel system while the ATV is in the vicinity of open flames, sparks or where someone is smoking. Gasoline vapors are actually more dangerous than liquid gasoline. Because these vapors are heavier than air, they collect in low areas and are easily ignited.
4. Allow the engine to cool completely before working on any fuel system component.
5. When draining the carburetor, catch the gasoline in a plastic container and then pour it into a safety-approved gas can.
6. Do not store gasoline in any type of glass container. If the glass should break, a serious explosion or fire could occur.
7. Wipe up spilled gasoline immediately with dry rags. Store the rags in a metal container with a lid until they can be properly disposed of, or put them outside in a safe place to dry.
8. Do not pour water onto a gasoline fire. Water spreads the fire and makes it more difficult to put out. Use a Class B, BC, or ABC fire extinguisher to smother the flames and put the fire out.
9. Always turn the engine off before refueling. Use a wide-mouth funnel to prevent spilling gasoline onto the engine, exhaust pipe or muffler. Do not overfill the fuel tank. Leave an air space at the top of the fuel tank to prevent fuel from spilling out when installing the cap.
10. Always refuel the ATV while it is parked outside and away from all open flames and sparks.
11. When transporting the ATV in another vehicle, keep it upright with the fuel valve turned off.
12. Do not perform a spark test (as described in Chapter Two) if there is any gasoline leaking from the fuel tank, fuel line or carburetor.

1

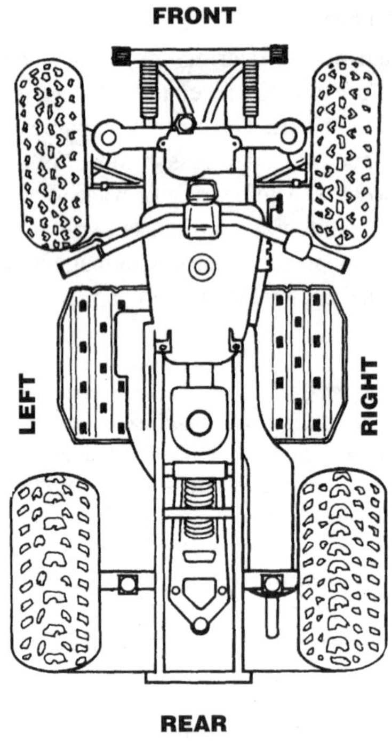

SERVICE HINTS

Most of the service procedures covered are straightforward and can be performed by anyone reasonably handy with tools. It is suggested, however, that the personal capabilities be carefully considered before attempting any operation involving major disassembly of the engine.

Take time and do the job right. Do not forget that a newly rebuilt engine must be broken in the same way as a new one. Refer to the *Engine Break-In* procedure listed in Chapter Four and Chapter Five.

1. Front, as used in this manual, refers to the front of the vehicle; the front of any component is the end closest to the front of the vehicle. The left and right sides refer to the position of the parts as viewed by a rider sitting on the seat facing forward. For example, the throttle control is on the right side. These rules are simple, but confusion can cause a major inconvenience during service. See **Figure 1**.
2. Whenever servicing an engine or suspension component, secure the vehicle in a safe manner.
3. Tag all similar internal parts for location and mark all mating parts for position. Record number

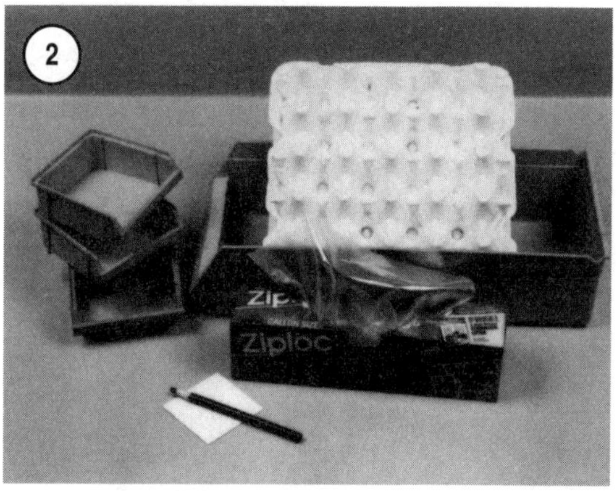

2

and thickness of any shims as they are removed. Small parts such as bolts can be identified by placing them in plastic sandwich bags (**Figure 2**). Seal and label them with masking tape.

4. Tag disconnected wires and connectors with masking tape and a marking pen. Again, do not rely on memory alone.

5. Protect finished surfaces from physical damage or corrosion. Keep gasoline and other chemicals off painted surfaces.

6. Use penetrating oil on frozen or tight bolts, then strike the bolt head a few times with a hammer and punch (use a screwdriver on screws). Avoid using heat where possible, as it can warp, melt or affect the temper of parts. Heat also ruins finishes, especially paint and plastics.

7. When a part is a press fit or requires a special tool to remove it, the necessary information or type of tool is called out in the text. Otherwise, if a part is difficult to remove or install, find out why before proceeding.

8. To prevent small objects and abrasive dust from falling into the engine, cover all openings after exposing them.

9. Read each procedure completely while looking at the actual parts before starting a job. Make sure the procedural steps are fully understood, then follow the procedure step by step.

10. Recommendations are occasionally made to refer service or maintenance to a Polaris dealership or a specialist in a particular field. In these cases, the work will be done more quickly and economically than by the home mechanic.

11. In procedural steps, the term *replace* means to discard a defective part and replace it with a new or rebuilt unit. *Overhaul* means to remove, disassemble, inspect, measure, repair and/or replace parts as required.

12. Some operations require the use of a hydraulic press. If a press is not available, it is wiser to have these operations performed by a shop equipped for such work, rather than to try to do the job yourself with makeshift equipment that may damage the machine.

13. Repairs go much faster and easier if the vehicle is clean before starting on the job. There are many special cleaners on the market, like Bel-Ray Degreaser, for washing the engine and related parts. Follow the manufacturer's directions on the container for the best results. Clean all oily or greasy parts with cleaning solvent as they are removed.

WARNING

***Never** use gasoline to clean parts or tools. It presents an extreme fire hazard. Be sure to work in a well-ventilated area when using cleaning solvent. Keep a fire extinguisher rated for gasoline fires near by in any case.*

CAUTION

If a car wash is used to clean the ATV, do not direct the high-pressure water hose at steering bearings, carburetor hoses, suspension components, wheel bearings, or electrical components. The water will flush grease out of the bearings or damage the seals.

14. Much of the labor charges for repairs made by dealerships are for the time involved during the removal, disassembly, assembly, and reinstallation of other parts in order to reach the defective part. When possible, perform the preliminary operations and take the defective unit to the dealer for repair at considerable savings.

15. When special tools are required, make arrangements to get them before starting on the job. It is frustrating and time-consuming to get partly into a job and then be unable to complete it. When special tools are required, they will be described (including part number) at the beginning of a procedure.

16. Make diagrams wherever similar-appearing parts are found. For instance, crankcase bolts are often not the same length. Do not rely on memory

alone to replace parts in their proper location. There is also the possibility of being sidetracked and not able to return to work for days or even weeks, during which time the carefully laid out parts may become disturbed.

17. When assembling parts, make sure all shims and washers are reinstalled exactly as they came out.

18. Whenever a rotating part contacts a stationary part, look for a shim or washer. Use new gaskets if there is any doubt about the condition of the old ones. A thin coating of oil on non-pressure type gaskets may help them seal more effectively.

19. Some components are held in place with self-locking nuts. The locking ability of these nuts is lessened every time they are installed or removed. It is recommended that they be replaced every time they are removed.

20. Use cold heavy grease to hold small parts in place if they tend to fall out during assembly. However, keep grease and oil away from electrical and brake components.

TORQUE SPECIFICATIONS

The materials used in the manufacture of the Polaris may be subjected to uneven stresses if the fasteners that hold the sub-assemblies are not installed and tightened correctly. Loose or missing fasteners can cause the cylinder head to warp, crankcase leaks, and premature bearing and seal failure and suspension failure from loose or missing fasteners. Therefore, use an accurate torque wrench (described in this chapter) together with the torque specifications listed at the end of most chapters.

Torque specifications throughout this manual are given in Newton-meters (N•m), foot-pounds (ft.-lb.) and, where applicable, in inch-pounds (in.-lb.).

Existing torque wrenches calibrated in meter kilograms can be used. Move the decimal point one place to the right; for example, 3.5 mkg = 35 N•m. The exact mathematical conversion is 3.5 mkg = 34.3 N•m.

To mathematically convert foot-pounds to Newton meters multiply the foot pounds specification by 1.3558 to achieve a N•m equivalent. For example 150 ft.-lb. × 1.3558 = 203 N•m.

Refer to **Table 5** for general torque specifications for various size screws, bolts and nuts not listed in the respective chapter tables. To use the table, first determine the size of the bolt or nut. Use a vernier caliper and measure the inside dimension of the threads of the nut (**Figure 3**) and across the threads for a bolt (**Figure 4**).

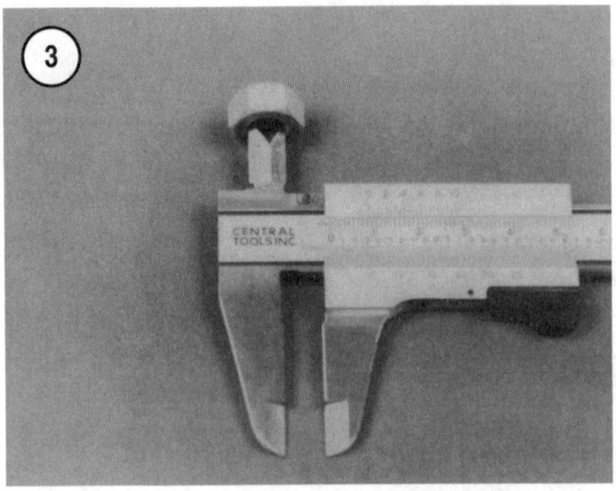

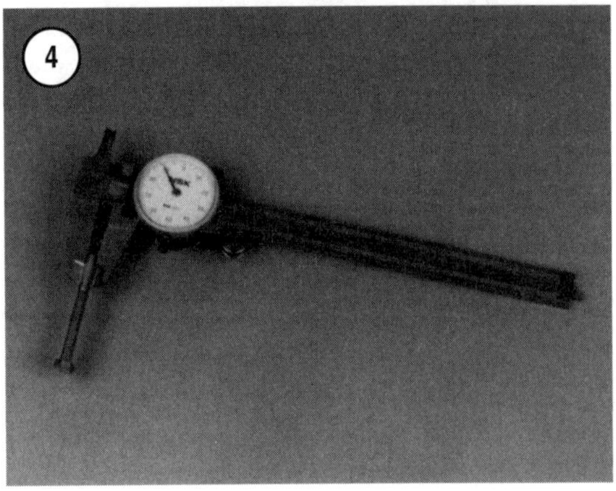

FASTENERS

The materials and designs of the various fasteners used on the Polaris are each designed for a specific purpose. Fastener design determines the type of tool required to work with the fastener. Fastener material is carefully selected to decrease the possibility of physical failure.

Nuts, bolts and screws are manufactured in a wide range of thread patterns. To join a nut and bolt, the diameter of the bolt and the diameter of the hole in the nut must be the same. It is just as important that the threads on both be properly matched.

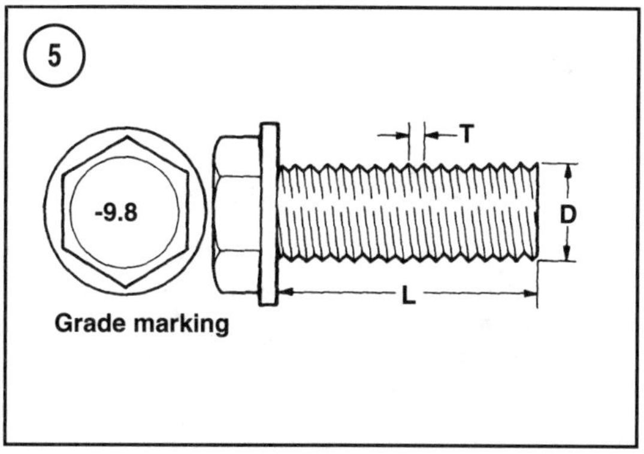

The best way to tell if two fasteners' threads match is to turn the nut on the bolt (or the bolt into the threaded hole in a piece of equipment) with fingers only. Be sure both pieces are clean. If excessive force is required, check the thread condition on each fastener. If the thread condition is good but the fasteners jam, the threads are not compatible. A thread pitch gauge can be used to determine pitch. Polaris vehicles are manufactured with ISO (International Organization for Standardization) metric as well as American fasteners. The threads are cut differently than those of American fasteners. All engine fasteners are metric threads while the frame components are secured with American threads

Most threads are cut so that the fastener must be turned clockwise to tighten it. These are called right-hand threads. Some fasteners have left-hand threads; they must be turned *counterclockwise* to be tightened. Left-hand threads are used in locations where normal rotation of the equipment would tend to loosen a right-hand threaded fastener.

ISO Metric Screw Threads (Bolts, Nuts and Screws)

ISO (International Organization for Standardization) metric threads come in three standard thread sizes: coarse, fine and constant pitch. The ISO coarse pitch is used for almost all common fastener applications. The fine pitch thread is used on certain precision tools and instruments. The constant pitch thread is used mainly on machine parts and not for fasteners. The constant pitch thread, however, is used on all metric thread spark plugs.

Metric screws and bolts are classified by length (L, **Figure 5**), nominal diameter (D) and distance between thread crests (T). The numbers 8 × 1.25—130 identifies a typical bolt, which would indicate that the bolt has a nominal diameter of 8 mm, the distance between thread crests is 1.25 mm and bolt length is 130 mm.

WARNING
Do not install screws or bolts with a lower strength grade classification than installed originally by the manufacturer. Doing so may cause engine or equipment failure and possible injury.

The measurement across two flats on the head of the bolt indicates the proper wrench size to use. **Figure 4** shows how to determine bolt diameter. When buying a bolt from a dealer or parts store, it is important to know how to specify bolt length. The correct way to measure bolt length is by measuring the length starting from underneath the bolt head to the end of the bolt. Always measure bolt length in this manner to avoid buying bolts that are of the wrong length.

Machine Screws

There are many different types of machine screws. The screw heads are also designed to protrude above the metal (round) or slightly recessed in the metal (flat). See **Figure 6**.

Nuts

Nuts are manufactured in a variety of types and sizes. Most are hexagonal (6-sided) and fit on bolts, screws and studs with the same diameter and pitch. The common nut is generally used with a lockwasher. Self-locking nuts have a nylon insert that prevents the nut from loosening; no lockwasher is required. Wing nuts are designed for fast removal by hand. Wing nuts are used for convenience in non-critical locations.

To indicate the size of a metric nut, manufacturers specify the diameter of the opening and the thread pitch. This is similar to bolt specifications, but without the length dimension. The measurement across two flats on the nut indicates the proper wrench size to be used.

(6) **MACHINE SCREWS**

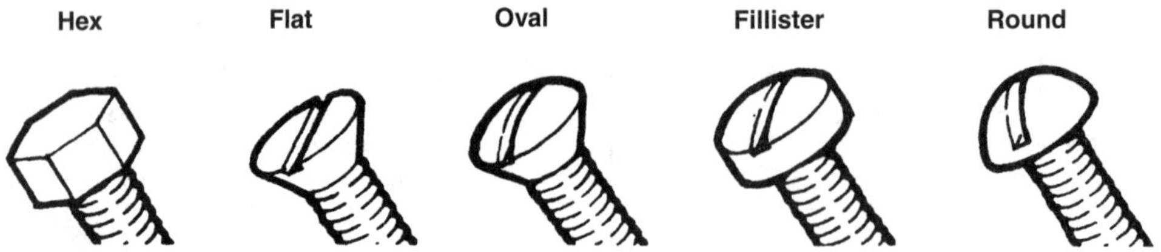

Self-Locking Fasteners

Several types of bolts, screws and nuts incorporate a system that develops interference between the bolt, screw, and nut or tapped hole threads. Interference is achieved in various ways: by distorting threads, coating threads with dry adhesive or nylon, distorting the top of an all-metal nut, using a nylon insert in the center or at the top of a nut.

Self-locking fasteners offer greater holding strength and better vibration resistance. The self-locking fasteners used on the Polaris ATV *cannot be reused*. Others, like the nylon insert nut, form an initial locking condition when the nut is first installed; the nylon forms closely to the bolt thread pattern, thus reducing any tendency for the nut to loosen. Always discard and replace self-locking fasteners after removal.

Washers

There are two basic types of washers: flat washers and lockwashers. Flat washers are simple discs with a hole to fit a screw or bolt. Lockwashers are designed to prevent a fastener from working loose due to vibration, expansion and contraction. Washers can be used in the following functions:

1. As spacers.
2. To prevent galling or damage of the equipment by the fastener.
3. To help distribute fastener load during tightening.
4. As seals.

Note that flat washers are often used between a lockwasher and a fastener to provide a smooth bearing surface. This allows the fastener to be turned easily with a tool.

NOTE

As much care should be given to the selection and purchase of washers as that given to bolts, nuts and other fasteners. Beware of washers that are made of thin and weak materials. These will deform and crush the first time they are used in a high-torque application.

Cotter Pins

In certain applications, a fastener must be secured so it cannot possibly loosen. The rear hub on an ATV is one of these applications. For this purpose, a cotter pin and slotted or castellated nut is often used. To use a cotter pin, first make sure the pin fits snugly, but not too tight. Then align the slot in the fastener with the hole in the bolt or axle.

Insert the cotter pin through the nut and bolt or axle and bend the ends over to secure the cotter pin tightly. If the holes do not align, tighten the nut just enough to obtain the proper alignment. Unless specifically instructed to do so, never loosen the fastener to align the slot and the hole. Because the cotter pin is weakened after installation and removal, never reuse a cotter pin. Cotter pins are available in several styles, lengths and diameters. Measure the cotter pin length from the bottom of its head to the tip of the shortest prong.

Circlips

Circlips can be internal or external in design. They are used to retain items on shafts (external type) or within tubes (internal type). In some applications, circlips of varying thicknesses are used to control the endplay of assemblies. These are often

7

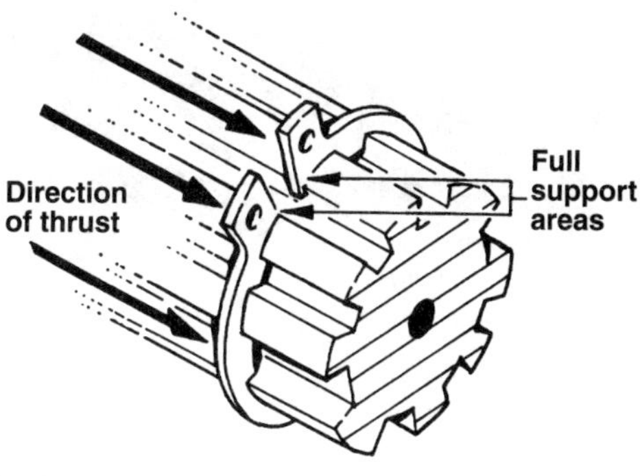

8

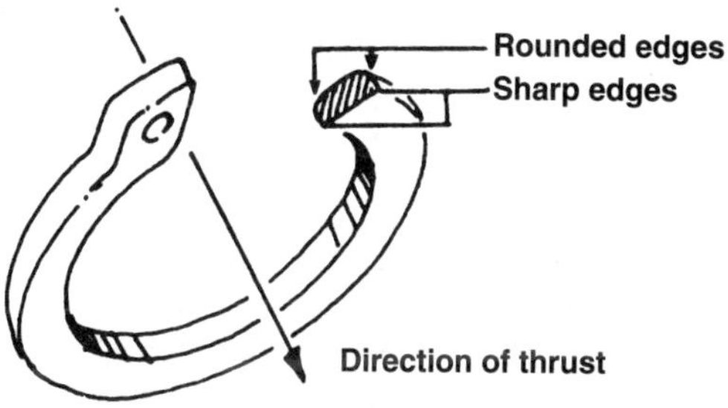

called selective circlips. Circlips should be replaced during installation, as removal weakens and deforms them.

Two basic styles of circlips are available: machined and stamped circlips. Machined circlips (**Figure 7**) can be installed in either direction (shaft or housing) because both faces are machined, thus creating two sharp edges. Stamped circlips (**Figure 8**) are manufactured with one sharp edge and one rounded edge. When installing stamped circlips in a thrust situation as on transmission shafts, the sharp edge must face away from the part producing the thrust. When installing circlips, observe the following:

1. Compress or expand circlips only enough to install them.

2. After the circlip is installed, make sure it is completely seated within its groove.

3. Transmission circlips become worn with use and increase side play. For this reason, always install new circlips whenever a transmission is reassembled.

LUBRICANTS

Periodic lubrication assures long life for any type of equipment. The type of lubricant used is just as important as the lubrication service itself, although in an emergency the wrong type of lubricant is better than none at all. The following paragraphs describe the types of lubricants most often used for ATVs. Be sure to follow the manufacturer's recommendations for lubricant types.

Generally all liquid lubricants are called oil. They may be mineral-based (including petroleum bases), natural-based (vegetable and animal bases), synthetic-based or emulsions (mixtures). Grease is oil to which a thickening base has been added so that the end product is semi-solid. Grease is often classified by the type of thickener added; lithium soap is commonly used.

Engine Oil

Engine oil is classified by two standards: the American Petroleum Institute (API) service classification and the Society of Automotive Engineers (SAE) viscosity rating. This information is on the oil container label. Two letters indicate the API service classification. The number or sequence of numbers and letter (10W-40 for example) is the oil's viscosity rating. The API service classification and the SAE viscosity index are not indications of oil quality.

The service classification indicates that the oil meets specific lubrication standards. The first letter in the classification *S* indicates that the oil is for gasoline engines. The second letter indicates the standard the oil satisfies. The classification started with the letter *A* and is currently at the letter *J*.

Always use an oil with a classification recommended by the manufacturer. Using an oil with a classification different than that recommended can cause engine damage.

Viscosity is an indication of the oil's thickness. Thin oils have a lower number while thick oils have a higher number. Engine oils fall into the 5- to 50-weight range for single-grade oils.

Most manufacturers recommend multigrade oil. These oils perform efficiently across a wide range of operating conditions. Multigrade oils are identified by a *W* after the first number, which indicates the low-temperature viscosity.

Engine oils are most commonly mineral (petroleum) based; however synthetic and semi-synthetic types are used more frequently. When selecting engine oil, follow the manufacturer's recommendation for type, classification and viscosity.

Grease

The National Lubricating Grease Institute (NLGI) grades greases. Greases are graded by number according to the consistency of the grease; these range from No. 000 to No. 6, with No. 6 being the most solid. Typical multipurpose grease is NLGI No. 2. For specific applications, equipment manufacturers may require grease with an additive such as molybdenum disulfide.

THREADLOCKING COMPOUND

A threadlocking compound should be used to help secure many of the fasteners used on the vehicle. A threadlock compound will lock fasteners against vibration loosening and seal against leaks. The following thread locking compounds are recommended for many threadlock requirements described in this manual.

1. ThreeBond TB1342 (blue): low-strength, frequent repair.
2. Loctite No. 242 (blue): low-strength, frequent repair.
3. ThreeBond TB1360 (green): medium-strength, high temperature.
4. ThreeBond No. 1333B (red): medium-strength, bearing and stud lock.
5. ThreeBond TB1303 (orange): high-strength, infrequent repair.
6. Loctite No. 271 (red): high-strength, infrequent repair.

There are other quality threadlock brands on the market.

RTV GASKET SEALANT

Room temperature vulcanizing (RTV) sealant is used on some preformed gaskets and to seal some components. RTV is a silicone gel supplied in tubes and is available at motorcycle and automotive supplies stores and major hardware stores.

Moisture in the air causes the RTV to cure. Always place the cap on the tube as soon as possible

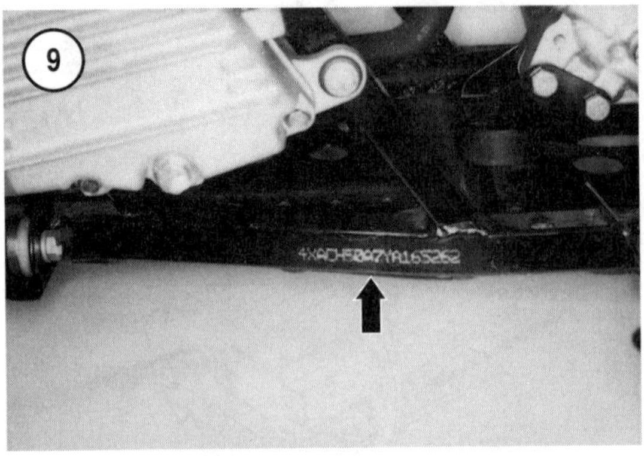

when using RTV. RTV has a shelf life of approximately one year and will not cure properly when the shelf life has expired. Check the expiration date on the RTV tube prior to purchasing a new tube and on using the sealant. Keep partially used tubes tightly sealed and discard them after the expiration date.

Applying RTV Sealant

Clean all old gasket residue from all mating surfaces. Remove all RTV gasket material from blind threaded holes; it can cause a hydraulic lock and affect bolt torque, leading to the bolt not being tightened to the correct torque specification. Finally, spray the mating surfaces with an aerosol parts cleaner and wipe with a lint-free cloth.

Apply RTV sealant in a continuous bead 2-3 mm (0.08-0.12 in.) thick. Circle all mounting holes unless otherwise specified. Do not allow any sealant to enter these holes. Assemble and tighten the fasteners to the specified torque within 10 minutes after application.

EXPENDABLE SUPPLIES

Certain expendable supplies are required during maintenance and repair work. These include grease, oil, and gasket cement, wiping rags and cleaning solvent. Ask the dealership for the special locking compounds, silicone lubricants and other products, which make vehicle maintenance simpler and easier. Cleaning solvent or kerosene is available at some service stations, paint or hardware stores.

Be sure to follow the manufacturer's instructions and warnings listed on the label of the product being used. Some cleaning supplies are very caustic and are dangerous if not used properly.

10

11

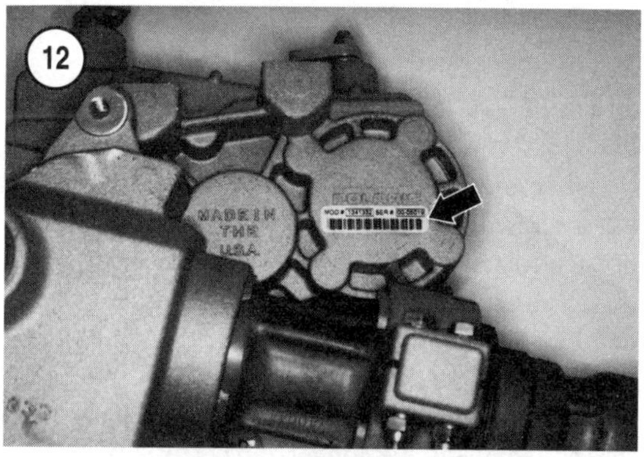

12

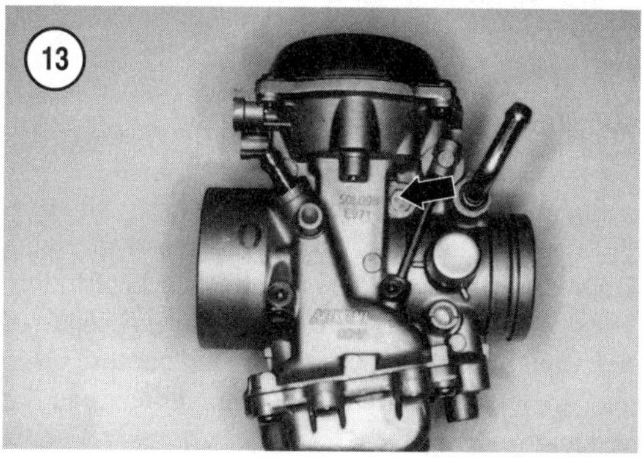

13

WARNING
Having a stack of clean shop rags on hand is important when performing engine and suspension service work. However, a pile of solvent-soaked rags presents a fire hazard. Store them in a sealed metal container until they can be washed or properly discarded.

NOTE
To prevent solvent and other chemicals from being absorbed into the skin, wear a pair of petroleum-resistant gloves when cleaning parts. These can be purchased through industrial supply houses or well-equipped hardware stores.

SERIAL NUMBERS

Polaris makes frequent changes during a model year—some minor, some relatively major. When ordering parts from the dealership or other parts distributor, always order by VIN and engine serial numbers. The serial number locations are as follows:

1. Model and VIN number (**Figure 9**) is stamped on the left lower frame rail near the rear portion of the front A-arm mount. On some models, a decal with the VIN number is located on the front fender cover (**Figure 10**).

2. Engine serial number (**Figure 11**) is stamped on a pad on the center top of the crankcase beneath the cylinder coolant elbow.

3. The transmission serial number is located on top of the transmission case below the shift bell crank and on a label on the right side (**Figure 12**).

4. The carburetor serial number (**Figure 13**) is located on the left side of the carburetor body.

Enter these numbers on the chart in the Quick Reference Data table at the front of this book and keep them for reference. Compare new parts to the old ones before buying them. If they are not alike, have the parts manager explain the difference. **Table 1** lists the model numbers for the models covered in this manual.

WARNING AND INFORMATION LABELS

A number of warning labels (**Figure 14**) are attached to the Polaris. These labels contain information that is important to personal safety when operating, transporting and storing the vehicle. Also refer to the informative labels fastened to the various components on the vehicle, as this information is very useful. Refer to the owner's manual for a description and location of each label. If a label is missing, order a replacement label from a Polaris dealership.

14

BASIC HAND TOOLS

Many of the procedures in this manual can be carried out with simple hand tools and test equipment familiar to the home mechanic. Keep all tools clean and in a toolbox. Keep them organized with the sockets and related drives together, the open-end combination wrenches together, etc. After using a tool, wipe off dirt and grease with a clean cloth and return the tool to its correct place.

Top quality tools are essential; they are also more economical in the long run. If just starting to build a tool collection, stay away from the advertised specials featured at some parts houses, discount stores and chain drug stores. These are usually poor grade tools that are made of inferior material, and are thick, heavy and clumsy to use. Their rough finish makes them difficult to clean and they usually do not last very long. The wrenches do not fit the heads of bolts and nuts correctly and may damage the fastener.

Quality tools are made of alloy steel and are heat-treated for greater strength. They are lighter and better balanced than inferior ones. Their surface is smooth, making them a pleasure to work with and easy to clean. The initial cost of good quality tools may be more, but they are more economical in the long run. Do not try to buy everything in all sizes in the beginning; buy a few at a time until all the necessary tools are on hand.

Screwdrivers

The screwdriver is a very basic tool, but if used improperly it will do more damage than good. The slot on a screw has a definite dimension and shape. A screwdriver must be selected to conform to that shape. Use a small screwdriver for small screws and a large one for large screws, or the screw head will be damaged.

Two basic types of screwdrivers are required: common (flatblade) screwdrivers and Phillips screwdrivers.

Screwdrivers are available in sets that often include an assortment of common and Phillips blades. If purchased individually, buy at least the following:

1. Common screwdriver—5/16 × 6 in. blade.
2. Common screwdriver—3/8 × 12 in. blade.
3. Phillips screwdriver—size 2 tip, 6 in. blade.
4. Phillips screwdriver—size 3 tip, 6 and 10 in. blade.

Use screwdrivers only for driving screws. Never use a screwdriver for prying or chiseling metal. Do not try to remove a Phillips or Allen head screw with a common screwdriver (unless the screw has a combination head that will accept either type); if the head is damaged, the proper tool will be unable to remove it. Keep screwdrivers in the proper condition and they will last longer and perform better. Always keep the tip of a common screwdriver in good condition.

Pliers

Pliers come in a wide range of types and sizes. Pliers are useful for cutting, bending and crimping. Do not use them to cut hardened objects or to turn bolts or nuts. Each type of pliers has a specialized function. Slip-joint pliers are general purpose pliers and are used mainly for holding things and for bending.

15

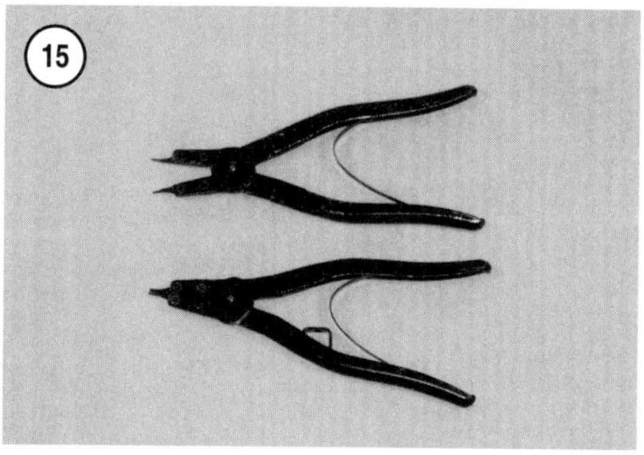

16

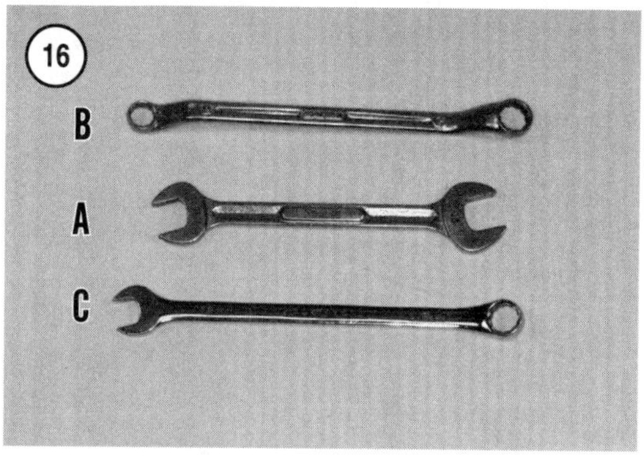

Needlenose pliers are used to hold or bend small objects. Water pump pliers can be adjusted to hold various sizes of objects; the jaws remain parallel to grip around objects such as pipe or tubing. There are many more types of pliers. The ones described here are most suitable for vehicle repairs.

Locking Pliers

Locking pliers are used to hold objects very tightly like a vise. But avoid using them unless necessary since their sharp jaws will permanently scar any objects that are held. Locking pliers are available in many types for more specific tasks.

Circlip Pliers

Circlip pliers (**Figure 15**) are made for removing and installing circlips. External pliers (spreading) are used to remove circlips that fit on the outside of a shaft. Internal pliers (squeezing) are used to remove circlips which fit inside a gear or housing.

WARNING
Because circlips can sometimes slip and fly off when removing and installing them, always wear safety glasses when using them.

Box, Open-End and Combination Wrenches

Open-end, box-end and combination wrenches are available in sets or separately in a variety of sizes. On open and box end wrenches, the number stamped near the end refers to the distance between two parallel flats on the hex head bolt or nut. On combination wrenches, the number is stamped near the center.

Open-end wrenches (A, **Figure 16**) are speedy and work best in areas with limited overhead access. Their wide, flat jaws make them unstable for situations where the bolt or nut is located in a bore or close to the edge of a casting. These wrenches grip only two flats of a fastener; if either the fastener head or the wrench jaws are worn, the wrench may slip off.

Box-end wrenches (B, **Figure 16**) require clear overhead access to the fastener but can work well in situations where the fastener head is close to another part. They grip on all six edges of a fastener for a very secure grip. They are available in either 6-point or 12-point. The 6-point gives superior holding power and durability but requires a greater swinging radius. The 12-point works better in situations where the swinging radius is limited.

Combination wrenches (C, **Figure 16**) have open-end on one side and box-end on the other with both ends being the same size. Professional mechanics favor these wrenches because of their versatility.

Adjustable Wrenches

An adjustable wrench (sometimes called crescent wrench) can be adjusted to fit nearly any nut or bolt head that has clear access around its entire perimeter. Adjustable wrenches are best used as a backup wrench to keep a large nut or bolt from turning while the other end is being loosened or tightened with a box-end or socket wrench.

Adjustable wrenches have only two gripping surfaces which make them more subject to slipping off the fastener and damaging the part and possibly causing injury. The fact that one jaw is adjustable only aggravates this shortcoming.

These wrenches are directional; the solid jaw must be the one transmitting the force. If the adjustable jaw is used to transmit the force, it will loosen and possibly slip off.

Socket Wrenches

This type of wrench is undoubtedly the fastest, safest and most convenient to use. Sockets, which attach to a ratchet handle, are available with 6-point (A, **Figure 17**) or 12-point (B, **Figure 17**) openings and 1/4, 3/8, 1/2 and 3/4 in. drives. The drive size indicates the size of the square hole which mates with the ratchet handle.

Allen Wrenches

Allen wrenches are available in sets or separately in a variety of sizes. These sets come in SAE and metric sizes. Allen bolts are sometimes called socket bolts. Sometimes the bolts are difficult to reach and it is suggested that a variety of Allen wrenches be purchased, such as the socket driven, T-handle and extension type.

Torque Wrench

A torque wrench is used with a socket to measure how tightly a nut or bolt is installed. They come with either 1/4, 3/8 or 1/2 in. square drive (**Figure 18**). The drive size indicates the size of the square drive that mates with the socket.

Impact Driver

This tool might have been designed with the ATV mechanic in mind. This tool makes removal of fasteners easy and eliminates damage to bolts and screw slots. Impact drivers (**Figure 19**) and interchangeable bits are available at most large hardware, vehicle or auto parts stores. Sockets can also be used with a hand impact driver; however, make sure that the socket is designed for use with an impact driver or air tool. Do not use regular hand sockets, as they may shatter during use.

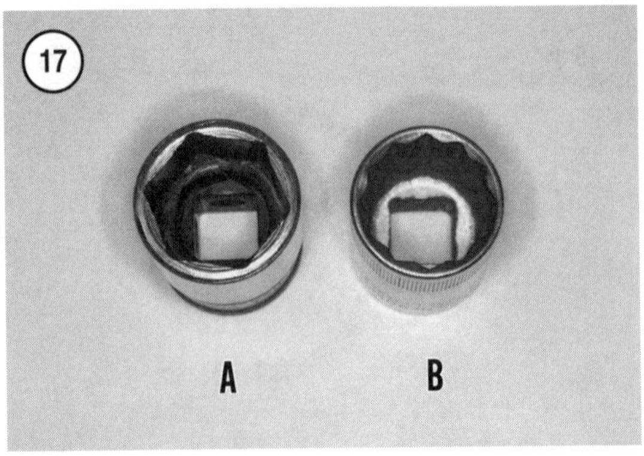

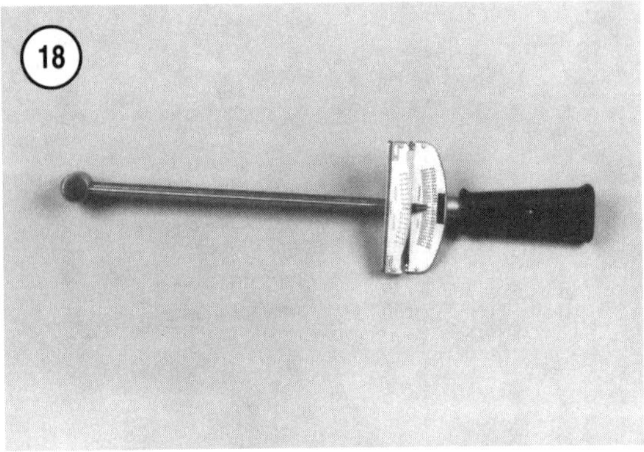

Hammers

The correct hammer is necessary for certain repairs. A hammer with a face (or head) of rubber or plastic or a soft-faced type filled with buckshot is sometimes necessary in engine disassembly. Never use a metal-faced hammer on engine or suspension parts, as severe damage will result in most cases. The same amount of force can be produced with a soft-faced hammer. The shock of a metal-faced hammer, however, is required for using a hand impact driver or cold chisel.

Support Jacks

The correct type of support jack is necessary for many routine service or major component replacement procedures on the vehicle. The centerstand scissor jack is suitable for most service procedures on this series of vehicles. It is adjustable and is very stable for use with the frame configuration of this vehicle.

Also, the standard floor jack may be used for some applications. To protect all engine and frame

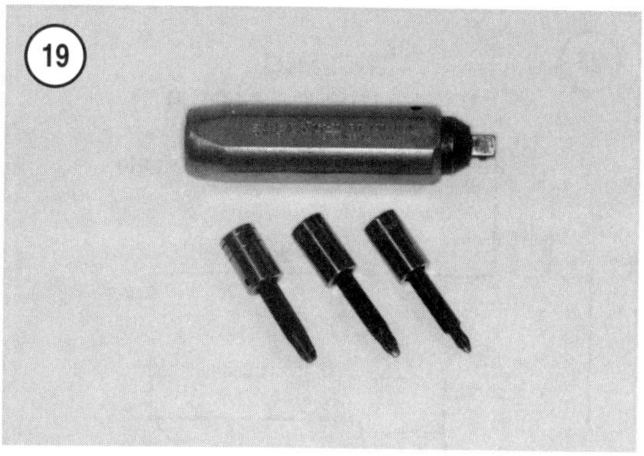

19

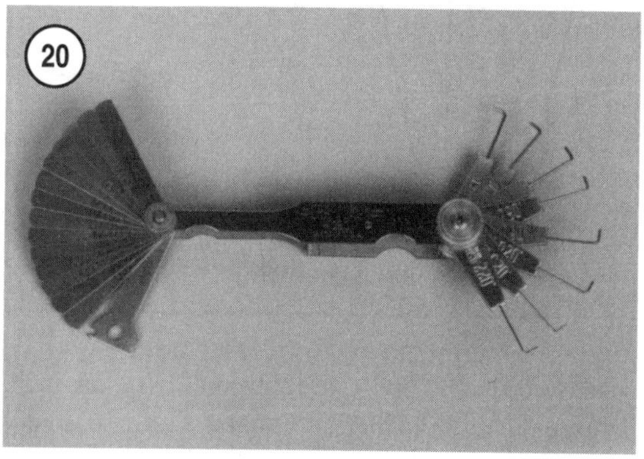

20

surfaces, always place a piece of wood between the jack pad and the supported component.

PRECISION MEASURING TOOLS

Measurement is an important part of engine and suspension service. When performing many of the service procedures in this manual, a number of measurements are required. These include basic checks such as engine compression and spark plug gap. As shop experience progresses into engine disassembly and service, many measurements are required to determine the size and condition of the piston and cylinder bore and crankshaft runout and other complex measurements. When making these measurements, the degree of accuracy will dictate which tool is required. Precision measuring tools are expensive. If this is the first experience at engine or suspension service, it may be more worthwhile to have the checks and measurements performed by a Polaris dealership, a competent independent vehicle repair shop or a machine shop. However, as skills and enthusiasm increase for doing service work, it may be desirable to buy some of these specialized tools. The following is a description of the measuring tools required to perform the service procedures described in the various chapters in this manual.

Feeler Gauge

Feeler gauges come in assorted sets and types (**Figure 20**). The feeler gauge is made of either a piece of a flat or round hardened steel of a specified thickness. Wire gauges are used to measure spark plug gap. Flat gauges are used for other measurements. Feeler gauges are also designed for specialized uses. For example, the end of a gauge can be small and angled to facilitate checking valve clearances on models requiring adjustment.

Vernier Caliper, Dial Caliper and Digital Electronic Caliper

These are valuable tools for reading inside, outside and depth measurements. Although this type of tool is not as precise as a micrometer, it allows reasonable, non-close tolerance measurements, typically to within 0.025 mm (0.001 in.). Common uses of a vernier caliper are measuring the length of the clutch springs, the thickness of clutch plates, shims and thrust washers, brake pad or lining thickness or the depth of a bearing bore. The jaws of the caliper must be clean and free of burrs at all times to obtain an accurate measurement. There are several types of vernier calipers available. The standard vernier caliper has a highly accurate graduated scale on the handle (**Figure 21**) in which the measurements must be calculated, following the manufacturer's instructions. The dial indicator caliper is equipped with a small dial and needle that indicates the measurement reading; the digital electronic type has an LCD display that shows the measurement on the small display screen. Some vernier calipers must be calibrated prior to making a measurement to ensure accuracy. Refer to the manufacturer's instructions for this procedure.

Outside Micrometers

An outside micrometer is a precision tool used to accurately measure parts using the decimal divisions of the inch or meter (**Figure 22**). While there are many types and styles of micrometers, this section describes how to use the outside micrometer. The outside micrometer is the most common type of micrometer used to service a vehicle. The outside micrometer is also used to measure the dimension taken by a small hole gauge or a telescoping gauge described later in this section.

Other types of micrometers include the depth micrometer and screw thread micrometer. **Figure 23** illustrates the various parts of the outside micrometer with its part names and markings identified.

Micrometer Range

A micrometer's size indicates the minimum and maximum size of a part that it can measure. The usual sizes are: 0-1 in.(0-25 mm), 1-2 in.(25-50 mm), 2-3 in. (50-75 mm) and 3-4 (75-100 mm). These micrometers use fixed anvils.

Some micrometers use the same frame with interchangeable anvils of different lengths. This allows the installation of the correct length anvil for a particular job. For example, a 0-4 in. interchangeable micrometer is equipped with four different length anvils. While purchasing one or two micrometers to cover a range from 0-4 in, or 0-6 inches is less expensive, its overall frame size makes it less convenient to use.

How To Read a Micrometer

When reading a micrometer, numbers are taken from different scales and added together. The following sections describe how to read the standard inch micrometer, the vernier inch micrometer, the standard metric micrometer and the metric vernier micrometer.

Standard inch micrometer

The standard inch micrometer is accurate to one-thousandth of an inch (0.001 in.). The heart of the micrometer is its spindle screw with 40 threads per inch. Every turn of the thimble will move the spindle 1/40 of an inch or 0.025 inch.

Before learning how to read a micrometer, study the markings and part names in **Figure 23**. Turn the micrometer thimble until its zero mark aligns with the zero mark on the sleeve line. Now turn the thimble counterclockwise and align the next thimble mark with the sleeve line. The micrometer now

(21) **METRIC VERNIER CALIPER**

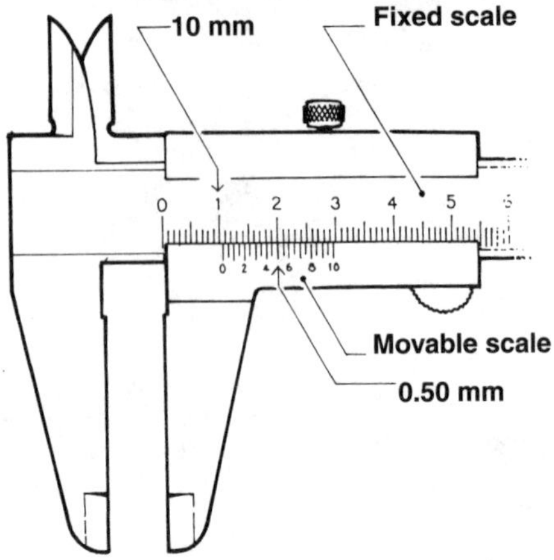

1. Reading on fixed scale: 10.00 mm
2. Reading on movable scale: +0.50 mm
Total reading: 10.50 mm

reads 0.001 in. (one one-thousandth) of an inch. Thus, each thimble mark is equal to 0.001 in. Every fifth thimble mark is numbered to help with reading: 0, 5, 15 and 20.

Reset the micrometer so that the thimble and sleeve line zero marks align. Then turn the thimble counterclockwise one complete revolution and align the thimble zero mark with the first line in the sleeve line. The micrometer now reads 0.025 in. (twenty-five thousands) of an inch. Thus, each sleeve line represents 0.025 inch.

Now turn the thimble counterclockwise while counting the sleeve line marks. Every fourth mark on the sleeve line is marked with a number ranging from one through nine. Manufacturers usually mark the last mark on the sleeve with a 0. This indicates the end of the micrometer's measuring range. Each sleeve number represents 0.1 in. For example, the number 1 represents 0.1 in. and the number 9 represents 0.9 inch.

When reading a standard micrometer, take the following three measurements described and add them together. The sum of the three readings will give the measurement in a thousandth of an inch (0.001 in.).

To read a micrometer, perform the following steps and refer to the example in **Figure 24**.

(22)

DECIMAL PLACE VALUES*

0.1	Indicates 1/10 (one tenth of an inch or millimeter)
0.010	Indicates 1/100 (one one-hundreth of an inch or millimeter)
0.001	Indicates 1/1,000 (one one-thousandth of an inch or millimeter)

*This chart represents the values of figures placed to the right of the decimal point. Use it when reading decimals from one-tenth to one one-thousandth of an inch or millimeter. It is not a conversion chart (for example: 0.001 in. is not equal to 0.001 mm).

(23)

STANDARD INCH MICROMETER

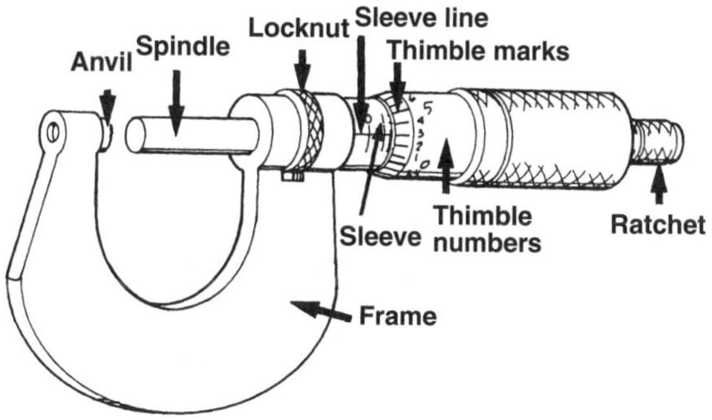

(24)

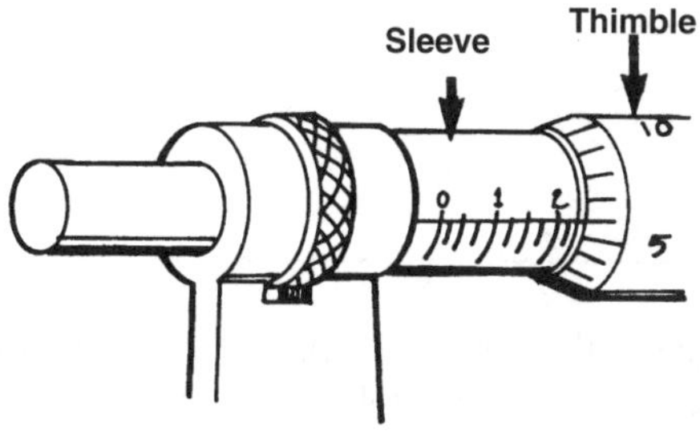

1. Largest number visible on the sleeve line	0.200 in.
2. Number on sleeve marks visible between the numbered sleeve mark and the thimble edge	0.025 in.
3. Thimble mark that aligns with sleeve line	0.006 in.
Total reading:	0.231 in.

(25)

VERNIER INCH MICROMETER

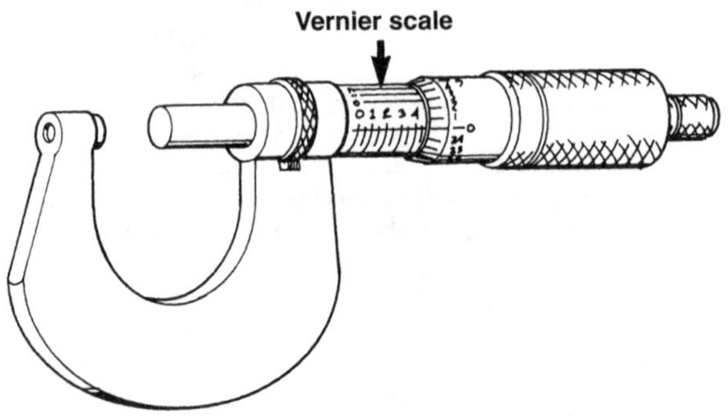

(26)

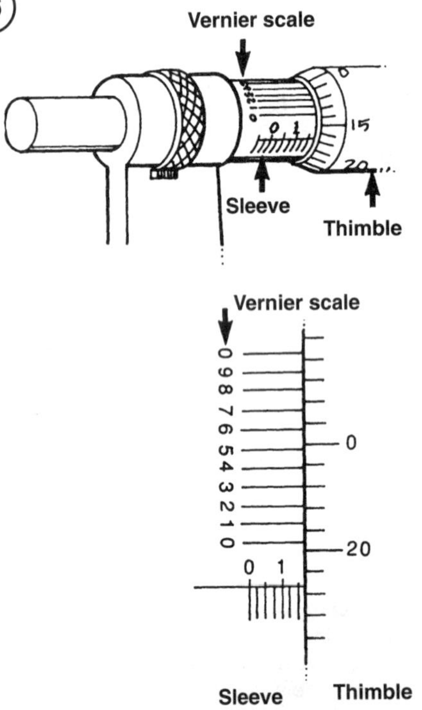

1. Largest number visible on sleeve line	0.100 in.
2. Number of sleeve marks visible between the numbered sleeve mark and the thimble edge	0.050 in.
3. Thimble is between 0.018 and 0.019 in. on the sleeve line	0.018 in.
4. Vernier line coinciding with thimble line	0.0003 in.
Total reading:	0.1683 in.

1. Read the sleeve line to find the largest number visible—each sleeve number mark equals 0.100 inch.

2. Count the number of sleeve marks visible between the numbered sleeve mark and the thimble edge—each sleeve mark equals 0.025 inch. If there is no visible sleeve marks, continue to Step 3.

3. Read the thimble mark that lines up with the sleeve line—each thimble mark equals 0.001 inch.

NOTE

If a thimble mark does not line up exactly with the sleeve line but falls between two lines, estimate the fraction of decimal amount between the lines.

(27) **STANDARD METRIC MICROMETER**

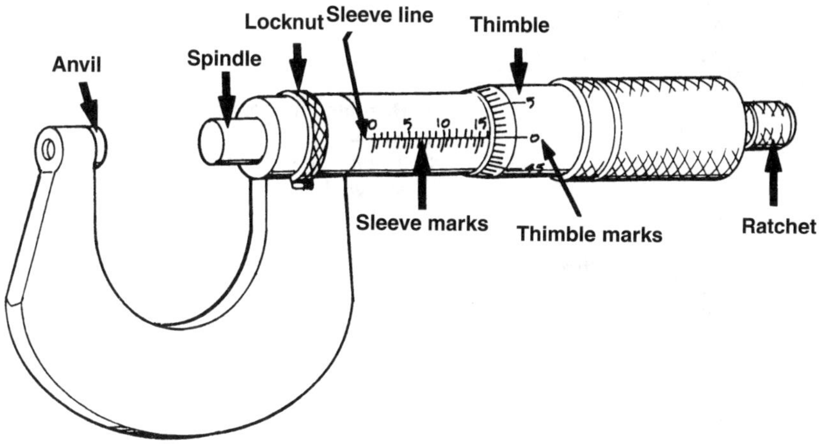

4. Adding the micrometer readings in Steps 1, 2 and 3 gives the actual measurement.

Vernier inch micrometer

A vernier micrometer can accurately measure in ten-thousandths of an inch (0.0001 in.). While it has the same markings as the standard inch micrometer, a vernier scale scribed on the sleeve (**Figure 25**) makes it unique. The vernier scale consists of eleven equally spaced lines marked 0-9 with a 0 on each end. These lines run parallel on the top of the sleeve where each line is equal to 0.0001 inch. Thus, the vernier scale divides a thousandth of an inch (0.001 in.) into ten-thousandths of an inch (0.0001 in.).

To read the vernier micrometer, perform the following steps and refer to the example in **Figure 26**:

1. Read the micrometer in the same way as on the standard inch micrometer. This is the initial reading.
2. If a thimble mark lines up exactly with the sleeve line, reading the vernier scale is not necessary. If a thimble mark does not line exactly with the sleeve line, read the vernier scale in Step 3.
3. Read the vernier scale to find which vernier mark lines up with the one thimble mark. The number of that vernier mark is the number of ten-thousandths of an inch to add to the initial reading taken in Step 1.

Metric micrometer

The metric micrometer is very similar to the standard inch micrometer. The differences are the graduations on the thimble and sleeve as shown in **Figure 27**.

The standard metric micrometer is accurate to one one-hundredth of an millimeter (0.01 mm). On the metric micrometer, the spindle screw is ground with a thread pitch of one-half millimeter (0.5 mm). Thus, every turn of the thimble will move the spindle 0.5 mm.

The sleeve line is graduated in millimeters and half millimeters. The marks on the upper side of the sleeve line are equal to 1.00 mm. Every fifth mark above the sleeve line is marked with a number. The actual numbers depend on the size of the micrometer. For example, on a 0-25 mm micrometer, the sleeve marks are numbered 0, 5, 10, 15, 20 and 25. On a 25-50 mm micrometer, the sleeve marks are numbered 25, 30, 35, 40, 45 and 50. This numbering sequence continues with larger micrometers (50-75 and 75-100). Each mark on the lower side of the sleeve line is equal to 0.5 mm.

28

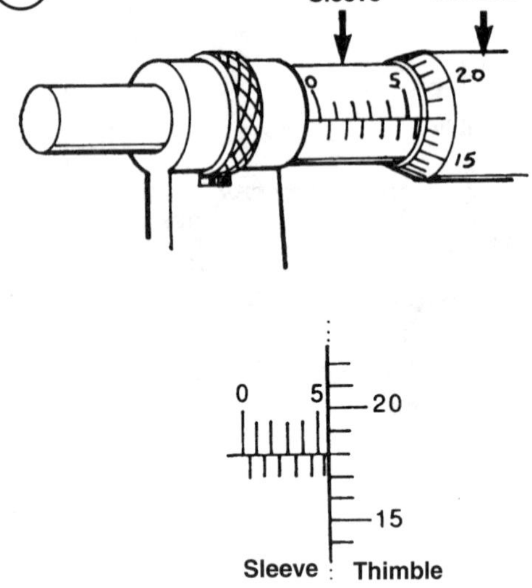

1. Reading on upper sleeve line	5.0 mm
2. Reading on lower sleeve line	0.50 mm
3. Thimble line coinciding with sleeve line	0.18 mm
Total reading:	5.68 mm

The thimble scale is divided into fifty graduations where one graduation is equal to 0.01 mm. Every fifth graduation is numbered to help with reading from 0-45. The thimble edge is used to indicate which sleeve markings to read.

To read the metric micrometer add the number of millimeters and half-millimeters on the sleeve line to the number of one-hundredth millimeters on the thimble. To do so, perform the following steps and refer to the example in **Figure 28**:

1. Take the first reading by counting the number of marks visible on the upper sleeve line. Record the reading.

2. Look below the sleeve line to see if a lower mark is visible directly past the upper line mark. If so, add 0.50 to the first reading.

3. Now read the thimble mark that aligns with the sleeve line. Record this reading.

NOTE

If a thimble mark does not align exactly with the sleeve line but falls between the two lines, estimate the decimal amount between the lines. For an accurate reading, a metric vernier micrometer must be used.

4. Adding the micrometer readings in Steps 1, 2 and 3 gives the actual measurement.

Metric vernier micrometer

A metric micrometer can accurately measure to two-thousandths of a millimeter (0.002 mm). While it has the same markings as the standard metric micrometer, a vernier scale scribed on the sleeve (**Figure 29**) makes it unique. The vernier scale consists of five equally spaced lines 0, 2, 4, 6 and 8. These lines run parallel on the top of the sleeve where each line is equal to 0.002 mm.

To read the metric vernier micrometer, perform the following steps and refer to the example in **Figure 30**:

1. Read the metric vernier micrometer the same way as with the standard metric micrometer. This is the initial reading.

2. If a thimble mark aligns exactly with the sleeve line, reading the vernier scale is not necessary. If a thimble line does not align exactly with the sleeve line, read the vernier scale in Step 3.

3. Read the vernier scale to find which mark aligns with one thimble mark. The number of the vernier mark is the number of thousands of a millimeter to add to the initial reading taken in Step 1.

Micrometer Accuracy Check

The micrometer must be checked frequently to assure accuracy as follows:

(29)

VERNIER METRIC MICROMETER

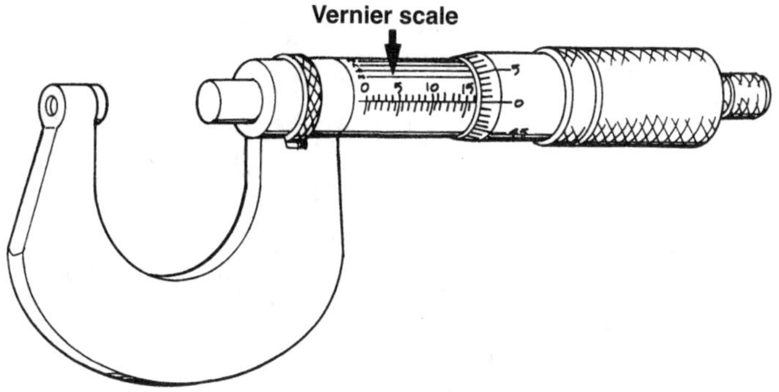

(30)

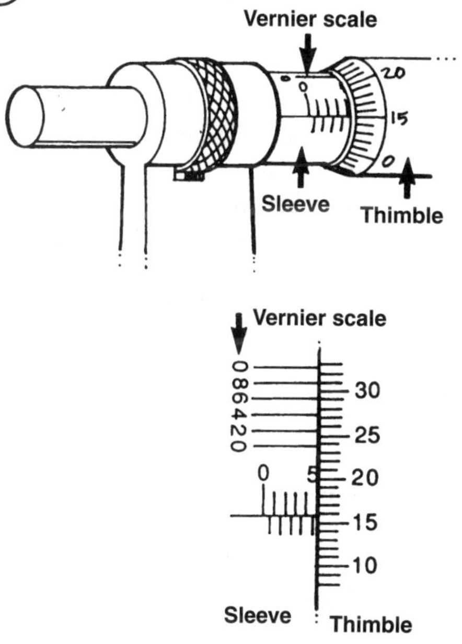

1.	Reading on upper sleeve line	4.0 mm
2.	Reading on lower sleeve line	0.5 mm
3.	Thimble is between 0.15 and 0.16 lines on the sleeve line	0.15 mm
4.	Vernier line coinciding with thimble line	0.008 mm
	Total reading:	4.658 mm

1. Make sure the anvil and spindle faces are clean and dry.
2. To check a 0-1 in. (0-25 mm) micrometer, perform the following:
   a. Turn the spindle until the spindle contacts the anvil. If the micrometer has a ratchet stop, use it to ensure that the proper amount of pressure is applied against the contact surfaces.
   b. Read the micrometer. If the adjustment is correct, the 0 mark on the thimble will be aligned exactly with the 0 mark on the sleeve line. If the 0 marks do not align, the micrometer is out of adjustment.
   c. To adjust the micrometer, follow the manufacturer's instructions provided with the micrometer.
3. To check the accuracy of a micrometer above the 1 inch (25 mm) size, perform the following:

a. Manufacturers usually supply a standard gauge with their micrometers. A standard is a steel block, disc or rod that is ground to an exact size to check the accuracy of the micrometer. For example, a 1-2 inch micrometer is equipped with a 1 inch standard gauge. A 25-50 mm micrometer is equipped with a 25 mm standard gauge.
b. Place the standard gauge between the micrometer's spindle and anvil and measure the outside diameter or length in the same manner as measuring a vehicle component. Read the micrometer. If the adjustment is correct, the 0 mark on the thimble will be aligned exactly with the sleeve line. If the 0 marks do not align, the micrometer requires calibration.
c. To adjust the micrometer, follow the manufacturer's instruction provided with the micrometer.

Proper Care of a Micrometer

Because the micrometer is a precision instrument, it must be used correctly and with great care. When using and storing a micrometer, refer to the following:

1. Store a micrometer in its box or in a protected place where dust, oil, or other debris cannot come in contact with them. Do not store micrometers in a drawer with other tools nor hang them on a tool board.
2. When storing a 0-1 in. (0-25 mm) micrometer, the spindle and anvil must not contact each other. If they do, this may cause rust to form on the contact ends or the spindle will be damaged by temperature changes.
3. Do not clean a micrometer with compressed air. Dirt forced under pressure into the tool can cause premature damage.
4. Occasionally lubricate the micrometer with lightweight oil to prevent rust and corrosion.
5. Before using a micrometer, check its accuracy. Refer to *Micrometer Accuracy Check* previously described in this section.

Cylinder Bore Gauge

The cylinder bore gauge is a very specialized precision tool comprising of a dial indicator, handle and a number of different length adapters (anvils) to adapt the gauge to different bore sizes. The bore gauge is used to make cylinder bore measurements such as bore size, taper and out-of-round. Depending on the bore gauge, it can sometimes be used to measure brake caliper and master cylinder bore sizes. In some cases, an outside micrometer must be used to calibrate the gauge to a specific bore diameter.

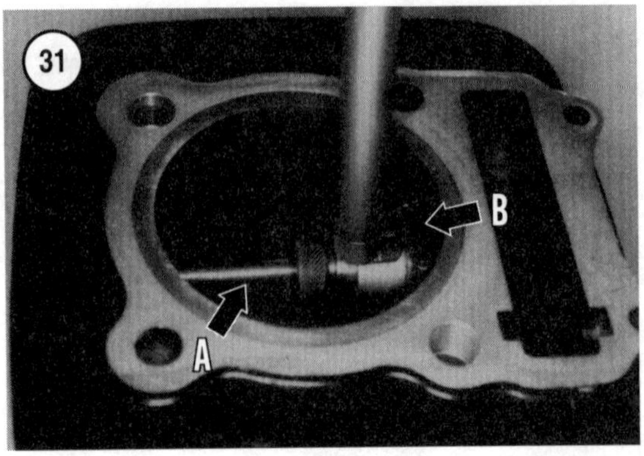

Select the correct length adapter (A, **Figure 31**) for the size of the bore to be measured. Zero the bore gauge according to manufacturer's instructions, insert the bore gauge into the cylinder, carefully move it around in the bore to make sure it is centered and that the gauge foot (B, **Figure 31**) sits correctly on the bore surface. This is necessary in order to obtain a correct reading. Refer to the manufacturer's instructions for reading the actual measurement obtained.

Small Hole Gauges

A set of small hole gauges, allows the measuring of a small hole, groove or slot. The small hole gauge is used for the smallest measurements and the telescoping gauges are used for slightly larger measurements. A small hole gauge is required to measure rocker arm bore and brake master cylinder bore diameters. The telescoping gauge does not have a scale for direct readings. An outside micrometer must be used together with the telescoping gauge to determine the bore dimension.

Carefully insert the small hole gauge into the bore of the component to be measured. Tighten the knurled end of the gauge to carefully expanded the gauge fingers to the limit within the bore. *Do not overtighten* the gauge, as it has no built-in release feature. If tightened too much, the gauge fingers can

32

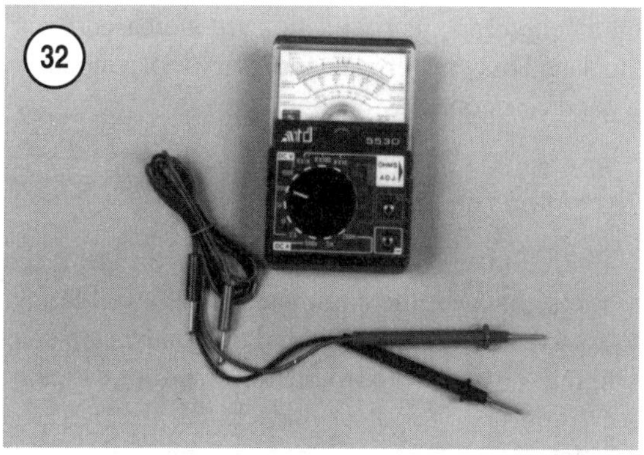

33

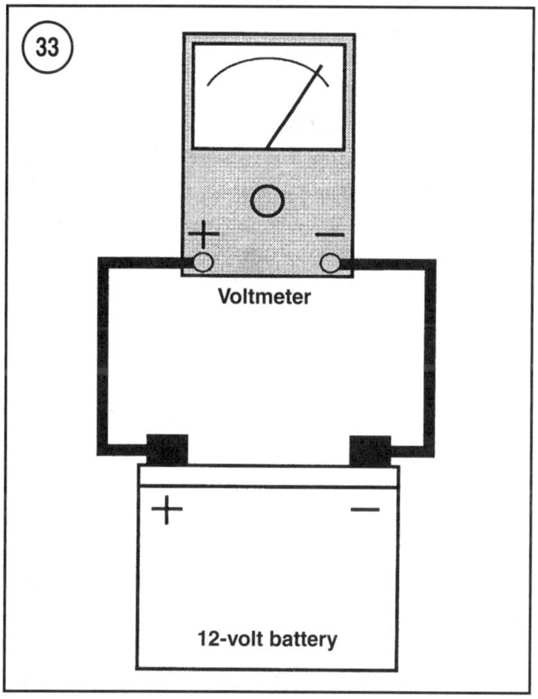

damage the bore surface. Carefully remove the gauge and measure the outside dimension of the gauge with a micrometer. See *Outside Micrometer* in this chapter.

Telescoping Gauges

A telescoping gauge is used to measure hole diameters from approximately 8 mm (5/16 in.) to 150 mm (6 in.). For example, they could be used to measure brake caliper bore and cylinder bore diameters. Like the small hole gauge, the telescoping gauge does not have a scale for direct readings. An outside micrometer must be used together with the telescoping gauge to determine the bore dimension.

Select the correct size telescoping gauge for the bore to be measured. Compress the movable side of the gauge post and carefully install the gauge into the bore of the component to be measured, then release the movable post against the bore. Carefully move the gauge around in the bore to make sure it is centered. Tighten the knurled end of the gauge to hold the movable gauge post in this position. Carefully remove the gauge and measure the outside dimension of the gauge posts with a micrometer. See *Outside Micrometer* in this chapter.

Multimeter

The multimeter is a valuable tool for all electrical system troubleshooting (**Figure 32**). The voltage application is used to indicate the voltage applied or available to various electrical components. The ohmmeter portion of the meter is used to check for continuity, or lack of continuity, and to measure the resistance of a component.

Voltage

Voltage is the pressure in an electrical circuit. The more pressure (voltage) in the circuit, the more work can be accomplished. Always measure voltage in a simple parallel connection. The connection of a voltmeter directly to the negative and positive terminals of a battery is an example of a parallel connection (**Figure 33**). Nothing must be disconnected to make a parallel connection.

Direct current (DC) voltage means that electricity flows in one direction only. All circuits powered by a battery are DC circuits.

Alternating current (AC) means that the electricity flows in one direction momentarily then switches to the opposite direction. The frequency at which AC voltage changes direction is referred to as hertz. In motorcycle, or ATV, applications, charging system output is AC voltage until the AC is converted to DC for storage in the battery.

Since resistance causes voltage to drop, resistance can be measured on an active circuit using a voltmeter. This is called a voltage drop test. Basically, a voltage drop test compares the voltage at the beginning of a circuit to the voltage available at the end of the circuit while the circuit is being operated. If the circuit has no resistance, there will be no voltage drop and the meter will read zero volts. The more resistance the circuit has, the higher the voltage meter reading will be. Generally, a voltage drop of one or more volts is considered excessive. The advantage to the voltage drop test over a resistance test is that the circuit is tested during operation. It is important to remember that a zero reading on a voltage drop test is desired while a reading of battery voltage indicates an open circuit.

When measuring voltage, select the meter voltage range one scale higher than the expected voltage of the circuit to prevent damage to the meter.

Resistance

NOTE

In most cases, to obtain an accurate resistance measurement, the component must be at approximately 20° C (68° F).

Resistance is the opposition to the flow of electricity in a circuit and is measured in ohms. Resistance causes a reduction in current flow and a reduction or drop in available voltage. Resistance is measured with an ohmmeter. To measure resistance, the ohmmeter sends a small amount of electricity in the circuit and measures how difficult it is push the electricity back to the ohmmeter.

CAUTION

An ohmmeter must only be used on circuit or component that is isolated from any other circuit or component and has no voltage present. The meter will be damaged if it is connected to a circuit with voltage present.

An ohmmeter, although useful, is not always a good indicator of a component's condition. This is primarily because resistance tests do not simulate actual operating conditions. For example, the power source in most ohmmeters is only 6-9 volts. The voltage in the secondary windings of an ignition coil, however, can be several thousand volts during normal operation. Such high voltage can cause coil insulation leakage that cannot be detected using an ohmmeter.

Because resistance generally increases with temperature, perform resistance tests with the component or circuit at room temperature. Resistance tests on a hot component will indicate increased resistance and may result in unnecessary replacement of a good component.

To calibrate an analog ohmmeter

Every time an analog ohmmeter is used or if the scale is changed, the ohmmeter must be calibrated to zero the needle. Most digital ohmmeters are auto ranging—when switched on they are automatically set to zero.

1. Make sure the meter battery power is at full power. If the battery condition is questionable, replace the battery.
2. Make sure the test probes are clean and free of corrosion.
3. Touch the two test probes together and observe the meter needle location on the ohm scale. The needle must be aligned with the 0 mark on the scale.
4. If necessary, rotate the *ohms adjust* knob on the meter in either direction until the needle is directly aligned with the 0 mark.

Continuity Test

A continuity test determines the integrity of a circuit or component. A broken wire or open circuit has no continuity, a complete circuit has continuity. Continuity can be checked using an ohmmeter or a self-powered test lamp. Using an ohmmeter, a low-resistance reading, usually 0 ohm, indicates continuity. An infinity reading indicates no continuity. Using a self-powered test lamp, continuity is indicated if the test lamp glows. If the lamp does not glow, no continuity is present.

The circuit or component must be isolated or disconnected from any other circuit to check continuity.

Amperage

Amperes (amps) are the units used to measure current flow in a circuit or through a component. Current is the actual flow of electricity. The more current that flows, the more work that can be accomplished. However, if excessive current flows through a wire, the wire will overheat and probably melt. Melted wires are caused by excessive current, not excessive voltage.

Amperes are measured using an ammeter attached in a simple series connection. Amperage

34

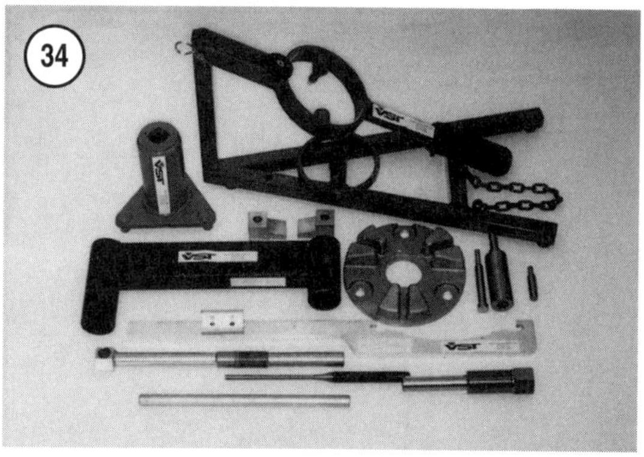

measurement requires that the ammeter be spliced into the circuit in a series connection. Always use an ammeter that can read higher that the anticipated current flow to prevent damage to the meter. Connect the red lead of the ammeter to the electrical source and the black lead to the electrical load.

SPECIAL TOOLS

A series of special tools are required to service the drive and driven pulleys of the Polaris Variable Transmission (PVT). These tools are required to remove, disassemble, assemble and install these components onto the engine and transmission. The special tools shown in **Figure 34** are available from Victor Specialty Tools (VST). They may be ordered directly from Victor Specialty Tools or through a Polaris dealership. The part numbers for each special tool is listed along with each specific service procedure in Chapter Eight.

FABRICATING TOOLS

Some of the procedures in this manual require using special tools. The resourceful mechanic can, in many cases, think of acceptable substitutes for special tools. This can be as simple as using a few pieces of threaded rod, washers and nuts to remove or install a bearing or as complicated as fabricating a tool from scrap material. If the special tool can be designed and safely made but requires some type of machine work, contact a local community college or high school that has a machine shop curriculum. Some shop teachers welcome outside work that can be used as practical shop application for advanced students.

MECHANIC'S TIPS

Removing Frozen Nuts and Screws

If a fastener rusts and cannot be removed, several methods may be used to loosen it. First, apply penetrating oil such as Liquid Wrench or WD-40 (available at hardware or auto supply stores). Apply it liberally and let it penetrate for 10-15 minutes. Rap the fastener several times with a small hammer; do not hit it hard enough to cause damage. Reapply the penetrating oil if necessary.

For frozen screws, apply penetrating oil as described, then insert a screwdriver in the slot and rap the top of the screwdriver with a hammer. This loosens the rust so the screw can be removed in the normal way. If the screw head is too damaged to use this method, grip the head with locking pliers and twist the screw out.

Avoid applying heat unless specifically instructed to do so, as it may melt, warp or remove the temper from parts.

Removing Broken Screws or Bolts

If the head breaks off a screw or bolt, several methods are available for removing the remaining portion. If a large portion of the remainder projects out, try gripping it with locking pliers. If the projecting portion is too small, file it to fit a wrench or cut a slot in it to fit a screwdriver.

If the head breaks off flush, use a screw extractor. To do this, centerpunch the exact center of the remaining portion of the screw or bolt. Drill a small hole in the screw and tap the extractor into the hole. Back the screw out with a wrench on the extractor (**Figure 35**).

Remedying Stripped Threads

Occasionally, threads are stripped through carelessness or impact damage. Often the threads can be cleaned up by running a tap (for internal threads on nuts) or die (for external threads on bolts) through the threads. To clean or repair spark plug threads, a spark plug tap can be used.

If an internal thread is damaged, it may be necessary to install a Helicoil or some other type of thread insert. Follow the manufacturer's instructions when installing their insert.

35

REMOVING BROKEN SCREWS AND BOLTS

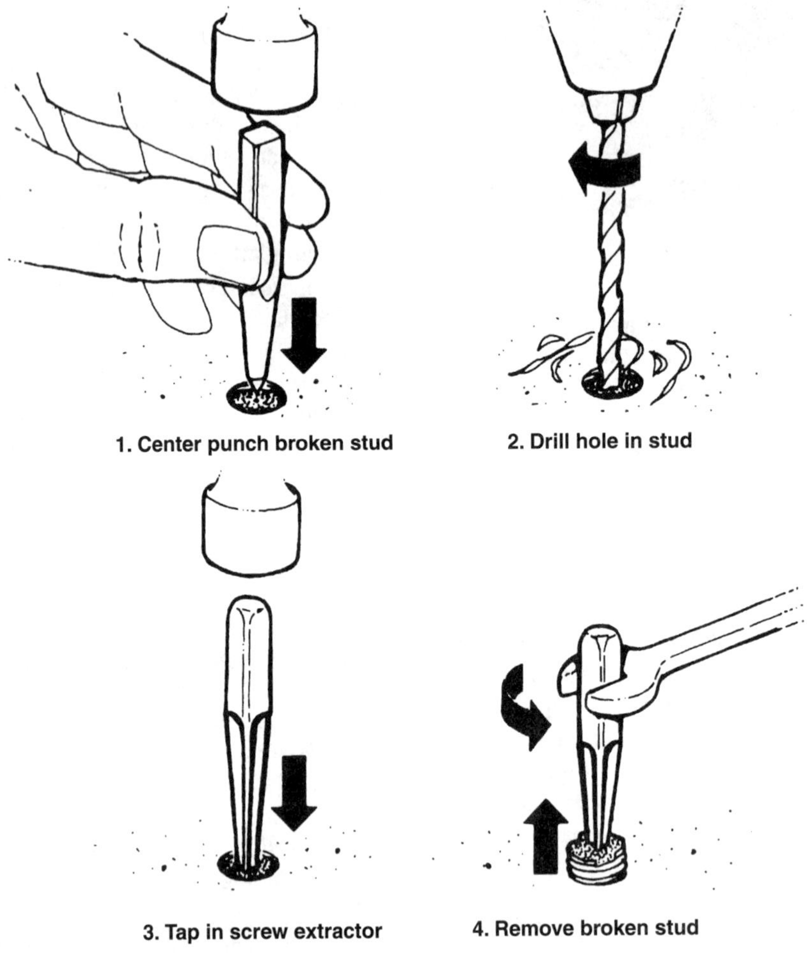

If it is necessary to drill and tap a hole, refer to **Table 8** for metric tap and drill sizes.

BEARING REPLACEMENT

Ball bearings are used in some locations in the engine and transmission assembly to reduce power loss, heat and noise resulting from friction. Because ball bearings are precision made parts, they must be maintained by proper lubrication and maintenance. If a bearing is damaged, it must be replaced immediately. However, when installing a new bearing, care should be taken to prevent damage to the new bearing. Bearing replacement is indicated in the individual chapters where applicable; however, use the following as a guideline.

NOTE
Unless otherwise specified, install bearings with the manufacturer's mark or number facing outward.

Bearing Removal

While bearings are normally removed only when damaged, there may be times when it is necessary to remove a bearing that is in good condition. How-

(36)

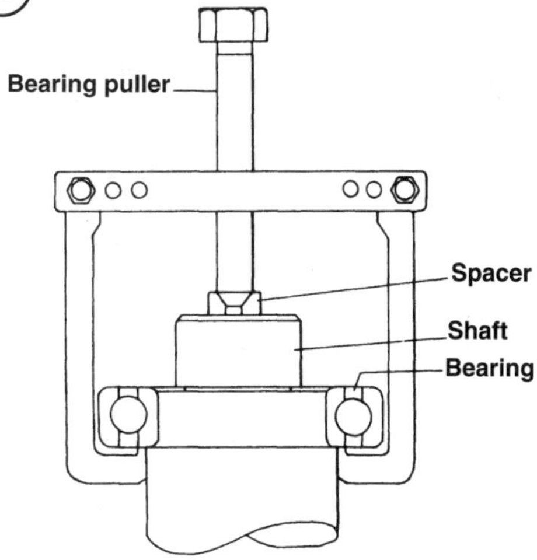

(37)

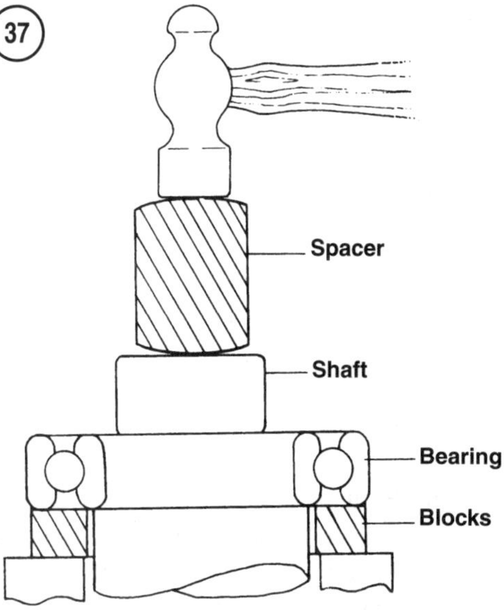

ever, improper bearing removal will damage the bearing and maybe the shaft or case half. Note the following when removing bearings.

1. When using a puller to remove a bearing from a shaft, take care that the shaft is not damaged. Always place a piece of metal between the end of the shaft and the puller screw. In addition, place the puller arms next to the inner bearing race. See **Figure 36**.

(38)

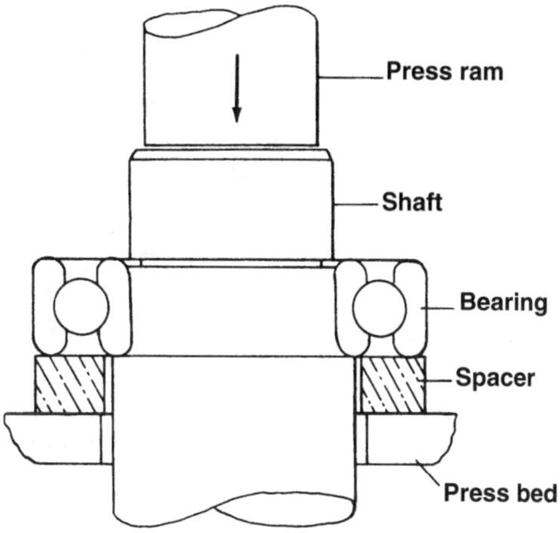

2. When using a hammer to remove a bearing from a shaft, do not strike the hammer directly against the shaft. Instead, use a brass or aluminum rod between the hammer and shaft (**Figure 37**) and make sure to support both bearing races with wooden blocks as shown.

3. The most ideal method of bearing removal is with a hydraulic press. However, certain procedures must be followed or damage may occur to the bearing, shaft or bearing housing. Note the following when using a press:

a. Always support the inner and outer bearing races with a suitable size wooden or aluminum ring (**Figure 38**). If only the outer race is supported, pressure applied against the ball bearings and/or the inner race will damage them.

b. Always make sure the press ram (**Figure 38**) aligns with the center of the shaft. If the ram is not centered, it may damage the bearing and/or shaft.

c. The moment the shaft is free of the bearing, it will drop to the floor. Secure or hold the shaft to prevent it from falling.

Bearing Installation

1. When installing a bearing in a housing, pressure must be applied to the *outer* bearing race (**Figure 39**). When installing a bearing on a shaft, pressure must be applied to the *inner* bearing race (**Figure 40**).
2. When installing a bearing as described in Step 1, some type of driver will be required. Never strike the bearing directly with a hammer or the bearing will be damaged. When installing a bearing, a piece of pipe or a socket with a diameter that matches the bearing race is required. **Figure 41** shows the correct way to use a socket and hammer when installing a bearing.
3. Step 1 describes how to install a bearing in a case half or over a shaft. However, when installing a bearing over a shaft and into a housing at the same time, a snug fit will be required for both outer and inner bearing races. In this situation, a spacer must be installed underneath the driver tool so that pressure is applied evenly across both races. See **Figure 42**. If the outer race is not supported as shown in **Figure 42**, the balls will push against the outer bearing track and damage it.

39

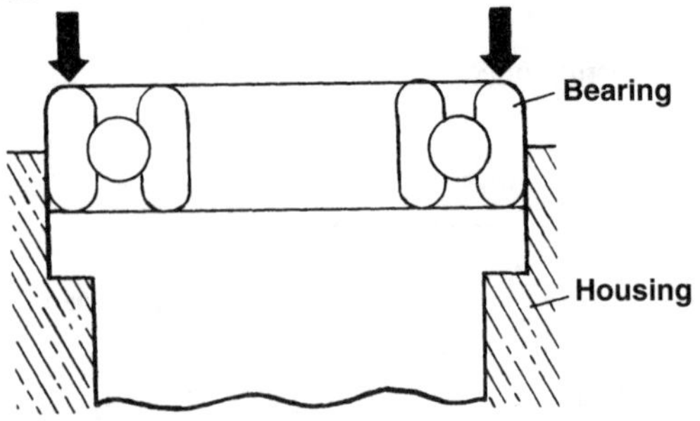

40

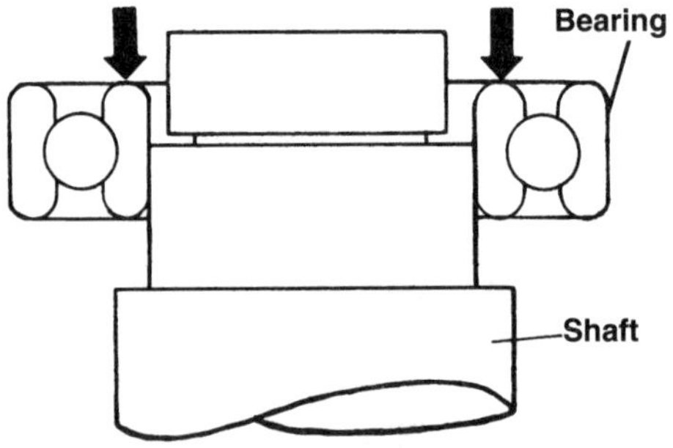

Shrink Fit

1. Installing a bearing over a shaft: When a tight fit is required, the bearing inside diameter will be smaller than the shaft. In this case, driving the bearing on the shaft using normal methods may cause bearing damage. Instead, the bearing should be heated before installation. Note the following:
   a. Secure the shaft so that it is ready for bearing installation.
   b. Clean all residue from the bearing surface of the shaft. Remove burrs with a file or sandpaper.
   c. Fill a suitable pot or beaker with clean mineral oil. Place a thermometer (rated higher than 120° C [248° F]) in the oil. Support the thermometer so that it does not rest on the bottom or side of the pot.
   d. Remove the bearing from its wrapper and secure it with a piece of heavy wire bent to hold it in the pot. Hang the bearing in the pot so that it does not touch the bottom or sides of the pot.
   e. Turn the heat on and monitor the thermometer. When the oil temperature rises to approximately 120° C (248° F), remove the bearing from the pot and quickly install it. If necessary, place a socket on the inner bearing race and tap the bearing into place. As the bearing chills, it will tighten on the shaft so work must be done quickly when installing it. Make sure the bearing is installed all the way.
2. Installing a bearing in a housing: Bearings are generally installed in a housing with a slight interference fit. Driving the bearing into the housing using normal methods may damage the housing or cause bearing damage. Instead, the housing should be heated before the bearing is installed. Note the following:

CAUTION

Before heating the crankcases in this procedure to remove the bearings, wash the cases thoroughly with detergent and water. Rinse and rewash the

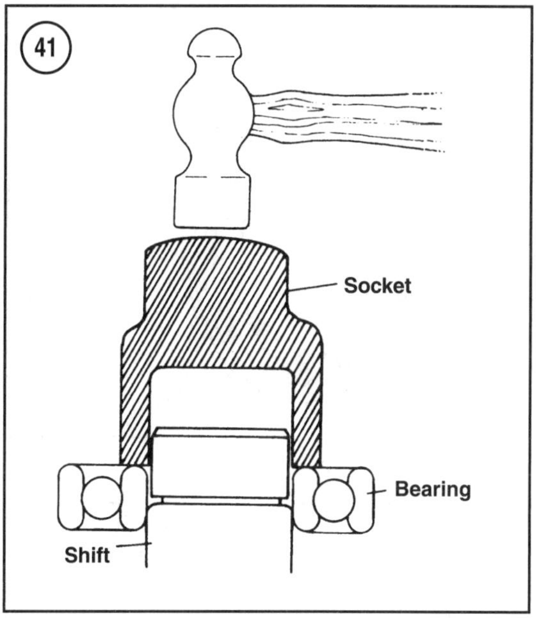

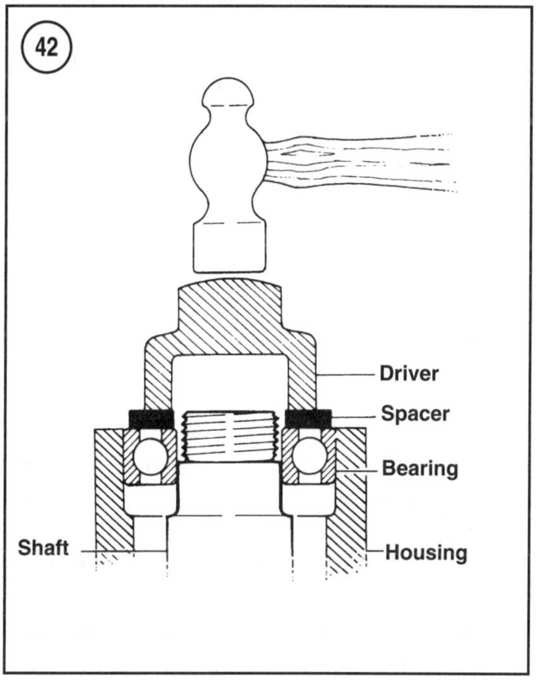

cases as required to remove all traces of oil and other chemical deposits.

a. The housing must be heated to a temperature of about 212° F (100° C) in an oven or on a hot plate. An easy way to check that it is at the proper temperature is to drop tiny drops of water on the case; if they sizzle and evaporate immediately, the temperature is correct. Heat only one housing at a time.

CAUTION
Do not heat the housing with a torch (propane or acetylene)—never bring a flame into contact with the bearing or housing. The direct heat will destroy the case hardening of the bearing and will likely warp the housing.

b. Remove the housing from the oven or hot plate and hold onto the housing with a kitchen pot holder, heavy gloves, or heavy shop cloth—it is hot.

NOTE
Removal and installation of bearings can be accomplished with a suitable size socket and extension.

c. Hold the housing with the bearing side down and tap the bearing out. Repeat for all bearings in the housing.
d. Prior to heating the bearing housing, place the new bearing in a freezer, if possible. Chilling a bearing will slightly reduce its outside diameter while the heated bearing housing assembly is slightly larger due to heat expansion. This will make bearing installation much easier.

NOTE
Always install bearings with the manufacturer's mark or number facing outward.

e. While the housing is still hot, install the new bearing(s) into the housing. Install the bearings by hand, if possible. If necessary, lightly tap the bearing(s) into the housing with a socket placed on the outer bearing race. Do not install new bearings by driving on the inner bearing race. Install the bearing(s) until it seats completely.

SEALS

Seals (**Figure 43**) are used to contain oil, water, grease or combustion gasses in a housing or shaft. Improper removal of a seal can damage the housing or shaft. Improper installation of the seal can damage the seal. Note the following:

1. Prying is generally the easiest and most effective method of removing a seal from a housing. However, always place a rag underneath the pry tool to prevent damage to the housing.
2. Pack waterproof grease in the seal lips before the seal is installed.
3. In most cases, oil seals should be installed so that the manufacturer's numbers or marks face out.
4. Install seals with a driver or socket placed on the outside of the seal as shown in **Figure 44**. Make sure the seal is driven squarely into the housing. Never install a seal by hitting against the top of the seal with a hammer.

43

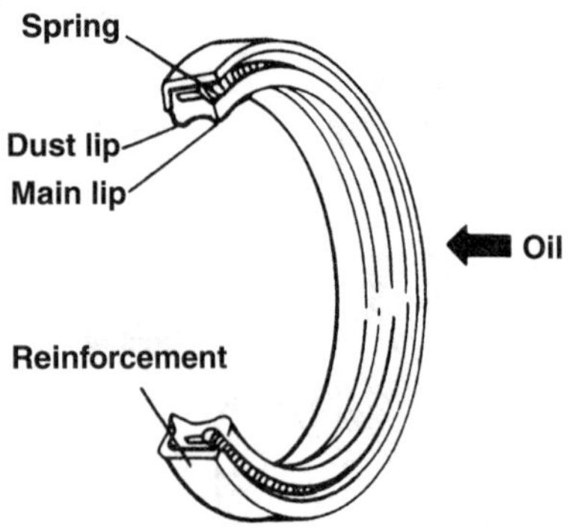

44

STORAGE

Several months of inactivity can cause serious problems and general deterioration of the vehicle. This is especially important in areas with cold winters. For winter storage, prepare the vehicle carefully.

Selecting a Storage Area

Most ATV riders store their vehicles in their home garage. If a garage is not available, there are other facilities for rent or lease in most areas. When selecting an area, consider the following points.

1. The storage area must be dry; there should be no dampness or excessive humidity. A heated area is not necessary, but it should be insulated to minimize extreme temperature variations.
2. Avoid buildings with large window areas. If this is not possible, mask the window to keep direct sunlight off the vehicle.
3. Avoid buildings in industrial areas where factories are liable to emit corrosive fumes. Also avoid buildings near large bodies of salt water.
4. Select an area where there is minimum risk of fire, theft or vandalism. Check with the insurance agent to make sure that the insurance policy covers the vehicle in storage.

Preparing Vehicle for Storage

Careful preparation will minimize deterioration and make it easier to restore the vehicle to service. Use the following procedure.

1. Wash the vehicle thoroughly. Make certain all the dirt and mud is thoroughly removed. Thoroughly clean all plastic and metal components. Apply a plastic preservative such as Armor-All to all the plastic parts and apply a tire dressing to all tires. Make sure to follow the manufacturer's instructions when applying the plastic preservative.
2. Run the engine until it reaches operating temperature. Drain the engine oil and transmission oil regardless of the riding time since the last change. Fill the engine and transmission with the recommended type and quantity of fresh oil.
3. Drain all the gasoline from the fuel tank, fuel line and carburetor. Run the engine at idle speed until all of the fuel is used up.
4. Remove the spark plug and add a small quantity of engine oil into the cylinder. Place a rag over the cylinder head openings and slowly roll the engine over a few times to distribute the oil, then reinstall the spark plug.
5. Check the tire pressures, reduce the normal inflation pressure by 20%, and move the machine to the storage area.

6. Place the vehicle securely on a stand, or wooden blocks, so all four wheels are off the ground. If not possible, place a piece of wood (plywood) under the tires to keep moisture away from the tire rubber.

After Storage

1. Before returning the vehicle to service, thoroughly check all fasteners, suspension components and brake components.

2. Check all controls and cables. Replace any cables that are frayed or kinked.

3. Make sure both brakes, the clutch and the throttle operate smoothly. Adjust the controls if necessary.
4. Ensure that all the wiring is correctly routed and all connections are tight and corrosion-free. Check that the auxiliary shutoff switch will stop the engine. Make sure the brake light is operational with both the hand lever and brake pedal. Make sure none of the wires are positioned against the exhaust pipe.
5. Before starting the engine, remove the spark plug and turn the engine over a few times to blow out the excess storage oil. Place a rag over the cylinder head openings to keep the oil off the engine. Install a new spark plug and connect the spark plug lead.

Table 1 MODEL YEAR AND NUMBER

Year	Model number
1996	
Sportsman 500	W969244
1997	
Sportsman 500 (U.S.)	W97CH50A
Sportsman 500 (Sweden)	S97750AE
Xplorer 500	W97CD50A
1998	
Sportsman 500 (U.S.)	W98CH50AB
Sportsman 500 (U.S.)	W98CH50AC
Sportsman 500 (U.S.)	W98CH50AD
Sportsman 500 (U.S.)	W98CH50AE
Sportsman 500 (U.S.)	W98CH50AF
Worker 500 (Sweden)	S98CH50E
Worker 500 (Sweden)	S98CH50EB
1999	
Sportsman 500 (U.S.)	A99CH50AA
Sportsman 500 (U.S.)	A99CH50AB
Worker 500 (Sweden)	A99CH50EA
Worker 500 (Sweden)	A98CH50EB
Sportsman 500 RSE*	A99CH50AC
2000	
Sportsman 500 (U.S.)	A00CH50A
Sportsman 500 (U.S.)	A00CH50AB
Worker 500 (Sweden)	A00CH50EA
Worker 500 (Sweden)	A00CH50EB
Sportsman 500 RSE*	A00CH50AC

* Sportsman 500 Remington Special Edition (Camouflage color scheme).

Table 2 GENERAL DIMENSIONS

Year	Height mm (in.)	Length mm (in.)	Width mm (in.)	Wheel base mm (in.)
1996	1194 (47)	1955.8 (77)	1168.4 (46)	1282.7 (50.50)
1997-1998	1194 (47)	2057.4 (81)	1168.4 (46)	1282.7 (50.50)
1999-on	1194 (47)	2159 (85)	1168.4 (46)	1282.7 (50.50)

Table 3 VEHICLE WEIGHT (DRY)

Year	kg	lb.
1996-1997	294.4	649
1998-on	316.1	697

Table 4 DECIMAL AND METRIC EQUIVALENTS

Fractions	Decimal in.	Metric mm	Fractions	Decimal in.	Metric mm
1/64	0.015625	0.39688	33/64	0.515625	13.09687
1/32	0.03125	0.79375	17/32	0.53125	13.49375
3/64	0.046875	1.19062	35/64	0.546875	13.89062
1/16	0.0625	1.58750	9/16	0.5625	14.28750
5/64	0.078125	1.98437	37/64	0.578125	14.68437
3/32	0.09375	2.38125	19/32	0.59375	15.08125
7/64	0.109375	2.77812	39/64	0.609375	15.47812
1/8	0.125	3.1750	5/8	0.625	15.87500
9/64	0.140625	3.57187	41/64	0.640625	16.27187
5/32	0.15625	3.96875	21/32	0.65625	16.66875
11/64	0.171875	4.36562	43/64	0.671875	17.06562
3/16	0.1875	4.76250	11/16	0.6875	17.46250
13/64	0.203125	5.15937	45/64	0.703125	17.85937
7/32	0.21875	5.55625	23/32	0.71875	18.25625
15/64	0.234375	5.95312	47/64	0.734375	18.65312
1/4	0.250	6.35000	3/4	0.750	19.05000
17/64	0.265625	6.74687	49/64	0.765625	19.44687
9/32	0.28125	7.14375	25/32	0.78125	19.84375
19/64	0.296875	7.54062	51/64	0.796875	20.24062
5/16	0.3125	7.93750	13/16	0.8125	20.63750
21/64	0.328125	8.33437	53/64	0.828125	21.03437
11/32	0.34375	8.73125	27/32	0.84375	21.43125
23/64	0.359375	9.12812	55/64	0.859375	22.82812
3/8	0.375	9.52500	7/8	0.875	22.22500
25/64	0.390625	9.92187	57/64	0.890625	22.62187
13/32	0.40625	10.31875	29/32	0.90625	23.01875
27/64	0.421875	10.71562	59/64	0.921875	23.41562
7/16	0.4375	11.11250	15/16	0.9375	23.81250
29/64	0.453125	11.50937	61/64	0.953125	24.20937
15/32	0.46875	11.90625	31/32	0.96875	24.60625
31/64	0.484375	12.30312	63/64	0.984375	25.00312
1/2	0.500	12.70000	1	1.00	25.40000

Table 5 GENERAL TORQUE SPECIFICATIONS

Thread diameter	N•m	ft.-lb.
5 mm	3.4-4.9	30-43
6 mm	5.9-7.8	52-69
8 mm	14-19	10-14
10 mm	25-39	18-29
12 mm	44-61	32-45
14 mm	73-98	54-72
16 mm	115-155	85-114
18 mm	165-225	122-166

Table 6 CONVERSION TABLES

	Multiply by:	To get the equivalent of:
Length		
Inches	25.4	Millimeter
Inches	2.54	Centimeter
Miles	1.609	Kilometer
Feet	0.3048	Meter
Millimeter	0.03937	Inches
Centimeter	0.3937	Inches
Kilometer	0.6214	Mile
Meter	0.0006214	Mile
Fluid volume		
U.S. quarts	0.9463	Liters
U.S. gallons	3.785	Liters
U.S. ounces	29.573529	Milliliters
Imperial gallons	4.54609	Liters
Imperial quarts	1.1365	Liters
Liters	0.2641721	U.S. gallons
Liters	1.0566882	U.S. quarts
Liters	33.814023	U.S. ounces
Liters	0.22	Imperial gallons
Liters	0.8799	Imperial quarts
Milliliters	0.033814	U.S. ounces
Milliliters	1.0	Cubic centimeters
Milliliters	0.001	Liters
Torque		
Foot-pounds	1.3558	Newton-meters
Foot-pounds	0.138255	Meters-kilograms
Inch-pounds	0.11299	Newton-meters
Newton-meters	0.7375622	Foot-pounds
Newton-meters	8.8507	Inch-pounds
Meters-kilograms	7.2330139	Foot-pounds
Volume		
Cubic inches	16.387064	Cubic centimeters
Cubic centimeters	0.0610237	Cubic inches
Temperature		
Fahrenheit	(F -32°) × 0.556	Centigrade
Centigrade	(C × 1.8) + 32	Fahrenheit
Weight		
Ounces	28.3495	Grams
Pounds	0.4535924	Kilograms
Grams	0.035274	Ounces
Kilograms	2.2046224	Pounds

(continued)

Table 6 CONVERSION TABLES (continued)

	Multiply by:	To get the equivalent of:
Pressure		
Pounds per square inch	0.070307	Kilograms per square centimeter
Kilograms per square centimeter	14.223343	Pounds per square inch
Kilopascals	0.1450	Pounds per square inch
Pounds per square inch	6.895	Kilopascals
Speed		
Miles per hour	1.609344	Kilometers per hour
Kilometers per hour	0.6213712	Miles per hour

Table 7 TECHNICAL ABBREVIATIONS

ABDC	After bottom dead center
ATDC	After top dead center
BBDC	Before bottom dead center
BDC	Bottom dead center
BTDC	Before top dead center
C	Celsius (Centigrade)
cc	Cubic centimeters
cid	Cubic inch displacement
CDI	Capacitor discharge ignition
cu. in.	Cubic inches
EBS	Engine Braking System
F	Fahrenheit
ft.	Feet
ft.-lb.	Foot-pounds
gal.	Gallons
H/A	High altitude
hp	Horsepower
in.	Inches
in.-lb.	Inch-pounds
I.D.	Inside diameter
kg	Kilograms
kgm	Kilogram meters
km	Kilometer
kPa	Kilopascals
L	Liter
m	Meter
MAG	Magneto
ml	Milliliter
mm	Millimeter
N•m	Newton-meters
O.D.	Outside diameter
oz.	Ounces
psi	Pounds per square inch
PTO	Power take off
PVT	Polaris Variable Transmission
pt.	Pint
qt.	Quart
rpm	Revolutions per minute
VST	Victory Specialty Tools

Table 8 METRIC TAP AND DRILL SIZES

Metric size	Drill equivalent	Decimal fraction	Nearest fraction
3 × 0.50	No. 39	0.0995	3/32
3 × 0.60	3/32	0.0937	3/32
4 × 0.70	No. 30	0.1285	1/8
4 × 0.75	1/8	0.125	1/8
5 × 0.80	No. 19	0.166	11/64
5 × 0.90	No. 20	0.161	5/32
6 × 1.00	No. 9	0.196	13/64
7 × 1.00	16/64	0.234	15/64
8 × 1.00	J	0.277	9/32
8 × 1.25	17/64	0.265	17/64
9 × 1.00	5/16	0.3125	5/16
9 × 1.25	5/16	0.3125	5/16
10 × 1.25	11/32	0.3437	11/32
10 × 1.50	R	0.339	11/32
11 × 1.50	3/8	0.375	3/8
12 × 1.50	13/32	0.406	13/32
12 × 1.75	13/32	0.406	13/32

NOTE: Refer to the Supplement at the back of this manual for information unique to 2001-on models, including the Sportsman 400.

CHAPTER TWO

TROUBLESHOOTING

The troubleshooting procedures described in this chapter provide typical symptoms and logical methods for isolating the cause(s). There may be several ways to solve a problem, but only a systematic approach will be successful in avoiding wasted time and possibly unnecessarily replacing parts.

Gather as much information as possible to aid in diagnosis. Never assume anything and do not overlook the obvious. Make sure there is fuel in the tank and the spark plug is connected. Learning to recognize symptoms will make troubleshooting easier. In most cases, expensive and complicated test equipment is not needed to determine whether repairs can be performed at home. On the other hand, be realistic and do not start procedures that are beyond the experience and equipment on hand. Many service departments will not take work that involves the reassembly of damaged or abused equipment. If they do, expect the cost to be high. If the ATV does require the attention of a professional, describe symptoms and conditions accurately and fully. The more information a technician has available, the easier it will be to diagnose the problem.

Proper lubrication, maintenance and periodic tune-ups reduce the chance that problems will occur. However even with the best of care, the motorcycle may require troubleshooting.

OPERATING REQUIREMENTS

An engine needs three basics to run properly: correct air/fuel mixture, compression and a spark at the right time. If one basic requirement is missing, the engine will not run. Four-stroke engine operating

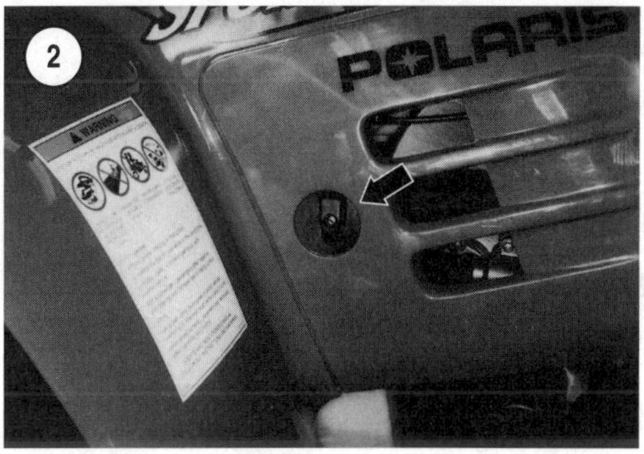

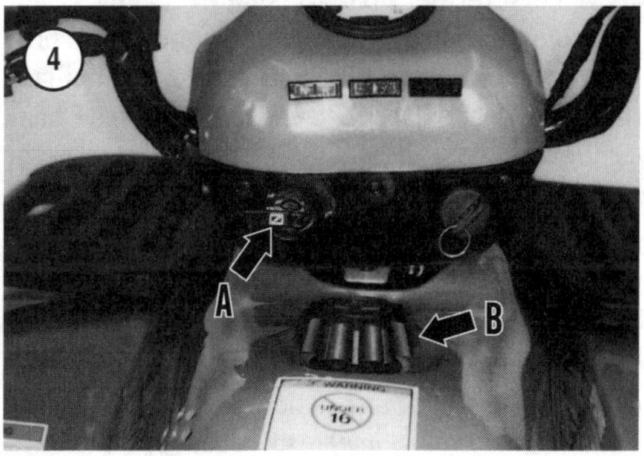

principles are described in Chapter Four under *Engine Principles*.

If the ATV has been sitting for any time and refuses to start, check and clean the spark plug. If the plug is not fouled, look to the fuel delivery system. This includes the fuel tank (**Figure 1**), fuel shutoff valve (**Figure 2**), fuel pump, fuel filter and fuel lines. If the ATV sat for awhile with fuel in the carburetor, fuel deposits may have gummed up carburetor jets and air passages. Gasoline tends to lose its potency after standing for long periods. Condensation may contaminate it with water. Drain the old gas and try starting with a fresh tankful.

TROUBLESHOOTING INSTRUMENTS

Chapter One lists the instruments needed and instruction for their use.

STARTING THE ENGINE

Use the following outline as a guide for basic starting procedures. In all cases, make sure that there is an adequate supply of fuel in the tank.

Starting a Cold Engine

1. Shift the transmission into NEUTRAL.

2A. On 1996-1998 models, perform the following:

   a. Move the engine auxiliary shutoff switch (A, **Figure 3**) to the RUN position.
   b. Turn the key, or ignition, switch to the ON position.
   c. Move the choke toggle lever (A, **Figure 4**) to the ON position (**Figure 4**).
   d. With the throttle completely closed, push the start button (B, **Figure 3**).

NOTE

On 1999 and later models, the start button is part of the engine stop switch. The engine stop switch moves from side-to-side and the start button portion of the switch moves UP to start the engine.

2B. On 1999-on models, perform the following:

   a. Move the engine auxiliary shutoff switch (**Figure 5**) to the run position.
   b. Turn the key, or ignition, switch to the ON position.

c. Move the choke toggle lever (A, **Figure 4**) to the ON position (**Figure 6**).

d. With the throttle completely closed, push the start button UP (**Figure 5**).

3. When the engine starts, work the throttle lever slightly to keep it running.

4. Idle the engine for approximately a minute or until the throttle responds cleanly, then push the choke toggle lever to the full OFF position.

Starting a Warm or Hot Engine

1. Shift the transmission into NEUTRAL.
2. Move the engine auxiliary shutoff switch to the RUN position.
3. Turn the key, or ignition, switch to the ON position.
4. Make sure the choke toggle lever is in the OFF position.
5. Open the throttle slightly and operate the start button.

Starting a Flooded Engine

If the engine will not start and there is a strong gasoline smell, the engine may be flooded. If so, open the throttle all the way and operate the starter. Do not open the choke. Holding the throttle open allows more air to reach the engine.

STARTING DIFFICULTIES

If the engine turns over but is difficult to start, or will not start, check for obvious problems first. Use the following list and review the *Operating Requirements* described earlier in this chapter.

If the engine still refuses to start, refer to the appropriate troubleshooting procedures in this chapter.

1. Make sure the choke toggle lever is in the correct position. Move the toggle lever to the ON position (**Figure 6**) for a cold engine and to the full OFF position (A, **Figure 4**) for a warm or hot engine.

WARNING
Do not use an open flame to check for fuel in the tank. A serious explosion is certain to result.

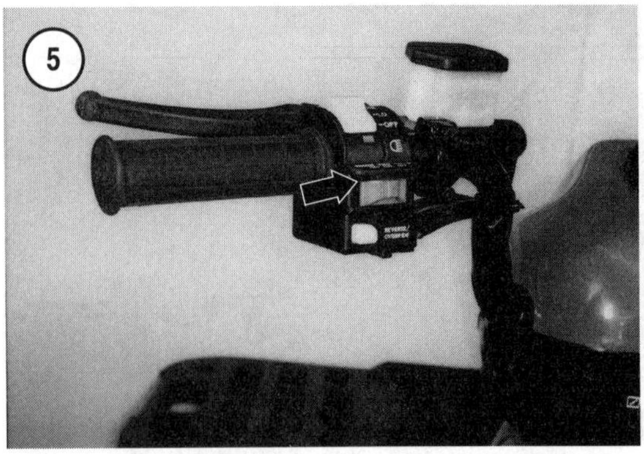
5

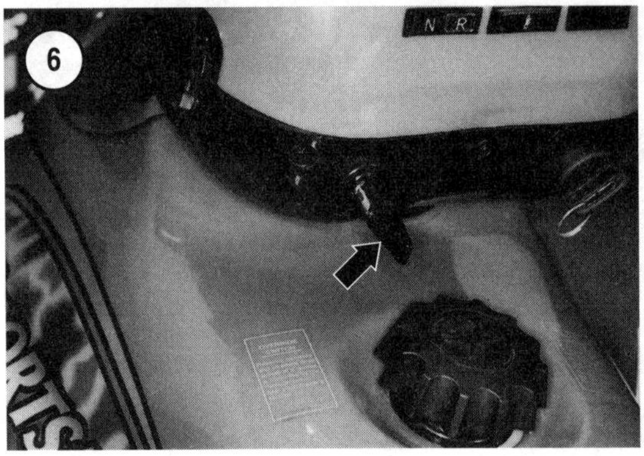
6

2. Make sure there is fuel in the tank. Open the fuel filler cap (B, **Figure 4**) and rock the ATV. Listen for the fuel sloshing around. Fill the tank if necessary. If the fuel is old, drain the tank and fill it with fresh fuel.

3. If there is a possibility that the cylinder is flooded, or there is a strong smell of gasoline, open the throttle all the way and operate the start button. If the cylinder is severely flooded (fouled or wet spark plug), remove the spark plug and dry the base and electrode thoroughly with a soft cloth, or use an aerosol parts cleaner. Reinstall the plug and attempt to start the engine.

4. Make sure the auxiliary shutoff switch is not stuck or working improperly or that the wire is broken and shorting out. If necessary, test the auxiliary shutoff switch as described under *Switches* in Chapter Eleven.

5. Make sure the spark plug wire is on tight. Push the wire and boot (**Figure 7**) on and slightly rotate it to clean the electrical connection between the plug and the connector. Push or screw the plug cap into the high-tension lead.

6. Perform a spark test as described under *Engine Fails to Start (Spark Test)* in this chapter. If there is a

7

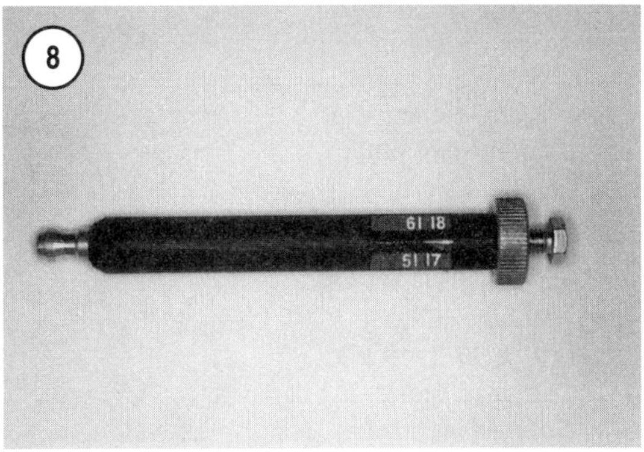

8

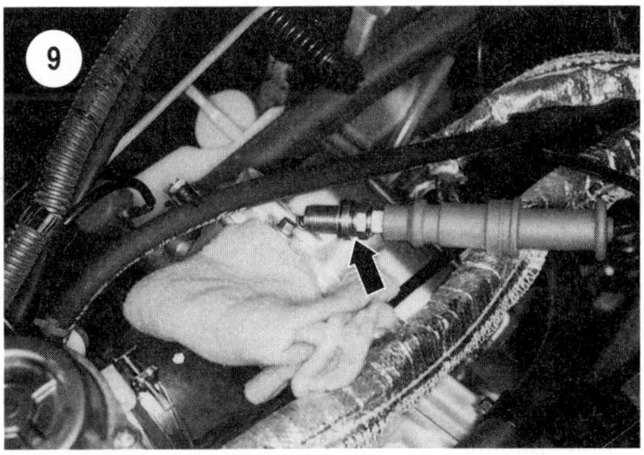

9

strong spark, perform Step 7. If there is no spark or if the spark is very weak, test the ignition system as described in Chapter Eleven.

7. Check cylinder compression as follows:

NOTE
Refer to Chapter Three for spark plug removal information.

a. Remove and ground the spark plug shell against the cylinder head cover.

CAUTION
To prevent damage to the ignition system, ground the spark plug when performing the following steps.

b. Place your finger over the spark plug hole.

c. Operate the start button. When the piston comes up on the compression stroke, pressure in the cylinder should be felt coming from the spark plug hole. If so, the cylinder probably has sufficient compression to start the engine.

NOTE
There may still be a compression problem even though it passes the previous test. The compression cannot be tested with a gauge on this engine due to the compression release mechanism within the camshaft.

d. Install the spark plug and cap.

Engine Fails to Start (Spark Test)

Perform the following spark test to determine if the ignition system is operating properly.

CAUTION
Before removing the spark plugs in Step 1, clean all dirt and debris away from the plug base. Dirt that falls into the cylinder will cause rapid engine wear.

1. Refer to Chapter Three and disconnect the spark plug wire and remove the spark plug.

NOTE
*A spark tester is a useful tool for testing the ignition systems spark output. **Figure 8** shows the Motion Pro Ignition System Tester (part No. 08-0122). This tool is inserted in the spark plug cap and its base is grounded against the cylinder head. The tool's air gap is adjustable, and it allows the visual inspection of the spark while testing the intensity of the spark. This tool is available through most motorcycle and ATV dealerships.*

2. Insert the spark plug (**Figure 9**), or spark tester (**Figure 10**), into its cap and touch the spark plug

base against the cylinder head to ground it. Position the spark plug so the electrode is visible.

NOTE
If not using a spark tester, always use a new spark plug for this test procedure.

WARNING
Mount the spark plug, or tester, away from the spark plug hole in the cylinder so that the spark or tester cannot ignite the gasoline vapors in the cylinder. If the engine is flooded, do not perform this test. The firing of the spark plug can ignite fuel that is ejected through the spark plug hole.

3. Turn the key, or ignition switch to the ON position.

WARNING
Do ***not*** *hold the spark plug, wire or connector, or a serious electrical shock may result.*

4. Turn the engine over with the electric starter. A crisp blue spark should be evident across the spark plug electrode or spark tester terminals. If there is strong sunlight on the plug, shade the plug with a hand to better see the spark.
5. If the spark is good, check for one or more of the following possible malfunctions:
   a. Obstructed fuel line or fuel filter or malfunctioning fuel pump.
   b. Low compression or engine damage.
   c. Flooded engine.
6. If the spark is weak or if there is no spark, refer to *Engine is Difficult to Start* in this chapter.

NOTE
If the engine backfires during starting attempts, the ignition timing may be incorrect. Refer to ***Ignition Timing*** *in Chapter Three for more information.*

ENGINE IS DIFFICULT TO START

The following section groups the three main engine operating systems with probable causes.

Electrical System

An often-overlooked source of electrical malfunctions is the wiring harness and electrical connectors. Check these carefully when troubleshooting.

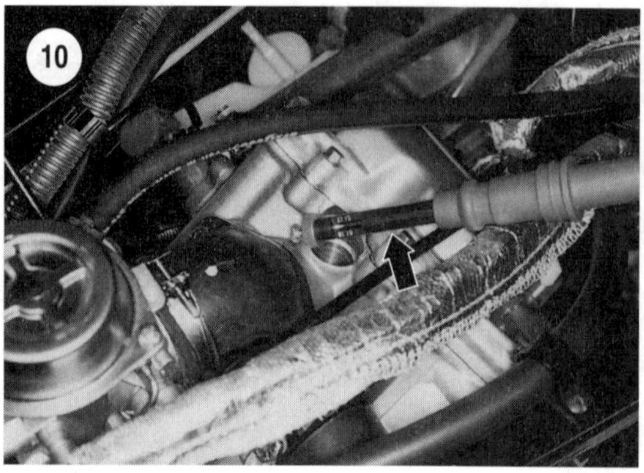

1. *Spark plug*—check for:
   a. Fouled spark plug.
   b. Incorrect spark plug gap.
   c. Incorrect spark plug heat range (Chapter Three).
   d. Worn or damaged spark plug electrodes.
   e. Damaged spark plug.
   f. Damaged spark plug cap or secondary wire.

NOTE
Refer to ***Reading Spark Plugs*** *in Chapter Three for additional information.*

2. *Ignition coil*—check for:
   a. Loose or damaged secondary or primary wire leads.
   b. Cracked ignition coil body.
   c. Loose or corroded ground wire.
3. *Switches and wiring*—check for:
   a. Dirty or loose-fitting terminals.
   b. Damaged wires or connectors.
   c. Damaged start switch.
   d. Damaged engine auxiliary shutoff switch.
   e. Damaged key, or ignition, switch.
4. *Electrical components*—check for:
   a. Damaged CDI stator.
   b. Damaged CDI unit.

Fuel System

A contaminated fuel system will cause engine starting- and performance-related problems. It only takes a small amount of dirt in the fuel valve, fuel line or carburetor to cause problems.

1. *Air filter*:
   a. Clogged air filter.
   b. Clogged air filter housing.
   c. Leaking or damaged air filter housing-to-carburetor air boot.
2. *Fuel shutoff valve*:
   a. Clogged fuel hose.
   b. Clogged fuel valve filter.
3. *Fuel tank*:
   a. No fuel.
   b. Clogged fuel filter.
   c. Contaminated fuel.
4. *Carburetor*:
   a. Clogged or damaged choke system.
   b. Clogged main jet.
   c. Clogged slow jet.
   d. Loose slow jet or main jet.
   e. Clogged slow jet air passages.
   f. Incorrect float level.
   g. Leaking or damaged float.
   h. Severely worn or damaged needle valve.
5. *Fuel pump*:
   a. Fuel pump filter clogged.
   b. Fuel pump electrical connector faulty, corroded or disconnected

Engine Compression

1. *Cylinder and cylinder head*:
   a. Loose spark plug.
   b. Missing spark plug gasket.
   c. Leaking cylinder head gasket.
   d. Leaking cylinder block base gasket.
   e. Severely worn or seized piston, piston rings and/or cylinder walls.
   f. Loose cylinder block and/or cylinder head fasteners.
   g. Cylinder head incorrectly installed and/or not tightened to the correct torque specification.
   h. Warped cylinder head.
   i. Blown head gasket.
   j. Blown cylinder block base gasket.
   k. Loose cylinder fasteners.
2. *Piston and piston rings*:
   a. Worn piston rings.
   b. Damaged piston rings.
   c. Piston seizure or piston damage.
3. *Crankcase and crankshaft*:
   a. Seized connecting rod.
   b. Damaged crankcase.
   c. Damaged oil seals.

Poor Idle Speed Performance

If the engine starts but off-idle performance is poor (engine hesitation, cutting out, etc.), check the following:
1. Clogged or damaged air filter.
2. *Carburetor*:
   a. Clogged slow jet.
   b. Loose slow jet.
   c. Damaged choke system.
   d. Incorrect throttle cable adjustment.
   e. Incorrect carburetor adjustment.
   f. Flooded carburetor (visually check carburetor overflow hose for fuel).
   g. Vacuum piston doesn't slide smoothly in carburetor bore.
3. *Fuel*:
   a. Water and/or alcohol in fuel.
   b. Old fuel.
4. *Engine*:
   a. Low engine compression.
5. *Electrical system*:
   a. Damaged spark plug.
   b. Damaged ignition coil.
   c. Damaged CDI trigger coil.
   d. Damaged CDI unit.

Poor Medium- and High-Speed Performance

Refer to *Engine is Difficult to Start*, then check the following:
1. *Carburetor*:
   a. Incorrect fuel level.
   b. Incorrect jet needle clip position (if adjustable).
   c. Clogged or loose main jet.
2. *Clogged air filter.*
3. *Other considerations*:
   a. Overheating.
   b. Clutch/drive belt slippage.
   c. Brake drag.
   d. Engine oil viscosity too high or oil level too high.

ENGINE STARTING SYSTEM

The starting system consists of the starter motor, battery, starter relay and switch. This section describes procedures for troubleshooting the system. A fully charged battery, ohmmeter and jumper cables are required for these tests.

If the starter does not operate, perform the following tests before going any farther. After each test, reconnect any connector that was disconnected before proceeding.

1. Make sure the battery is fully charged and that all cables and connections are correct, undamaged, clean and secure.
2. Make sure all electrical connections are clean and secure. Inspect the wiring harness for damage.

Starter Troubleshooting

If the starter does not operate, perform the following. When operating the starter button, turn the engine shutoff switch to RUN and the key switch to ON.

CAUTION

Do not operate an electric starter motor continuously for more than 5 seconds. Allow the motor to cool for at least 15 seconds between attempts to start the engine.

1. Check the 20A circuit breaker (**Figure 11**) next to the battery. If necessary, open the pouch and reset the breaker, then go on to the next step.
2. Test the battery as described under *Battery* in Chapter Three. If the battery voltage is not within the prescribed range, clean and recharge the battery as described under *Battery* in Chapter Three. Replace a damaged battery.
3. Disconnect the following switches one by one (in the sequence provided) and test them as described under *Switches* in Chapter Eleven. If the switch operates correctly, reinstall the switch and test the next one. If the switch does not operate correctly, replace it.
   a. Key (or ignition) or start switch.
   b. Start switch.
   c. Engine auxiliary shutoff switch.
4. Disconnect the red/white electrical connector from the starter solenoid. Connect a voltmeter black test lead to ground and the red test lead to the red/white connector on the harness side. Turn the key switch to the ON position and depress the start button. There should be battery voltage. Connect an ohmmeter between the red wire terminal and the solenoid mounting plate. The specified resistance is 3.4 ohms.
   a. If the starter circuit solenoid tested correctly, perform Step 5.
   b. If the starter circuit solenoid did not test correctly, replace the solenoid and retest.
5. If the switches and solenoid tested successfully, recheck the wiring for dirty or loose-fitting terminals or damaged wires; clean and repair as required. If all the connectors and wires are in good condition, the starter motor is probably defective. Remove and overhaul the starter motor as described under *Starter* in Chapter Eleven.
6. Make sure all connectors disassembled during this procedure are free of corrosion and are reconnected properly.

11

CHARGING SYSTEM

A malfunction in the charging system generally causes the battery to remain undercharged.

Troubleshooting

Before testing the charging system, visually check the following.

1. Check the battery connections at the battery. If polarity is, or was, reversed, check for a damaged regulator/rectifier.
2. Check for loose or corroded battery cable connectors.
3. Inspect all wiring between the battery and CDI stator for worn or cracked insulation or loose connections. Replace wiring or clean and tighten connections as required.
4. Check battery condition. Clean and recharge as required. See *Battery* in Chapter Three.

5. Perform the *Charging System Output Test* listed under *Charging System* in Chapter Eleven.
6. Test the regulator/rectifier as described under *Regulator/Rectifier* in Chapter Eleven.

IGNITION SYSTEM

All models are equipped with a transistorized ignition system (**Figure 12**). Refer to the wiring diagrams at the end of this book for the specific model and year being worked on.

Because of the solid-state design, problems with the transistorized system are rare. If a problem occurs, it generally causes a weak spark or no spark at all. An ignition system with a weak spark or no spark is relatively easy to troubleshoot. It is difficult, however, to troubleshoot an ignition system that only malfunctions when the engine is hot or under load.

Ignition System Precautions

Certain measures must be taken to protect the ignition system.

1. Never disconnect any of the electrical connectors while the engine is running.
2. Apply dielectric grease to all electrical connectors prior to reconnecting them. This will help seal out moisture.
3. Make sure all electrical connectors are free of corrosion and are securely coupled.
4. The CDI unit must always be mounted securely to the frame.

Troubleshooting Preparation

Refer to the wiring diagrams at the end of this book for the specific model being worked on when performing the following.

1. Check the wiring harness for visible signs of damage.
2. Make sure all connectors are properly attached to each other and locked in place.
3. Check all electrical components for a good ground to the engine.
4. Check all wiring for short circuits or open circuits.
5. Make sure the fuel tank has an adequate supply of fresh gasoline and is full.
6. Make sure the spark plug cable is properly connected to the spark plug.
7. Remove the spark plug and examine it as described in Chapter Three.

Switch Test

Test the ignition switch and the engine auxiliary shutoff switch as described in Chapter Eleven.

Ignition Coil Test

The ignition coil is located under the front fender cover.

1. Remove the front fender cover (**Figure 13**) as described in Chapter Fifteen.
2. Disconnect the white/blue primary electrical connector from the ignition coil (**Figure 14**).
3. Measure the ignition coil primary resistance using an ohmmeter set at R × 1. Measure resistance between the primary wire terminal and the coil ground lug (**Figure 15**). Refer to **Table 1** for test specifications.
4. To measure the secondary resistance as follows:
   a. Remove the spark plug cap from the secondary cable.
   b. Using an ohmmeter set at R × 1K, measure resistance between the secondary cable and the coil ground lug (**Figure 15**). Refer to **Table 1** for test specifications.
   c. Install the cap onto the secondary cable.
5. Connect the white/blue primary electrical connector (**Figure 14**) onto the ignition coil.
6. If the ignition coil does not meet any of these specifications, the coil must be replaced. If the coil exhibits visual damage, replace the coil as described in Chapter Eleven.
7. Install the front fender cover (**Figure 13**) as described in Chapter Fifteen.

Exciter (Stator) Coil and Trigger Coil Test

Refer to **Table 1** for test specifications.

1. Locate the electrical cables leading from the engine flywheel CDI stator to the CDI unit. Carefully disconnect the exciter coil and trigger coil connectors from the CDI unit.
2. Measure the exciter coil resistance using an ohmmeter set at R × 100. Measure resistance be-

(12)

IGNITION SYSTEM

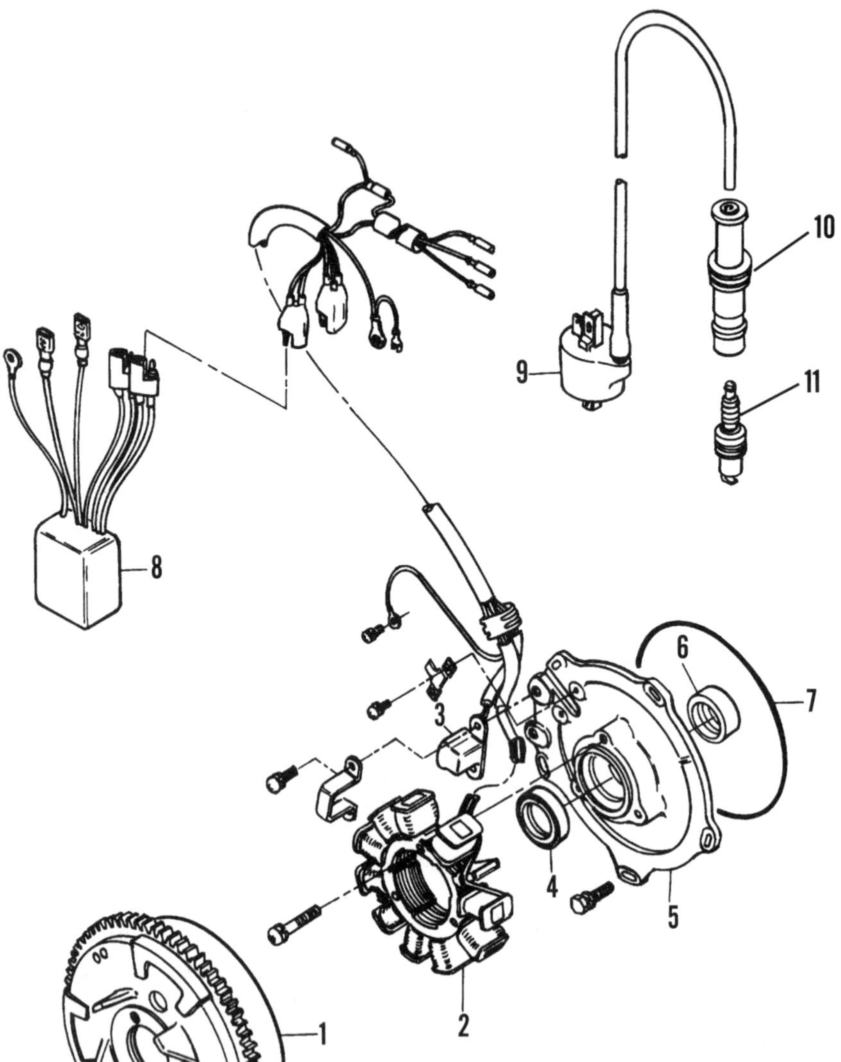

1. Flywheel
2. Stator coils
3. Trigger coil
4. Seal
5. Stator plate
6. Bushing
7. O-ring
8. CDI unit
9. Ignition high tension coil
10. Spark plug cap
11. Spark plug

13

14

15

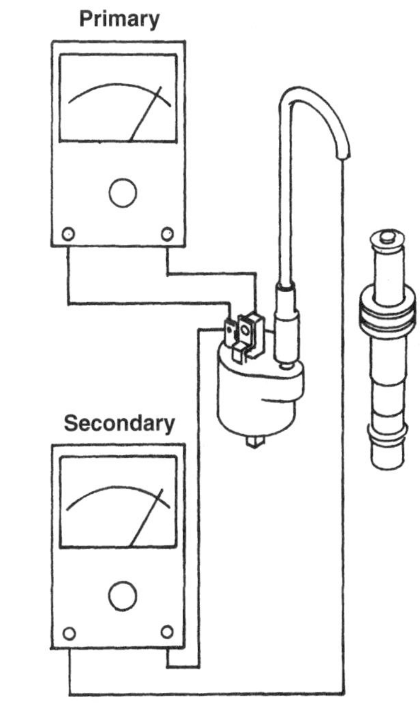

tween the following terminals on the alternator side of the connectors and check the resistance:

a. Between red and green terminals.
b. Between black/red and green terminals.

3. Measure the CDI trigger coil resistance using an ohmmeter set at R × 100. Measure resistance between the white and white/red terminals on the CDI magneto side.
4. If either the exciter coil and/or trigger coil does not meet any of these specifications, the CDI stator assembly must be replaced. The individual coils cannot be replaced.
5. If the coils test acceptably, reconnect the exciter coil and trigger coil connectors to the CDI unit.

ELECTRONIC THROTTLE CONTROL

The electronic throttle control (ETC) disables the vehicle if there is a mechanical problem in the throttle mechanism. When the throttle is operating normally, throttle cable tension holds the ETC switch in the open position. If a mechanical failure occurs in the throttle mechanism and cable tension is lost, the switch contacts close. This grounds the CDI unit and disables the ignition system. The ETC is an important safety device. Do not operate the ATV with the ETC disabled.

Electronic Throttle Control Switch Testing

1. Use a screwdriver to remove the throttle control cover.
2. Shift the transmission into NEUTRAL and apply the parking brake.
3. Block the rear wheels so the vehicle will not roll in either direction.
4. Start the engine and open the throttle lever slightly to increase engine RPM just above idle speed.
5. Use a finger and hold the throttle cable (A, **Figure 16**) stationary, then release the throttle lever (B, **Figure 16**).

6A. On 1996-1998 models, the engine rpm should be limited to the specified ECT limit of 1400 rpm. If the engine continues to run at a higher rpm, the switch is faulty and must be replaced. Refer to Chapter Eleven.

6B. On 1999-on models, the engine should lose spark and stop. If the engine continues to run, the switch (C, **Figure 16**) is faulty and must be replaced. Refer to Chapter Eleven.

7. Install the throttle control cover.

FUEL SYSTEM

Do not automatically assume that the carburetor is at fault when the engine does not run properly. While fuel system problems are not uncommon, carburetor adjustment is seldom the answer. In many cases, adjustment will only compound the problem by making the engine run worse.

Begin fuel system troubleshooting with the fuel tank and work through the system, reserving the carburetor as the final point. Most fuel system problems result from an empty fuel tank, a plugged fuel filter or fuel valve, fuel pump failure or old fuel. Fuel system troubleshooting is covered thoroughly under *Engine Is Difficult To Start*, *Poor Idle Speed Performance* and *Poor Medium- and High-Speed Performance* in this chapter.

ENGINE OVERHEATING

Engine overheating is a serious problem that can quickly cause engine seizure and damage. The following section groups five main systems with probable causes that can cause engine overheating.

1. *Ignition system*:
   a. Incorrect spark plug gap.
   b. Incorrect spark plug heat range (Chapter Three).
   c. Defective CDI unit/incorrect ignition timing.
2. *Engine compression system*:
   a. Cylinder head gasket leakage.
   b. Heavy carbon buildup in combustion chamber.
3. *Engine cooling system*:
   a. Improper spark plug heat range.
   b. Cooling system malfunction.
   c. Clogged radiator.
   d. Thermostat stuck closed.
   e. Worn or damaged radiator cap.
   f. Fan switch malfunction.
   g. Damaged cooling fan blades.
   h. Clogged or blocked coolant passages in radiator, hoses or engine.
   i. Oil level low.

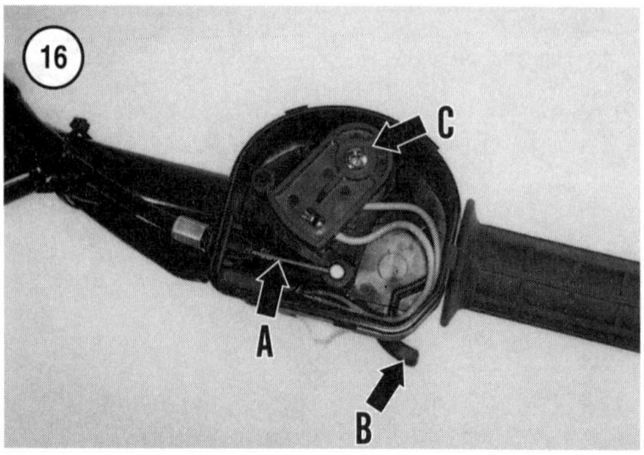

   j. Oil not circulating properly.
   k. Valves leaking.
   l. Dragging brakes.
   m. Clutch/drive belt slippage.
   n. Heavy carbon buildup in combustion chamber.
4. *Fuel system*:
   a. Clogged air filter element.
   b. Carburetor fuel level too low.
   c. Incorrect carburetor adjustment or jetting.
   d. Loose carburetor hose clamps.
   e. Leaking or damaged carburetor-to-air filter housing air boot.
   f. Incorrect air/fuel mixture.
5. *Engine load*—check for:
   a. Dragging brake(s).
   b. Damaged drive train components.
   c. Slipping clutch/drive belt.
   d. Engine oil level too high.

ENGINE

Preignition

Preignition is the premature burning of fuel and is caused by hot spots in the combustion chamber. Glowing deposits in the combustion chamber, inadequate cooling or an overheated spark plug can all cause preignition. This is first noticed as a power loss but will eventually result in damage to the internal parts of the engine because of higher combustion chamber temperatures.

Detonation

Commonly called *spark or fuel knock*, detonation is the violent explosion of fuel in the combustion chamber before the proper time of combustion. Severe engine damage can result if this condition persists. Use of low-octane gasoline is a common cause of detonation.

Even when using a high-octane gasoline, detonation can still occur. Other causes are over-advanced ignition timing, lean fuel mixture at or near full throttle, inadequate engine cooling, or the excessive accumulation of carbon deposits in the combustion chamber.

Power Loss

Several factors can cause a lack of power and speed. Look for a clogged air filter or a fouled or damaged spark plug. Galled piston or cylinder, incorrect piston clearance or worn or sticky piston rings may be responsible for any power loss. Look for loose bolts, defective gaskets or leaking machined mating surfaces on the cylinder head, cylinder block or crankcase.

Piston Seizure

This is caused by incorrect bore clearance, piston rings with an improper end gap, compression leak, incorrect air/fuel mixture, a spark plug of the wrong heat range or incorrect ignition timing. Overheating from any cause may result in piston seizure.

Piston Slap

Piston slap is an audible slapping or rattling noise resulting from excessive piston-to-cylinder clearance. When allowed to continue, piston slap will eventually cause the piston skirt to shatter.

To prevent piston slap, clean the air filter on a regular schedule. When piston slap can be heard, disassemble the engine top end and measure the cylinder bore and piston diameter and check for excessive clearance. Replace parts that exceed wear limits or show damage.

ENGINE NOISES

1. *Knocking or pinging during acceleration* can be caused by using a lower octane fuel than recommended or a poor grade of fuel. Incorrect carburetor jetting and a too hot spark plug can cause pinging. Refer to *Spark Plug Heat Range* in Chapter Three. Check also for excessive carbon buildup in the combustion chamber or a defective ignition system CDI unit.
2. *Slapping or rattling noises at low speed or during acceleration* can be caused by excessive piston-to-cylinder wall clearance. Check also for a bent connecting rod or worn piston pin and/or piston pin hole in the piston.
3. *Knocking or rapping while decelerating* usually caused by excessive rod bearing clearance.
4. *Persistent knocking and vibration or other noise* usually caused by worn main bearings. If the main bearings are acceptable, consider the following:
   a. Loose engine mounts.
   b. Cracked frame.
   c. Leaking cylinder head gasket.
   d. Exhaust pipe leakage at cylinder head.
   e. Stuck piston ring(s).
   f. Broken piston ring(s).
   g. Partial engine seizure.
   h. Excessive connecting rod bearing clearances.
   i. Excessive connecting rod big end side clearance.
   j. Excessive crankshaft runout.
   k. Worn or damaged primary drive gear.
5. *Rapid on-off squeal* indicates a compression leak around cylinder head gasket or spark plug.

CYLINDER LEAKDOWN TEST

A cylinder leakdown test can isolate an engine malfunction caused by a leaking valve, defective cylinder head gasket, worn, stuck or broken piston ring(s), or defective piston. Perform a cylinder leakdown test by applying compressed air into the cylinder, then measuring the percent of leakage. A cylinder leakage tester (**Figure 17**) and an air compressor are required to perform this test.

Follow the manufacturer's directions along with the following information when performing a cylinder leak down test.

1. Start and run the engine until it reaches normal operating temperature, then turn off the engine.
2. Remove the air filter assembly. Open and secure the throttle so that it is at its wide-open position.
3. Set the piston to TDC on its compression stroke. See *Valve Clearance Check and Adjustment* in Chapter Three.

17

LEAKDOWN TESTER

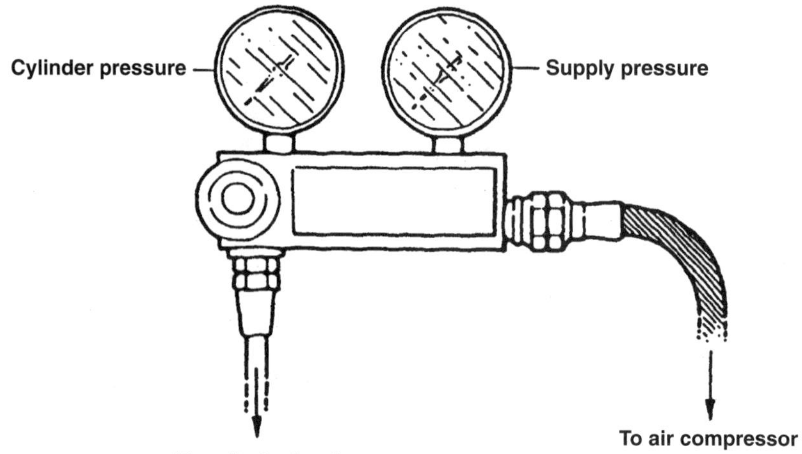

4. Remove the spark plug cap and the spark plug as described in Chapter Three.

NOTE
The engine may turn over when air pressure is applied to the cylinder. To prevent this from happening, shift the low range and set the parking brake.

5. Install the leakdown tester into the cylinder spark plug hole (**Figure 18**).
6. Apply pressure to the cylinder following the manufacturer's instructions. Listen for air leaking while noting the following:
   a. Air leaking through the exhaust pipe indicates a leaking exhaust valve.
   b. Air leaking through the carburetor or throttle body indicates a leaking intake valve.
   c. Air leaking through the crankcase breather tube indicates worn piston rings.
7. A cylinder with 10% cylinder leakdown requires further service.
8. Install the spark plug and the air filter assembly.

POWER TRAIN

The following items provide a starting point from which to troubleshoot power train malfunctions. The possible causes for each malfunction are listed in a logical sequence.

Low Engine Operating Speed (Engine Running Properly, but Lugs)

1. Drive pulley spring is broken or wrong spring.
2. Drive pulley weight is too heavy.
3. Drive belt is slipping.

Engine Operating Speed Too High

1. Incorrect drive pulley spring.
2. Drive pulley weights are too light.
3. Drive pulley is binding.
4. Driven pulley is binding.

Engine Speed Erratic During Speed or Load Changes

1. Drive pulley is binding.
2. Driven pulley is binding.
3. Pulley grooves are worn.

Harsh Engagement

1. The drive belt is worn (too narrow).
2. Incorrect pulley-to-pulley clearance (1996-1998 models).

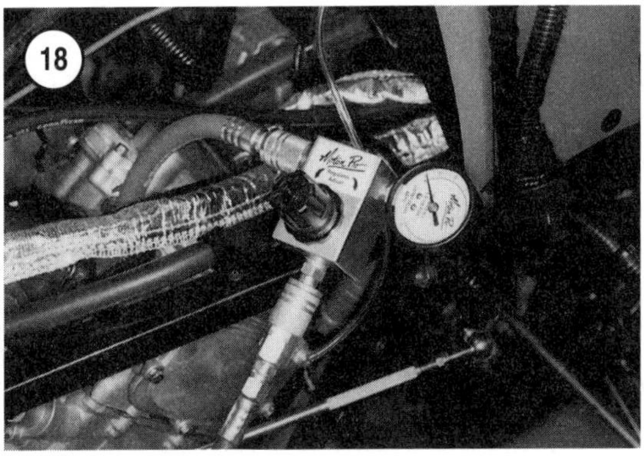

Drive Belt Not Operating Smoothly in Primary Sheave

1. The drive pulley face is rough, grooved, pitted or scored.
2. The drive belt is worn and/or defective.

Drive Belt Edge Cord Failure or Uneven Drive Belt Wear

1. The drive and driven pulleys are misaligned.
2. The engine mounts are loose.

Glazed Drive Belt

1. Excessive slippage. May be caused by sticking brakes.
2. Engine idle speed set too high.

Drive Belt Too Tight at Idle

1. Engine idle speed set too high.
2. Incorrect distance between pulleys.
3. Incorrect drive belt length.

Drive Belt Turns Over

1. Incorrect drive belt.
2. Incorrect drive belt alignment.
3. Engine mount broken or loose.

Brake Not Holding Properly

1. Incorrect brake adjustment.
2. Worn brake pads.
3. Worn brake disks.
4. Contaminated brake pads.
5. Sheared key on brake disc.
6. Air in brake lines.

Leaking Transmission

1. Loose bolts.
2. Damaged gasket seal.
3. Damaged seals.
4. Cracked or broken case and/or cover.

Drive Clutch Engages Before Specified Engagement RPM

1. Worn spring.
2. Incorrect width.

Drive Clutch Engages After Specified Engagement RPM

1. Incorrect spring.
2. Worn or damaged secondary sheave buttons.

Erratic Shifting

1. Worn rollers and bushings.
2. Scuffed or damaged weights.
3. Dirty drive pulley assembly.
4. Worn or damaged driven pulley ramps.

Engine Bogs Down During Engagement

1. Incorrect driven pulley width adjustment.
2. Drive belt worn too thin.
3. Incorrect distance between drive and driven pulleys.

Drive or Driven Pulley Sticks

1. Damaged pulley assembly.
2. Movable pulley damaged.
3. Dirty pulley assembly.

STEERING

Description of handling problems are subjective, but the following items will provide a starting point from which to troubleshoot handling and steering problems. Some possible causes for each malfunction are listed in a logical sequence.

19

DISC BRAKE TROUBLESHOOTING

Disc brake fluid leakage	Check: • Loose or damaged line fittings • Worn caliper piston seals • Scored caliper piston and/or bore • Loose banjo bolts • Damaged washers • Leaking master cylinder diaphragm • Leaking master cylinder secondary seal • Cracked master cylinder housing • Brake fluid level too high • Loose or damaged master cylinder cover
Brake overheating	Check: • Warped brake disc • Caliper piston and/or brake pads sticking • Riding brakes
Brake chatter	Check: • Warped brake disc • Loose brake disc • Incorrect caliper alignment • Loose caliper mounting bolts • Loose front axle nut and/or clamps • Worn wheel bearings • Damaged hub • Restricted brake hydraulic line • Contaminated brake pads
Brake locking	Check: • Incorrect brake fluid • Plugged passages in master cylinder • Incorrect front brake adjustment • Caliper piston and/or brake adjustment • Warped brake disc
Insufficient brakes	Check: • Air in brake lines • Worn brake pads • Low brake fluid • Incorrect brake fluid • Worn brake disc • Worn caliper piston seals • Glazed brake pads • Leaking primary cup seal in master cylinder • Contaminated brake pads and/or disc
Brake squeal	Check: • Contaminated brake pads and/or disc • Dust or dirt collected behind brake pads • Loose parts

Generally Poor or Unpredictable Handling

1. Improper tire inflation pressure.
2. Improperly adjusted wheel alignment.
3. Worn or damaged steering components.
4. Worn or damaged suspension components.
5. Bent or broken frame.

Loose Steering

1. Loose steering shaft, bushings or steering shaft fasteners.
2. Loose tie rod ends.
3. Worn spindle bushings.

Unequal Steering

1. Improperly adjusted tie rods.
2. Improperly adjusted steering stops.
3. Damaged steering components.
4. Uneven front tire pressure.

Steering Wanders

1. Loose or worn steering components.
2. Improperly adjusted wheel alignment (toe out).
3. Worn or damaged tires.
4. Damaged shock absorber(s).
5. Bent or broken frame.

FRAME NOISE

Noises traced to the frame or suspension are usually caused by loose, worn or damaged parts. Various noises that are related to the frame are listed below:

1. *Disc brake noise*—A screeching sound during braking is the most common disc brake noise. Some other disc brake associated noises can be caused by:
   a. Glazed brake pad surface.
   b. Excessively worn brake pads.
   c. Warped brake disc(s).
   d. Loose brake disc mounting bolts.
   e. Loose or missing caliper mounting bolts.
   f. Damaged caliper(s).
   g. Cracked wheel flange or bosses, where the brake disc mounts to the hub flange.
2. *Front shock absorber noise*:
   a. Cracked or broken shock spring(s).
   b. Damage shock absorber(s).
   c. Loose shock absorber mounting bolts and nuts.
3. *Rear shock absorber noise*:
   a. Loose shock absorber mounting bolts and nuts.
   b. Cracked or broken shock spring.
   c. Damaged shock absorber(s).
4. Some other frame associated noises can be caused by:
   a. Cracked or broken frame.
   b. Cracked or broken rear upper and lower suspension control arms.
   c. Loose engine mounting bolts.
   d. Damaged steering shaft bearings.
   e. Loose mounting bracket.

BRAKES

The front and rear brake units are critical to riding performance and safety. Inspect the brake system frequently and repair any problem immediately. When replacing or refilling the disc brake fluid, use only DOT 3 brake fluid from a closed and sealed container. See Chapter Fourteen for additional information on brake fluid selection and disc brake service. The troubleshooting procedures in **Figure 19** will help to isolate the majority of disc brake troubles.

When checking brake pad wear, check that the brake pads in each caliper contact the disc squarely. If one of the brake pads is wearing unevenly, suspect a warped or bent brake disc or damaged caliper.

Table 1 is on the following page.

Table 1 ELECTRICAL SPECIFICATIONS

Item	Specification
Alternator stator coils	
Exciter coils (1996-1998)	
Between red and green	3.2 ohms
Between black/red and green	446 ohms
Exciter coils (1999-on)	
Between red and green	1.6 ohms
Between black/red and green	446 ohms
Trigger coil	
Between white and white/red	97 ohms
Charge coil (1996-1998)	
Yellow to yellow/brown	0.17 ohm
Yellow/red to yellow/brown	0.17 ohm
Charge coil (1999-on)	
Yellow to yellow/red	0.13 ohm
Yellow to ground	infinity
Ignition coil	
Primary resistance	0.3 ohm
Secondary resistance	6.3K ohms
Starter solenoid resistance	3.4 ohms

NOTE: Refer to the Supplement at the back of this manual for information unique to 2001-on models, including the Sportsman 400.

3

CHAPTER THREE

LUBRICATION, MAINTENANCE AND TUNE-UP

This chapter covers lubrication, maintenance and tune-up procedures. A maintenance schedule, specifications, lubricants and capacities are listed in **Tables 1-6** at the end of this chapter.

To maximize the service life of the ATV and gain the utmost in safety and performance, it is necessary to perform periodic inspections and maintenance. Minor problems found during routine service can be corrected before they develop into major ones.

The recommended maintenance schedule (**Table 1**) is to be considered as a guideline. If the ATV is operated under severe conditions (high humidity, partial water submersion, muddiness, etc.) perform the services more frequently.

Most of the service procedures in the schedule are described in this chapter, however, those that require more than minor disassembly or adjustment are covered in the appropriate chapters.

PRE-RIDE CHECKLIST

Perform the following checks prior to the first ride of the day. All of these checks are described in this chapter. If a component requires service, refer to the appropriate section.

At the end of each riding day, clean the ATV thoroughly and inspect it carefully. Then give it a good general lubrication and make any adjustments necessary.

1. Check the engine oil level in the oil tank. Remove the oil fill cap/dipstick (**Figure 1**). Wipe it clean. Reinsert the dipstick and remove it. The oil

level must be between the upper and lower lines on the dipstick (**Figure 2**). If necessary, add the correct type of oil to bring the level up to the upper line. Refer to **Table 3**.

2. Check the transmission oil level as follows:
   a. Remove the oil fill dipstick (**Figure 3**) and wipe it clean. Reinsert the dipstick and remove it.
   b. The oil level must be within the knurled section of the dipstick (**Figure 4**).
   c. If necessary, add the correct type of oil to bring the level within the knurled section of the dipstick. Refer to **Table 3**.
   d. Install the oil fill cap/dipstick.

WARNING
*When performing any service work to the engine or cooling system, never remove the radiator cap (**Figure 5**), coolant drain screws or disconnect any coolant hose when the engine and radiator are hot. Scalding fluid and steam are under pressure and will cause serious injury if allowed to escape.*

3. Check the coolant level with the engine cold. Check the cooling system for leaks and make sure the coolant is up to the FULL mark on the coolant reservoir (**Figure 6**). Always add coolant to the reservoir tank, not the radiator.

4. Turn the handlebar from side to side and check for steering play. Check that the control cables are properly routed and do not interfere with the handlebar or the handlebar controls.

5. Check the throttle operation. Open the throttle all the way and release it. The throttle should close quickly with no binding or roughness. Repeat this step with the handlebar facing straight ahead and both full lock positions.

6. Check that the front master cylinder brake lever and rear master cylinder pedal operate properly with no binding. Replace any broken lever or pedal. Check the lever and pedal housings for damage.

WARNING
When checking the brake lever, check the ball on the end of the lever. If it is broken off, replace the lever immediately. The lever balls help to prevent the lever from puncturing a hand or arm during a fall or crash.

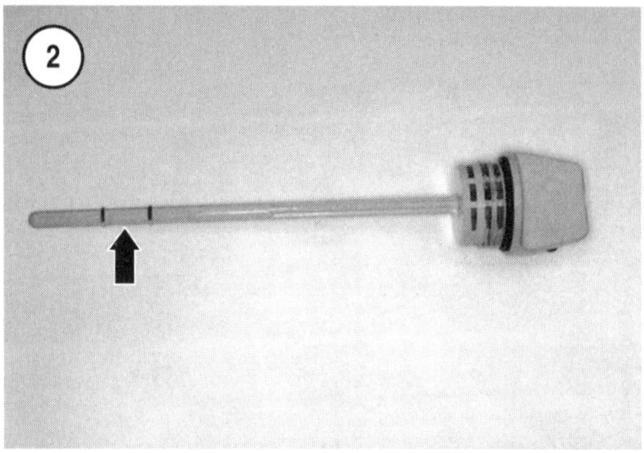

7. Inspect the front and rear suspension; make sure they have a good solid feel with no looseness.

8. Check all four wheels and tires for damage.

9. Make sure the air filter element is clean and that the air box and carburetor or throttle body boots are secured tightly.

10. Check tire pressure as listed in **Table 2**.

11. Check the exhaust system for looseness or damage.

12. Check the tightness of all fasteners, especially engine, steering and suspension mounting hardware.

13. Make sure the fuel tank is full of fresh gasoline.

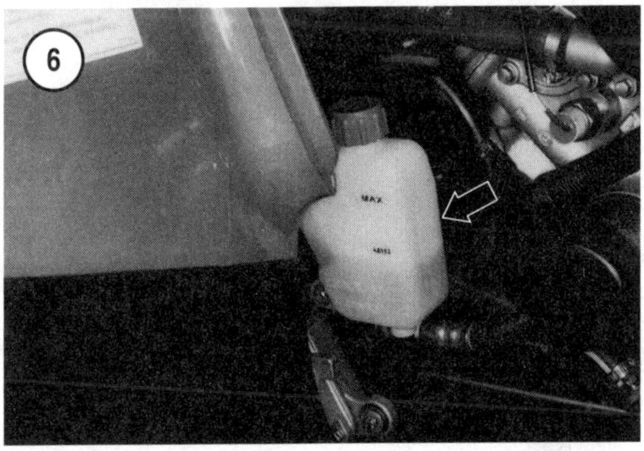

14. Inspect the fuel lines and fittings for wetness.
15. Check the brake fluid level in both brake master cylinder reservoirs. If necessary, add DOT 3 brake fluid to bring the level up to the maximum line. Refer to **Table 3**.

TIRES AND WHEELS

Tire Pressure

Check and adjust the tire pressure to achieve good traction and handling, and to get the maximum life out of the tires. Carry a simple, accurate low-pressure gauge in the toolbox. The appropriate tire pressures are listed in **Table 2**. Check tire pressure when the tires are cold.

WARNING
Always inflate both tire sets (front and rear) tires to correct air pressure. If the vehicle is run with unequal air pressures, the vehicle will run toward one side, causing poor handling.

CAUTION
Do not over-inflate the tires, as they will be permanently distorted and damaged. Over-inflated tires will cause poor handling and abnormal tire wear.

NOTE
*The tire pressure specifications listed in **Table 2** are for the original tires. If different tires have been installed, follow the tire pressure recommendations specified by the tire manufacturer.*

NOTE
After checking and adjusting the air pressure, make sure to reinstall the air valve cap. The cap prevents small pebbles from collecting in the valve stem; this could allow air leakage or result in incorrect tire pressure reading.

Tire Inspection

The tires take a lot of punishment due to the variety of terrain they are subjected to. Inspect them periodically for excessive wear, cuts, abrasions, etc. If a nail or other object is found in the tire, mark its location with a light crayon prior to removing it. This will help locate the hole for repair. Refer to Chapter Twelve for tire changing and repair information.

To gauge tire wear, inspect the shape of the tread knobs. To get an accurate measurement of tire wear, measure a number of different knobs around the tire. If the drive knob vertical sides (**Figure 7**) are worn to less than 3 mm (1/8 in.), replace the tire as described in Chapter Twelve.

WARNING
Do not ride the vehicle with damaged or severely worn tires. Replace dam-

aged or severely worn tires immediately.

Rim Inspection

Frequently inspect the condition of the wheel rims, especially the outer side. If the wheel has hit a tree or large rock, rim damage may be sufficient to cause an air leak or knock it out of alignment. Improper wheel alignment can cause severe vibration and result in an unsafe riding condition.

Make sure the wheel lug nuts are securely in place on all wheels. If they are loose, the wheel could damage the hub studs or fall off. Tighten wheel lug nuts to the torque specification listed in **Table 5**.

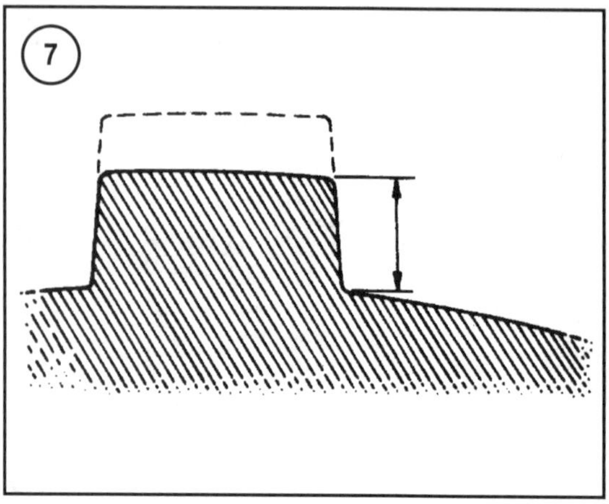

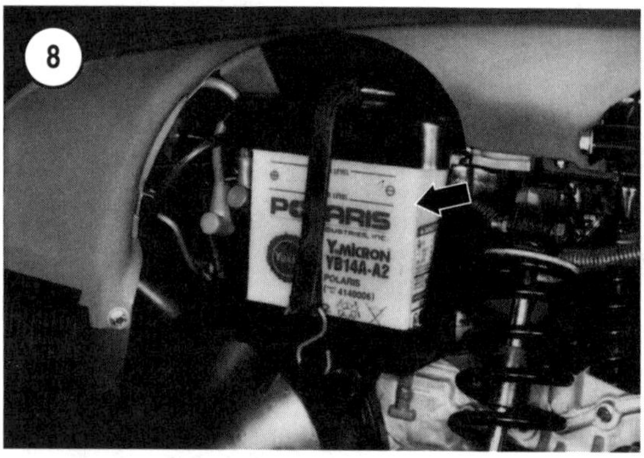

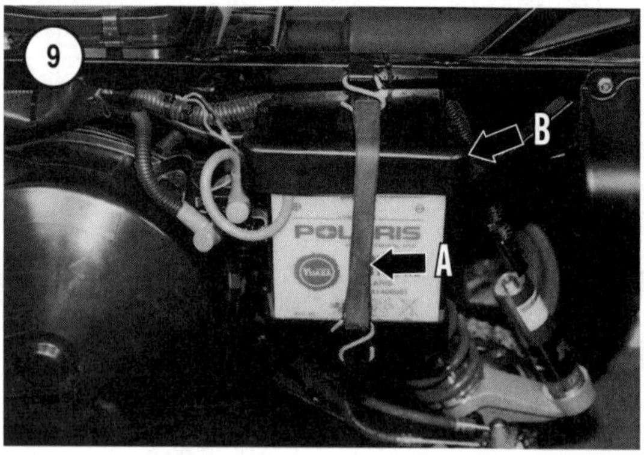

BATTERY

The battery is an important component in the electrical system. Yet most electrical system troubles can be traced to battery neglect. Therefore, clean and inspect the battery and electrolyte level once each week.

On all models covered in this manual, the negative side is grounded. When removing the battery, disconnect the negative cable first, then the positive cable. This minimizes the chance of a tool shorting to ground when disconnecting the positive battery cable.

Safety Precautions

When working with a battery, use extreme care to avoid spilling or splashing the electrolyte. This solution contains sulfuric acid, which will ruin clothing and cause serious chemical skin burns. If any electrolyte is spilled or splashed on clothing or skin, immediately neutralize it with a solution of baking soda and water, then flush with an abundance of clean water.

WARNING

Electrolyte splashed into the eyes is extremely harmful. Always wear eye protection while working with a battery. If electrolyte gets into the eyes, call a physician immediately. Force the eyes open and flood them with cool, clean water for approximately 15 minutes.

While a battery is being charged, highly explosive hydrogen gas forms in each cell. Some of this gas escapes through filler cap openings and may form an explosive atmosphere in and around the battery. This condition can persist for several hours. Sparks, an open flame or a lit cigarette can ignite the gas, causing an explosion and possible serious personal injury.

Note the following precautions to prevent an explosion:

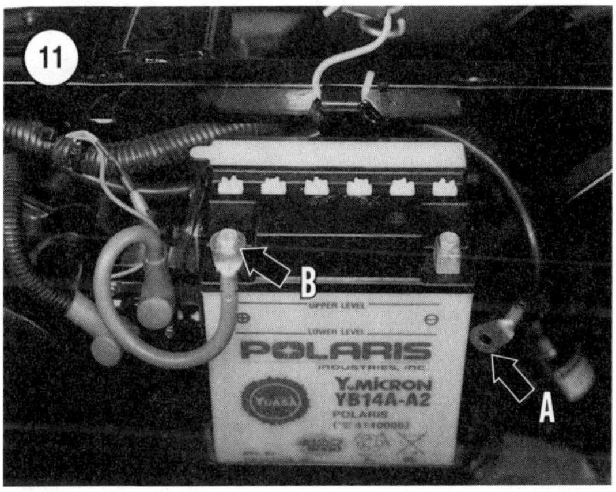

1. Do not allow anyone to smoke or permit any open flame near any battery being charged or recently charged battery.

2. Do not disconnect live circuits at battery terminals since a spark usually occurs when a live circuit is broken.

3. Be careful when connecting or disconnecting any battery charger. Make sure the main key switch is in the off position before making or breaking connections. Poor connections are a common cause of electrical arcs that cause explosions.

4. Keep children and pets away from charging equipment and batteries.

WARNING
When performing the following procedures, protect the eyes, skin and clothing. If electrolyte gets into the eyes, flush the eyes thoroughly with clean water and get prompt medical attention.

Electrolyte Level Check

1. Maintain the electrolyte level between the two marks on the battery case (**Figure 8**).
2. To adjust the electrolyte level, remove the battery from the frame as described in the next procedure. Do not add water while the battery is still in the frame as any spilled water along with electrolyte will flow onto the rear frame resulting in corrosion.
3. Make sure all cell caps are in place and are tight; tighten if necessary.
4. If the electrolyte level is correct, reinstall the battery.

Battery Removal/Installation

NOTE
The battery can be removed with the rear fender in place by removing the rear wheel, but the working room is very limited. Remove whatever component is most convenient.

1A. Remove the rear fender as described in Chapter Fifteen.
1B. Remove the left-hand rear wheel as described in Chapter Thirteen.
2. Use a stiff whiskbroom or brush and thoroughly clean off any debris from the top of the battery cover prior to removing any parts or connectors.
3. Unhook and remove the battery hold down strap (A, **Figure 9**).
4. Remove the battery cover (B, **Figure 9**).
5. Disconnect the battery vent hose (**Figure 10**) from the battery. Leave the vent hose routed through the frame.
6. Disconnect the negative battery cable (A, **Figure 11**) from the battery.
7. Disconnect the positive battery cable (B, **Figure 11**) from the battery.
8. Carefully lift the battery out of the battery frame tray and remove the battery.

CAUTION
Be careful not to spill battery electrolyte on painted or polished surfaces. The liquid is highly corrosive and will damage the finish. If it is spilled, wash it off immediately with soapy water and thoroughly rinse with clean water.

9. Inspect the cushion pads (**Figure 12**) in the battery frame tray for wear or deterioration. Replace if necessary.
10. Position the battery with the negative battery terminal toward the rear of the ATV.
11. Reinstall the battery into the battery frame tray.
12. Install and tighten the positive battery cable (B, **Figure 11**).
13. Install and tighten the negative battery cable (A, **Figure 11**).

CAUTION

Be sure the battery cables are connected to their proper terminals. The red battery cable must be connected to the positive battery terminal and the black battery cable must be connected to the negative battery terminal. Connecting the battery backwards will reverse the polarity and damage the voltage regulator/rectifier and CDI unit.

14. Coat the battery connections with dielectric grease or petroleum jelly to retard corrosion.
15A. If removed, install the rear fender as described in Chapter Fifteen.
15B. If removed, install the left-hand rear wheel as described in Chapter Thirteen.

Cleaning, Inspection and Adding Water

1. Inspect the battery pads in the battery frame tray for contamination or damage. Clean with a baking soda and water solution.
2. Check the entire battery case for cracks or other damage. If the battery case is warped, discolored or has a raised top, the battery has been suffering from overcharging or overheating.
3. Check the battery terminal bolts, spacers and nuts for corrosion, deterioration or damage. Clean parts thoroughly with a baking soda and water solution. Replace severely corroded or damaged parts.

NOTE

Keep cleaning solution out of the battery cells, or the electrolyte level will be seriously weakened.

4. Clean the top of the battery with a stiff bristle brush using the baking soda and water solution.

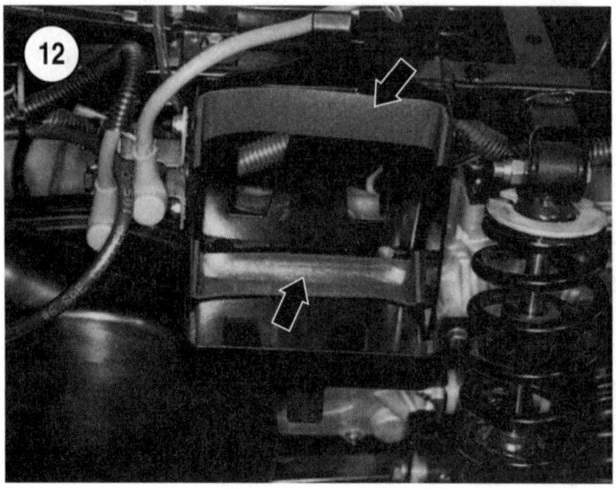

Thoroughly rinse off all baking soda residue with freshwater.

5. Check the battery cable clamps for corrosion and damage. If corrosion is minor, clean the battery cable clamps with a stiff wire brush. Replace severely worn or damaged cables.

NOTE

Do not overfill the battery cells in Step 6. The electrolyte expands due to heat

15

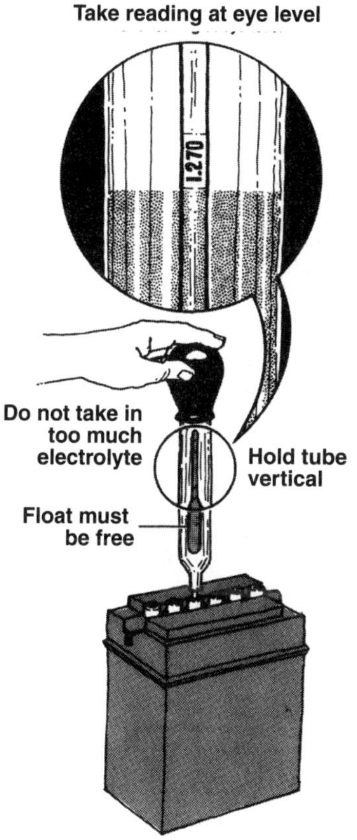

from charging and will overflow if the level is above the upper level line.

6. Remove the fill caps (**Figure 13**) from the battery cells and check the electrolyte level in each cell. Add distilled water, if necessary, to bring the level within the upper and lower level lines on the battery case (**Figure 14**). Install the caps and tighten securely.

CAUTION

Adding water to the cells will dilute the electrolyte. The diluted electrolyte can freeze and damage the battery during sub-freezing temperatures. Therefore, during cold weather, charge the battery after adding water to the cells.

Battery Testing

Checking the specific gravity of the battery electrolyte is the best way to check the state of charge of the battery. Specific gravity is the density of the electrolyte as compared to pure water. To check the specific gravity, use a hydrometer with numbered graduations from 1.100 to 1.300 rather than one with just color-coded bands. To use the hydrometer, squeeze the rubber ball, insert the tip into the cell and release the ball (**Figure 15**).

NOTE

Adding water to the cells will lower the specific gravity (density) of the electrolyte. After adding water charge the battery for 15-20 minutes at a rate high enough to cause vigorous gassing.

Draw sufficient electrolyte to float the weighted float inside the hydrometer. When using a temperature-compensated hydrometer, release the electrolyte and repeat this process several times to make sure the thermometer has had time to adjust to the electrolyte temperature before taking the reading.

Hold the hydrometer vertically and note the number in line with the surface of the electrolyte (**Figure 15**). This is the specific gravity for this cell. Return the electrolyte to the cell from which it came. The specific gravity of the electrolyte in each battery cell is an excellent indication of that cell's condition. Refer to **Figure 16**. A fully charged cell will read 1.260-1.280 while a cell in good condition reads from 1.230-1.250 and anything below 1.140 is discharged. Charging is also necessary if the specific gravity varies more than 0.050 from cell to cell. After charging, if the specific gravity still varies more than 0.050, the battery has failed.

NOTE

If a temperature-compensated hydrometer is not used, add 0.004 to the specific gravity reading for every 10° above 80° F (25° C). For every 10° below 80° F (25° C), subtract 0.004.

16

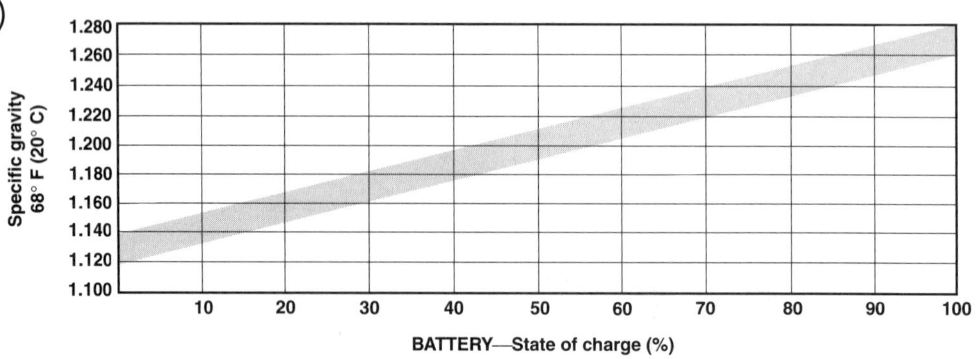

Charging

Maintain a good state of charge in a battery used for starting. When charging the battery, the electrolyte will begin to bubble. This is called gassing.

If one cell does not bubble, it is probably defective. Also, if the specific gravity of the cell is considerably lower than the other cells (0.050 points or more) after the battery is charged, the cell is defective.

If a battery not in use loses its charge within a week after charging or if the specific gravity drops quickly, the battery is defective. A good battery should only self-discharge approximately 1% each day.

WARNING
During charging, highly explosive hydrogen gas is released from the battery. Charge the battery only in a well-ventilated area, and away from open flames (including pilot lights on some gas home appliances). Do not allow any smoking in the area. Never check the charge of the battery by arcing across the terminals; the resulting spark can ignite the hydrogen gas.

CAUTION
Always remove the battery from the vehicle before connecting the charging equipment.

1. Remove the battery from the vehicle as described in this chapter.
2. Connect the positive charger lead to the positive battery terminal and the negative charger lead to the negative battery terminal.
3. Remove all fill/vent caps (**Figure 13**) from the battery, set the charger at 12 volts, and switch it on. Normally, a battery should be charged at a slow charge rate of 1/10 its given capacity.

CAUTION
Maintain the electrolyte level at the upper level during the charging cycle; check and refill with distilled water as necessary.

4. The charging time depends on the discharged condition of the battery.
5. After the battery has been charged for the pre-determined time, turn the charger off, disconnect the leads and check the specific gravity. It should be within the limits specified in *Battery Testing*. If it is, and remains stable for one hour, the battery is charged.

New Battery Installation

A new battery must be *fully* charged (specific gravity of 1.260-1.280) before installing it in the vehicle. When electrolyte is added to a new battery, its charge or capacity at that time is approximately 80%. To bring the battery to a full charge, it must receive an initial or boost charge. Using a new battery without an initial charge will cause permanent battery damage. That is, the battery will never be able to hold more than an 80% charge. Charging a new battery after it has been used will not bring its charge to 100%. When purchasing a new battery,

verify its charge status. If necessary, have the parts supplier perform the initial or booster charge to bring the battery up to 100% charge.

NOTE
***Recycle the old battery**. When the new battery is purchased, return the old one for recycling. The lead plates and the plastic case can be recycled. Most vehicle dealerships will accept the old battery in trade when the new one is purchased. Never place an old battery in the household trash. It is illegal to place any acid or lead (heavy metal) contents in landfills.*

BATTERY ELECTRICAL CABLE CONNECTORS

To ensure good electrical contact between the battery and the electrical cables (**Figure 17**), the cables must be clean and free of corrosion.

1. If the electrical cable terminals are badly corroded, disconnect them from the ATV's electrical system.

2. Thoroughly clean each connector with a wire brush and then with a baking soda solution. Rinse thoroughly with clean water and wipe dry with a clean cloth.

3. After cleaning, apply a thin layer of dielectric grease to the battery terminals before reattaching the cables.

4. After connecting the electrical cables, apply a light coating of dielectric grease to the electrical terminals of the battery to retard corrosion.

PERIODIC LUBRICATION

Perform the services listed in this section at the maintenance intervals listed in **Table 1**. Refer to **Table 3** for fluid types and capacities. If the vehicle is exposed to harder than normal use with constant exposure to water and high humidity, perform the services more frequently.

The Polaris engine is a dry-sump design with an oil tank (**Figure 18**) located on the left side of the engine. This tank must always be filled with the recommended type of engine oil listed in **Table 3**. The oil within the tank is circulated throughout the engine and then is returned to this tank for cooling.

Refer to *Lubricants* in Chapter One.

Engine Oil Level Check

Check the engine oil level using the oil fill cap/dipstick located on the top of the oil tank.

1. Start the engine and let it warm up approximately 2-3 minutes.

2. Park the ATV on level ground and set the parking brake.

3. Shut off the engine and let the oil settle for 2-3 minutes.

4. Remove the oil fill cap/dipstick (**Figure 19**) and wipe it clean. Reinsert the dipstick and remove it. The oil level must be between the upper and lower lines on the dipstick (**Figure 20**). If necessary, add the correct type (**Table 3**) of oil to bring the level up to the upper line.

5. Install the oil fill cap/dipstick and tighten securely.

3

Engine Oil and Filter Change

Regular oil and filter changes will contribute more to engine longevity than any other maintenance performed.

The manufacturer recommends using Polaris Premium 4 synthetic SAE 10W-40 engine oil or 10W-40 engine oil. Use the same brand of oil at each oil change.

To change the engine oil and filter the following is required:

a. Drain pan.
b. Funnel.
c. Wrench and sockets.
d. Two quarts (1.89 L) of oil (see **Table 3**).
e. New oil filter.
f. Socket-type oil filter wrench.

NOTE
A socket-type oil filter wrench must be used to remove the oil filter because of the small working area surrounding the oil filter.

NOTE
Never dispose of motor oil in the trash, on the ground, or down the storm drain. Many service stations accept used motor oil and waste haulers provide curbside used motor oil collection. Do not combine other fluids with motor oil to be recycled. To locate a recycler, contact the American Petroleum Institute (API) at ***www.recycleoil.org***.

NOTE
Warming the engine allows the oil to heat up; thus it flows freely and carries contamination and any sludge buildup out with it.

1. Start the engine and let it warm up approximately 2-3 minutes. Shut the engine off.
2. Place the ATV on level ground and set the parking brake.
3. Place a drain pan under the oil tank drain plug.

WARNING
The oil draining out of the oil tank is very hot; protect hands accordingly.

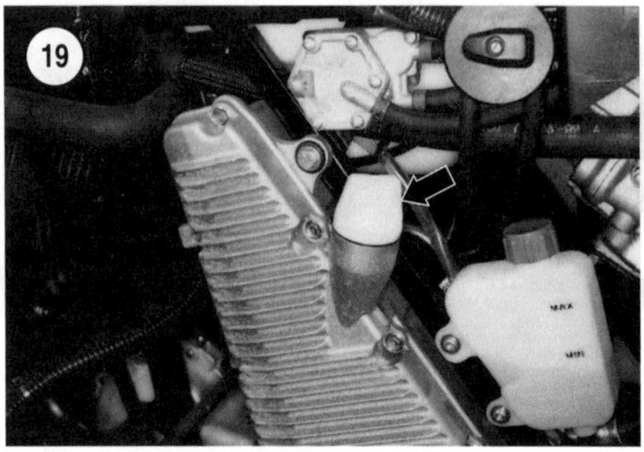

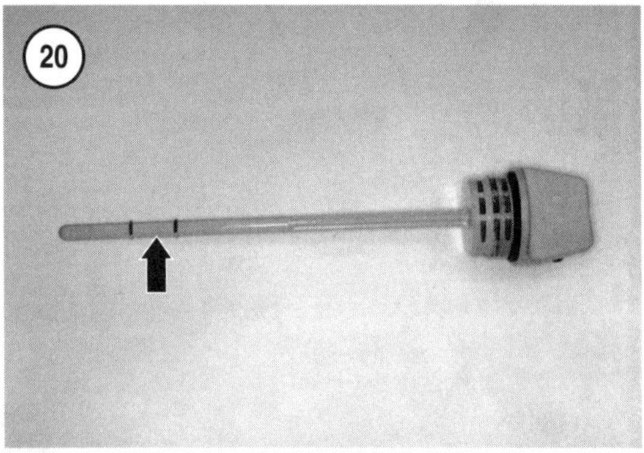

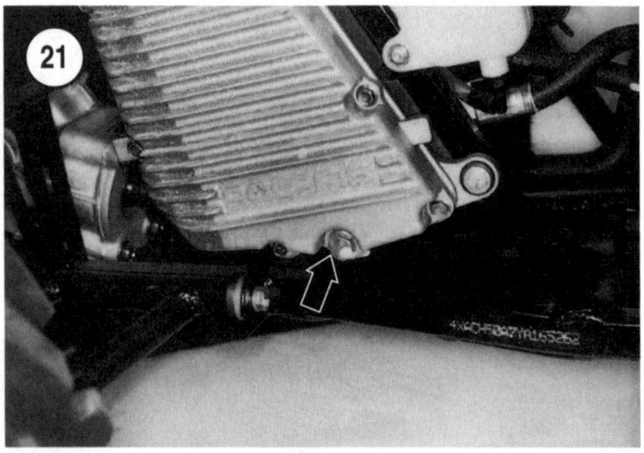

4. Loosen the drain plug (**Figure 21**) mounted on the bottom of the oil tank. Then remove the drain plug and gasket.
5. Loosen the oil fill cap/dipstick (**Figure 19**), as this will speed up the flow of oil.
6. Allow the oil to completely drain.
7. Inspect the condition of the drained oil for contamination after it has cooled down. If any particles are found, this indicates some sort of internal engine damage is occurring. Refer to Chapter Four and Chapter Five.

22

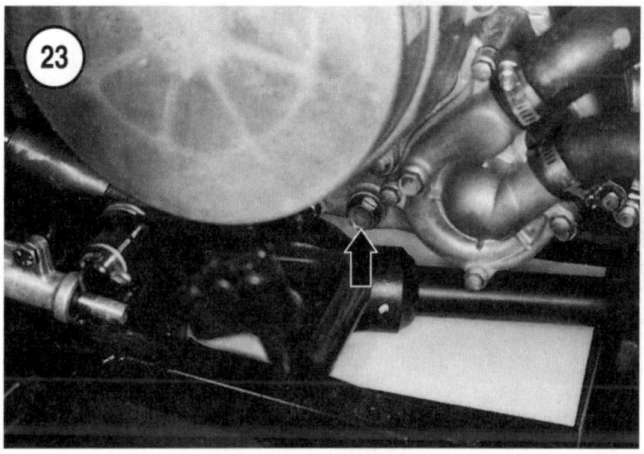

23

24

8. Remove the screen from the backside of the oil tank as follows:
   a. Loosen and remove the banjo bolt (**Figure 22**) and sealing washers securing the oil hose and disconnect the hose from the fitting.
   b. Unscrew the fitting and screen from the oil tank.
   c. Thoroughly clean the screen with solvent and check for damage.
   d. Apply Loctite PST505, or equivalent thread sealant, to the thread fittings.
   e. Install the screen and fitting onto the oil tank and tighten to the torque specification listed in **Table 5**.
   f. Install the hose, with a sealing washer on each side, and banjo bolt onto the fitting and tighten securely.
9. There is approximately 1 cup of engine oil that will remain in the crankcase after the oil tank is drained. Drain this oil as follows:
   a. Move the drain pan under the right side of the crankcase below the recoil starter assembly.
   b. On the right side, remove the drain plug and gasket (**Figure 23**) from the crankcase and allow the oil to completely drain.
   c. Check that the sealing surface on the crankcase and the drain plug are free of burrs and damage. Clean off if necessary to maintain a leak-free seal.
   d. Install a new gasket on the drain plug and install the drain plug. Tighten to the torque specification listed in **Table 5**.
10. To replace the oil filter, perform the following:
   a. Move the drain pan under the oil filter, as residual oil will drain out when the filter is loosened and removed. Place a shop cloth under the oil filter to catch residual oil as the oil filter is loosened.
   b. Install a socket-type oil filter wrench onto the oil filter (**Figure 24**) and turn the filter *counterclockwise* until oil begins to run out onto the shop cloth. Wait until the oil stops then loosen the filter until it is easy to turn.
   c. Due to limited space, remove the oil filter wrench from the end of the filter then completely unscrew and remove the filter holding it with the open facing up.
   d. Hold the filter over the drain pan and pour out any remaining oil. Place the old filter in a heavy-duty plastic bag and close the bag. Discard the old filter properly.
   e. Thoroughly clean the sealing surface of the crankcase where the filter's rubber seal seats. This surface must be clean to achieve a good oil seal when the filter is installed and tightened.
   f. Apply a light coat of clean engine oil to the rubber seal on the new filter.
   g. Install a new oil filter onto the threaded fitting on the crankcase.

h. Tighten the filter by hand until the rubber gasket contacts the crankcase surface, then tighten it an additional 1/2 turn.

11. Install a new gasket on the oil tank drain plug.

12. Install the drain plug (**Figure 21**) and its gasket. Tighten to the torque specification in **Table 5**.

13. Insert a funnel into the oil fill hole and fill the oil tank and engine with the correct weight (**Table 3**) and quantity of oil (**Table 4**).

14. Remove the funnel, install the oil fill cap/dipstick and tighten securely.

15. Usually some oil will find its way onto the frame and floorboards during this procedure. Wipe as much as possible off with a shop rag, then spray some aerosol parts cleaner to remove most of the oil residue.

16. Place the gear selector in NEUTRAL and make sure the parking brake is still applied.

17. Start the engine and allow it to idle.

18. Check the oil filter and both drain plugs for leaks. Tighten, if necessary.

19. Turn off the engine and allow the oil to settle. Then check the engine oil level as described in this chapter. Adjust the oil level if necessary.

WARNING
Contact with oil may cause cancer. Wash both hands thoroughly with soap and water as soon as possible after handling or coming in contact with motor oil.

Engine Oil Pressure Test

Use this procedure to check the engine oil pressure after reassembling the engine or when troubleshooting the lubrication system.

An oil pressure gauge and 1/8 NPT oil pressure gauge and adapter or an equivalent, are required.

1. Place the ATV on level ground and set the parking brake.

2. Remove the front fender as described in Chapter Fifteen.

3. Check that the engine oil level is correct as described in this chapter. Add oil if necessary.

4. Start the engine and allow it to reach normal operating temperature. Shut the engine off.

5. Place a drain pan under the blind plug on the cylinder head as some oil will drain out.

NOTE
***Figure 25** shows the engine removed for clarity.*

6. On the front left corner of the cylinder head, unscrew and remove the blind plug (**Figure 25**) from the cylinder head.

7. Install the adapter into the blind plug hole. Make sure the fitting is tight to avoid an oil loss. Install the gauge into the adapter.

CAUTION
Keep the oil pressure gauge hose away from the exhaust pipe during this test. If the hose makes contact with the exhaust pipe, it may melt and spray hot oil onto the hot exhaust pipe, resulting in a dangerous fire.

8. Place the gear selector in NEUTRAL and make sure the parking brake is still applied.

9. Start the engine and increase engine speed to 5000 rpm. The oil pressure should be approximately 138 kPa (20 psi). The minimum oil pressure is 83 kPa (12 psi).

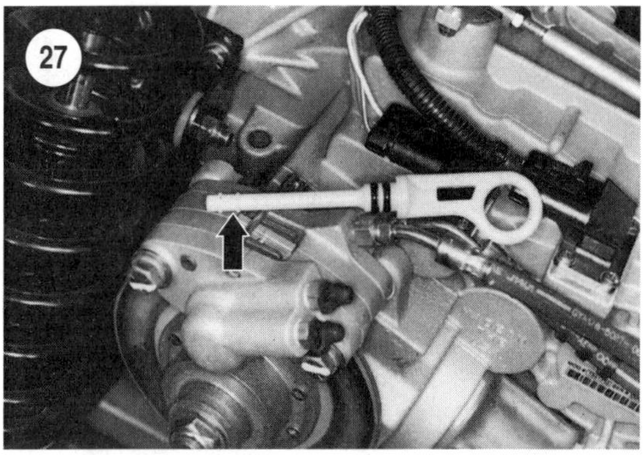
27

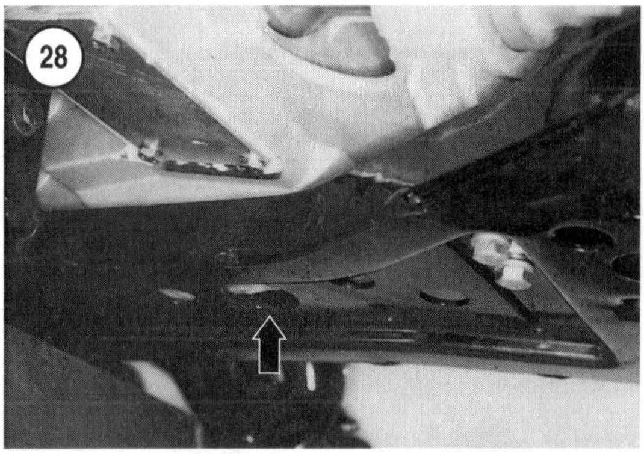
28

10. If the oil pressure is lower than specified check the following:

a. Clogged oil filter and/or screen.
b. Oil leak from oil passageway.
c. Damaged oil seal(s).
d. Defective oil pump.
e. Combination of the above.

11. If the oil pressure is higher than specified check the following:

a. Oil viscosity is too heavy; drain the oil and refill with lighter weight oil.
b. Clogged oil passageway.
c. Combination of the above

12. Shut off the engine and remove the test equipment.

13. Apply a light coat of gasket sealer to the blind plug, then install the plug (**Figure 25**) onto the cylinder head and tighten securely.

14. Check the oil level and adjust if necessary.

15. Install the front fender as described in Chapter Fifteen.

Transmission Oil Level Check

1. Park the ATV on level ground and set the parking brake.
2. Remove the oil fill dipstick (**Figure 26**) and wipe it clean. Reinsert the dipstick and remove it.
3. The oil level must be within the knurled section of the dipstick (**Figure 27**).
4. If necessary, add the correct type of oil (**Table 3**) to bring the level within the knurled section of the dipstick.
5. Install the oil fill cap/dipstick.

Transmission Oil Change

Polaris recommends the use of a synthetic gearcase lubricant, or equivalent, listed in **Table 3**.

To change the transmission oil and filter, the following is required:

a. Drain pan.
b. Funnel.
c. Can opener or pour spout.
d. Wrench and sockets.
e. 24 oz. bottle of lubricant.

NOTE
*Never dispose of oil in the trash, on the ground, or down the storm drain. Many service stations accept used oil and waste haulers provide curbside used oil collection. To locate a recycler, contact the American Petroleum Institute (API) at **www.recycleoil.org.***

NOTE
Warming the transmission allows the oil to heat up. This causes it to flow freely and carry contamination and any sludge buildup out with it.

1. Ride the ATV for 10-15 minutes and shift through both transmission ranges. Shut off the engine.
2. Place the ATV on level ground and set the parking brake.
3. Place a drain pan under the transmission drain plug.

WARNING
The oil draining out of the transmission is very hot; protect both hands accordingly.

4. Loosen the drain plug (**Figure 28**). Remove the drain plug and gasket.

5. Remove the oil fill/dipstick (**Figure 27**), as this will speed up the flow of oil.
6. Allow the oil to completely drain.
7. Inspect the condition of the drained oil for contamination after it has cooled down. If any particles are found, some type of internal transmission damage has occurred. Refer to Chapter Nine.
8. Install a new gasket on the oil tank drain plug.
9. Install the drain plug (**Figure 28**) and its gasket. Securely tighten the drain plug.
10. Insert a funnel into the oil fill hole and fill the transmission with the correct weight (**Table 3**) and quantity of oil (**Table 4**).
11. Remove the funnel, install the oil fill cap/dipstick and tighten securely.
12. Ride the ATV for 10-15 minutes and shift through all transmission ranges. Shut off the engine.
13. Place the ATV on level ground and set the parking brake.
14. Check for leaks. Tighten if necessary.
15. Check the transmission oil level as described in this chapter. Adjust the oil level if necessary.

WARNING

Contact with oil may cause cancer. Wash both hands thoroughly with soap and water as soon as possible after handling or coming in contact with transmission oil.

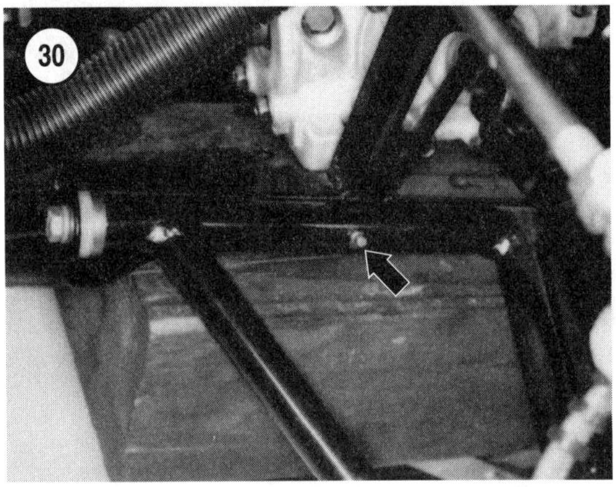

Front Gearcase (1996-1997 Models) Oil Level Check

1. Unscrew the oil fill plug and check the transmission oil level. The oil level is correct if it reaches the bottom of the oil fill hole.
2. If necessary, add the correct type of oil to bring the level up to the bottom of the oil fill hole. Refer to **Table 3**.
3. Install the oil fill plug and sealing washer and tighten securely.

Front Gearcase (1998 and Later Models) Oil Level Check

The oil level cannot be checked on these models. The gearcase must be drained and refilled with the correct quantity of oil to ensure correct oil level. Refer to the following procedure.

Front Gearcase Oil Change (All Models)

NOTE

This procedure is shown on a 2000 model and relates to all models covered in this manual. The only variation is the location of the oil fill plug on the gearcase.

32

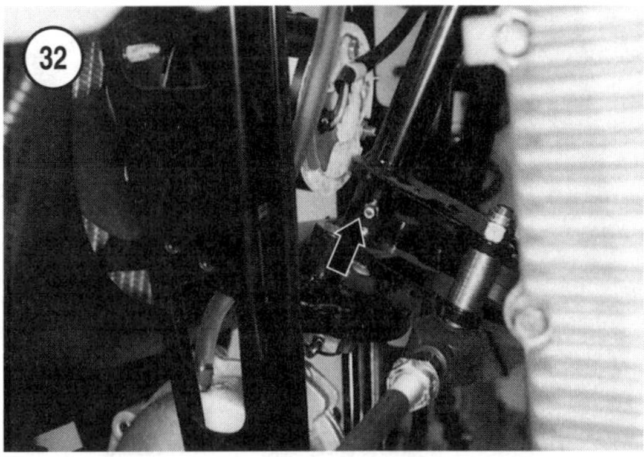

33

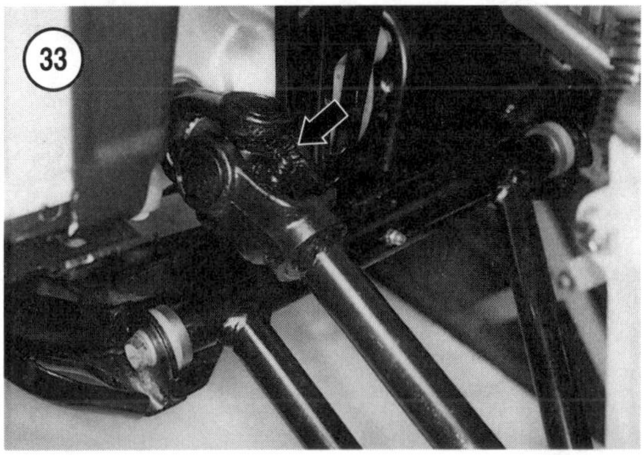

34

1. Ride the ATV for 10-15 minutes and shift through both transmission ranges. Shut off the engine.

2. Place the ATV on level ground and set the parking brake.

NOTE
Access to the front gearcase can be achieved with the front fender in place by removing the right front wheel but the working room is very limited. Remove whatever component is most convenient.

3A. Remove the front fender as described in Chapter Fifteen.

3B. Remove the right front wheel as described in Chapter Twelve.

4. Place a drain pan under the front gearcase drain plug.

5. Loosen the drain plug. Then remove the drain plug and gasket.

6. Unscrew the oil fill plug (**Figure 29**) as this will speed up the flow of oil

7. Allow the oil to completely drain.

8. Inspect the condition of the drained oil for contamination after it has cooled down. If any particles are found, some type of internal front gearcase damage has occurred. Refer to Chapter Ten.

9. Install a new gasket on the drain plug.

10. Install the drain plug and its gasket. Tighten the drain plug to the torque specification listed in **Table 5**.

11. Insert a funnel into the oil fill hole and fill the gearcase with the correct weight (**Table 3**) and quantity of oil (**Table 4**).

12. Remove the funnel and install the oil fill plug (**Figure 29**). Tighten the plug securely.

13. Check for leaks. Tighten if necessary.

Grease Service

Various suspension and drive train components require periodic lubrication.

Wipe the grease fitting clean prior to installing the grease gun. Use the recommended grease listed in **Table 3** and inject the grease into the fitting with a grease gun. Wipe off any excess grease from the fitting.

Apply grease to the following fittings:

1. The front suspension arms (**Figure 30**).
2. The front struts (**Figure 31**).
3. The lower end of the steering shaft (**Figure 32**).
4. The front drive axle inner U-joints (**Figure 33**).
5. The front propeller shaft, front U-joint (**Figure 34**) and the rear U-joint (**Figure 35**).
6. Upper (**Figure 36**) and lower (**Figure 37**) rear suspension arms.
7. Rear stabilizer bar assembly (**Figure 38**).

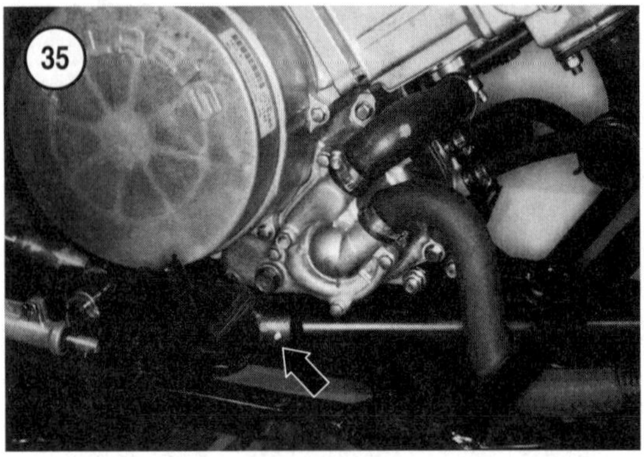

Front Hub

Oil level check

1. Place the ATV on level ground and set the parking brake.
2. Remove the front wheel as described in Chapter Twelve.
3. Place a drain pan under the front hub.
4. Rotate the front hub until the fill/check plug (**Figure 39**) is at the 12 o'clock position, then remove the fill/check plug (**Figure 40**).
5. Slowly rotate the front hub until the fill/check plug opening is located at either the 4 o'clock or 8 o'clock position. If the oil starts to trickle out with the hub in this position, the oil level is correct. If not, proceed to Step 3.

CAUTION
Do not overfill the front hub and do not force the oil into the hub as the internal seals will be damaged.

6. Add the recommended lubricant listed in **Table 3** to the front hub. Fill the hub (**Figure 41**) until the oil starts to trickle out of the fill/check plug opening.
7. Rotate the front hub until the fill/check plug is once again at the 12' clock position.
8. Install the fill/check plug (**Figure 40**) and tighten securely.
9. Install the front wheel as described in Chapter Twelve.

Oil change

1. Place the ATV on level ground and set the parking brake.

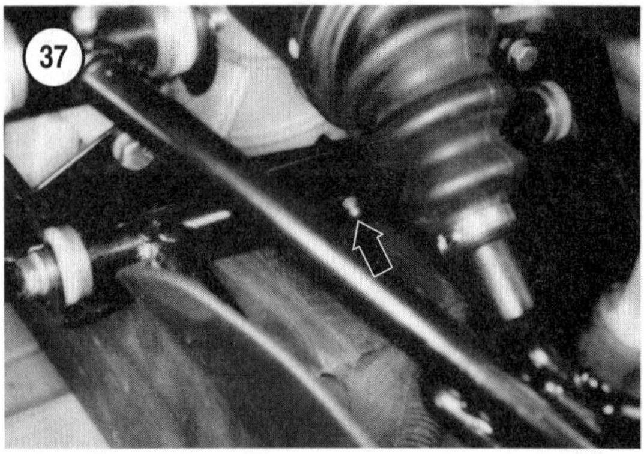

40

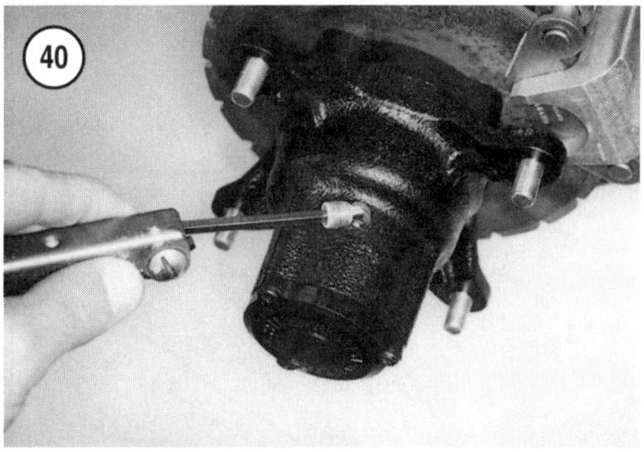

41

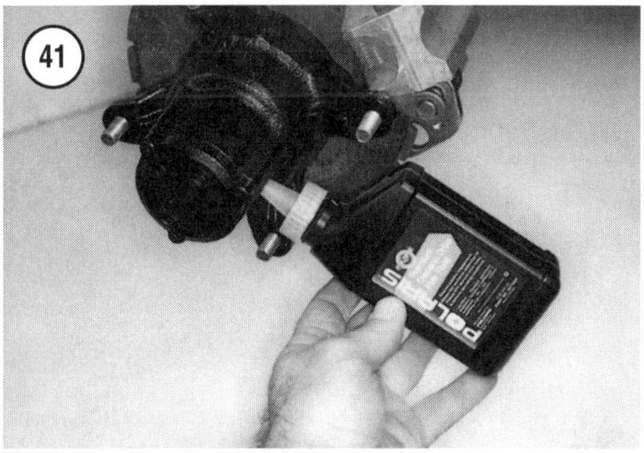

42

43

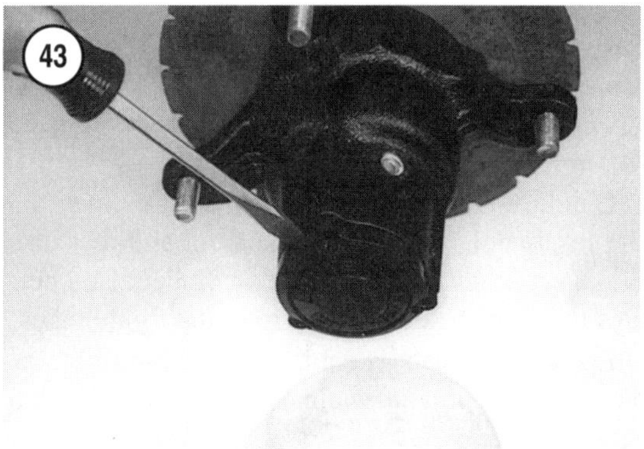

44

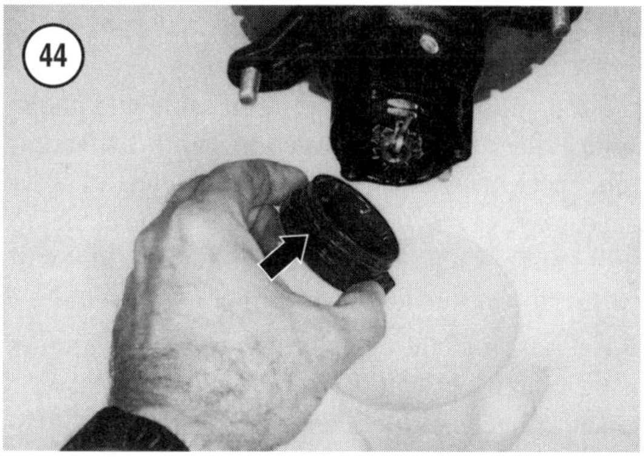

2. Remove the front wheel as described in Chapter Twelve.
3. Place a drain pan under the front hub.
4. Remove the three T-25 Torx bolts (**Figure 42**) securing the hubcap. Carefully remove the hubcap (**Figure 43**).
5. Allow the oil to completely drain from the front hub. Slowly rotate the hub back and forth to help drain out all fluid.
6. If the vehicle has been ridden in water or if water has entered the front hubs, drain the oil, flush the front hub with clean oil and drain again. Observe the drained oil. If water is still present, continue to flush the hub until all moisture is removed.
7. Remove the fill/check plug (**Figure 40**).
8. Inspect the hubcap O-ring seals (**Figure 44**) for nicks, cuts and deterioration. Replace as necessary.
9. Install the hubcap and tap it into place until it is completely seated. Install the three Torx bolts and tighten securely.
10. Rotate the front hub until the fill/check plug hub opening is located at the 4 o'clock or 8 o'clock position.

CAUTION
Do not overfill the front hub and do not force the oil into the hub, as the internal seals will be damaged.

11. Fill the front hub (**Figure 41**) with the recommended lubricant (**Table 3**). Fill the hub until the oil starts to trickle out of the fill/check plug opening.
12. Install the fill/check plug (**Figure 39**) and tighten securely.
13. Install the front wheel as described in Chapter Twelve.
14. Ride the vehicle for 10-15 minutes and check for oil leakage.

Control Cable Lubrication

Clean and lubricate the throttle cable and choke cable at the intervals indicated in **Table 1**. In addition, check the cables for kinks and signs of wear and damage or fraying that could cause the cables to fail or stick. Cables are expendable items and will not last forever under the best of conditions.

The best method of control cable lubrication is using a cable lubricator (**Figure 45**) or, if necessary, an aerosol general lubricant can be substituted. Do *not* use chain lube as a cable lubricant.

1. Remove the seat as described in Chapter Fifteen.
2. Remove the fuel tank as described in Chapter Six. This is necessary to access the lower end of the cables.
3. Disconnect the throttle cable from the throttle housing. Refer to Chapter Six.
4. Disconnect the choke cable from the toggle lever on the indictor panel.
5. Attach a cable lubricator to the end of the cable following the manufacturer's instructions.
6. Insert the lubricant can nozzle into the lubricator, press the button on the can and hold down until the lubricant begins to flow out of the other end of the cable. If the cable lube will not flow through the cable at one end, remove the lubricator, disconnect the cables from the carburetor assembly, and try at the opposite end of the cable.

NOTE
Place a shop cloth at the end of the cables to catch the oil as it runs out.

7. Disconnect the lubricator.
8. Apply a light coating of grease to the cable ends before reconnecting them. Reconnect the cables and adjust as described in this chapter.
9. After lubricating the throttle cable, operate the throttle lever at the handlebar. It should open and close smoothly with no binding.
10. After lubricating the choke cable, operate the choke toggle lever. It should open and close smoothly with no binding.

PERIODIC MAINTENANCE

Maintenance intervals are listed in **Table 1**.

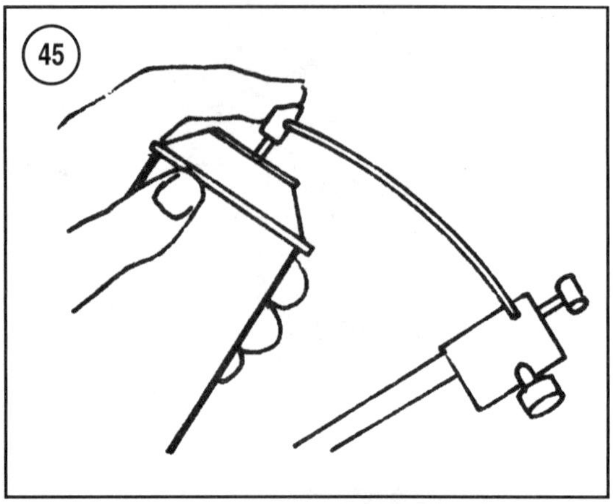

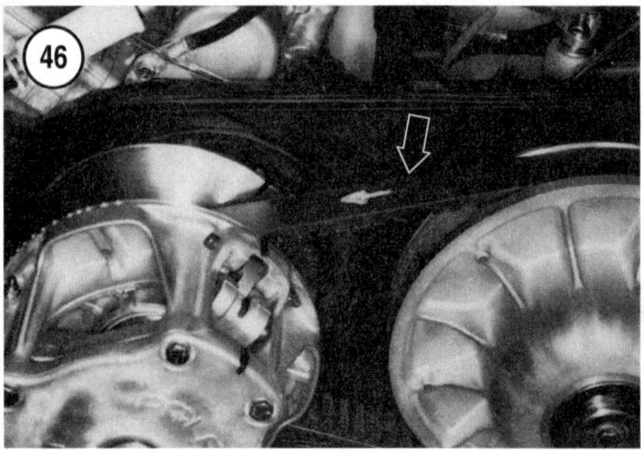

Drive Belt Inspection

1. Remove the drive belt outer cover as described in Chapter Eight.
2. Check the drive belt (**Figure 46**) for cracks, fraying or unusual wear as described in Chapter Eight.
3. Replace a worn or damaged drive belt as described in Chapter Eight.
4. Install the drive belt outer cover as described in Chapter Eight.

Disc Brake System Inspection

Check the disc brake system at the interval listed in **Table 1**.

On all models, a single brake master cylinder on the left handlebar operates the front and rear disc brake systems. The rear master cylinder also operates the rear brake independent of the front brakes.

Each front wheel is equipped with a disc brake. The rear disc brake is mounted on the transmission output shaft.

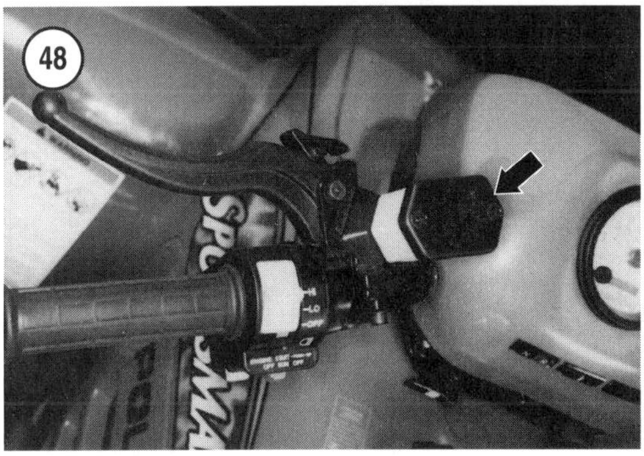

Visually inspect each brake disc for cracks, deep scoring, heat distortion, checking and excessive wear. Inspect the brake pads for uneven wear (**Figure 47**, typical) and overheating. Install new brake pads if worn to the brake pad service limit groove or to the dimension listed in **Table 6**.

Bleeding the system, servicing the brake system components and replacing the brake pads are covered in Chapter Fourteen.

Disc Brake Fluid Level Check and Fill

Maintain the hydraulic brake fluid in the reservoir at its maximum level. If necessary, correct the level by adding fresh brake fluid.

CAUTION

Do not spill brake fluid on plastic, painted or plated surfaces, as it will destroy the finish. Wash off the area immediately with soapy water and thoroughly rinse it off with clean water.

1. Place the ATV on level ground and set the parking brake.
2. Clean any dirt from the area around the cover prior to removing the cover.

NOTE

To control the small flow of hydraulic fluid, punch a small hole into the seal of a new container of brake fluid next to the edge of the pour spout. This will help eliminate fluid spillage, especially while adding fluid to the very small reservoirs.

WARNING

Use brake fluid clearly marked DOT 3 from a sealed container. Other types may vaporize and cause brake failure. Always use the same brand name; do not intermix as many brands are not compatible. Do not intermix silicone-based (DOT 5) brake fluid, as it can cause brake component damage leading to brake system failure.

3A. On the front master cylinder, perform the following:
   a. Position the handlebar so the front master cylinder is horizontal.
   b. Remove the screws securing the reservoir cap and remove the reservoir cover (**Figure 48**).
   c. Refill the master cylinder reservoir, if necessary, to maintain the correct fluid level as indicated on the side of the reservoir.
   d. Install the diaphragm and cover. Tighten the cover screws securely.

3B. On the rear master cylinder, perform the following:
   a. Remove the seat as described in Chapter Fifteen.
   b. Unscrew and remove the reservoir cap (**Figure 49**).
   c. Refill the remote reservoir, if necessary, to maintain the correct fluid level as indicated on the side of the reservoir.
   d. Install the reservoir cap and tighten securely.

Disc Brake Hoses

Check the brake hoses between the master cylinder and each brake caliper assembly. If there is any leakage, tighten the connections and bleed the brakes as described under *Bleeding the System* in

Chapter Fourteen. If tightening the connection does not stop the leak or if the brake hose(s) is obviously damaged, cracked or chafed, replace the brake hose(s) and bleed the system as described in Chapter Fourteen.

Auxiliary Brake Testing and Adjustment (1996-1997 Models)

The auxiliary brake is intended for use as a backup if the hydraulic system should fail. Depressing the foot pedal on the right floorboard activates the rear brake, located on the transmission output shaft.

Testing

1. Shift the transmission into NEUTRAL.
2. Support the vehicle with the rear wheels off the ground. Block the front wheels so the vehicle cannot roll in either direction.
3. Rotate the rear wheels by hand and depress the auxiliary brake pedal.
4. The rear wheel should stop rotating when the brake pedal has traveled midway between the at-rest position and bottoming out on the floorboard.
5. If the rear wheel does not stop rotating within this pedal travel, adjust the auxiliary portion of the rear brake.
6. If adjustment is not necessary, lower the vehicle.

Adjusting

1. Shift the transmission into NEUTRAL.
2. Support the vehicle with the rear wheels off the ground. Block the front wheels so the vehicle cannot roll in either direction.
3. Remove the bolts and washers securing the drive chain guard and remove the chain guard.
4. At the rear brake caliper, loosen the locknut (A, **Figure 50**).
5. Rotate the rear wheels by hand.
6. Turn the adjust bolt (B, **Figure 50**) clockwise until the rear wheel rotation becomes difficult, then stop.
7. Continue to rotate the rear wheels and turn the adjust bolt (B, **Figure 50**) counterclockwise and have an assistant apply the rear brake. When the

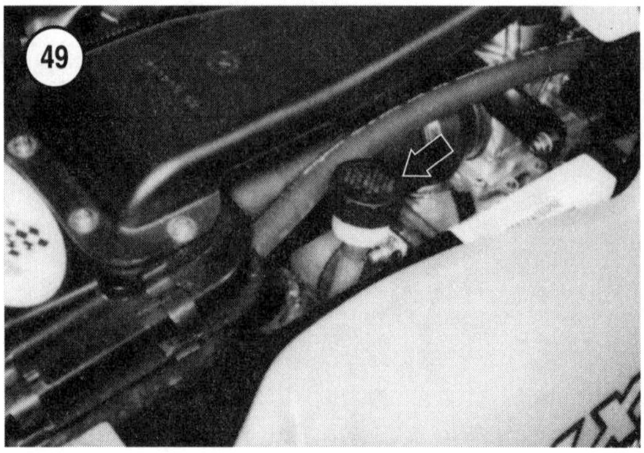

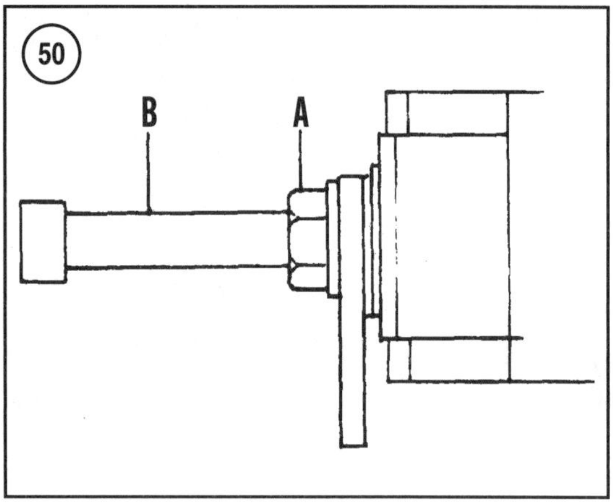

brake pedal has traveled to the mid-way point stop turning the adjust bolt. Tighten the locknut.
8. Once again rotate the rear wheels by hand and apply the rear brake. The rear wheels should stop once the rear brake pedal has traveled to the mid-way point. Readjust if necessary.
9. Tighten the locknut (B, **Figure 50**) securely.
10. Install the drive chain guard and tighten the bolts securely.
11. Lower the vehicle and test drive it to make sure the auxiliary brake is operating correctly. Also, make sure the rear brake is not dragging. Readjust if necessary.

Throttle Cable/Electronic Throttle Control Adjustment

All models require some throttle cable play to prevent changes in the idle speed when the handlebar is turned. The recommended amount of cable free play is 1.6 mm (1/16 in.) when measured at the

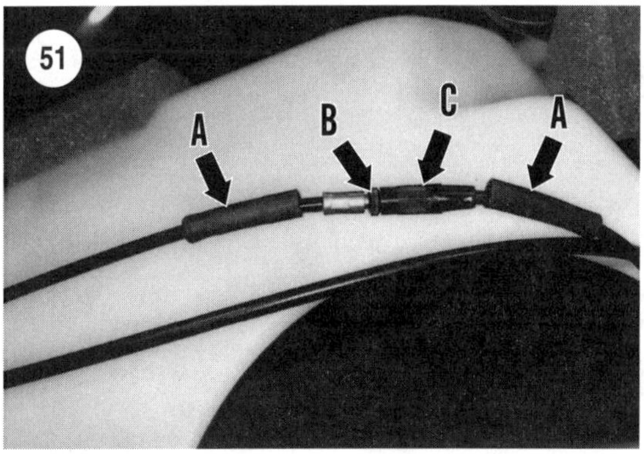

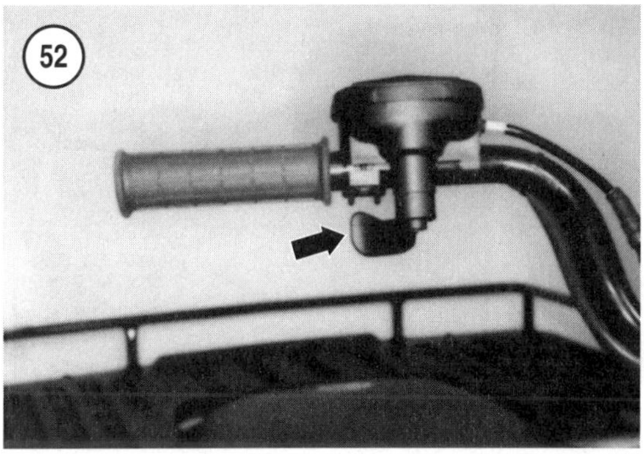

end of the throttle lever. In time, the cable will stretch and the free play will become excessive.

NOTE
Check throttle cable free play at the handlebar lever. It is important that the throttle cable has the correct amount of free play as described in this procedure.

1. Set the engine idle speed as described under *Idle Speed Adjustment* in this chapter.
2. Shift the transmission into NEUTRAL.
3. Block the front wheels so the vehicle cannot roll in either direction.
4. Start the engine and allow it to idle. Make sure the handlebar mounted speed control lever is at its slowest speed position.
5. Slide both rubber boots (A, **Figure 51**) off the in-line cable adjuster.
6. Loosen the locknut (B, **Figure 51**).
7. Turn the cable adjuster (C, **Figure 51**) out until engine rpm starts to increase, then stop.
8. Turn the cable adjuster back in until the throttle lever (**Figure 52**) has 1.6 mm (1/16 in.) of travel before the engine speed increases.
9. Securely tighten the locknut (B, **Figure 51**).
10. Shut off the engine.
11. Slide both rubber boots (A, **Figure 51**) back onto the cable adjuster.
12. Turn the handlebar from side-to-side in the full turning range. If the idle speed increases, the throttle cable free play must be increased or the throttle cable is routed incorrectly.
13. Check for smooth throttle operation in all handlebar positions. The throttle lever should move smoothly and return without binding.

Throttle Cable Adjustment (At Carburetor—1996-1998 Models)

NOTE
The 1999 and later models are not equipped with a cable adjuster at the carburetor end of the throttle cable.

1. Remove the fuel tank as described in Chapter Six.
2. At the carburetor, slide the rubber boot up and off the throttle cable adjuster.
3. Loosen the locknut and turn the adjuster (**Figure 53**) until the correct amount of cable free-play is obtained.
4. Securely tighten the locknut.
5. Slide the rubber boot back down onto the throttle cable adjuster.
6. If necessary, perform a fine adjustment at the throttle housing as previously described.
7. Install the fuel tank as described in Chapter Six.

Air Filter Element

Remove and replace the air filter at the interval indicated in **Table 1**. Replace the element immediately if it is damaged or starting to deteriorate.

The air filter removes dust and abrasive particles before the air enters the carburetor and the engine. Without the air filter, very fine particles could enter into the engine and cause rapid wear of the piston rings, cylinder bores and bearings. They also might clog small passages in the carburetor. Never run the ATV without the element installed.

1. Place the ATV on level ground and set the parking brake.
2. Remove the seat as described in Chapter Fifteen.
3. Thoroughly clean any road debris from the area surrounding the air filter air box cover.
4. Unhook the spring clip securing the air filter air box cover and remove the cover (**Figure 54**).
5. Loosen the clamp screw (A, **Figure 55**) and remove the air filter element (B, **Figure 55**) from the air box.
6. Place a clean shop cloth into the opening in the air filter air box to prevent the entry of debris.
7. Slide off the foam pre-filter, or pre-filter sleeve (A, **Figure 56**) from the air filter element (B, **Figure 56**).

NOTE

If the air filter element is extremely dirty or if there are any holes in the element, wipe out the interior of the air box with a shop rag dampened in cleaning solvent. Remove any debris that may have passed through a broken element.

8. Gently tap the air filter element to loosen the trapped dirt and dust.

NOTE

Cleaning the air filter element is not recommended. Replace the air filter element if dirty or damaged.

9. Thoroughly and carefully inspect the filter element (**Figure 57**). If it is torn or broken in any area, replace the air filter element. Do not run the ATV with a damaged element as it may allow dirt to enter the engine. If the element is good, it can be used until replacement is required.
10. Clean the foam pre-filter, or pre-filter sleeve, with warm water and mild soap. Wash several times

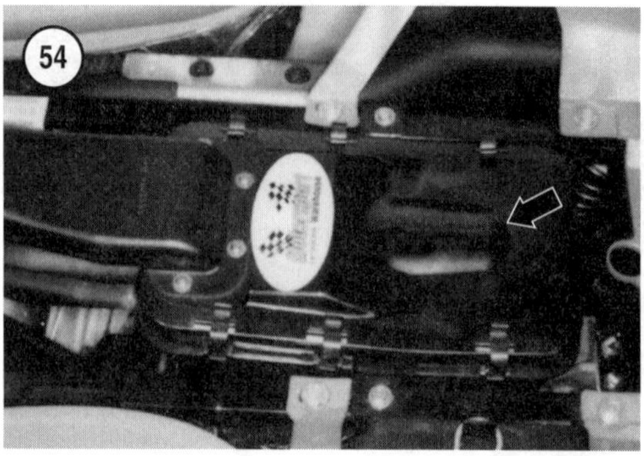
54

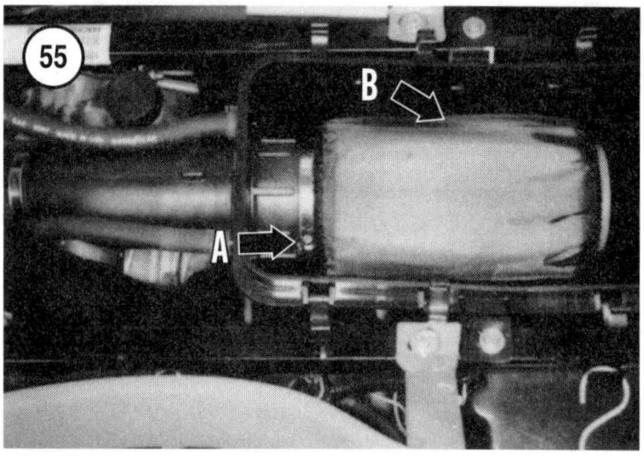

55

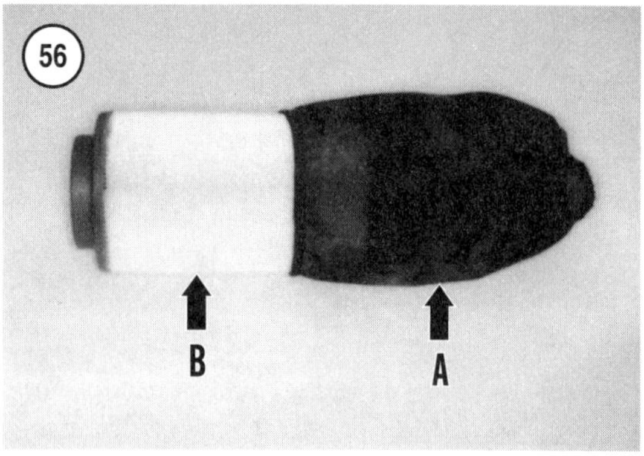

56

57

58

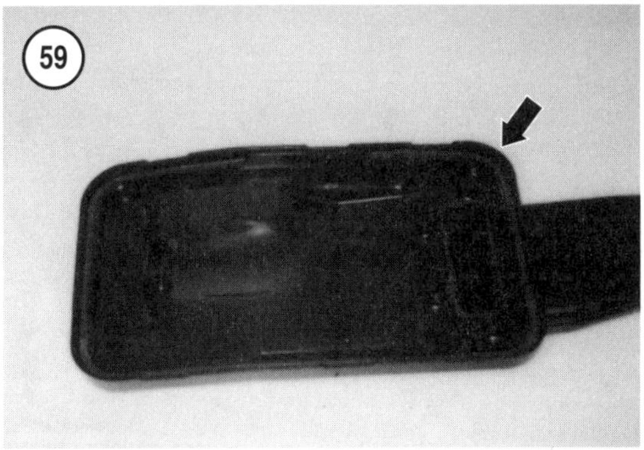
59

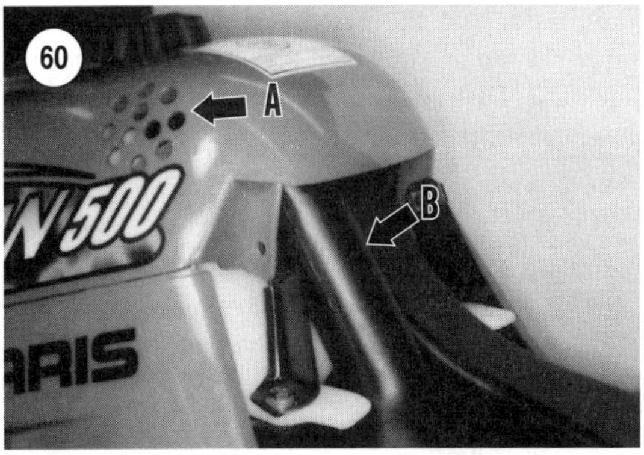

60

61

if necessary to remove all dirt and rinse in clean water. Thoroughly dry the pre-filter prior to installation.

11. Install the pre-filter onto the air filter element.
12. Inspect the air box (**Figure 58**) for any debris. Thoroughly clean out the air box.
13. Install the air filter element assembly onto the air box intake and tighten the clamp screw securely. Make sure the clamp is seated correctly and that the clamp screw is tight (A, **Figure 55**).
14. Inspect the air filter element cover gasket seal (**Figure 59**) for damage or deterioration. Replace if necessary.
15. Check the air intake holes (A, **Figure 60**) in the rear left side of the front fender for any debris that may obstruct intake air flow.
16. Install the air filter element cover and seal. Make sure it is seated correctly and secure it with the six spring clips. Make sure the air intake tube is positioned correctly within the rear portion of the front fender (B, **Figure 60**).
17. Check the air box sediment drain as follows:
    a. At the rear of the air box, place a rag under the drain cap and remove it (**Figure 61**). Drain out water and other debris collected in the air box.
    b. Reinstall the drain cap and make sure the clamp is in place.
18. Install the seat as described in Chapter Fifteen.

Coolant Inspection

The ATV is equipped with a liquid cooling system. The cooling system is small; even a slight leak can cause the engine to overheat. Therefore, check the coolant level and condition of the radiator and hoses frequently.

WARNING

Never remove the radiator cap, open the coolant drain or disconnect any hose while the engine is hot. Scalding fluid and steam may be blown out under pressure and cause serious injury.

Check the following items once a year, or whenever troubleshooting the cooling system. If the test equipment is not available, have the tests performed by a Polaris dealership, radiator shop or service station.

1. Remove the front fender cover as described in Chapter Fifteen.

2. Loosen the radiator cap (**Figure 62**) to its first detent and release the system pressure, then turn the cap to its second detent and remove it from the radiator.
3. Check the rubber washers on the radiator cap (**Figure 63**) for tears or cracks. Check for a bent or distorted cap. Raise the vacuum valve and rubber seal and rinse the cap under warm tap water to flush away any loose rust or dirt particles.
4. Inspect the radiator cap neck seat on the coolant tank for dents, distortion or contamination. Wipe the sealing surface with a clean cloth to remove any rust or dirt.

CAUTION
Do not exceed 89 kPa (13 psi) when performing Steps 4 and 5, or damage to the cooling system will occur.

5. Have the radiator cap pressure-tested. The specified radiator cap relief pressure is 89 kPa (13 psi). The cap must be able to sustain this pressure for 5 minutes or longer. Replace the radiator cap if it does not hold pressure.
6. Leave the radiator cap off and pressure-test the cooling system to 69 kPa (10 psi). The system must be able to hold this pressure. Replace or repair any components that fail this test.
7. Check all cooling system hoses for damage or deterioration. Replace any hose that is in questionable condition. Make sure all hose clamps are tight.
8. Check the radiator for leaks or other damage. Repair or replace the radiator as necessary.
9. Install the front fender cover as described in Chapter Fifteen.

Coolant Change

Drain and refill the cooling system at the interval listed in **Table 1**.

It is sometimes necessary to drain the coolant from the system to perform a service procedure on some part of the engine. If the coolant is still in good condition and it is not time to replace the coolant, the coolant can be reused if it remains clean. Drain the coolant into a *clean* drain pan and then pour the coolant into a *clean* sealable container such as a plastic milk or bleach bottle and screw on the cap.

Only use a high-quality ethylene glycol-based coolant compounded for aluminum radiators and engines. Mix the coolant with distilled water at a 50:50 ratio. Coolant capacity is listed in **Table 4**. *Never* use tap or salt water, as this will damage engine parts. Distilled (or purified) water can be purchased at supermarkets.

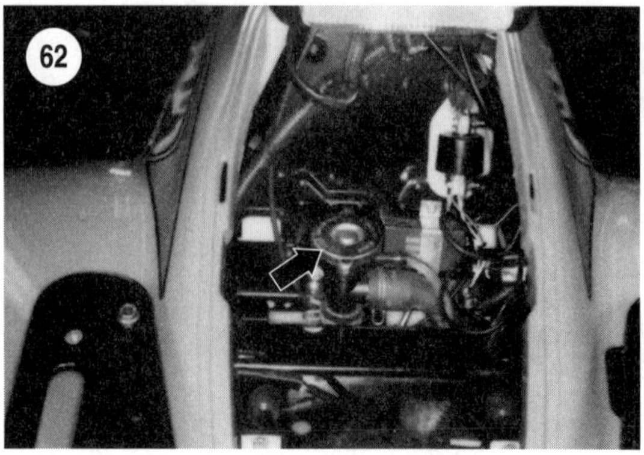

WARNING
Antifreeze is an environmental toxin and cannot legally be disposed of by flushing down a drain or pouring it onto the ground. Place old antifreeze into a suitable container and dispose of it according to EPA regulations. Do not store coolant where it is accessible to children or animals.

WARNING
Do not remove the radiator fill cap when the engine is hot. The coolant is very hot and is under pressure. Severe scalding could result if the coolant comes in contact with skin.

CAUTION
Coolant can stain concrete and will damage or kill plants. Do not drain the coolant onto a driveway or allow it to drain into a planted area. Be

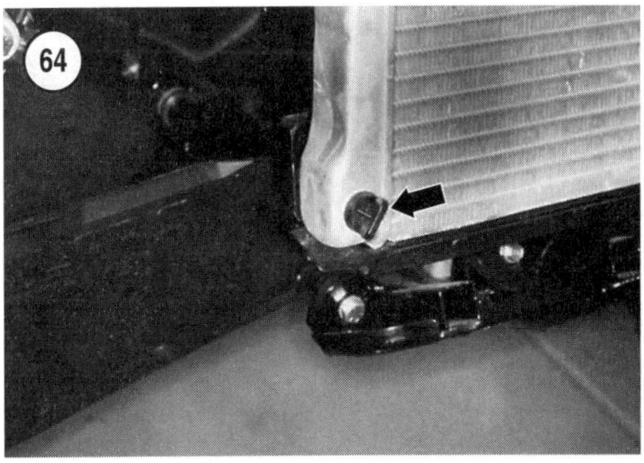
64

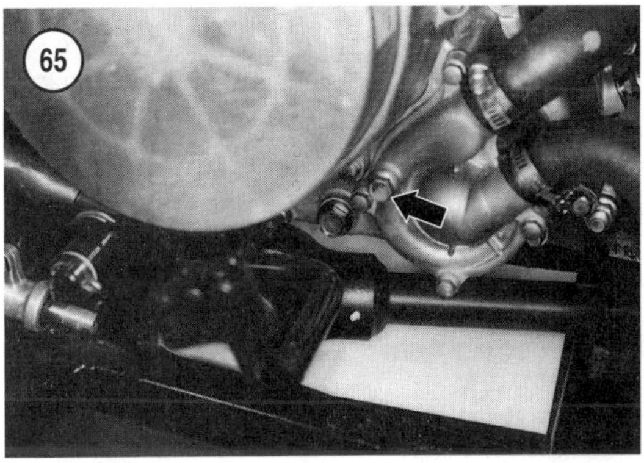
65

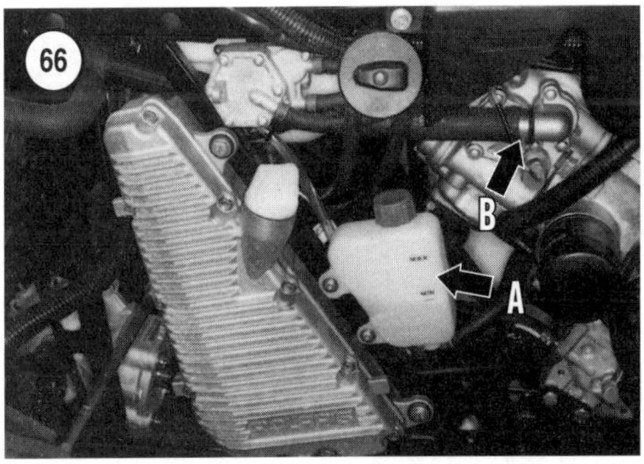

66

careful not to spill coolant on painted, plated or plastic surfaces, as it will damage the finish and/or surface. Wash any applicable area with soapy water and rinse thoroughly with clean water.

Perform the following procedure when the engine is *cold*.

1. Place the ATV on level ground and set the parking brake.
2. Remove the front fender and right side footwell as described in Chapter Fifteen.
3. With the engine *cold*, remove the radiator cap (**Figure 62**).
4. Place a drain pan under the drain fitting on the base of the radiator.

NOTE
***Figure 64** shows a 2000 model with the radiator shroud removed to better illustrate the step. The drain valve on prior years is located on the back side of the radiator.*

5. Open the drain valve on the base of the radiator (**Figure 64**) and drain the coolant.
6. Move the drain pan under the water pump drain bolt.
7. Remove the drain screw and sealing washer (**Figure 65**) and drain the coolant from the pump and hoses.
8. Rock the ATV from side to side to drain any residual coolant from the cooling system. Correctly dispose of the coolant.

NOTE
If the coolant is dirty, place a different drain pan under the radiator and flush out the system with clean water. Drain out all water from the system.

9. Tighten the radiator drain valve and install the water pump drain screw and sealing washer. Tighten the drain screw securely.
10. Remove the coolant reservoir (A, **Figure 66**) mounting bolts. Partially pull the reservoir away from the frame and disconnect the hoses from it. Place a plug in the lower fitting to prevent the loss of coolant in the tank.
11. Remove the coolant reservoir cap and empty out the old coolant into a suitable container.
12. If necessary, clean the inside of the reservoir with a liquid detergent and thoroughly rinse with clean water. Remove all detergent residue from the reservoir.
13. Attach both hoses to the coolant reservoir. Reinstall the reservoir and bolts and tighten securely.

CAUTION
Do not use a higher ratio of coolant-to-water than recommended for the ambient temperature. A higher concentration of coolant (60% or

*greater) will actually **decrease** the performance of the cooling system.*

14. Place a funnel into the radiator filler neck and refill the radiator and engine.
15. Slowly add the 50% coolant and 50% distilled water mixture through the radiator filler neck. Add it slowly so it will expel as much air as possible from the engine and radiator. Top off the coolant to the bottom of the filler neck. Do not install the radiator cap at this time.
16. Be sure to fill the system completely. If the system is completely drained, loosen the clamp (B, **Figure 66**) on the hose to the thermostat housing. Pull the hose loose and fill the system with coolant at the radiator, while allowing air to escape from the loosened hose. When coolant begins to flow from the thermostat and hose connection, reattach the hose and tighten the clamp securely.
17. Squeeze the coolant hoses to purge air from the cooling system while filling with coolant.
18. Remove the fill cap, then refill the coolant reservoir to the FULL mark, install the cap and tighten securely.

NOTE

Fill the cooling system slowly so the coolant can expel the air within the radiator and engine.

19. Rock the ATV about 20° to the left and then to the right several times. This will help bleed off some of the air trapped in the cooling system. If necessary, add additional coolant mixture to the system until the coolant level is to the bottom of the filler neck.
20. Install the radiator cap (**Figure 62**). Turn the radiator cap clockwise to the first stop. Then push down and turn it clockwise until it stops.

CAUTION

If the radiator cap is not installed correctly, coolant loss and engine overheating will occur.

21. Start the engine and run it at idle until it reaches operating temperature. Make sure there are no air bubbles in the coolant and that the coolant level stabilizes at the correct level. Add coolant if necessary.
22. Test ride the ATV and readjust the coolant level in the reservoir if necessary.

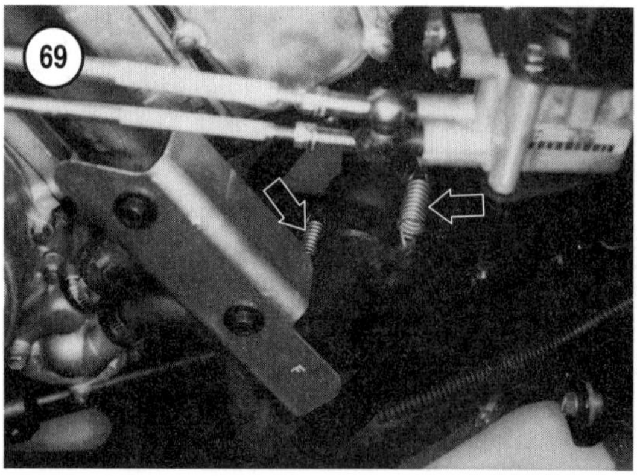

Exhaust System

1. Inspect the exhaust system for cracks or dents that could alter performance.
2. Remove the rear fender as described in Chapter Fifteen.
3. Check the tightness of the muffler mounting bolts (**Figure 67**) and the attaching springs (**Figure 68**).
4. Make sure the front springs (**Figure 69**) are secure.

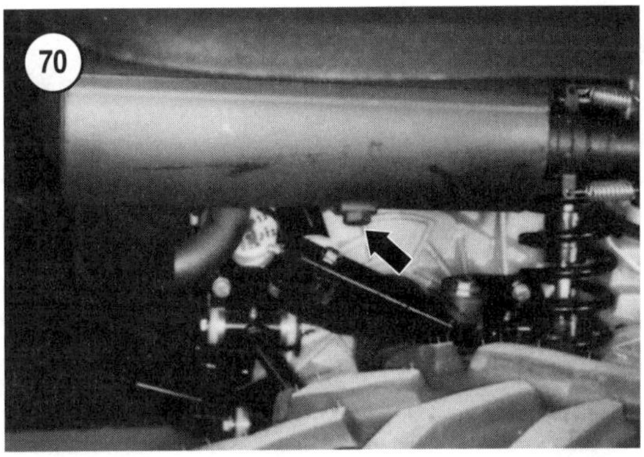

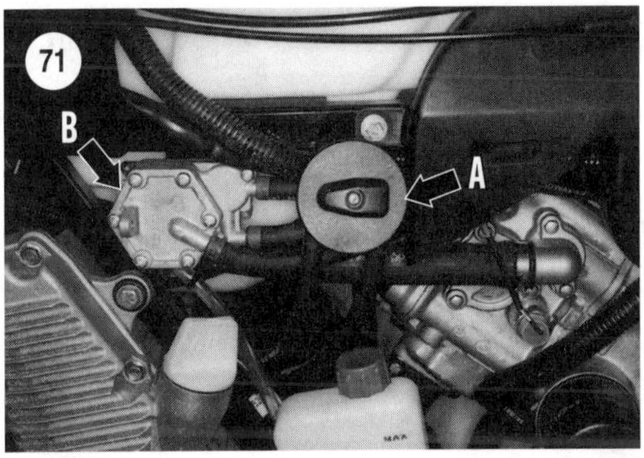

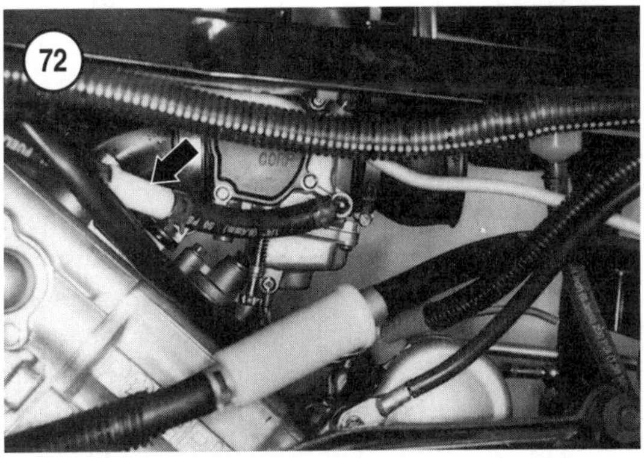

5. On models so equipped, remove the plug and washer (**Figure 70**) at the base of the muffler. Drain out any residue. Install a new washer and tighten the plug securely.

Fuel Hose Inspection

Inspect the fuel hoses (**Figure 71**) from the fuel tank to the fuel shutoff valve (A), the fuel pump (B) and the carburetor. Replace any hoses that are cracked or starting to deteriorate. Make sure the small hose clamps are in place and secure.

WARNING
A damaged or deteriorated fuel line presents a very dangerous fire hazard to both the rider and the ATV.

Fuel Filter Replacement

An inline fuel filter is located between the fuel pump and the carburetor. The fuel filter traps particles that might otherwise enter the carburetor. Minute particles can cause the float valve and fuel inlet needle to stick or clog one of the jets.

1. Remove the front fender as described in Chapter Fifteen.
2. Disconnect the negative battery cable as described in this chapter.
3. Turn the fuel valve to the OFF position.
4. Place several cloths under the fuel filter, as gasoline still present in the fuel line will drain out once the fuel filter is removed.
5. Below the left side of the carburetor, loosen one of the clamps securing the fuel filter (**Figure 72**) to the outlet hoses.
6. Disconnect that hose and plug it to stop the flow of gasoline.
7. Disconnect the other fuel line from the fuel filter and plug it.
8. Remove the fuel filter.
9. Position the new fuel filter with the arrow pointing in the direction of fuel flow. Install both fuel hoses and tighten the clamps securely.
10. Turn the shut-off valve to the ON position and check for fuel leakage.
11. Install the front fender as described in Chapter Fifteen.

Steering System and Front Suspension Inspection

Check the steering system and front suspension at the intervals listed in **Table 1** following any hard spill or collision or if a problem with operation is suspected.

1. Park the vehicle on level ground and set the parking brake.
2. Visually inspect all components of the steering and front suspension for obvious problems. Pay

close attention to the tie rods, steering shaft and front struts. Some suggested indicators of damage are:

a. Bent or broken components. Especially check areas where paint is flaking or missing.
b. Loose fasteners or locknuts.
c. Excessively loose components.
d. Stiff or frozen components that normally move freely.

3. Check the handlebar holder (**Figure 73**) bolts for tightness. See **Table 5**.
4. Make sure the front wheel lug nuts are tight. See **Table 5**.
5. Make sure the cap is in place on both front hubs.
6. Make sure the front hub nut is tight and that the cotter pin is in place. See Chapter Ten.
7. Check steering play as follows:

a. To check the steering shaft for radial play, move the handlebar from side to side (without attempting to turn the wheels). If play is excessive, the upper bearings are probably worn and should be replaced.

NOTE
***Figure** 74 shows the tie rods removed to better show the cotter pin and nut.*

b. To check the steering shaft for axial (vertical) play, lift up and push down on the handlebar. If excessive play is noticed, check the nut and cotter pin (**Figure 74**) located at the bottom of the steering shaft. If the nut and cotter pin are in place and in good condition, check the thrust bearings located at the lower end of the steering shaft.

8. Turn the handlebar quickly from side to side and notice the following:

a. If there is appreciable looseness at the tie rod ends, the ends may be worn.
b. Observe the joint between the lower end of the strut and the A-arm. Noticeable looseness may indicate a worn ball-joint.
c. Observe the joints at the inner ends of the A-arms. Noticeable looseness may indicate worn bushings.
d. Check for missing cotter pins and loose or missing fasteners.

Front Wheel Toe-Out

Toe-out is adjusted by placing the front of the tires farther apart than the back. This is accomplished by changing the length of the tie rods. Check and adjust the toe-out periodically or when the steering is imprecise or unpredictable. Inspect the steering assembly for damage and wear before adjusting the toe-out. Inflate the tires to the pressure listed in **Table 2**, then check the tires and wheels for damage. If a wheel appears bent, raise that wheel off the ground and rotate it to check more carefully.

To check the toe adjustment, proceed as follows:

1. Position the vehicle on a flat, smooth surface and set the handlebar straight ahead.
2. Raise one front wheel, rotate the tire and use chalk to mark the centerline all around the tire. Lift the other front wheel and mark the centerline of that tire in the same way.
3. Use a tape measure to measure the distance between the centerline at the front, then at the rear of the tires. The distance between the centerlines of the tires should be 3.18-6.35 mm (1/8-1/4 in.) more at the front than at the rear.

75

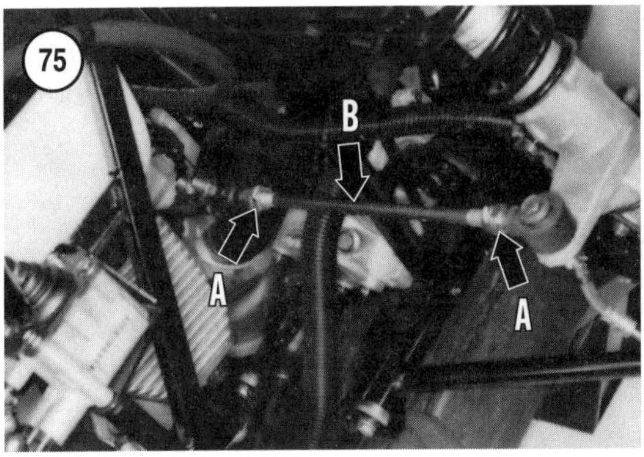

4. If the measured distance is incorrect, adjust as follows:
   a. Loosen the inner and outer tie rod end lock nuts (A, **Figure 75**) on both tie rods. Both tie rods must be adjusted.
   b. Rotate the tie rods (B, **Figure 75**) the same amount on both sides to establish the recommended toe-out. The distance between the ball ends of the two tie rods should be the same to center the steering.
   c. Tighten the lock nuts (A, **Figure 75**) securely when adjustment is correct. Recheck to make sure toe-out is correct after tightening the lock nuts. Make sure the tie rod has full movement after tightening the lock nuts. The tie rod ends should be square with each other (not cocked) after the lock nuts are tightened.

CAUTION

The fasteners that attach the tie rod ends must be installed in a certain direction to prevent steering system interference and binding. In addition, the tie rod ends must be correctly positioned or interference can occur. Refer to Chapter Twelve for correct installation of the inner tie rod to the plates on the base of the steering shaft. The threaded stud on the outer tie rod end must face down with the nut on the bottom.

Front Hub Wheel Bearings

Inspect the front hub bearings for excessive wear or damage at the intervals specified in **Table 1**. Refer to *Front Hub* in the *Periodic Lubrication* section of this chapter for lubrication requirements. Refer to Chapter Twelve for removing and installing the bearings and seals.

1. Support the vehicle with both front wheels off the ground. Block the rear wheels so the vehicle cannot roll in either direction.
2. Turn both wheels by hand. The wheels should rotate smoothly without excessive noise or excessive play.
3. If necessary, service the front hub bearings as described in Chapter Twelve.

3

Rear Suspension

1. Place the vehicle on level ground and set the parking brake.
2. Push down on the rear of the vehicle and observe the movement of all rear suspension components.
3. Check the rubber bushings on the stabilizer linkage rods for wear or deterioration.
4. Inspect the rear drive axle rubber boots for hardness or tears.
5. If necessary, service the rear suspension components as described in Chapter Thirteen.

Nuts, Bolts, and Other Fasteners

Check the tightness of fasteners. Constant vibration can loosen many of the fasteners and all should be checked for tightness, especially:

1. Engine mounting hardware.
2. Engine covers.
3. Handlebar mounting.
4. Exhaust system.

Wire Harness, Control Cables and Hose Lines

Inspect all wiring, cables and hoses for proper routing. The spark plug wire must be routed directly to the front.

Secure hoses, cables and wires to the frame with cable ties. Tighten cable ties only enough to hold the components, but not tight enough to collapse the hoses.

Replace damaged wires, hoses and cables as required, following the original routing. Attach a string to the old wire, cable or hose before withdrawing it to make following the original routing easier. If carefully removed, the string can then be used to pull the new component through the same path as the old one.

UNSCHEDULED INSPECTION AND MAINTENANCE

Recoil Starter

Pull out the starter rope and inspect it for fraying. If its condition is questionable, replace the rope as described in Chapter Five. Check the action of the starter. It should be smooth, and when the rope is released, it should return all the way. If the starter action is rough or if the rope does not return, service the starter as described in Chapter Five.

Body Fasteners

Tighten any loose body fasteners. Replace loose rivets by first drilling out the old rivet and installing a new pop rivet. This tool, along with an assortment of rivets, is available at most hardware and auto parts stores. Follow the manufacturer's instructions for installing rivets.

Check welded joints for cracks and damage. Have damaged welded joints repaired by a competent welding shop.

Fuel Tank and Lines

Inspect the fuel tank for cracks and abrasions. If the tank is damaged and leaking, replace it. See Chapter Six.

Oil Tank

Inspect the oil tank for cracks, abrasions or leaks. Replace the tank if its condition is in doubt.

Electrical System

Check all of the switches for proper operation. Refer to Chapter Eleven.

Electrical Connectors

Inspect the high-tension lead to the spark plug (**Figure 76**) for cracks and breaks in the insulation and replace the lead if it is not perfect. Breaks in the insulation allow the spark to arc to ground and will impair engine performance.

Check primary ignition wiring and lighting wiring for damaged insulation. In some cases, minor damage can be repaired by wrapping the damaged area with electrical insulating tape. If insulation damage is extensive, replace the damaged wires.

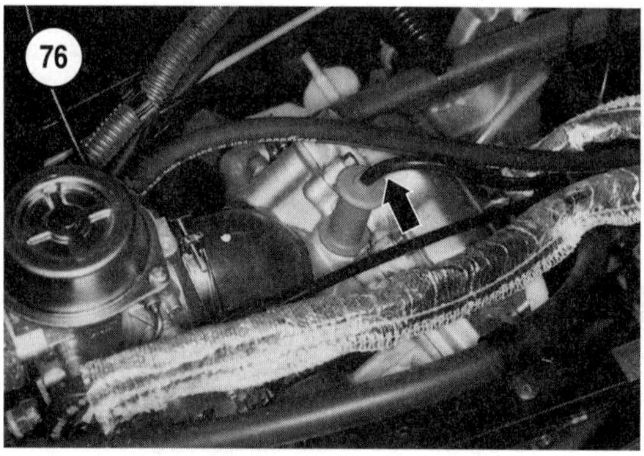

Abnormal Engine Noise

Start the engine and listen for abnormal noises. Often the first indication of developing trouble is a change in sound. An unusual rattle might indicate a loose fastener that can be easily repaired, or it could be the first indication of severe engine damage. After becoming familiar with the vehicle and with practice, it will be possible to identify most new sounds. Periodic inspections and quick identification of abnormal engine noises can prevent a complete engine failure.

ENGINE TUNE-UP

The following procedures cover each phase of a tune-up. Unless otherwise specified, make sure the engine is cool before starting any procedure. A spark plug wrench with a long reach is required to

remove the spark plug. Perform the procedures in the following order:

1. Replace the air filter element. Clean the foam pre-filter element if necessary.
2. Check and adjust the valve clearances.
3. Check or replace the spark plugs.
4. Check and adjust the carburetor idle speed.

Air Filter Element

If necessary, replace the air filter and clean the pre-filter, as described in this chapter, before performing the following tune-up procedures.

Valve Clearance Measurement

The correct valve clearance is listed in **Table 6**. The exhaust valves are located at the front of the engine and the intake valves are located at the rear of the engine.

The photographs in the following procedures show the engine removed from the frame for clarity. It is not necessary to remove the engine to adjust the valves.

NOTE

Valve clearance measurement and adjustment must be performed with the engine cool, at room temperature (below 35° C/95° F).

1. Place the ATV on a level surface and apply the parking brake. Block the wheels to keep it from rolling in either direction.
2. Remove the seat and front fender as described in Chapter Fifteen.
3. Remove the fuel tank as described in Chapter Six.
4. Remove spark plug as described in this chapter. This will make it easier to rotate the engine. Place a piece of duct tape over the spark plug hole to prevent the entry of debris.
5. Remove the screws securing the cylinder head cover (**Figure 77**) and remove the cylinder head cover and gasket.
6. Remove the plug from the timing inspection hole (**Figure 78**).
7. Position the piston at top dead center (TDC) on the compression stroke as follows:
   a. Using the recoil starter, slowly pull on the recoil handle and observe the opening and closing of both sets of valves.
   b. Stop rotating the engine when both sets of intake and exhaust valves are closed.
   c. Verify that the two raised pins on the camshaft sprocket are parallel with the rocker arm cover gasket surface (**Figure 79**). The camshaft lobes should be facing down away from the rocker arms.
   d. Wiggle all four rocker arms, there should be free play indicating that all four valves are closed. This indicates that the piston is at top dead center (TDC) on the compression stroke and all four valves are closed.
   e. Check that the flywheel timing mark is aligned with the center line mark in the timing inspection hole (**Figure 80**) in the recoil starter cover.
8. Insert metric feeler gauges of various thicknesses between the rocker arm adjust screw and intake valve stem (A, **Figure 81**).
   a. When the correct gauge is selected, there will be a slight resistance on the feeler gauge when it is inserted and withdrawn.
   b. Record the clearance and identify the valve checked (right or left intake valve).

3

9. Check the clearance of the remaining intake valve.

NOTE
*A single common rocker arm (**Figure 82**) controls both exhaust valves. Two flat feeler gauges are necessary to check the exhaust valve clearance. This will prevent the rocker arm from tilting slightly during the next step.*

10. Insert metric feeler gauges of various thicknesses between each exhaust valve stem and rocker arm adjust screws.
   a. When the correct gauge is selected, there will be a slight resistance on the feeler gauge when it is inserted and withdrawn.
   b. Record the clearance and identify the valve checked (right or left exhaust valve).

11. If adjustment is required, refer to the *Valve Clearance Adjustment* procedure.

12. If the valve clearance is correct on all four valves, perform the following:
   a. Clean the gasket surfaces of the cylinder head and the cover. Install a new gasket to the cylinder head cover (**Figure 83**).
   b. Install the cylinder head cover and tighten the retaining screws to the torque listed in **Table 5**.
   c. Install all remaining components removed.

Valve Clearance Adjustment

1. Use a 10 mm wrench (B, **Figure 81**) to loosen the valve adjuster locknut.

2. On the *exhaust valves*, leave both flat feeler gauges in place between *each* rocker arm adjuster screw and valve stem end. This will prevent the rocker arm from tilting slightly during the tightening of the locknuts.

3. Use a screwdriver and turn the adjuster in or out to obtain the correct clearance (**Table 6**).

4. Hold the adjuster with the screwdriver (A, **Figure 84**) to prevent it from turning.

5. Install a 10 mm offset adapter (B, **Figure 84**) onto the valve adjuster locknut.

NOTE
Use an offset adapter to prevent overtightening the adjuster locknut.

80

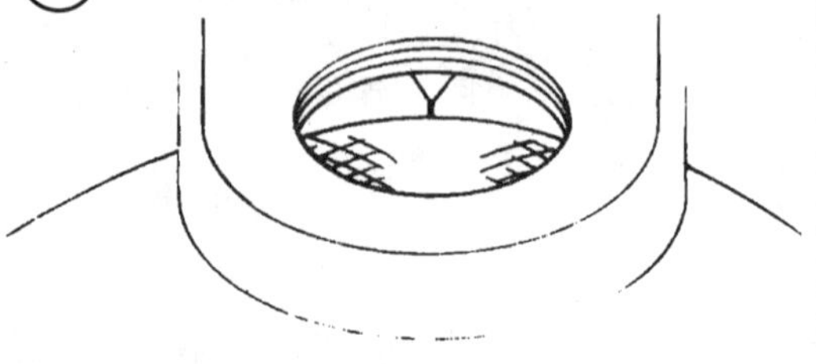

81

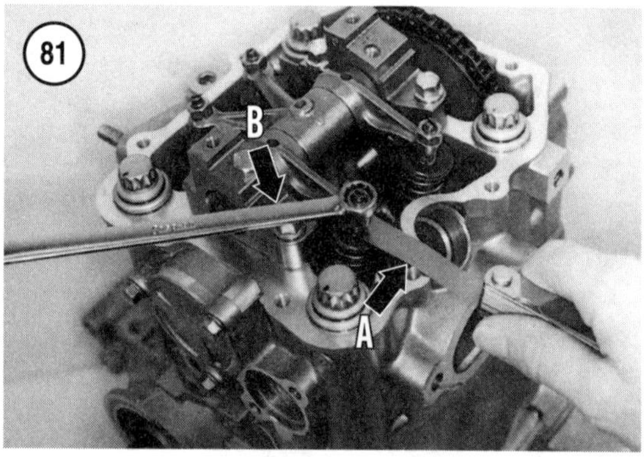

82

83

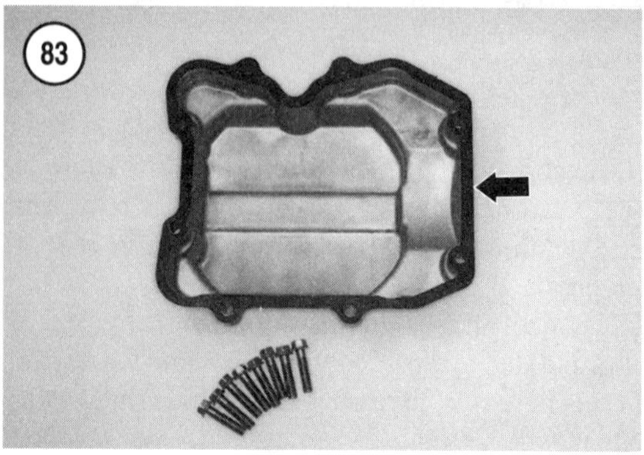

84

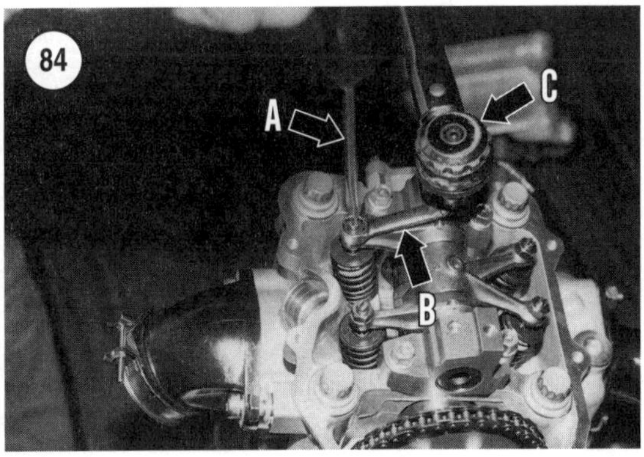

85

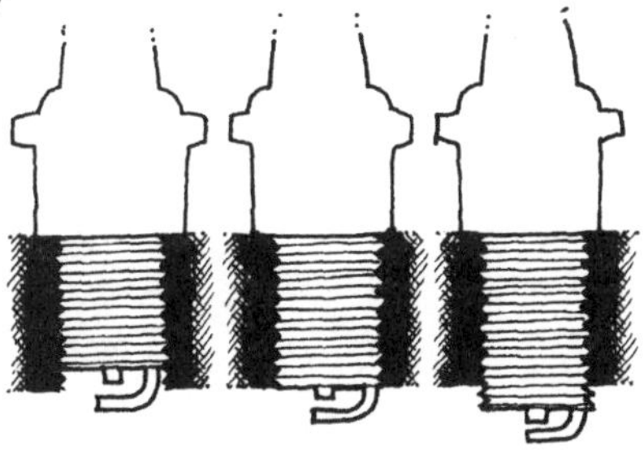

6. Install a torque wrench (C, **Figure 84**) onto the offset adapter at a 90° angle and tighten the adjuster locknut to the torque specification listed in **Table 5**.

7. Recheck the clearance to make sure the adjusters did not move when the locknut was tightened. Readjust the valve clearance if necessary.

8. Clean the gasket surfaces of the cylinder head and cover, then install a new gasket to the cylinder head cover (**Figure 83**).

9. Install the cylinder head cover and tighten the retaining screws to the torque listed in **Table 5**.

10. Install all remaining components removed.

Cam Chain Adjustment

The engine is equipped with an automatic cam chain tensioner assembly. No adjustment is possible or required.

Spark Plug Heat Range

Spark plugs are available in various heat ranges, hotter or colder than the plugs originally installed.

Select a plug of the heat range designed for the loads and conditions under which the vehicle will be operated.

In general, use a hot plug for low speeds and low temperatures. Use a cold plug for high speeds, high engine loads and high temperatures. The plug should operate hot enough to burn off unwanted deposits, but not so hot that it is damaged or causes preignition. A spark plug of the correct heat range will show a light tan color on the portion of the insulator within the cylinder after the plug has been in service.

The reach or length of a plug is also important. A longer than normal plug could interfere with the piston, causing permanent and severe damage; refer to **Figure 85**.

Refer to **Table 6** for recommended spark plug heat ranges.

Spark Plug Removal

CAUTION
Whenever the spark plug is removed, dirt around it can fall into the plug hole. This can cause serious engine damage.

1. Remove the seat as described in Chapter Fifteen.
2. Remove the fuel tank as described in Chapter Six.
3. Blow away all loose dirt then wipe off the cylinder head. Remove all loose debris that could fall into the cylinder head spark plug tunnel.
4. Grasp the spark plug lead, twist from side-to-side to break the seal loose. Then pull the cap off the spark plug and out of the cylinder head (**Figure 86**). If the cap is stuck to the plug, twist it slightly to break it loose.

NOTE
Use a special spark plug socket equipped with a rubber insert that contacts the side of the spark plug. This type of socket is included in the standard tool kit. It is necessary for both removal and installation since the spark plug is recessed in the cylinder head. The spark plug cannot be removed or installed with fingers.

5. Install the special 5/8 in. spark plug socket onto the spark plug. Make sure it is correctly seated and install an open end wrench (tool kit) or socket handle to remove the spark plug.
6. Inspect the plug carefully. Look for a broken center porcelain, excessively eroded electrodes and excessive carbon or oil fouling.

NOTE
Spark plug cleaning with the use of a sand-blast type device is not recommended. While this type of cleaning is thorough, the plug must be completely free of all abrasive cleaning material when done. If not, it is possible for the cleaning material to fall into the cylinder during operation and cause damage.

Gapping and Installing the Spark Plug

Carefully adjust the electrode gap of a new spark plug to ensure a reliable, consistent spark. Use a special spark plug gapping tool and a wire feeler gauge.
1. Make sure the small terminal (**Figure 87**) is attached to the end of the plug.
2. Insert a wire feeler gauge between the center and side electrode of the plug (**Figure 88**). The correct gap is listed in **Table 6**. If the gap is correct, there will be a slight drag felt as the wire is pulled through. If there is no drag, or the gauge will not pass through, bend the side electrode with a gapping tool (**Figure 89**) to set the proper gap listed in **Table 6**.
3. Apply a light coating of antiseize compound to the threads of the spark plug before installing it. Do not use engine oil on the plug threads.

CAUTION
The cylinder head is aluminum and cross-threading of the spark plug can easily damage it.

4. Use the same tool set-up used during removal and screw the spark plug in by hand until it seats. Very little effort is required. If force is necessary, the plug is cross-threaded—stop, unscrew it and try again.
5. Tighten the plug until it seats on the spark plug hole in the cylinder head, then tighten it an additional 1/4 to 1/2 turn.

86

87

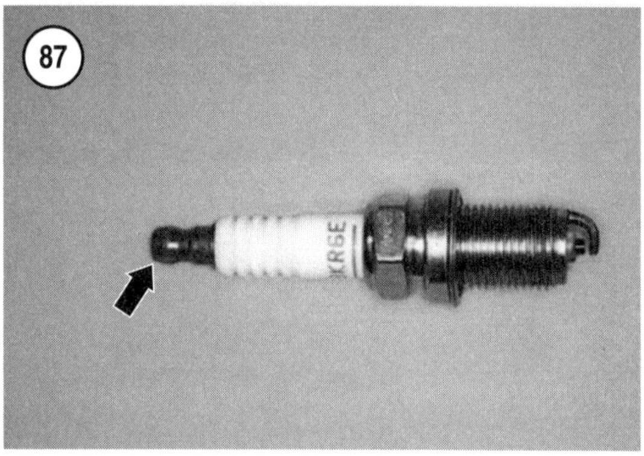

NOTE
Do not overtighten. This will only squash the gasket and destroy its sealing ability.

6. Install the spark plug cap and lead and cap onto the spark plug. Rotate the cap slightly in both directions and make sure it is attached to the spark plug as well as the sealing surface of the cylinder head.

Reading Spark Plugs

Reading the spark plug can provide a significant amount of information regarding engine performance. A careful examination of a plug that has been in use will provide an indication of spark plug operation (heat range), air/fuel mixture composition and engine condition (oil consumption, piston, etc.). If the plug is new, operate the ATV under a medium load for a short period. Avoid prolonged idling before shutting off the engine. Remove the spark plug as described in this chapter. Examine the plug and compare it to those in **Figure 90**.

If the plug is being read to determine if the carburetor jetting is correct, start with a new plug and op-

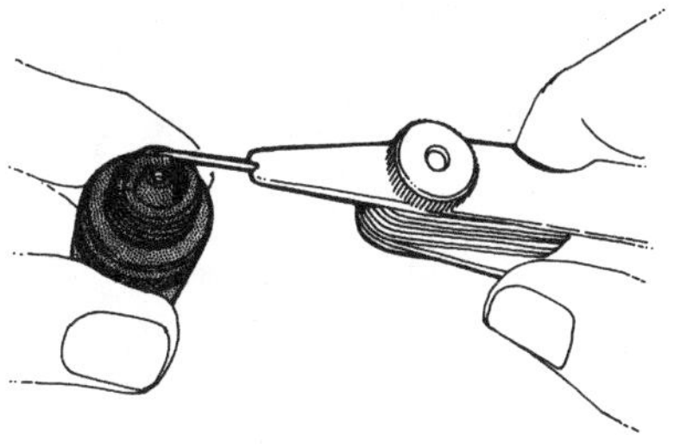

88

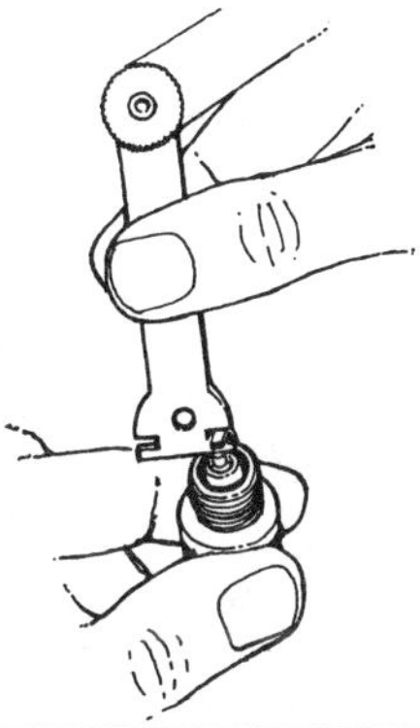

89

erate the ATV at the load that corresponds to the jetting information desired. For example, if the main jet is in question, operate the ATV at full throttle and shut the engine off and coast to a stop.

Normal condition

If the plug has a light tan- or gray-colored deposit and no abnormal gap wear or erosion, good engine, air/fuel mixture and ignition condition are indicated. The plug in use is of the proper heat range and may be serviced and returned to use.

Carbon-fouled

Soft, dry, sooty deposits covering the entire firing end of the plug are evidence of incomplete combustion. Even though the firing end of the plug is dry, the plug's insulation decreases when in this condition. An electrical path is formed that bypasses the electrodes resulting in a misfire condition. One or more of the following can cause carbon fouling:

1. Too rich fuel mixture.
2. Spark plug heat range too cold.
3. Clogged air filter.
4. Improperly operating ignition component.
5. Ignition component failure.
6. Low engine compression.
7. Prolonged idling.

Oil-fouled

The tip of an oil-fouled plug has a black insulator tip, a damp oily film over the firing end and a carbon layer over the entire nose. The electrodes are not worn. Common causes for this condition are:

1. Incorrect air/fuel mixture.
2. Low idle speed or prolonged idling.
3. Ignition component failure.
4. Spark plug heat range too cold.
5. Engine still being broken in.
6. Valve guides worn.
7. Piston rings worn or broken.

An oil-fouled spark plug may be cleaned in an emergency, but it is better to replace it. It is important to correct the cause of fouling before the engine is returned to service.

Gap bridging

Plugs with this condition exhibit gaps shorted out by combustion deposits between the electrodes. If this condition is encountered, check for excessive carbon or oil in the combustion chamber. Be sure to locate and correct the cause of this condition.

Overheating

Badly worn electrodes and premature gap wear are signs of overheating, along with a gray or white blistered porcelain insulator surface. The most common cause for this condition is using a spark plug of the wrong heat range (too hot). If a hotter plug has not been installed and the plug is overheated, consider the following causes:

1. Lean air/fuel mixture.
2. Improperly operating ignition component.
3. Engine lubrication system malfunction.
4. Cooling system malfunction.
5. Engine air leak.
6. Improper spark plug installation (overtightening).
7. No spark plug gasket.

90

SPARK PLUG CONDITION

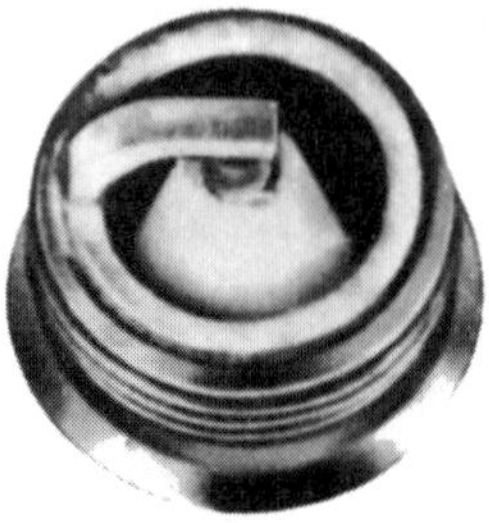

NORMAL

- Identified by light tan or gray deposits on the firing tip.
- Can be cleaned.

GAP BRIDGED

- Identified by deposit buildup closing gap between electrodes.
- Caused by oil or carbon fouling. If deposits are not excessive, the plug can be

OIL FOULED

- Identified by wet black deposits on the insulator shell bore and electrodes.
- Caused by excessive oil entering combustion chamber through worn rings and pistons, excessive clearance between valve guides and stems or worn or loose bearings. Can be cleaned. If engine is not repaired, use a hotter plug.

CARBON FOULED

- Identified by black, dry fluffy carbon deposits on insulator tips, exposed shell surfaces and electrodes.
- Caused by too cold a plug, weak ignition, dirty air cleaner, too rich fuel mixture or excessive idling. Can be cleaned.

LEAD FOULED

- Identified by dark gray, black, yellow or tan deposits or a fused glazed coating on the insulator tip.
- Caused by highly leaded gasoline. Can be cleaned.

WORN

- Identified by severely eroded or worn electrodes
- Caused by normal wear. Should be replaced.

FUSED SPOT DEPOSIT

- Identified by melted or spotty deposits resembling bubbles or blisters.
- Caused by sudden acceleration. Can be cleaned.

OVERHEATING

- Identified by a white or light gray insulator with small black or gray brown spots with bluish-burnt appearance of electrodes.
- Caused by engine overheating, wrong type of fuel, loose spark plugs, too hot a plug or incorrect ignition timing. Replace the plug.

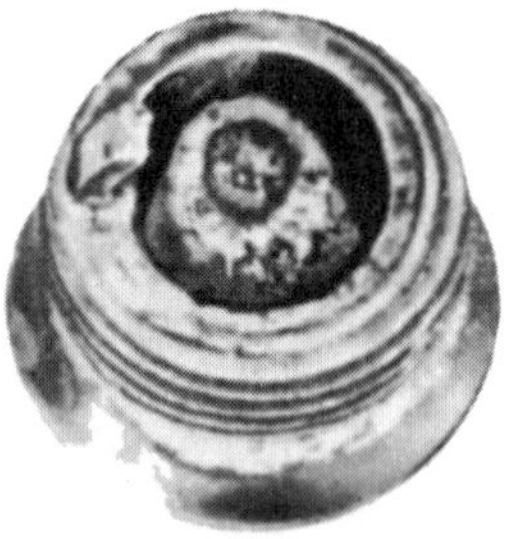

PREIGNITION

- Identified by melted electrodes and possibly blistered insulator. Metallic deposits on insulator indicate engine damage.
- Caused by wrong type of fuel, incorrect ignition timing or advance, too hot a plug, burned valves or engine overheating. Replace the plug.

Worn

Corr voltage plug in under h plug.

Preigni

If the certainly over-adv that a plu used. Fir turning tl mation c Chapter 1

Checking Ignition 1

All moc charge ign used. This to failures breaker-poi

Change i ... relocating the stator plate located under the engine flywheel. When disassembling, note that the holes for the stator plate attaching screws are elongated.

When assembling the stator plate, align the mark on the stator plate with the mark on the crankcase as shown in **Figure 91**. It may be necessary to move the stator plate slightly when timing as described in this chapter.

NOTE

Because ignition components are temperature-sensitive, check ignition timing while the engine is cold. Timing may change as much as 2° when the engine warms.

ce the ATV on a level surface and apply the g brake. Block the wheels to keep it from roll- either direction.

nove the plug from the timing hole in the re- rter cover (**Figure 78**).

ch a stroboscopic timing light to the spark ad following the manufacturer's instruc-

h a portable tachometer according to its turer's instructions.

the transmission to NEUTRAL.

WARNING

not allow anyone to stand behind in front of the vehicle when the en- ie is running. Keep hands, feet and thing away from the engine, belt d drive chains.

ie engine, allow it to idle for approxi- -15 seconds, then increase the engine e *ignition timing speed* rpm listed in **Ta-**

e timing light at the recoil starter cover ection hole (**Figure 78**) and observe the ning mark.

NOTE

timing light will flash, appearing op the timing marks at the instant nition.

the engine speed briefly and observe mark that is aligned with the timing ure 92).

is not correct, adjust it as described in the following procedure.

10. When timing is correct, turn the engine off, remove the timing light and tachometer. Install all of the covers that were removed.

Adjusting Ignition Timing

The ignition must occur at a specific time to achieve optimum engine performance.

Walmart
Save money. Live better.

Walmart
MANAGER DIANE MAXWELL
(719) 484 - 0912
ST# 3227 OP# 00000247 TE# 90 TR# 09425
BATT ES14AA2 068113131914 45.00 X
BATT CORE FE 068113107867 10.00 O
** VOIDED ENTRY **
BATT CORE FE 068113107867 10.00-O
SUBTOTAL 45.00
TAX 1 7.900 % 3.56
TOTAL 48.56
ECA CHECK TEND 48.56
CHANGE DUE 0.00

When you pay by check, you authorize us to use its information to process an Electronic Funds Transfer (EFT) or a draft drawn on your account, or to process the payment as a check. If payment is returned unpaid, you authorize collection of your payment and the Return Fee below by EFT(s) or draft(s) drawn on your account. Call 888-905-3388 with any questions
RETURN FEE AMOUNT 20.00

ITEMS SOLD 1

TC# 9353 0125 3448 2719 2361

Find us on Facebook!
www.facebook.com/walmart

THANK YOU FOR SHOPPING WITH US
10/30/10 15:02:15

92

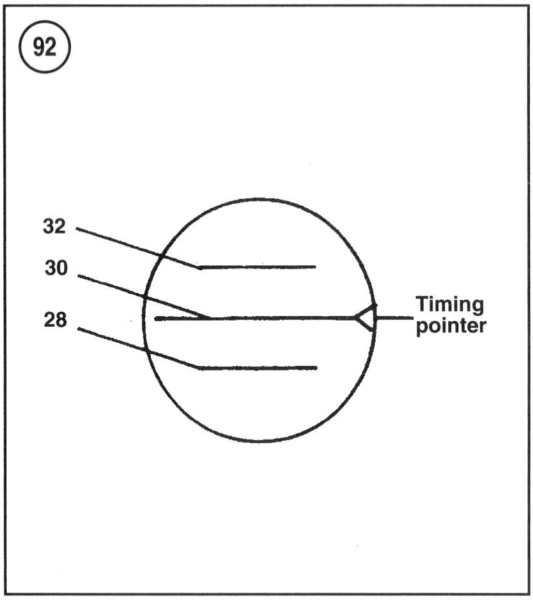

1. Remove the recoil starter assembly as described in Chapter Five.

2. Remove the flywheel as described in Chapter Five.

3. Loosen the stator plate mounting screws (**Figure 93**) and rotate the stator plate to adjust ignition timing. Turn the stator plate *clockwise* to retard ignition timing or *counterclockwise* to advance timing.

4. Tighten the stator plate retaining screws.

5. Reinstall the flywheel, starter pulley and recoil starter assembly.

Carburetor Idle Mixture Adjustment

The pilot air screw controls the air/fuel mixture at idle speed. Turning the pilot air screw *clockwise* reduces the amount of air and richens the mixture.

The pilot air screw is preset by the manufacturer. The following procedure is to be used only after the carburetor has been disassembled and cleaned or if the pilot air screw is replaced.

1. The pilot air screw (**Figure 94**) is located on the bottom of the carburetor, nearest the engine.

2. Turn the pilot air screw in *clockwise*) until it seats lightly.

93

94

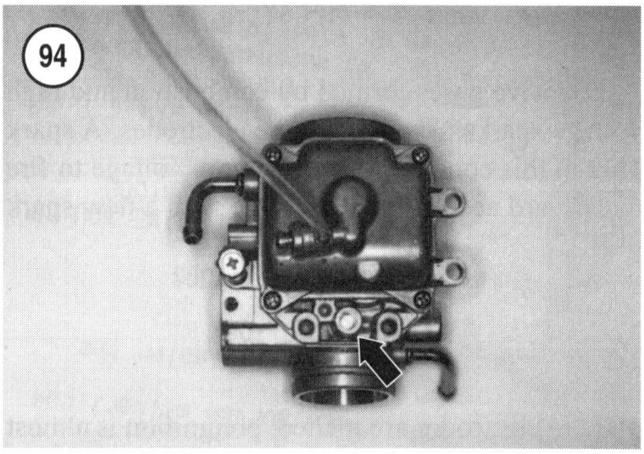

95

NOTE
Do not damage the seat or the tip of the pilot air screw by forcing it into its seat.

3. Back the pilot air screw out the number of turns specified in **Table 6**.

4. Start the engine and allow it to warm up to normal operating temperature (about 10 minutes).

5. Connect an accurate portable tachometer capable of reading increments of ± 50 rpm.

6. Set the idle speed to 1200 rpm by turning the throttle adjust knob (**Figure 95**).
7. Slowly turn the pilot air screw clockwise until the engine speed begins to decrease by 50 rpm or greater, stop and note the screw location.
8. Slowly turn the pilot air screw counterclockwise until idle speed increases to maximum rpm. Continue to turn the pilot air screw counterclockwise until idle RPM begins to drop. Stop and note the screw location.
9. Center the pilot air screw between the screw settings achieved in Step 7 and Step 8.
10. Readjust idle speed if not within the idle speed listed in **Table 6**.

Idle Speed

CAUTION

Do not use the pilot air screw to change the engine idle speed. The pilot air screw must be set as described in this chapter or the engine may be damaged by excessively lean air/fuel mixture.

1. Connect a tachometer according to its manufacturer's instructions.
2. Refer to **Table 6** for the correct idle speed.
3. Turn the throttle stop knob (**Figure 95**) in to increase or out to decrease idle speed.

Table 1 MAINTENANCE AND LUBRICATION SCHEDULE

Pre-ride check	Check tire condition and inflation pressure Check wheel rim condition Check brake fluid level; add fluid if necessary Check brake lever operation and travel Check tightness of nuts, bolts and fasteners Check fuel level in fuel tank; top off if necessary
Daily checks	Check air filter element Check air filter air box sediment tube Check coolant level in reservoir Check operation of headlight and brake lamp Check drive chain tension and condition
Weekly	Check for moisture in recoil starter housing Check air filter element
Every month or after 10-25 hours of operation	Check battery condition Check transmission oil level Check front drive unit oil level Check engine breather filter Check brake pad wear
Every six months or after 50 hours of operation	General lubrication of chassis components Lubricate steering shaft bushing Change engine oil and filter Check throttle operation; lubricate cable if necessary Check ETC switch operation Check choke operation; lubricate if necessary Drain carburetor float bowl Inspect all air intake ducts and fittings Check coolant-to-water ratio Check front hub lubrication Check drive belt (EBS models) Check and adjust drive belt (non-EBS models) Check and adjust shift linkage Check steering operation; lubricate if necessary Check front suspension mounting fittings; lubricate if necessary

(continued)

Table 1 MAINTENANCE AND LUBRICATION SCHEDULE (continued)

Every twelve months or after 100 hours of operation	Check oil tank vent hose routing and condition Check and adjust valve clearance Check entire fuel system for leaks and hose deterioration Replace fuel filter Check radiator and hoses for leakage and damage Check engine mounting hardware Inspect spark plug; replace if necessary Check ignition timing; adjust if necessary Change lubricant in front hubs Change transmission fluid Check front hub bearings for excessive wear Inspect clutch drive pulley for correct engagement Check auxiliary brake pedal operation and adjustment Check headlight aim; adjust if necessary Check front wheel toe-out adjustment Check exhaust system mounts for tightness Remove the drain plug on muffler and drain out any residue
Every twenty four months or after 200 hours of operation	All of the above checks plus the following Change brake fluid Check tightness of front hub nut

Table 2 TIRE INFLATION PRESSURE (COLD)*

Model	kPa	PSI
Front wheels	34.5	5
Rear wheels	34.5	5

* Tire pressure for original equipment tires. Aftermarket tires may require different inflation pressure.

Table 3 RECOMMENDED LUBRICANTS AND FLUIDS

Item	Lubricant or fluid type
Engine oil	Polaris Premium 4 Synthetic 10W/40 or 10W/40 motor oil
Transmission oil	Polaris synthetic gear case oil (part No. 2871478)
Front gear case	Polaris front gearcase lube (part No. 2871653), or API GL5 80-90 gear lube
Front hubs	Polaris demand drive hub fluid (part No. 2871654), or ATF Type F
Brake fluid	DOT 3 brake fluid
Coolant	50:50 mixture high-quality ethylene glycol-based coolant compounded for aluminum radiators and engines
Grease	Polaris all season grease, or equivalent

Table 4 CAPACITIES

Item	Quantity
Engine oil	1.89 L (2 U.S. qts.)
Transmission oil	946.3 cc (32 U.S. oz.)
Front gear case (all years)	96 cc (3.25 U.S. oz.)
Front hubs	75 cc (2.5 U.S. oz.)
Coolant	Approx. 2.16 L (2.25 U.S. qts.)

Table 5 MAINTENANCE AND TUNE-UP TORQUE SPECIFICATIONS

Item	N•m	in.-lb.	ft.-lb.
Crankcase oil drain plug	19	–	14
Cylinder head cover screws	8.2	72	–
Front gear case drain plug	9.4	83	–
Handlebar upper holder bolts	13-17	115-150	–
Oil tank drain plug	19	–	14
Oil tank screen and fitting	20	–	15
Valve adjuster locknuts	6-7	53-62	–
Wheel lug nuts			
Front	21	–	15
Rear	21	–	15

Table 6 MAINTENANCE AND TUNE-UP SPECIFICATIONS

Item	Specification
Disc brake pad thickness wear limit	
All calipers	3.81 mm (0.150 in.)
Valve clearance (cold)	
Intake and exhaust	0.15 mm (0.006 in.)
Spark plug	
Heat range	
1996-1997	NGK BKR5ES
1998-on	NGK BKR5E
Gap	
1996-1998	0.6-0.7 mm (0.024-0.028 in.)
1999-on	0.7 mm (0.028 in.)
Idle speed	
1996-1998	1100-1300 rpm
1999-on	1000-1400 rpm
Ignition timing/speed	30° @ 3500 rpm
Carburetor pilot air screw	
1996	1 1/2 turns out
1997-1998	2 turns out
1999-on	2 5/8 turns out
Oil pressure @5500 rpm	
Standard	138 kPa (20 psi)
Minimum	83 kPa (12 psi)

CHAPTER FOUR

ENGINE TOP END

This chapter covers top end engine service and repair procedures. Specifications are provided in **Tables 1-4** at the end of the chapter.

The ATV is equipped with a liquid-cooled single cylinder engine. The engine features a single overhead camshaft (SOHC), which is chain driven from the crankshaft and a four-valve cylinder head. Valve actuation and adjustment is by means of adjustable rocker arms.

One of the most important aspects of a successful engine overhaul is preparation. Read all of the procedures before starting and review the information in Chapter One regarding tools and methods. The accurate use of precision measuring equipment is vital to a successful overhaul. Before removing the engine and disassembling the crankcase, degrease the engine and frame. Have all the necessary hand and special tools available. Make sure the work area is clean and well lit. Identify and store individual parts and assemblies in appropriate storage containers (**Figure 1**).

References to the left and right sides refer to the position of the parts as viewed by the rider siting on the seat facing forward, not how the engine may sit on the workbench.

ENGINE PRINCIPLES

Figure 2 explains four-stroke engine operation.

1

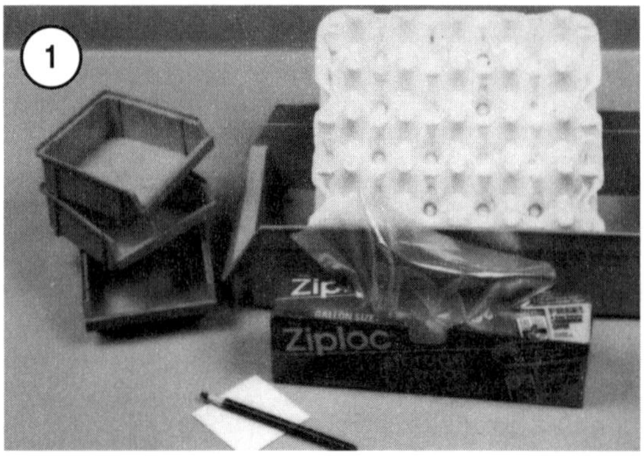

ENGINE COOLING

A mixture of antifreeze and distilled water cools the engine. The coolant is circulated through the engine and radiator by a shaft-driven pump. Refer to Chapter Three for cooling system maintenance and to Chapter Seven for service to the engine cooling system.

NOTE

Cooling is also assisted by the fins (A, ***Figure 3****) on the oil tank located on the left side. Some of the heat from the engine is transferred to the oil, then radiated to the air flowing past the cooling fins on the reservoir. Service to the lubrication system is covered in Chapter Five.*

4

(1)

FOUR-STROKE OPERATING PRINCIPLES

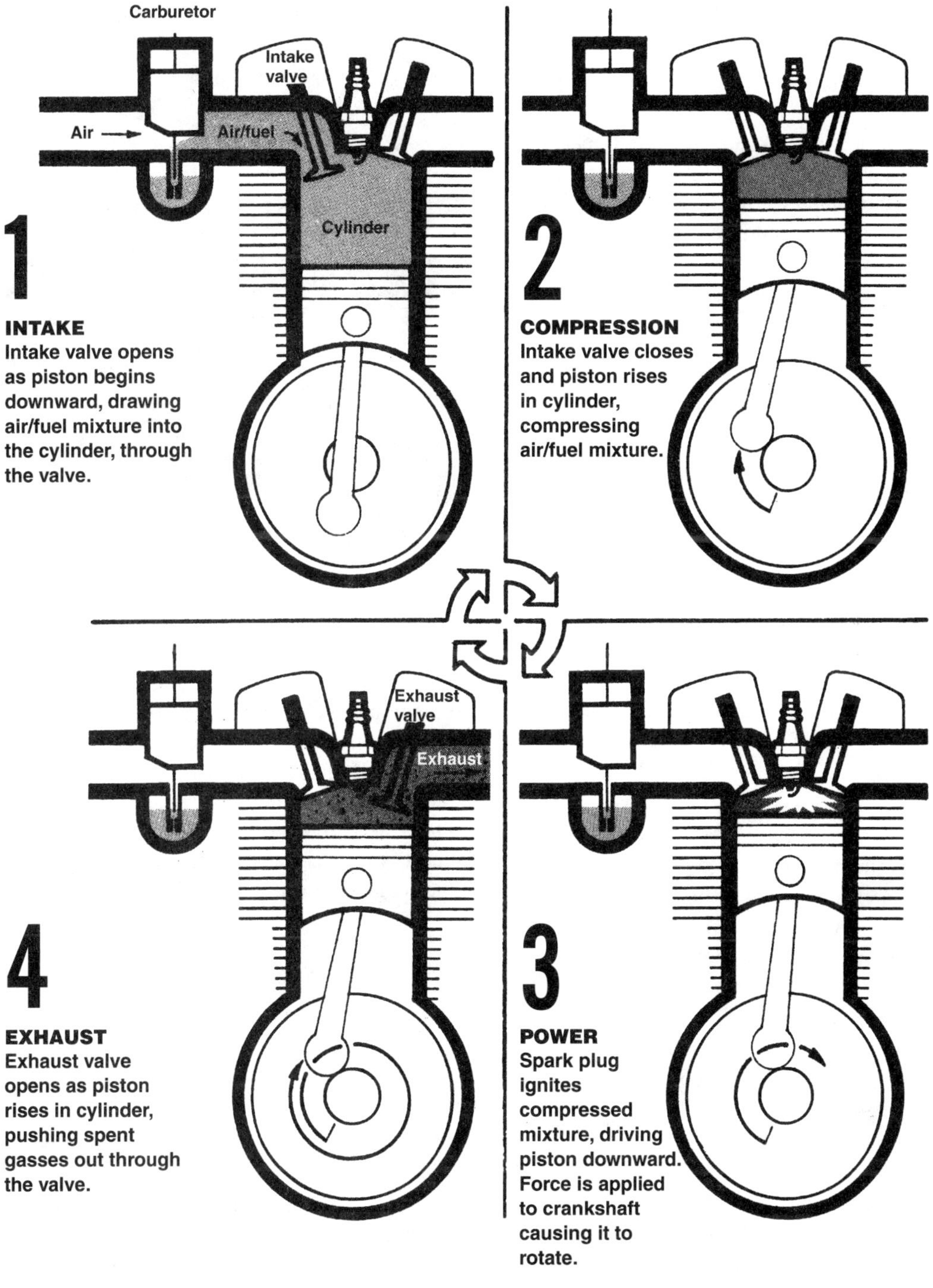

ENGINE LUBRICATION

The engine is equipped with a dry sump-type lubrication system that contains only a small amount of oil. The various components of the engine are lubricated by the oil as it is circulated within the engine, then back to the oil tank. Engine heat is transferred to the oil, then the oil is allowed to cool while it is in the oil tank (A, **Figure 3**).

The oil flows through a screen in the bottom of the oil tank, then through the supply hose to the oil pump. The oil pump forces oil through a one-way check valve that keeps the oil from draining from the oil tank into the engine when it is not running. After passing the check valve, oil flows to the oil filter for cleaning. If the oil filter (B, **Figure 3**) is obstructed, a bypass valve in the filter allows the oil to pass without being filtered. After flowing through (or around) the oil filter, the oil is divided into two separate paths.

Part of the pressurized oil flows through the stud at the left front of the cylinder head to lubricate the camshaft and valve operating mechanism. The remaining oil is directed to the crankcase main oil gallery. Oil from the main oil gallery is used to lubricate the crankshaft, connecting rod and engine balancer assembly. This oil also lubricates the cylinder, piston and piston rings, connecting rod, piston pin bearing, oil/coolant pump drive gears, cam chain and drive sprockets.

Oil pump service is covered in Chapter Five.

Refer to Chapter Three to service the engine oil and the oil filter and to check the oil pressure.

SERVICING THE ENGINE IN THE FRAME

The ATV's frame is a great holding fixture, especially when breaking loose stubborn bolts and nuts. The following components can be serviced while the engine is mounted in the frame.

1. Flywheel and alternator stator.
2. Rocker arm assembly.
3. Camshaft, chain and sprockets.
4. Camshaft chain tensioner and guide.
5. Cylinder head.
6. Cylinder block.
7. Piston and rings.
8. Starter motor and drive.

Some of the photographs in this chapter are shown with the engine removed from the frame to better illustrate the steps.

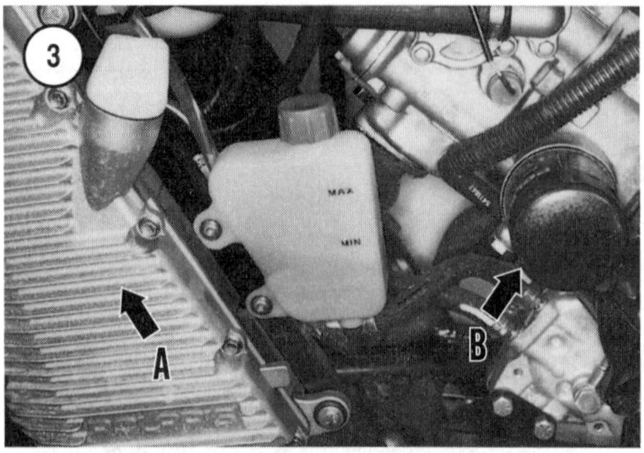

EXHAUST SYSTEM

Check the exhaust system for deep dents or fractures and repair or replace parts as required. Check the mounting flanges on the muffler and the frame for fractures. Replace broken or missing springs (**Figure 4**). Replace or tighten any missing or loose bolts. Check the mounting flange attached to the cylinder head for tightness. A loose exhaust pipe connection will cause excessive exhaust noise and reduce engine power.

Removal/Installation

Refer to **Figure 5**.

1. Place the vehicle on level ground and set the parking brake.
2. Remove the front and rear fenders as described in Chapter Fifteen.
3. Remove the muffler mounting bolts (**Figure 6**) and unhook the attaching springs (**Figure 7**). Do not lose the washers, bushings and collars on the mounting bolts.

5

EXHAUST SYSTEM

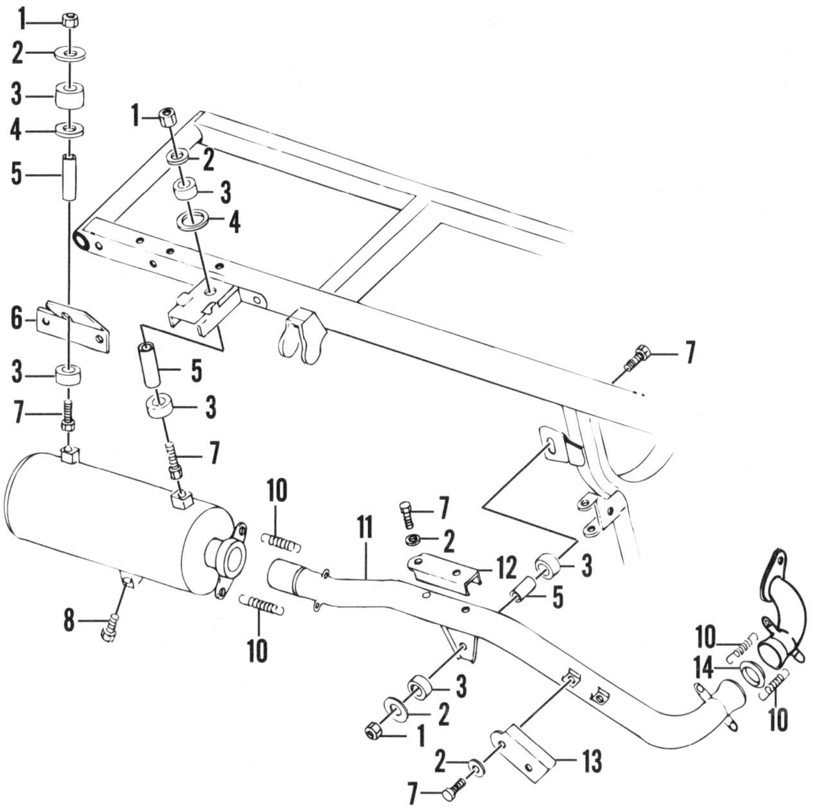

1. Nut
2. Washer
3. Rubber cushion
4. Washer
5. Collar
6. Mounting bracket
7. Bolt
8. Drain bolt
9. Muffler
10. Spring
11. Exhaust pipe
12. Heat shield
13. Heat shield
14. Gasket

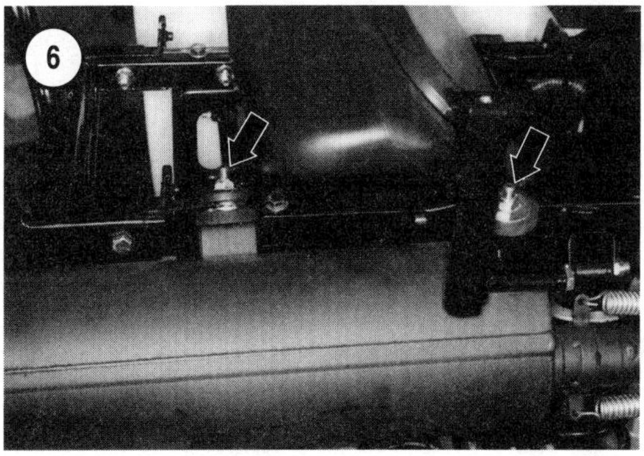

6

7

4. Pull the muffler to the rear and disengage it from the exhaust pipe. Remove the muffler.

WARNING
Use caution when unhooking the springs at the cylinder head exhaust fitting. Attaching a spring hook onto the inner spring is very difficult due to the limited work area. Protect your hands accordingly.

5. Unhook the springs (**Figure 8**) securing the exhaust pipe to the cylinder head exhaust fitting.
6. Remove the nut and washer (**Figure 9**) securing the exhaust pipe to the frame mounting bracket.
7. Disengage the exhaust pipe from the fitting.
8. Lift up on the rear portion of the exhaust pipe until it is almost vertical (**Figure 10**), then carefully pull the exhaust pipe out from behind the shift levers (**Figure 11**).
9. Install by reversing these removal steps while noting the following:
   a. Inspect the gasket between the cylinder head exhaust fitting and exhaust pipe and the one between the exhaust pipe and the muffler. Replace any gasket(s) that are damaged or leaking.
   b. After installation is complete, start the engine and make sure there are no exhaust leaks.

Inspection

Replace parts that show excessive wear or damage as described in this section.

1. Inspect the springs for damage. Replace weak or damaged springs.
2. Inspect the exhaust pipe mounting bracket (**Figure 12**) for missing parts or damage.

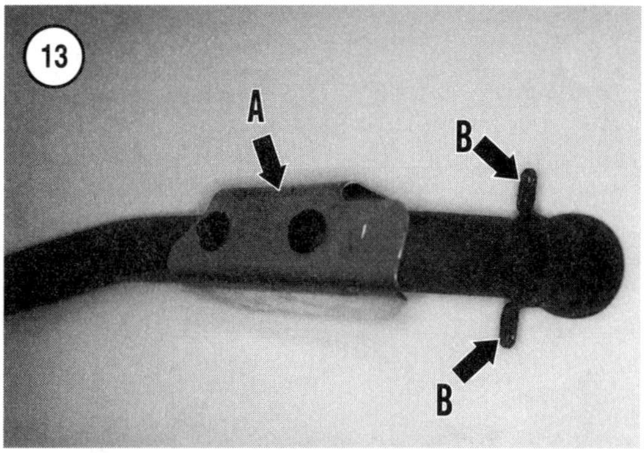

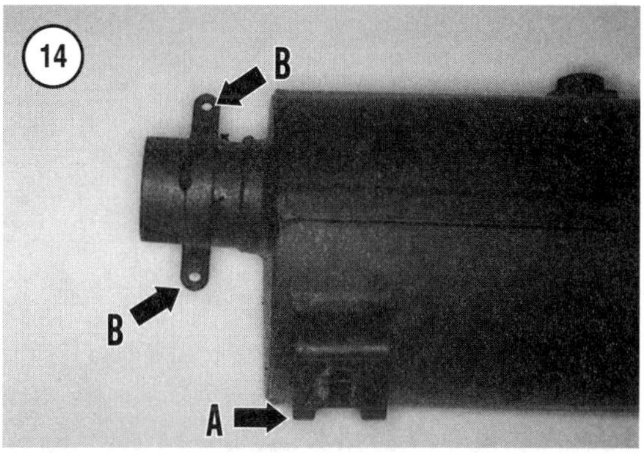

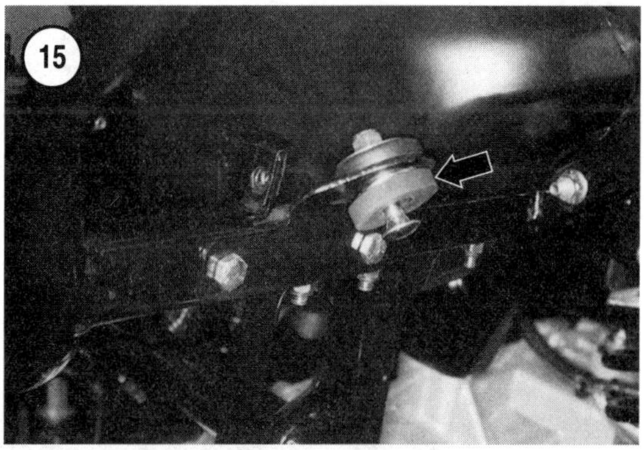

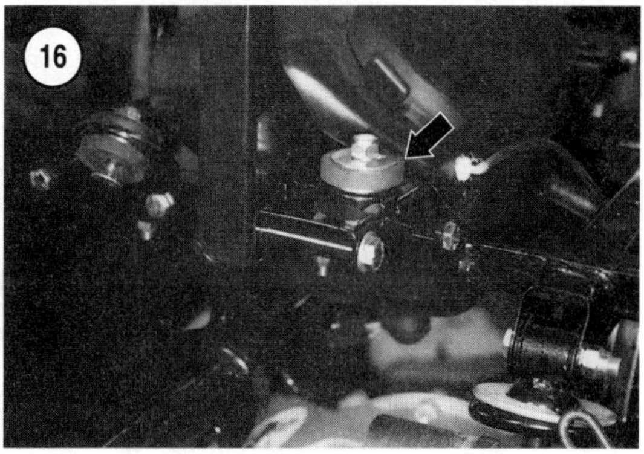

3. Inspect the exhaust pipe heat shield (A, **Figure 13**) and spring brackets (B, **Figure 13**) for cracks or other damage.

4. Inspect the muffler mounting bracket (A, **Figure 14**) and spring brackets (B, **Figure 14**) for cracks or other damage.

5. Inspect the muffler mounting brackets on the frame. Refer to **Figure 15** and **Figure 16**. Check for cracks or other damage to the rubber cushions. Replace as necessary.

6. Inspect the muffler for rust and damage.

CYLINDER HEAD COVER

Removal/Installation

1. Place the ATV on a level surface and set the parking brake. Block the wheels to keep it from rolling in either direction.

2. Remove the seat and front fender as described in Chapter Fifteen.

3. Remove the fuel tank as described in Chapter Six.

4. Remove the screws securing the cylinder head cover (**Figure 17**), then remove the cover and gasket.

5. Install by reversing these removal steps. Install a new gasket (**Figure 18**) and tighten the screws securely.

ROCKER ARM ASSEMBLY

Removal

1. Remove the cylinder head cover as described in this chapter.

2. Disconnect the negative battery cable as described in Chapter Three. Secure the cable so it will

not accidentally make contact with the battery terminal.

3. Remove the spark plug as described in Chapter Three. This will make it easier to rotate the engine.

4. Remove the plug from the timing inspection hole (**Figure 19**).

5. Position the piston at top dead center (TDC) on the compression stroke as follows:

   a. Using the recoil starter, slowly pull on the recoil handle and observe the opening and closing of the valves.

   b. Stop rotating the engine when both sets of intake and exhaust valves are closed.

   c. Verify that the two raised pins on the camshaft sprocket are parallel with the rocker arm cover gasket surface (**Figure 20**). The camshaft lobes should be facing down away from the rocker arms.

   d. Wiggle all four rocker arms, there should be free play indicating that all four valves are closed. This indicates that the piston is at top dead center (TDC) on the compression stroke and all four valves are closed.

   e. Check that the flywheel timing mark is aligned with the center line mark in the timing inspection hole (**Figure 21**) in the recoil starter cover.

6. If the rocker arm assembly is going to be serviced, loosen the rocker shaft retaining screw (**Figure 22**).

CAUTION
Account for the dowel pins when removing the rocker arm assembly.

7. Remove the four bolts (**Figure 23**) securing the rocker arm shaft brackets.

CAUTION
Hold onto the rocker arm assembly, as it will separate after being removed from the cylinder head. Do not drop any of the components.

8. Pull straight up and lift the rocker arms and shaft assembly from the cylinder head. Do not lose the locating dowels.

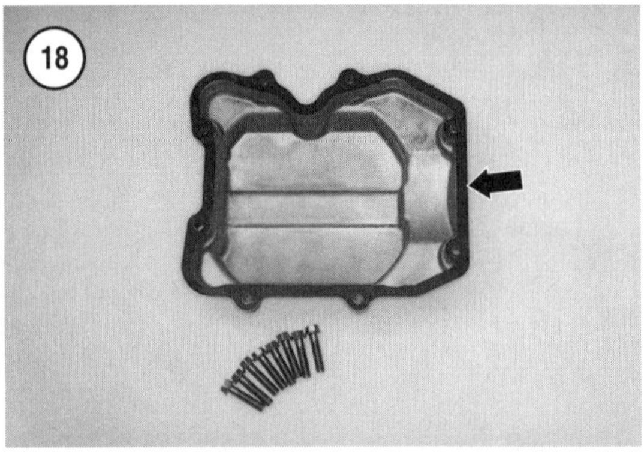
18

19

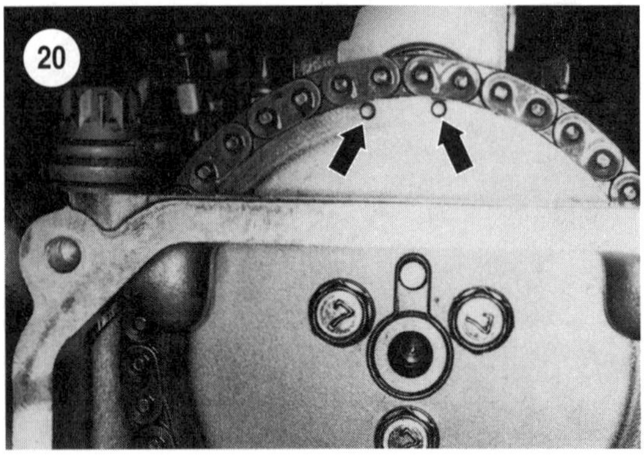
20

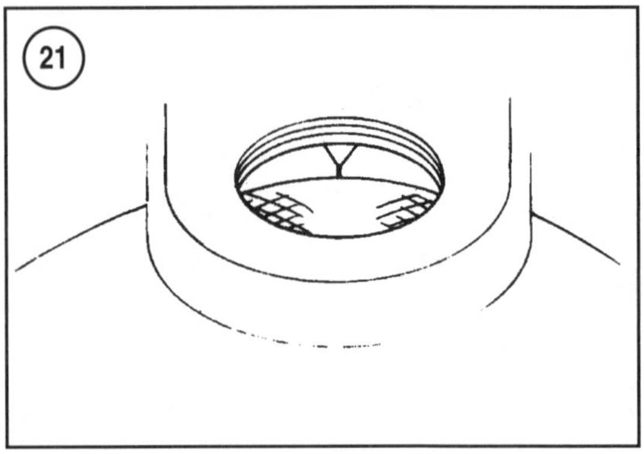
21

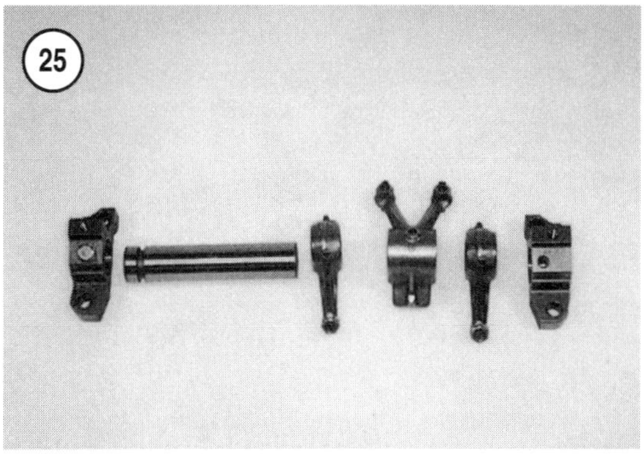

Installation

1. Coat the cam lobes and cam follower surfaces with molybdenum disulfide grease before installing the rocker arm assembly. Coat the mounting bolt threads with a light film of engine oil.

NOTE

*If the camshaft has turned from top dead center on the compression stroke, repeat Step 5 in **Removal** to return the engine to TDC on the compression stroke.*

2. If removed, install the locating dowels (**Figure 24**) into the cylinder head.
3. Correctly position the rocker arm assembly and install the rocker arm assembly onto the locating dowels and the cylinder head. Push the assembly down until it is flush with the mating surface of the cylinder head.
4. Install the four support bolts (**Figure 23**) and tighten in a crisscross pattern to the torque value listed in **Table 3**.
5. If loosened or removed, tighten the rocker shaft retaining screw (**Figure 22**) securely.
6. Adjust valve clearance as described in Chapter Three.
7. Clean the gasket surfaces of the cylinder head and cover, then install a new gasket (**Figure 18**) on the cylinder head cover.
8. Install the cylinder head cover as described in this chapter.
9. Install the plug into the timing inspection hole and tighten securely.
10. Install the spark plug as described in Chapter Three.
11. Connect the negative battery cable.

Rocker Arm Disassembly/Inspection/Assembly

1. Remove the rocker arm assembly as described in this chapter.
2. Separate the bracket, rocker arms and shaft (**Figure 25**).
3. Thoroughly clean all parts in solvent and dry with compressed air.
4. Make sure the rocker arm oil holes are clear (**Figure 26**). Clean out if necessary.

4

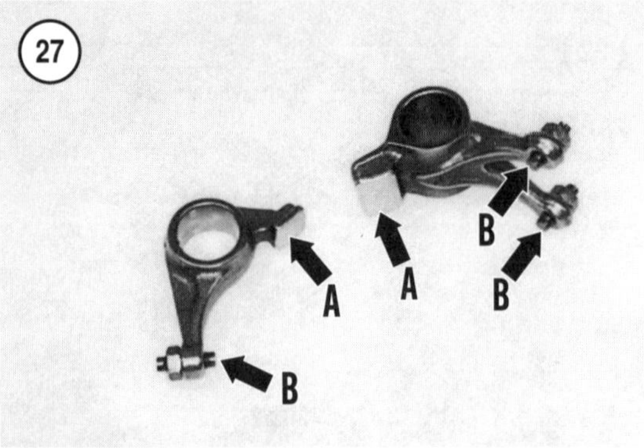

5. Inspect each rocker arm pad (A, **Figure 27**) where it contacts the camshaft lobe and where the adjuster (B, **Figure 27**) contacts the valve stem. Check for scratches, flat spots, uneven wear and scoring and replace if necessary.

NOTE
The valve adjuster screw is hardened. It cannot be re-faced if damaged.

6. Inspect the valve adjuster screw for flat spots, cracks or other damage. Inspect the locknuts for damage. Replace the valve adjuster screw and locknuts if necessary.
7. Inspect the rocker arm shaft surface (**Figure 28**) for wear, scoring, cracks or other damage and replace if necessary.
8. Unscrew the rocker shaft retaining screw and separate the shaft from the support (**Figure 29**).
9. Inspect rocker arm bores (**Figure 30**) and the shaft support bore (**Figure 31**) for wear or scoring.
10. Measure the rocker arm bore diameter with a snap gauge (**Figure 32**). Record the dimension.
11. Measure the rocker arm shaft outside diameter with a micrometer (**Figure 33**). Record the dimension.
12. Calculate the rocker arm-to-shaft clearance as follows:
   a. Subtract the rocker arm shaft diameter (Step 11) from the rocker arm bore diameter (Step 10).
   b. Replace the rocker arm and/or shaft if the clearance exceeds the service limit in **Table 4**.
13. Repeat for the other rocker arm.
14. Apply clean engine oil to all sliding parts and install the rocker arms onto the shaft, then install the support. Refer to **Figure 34** for the correct placement of all parts on the shaft.
15. Install the rocker arm assembly as described in this chapter.

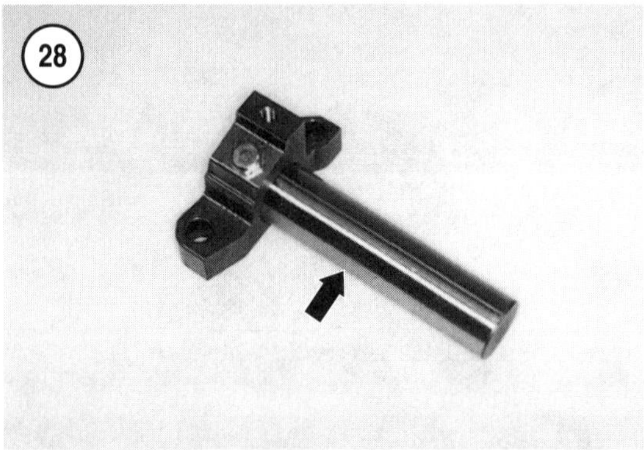

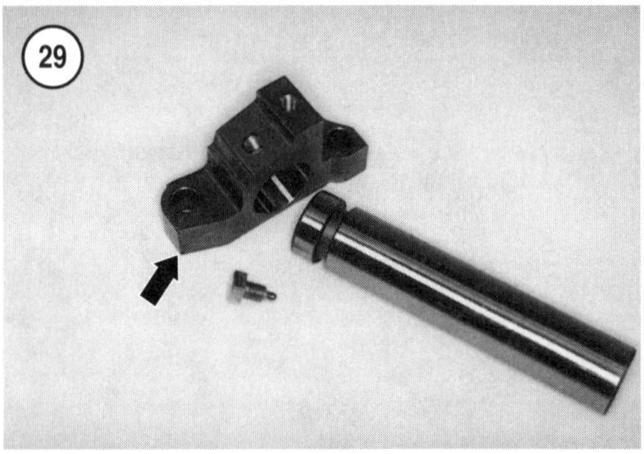

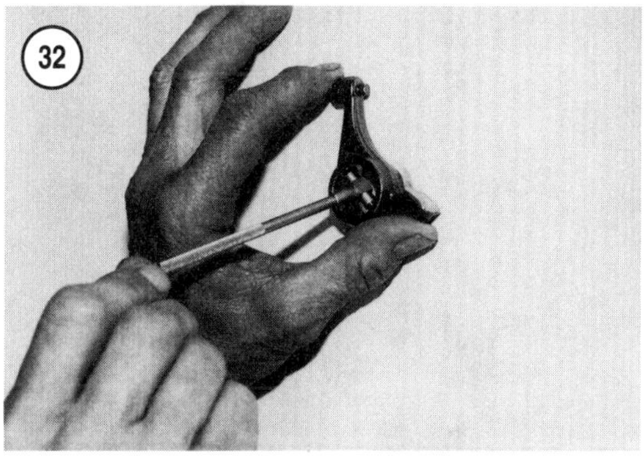

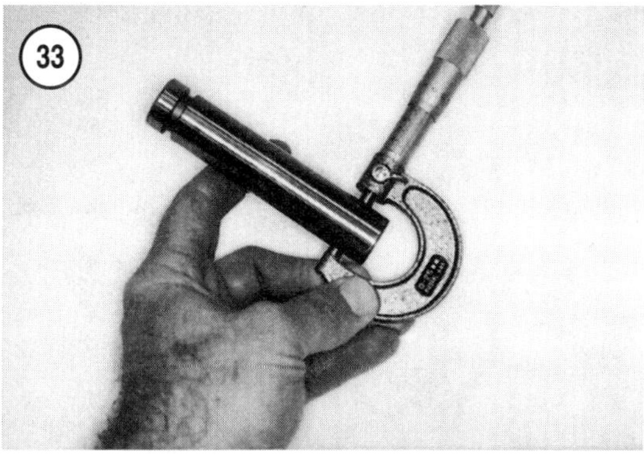

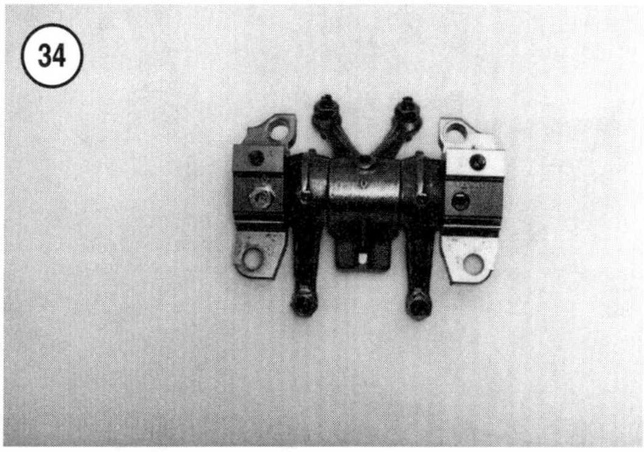

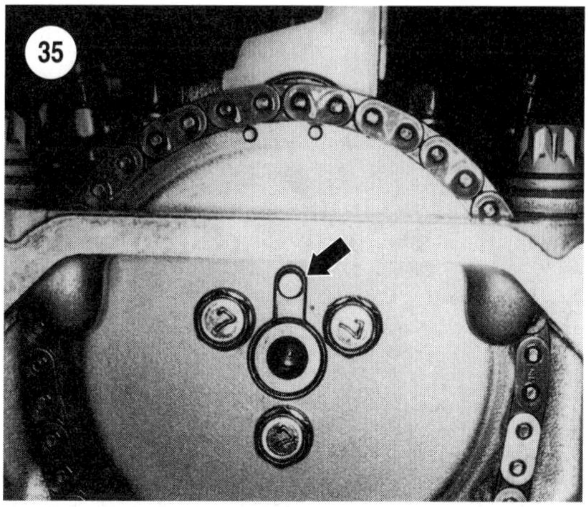

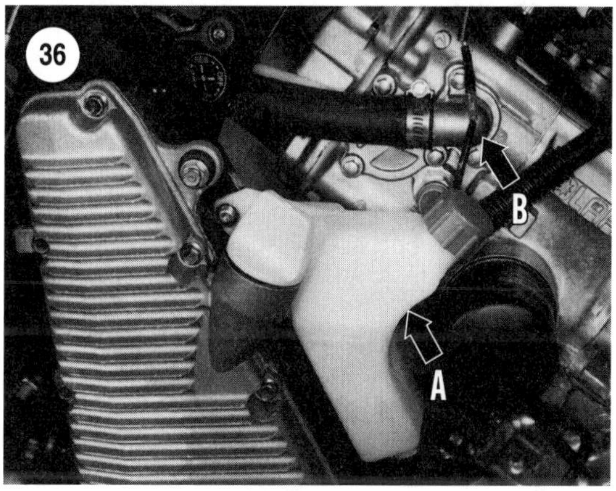

4

CAMSHAFT

Removal

1. Remove the cylinder head cover and rocker arm assembly as described in this chapter.

2. Position the piston at TDC on its compression stroke as described under *Rocker Arm Assembly* in in this chapter. When the piston is at TDC on the compression stroke, the sprocket alignment pin (**Figure 35**) will be located at the top of the camshaft.

3. Remove the coolant reservoir (A, **Figure 36**) as described in Chapter Six.

4. Remove the thermostat housing (B, **Figure 36**) as described in Chapter Six.

5. On the left side, remove the bolts securing the camshaft end cap (**Figure 37**) and remove the end cap and O-ring.

6. On the right side, remove the bolts securing the camshaft sprocket cover (**Figure 38**) and remove the cover and gasket.

CAUTION
The bolt is under spring pressure. While removing, push against the bolt to keep it from flying off.

7. Remove the bolt and washer (**Figure 39**) from the camshaft chain tensioner, then withdraw the spring (**Figure 40**).

8. Remove the two bolts (A, **Figure 41**) securing the camshaft chain tensioner and remove the tensioner assembly and gasket (B, **Figure 41**) from the cylinder block.

9. Place a clean shop cloth in the cavity below the cam sprocket, then remove the three sprocket mounting bolts (**Figure 42**).

10. Hold onto the sprocket, then slide the camshaft in and away from the sprocket being careful not to dislodge the dowel pin in the end of the camshaft.

11. Disengage the sprocket from the camshaft chain and remove the sprocket.

12. Secure the camshaft chain to the exterior of the engine with a piece of wire.

13. Remove the camshaft from the left side of engine (**Figure 43**).

Inspection

When measuring the camshaft in this section, compare the actual measurements to the new and service limit specifications listed in **Table 4**. Replace worn or damaged parts as described in this section.

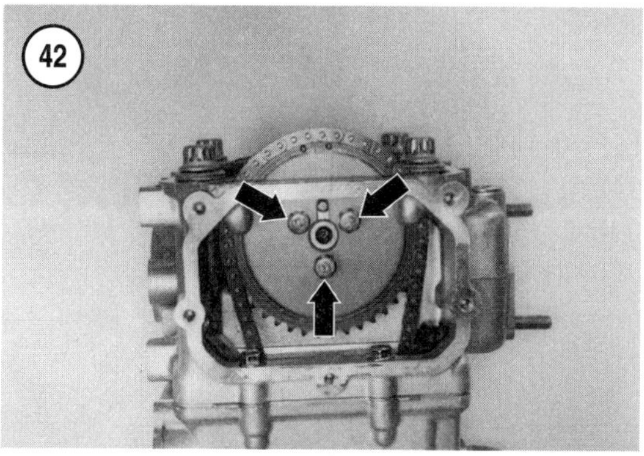

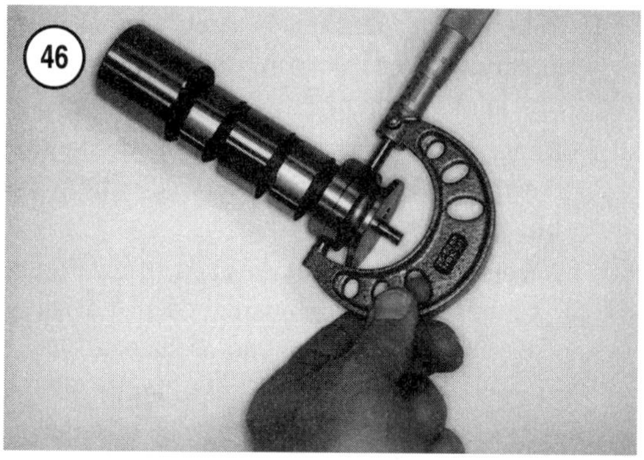

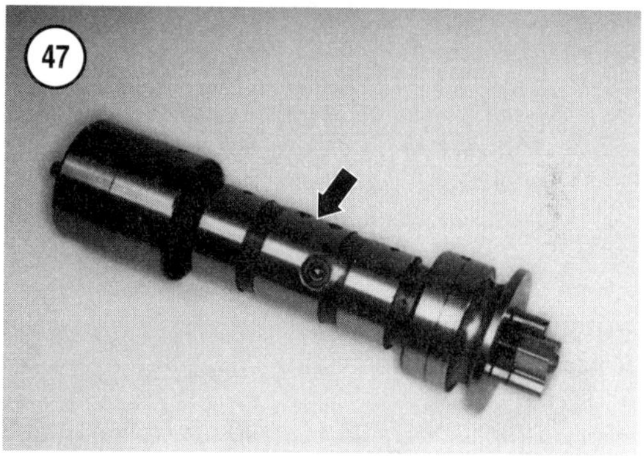

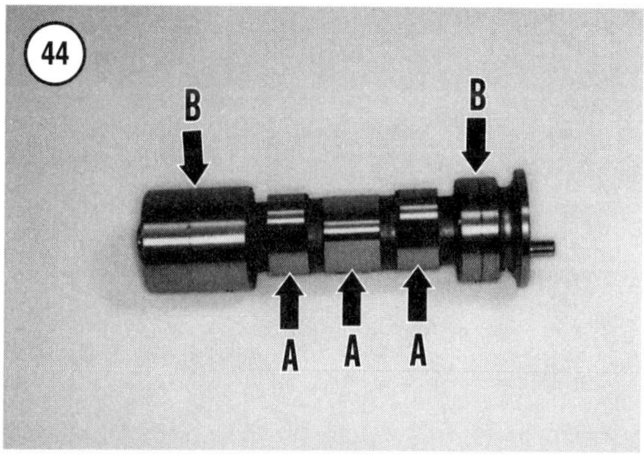

1. Thoroughly clean the camshaft in solvent, then thoroughly dry. Apply engine oil to all bearing surfaces.

2. Check the camshaft lobes (A, **Figure 44**) for wear. The lobes should not be scored and the edges should be square.

3. Measure the height of each lobe (**Figure 45**) with a micrometer.

4. Check each camshaft bearing journal (B, **Figure 44**) for wear and scoring.

5. Measure each camshaft bearing journal (**Figure 46**) with a micrometer.

6. If the bearing journals are severely worn or damaged, check the bearing journals in the cylinder head. They should not be scored or excessively worn. If any of the bearing surfaces are worn or scored, replace the cylinder head.

7. Make sure the camshaft oil holes are open and clear (**Figure 47**), clean them out if necessary.

8. Measure the camshaft bearing bore inner diameter (**Figure 48**) in the cylinder head with a bore gauge.

9. Calculate the camshaft-to-cylinder head bore clearance as follows:

a. Subtract the camshaft bearing journal outer diameter (Step 5) from the cylinder head bearing bore diameter (Step 8).

b. Replace the camshaft and/or cylinder head if the clearance exceeds the service limit in **Table 4**.

10. Inspect the thrust face of the end cap (A, **Figure 49**) for wear. If the end cap is damaged, install a new cap and carefully inspect the end of the camshaft.

11. Inspect the camshaft sprocket (**Figure 50**) for damaged teeth. If the camshaft sprocket is damaged or severely worn, replace it. Also, inspect the crankshaft drive sprocket as described in Chapter Five.

NOTE
If the camshaft sprockets are worn, check the camshaft drive chain, chain guides and chain tensioner for excessive wear or damage.

Automatic Compression Release Mechanism Testing

The automatic compression release mechanism located within the center of the camshaft can be inspected without removing the camshaft from the engine.

1. Twist the release mechanism inside the camshaft and observe the smoothness of operation. There should be no roughness and the spring should return the weight against the stop pin.

2. The actuator ball (**Figure 51**) must be held outward when the release mechanism is in the compression release position.

3. Withdraw the release mechanism (**Figure 52**) from the camshaft. Inspect the shaft and spring for wear or damage.

4. Inspect the lobe at the end of the release lever shaft and the actuator ball for wear or damage. The actuator ball is not available separately from the camshaft.

NOTE
To install the automatic compression release mechanism ***(Figure 53)****, the actuator ball* ***(Figure 51)*** *must be held out. If necessary, use a small magnet to hold the actuator ball out while installing the compression release into the camshaft.*

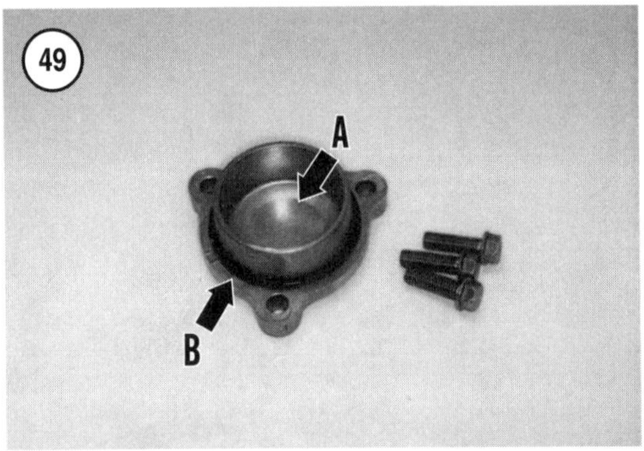

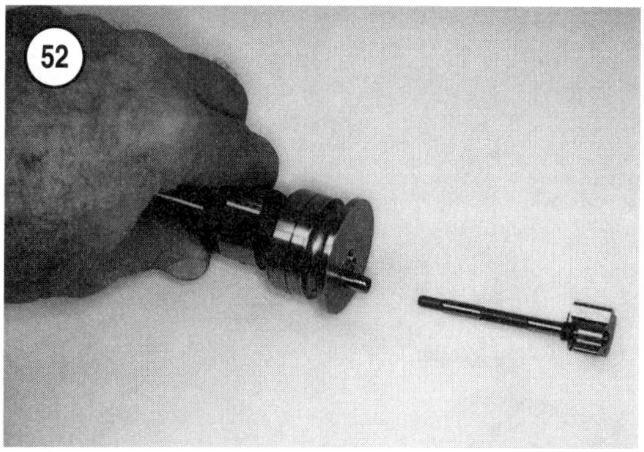

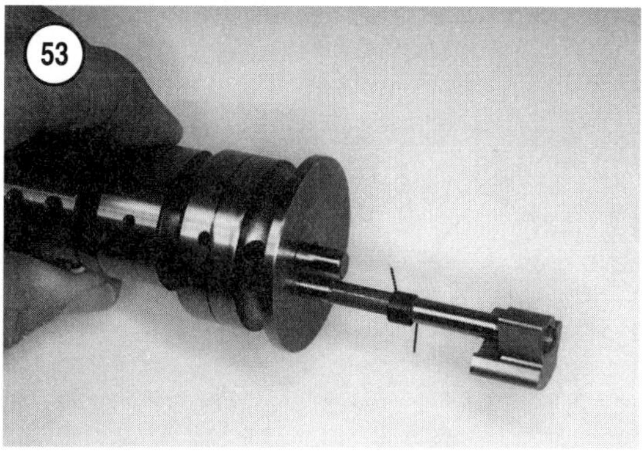

NOTE
Do not prewind the spring one full turn or the compression release will not disengage when the engine is started.

5. Lubricate the automatic compression release with clean engine oil and install the mechanism into the camshaft with the ends of the spring positioned as shown in **Figure 54**. Check for correct operation before continuing assembly. When installed correctly, the actuator ball will be held in the out position with light spring pressure.

Installation

NOTE
The engine must be at top dead center (TDC) on the compression stroke before installing and timing the camshaft.

CAUTION
The camshaft must be correctly synchronized in relation to the position of the crankshaft. The camshaft chain must be installed on the crankshaft driven sprocket and camshaft drive sprocket in the correct locations. Very expensive damage could result from improper installation.

NOTE
*To install the automatic compression release mechanism (**Figure 53**), the actuator ball (**Figure 51**) must be held out. If necessary, use a small magnet to hold the actuator ball out while installing the compression release into the camshaft.*

1. Lubricate the automatic compression release with clean engine oil and install the mechanism with the ends of the spring positioned as shown in **Figure 54**. Check for correct operation before continuing assembly.

2. Coat the camshaft lobes and journals with molybdenum disulfide or Polaris low temp grease (part No. 2870577). Also coat the bearing journals in the cylinder head.

3. Position the camshaft until the lobes are facing down, toward the cylinder head and insert the camshaft into the cylinder head (**Figure 55**). The sprocket drive pin must be straight up (**Figure 56**).

4A. If the alternator stator is in place on the crankcase perform the following:

CAUTION
To prevent damage to the crankshaft and crankcase when rotating the crankshaft, keep the camshaft chain taut and properly meshed with the drive sprocket on the crankshaft.

4

a. Make sure that the flywheel TDC timing mark is aligned with the center of the timing port (**Figure 57**).
b. If necessary, turn the engine with the recoil starter while guiding the timing chain as required.

4B. If the alternator stator plate is removed, rotate the crankshaft until the mark (A, **Figure 58**) on the crankshaft sprocket is facing down and is aligned with the crankcase projection (B, **Figure 58**).

5. Remove the wire from the camshaft chain and loop it over the end of the camshaft (**Figure 59**).

6. Position the camshaft driven sprocket with the two dots (**Figure 60**) facing away from the engine and at the 12 o'clock position.

7. Properly mesh the driven sprocket with the camshaft chain as follows:
   a. Pull up on the camshaft chain and make sure it is properly meshed with the crankshaft drive sprocket.
   b. Align the driven sprocket two dots (A, **Figure 61**) with the *two plated links* (B, **Figure 61**) on the camshaft chain and mesh the chain with the driven sprocket. After meshing the chain, recheck for correct alignment of the two parts. Reposition the sprocket if necessary until alignment is correct.

NOTE

When installing the driven sprocket onto the camshaft, do not knock the dowel pin loose from the camshaft or it will fall into the crankcase.

8. Install the driven sprocket onto the camshaft and position it correctly with the dowel pin. If necessary, slightly rotate the camshaft in either direction and align the mounting bolt holes. Temporarily in-

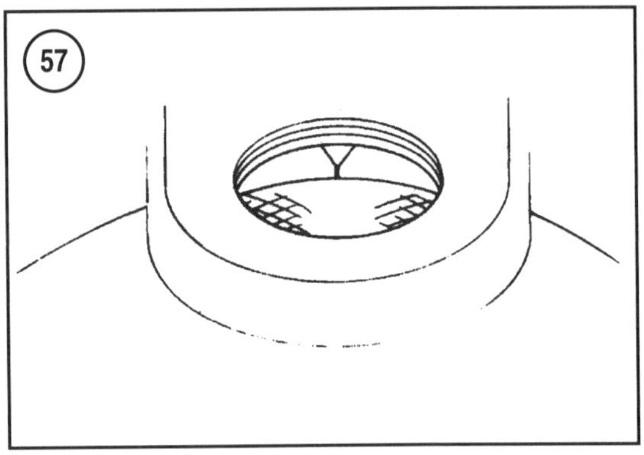

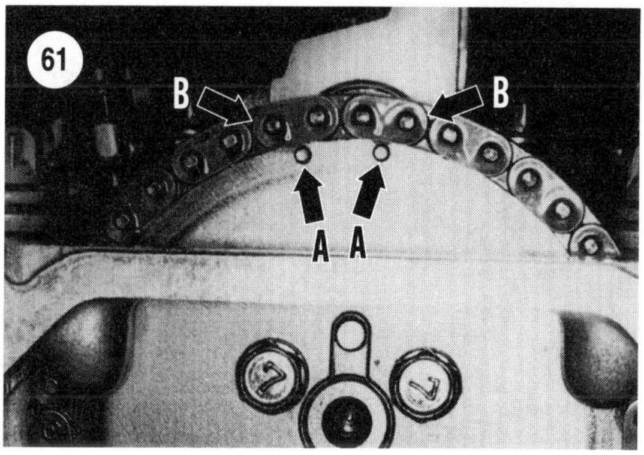

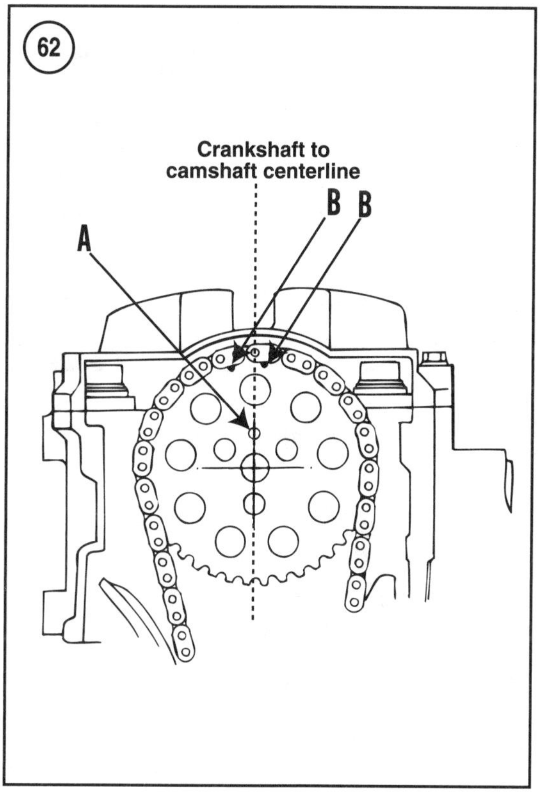

stall the two mounting bolts and tighten finger-tight.

9A. If the alternator stator plate was not removed, check for proper alignment as follows:

a. The flywheel TDC mark will be centered in the timing port hole (**Figure 57**).

b. The camshaft sprocket drive pin (A, **Figure 62**) will be straight up as shown.

c. The camshaft sprocket dots will be facing up (B, **Figure 62**).

9B. If the alternator stator plate is removed, check for proper alignment as follows:

a. The mark (A, **Figure 58**) on the crankshaft sprocket is facing down and is aligned with the crankcase projection (B, **Figure 58**).

b. The camshaft sprocket drive pin (A, **Figure 62**) will be straight up as shown.

c. The camshaft sprocket dots will be facing up (B, **Figure 62**).

10. When the camshaft timing is correct as checked in Step 9, perform the following:

a. Remove one of the camshaft driven sprocket bolts.

b. Apply ThreeBond TB1342, Loctite 242, or equivalent, to the bolt threads and reinstall it.

c. Repeat for the remaining two bolts, then tighten all three bolts to the torque specification listed in **Table 3**.

11. Install a new O-ring (B, **Figure 49**) onto the camshaft end cap.

12. Apply Loctite 525, Loctite 518 Gasket Eliminator or equivalent to the camshaft end cap, then install the end cap and bolts (**Figure 63**). Tighten the bolts securely.

13. Install the camshaft chain tensioner body as follows:

a. Lift the ratchet (A, **Figure 64**), then push the plunger (B, **Figure 64**) all the way into the body. Release the ratchet to hold the plunger in the correct position (**Figure 65**).
b. Install a new gasket (**Figure 66**) and install the tensioner body (B, **Figure 41**) into the cylinder block and against the camshaft chain.
c. Push the tensioner against the cylinder block and install the mounting bolts (A, **Figure 41**). Tighten the bolts to the torque specification listed in **Table 3**.
d. Install the spring (**Figure 40**) into the body.
e. Install a new gasket, then install the bolt (**Figure 39**). Tighten the bolt to the torque specification listed in **Table 3**.

NOTE
The plated links and dots on the sprocket are aligned during the initial camshaft timing procedure. After turning the crankshaft the same alignment only occurs infrequently. Therefore, during Step 14, reference the timing marks on the sprockets, not the two plated camshaft links.

14. Rotate the engine crankshaft two or more revolutions and recheck alignment of the timing marks (**Figure 58** and **Figure 61**). If the alignment marks changed after installing the chain tensioner, remove the tensioner and repeat Steps 3-5.
15. On the right, install a new gasket (**Figure 67**) and the camshaft sprocket cover (**Figure 68**). Install the bolts and tighten securely.
16. Install the thermostat housing as described in Chapter Six.
17. Install the coolant reservoir as described in Chapter Six.
18. Install the rocker arm assembly and the cylinder head cover as described in this chapter.

CYLINDER HEAD

Removal

1. Remove the cylinder head cover, rocker arm assembly and the camshaft as described in this chapter.
2. Remove the carburetor and exhaust pipe from the cylinder head as described in Chapter Six.
3. Loosen the two flange bolts (A, **Figure 69**) in 2-3 stages then remove them.

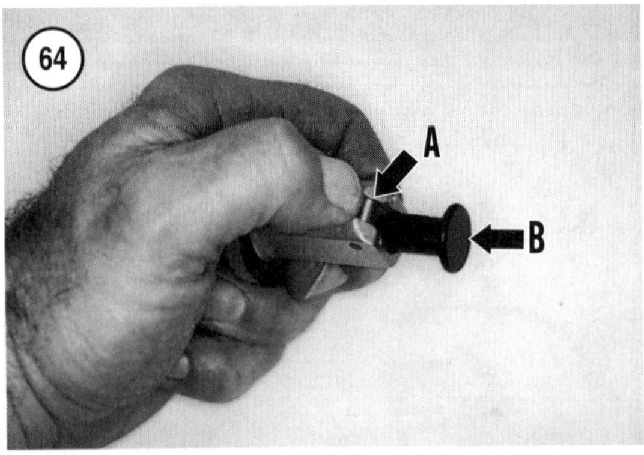

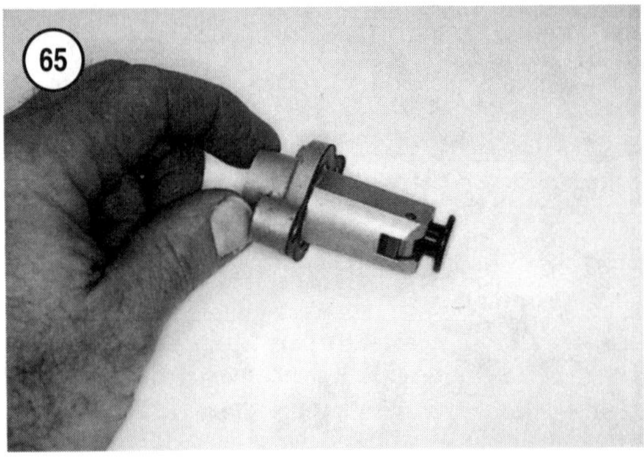

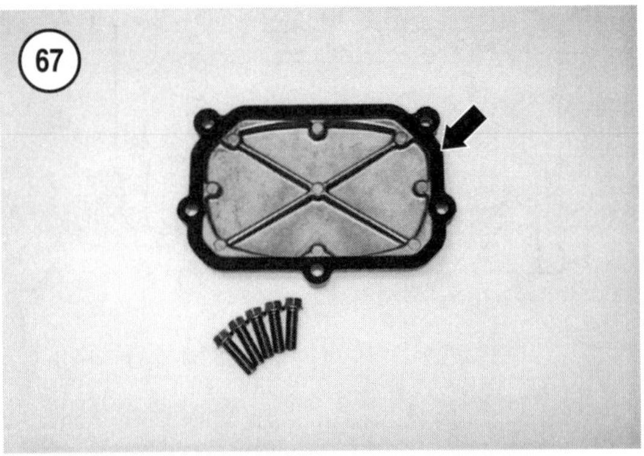

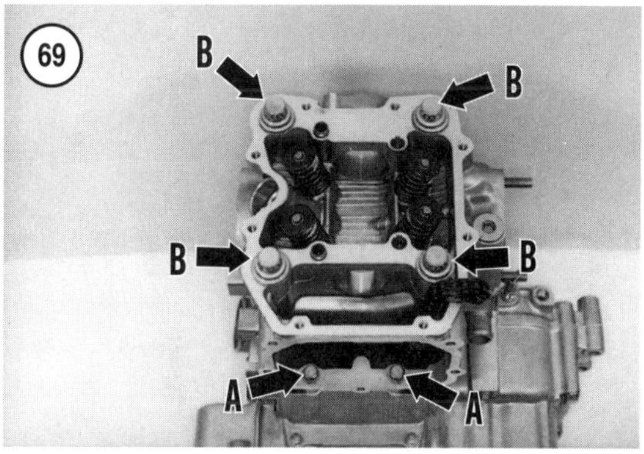

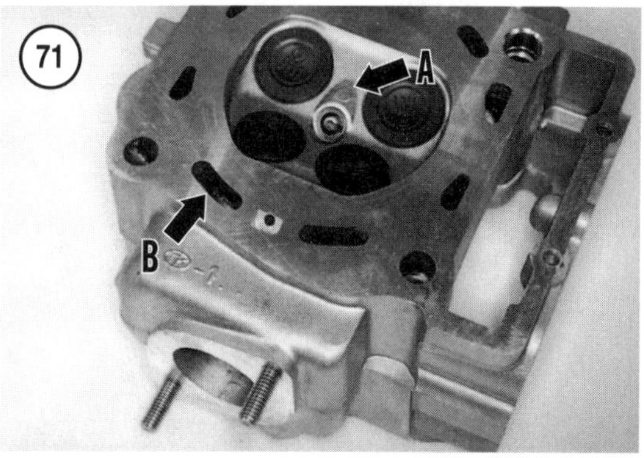

4. Loosen the four mounting bolts and washers (B, **Figure 69**) in 2-3 stages in a crossing pattern, then remove the bolts.

5. Tap the cylinder head with a soft-faced mallet to break it loose from the cylinder head gasket.

6. Pull straight up and remove the cylinder head from the cylinder block.

7. Secure the camshaft chain to the exterior of the engine (**Figure 70**).

8. Remove and discard the cylinder head gasket.

9. Remove the two locating dowels if loose.

10. Cover the cylinder block with a clean shop cloth or paper towels.

Inspection

1. Remove all traces of gasket material from the cylinder head and block mating surfaces.

2. Before removing the valves, remove all carbon deposits from the combustion chamber (A, **Figure 71**) and valve ports with a wire brush. Use a blunt screwdriver or similar scraper and be careful not to damage the cylinder head, valves or spark plug threads.

3. After the carbon is removed from the combustion chamber and ports, clean the entire cylinder head with solvent. Blow dry with compressed air.

4. Make sure all coolant passages (B, **Figure 71**) are clean. Clean out if necessary and apply compressed air to all passages.

5. Inspect the cylinder head (**Figure 72**) for cracks, erosion, stripped threads or other damage.

6. Clean all carbon from the piston crown.

7. Place a straightedge across the cylinder head gasket surface. Check for warp by inserting a flat feeler gauge between the straightedge and the cylin-

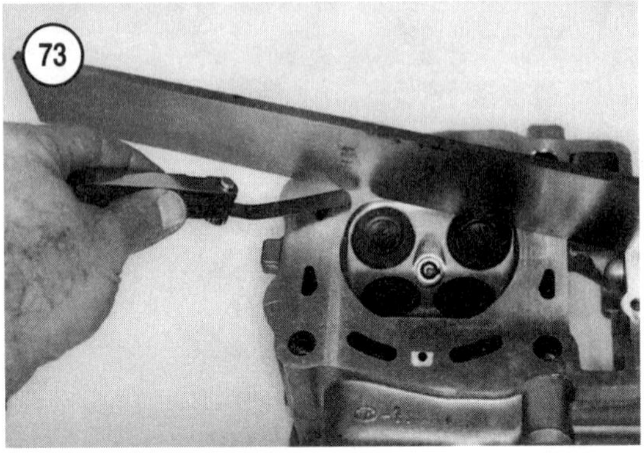

der head at several locations (**Figure 73**). Compare the reading with the warp limit listed in **Table 4**.

8. Inspect the camshaft bearing surfaces (**Figure 74**) in the cylinder head for wear or scoring. Also check the oil delivery port (**Figure 75**) for blockage.

9. Remove the oil pressure blind plug (**Figure 76**) in front of the oil delivery port to assist with cleaning. Coat the threads of the blind plug with sealer before installing, then tighten securely.

10. Inspect the mounting bolts for thread damage and stretching (**Figure 77**). Replace as a set if any are damaged.

Installation

1. If removed, install the two locating dowels (A, **Figure 78**) in the cylinder block.

2. Position the new gasket (B, **Figure 78**) onto the cylinder block and over the locating dowels. Make sure all coolant and bolt holes are aligned correctly.

3. Position the cylinder head over the dowels in the cylinder block and push it down until it completely seats.

4. Use a piece of wire to pull the camshaft chain up through the top of the cylinder block chain cavity. Pull up on the camshaft chain and make sure it is properly meshed with the crankshaft drive sprocket. Secure the chain to the exterior of the engine (A, **Figure 79**).

5. Apply engine oil to the four large mounting bolts and two smaller bolt threads. Also apply oil to both sides of the large washers (**Figure 80**).

6. Install the small bolts (B, **Figure 79**) and tighten finger-tight.

7. Install the four large bolts and washers (**Figure 81**) and tighten finger-tight.

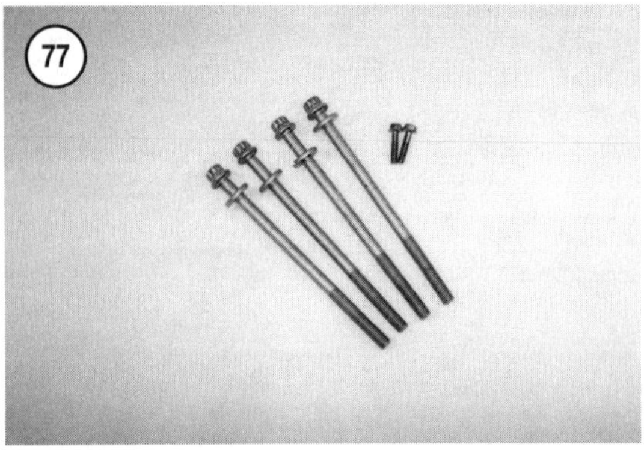

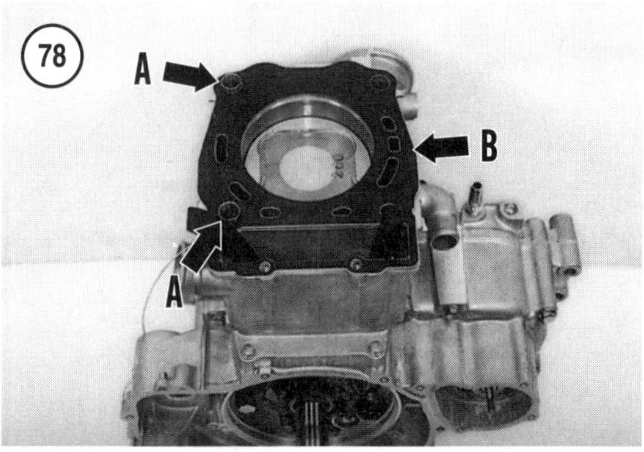

CAUTION

The four large bolts must be tightened, loosened, then tighten again in the following sequence to provide a good seal and to prevent damage.

8. Tighten the four larger bolts (**Figure 81**) in a crossing pattern evenly in the following steps. Mark a line on the large bolts (**Figure 82**) for a degree reference:
   a. Tighten to 30 N•m (22 ft.-lb.).
   b. Tighten to 70 N•m (51 ft.-lb.).
   c. Loosen each of the four bolts exactly 180° (1/2 turn).
   d. Loosen each of the four bolts again exactly 180° (1/2 turn).
   e. Tighten to 15 N•m (11 ft.-lb.).
   f. Tighten each of the four bolts exactly 90° (1/4 turn).
   g. Finally, tighten each of the four bolts exactly 90° (1/4 turn) more.
9. Tighten the two small 6 mm bolts (B, **Figure 79**) to 8 N•m (71 in. lb.).
10. Install the camshaft (Chapter Six), rocker arm assembly and cylinder head cover (this chapter).
11. Install the carburetor (Chapter Six) and the exhaust pipe to the cylinder head.

VALVES AND VALVE COMPONENTS

Complete valve service requires a number of special tools. The following procedures describe how to check for valve component wear and to determine what type of service is required. A valve spring compressor is required to remove and install the valves.

Solvent Test

Before removing the valves from the cylinder head, perform this solvent test to check the valve face seal against the cylinder head seat.

1. Remove the cylinder head as described in this chapter.
2. Support the cylinder head so the exhaust port faces up (**Figure 83**). Then pour kerosene or solvent into the exhaust port as shown in **Figure 83**. Check the combustion chamber for fluid leaking past the exhaust valves.
3. Repeat Step 2 for the intake port and intake valves.
4. Discard the used kerosene or solvent in a safe manner.
5. If any of the valves are leaking, check for the following conditions that can cause poor valve seating:
   a. A bent valve stem.
   b. A worn or damaged valve seat.
   c. A worn or damaged valve face.
   d. A crack in the combustion chamber.

Valve Removal

1. Install a valve spring compressor squarely over the valve spring retainer and the valve head.

CAUTION
To avoid loss of spring tension, do not compress the spring any more than necessary to remove the valve keepers.

2. Tighten valve spring compressor until the valve keepers separate from the valve stem. Lift the valve keepers (**Figure 84**) out through the valve spring compressor with a magnet or needlenose pliers.
3. Gradually loosen the valve spring compressor and remove it from the cylinder head.
4. Remove the spring retainer and the valve spring.

CAUTION
*Remove any burrs from the valve stem groove before removing the valve (**Figure 85**); otherwise, the valve guide will be damaged as the valve stem passes through it.*

5. Remove the valve from the cylinder head while rotating it slightly.
6. Remove the spring seat.

81

82

83

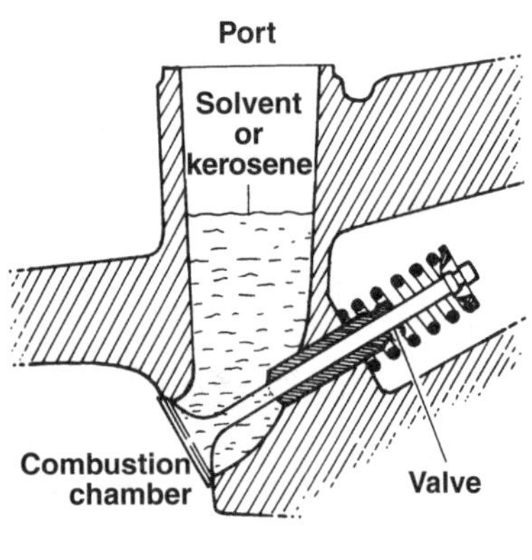

7. Pull the oil seal (**Figure 86**) off of the valve guide.

CAUTION
Keep all component parts of each valve assembly together. Place each set in a divided carton, separate small boxes or small reclosable bags. Identify the sets as right or left and either

84

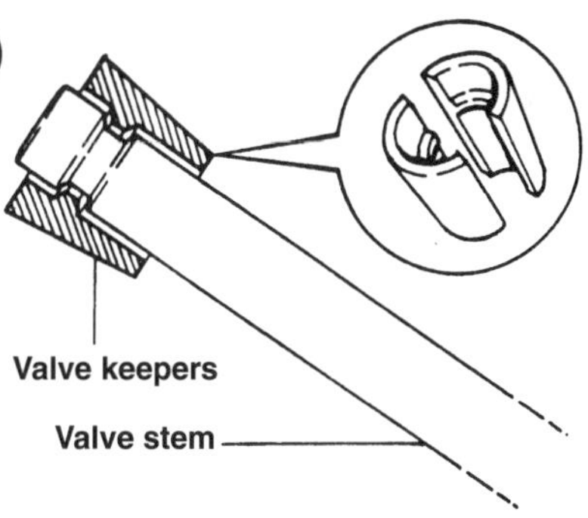

85

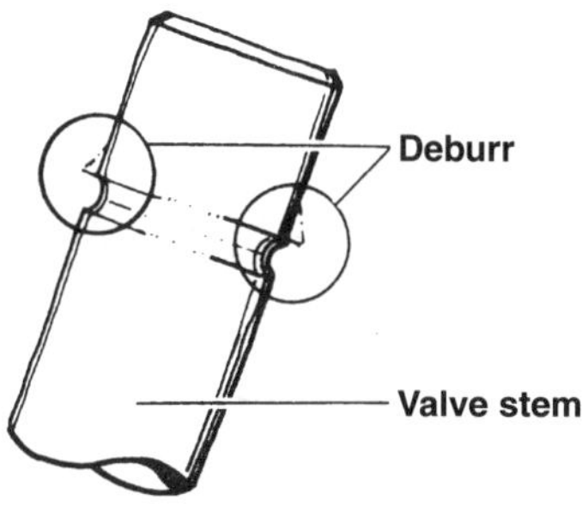

86

intake or exhaust valves. Do not intermix components from the valves, or excessive wear may result.

8. Repeat Steps 2-7 and remove the remaining valves—keep all valve sets separate.

Valve Inspection

Refer to the troubleshooting chart in **Figure 87** when performing valve inspection procedures in this section. Valve service specifications are listed in **Table 4**.

1. Clean valves in solvent. Do not gouge or damage the valve face surface.
2. Carefully inspect the valve face. Minor roughness and pitting can be removed by lapping the valve as described in this chapter. Excessive unevenness to the contact surface is an indication that the valve is not serviceable.
3. Inspect the valve stem for wear and roughness. Then measure the valve stem outer diameter with a micrometer (**Figure 88**). Compare to the dimension in **Table 4** and replace the valve if the stem diameter is less than the service limit.
4. Remove all carbon and varnish from the valve guides with a stiff spiral wire brush.

NOTE

If the required measuring tools are not available, proceed to Step 6.

5. Measure the valve guide inner diameter with a small hole gauge (**Figure 89**). Measure at the top, center and bottom positions. Then measure the small hole gauge and check against the dimension in **Table 4**. Replace the valve guide if the diameter exceeds the service limit.
6. If a small hole gauge is not available, insert each valve in its guide. Attach a dial indicator to the valve stem next to the head (**Figure 90**). Hold the valve just slightly off its seat and rock it sideways on both directions. If the valve rocks more than slightly, the guide is probably worn. However, as a final check, take the cylinder head to a Polaris dealership or machine shop and have the valve guides measured.
7. Check the valve springs as follows:
   a. Check each of the valve springs for visual damage.
   b. Use a square to visually check spring for distortion or tilt (**Figure 91**).
   c. Measure the valve spring free length with a vernier caliper (**Figure 92**) and check against the dimension in **Table 4**. Replace the spring if its free length is less than the service limit.
   d. Repeat for each valve spring.
8. Check the valve keepers for cracks or other damage.
9. Inspect the valve seats in the cylinder head. If worn or burned, they may be reconditioned as described in this chapter. Seats and valves in good

4

87

VALVE TROUBLESHOOTING

Valve deposits

Check:
- Worn valve guide
- Carbon buildup from incorrect engine tuning
- Carbon buildup from incorrect carburetor adjustment
- Dirty or gummed fuel
- Dirty engine oil

Valve sticking

Check:
- Worn valve guide
- Bent valve stem
- Deposits collected on valve stem
- Valve burning or overheating

Valve burning

Check:
- Valve sticking
- Cylinder head warped
- Valve seat distorted
- Valve clearance incorrect
- Incorrect valve spring
- Valve spring worn
- Worn valve seat
- Carbon buildup in engine
- Engine ignition and/or carburetor adjustments incorrect

Valve seat/face wear

Check:
- Valve burning
- Incorrect valve clearance
- Abrasive material on valve face and seat

Valve damage

Check:
- Valve burning
- Incorrectly installed or serviced valve guides
- Incorrect valve clearance
- Incorrect valve, spring seat and retainer assembly
- Detonation caused by incorrect ignition and/or carburetor adjustments

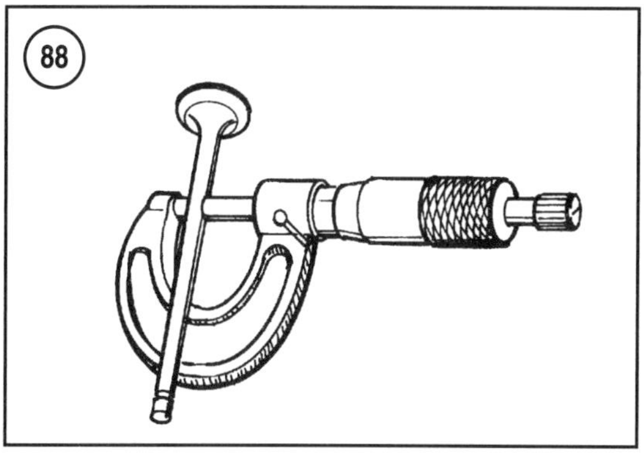

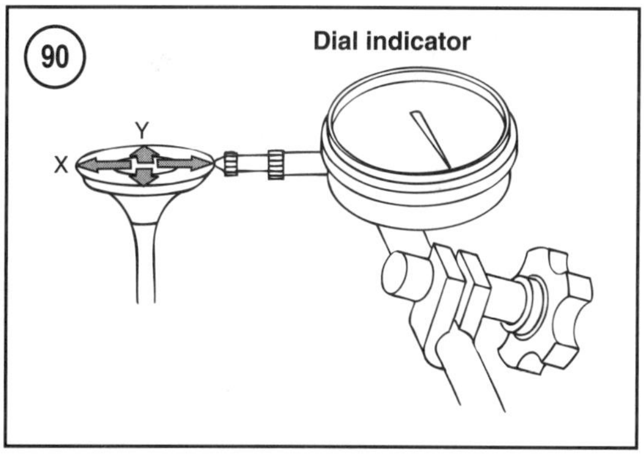

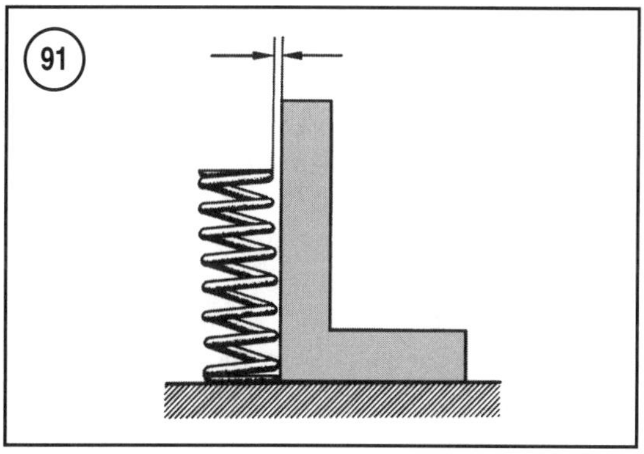

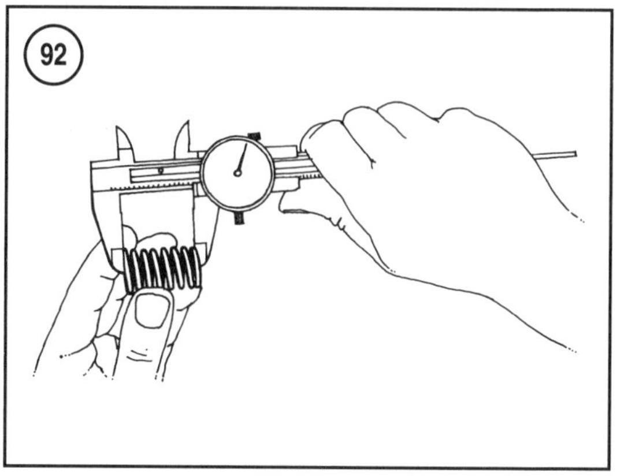

condition can be reconditioned by lapping with fine carborundum paste. Check as follows:

a. Clean the valve seat and corresponding valve mating areas with contact cleaner.
b. Coat the valve seat with marking compound.
c. Install the valve into its guide and rotate it against its seat with a valve lapping tool. See *Valve Lapping* in this chapter.
d. Lift the valve out of the guide and measure the width of the impression the marking compound makes on the valve face.
e. The contact seat width specifications for the valves are listed in **Table 4**. If the seat width exceeds the specifications, recondition the seats as described in this chapter.
f. Clean all marking compound from the seats and valves.

Valve Installation

1. Clean the end of the valve guide.
2. Oil the inside of the *new* valve stem oil seal and install it over the end of the valve guide (**Figure 86**). Push it down until it is completely seated on the cylinder head surface.
3. Coat a valve stem with molybdenum disulfide paste. Install the valve part way into the guide, then slowly turn the valve as it enters the oil seal and continue turning it until the valve is installed all the way.
4. Position the valve spring with the *closer* wound coils facing the cylinder head.
5. Install the valve spring. Make sure it is properly seated on the cylinder head surface.

6. Install the retainer on top of the valve spring.

CAUTION
To avoid loss of spring tension, do not compress the spring any more than necessary to install the valve keepers.

7. Compress the valve spring with a valve spring compressor and install the valve keepers (**Figure 84**).
8. When both valve keepers are in place, make sure they are seated around the valve stem (**Figure 93**) prior to releasing the compressor.
9. Slowly release the tension from the compressor and remove it. After removing the compressor, inspect the valve keepers to make sure they are properly seated. Then tap the end of the valve stem with a soft-faced hammer. This will ensure that the keepers are properly seated.
10. Repeat Steps 1-9 for the remaining valves.
11. Install the cylinder head as described in this chapter.
12. After installing the cylinder head, adjust the valve clearance as described in Chapter Three.

93

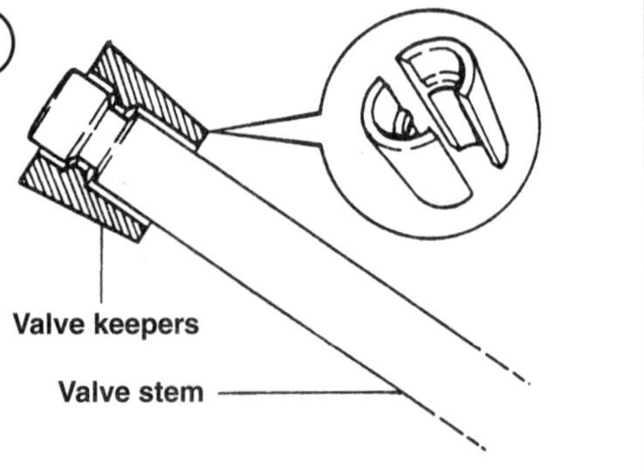

94

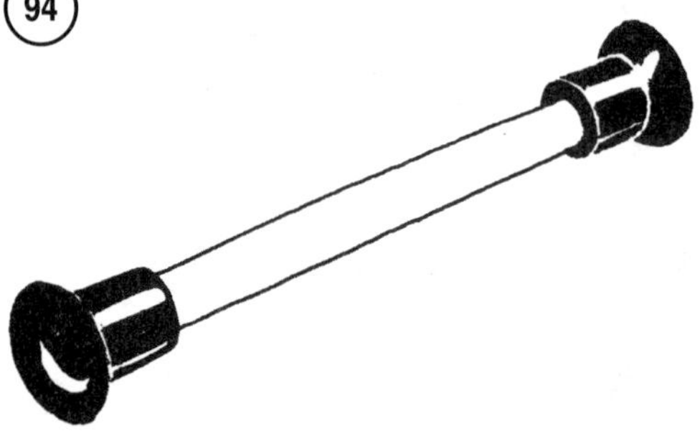

95

Valve Guide Replacement

If excessive valve stem-to-guide clearance is present, replace the valve guides and valves. Entrust valve guide replacement to a Polaris dealership or qualified machine shop.

Valve Lapping

Valve lapping is a simple operation that can restore the valve seal without machining if the amount of wear or distortion is not too great.

Perform this procedure after determining that valve seat width and outside diameter are within specifications. A lapping tool (**Figure 94**) is required.

1. Remove the valve as previously described in this chapter.
2. Apply a light coating of fine-grade valve lapping compound on the seating surface of the valve.
3. Insert the valve into the cylinder head.
4. Wet the suction cup of the lapping tool and stick it onto the head of the valve. Spin the stick in both directions, while pressing it against the valve seat and lap the valve to the seat. Every 5 to 10 seconds, rotate the valve 180° in the valve seat. Continue with this action until the mating surfaces on the valve and seat are smooth and equal in size.
5. Closely examine the valve seat in the cylinder head. It should be smooth and even with a smooth, polished seating ring.
6. Repeat Steps 1-5 for the other valves.
7. Thoroughly clean the valves and cylinder head in solvent or detergent and hot water to remove all valve grinding compound. Dry thoroughly. Apply a light coating of engine oil to all bare metal surfaces to prevent rust.

96

97

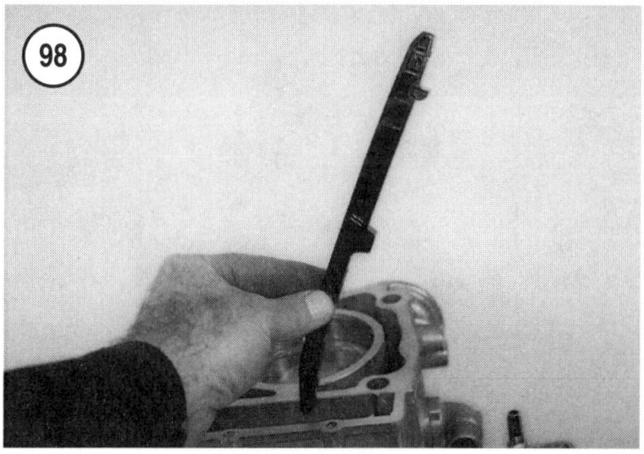
98

99

CAUTION
Any compound left on the valves or the cylinder head will end up in the engine and cause wear and damage.

8. Install the valve assemblies as described in this chapter.

9. Perform the *Solvent Test* as described in this chapter to check the valve seating ability.

NOTE
This solvent test does not ensure long-term durability or maximum power. It merely ensures maximum compression will be available on initial start-up after reassembly.

CYLINDER BLOCK

Removal

1. Remove the cylinder head cover, rocker arm assembly, camshaft and cylinder head (A, **Figure 95**) as described in this chapter.

2. Loosen the banjo bolts at each end of both oil pipes (**Figure 96**). Remove the two banjo bolts and two sealing washers at each end of the oil pipe. Remove the oil pipe and place in a reclosable plastic bag along with the banjo bolts and sealing washers to keep them clean.

3. Repeat Step 2 for the remaining oil pipe.

4. Loosen the clamp screw (B, **Figure 95**), then disconnect the coolant hose from the cylinder inlet fitting.

5. Remove the two 6mm bolts (**Figure 97**) from the right side of the cylinder.

6. If still in place, remove the camshaft front chain guide (**Figure 98**).

7. If still in place, remove the cylinder head gasket (**Figure 99**) from the top of the cylinder block to expose the four cylinder block mounting bolts.

8. Loosen each of the four cylinder block base bolts (**Figure 100**) in a crisscross pattern 1/4 turn at a time. Remove all four bolts (**Figure 101**).

NOTE
The piston should slide smoothly in the cylinder bore and only light taps should be required to release the cylinder from the crankcase.

9. Tap the cylinder block (**Figure 102**) with a soft-faced mallet to break it loose from the mating surface of the crankcase.

10. Pull straight up and partially remove the cylinder block from the piston and the crankcase.

CAUTION

Place a clean shop cloth around the connecting rod before the cylinder block is completely removed to prevent any loose parts from falling into the crankcase opening. The shop cloth will also keep the connecting rod and piston from falling against the crankcase after the cylinder block is removed.

11. Lift the cylinder block from the piston and crankcase.

12. Remove the cylinder base gasket.

13. If loose, remove the two dowel pins from the crankcase.

14. Install a piston holding fixture under the piston to protect the piston skirt from damage. This fixture (**Figure 103**) may be purchased or fabricated from wood.

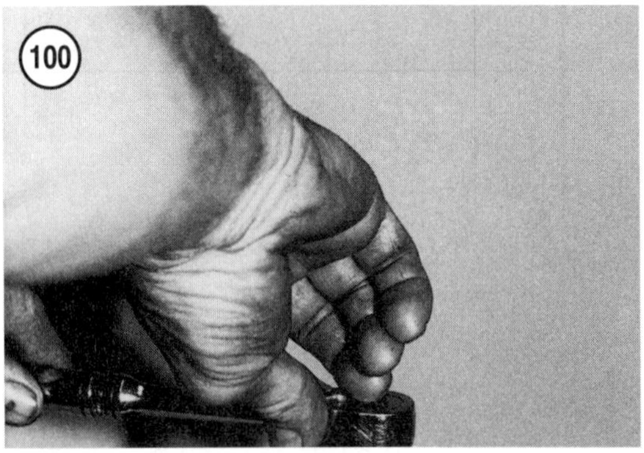

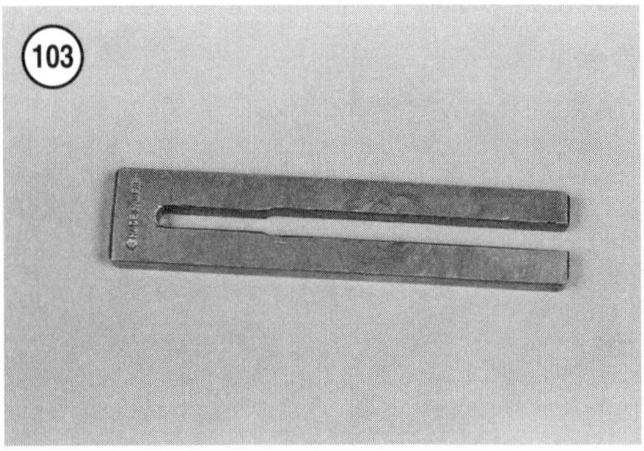

Inspection

A bore gauge and micrometer are required to accurately measure the cylinder bore. If these tools are not available, have the measurements performed by a Polaris dealership or machine shop.

1. Remove all gasket residue from the cylinder block top and bottom gasket surfaces. Both surfaces must be free of all residue.

2. Wash the cylinder block in solvent. Dry with compressed air.

3. Check the locating dowels holes for cracks or other damage.

4. Check the cylinder block bore (**Figure 104**) for scoring, rust or other visible damage.

5. Measure the cylinder block bore diameter, taper and out-of-round with a bore gauge (**Figure 105**) or inside micrometer. Measure the cylinder bore at the following locations:

   a. 12.7 mm (0.50 in.) down from the top of the cylinder block.

   b. At the center of the bore.

   c. 12.7 mm (0.50 in.) up from the bottom of the cylinder block.

104

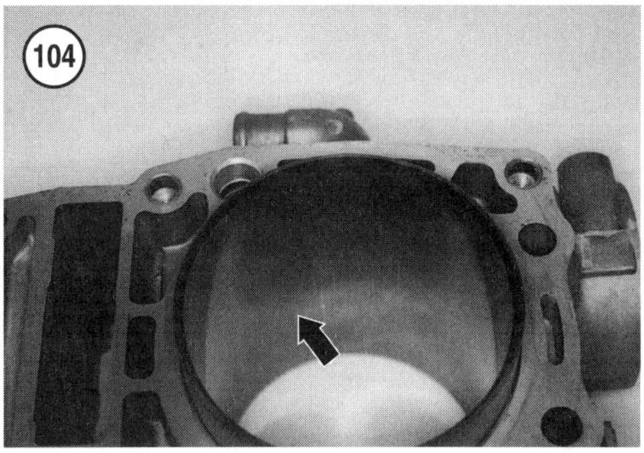

105

106

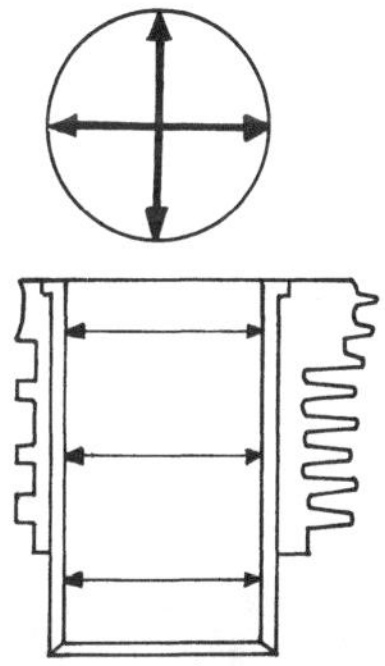

107

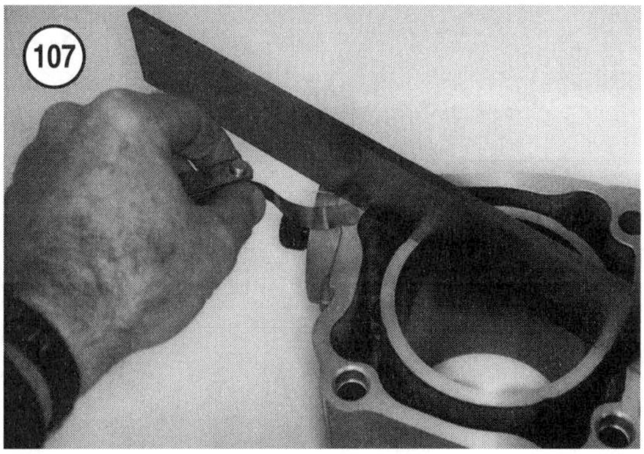

6. To check for excessive bore out-of-round, take measurements aligned with the piston pin and 90° to the pin (**Figure 106**).
7. If the cylinder bore is excessively worn, scored, or damaged or has excessive taper or is out-of-round, bore the cylinder to the next oversize and install a new piston and rings.

NOTE
*The recommended piston-to-cylinder clearance is provided in **Table 4**. Prior to boring the cylinder oversize, purchase and measure the oversize piston to establish the correct finished bore diameter to provide the correct piston clearance.*

8. Determine the piston-to-cylinder clearance as described under *Piston Clearance* in this chapter.
9. After servicing the cylinder block, thoroughly wash the bore in hot soapy water. After washing the cylinder bore, run a clean white cloth through it. The cylinder wall should show no traces of grit or other debris. If the rag is dirty, the cylinder wall is not clean and must be re-washed. When the cylinder bore is thoroughly clean, lubricate the cylinder bore with clean engine oil to prevent it from rusting.

CAUTION
A combination of soap and water is the only solution that will completely clean the cylinder bore. Solvent and kerosene cannot wash fine grit out of the cylinder crevices. Grit left in the cylinder bore will act as a grinding compound and cause premature wear to the new rings.

10. After thoroughly cleaning the cylinder block, place a straightedge across the cylinder head-to-cylinder gasket surface at several points. Measure warp by attempting to insert a feeler gauge between the straightedge (**Figure 107**) and cylinder head at each location. Maximum allowable warp is listed in **Table 4**. A warped or nicked cylinder block surface could cause a coolant leak and result in overheating. If warp exceeds the limit, the cylinder block must be resurfaced or replaced. Consult a Polaris dealership or machine shop experienced in this type of work.
11. Check the cylinder block coolant fitting (**Figure 108**) for corrosion or damage. Remove any corrosion or oxidation from the fitting.

4

12. Check the threaded fitting for the oil filter (**Figure 109**) for wear or damage. Replace the fitting if necessary.

Installation

To make installation of the cylinder block over the piston safer and easier, two special tools are very helpful. Cylinder block installation can be accomplished without these tools, but is more difficult and also increases the chance of damage to both the cylinder wall surfaces and to the piston rings and skirt. The special tools are a piston holding fixture (A, **Figure 110**) and a ring compressor (B, **Figure 110**) and are available through Polaris dealerships or aftermarket parts suppliers.

1. Clean the crankcase mating surface of all gasket residue (**Figure 111**).
2. Check that the top and bottom of the cylinder block surfaces are clean of all gasket residue.
3. If removed, install the cylinder block locating dowels (A, **Figure 112**).
4. Install a new cylinder block base gasket (B, **Figure 112**). Make sure all holes align.
5. If removed, install the piston as described in this chapter.
6. Insert the piston holding fixture (**Figure 113**) under the piston.
7. Check that both piston pin clips are installed and seated correctly.
8. Lubricate the cylinder wall, piston and rings liberally with clean engine oil prior to installation.
9. Make sure the oil ring top rail is correctly positioned in the notch as shown in **Figure 114**. The gaps in the remaining rings should be spaced evenly around the piston.

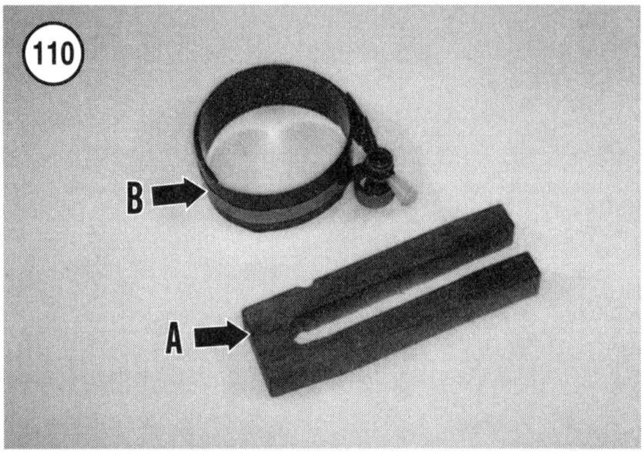

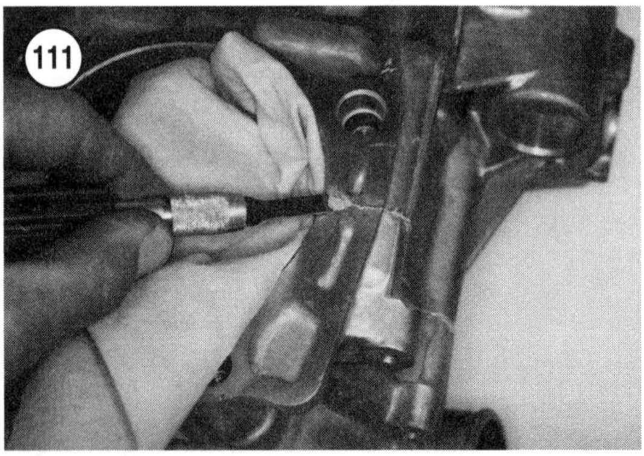

NOTE
The piston ring compressor must be the correct size and must be of the type that can be removed from the piston after the piston starts to enter the cylinder bore.

10. Install a piston ring compressor over the piston rings (**Figure 115**).
11. Carefully align the cylinder block onto the top of the piston.
12. Slowly slide the cylinder block down onto the piston until it *lightly* bottoms out on the ring compressor (**Figure 116**).
13. Slowly and carefully slide the cylinder block down past the piston rings, then remove the piston ring compressor.
14. Slide the cylinder block down until it almost contacts the piston holding fixture. Carefully slide the holding fixture (**Figure 117**) out from under the piston.
15. Carefully push the cylinder block down until it bottoms out on the base gasket and the upper crankcase (**Figure 118**). Make sure the locating dowels correctly enter the cylinder block.

16. Apply clean engine oil to the threads and to the underside of the four cylinder block base bolt flanges. Install the four bolts and tighten finger-tight.
17. Use a piece of wire to pull the camshaft chain up through the top of the cylinder block chain cavity. Pull up on the camshaft chain and make sure it is properly meshed with the crankshaft drive sprocket.
18. Rotate the crankshaft until the piston is at bottom dead center. Reattach the chain to the exterior of the engine.
19. Tighten each of the four cylinder block base bolts (**Figure 101**) in a crisscross pattern to the torque specification listed in **Table 3**.
20. Install the two 6 mm bolts (**Figure 97**) onto the right-hand side of the cylinder and tighten to the torque specification listed in **Table 3**.
21. Connect the coolant hose onto the cylinder inlet fitting. Move the clamp into position and tighten the screw (B, **Figure 95**) securely.
22. Install both external oil pipes to the cylinder block and crankcase. Install the banjo bolt and new sealing washers (**Figure 119**) at each end of the oil pipe. Refer to **Figure 120** and **Figure 121**. Tighten the banjo bolts to the torque specification listed in **Table 3**.
23. Insert the camshaft front chain guide (**Figure 98**) down through the camshaft chain tunnel. Make sure the lower end seats correctly in the guide recess in the crankcase (**Figure 122**) and into the receptacle at the top (**Figure 123**) of the cylinder block.
24. Install the cylinder head, rocker arm assembly and cylinder head cover as described in this chapter.

119

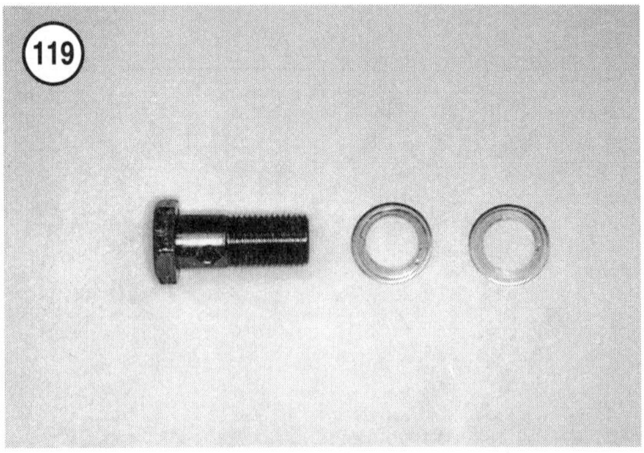

120

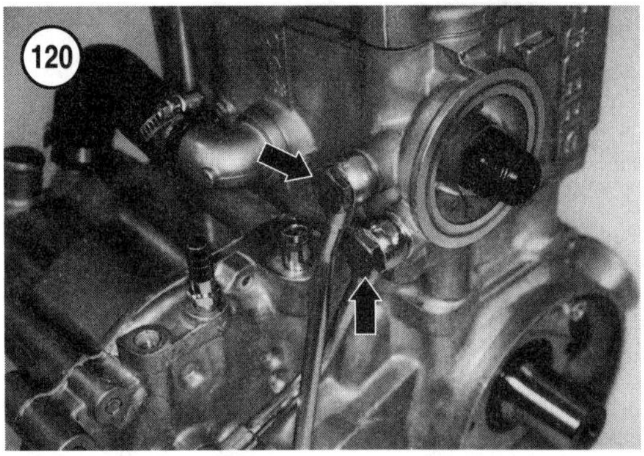

121

122

PISTON AND PISTON RINGS

The piston is made of an aluminum alloy. The piston pin is made of steel and is a precision fit in the piston pin bore. The piston pin is held in place by a clip at each end of the bore in the piston.

Piston Removal

1. Remove the cylinder head cover, cylinder head and cylinder block as described in this chapter.
2. Before removing the piston, hold the rod tightly and rock the piston (**Figure 124**) to detect excessive clearance between the piston, piston pin and connecting rod. Do not confuse the normal sliding motion of the piston on the pin with rocking motion. Any perceptible rocking motion indicates wear to

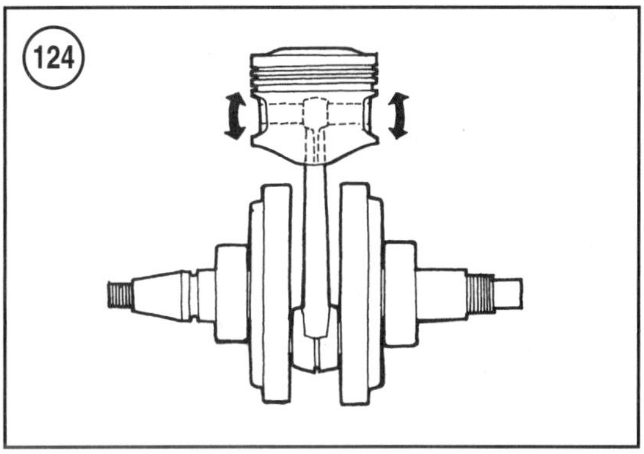

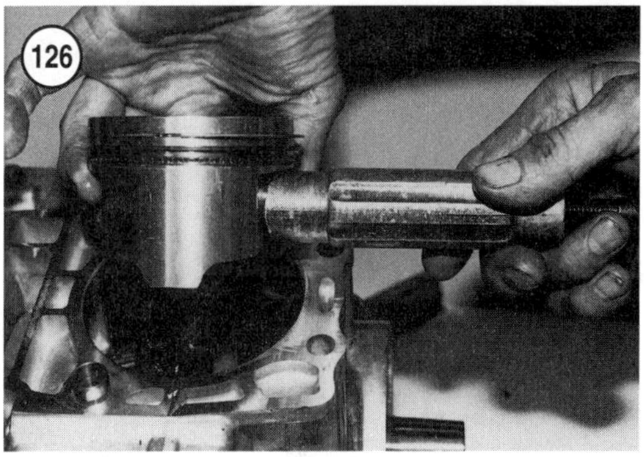

the piston pin, piston, connecting rod bore or, in most cases, a combination of all of three.

NOTE
Do not reuse the piston pin retaining clips. The clips are damaged during removal and severe engine damage will result if a clip becomes loose while the engine is running.

3. Cover the crankcase with a clean shop cloth (A, **Figure 125**) to prevent the piston pin retaining clip from falling into the crankcase.
4. Remove the retaining clip (B, **Figure 125**) from each side of the piston pin bore. Be careful to prevent the clip from springing out.
5. Use a proper size wooden dowel or suitable tool (**Figure 126**) to push the piston pin from the bore in the piston.

CAUTION
Be careful when removing the piston pin to avoid damaging the connecting rod. The piston must be supported when either pushing or pulling the pin from the piston pin bore. Be sure that lateral loads are not transmitted to the lower connecting rod bearing.

6. Lift the piston from the connecting rod.

NOTE
If the piston is to be left off for some time, protect the connecting rod by placing a piece of foam insulation tube over its end. Place a clean, lint-free shop towel around the connecting rod to keep dirt from entering the crankcase.

Piston Inspection

1. If necessary, remove the piston rings as described in this chapter.
2. Carefully clean the carbon from the piston crown with a soft scraper or wire wheel mounted in a drill. Large carbon accumulations reduce piston cooling and result in detonation and piston damage.

CAUTION
Be careful not to gouge or otherwise damage the piston when removing carbon. Never use a wire brush to clean the piston skirt or ring grooves.

4

Do not attempt to remove carbon from the sides of the piston above the top ring or from the cylinder bore near the top. Removal of carbon from these two areas may cause increased oil consumption.

3. After cleaning the piston, examine the crown (**Figure 127**). The crown should show no signs of wear or damage. If the crown appears pecked or spongy-looking, also check the spark plug, valves and combustion chamber for aluminum deposits. If these deposits are found, the engine is overheating.
4. Examine each ring groove (A, **Figure 128**) for burrs, dented edges or other damage. Pay particular attention to the top compression ring groove as it usually wears more than the others. Because the oil rings are constantly bathed in oiled, these rings and grooves wear little compared to compression rings and their grooves. If there is evidence of oil ring groove wear or if the oil ring assembly is tight and difficult to remove, the piston skirt may have collapsed due to excessive heat and is permanently deformed. Replace the piston.
5. Check the oil control holes in the piston (**Figure 129**) for carbon or oil sludge buildup. Clean the holes with wire and blow out with compressed air.
6. Check the piston skirt (B, **Figure 128**) for cracks or other damage. If a piston shows signs of partial seizure (bits of aluminum build-up on the piston skirt), replace the piston and bore the cylinder oversize if necessary to reduce the possibility of engine noise and further piston seizure.

NOTE

If the piston skirt is worn or scuffed unevenly from side to side, the connecting rod may be bent or twisted.

7. Check the retaining clip groove (**Figure 130**) on each side for wear, cracks or other damage. If the grooves are questionable, check the retaining clip fit by installing a new retaining clip into each groove and then attempt to move the retaining clip from side-to-side. If the retaining clip has any side play, the groove is worn. Replace the piston.
8. To check the piston pin-to-piston clearance, perform the following:
   a. Measure the outer diameter of the piston pin with a micrometer (**Figure 131**).
   b. Measure the piston pin bore inner diameter in the piston with a snap gauge (**Figure 132**).

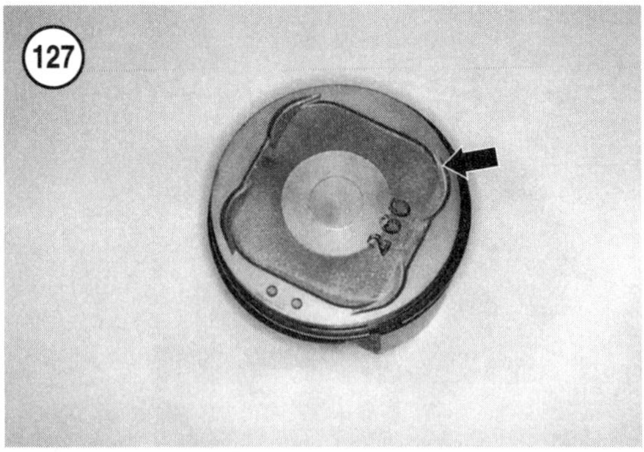

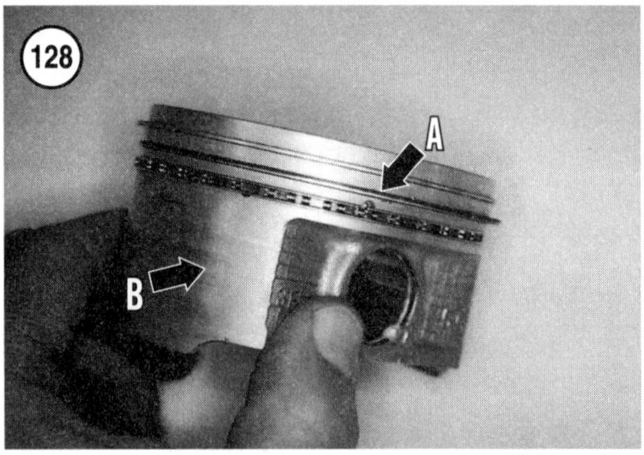

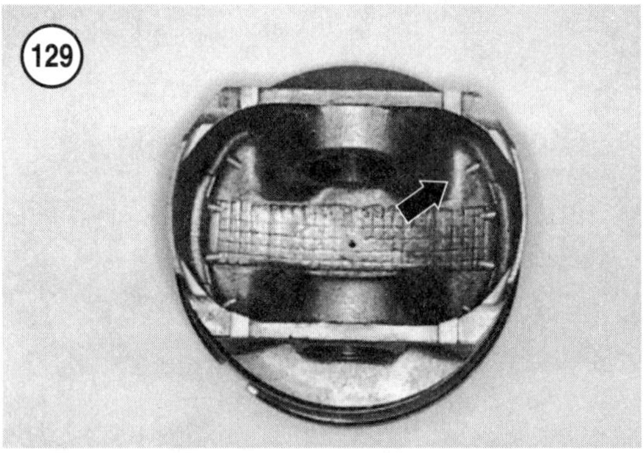

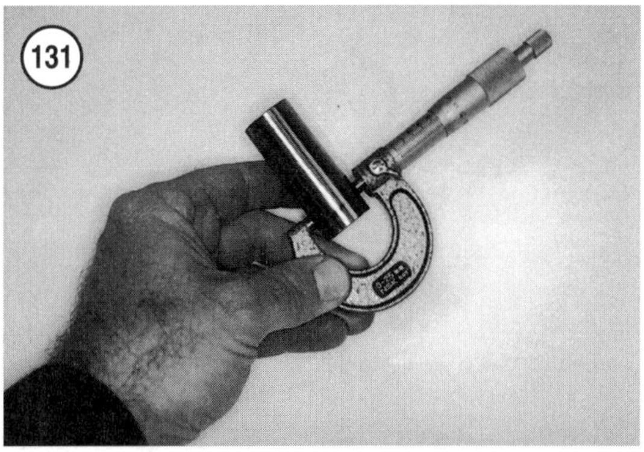

131

132

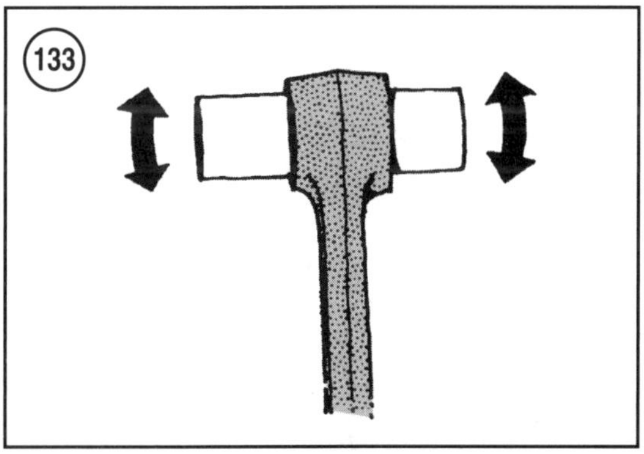

133

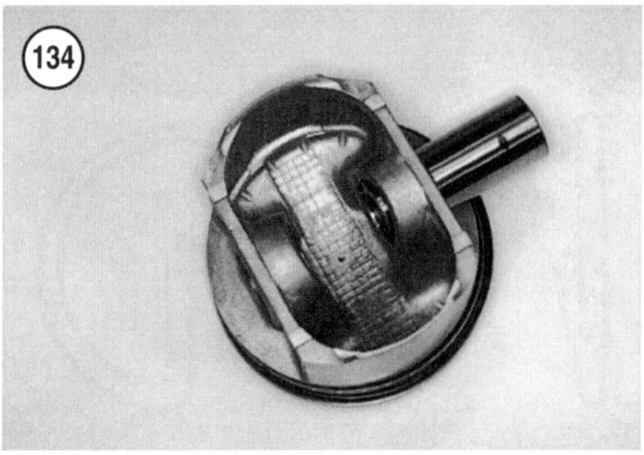

134

c. Subtract the outer diameter of the piston pin from the inside diameter of the piston pin bore. This will determine the piston pin-to-piston clearance.

d. Refer to the specification listed in **Table 4**. If clearance exceeds the specification in **Table 4**, replace any worn part(s).

9. Measure piston-to-cylinder clearance as described under *Piston Clearance* in this chapter.

10. If damage or wear indicate piston replacement, select a new piston as described under *Piston Clearance* in this chapter. If the piston, rings and cylinder are not damaged and are dimensionally correct, they can be reused.

Piston Pin Inspection

1. Clean the piston pin in solvent and dry thoroughly.
2. Inspect the piston pin for chrome flaking or cracks. Replace if necessary.
3. Oil the piston pin and install it in the connecting rod. Slowly rotate the piston pin and check for radial play (**Figure 133**).
4. Oil the piston pin and install it in the piston. Check the piston pin for excessive play (**Figure 134**).
5. Replace the piston pin and/or piston or connecting rod if necessary.

Piston Clearance

1. Make sure both the piston skirt and cylinder wall are clean and dry.
2. Measure the cylinder bore diameter and check for excessive taper and out-of-round using a bore gauge, inside micrometer or telescoping gauge (**Figure 135**). To determine if the cylinder is excessively tapered, take three measurements:
   a. 12.7 mm (0.50 in.) down from the top of the cylinder block.
   b. At the center of the cylinder bore.
   c. 12.7 mm (0.50 in.) up from the bottom of the cylinder block.
3. To determine if the cylinder is out-of-round, perform the measurements aligned with the piston pin, then at 90° to the piston pin.
4. If the cylinder bore diameter is excessively worn, tapered or out-of-round, bore the cylinder to the next oversize and replace the piston and rings.

5. Next, measure the piston diameter at a right angle to the piston pin bore at a point 5.0 mm (0.196 in.) from the bottom edge of the piston skirt (**Figure 136**).
6. Subtract the piston diameter from the largest bore diameter; the difference is piston-to-cylinder clearance. If clearance is excessive (**Table 4**), bore the cylinder to the next oversize and replace the piston and rings. Prior to boring the cylinder oversize, purchase and measure the oversize piston to establish the correct finished bore diameter to provide the correct piston clearance (**Table 4**).

135
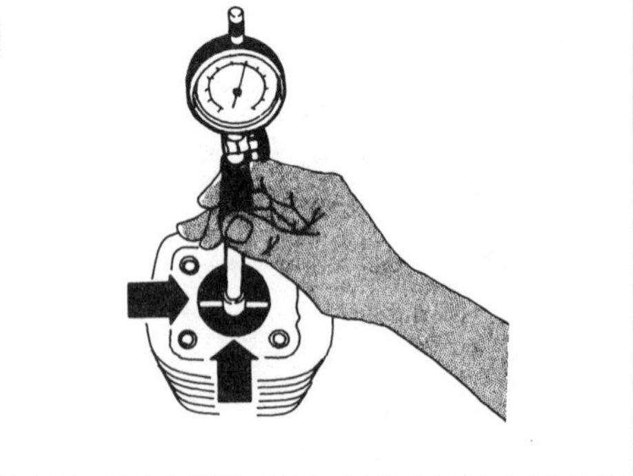

Piston Installation

1. Coat the connecting rod, piston pin and the piston pin bore with clean engine oil.
2. Install a new retaining clip (**Figure 137**) into one of the piston pin bore grooves. Position the tang on the retaining clip outward as shown in **Figure 138**. The tang can be directed to either the top or bottom of the piston. Make sure it is correctly seated in the piston pin bore groove.
3. Slide the piston pin into the piston until its end is flush with the piston pin boss (**Figure 134**).
4. Place a clean shop cloth (A, **Figure 139**) into the crankcase cavity to catch the piston retaining clip should it work loose during installation.
5. Place a piston holding fixture (B, **Figure 139**) under the connecting rod.
6. Place the correct piston over the connecting rod so that the arrow, or two dots, on the piston crown face toward the right side or alternator side, of the engine (**Figure 140**).
7. Line up the piston pin with the hole in the connecting rod. Push the piston pin (**Figure 141**) through the connecting rod and into the other side of the piston until it is centered in the piston.
8. Install a new piston retaining pin clip to the other side of the pin boss. Make sure the clip is seated correctly in the piston pin bore groove.
9. If removed, install the piston rings as described in this chapter.
10. Remove the piston holding fixture and shop cloth.

136
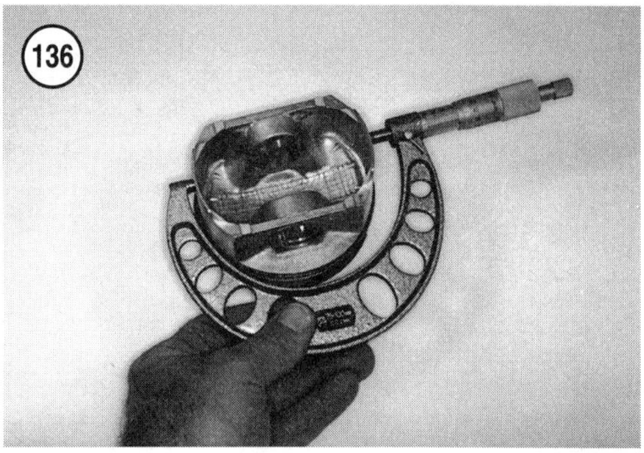

137
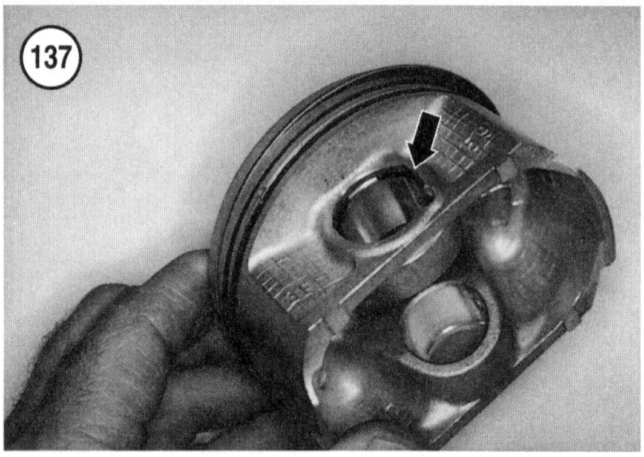

138
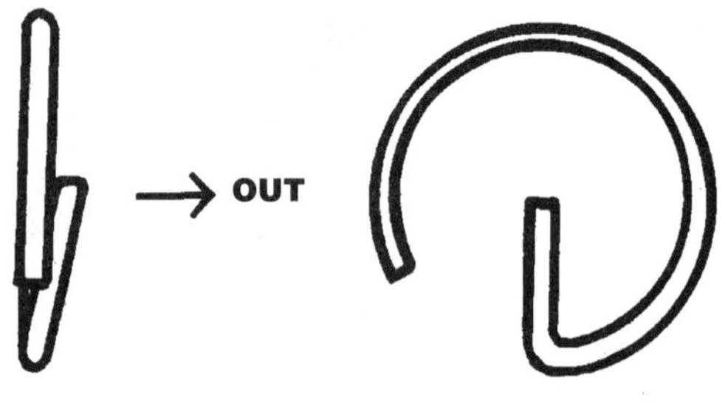

Piston Ring Inspection and Removal

A three-ring type piston and ring assembly is used. The top and second rings are compression

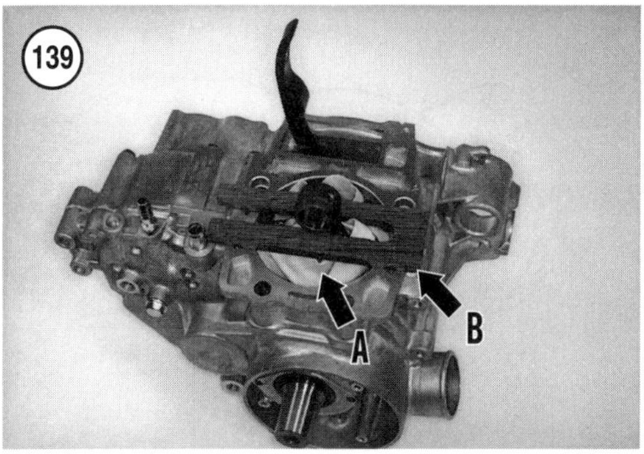

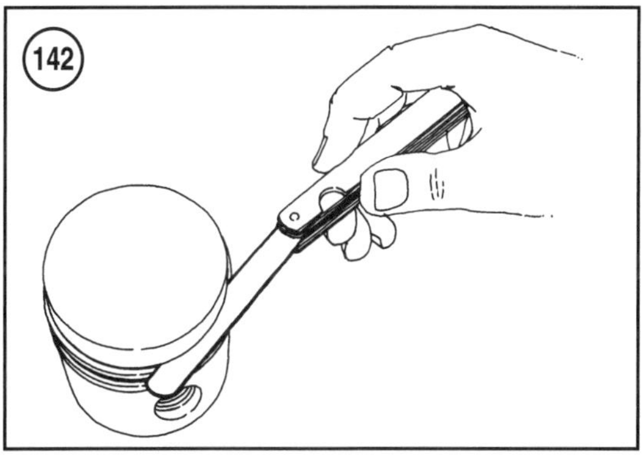

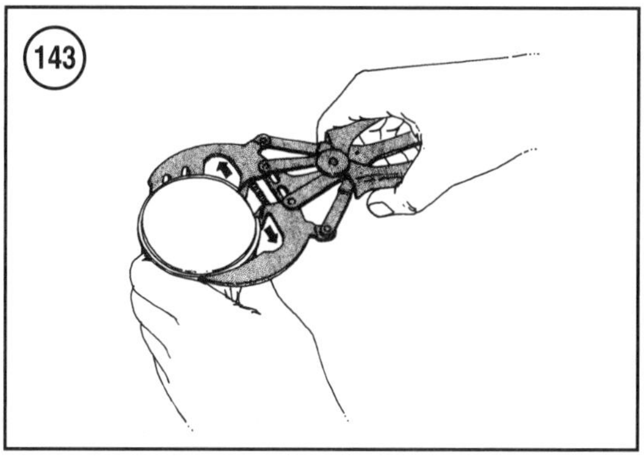

rings. The lower ring is an oil control ring assembly consisting of two ring rails and an expander spacer.

When measuring the piston rings and piston in this section, compare the actual measurements to the new and service limit specifications in **Table 4**. Replace parts that are out of specification or show damage as described in this section.

1. Measure the side clearance of each compression ring in its groove with a flat feeler gauge (**Figure 142**). If the clearance is still excessive with new rings, replace the piston and rings.

WARNING
The edges of all piston rings are very sharp. Be careful when handling them to avoid cutting fingers.

NOTE
Store the old rings in the order in which they are removed.

2. Remove the compression rings with a ring expander tool (**Figure 143**) or by spreading the ring ends by hand and lifting the rings up evenly (**Figure 144**).
3. Remove the oil ring assembly by first removing the upper and then the lower ring rails. Then remove the expander spacer.
4. Using a broken piston ring, carefully remove carbon and oil residue from the piston ring grooves (**Figure 145**). Do not remove aluminum material from the ring grooves, as this will increase ring side clearance.
5. Inspect grooves carefully for burrs, nicks or broken or cracked lands. Replace the piston if necessary.
6. Insert the ring into the bottom of the cylinder bore and square it with the cylinder wall by tapping it with the piston. Measure the end gap with a feeler gauge (**Figure 146**). Replace the rings if the end gap

exceeds the specification in **Table 4**. If the gap on a new compression ring is smaller than specified, place a small file in a vise (**Figure 147**), grip the ends of the ring with two fingers and enlarge the gap.

Piston Ring Installation

1. If new rings are installed, the cylinder must be deglazed or honed. This will help to seat the new rings. If necessary, refer honing service to a Polaris dealership or motorcycle repair shop. After honing, measure the end gap of each ring and compare to specifications in **Table 4**.

NOTE
If the cylinder was deglazed or honed, clean the cylinder as described under Cylinder Block Inspection in this chapter.

2. Clean the piston and rings. Dry with compressed air.
3. Install piston rings as follows:

NOTE
*Install the piston rings—first the bottom, then the middle, then the top ring by carefully spreading the ends by hand (**Figure 144**) and slipping the rings over the top of the piston. Remember that the piston rings must be installed with the marks on them facing up toward the top of the piston. Incorrectly installed piston rings can wear rapidly and/or allow oil to escape past them.*

a. Install the oil ring assembly into the bottom ring groove. First install the expander spacer so that the ends butt together. Do not overlap the ends. Then install the top and bottom ring rails.
b. Install the compression rings with the manufacturer's mark facing up.

NOTE
When installing aftermarket piston rings, follow the manufacturer's directions.

c. Install the second or middle compression ring.
d. Install the top compression ring.

4. Make sure the rings are seated completely in their grooves all the way around the piston and that

144

145

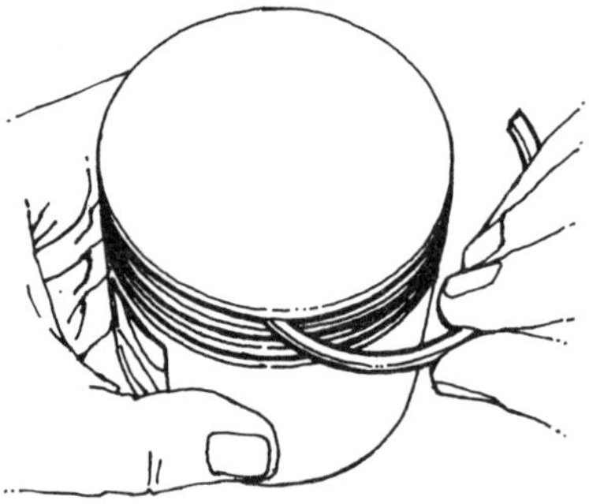

146

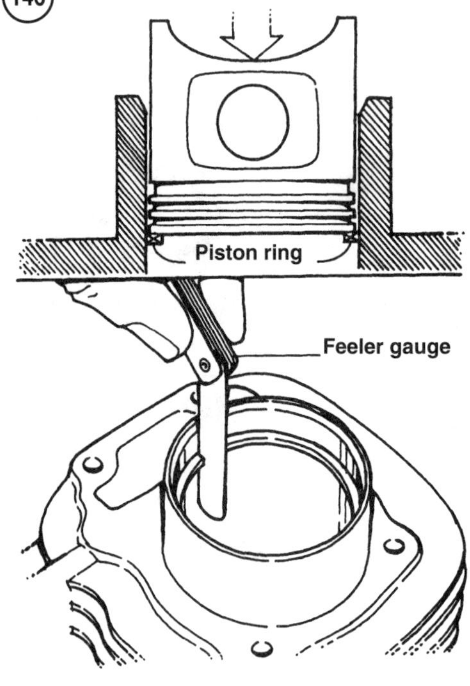

147

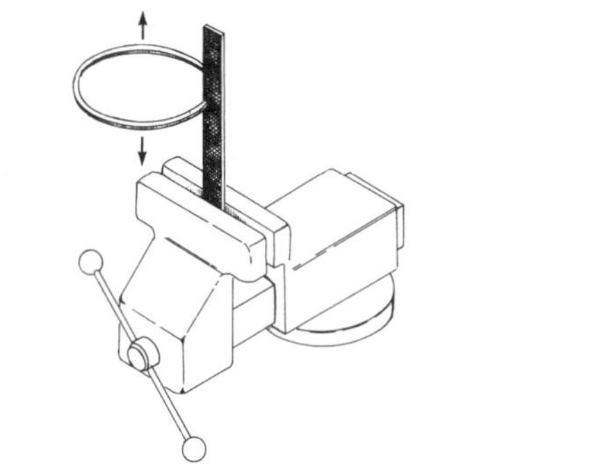

148

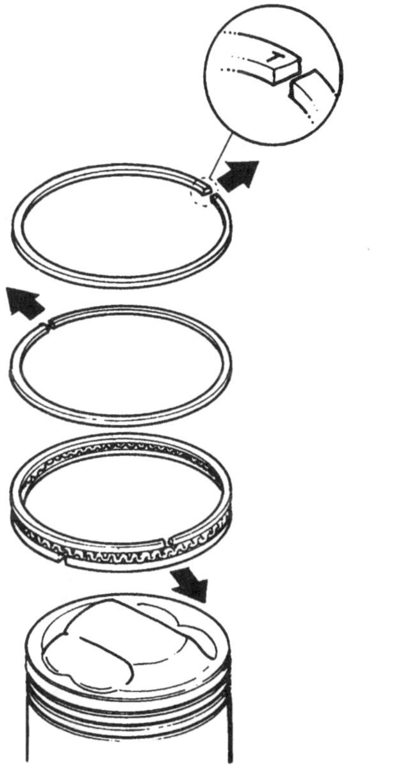

149

the end gaps are distributed around the piston as shown in **Figure 148**. It is important that the ring gaps are not aligned with each other when installed to prevent compression pressures from escaping past them.

5. If installing oversize compression rings, check the number to make sure the correct rings are being installed. The ring numbers should be the same as the piston oversize number.

6. If new parts were installed, the engine should be broken in the same as a new one. Refer to *Engine Break-In* in this chapter.

CAMSHAFT CHAIN AND SPROCKETS

The camshaft is driven by a chain located in a cavity in the right side of the engine.

WARNING

The original chain is a continuously closed loop without a master link. To prevent chain failure, do ***not*** *cut and then reinstall this type of chain. Install only a new continuous closed loop chain.*

Removal

1. Remove the cylinder head cover and rocker arm assembly as described in this chapter.
2. Remove the camshaft as described in this chapter.
3. Remove the recoil starter assembly as described in Chapter Five.
4. Remove the flywheel and the alternator stator plate as described in Chapter Five.
5. Remove the bolt (**Figure 149**) securing the camshaft chain rear tensioner slider. Remove the slider out thorough the top of the chain tunnel in the cylinder block and cylinder head.
6. Remove the driven sprocket from the chain.
7. Partially lower the camshaft chain (A, **Figure 150**) through the chain tunnel in the cylinder head and cylinder block.
8. Disengage the camshaft chain from the drive sprocket (B, **Figure 150**) and crankshaft, then remove the chain.
9. If still in place, remove the nut and washer (C, **Figure 150**) from the end of the crankshaft,

150

151

152

153

154

CAUTION
The slotted nut has left-hand threads. Turn the special wrench ***clockwise*** *to loosen the nut.*

10. Install the special tool (**Figure 151**) onto the slotted nut. Press hard on the tool to engage the tool tabs into the nut slots. Turn the special tool *clockwise* and loosen the slotted nut. Remove the special tool.
11. Unscrew and remove the slotted nut (**Figure 152**).
12. Slide the drive sprocket (**Figure 153**) off the crankshaft, then remove the Woodruff key (**Figure 154**) from the crankshaft.

Inspection

1. Clean the chain and sprockets in solvent and thoroughly dry.
2. Place the chain on a flat surface and pull the chain tight with no slack between the pins, exerting approximately 4.53 kg (10 lb.) force.
3. Measure the length of any 20-pitch section with a vernier caliper (**Figure 155**). Measure at several locations on the chain, as a chain usually does not wear equally.
4. If the length of 20 pitches exceeds 13.7 cm (5.394 in.) (**Figure 156**), replace the chain and sprockets.

CAUTION
Never install a new drive or driven sprocket or a new chain without replacing all three components as a set. If only one of the components is replaced, it will wear out prematurely.

5. Inspect both the drive (A, **Figure 157**) and driven (**Figure 158**) sprocket teeth for wear or other

155

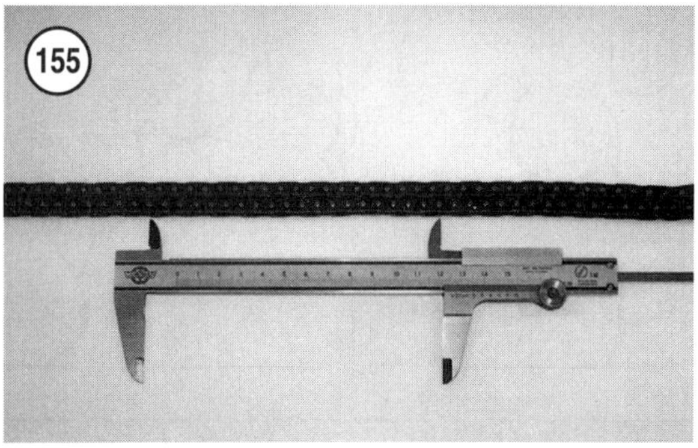

156

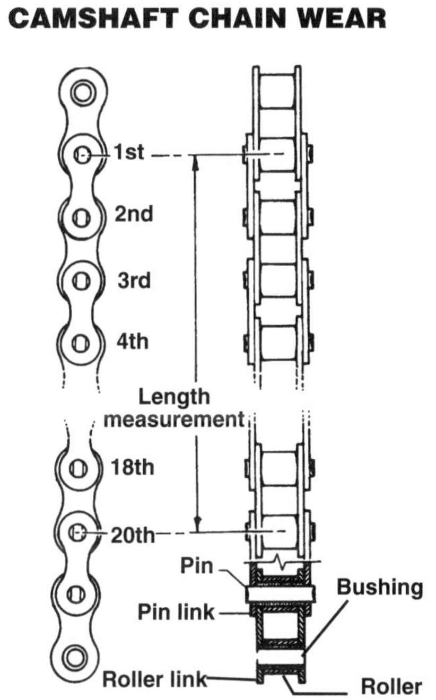

damage (**Figure 159**). If one of the sprockets is worn or damaged, replace both sprockets as well as the chain. A damaged sprocket can quickly damage a new chain.

6. Inspect the slotted nut (B, **Figure 157**) for thread damage. Replace if necessary.

7. Check the Woodruff key and the crankshaft key slot for wear or damage. Replace the Woodruff key if necessary.

8. Check the Woodruff key slot in the drive sprocket for wear or damage.

9. Inspect the rear tensioner slider (**Figure 160**) for wear or damage. Replace if necessary.

157

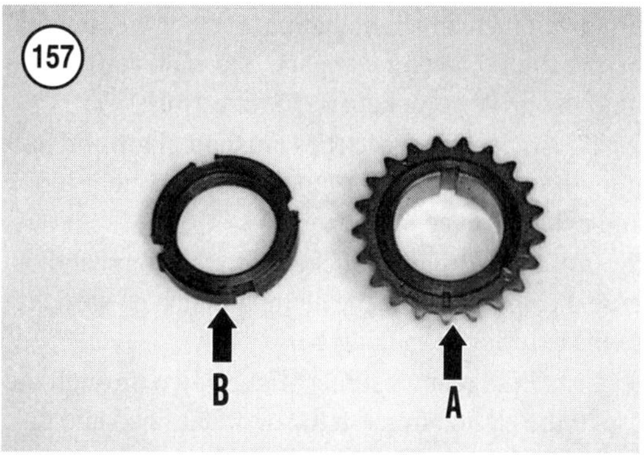

158

Installation

1. Install the Woodruff key (**Figure 154**) into the slot in the crankshaft. Make sure it is seated correctly and is not cocked.
2. Position the drive sprocket with the sprocket teeth side going on last. Slide the drive sprocket (**Figure 153**) onto the crankshaft and index in onto the Woodruff key. Push the drive sprocket on until it bottoms.

CAUTION
The slotted nut has left-hand threads. Turn the special wrench ***counter-clockwise*** *to tighten the nut.*

3. Install the slotted nut (**Figure 152**) onto the crankshaft and tighten finger tight making sure the drive sprocket is properly seated on the Woodruff key and the crankshaft.
4. Install the special tool (**Figure 151**) onto the slotted nut. Press hard on the tool to engage the tool tabs into the nut slots. Turn the special tool *counter-clockwise* and tighten to the torque specification listed in **Table 3**. Remove the special tool.
5. Install the washer and nut (C, **Figure 150**) onto the end of the crankshaft. Tighten finger tight at this time.

4

6. Install the camshaft chain into the lower portion of the crankcase and engage the camshaft chain onto the drive sprocket (B, **Figure 150**).
7. Tie a piece of wire to the camshaft chain and pull it up through the chain tunnel in the cylinder block and cylinder head.
8. Install the driven sprocket onto the chain and secure the upper end of the chain and driven sprocket to the exterior of the engine.
9. Install the rear tensioner slider down through the top of the chain tunnel in the cylinder head and cylinder block.
10. Install the bolt (**Figure 149**) securing the camshaft chain rear tensioner slider to the crankcase. Tighten to the torque specification listed in **Table 3**.
11. Install the alternator stator plate and flywheel as described in this chapter.
12. Install the recoil starter assembly as described in this chapter.
13. Install the camshaft as described in this chapter.
14. Install rocker arm assembly and the cylinder head cover as described in this chapter.

159

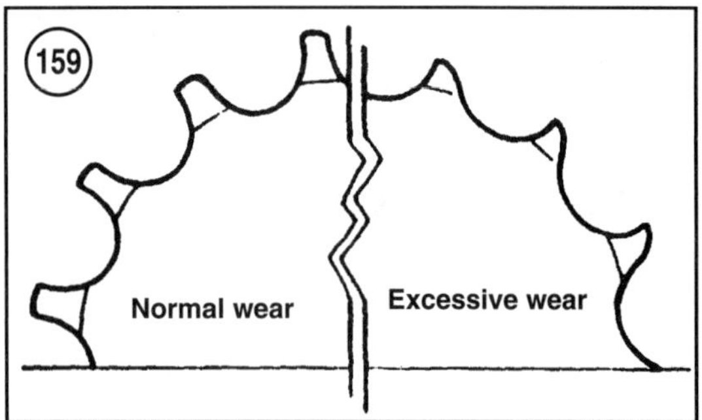

160

BREAK-IN PROCEDURE

If the piston rings were replaced, a new piston installed, the cylinder rebored or honed, break the engine in as though it were new. The performance and service life of the engine depends greatly on a careful and sensible break-in.

For the first 5-10 hours of operation, use no more than 1/3 throttle, and vary the speed as much as possible within the 1/3 throttle limit. Avoid hard acceleration in addition to prolonged steady running at one speed, no matter how moderate.

After the initial 5-10 hours of operation, use progressively more throttle with short bursts of speed until the ATV has run for 10-15 hours.

Table 1 GENERAL ENGINE SPECIFICATIONS

Item	Specifications
Engine type	Four-stroke, SOHC, single cylinder
Cooling system	Liquid
Bore and stroke	92 × 75 mm (3.622 × 2.953 in.)
Displacement	498 cc
Compression ratio	10 to 1

Table 2 ENGINE LUBRICATION SYSTEM

Item	Specification
Dry sump	
Engine oil	
Type	SE or SF
Viscosity	Polaris Premium 4 Synthetic 10W/40 or SAE 10W/40 motor oil
Oil capacity	1.89 L (2 U.S. qts.)
Oil pressure at 5500 rpm	
Standard	138 kPa (20 psi)
Minimum	83 kPa (12 psi)

Table 3 ENGINE TOP END TIGHTENING TORQUE SPECIFICATIONS

Item	N•m	in-lb.	ft.-lb.
Cylinder head bolts			
Large bolts*			
Small 6 mm bolts	8	71	–
Cylinder block bolts			
10 mm bolts	63	–	46
6 mm bolts	8	71	–
Crankcase bolts	19-21	–	14-15
Camshaft chain			
Drive sprocket slotted nut	48-70	–	35-52
Driven sprocket bolt	7-8	62-71	–
Rear tensioner			
Mounting bolts	7-8	62-71	–
Center bolt	17	–	12
Oil delivery pipe	25-34	–	18-25
Oil pressure blind plug	9-15	80-133	–
Rocker arm support bolts	11-12	97-106	–
Rocker arm adjuster locknut	6-7	53-71	–
Spark plug	19	–	14

* See text in this chapter for torque procedure.

4

Table 4 ENGINE TOP END SPECIFICATIONS

Item	New mm (in.)	Service limit mm (in.)
Rocker arm outside diameter	22.020-22.041 (0.8669-0.8678)	–
Rocker arm shaft outer diameter	21.987-22.000 (0.8656-0.8661)	–
Rocker arm-to- shaft clearance	0.020-0.054 (0.0008-0.0021)	0.10 (0.0039)
Camshaft		
Lobe height		
Intake and exhaust	32.726-32.826 (1.2884-1.2924)	32.426 (1.2766)
Journal outside diameter		
Both sides	37.935-37.9500 (1.4935-1.4941)	–
Journal bore outside diameter		
Both sides	38.005-38.025 (1.4963-1.4970)	–
Journal-to-bore clearance	0.055-0.090 (0.0022-0.0035)	0.10 (0.0039)
Cylinder head		
Top surface warp	–	0.050 (0.0020)
Valves		
Contact seat width		
Intake	0.7 (0.028)	1.4 (0.055)
Exhaust	1.0 (0.039)	1.9 (0.075)
Margin thickness		
Intake	1.0 (0.039)	0.8 (0.031)
Exhaust	1.2 (0.047)	0.8 (0.031)
Valve clearance (cold)		
Intake and exhaust	0.15 (0.006)	–

(continued)

Table 4 ENGINE TOP END SPECIFICATIONS (continued)

Item	New mm (in.)	Service limit mm (in.)
Valve stem outer diameter		
Intake	5.9950-5.965 (0.2360-0.2348)	–
Exhaust	5.945-5.960 (0.2341-0.2346)	–
Valve guide (intake and exhaust)		
Inside diameter	6.0-6.012 (0.2362-0.2367)	–
Protrusion above head	17.5-18.0 (0.689-0.709)	–
Valve stem-to-guide clearance		
Intake	0.035-0.062 (0.0014-0.0024)	0.15 (0.0059)
Exhaust	0.040-0.067 (0.0016-0.0026)	0.15 (0.0059)
Valve overall length		
Intake	101.0 (3.976)	–
Exhaust	101.2 (3.984)	–
Valve springs free length		
Orange paint mark	44.05 (1.7342)	42.05 (1.656)
Yellow paint mark	42.0 (1.654)	40.0 (1.575)
Cylinder block		
Bore	91.988-92.009 (3.6216-3.6224)	–
Bore limit	–	0.5 (0.020)
Taper	–	0.050 (0.0020)
Out of round	–	0.050 (0.0020)
Top surface warp	–	0.050 (0.0020)
Piston		
Outer diameter		
Standard	91.96-91.97 (3.6206-3.6210)	–
0.25 mm oversize	92.21-92.23 (3.6304-3.6310)	–
0.50 mm oversize	92.46-92.47 (3.6403-3.6407)	–
Piston pin bore inside diameter	23.0-23.006 (0.99055-0.9057)	–
Piston pin-to-piston clearance	0.004-0.008 (0.0002-0.0003)	–
Piston-to-cylinder clearance	0.015-0.045 (0.0006-0.00181)	0.060 (0.0024)
Piston rings		
End gap-installed		
Top and second	0.20-0.36 (0.0079-0.0138)	1.0 (0.039)
Oil ring	0.20-0.70 (0.0079-0.0276)	1.5 (0.059)
Side clearance		
Top ring	0.040-0.080 (0.0016-0.0031)	0.15 (0.0059)
Second ring	0.030-0.070 (0.0012-0.0028)	0.15 (0.0059)

NOTE: Refer to the Supplement at the back of this manual for information unique to 2001-on models, including the Sportsman 400.

CHAPTER FIVE

ENGINE LOWER END

5

This chapter covers service and overhaul procedures for the lower end engine components. Specifications are in **Table 1** and **Table 2** at the end of the chapter.

One of the most important aspects of a successful engine overhaul is preparation. Read all of the procedures before starting and review the information in Chapter One regarding tools and methods. The accurate use of precision measuring equipment is vital to a successful overhaul. Before removing the engine and disassembling the crankcase, degrease the engine and frame. Have all the necessary hand and special tools available. Make sure the work area is clean and well lit. Identify and store individual parts and assemblies in appropriate storage containers (**Figure 1**).

References to the left and right sides refer to the position of the parts as viewed by the rider sitting on the seat facing forward, not how the engine may sit on the workbench.

ENGINE

The following procedure describes removal and installation. If service work requires only the removal of a top end component (Chapter Four), leave the engine in the frame and disassemble the top end only as far as necessary to remove the desired subassembly.

It may be easier in some cases to remove as many engine components as possible before removing the lower end from the frame. Following this method reduces the weight of the engine and allows the frame to be used as a holding fixture. Disassembling the engine on the workbench without some type of holding fixture can be difficult, time consuming and may require an assistant to hold the engine when loosening large fasteners.

The engine must be removed from the frame to service the following components.

1. Counter balance system.
2. Crankcase.
3. Crankshaft and connecting rod.
4. Main bearings.
5. Oil pump.

Removal

1. Place the ATV on a level surface and set the parking brake. Block the wheels to keep it from rolling in either direction.
2. Remove the fuel tank as described in Chapter Six.
3. Remove the seat, front fender and side covers as described in Chapter Fifteen.
4. Disconnect the negative battery cable as described in Chapter Three. Secure the cable so it will not accidentally make contact with the battery terminal.
5. Drain the engine coolant as described in Chapter Three.
6. Drain the engine and oil tank as described in Chapter Three.
7. Disconnect the spark plug high tension lead (A, **Figure 2**) and move it out of the way.
8. Disconnect the engine breather hose from the engine.
9. Remove the air filter and air box as described in Chapter Six.
10. Remove the carburetor as described in Chapter Six. Insert a clean, lint free shop towel or plug (B, **Figure 2**) in the exposed intake port to prevent dirt from entering.
11. Remove the exhaust system as described in Chapter Four.
12. On 1997 models, remove the center drive and driven sprockets, and chain as described in Chapter Ten.

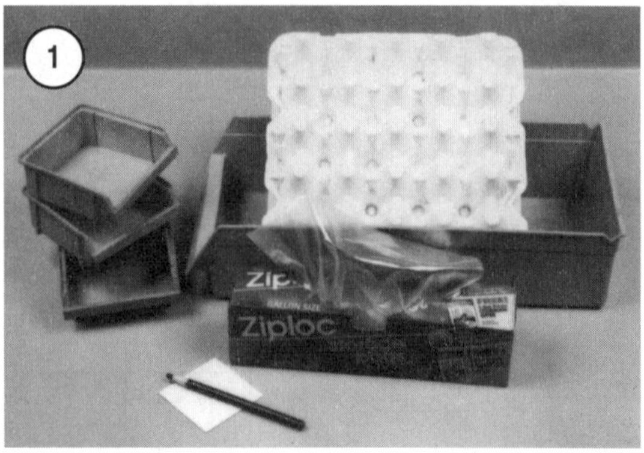

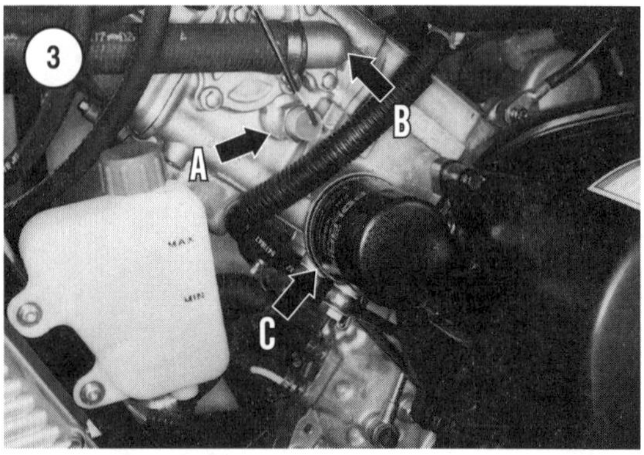

CAUTION
Do not lose the spacers or the spacer retaining O-rings from the threaded ends of the screws that attach the PVT inner cover.

13. Remove the PVT (Polaris variable transmission), drive belt, drive pulley, driven pulley and inner cover as described in Chapter Eight.
14. Remove the recoil starter as described in this chapter.

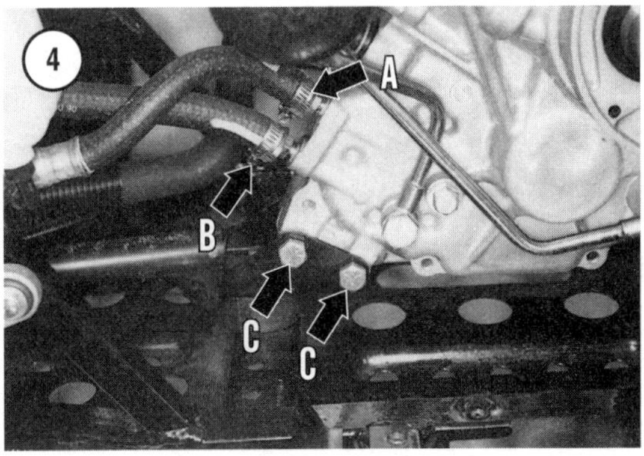

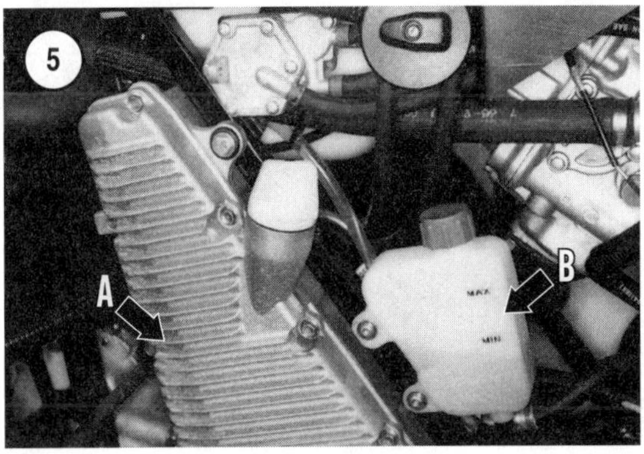

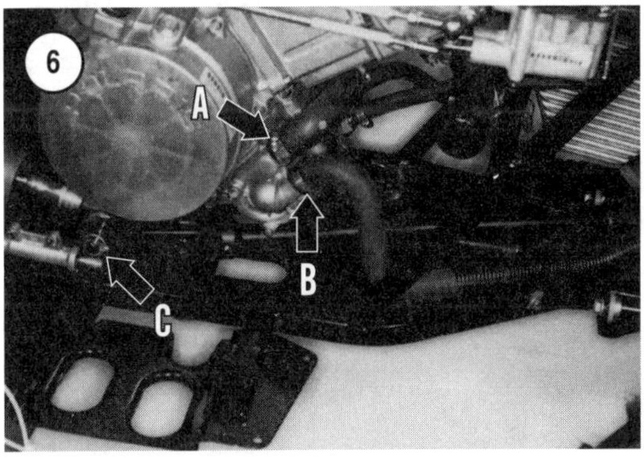

15. Remove the flywheel and stator plate as described in this chapter.

16. Cover the end of the crankshaft with a clean, lint-free shop towel to keep it clean.

17. Refer to Chapter Nine and disconnect the transmission shift linkage from the shift selector. Move the linkage out of the way and secure it to the frame.

18. Disconnect the electrical wire from the coolant temperature sender (A, **Figure 3**).

NOTE
Note the location of the starter motor cable before disconnecting it from the starter motor. The cable must be reconnected without any sharp turns or binding that could cause it to short out.

19. Remove the electric starter motor as described in Chapter Eleven.

20. Place a shop cloth under the oil hoses as some residual oil will drain out when the hoses are disconnected.

21. Loosen the hose clamp screws, then disconnect the oil delivery hose (A, **Figure 4**) and oil return hose (B, **Figure 4**) from the crankcase fittings. Cover the fittings and plug the lines to keep them clean and prevent oil leakage.

22. Remove the bolts securing the oil tank (A, **Figure 5**). Remove the oil tank and store it in the upright position.

23. Remove the bolts securing the coolant reservoir (B, **Figure 5**). Move the coolant reservoir out of the way and secure it to the frame.

24. Place a shop cloth under the coolant hose as some residual coolant will drain out when the hose is disconnected. Loosen the hose clamp screw and disconnect the cooling hose from the thermostat housing (B, **Figure 3**).

25. Remove the engine oil filter (C, **Figure 3**) as described in Chapter Three.

26. Place a drain pan under the coolant hose connections at the coolant pump.

27. Loosen the clamp on the upper coolant hose (A, **Figure 6**), detach the hose from the coolant pump outlet and allow the remaining coolant to drain. Reconnect the hose after the coolant has drained.

28. Loosen the clamp and remove the coolant pump lower inlet hose (B, **Figure 6**).

29. Remove the rear auxiliary brake master cylinder assembly (C, **Figure 6**) mounting bolts. Do not disconnect the hydraulic brake line, just move the master cylinder out of the way.

NOTE
Make centerline alignment marks at the location of the engine mount bolts and studs prior to removal. This will make reinstalling the engine easier.

5

30. Remove the bolts and self-locking nuts (C, **Figure 4**) that secure the front engine mounts to the bracket.

NOTE
***Figure** 7 is shown with the transmission assembly removed to better illustrate this step. Be sure to remove both self-locking nuts, as only one is shown in the illustration.*

31. Remove the two self-locking nuts and frame support strap (**Figure 7**) securing the rear engine mount.
32. Remove the self-locking nut and washer (**Figure 8**) securing the upper right side engine mount. On some models, the ground strap is also attached to this engine mount (**Figure 9**).
33. Lift and rotate the engine *clockwise* until the engine mount stud at the left front is withdrawn from the frame mount and the coolant hoses (on the lower right side), are clear of the frame.
34. Place a board across the frame to support the engine.
35. Lift the back of the engine while rotating the front clockwise, then remove the engine from the right side.

Installation

1. Install the engine onto the frame from the right side.
2. Install the rear engine mount washer and nut loosely before inserting it into the slotted plate.
3. Connect the coolant hoses to the coolant pump inlet and outlet, before final positioning of the engine.

NOTE
Make sure that coolant hoses and clamps are clear of the frame when the engine is in the correct position.

4. Locate the rear mount stud in the slotted plate, then move the engine into position in the reverse of the removal procedure.
5. Refer to the alignment marks made during removal and install the engine mounts. Tighten all bolts and nuts finger-tight until all mounting components are in place.

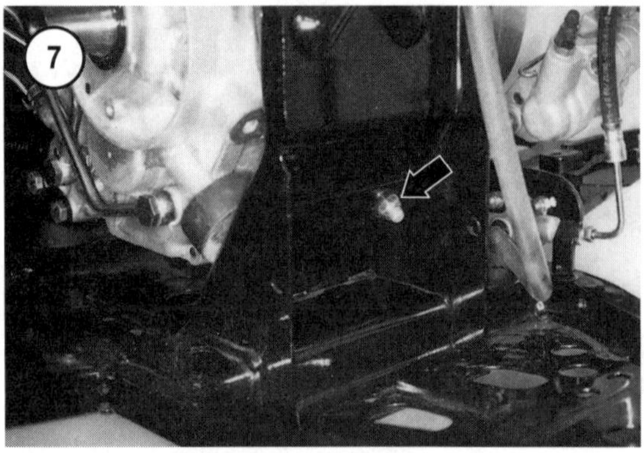

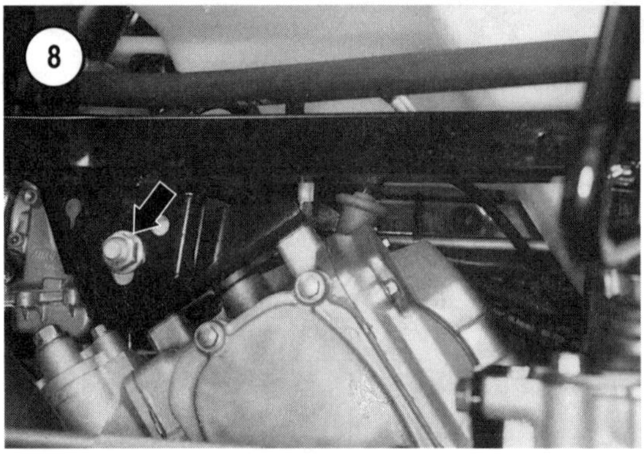

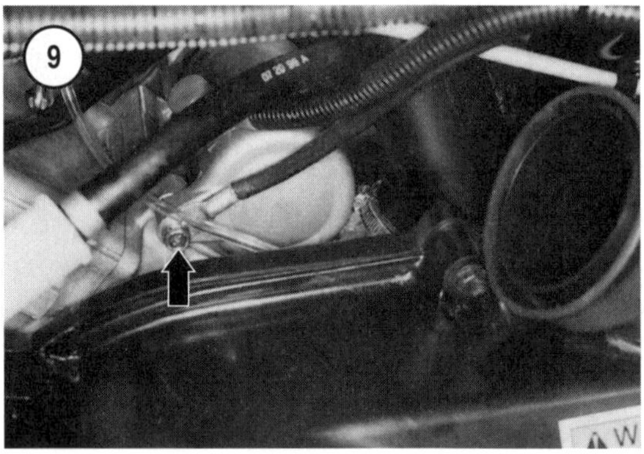

NOTE
The PVT drive pulleys should be temporarily installed to check the alignment of the engine in it mounts. If not aligned, it may be necessary to relocate the engine mounts.

6. Refer to Chapter Eight and temporarily install and align the PVT drive pulleys.
7. Tighten all engine mounting bolts and nuts securely.
8. Remove the drive pulleys.

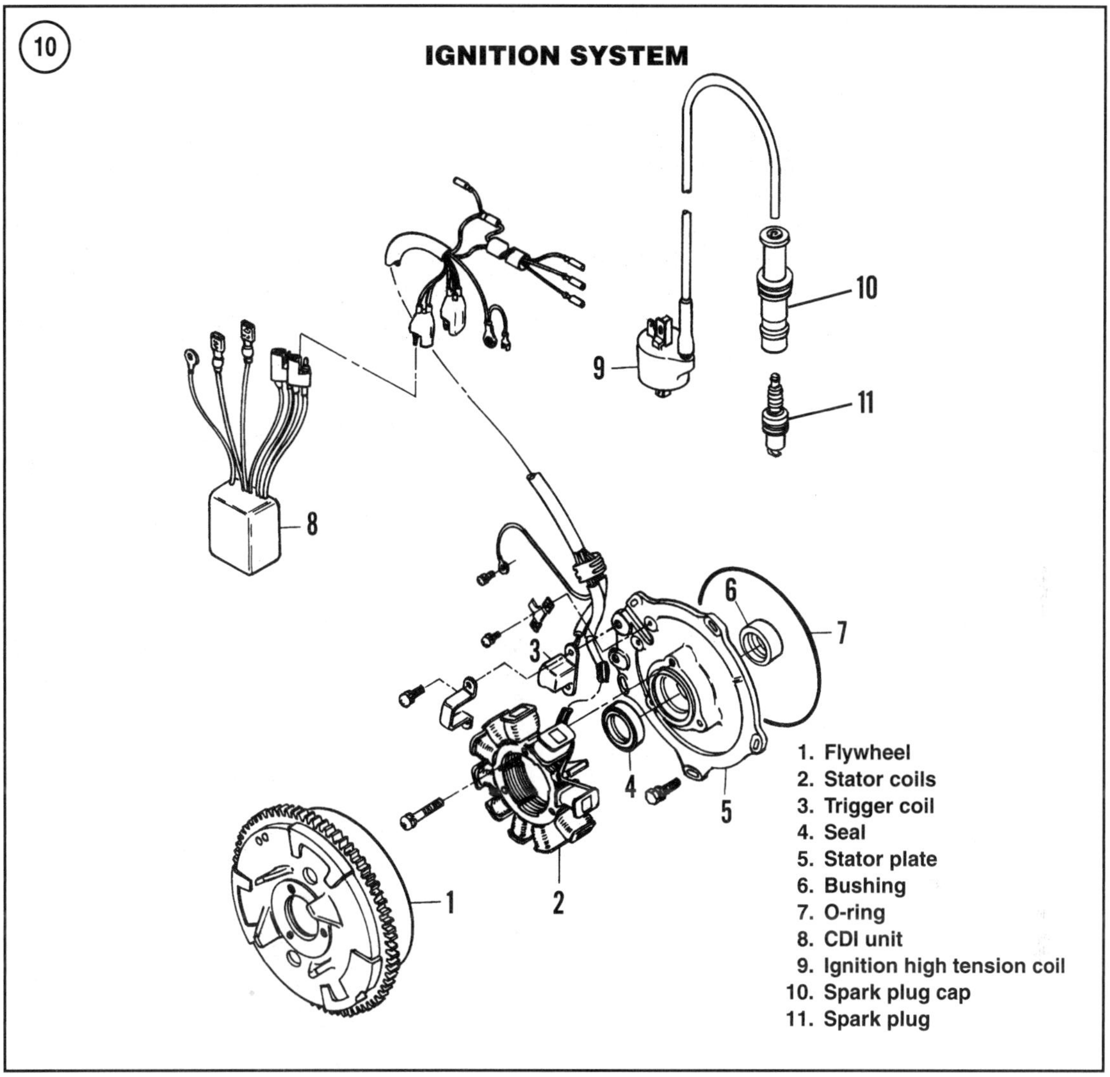

9. Complete assembly by reversing the removal procedure and observing the following.
   a. Install the flywheel and stator plate as described in this chapter.
   b. Refer to Chapter Three to fill and bleed the cooling system.
   c. Be sure that the oil delivery hose from the oil tank is attached to the upper fitting (A, **Figure 4**) and the return hose to the oil tank is attached to the lower fitting (B, **Figure 4**).
   d. Refer to Chapter Three and install the oil filter and refill the engine with oil.
   e. Refer to Chapter Nine and adjust the transmission shift linkage.
   f. Check and adjust the engine and the transmission controls if necessary.

FLYWHEEL AND STATOR PLATE

Removal

Before removing the flywheel and stator plate, clean the engine, frame and work area thoroughly. If water is used, be sure blow or wipe the engine dry before beginning removal.

Refer to **Figure 10**.

1. Place the ATV on a level surface and apply the parking brake. Block the wheels to keep it from rolling in either direction.
2. Disconnect the negative battery cable as described in Chapter Three. Move the cable out of the way so it will not accidentally make contact with the battery terminal.

3. Drain the engine oil and oil tank as described in Chapter Three.

4. Disconnect the spark plug high-tension lead and secure it out of the way.

5. Remove the recoil starter as described in this chapter.

6. Loosen, then remove the flywheel nut and washer (**Figure 11**).

CAUTION
Do not thread the puller attaching bolts into the flywheel more than 6 mm (1/4 in.), or the stator coils may be damaged.

7. Install a suitable puller (**Figure 12**) onto the flywheel. Tighten the center bolt and remove the engine flywheel from the crankshaft.

NOTE
Do not lose the thrust washer located between the electric starter drive and the crankcase.

8. Remove the electric starter drive (**Figure 13**) and the thrust washer (**Figure 14**).

9. Mark the position of the stator plate on the crankcase (A, **Figure 15**), so the stator can be reinstalled in the same timing position.

CAUTION
Use care to prevent damage to seals, crankshaft, stator plate, armature wires or other parts when removing the stator plate and stator assembly.

10. Remove the stator mounting bolts (B, **Figure 15**), then remove the stator plate and stator assembly.

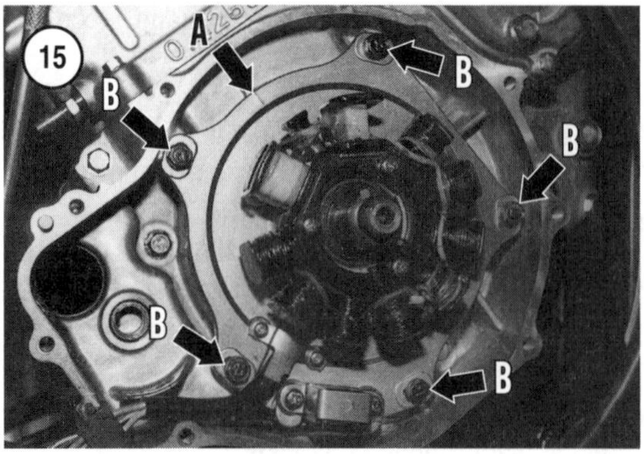

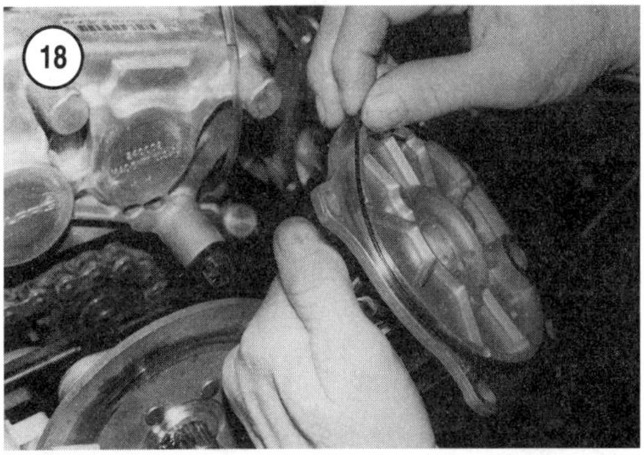

11. Remove the oil passage O-ring (**Figure 16**) from the crankcase.

12. Check the bearing and seal surfaces for scratches or burrs.

Installation

1. Apply a light coating of grease to the crankshaft and the seal (A, **Figure 17**) located in the stator plate.

2. Coat the bushing (B, **Figure 17**) in the stator plate with molybdenum disulfide grease or assembly lube.

3. Install a *new* O-ring (**Figure 16**) in the recess of the engine crankcase.

4. Apply Loctite 515, Loctite 518 or equivalent sealer to the outer diameter of the stator and position a *new* O-ring (**Figure 18**) on the stator plate.

5. Install the stator plate, making sure the previously affixed timing marks are aligned. Be sure the stator is fully seated and tighten the retaining bolts to the torque listed in **Table 1**.

6. Seal the stator wire grommet (A, **Figure 19**) with an appropriate sealer.

7. Be sure the thrust washer is located on the back of the starter reduction gear (B, **Figure 19**). Apply a coating of grease to the bushing, then install the gear.

8. Make sure the Woodruff key is in place, then install the flywheel. Push the flywheel on until it bottoms.

9. Install the washer and nut. Secure the flywheel with a suitable tool (A, **Figure 20**) to keep it from rotating in the following step.

10. Tighten the flywheel nut (B, **Figure 20**) to the torque specification listed in **Table 1**.

11. Install the recoil starter as described in this chapter.

RECOIL STARTER

Removal/Installation

1. Place the ATV on a level surface and apply the parking brake. Block the wheels to keep it from rolling in either direction.
2. On 1998 and later models, remove the rear auxiliary brake master cylinder and rear brake assembly (A, **Figure 21**) as described in Chapter Fourteen. Do not disconnect the hydraulic brake line, just move the master cylinder out of the way.
3. Remove the bolts securing the recoil starter (B, **Figure 21**) to the crankcase, then remove the recoil starter and gasket.

NOTE
The electric starter reduction drive assembly should remain with the engine. One end of the reduction drive assembly pivots in the rewind starter housing.

4. Install the recoil starter assembly and tighten the mounting bolts to the torque specification listed in **Table 1**.

Disassembly and Starter Rope Removal

Refer to **Figure 22**.

1. If the rope is not broken, pull it from the housing and tie a loose knot to keep the rope from rewinding.
2. Remove the anchor from the starter handle, untie the knot and remove the handle from the end of the rope.
3. Allow the rope to wind slowly into the housing.
4. Remove the center bolt (**Figure 23**).
5. Remove the friction plate (A, **Figure 24**), ratchet pawl (B), pawl spring (C) and friction spring (D).

CAUTION
The recoil spring is under pressure and may jump from the housing during disassembly. Its edges are sharp and may cut or cause eye injury. Wear hand and eye protection when disassembling and assembling.

6. Carefully lift the starter pulley and rope from the housing. Make sure the recoil spring remains in the starter housing.
7. Unwind and remove the rope from the starter pulley if replacement is necessary.

21

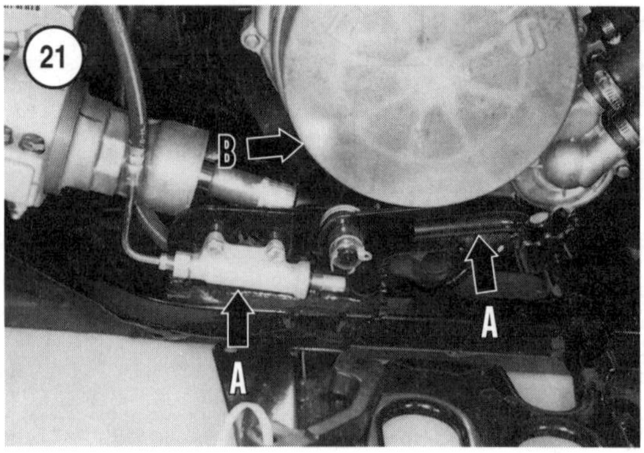

8. To remove the recoil spring, invert the starter housing and tap it on a solid surface. The spring will fall free and unwind inside the starter housing.

Inspection and Assembly

1. Clean all parts in solvent and dry them thoroughly.
2. Inspect the friction plate (A, **Figure 24**), ratchet pawl (B), pawl spring (C) and friction spring (D) for damage. The friction spring should grip the friction plate securely.
3. Check the rope for fraying or other damage.
4. Inspect the tabs at the ends of the recoil spring.

5A. Reinstall the old recoil spring as follows:
   a. Hook the outer end of the recoil spring in the housing.
   b. Wind the spring into the housing in a *counterclockwise* direction until the spring is completely in the housing. Hold the coils in place while winding the spring into the hosing.
   c. The installed spring should be positioned as shown in **Figure 25**.

5B. New recoil springs are held compressed by a wire. Use the following instructions to install the new spring.
   a. Position the new spring in the housing so that it spirals inward in a *counterclockwise* direction and attach the outer end of the spring to the housing.
   b. Hold the spring in place and cut the retaining wire. The installed spring should be positioned as shown in **Figure 25**.

6. Lubricate the spring with a light, low-temperature lubricant such as Polaris Cable Lube (part No. 2870510).
7. If the rope is detached from the pulley, attach the rope as follows:

(22)

RECOIL STARTER

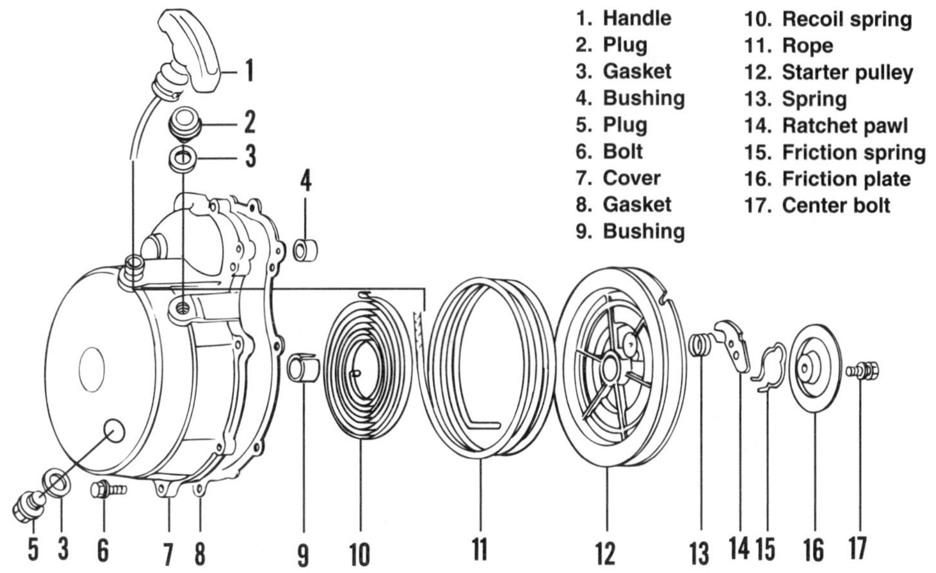

(23)

(25)

(24)

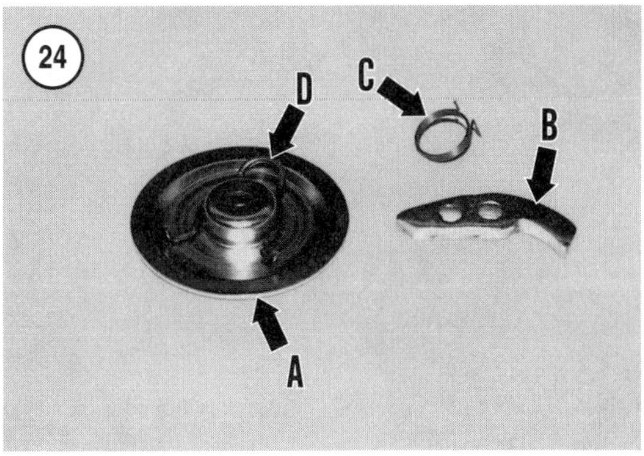

a. Tie a secure knot at one end of the rope and insert the other end through the hole (A, **Figure 26**).

b. Pull the rope through the pulley until the knot seats firmly in the pocket of the pulley.

c. Wind the rope into the pulley groove *counter-clockwise* as viewed from the side shown in **Figure 26**. The rope should be wound fairly tightly into the groove.

d. When the rope is almost completely wound into the pulley, pull the end up through the notch (B, **Figure 26**). The end of the rope should lock into the notch.

8. Apply a small amount of Polaris low-temperature grease, or equivalent, to the center post in the starter housing and to the bushing in the center of the starter pulley.

9. Install the starter pulley over the center post making sure the inner end of the recoil spring engages the tab at the center of the pulley (**Figure 27**). Make sure the pulley is fully seated (down) in the housing.

10. Preload the recoil spring as follows:

   a. Hold the pulley down in the housing.
   b. Grasp the end of the rope that extends from the notch (B, **Figure 26**) in the pulley and wind the pulley counterclockwise four turns.
   c. Hold the pulley to prevent the spring from pulling the rope back into the housing.
   d. Route the end of the rope out through the housing, while continuing to hold the pulley.
   e. When the rope exits the housing, pull enough rope out to tie a large knot in the rope to keep it from winding into the housing.

11. Install the pawl spring (**Figure 28**).

12. Install the pawl as shown in **Figure 29**.

13. Install the friction plate and spring (**Figure 30**) with each end of the spring located on the drive side of the ratchet.

14. Install the spring washer and center screw (**Figure 23**). Tighten the bolt securely.

15. Attach the handle to the starter rope and tie a knot. Check operation of the recoil starter. If the rope is the correct length, but the recoil spring does not hold the handle against the housing, refer to Step 10 and preload the spring an additional turn. If the rope is too long, the coils of the rope may extend outside the pulley groove and bind against the housing.

CRANKCASE

The crankcase is a two-piece precision-cast aluminum alloy assembly. The two case halves are only available as a matched set. If one is damaged, both must be replaced. Do not hammer or pry on any of the projecting walls. Treat the sealing surfaces with extreme care. These areas are sealed with a gasket sealer; any small imperfections in the surfaces will cause oil leakage.

The following procedure has many references to the right and left sides of the engine. This refers to the engine while mounted in the frame, *not* as it may

26

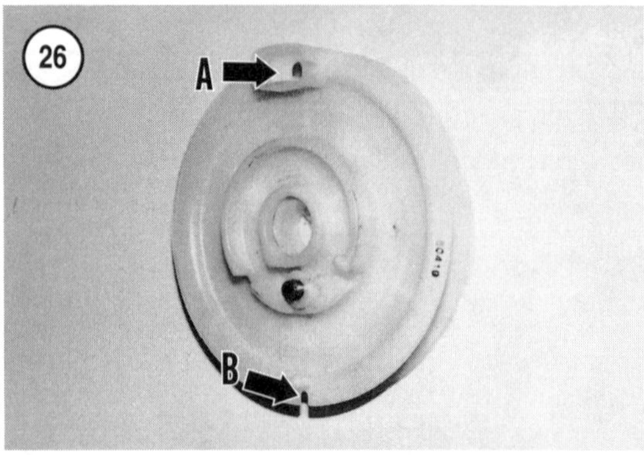

27

28

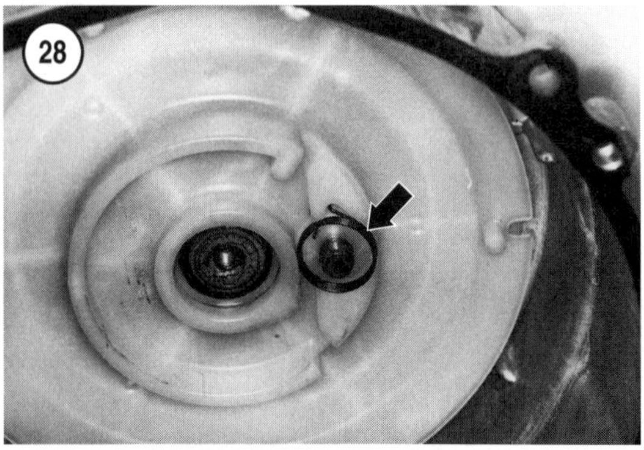

29

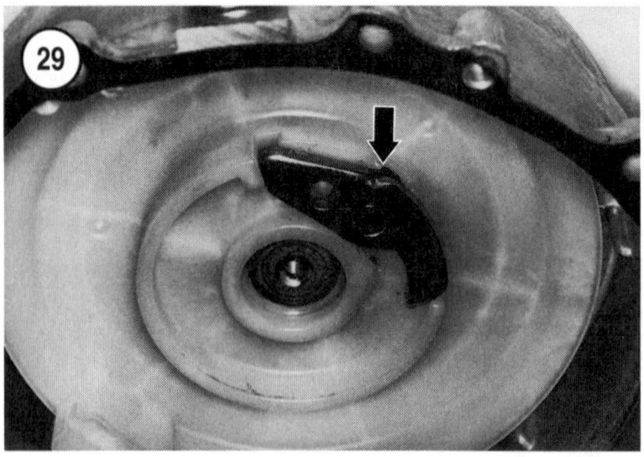

30

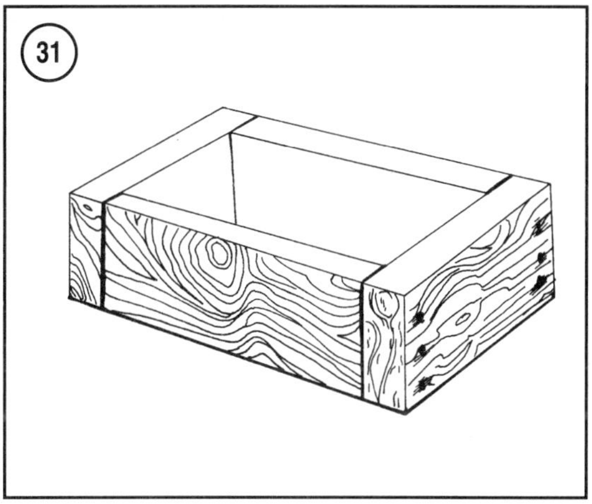
31

32

sit on the workbench. Keep this in mind when the crankcase is on the workbench.

Crankcase Separation

NOTE
A crankcase separation tool is required to remove the crankshaft assembly from the left crankcase half. A special Polaris crankshaft installation tool set (part No. 2871283) is necessary to draw the crankshaft back into the left case half and to assemble the crankcase halves.

1. Remove the engine as described in this chapter.
2. Remove all exterior engine assemblies from the crankcase as described in this chapter and other related chapters.
3. Remove the camshaft drive gear from the crankshaft as described under *Camshaft Chain and Sprockets* in Chapter Four.
4. Place the crankcase on wooden blocks, or a fabricated wooden box as shown in **Figure 31**, with the right side facing up (**Figure 32**).

NOTE
Keep track of the crankcase bolts by drawing the crankcase outline on a piece of cardboard, then number and punch holes to correspond with each bolt location. After removal, insert the bolts in their appropriate locations. Leave cable clamps on their respective bolts.

5. Loosen the ten crankcase mounting bolts one-quarter of a turn and in a crisscross pattern. Repeat until all bolts are loose.
6. Remove all ten bolts and store them in the cardboard fixture in the correct location.
7. If still in place, remove the Woodruff key from the right-hand end of the crankshaft.

NOTE
The crankcase separation tool is attached to one side of the crankcase with the pressure bolt placed at the center of the crankshaft. The tool pushes the crankshaft out of the right crankcase main bearing without damaging the crankshaft. Pounding on the end of the crankshaft can knock the crankshaft out of alignment as well as damage the threaded end.

8. Install the crankcase separating tool into the threaded holes on the right crankcase. Center the pressure bolt on the end of the crankshaft. Tighten the securing bolts into the crankcase making sure the tool is parallel with the crankcase. If necessary, back out one of the mounting bolts.

33

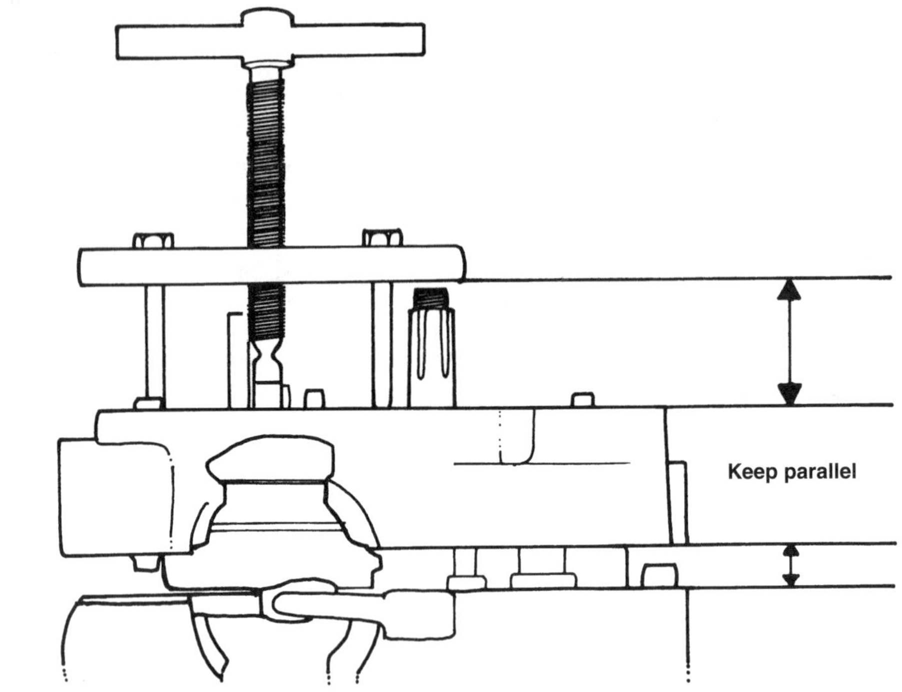

9. Tighten the pressure bolt *clockwise* until both crankcase halves begin to separate.

CAUTION

While tightening the separating tool make sure the body is kept parallel to the top surface of the right-hand crankcase during this operation ***(Figure 33)****.*

10. Use a plastic or rubber mallet and tap gently on the coolant pump shaft while tightening the center bolt to help during separation.

11. Insert a small drift into the right crankcase opening and tap on the end of the balancer shaft to ensure the balancer shaft stays with the left crankcase half.

CAUTION

Crankcase separation requires only light pressure on the separator pressure bolt. If extreme pressure seems to be needed, or if both crankcase halves do not remain parallel, ***stop immediately****. Check for crankcase bolts not removed, any part that is still at-*

34

35

tached, or a shaft that is hung up on a bearing. Relieve pressure immediately and correct the problem before proceeding.

CAUTION
Never pry the crankcase halves apart. Doing so will result in oil leaks, requiring the replacement of the crankcase.

12. Pull the right crankcase straight up and off the left crankcase half and shafts. Set the right crankcase aside and remove the separating tool from it.

13. Remove the locating dowels. Refer to **Figure 34** and **Figure 35**.

14. Remove the thrust washer from the pump shaft, then slide the drive gear (A, **Figure 36**) from the pump shaft.

15. Remove the three mounting bolts (A, **Figure 37**) securing the oil pump to the crankcase. Lift up and remove the oil pump (B, **Figure 37**).

CAUTION
The balance shaft may be equipped with a shim(s). Be careful not to loose or damage the shim(s).

16. Lift the balance shaft (B, **Figure 36**) straight up and out of the left crankcase. Keep the shims with the shaft as they must be reinstalled.

17. If so equipped, remove the shim (C, **Figure 36**) from the end of the crankshaft.

18A. If a press is available, perform the following:

CAUTION
Place wooden blocks on the press bed to protect the sealing surface of the left crankcase half during the press operation.

a. Place the left crankcase on the press bed with the sealing surface facing down.
b. Position the crankcase on the press bed so the crankshaft is centered under the press post (**Figure 38**).
c. Slowly apply pressure to the end of the crankshaft while holding onto the right end under the press bed.

CAUTION
Do not drop the crankshaft when it is released from the bearing.

d. Continue to apply pressure until the crankshaft is released from the bearing in the left crankcase. Remove the crankshaft (**Figure 39**).
e. Remove the left crankcase half from the press bed.

18B. If a press is not available, take the left side crankcase/crankshaft assembly to a Polaris dealership, or machine shop, and have the crankshaft pressed out.

19. Inspect all components of the crankcase as described in this chapter.

Crankcase Inspection

1. Clean both crankcase halves inside and out and all crankcase bearings with cleaning solvent. Thoroughly dry with compressed air.
2. Using a scraper, *carefully* remove any remaining sealer residue from all crankcase mating surfaces.
3. Carefully check the sealing surface of both crankcase halves. Check for gouges or nicks that may lead to an oil leak.
4. Clean all crankcase oil passages (**Figure 40**) with compressed air.
5. Make sure the oil pump inlet and outlet fittings are clear (**Figure 41**).
6. Inspect the cases for cracks and fractures, especially in the lower areas (**Figure 42**) where they are vulnerable to rock damage. Check the areas around the stiffening ribs, around bearing bosses and threaded holes for damage. If damage is found, have it repaired by a shop specializing in the repair of precision aluminum castings or replace the damaged crankcase.
7. Check the threaded holes in both crankcase halves for thread damage, dirt or oil buildup. If necessary, clean or repair the threads with a suitable size metric tap. Coat the tap threads with kerosene or an aluminum tap fluid before use.
8. Check the bearings (**Figure 43**) in each case half for wear. Rotate the inner race of the bearing by hand. The bearing must rotate freely with no signs of binding. If necessary, replace the bearing as described in Chapter One.
9. Make sure the locating dowels are a tight-fit. Refer to **Figure 44** and **Figure 45**. Replace the locating dowels if loose or severely corroded.
10. Inspect the crankshaft oil seal (**Figure 46**) and replace as described in the following procedure.

Crankshaft Seal Replacement

When removing the crankshaft seal from the right side case half, note and record the direction the seal faces and its depth from the crankcase surface (**Figure 47**) for proper installation.

Install new crankcase seals before reassembling the engine.

Refer to **Figure 48**.

1. Pry the old seal out with a flat bladed screwdriver or seal removal tool (**Figure 49**). Pad the pry-

39

40

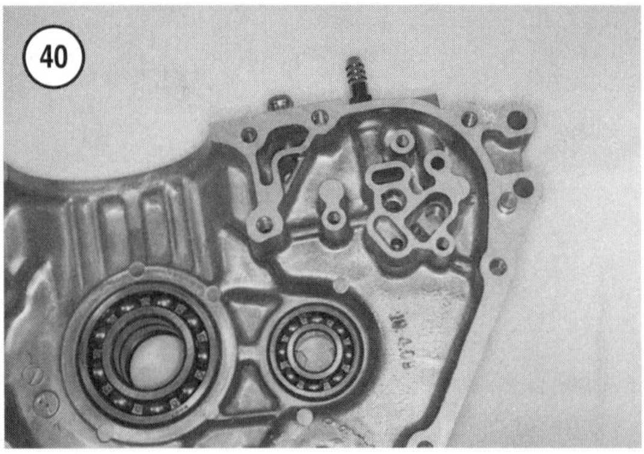

41

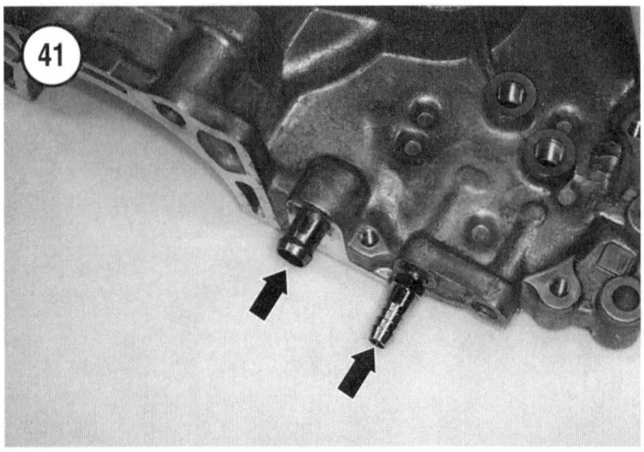

42

43

44

45

46

47

ing area under the tool with a shop cloth to avoid damaging the crankcase seal mounting bore.

2. Inspect the engine case bearings and replace damaged bearings before installing new seals. Refer to *Crankcase Bearing Replacement* in this section.

3. Pack high-temperature grease between the lips of each seal.

CAUTION
The oil seal must be installed after the crankcase has been assembled to prevent damage to the seal lips.

4. Assemble the crankcase as described in this chapter.

5. Correctly position the seal, as noted during removal, over the crankshaft (**Figure 50**) and onto the crankcase mounting bore.

6. Place a suitable size socket or bearing driver over the seal. Drive the seat into its mounting bore (**Figure 51**) until it is installed to the correct depth as noted prior to removal.

Crankcase Bearing Replacement

When removing the bearings, note and record the direction of the bearings, the manufacturer's name and size code. The bearings must be reinstalled in the same direction.

Refer to **Figure 48**.

1. If a bearing came off with the crankshaft, remove it with a bearing splitter and press as follows:
   a. Mount a bearing splitter against the main bearing.
   b. Place the connecting rod at bottom dead center (BDC) and install the crankshaft jig be-

48

CRANKCASE

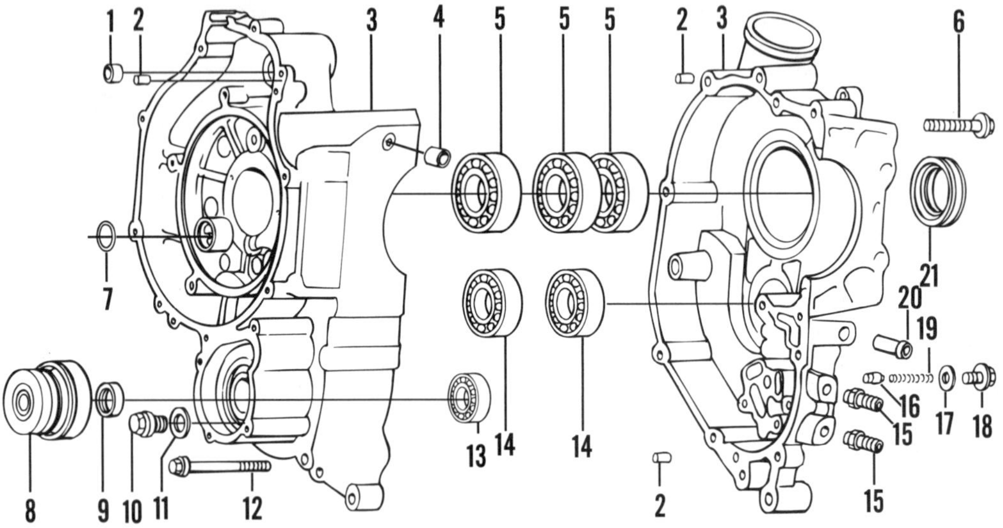

1. Starter bushing
2. Dowel pin
3. Crankcase half assembly
4. Dowel pin
5. Bearing
6. Bolt
7. O-ring
8. Mechanical seal (water pump)
9. Oil seal
10. Drain plug
11. Gasket
12. Bolt
13. Bearing
14. Bearing
15. Oil hose union
16. One-way valve
17. Aluminum gasket
18. Plug
19. Spring
20. Breather fitting
21. Oil seal

49

50

51

52

tween the crankshaft wheels. Position the tool with its arms contacting the inside of the crank wheels evenly (in four places), then tighten the wing nut securely.

c. Mount the sides of the bearing splitter on two wooden blocks in the press. Center the crankshaft under the press ram.

CAUTION
Make sure the wooden blocks are tall enough so the crankshaft has room to press out of its bearing without it or the connecting rod contacting the press bed.

WARNING
The crankshaft will fall once it is free of the bearing. Hold the crankshaft so it will not fall to the floor.

d. Press the crankshaft off its bearing.
e. Repeat for the other bearing, if necessary.

NOTE
*Two methods of replacing the crankcase bearings are described in the following procedure. Before starting, read the **Bearing Replacement** section in Chapter One for additional information on bearing removal.*

2A. To replace the bearings using heat, perform the following steps:

a. Read this step through completely and have all of the correct size bearing drivers or sockets on hand before starting. Have all tools and supplies on hand to be able to quickly replace the bearings while the crankcase is hot.

NOTE
Prior to removing the right side crankcase main bearings, the seal must be removed.

b. Before heating the crankcases to replace the bearings, place the new bearings in a freezer. Chilling them will slightly reduce their overall diameter while the hot crankcase is slightly larger due to heat expansion. This will make installation much easier.
c. Wash the cases thoroughly to remove all traces of oil and other chemical deposits.
d. The bearings are installed with a slight interference fit. Heat the crankcase to a temperature of about 212° F (100° C) in a shop oven or on a hot plate. Heat only one case at a time.

CAUTION
Do not heat the cases with a torch (propane or acetylene); never bring a flame into contact with the bearing or case. The direct heat will destroy the case hardening of the bearing and will likely warp the case half.

e. Remove the case from the shop oven or hot plate and hold onto the crankcase with welding gloves—*it is hot.*

NOTE
Suitable size sockets and extensions can be used for removing and installing bearings.

f. Support the crankcase on wooden blocks and then drive the bearing out from its opposite side (**Figure 52**). Use a bearing driver or socket to remove the bearing. Use a blind

53

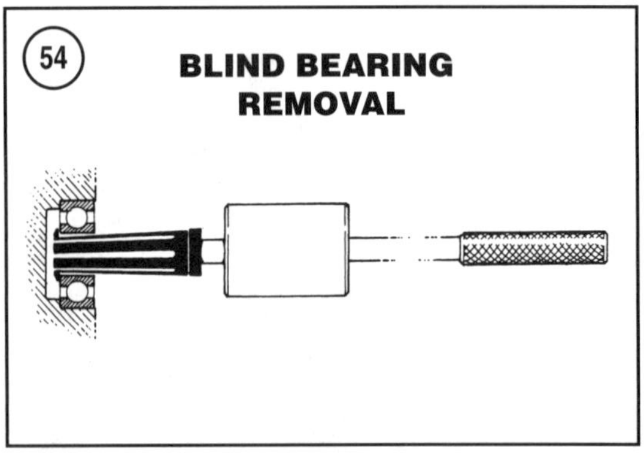
54

bearing removal tool to remove bearings installed in blind holes.

NOTE
Install new bearings so their manufacturer's name and size code face in the same direction recorded during disassembly. If this information was not recorded during removal, install the new bearings so their marks will be visible after the bearings have been installed.

g. While the crankcase is still hot, install the new bearing(s) into the crankcase. Install the bearings by hand, if possible. If necessary, lightly tap the bearing(s) into the case with a bearing driver or socket placed on the outer bearing race. *Do not* install the bearings by driving on their inner race. Install the bearing(s) until it seats completely in its mounting bore.

2B. To replace bearings with a press:
a. Remove the right side seal as described in this chapter.
b. Support the crankcase on two wooden blocks and center the bearing under the press ram.
c. Press the bearing out of the crankcase.
d. Support the crankcase on two wooden blocks and center the bearing and bearing bore under the press ram.
e. Place a bearing driver on the outer bearing race and press the bearing into the crankcase until it bottoms.

3. To remove a blind bearing(s) (**Figure 53**), a special bearing removal tool is required (**Figure 54**). Occasionally, it is possible to remove a blind bearing by heating the crankcase half and then tapping the crankcase on a soft wooden surface. If the bearing does not fall out, remove it with the proper tool.

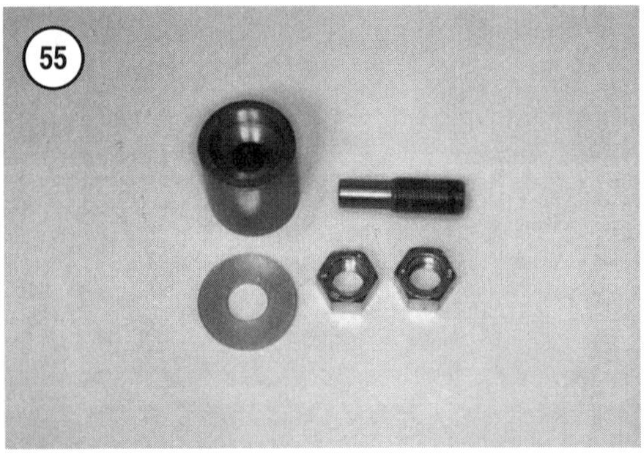
55

56

57

58

59
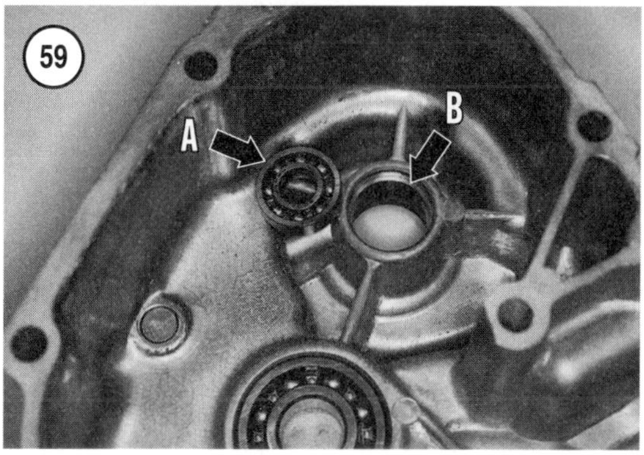

60
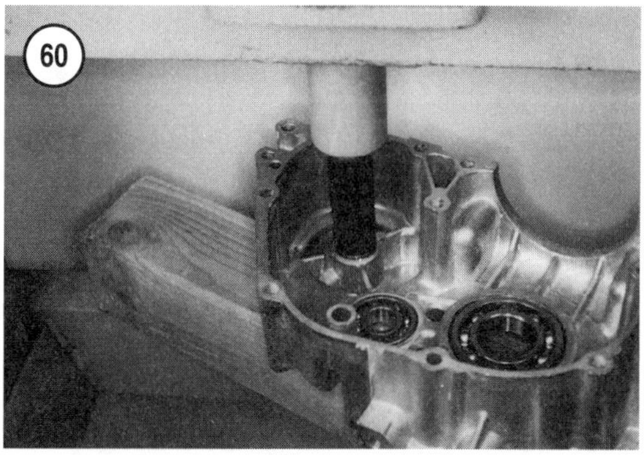

61

62

Do not force or pry the bearing out of the receptacle. This may damage the crankcase half.

Water Pump Mechanical Seal and Bearing Replacement

A Polaris special tool set (part No. 5131135) is required to pull the mechanical seal back into the crankcase (**Figure 55**).

1. Install a bearing puller onto the bearing (**Figure 56**) and withdraw the bearing.
2. Pry the old seal out with a flat-bladed screwdriver (**Figure 57**) or seal removal tool. If using a screwdriver, pad the prying area under the screwdriver with a shop cloth to avoid damaging the crankcase seal mounting bore.
3. Place a suitable size socket over the mechanical seal. Drive the mechanical seal out of the crankcase.
4. Insert a scribe through the crankcase weep hole (**Figure 58**) to ensure the hole is open. Clean out if necessary.
5. Place the new bearing (A, **Figure 59**) over the mounting bore (B).
6. Place a suitable size socket over the bearing and drive it into the crankcase until it bottoms (**Figure 60**).
7. Install the water pump seal as follows:
   a. Turn the crankcase over and correctly position the seal (**Figure 61**), as noted during removal.
   b. Place a socket with a 24.5 mm outer diameter over the seal and drive it into the crankcase until it bottoms (**Figure 62**).
8. Assemble the crankcase as described in this chapter.
9. Install the mechanical seal as follows:

a. Position the new seal as shown in **Figure 63** and install it onto the water pump shaft. Push it down until it bottoms (A, **Figure 64**).
b. Install the push piece (B, **Figure 64**) and center it over the mechanical seal (**Figure 65**).
c. Screw the threaded shaft onto the water pump shaft (**Figure 66**) and tighten it securely.
d. Install the flat washer and nut (A, **Figure 67**) and tighten securely.
e. Use an open-end wrench (B, **Figure 67**) to tighten the nut to press the seal into the crankcase bore.
f. Remove the special tool and check that the seal is seated correctly (**Figure 68**).

Crankcase Assembly

1. Replace the right side oil seal prior to reassembling the case halves.
2. Apply clean engine oil to all bearing surfaces in both case halves.
3. Prior to installing any components into the left crankcase, perform *Shaft End Float Measurement and Shim Selection* in this chapter. This will determine the correct thickness of shims to install on the water pump shaft, crankshaft and balance shaft.

CAUTION
The special crankshaft installation tool set (part No. 2871283) is required to pull the crankshaft into the left crankcase half bearing. Do not drive the crankshaft into the bearing, as the crankshaft will be misaligned.

4A. If using the special tool set, perform the following:
a. Place the left crankcase half on wooden blocks and partially install the crankshaft into the crankcase bearing (**Figure 69**).
b. Make a mark on the threaded rod 25.4 mm (1.0 in.) from the end (**Figure 70**).
c. Screw the threaded rod into the crankshaft up to the mark made in substep b (A, **Figure 71**).
d. Install the collar (B, **Figure 71**), washer and nut onto the threaded rod (**Figure 72**).
e. Center the connecting rod within the crankcase opening (**Figure 73**).
f. Hold onto the crankshaft and tighten the nut (**Figure 74**) to draw the crankshaft into the

63

64

65

66

67
A
B

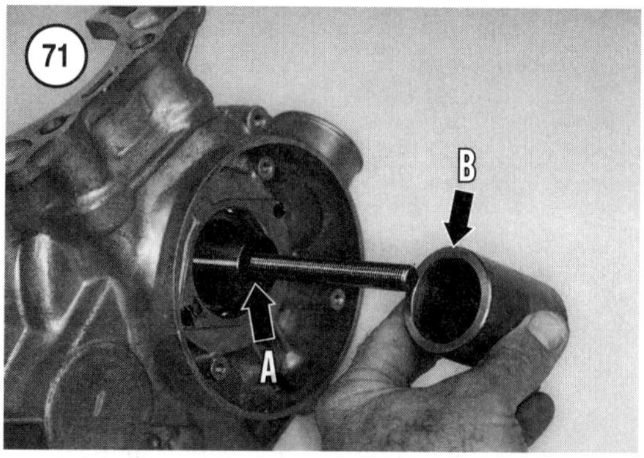
71
B
A

68

72

69

73

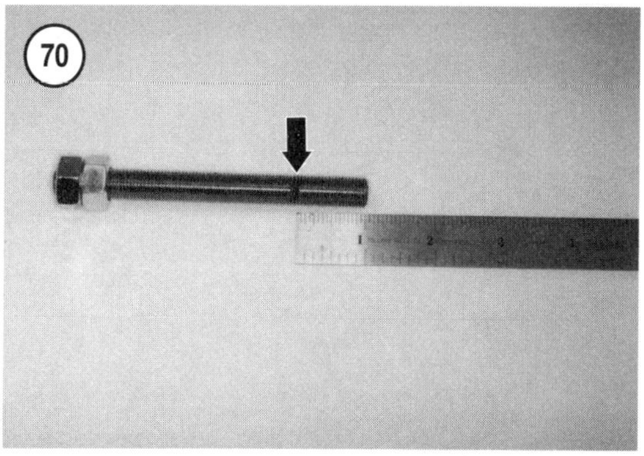
70

74

bearing until it is fully seated on the bearing (**Figure 75**).

NOTE
If it is difficult to unscrew the threaded rod from the crankshaft, install two nuts onto the threaded rod and tighten them securely against each other. Using these nuts, unscrew the threaded rod.

g. Loosen the nut and remove the threaded rod, washer and collar from the crankshaft.

4B. If the special tools are not available, take the crankshaft and left side crankcase to a Polaris dealership, or machine shop, and have them properly install the crankshaft.

5. Place the left crankcase on a couple of wooden blocks (**Figure 76**), or the wooden box used during separation with the mating surface facing up.

6. If so equipped, install the proper shim (**Figure 77**) onto the crankshaft. Make sure it is properly seated (**Figure 78**).

7. Rotate the crankshaft so the timing mark (**Figure 79**) is facing in the direction of the balance shaft.

8. Install the balance shaft part way into the left crankcase.

CAUTION
Improper alignment of the balance shaft gear to the crankshaft gear will result in severe engine vibration leading to expensive engine damage.

9. Rotate the balance gear until the timing mark is aligned with the timing mark on the crankshaft gear (**Figure 80**). Push the balance shaft and gear down until they are fully seated on the bearing. Recheck the alignment of the timing marks (**Figure 81**), readjust if necessary.

10. If so equipped, install the proper shim onto the balance shaft (**Figure 82**) make sure it is properly seated (**Figure 83**).

11. Fill the oil pump cavity in the crankcase with clean engine oil (**Figure 84**).

NOTE
Do not use any gasket sealer on the oil pump mating surfaces.

12. Apply a light film of engine oil to the oil pump and crankcase mounting surface (**Figure 85**) and install the oil pump (**Figure 86**).

75

76

77

78

79

83

80

84

81

85

82

86

13. Install the three bolts and tighten to the torque specification listed in **Table 1**.

14. Align the oil pump drive gear pin receptacle (**Figure 87**) with the raised pin (**Figure 88**) on the oil pump shaft and install the drive gear (A, **Figure 89**). Make sure the drive gear is properly meshed with the drive pin (**Figure 90**).

NOTE

*When all shafts have been correctly installed in the crankcase, the top surfaces of each mating gear will be flush with each other (B, **Figure 89**).*

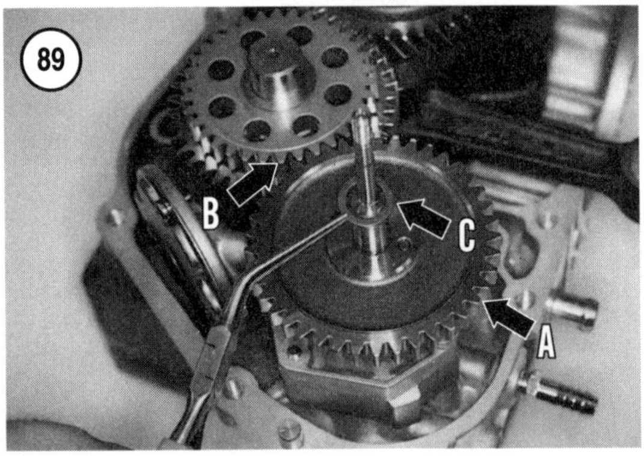

15. Install the correct shim thickness for the pump shaft (C, **Figure 89**). Make sure it is properly seated (**Figure 90**).

16. If removed, install the locating dowels onto the left crankcase half. Refer to **Figure 91** and **Figure 92**. Make sure they are correctly seated.

17. The crankcase assemblies are now ready to be joined.

18. Make sure both crankcase sealing surfaces are free of old sealant material or other residue.

19. Apply a light coating of non-hardening liquid gasket sealer, such as ThreeBond No. 1104, or equivalent, onto the left crankcase mating surface. When selecting an equivalent, avoid thick and hard-setting materials. Make sure the coating is as thin as possible, but still completely covering the surface.

CAUTION

When properly lined up, the right crankcase half will slide over the shafts and seat against the left case half. If the crankcase halves do not fit together completely, do not attempt to pull them together with the crankcase bolts. Separate the crankcase halves

92

93

94

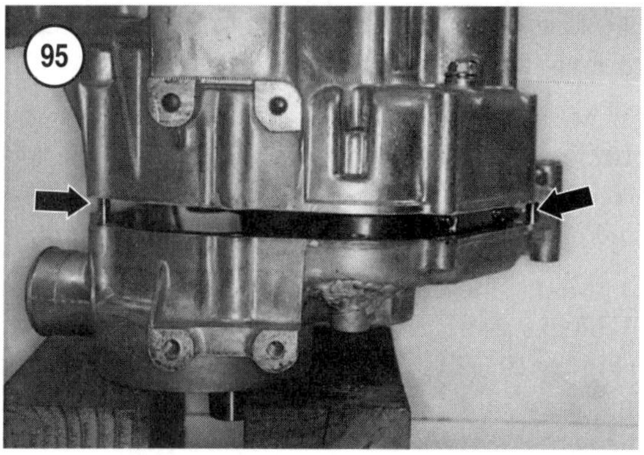
95

96

and investigate the cause of the interference. Check the shafts and gears for proper installation. Crankcase halves are a matched set and are very expensive. Do not risk damage by trying to force them together.

CAUTION
*The special crankshaft installation tool set (**Figure 93**) (part No. 2871283) is required to pull the crankshaft into the right crankcase half bearing. Do not try to pull the crankshaft into the bearing by tapping on the right crankcase as the crankcase and the crankshaft will be damaged and misaligned.*

20A. If using the special tool set, perform the following:

a. Install the threaded stud (**Figure 94**) onto the crankshaft. Screw it on until it stops and tighten it securely. Do not overtighten.
b. Position the right crankcase half onto the left crankcase assembly and align the locating dowels (**Figure 95**).
c. Install the adapter, washer and nut onto the threaded stud on the crankshaft (**Figure 96**).
d. Slowly tighten the nut with a wrench (**Figure 97**) and pull the crankshaft through the right side main bearing. Make sure the case halves are parallel to each other (**Figure 98**).
e. Gently tap the case around the water pump to fully seat the case halves (**Figure 99**).
f. If it is necessary to join both halves, carefully tap them together lightly with a plastic or soft-faced mallet—do not use a metal hammer, as it will damage the cases.

5

g. Remove the special tools from the crankshaft.

NOTE
After the crankcase has been assembled the crankshaft will ***usually not rotate freely****. This is normal with this engine. After the crankcase bolts are installed and tightened, carefully tap on the PVT end of the crankshaft with a brass mallet to help reposition the crankshaft within the bearings. The PVT side is normally the tight side since there are two bearings on this side. If it is still a little tight, the crankshaft will center itself after the engine first starts to run.*

h. Before installing the crankcase bolts, slowly spin the crankshaft to make sure there is no binding.
i. Remove the bolts from the cardboard template and install the right crankcase mounting bolts in the correct locations. Tighten all bolts finger-tight at this time.
j. Tighten the bolt in 2-3 steps using a crossing pattern. Tighten to the torque specification listed in **Table 1**.

20B. If the special tools are not available, take the crankcase assembly to a Polaris dealership or a machine shop, and have them properly install the right side crankcase half.

21. If removed, install the oil/coolant pump shaft mechanical seal as previously described in this chapter.

22. Install the camshaft drive gear as described in Chapter Four.

23. Install all exterior engine assemblies onto the crankcase as described in this chapter and other related chapters.

24. Install the engine as described in this chapter

CRANKSHAFT INSPECTION

Refer to **Figure 100**.

1. Check the condition of the connecting rod bearing. It is difficult to clean this bearing and its condition is usually determined by turning the connecting rod and noting any roughness or noise. Additional tests are as follows:

2. Measure connecting rod side play with a flat feeler gauge as shown in **Figure 101**. Compare the side play with the specification listed in **Table 2**. Replace the connecting rod or the crankshaft if worn to the service limit.

3. Measure connecting rod radial play (**Figure 102**) with a dial indicator and compare to the service limit listed in **Table 2**. Replace the connecting rod or the crankshaft if worn to the service limit.

4. Mount the crankshaft in a truing stand or in V-blocks and measure the runout at the shaft ends (**Figure 103**). If the runout exceeds the service limit listed in **Table 2**, take the crankshaft to a Polaris dealer for service.

(100) CRANKSHAFT AND BALANCER

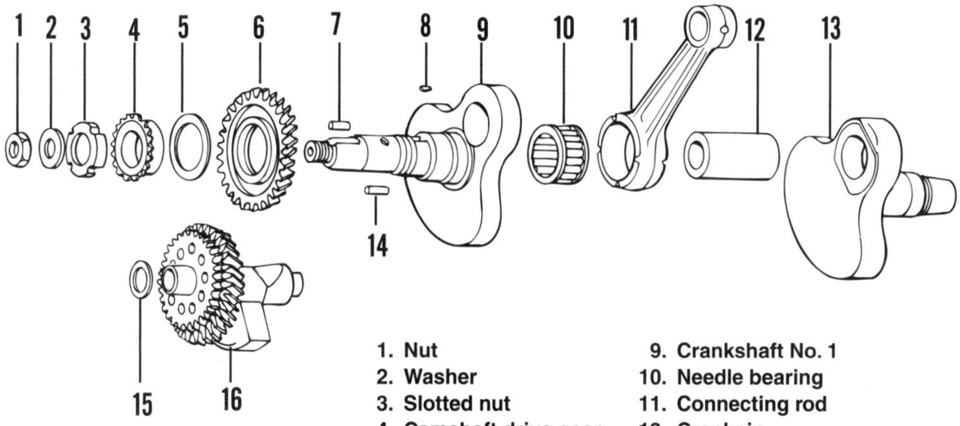

1. Nut
2. Washer
3. Slotted nut
4. Camshaft drive gear
5. Spacer
6. Balancer drive gear
7. Key
8. Woodruff key
9. Crankshaft No. 1
10. Needle bearing
11. Connecting rod
12. Crankpin
13. Crankshaft No. 2
14. Dowel pin
15. Spacer
16. Balancer shaft

(101)

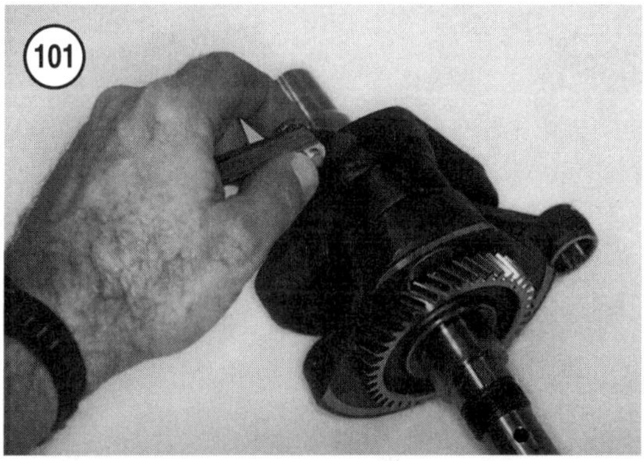

5. Measure the connecting rod piston pin bore diameter (**Figure 104**) with a telescoping gauge or inside micrometer and check against the specification listed in **Table 2**. Replace the connecting rod or the crankshaft if the diameter exceeds the new dimension.
6. Check the crankshaft bearing journals (**Figure 105**) for scratches, heat distortion or other defects.
7. Check the threaded portions (**Figure 106**) for wear or damage. Repair the threads if necessary.
8. Inspect the balancer gear (**Figure 107**) for worn, chipped or missing teeth. If any teeth are damaged, also check the teeth on the balancer gear. The gear is pressed onto the crankshaft and if damaged, it can be replaced.

BALANCER SHAFT INSPECTION

1. Inspect the balancer shaft bearing journals (**Figure 108**) for deep scoring, excessive wear, heat distortion or cracks.
2. Inspect the gears (**Figure 109**) for worn, chipped or missing teeth. If any teeth are damaged, also check the balancer gear teeth on the crankshaft.
3. Replace the balancer shaft if it is damaged.

SHAFT END FLOAT MEASUREMENT AND SHIM SELECTION

NOTE

*The following measurements must be accurate to avoid damage to the internal components of the crankcase. A machined straightedge and an accurate dial-type vernier caliper is required for this procedure (**Figure 110**). If the measuring equipment is*

102

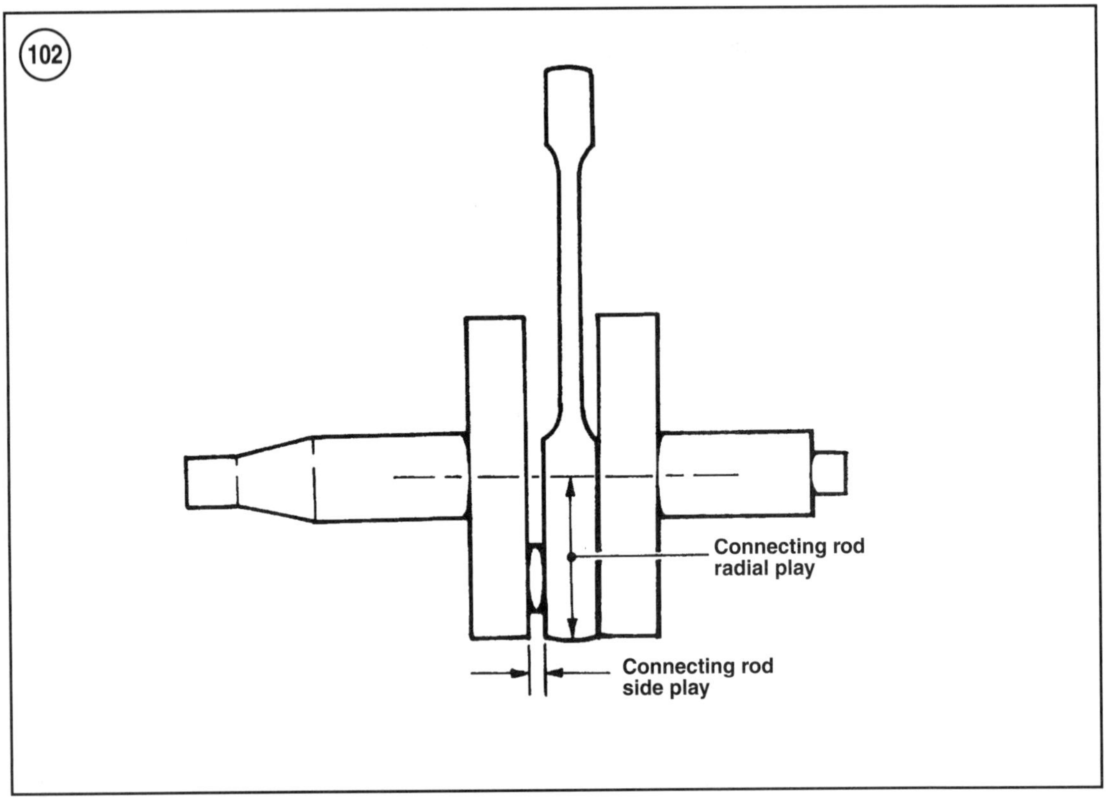

103

105

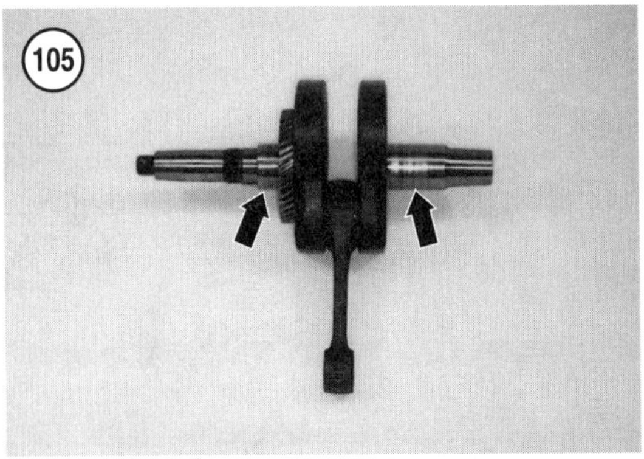

104

106

107

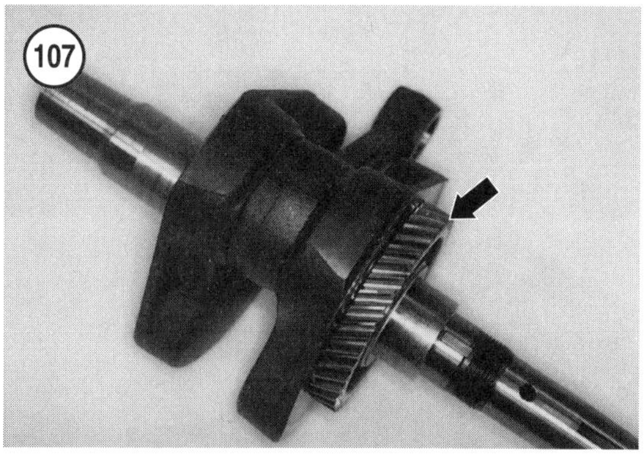

108

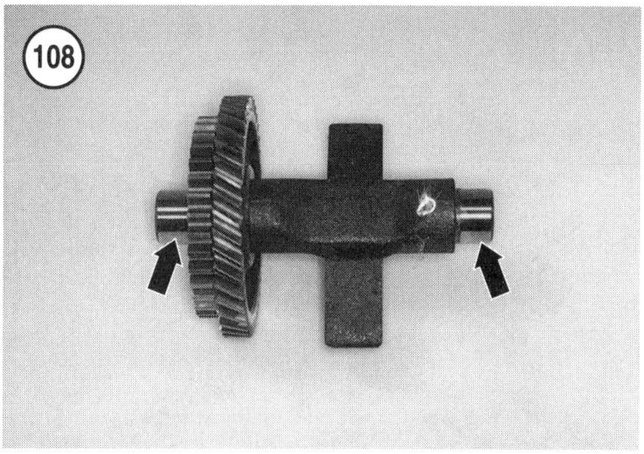

109

110

111

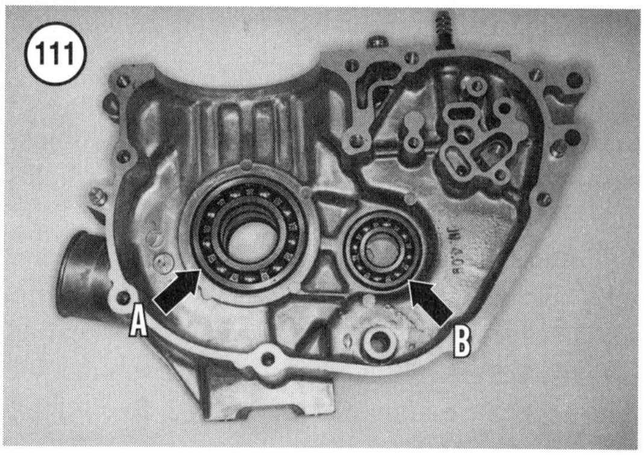

112

not available to perform this procedure, take the components to a Polaris dealership.

This procedure is necessary to determine the correct shim thickness required to establish the correct end play within the crankcase for the crankshaft, balance shaft and oil pump shaft. This is accomplished by accurately measuring the distance between the inner races of the bearings for each specific shaft assembly.

Crankshaft end play

1. Make certain the crankshaft bearings (A, **Figure 111**) are fully seated in both crankcase halves.
2. Measure the thickness of the straightedge as shown in **Figure 112**. This dimension will be used in the following steps.
3. Use a dial vernier caliper and measure the width of the crankshaft, including the balancer gear, at the machined surfaces where it rides on the bearing inner race (**Figure 113**). Record this measurement.
4. Position a straightedge across the sealing surface of the left-hand crankcase half.

5. Using a dial vernier caliper or depth gauge, carefully measure the distance from the top of the straightedge to the left side crankshaft bearing (**Figure 114**). Note the dimension and subtract the thickness of the straightedge in Step 2. Record this measurement.
6. Using a dial vernier caliper or depth gauge, carefully measure the distance from the top of the straightedge to the right side crankshaft bearing (**Figure 115**). Note the dimension and subtract the thickness of the straightedge in Step 2. Record this measurement.
7. The specified crankshaft end play is listed in **Table 2**. Use the following equation to select the correct shim thickness to obtain the specified end play.

$a = (b + c) - (d + e)$

a = the new shim thickness.

b = the distance recorded in Step 5.

c = the distance recorded in Step 6.

d = the width of the crankshaft (Step 3).

e = the specified end play in **Table 2**.

Balancer shaft end play

1. Make certain the balancer shaft bearings (B, **Figure 111**) are fully seated in both crankcase halves.
2. Measure the thickness of the straightedge as shown in **Figure 112**. This dimension will be used in the following steps.
3. Use a dial vernier caliper to measure the width of the balancer shaft at the machined surfaces where it contacts the bearing inner race (**Figure 116**). Record this measurement.
4. Position a straightedge across the sealing surface of the left side crankcase half.
5. Using a dial vernier caliper or depth gauge, carefully measure the distance from the top of the straightedge to the left side balancer shaft bearing (**Figure 117**). Note the dimension and subtract the thickness of the straightedge in Step 2. Record this measurement.
6. Using a dial vernier caliper or depth gauge, carefully measure the distance from the top of the straightedge to the right side balancer shaft bearing (**Figure 118**). Note the dimension and subtract the thickness of the straightedge in Step 2. Record this measurement.
7. The specified balancer shaft end play is listed in **Table 2**. Use the following equation to select the correct shim thickness to obtain the specified end play.

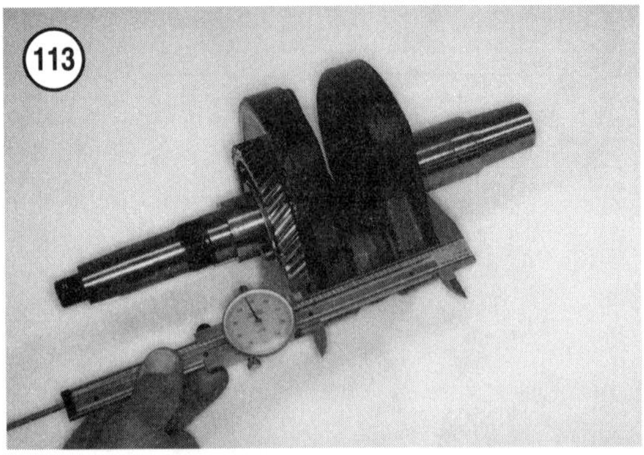

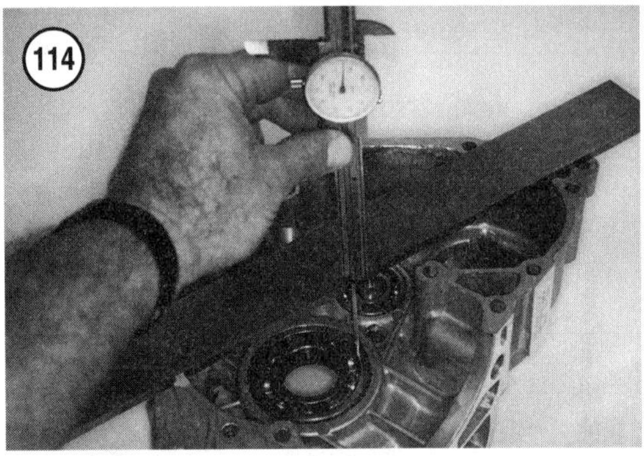

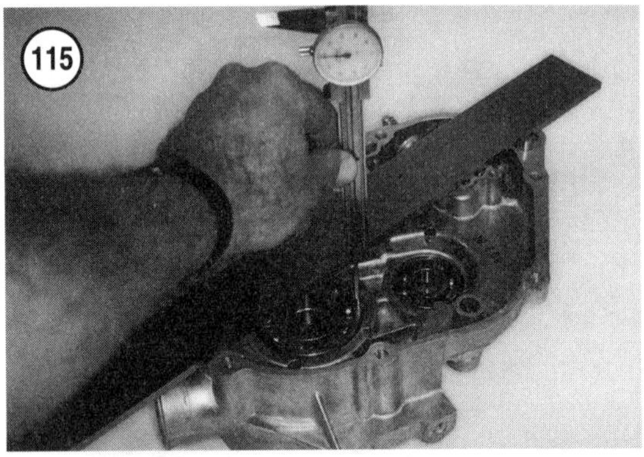

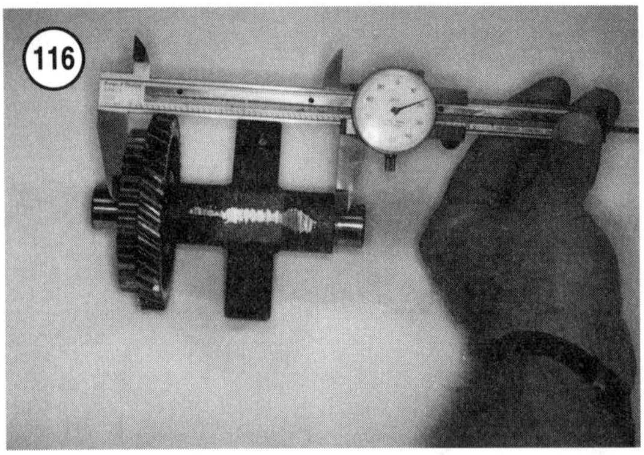

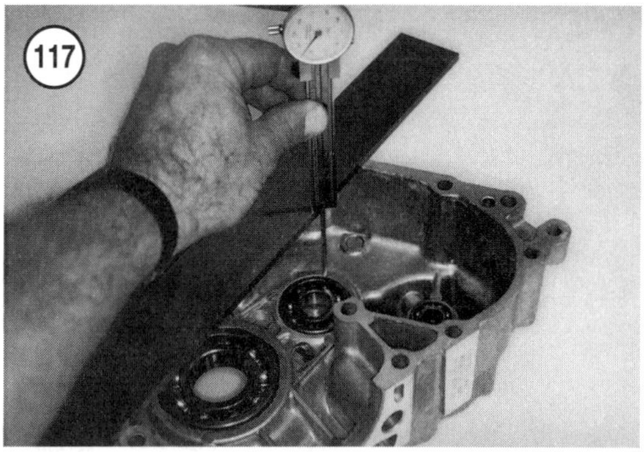

117

118

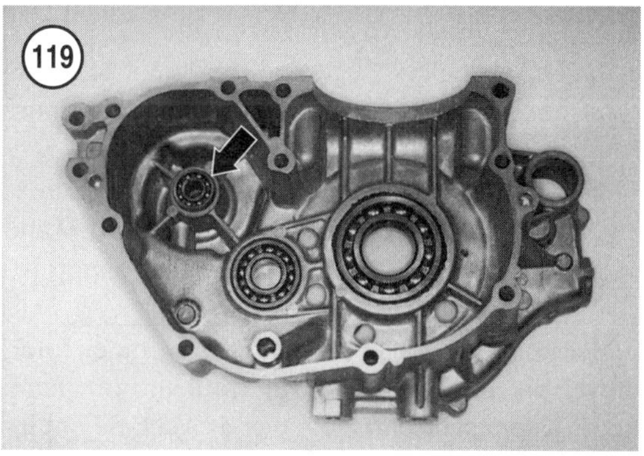

119

120

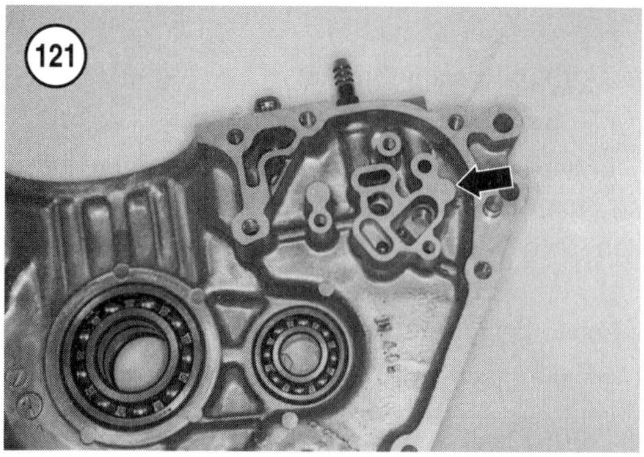

121

$a = (b + c) - (d + e)$

a = the new shim thickness.

b = the distance recorded in Step 5.

c = the distance recorded in Step 6.

d = the width of the balancer shaft (Step 3).

e = the specified end play in **Table 2**.

Oil pump shaft end play

1. Make certain the oil pump shaft bearing (**Figure 119**) is fully seated in the right side crankcase half.
2. Measure the thickness of the straightedge as shown in **Figure 112**. This dimension will be used in the following steps.
3. Position a straightedge across the sealing surface of the right side crankcase half.
4. Using a dial vernier caliper or depth gauge, carefully measure the distance from the top of the straightedge to the left side oil pump shaft bearing (**Figure 120**). Note the dimension and subtract the thickness of the straightedge in Step 2. Record this measurement.
5. Using a dial vernier caliper or depth gauge, carefully measure the distance from the top of the straightedge to the oil pump mounting surface (**Figure 121**) in the right side crankcase. Note the dimension and subtract the thickness of the straightedge in Step 2. Record this measurement.
6. With the oil pump removed from the crankcase, install the oil pump drive gear onto the oil pump drive. Using a dial vernier caliper, measure the thickness from the mating surface of the oil pump to the top machined surface of the gear where the shim is located (**Figure 122**). Record this measurement.
7. The specified oil pump end play is listed in **Table 2**. Use the following equation to select the correct shim thickness to obtain the specified end play.

a = (*b* + *c*) – (*d* + *e*)

a = the new shim thickness.

b = the distance recorded in Step 4.

c = the distance from the top of the straightedge to oil pump mounting surface in the right crankcase half (Step 5).

d = the distance from the mating surface of the oil pump to the top surface of the gear (Step 6).

e = the specified end play in **Table 2**.

OIL PUMP

The crankcase must be separated to access the oil pump assembly.

There are two chambers in the oil pump; one is the feed side (thin rotors) and the other is the side (thicker rotors). The specification listed in **Table 2** relates to the rotors in both chambers.

Removal/Disassembly

Refer to **Figure 123**.

1. Separate the crankcase halves as described in this chapter.
2. Remove the bolts (A, **Figure 124**) securing the oil pump and remove the oil pump (B, **Figure 124**) from the right crankcase half.
3. Remove the three screws attaching the pump intake screen and remove the screen from the pump (**Figure 125**).
4. Remove the screw securing the feed chamber cover and remove the cover (**Figure 126**) from the middle cover.
5. Inspect the feed chamber components as described in the following procedure.
6. Remove the feed chamber inner and outer rotors and dowel pin (A, **Figure 127**).
7. Remove the middle cover (B, **Figure 127**) from the oil pump body.
8. Inspect the scavenge chamber components as described in the following procedure.
9. Remove the scavenge chamber inner and outer rotors and dowel pin (A, **Figure 128**) from oil pump body (B, **Figure 128**).
10. Inspect all components as described in the following procedure.

122

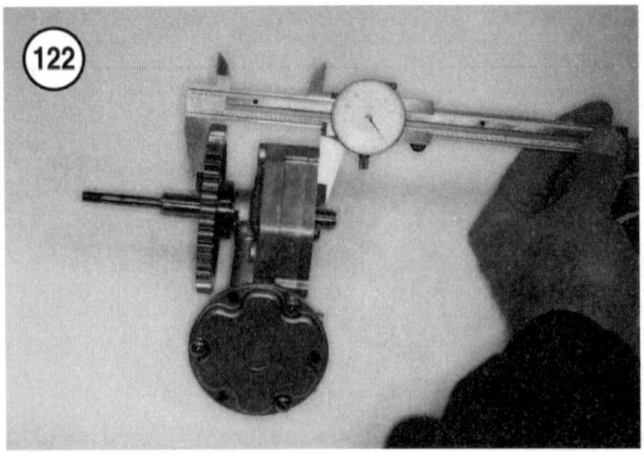

Inspection

Refer to the service limit dimension listed in **Table 2**. Replace worn or damaged parts. If several parts require replacement, it is recommended that the entire oil pump be replaced.

1. Clean and inspect the screen (**Figure 129**). Check for damage to the screen and for other damage indicated by metal particles in the screen.
2. Check the clearance of the *feed side* rotors as follows:
   a. Use a feeler gauge to measure the clearance between the outer rotor and the middle cover, as shown in **Figure 130**.
   b. Use a feeler gauge and measure the clearance between the tip of the inner rotor and the outer rotor as shown in **Figure 131**.
   c. Use a straightedge and feeler gauge across the middle cover as shown in **Figure 132** and measure the end play of the feed pump rotors.
3. Remove the feed side inner rotor, outer rotor, dowel pin and middle cover from the oil pump body. Keep these parts together as a set; do not intermix them with scavenge rotors.
4. Check the clearance of the *scavenge side* rotors as follows:
   a. Use a feeler gauge to measure the clearance between the outer rotor and the oil pump body as shown in **Figure 133**.
   b. Use a feeler gauge and measure the clearance between the tip of the inner rotor and the outer rotor as shown in **Figure 134**.
   c. Use a straightedge and feeler gauge across the oil pump body and measure the end play of the scavenge pump rotors as shown in **Figure 135**.

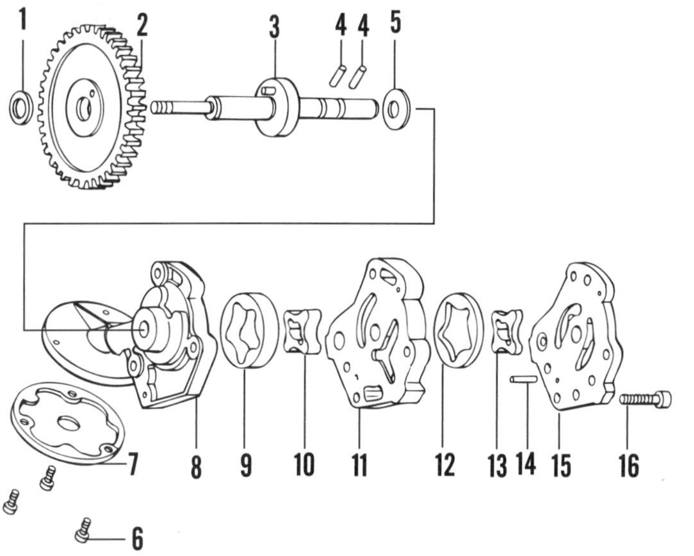

1. Shim
2. Drive gear
3. Drive shaft
4. Dowel pin
5. Washer
6. Screw
7. Intake screen
8. Body
9. Outer rotor—scavenge
10. Inner rotor—scavenge
11. Middle cover
12. Outer rotor—feed
13. Inner rotor—feed
14. Dowel pin
15. Feed chamber cover
16. Bolt

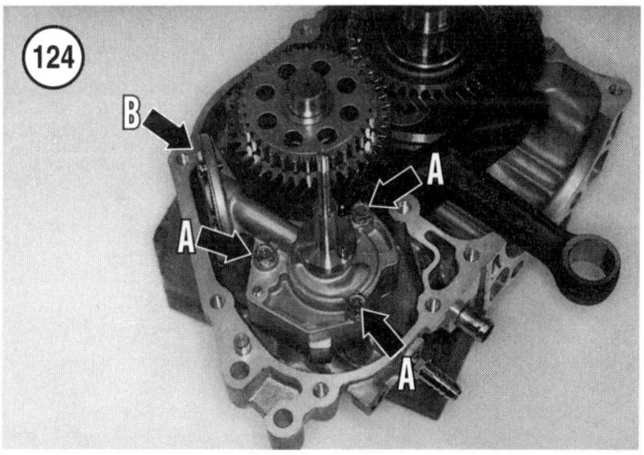

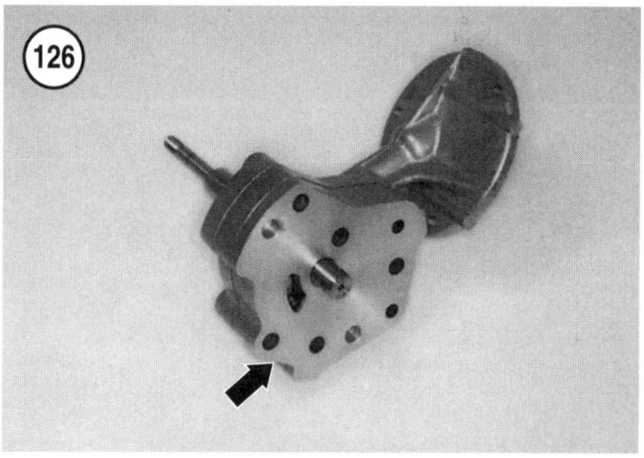

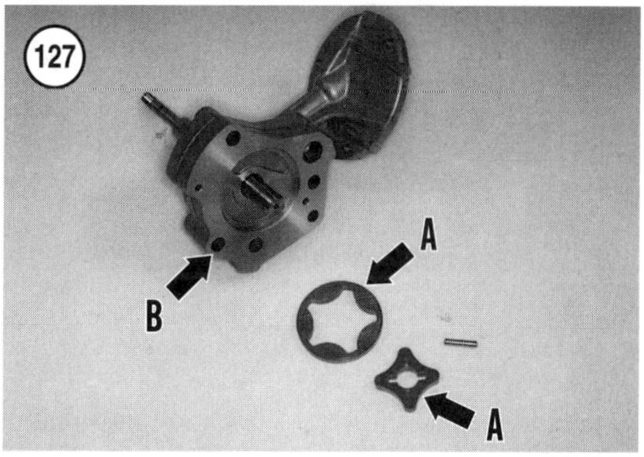

5

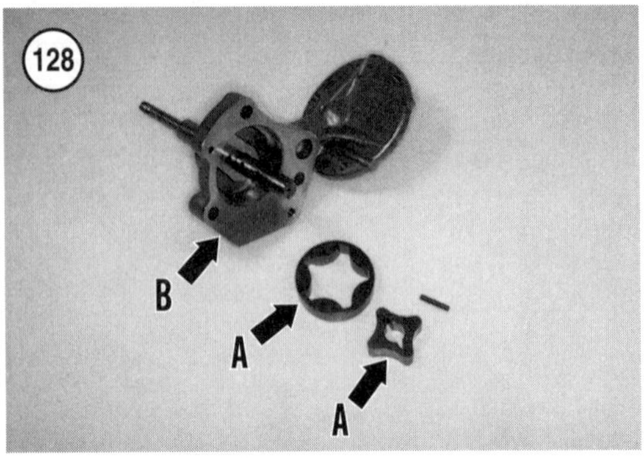
128
B
A
A

129

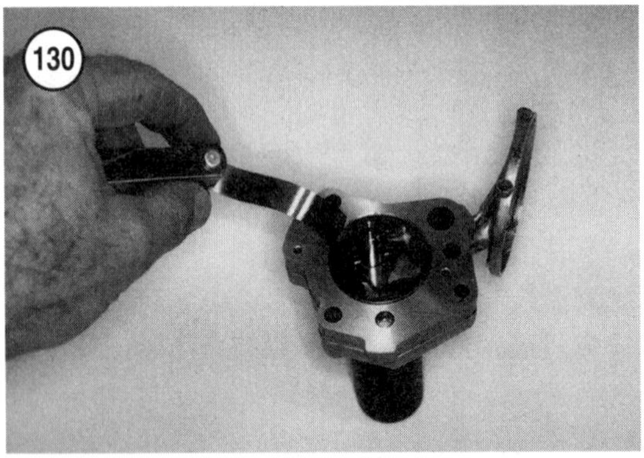
130

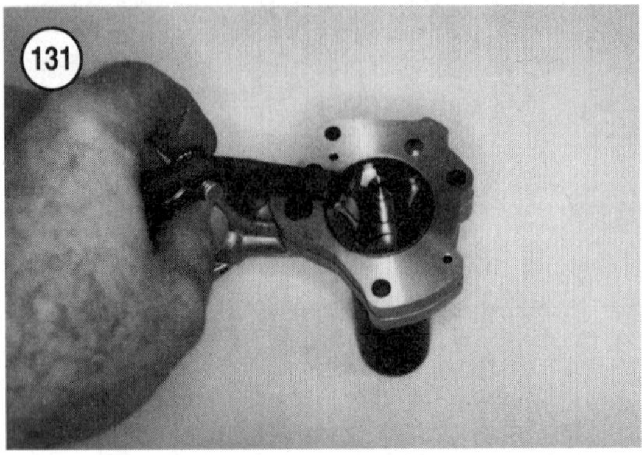
131

132

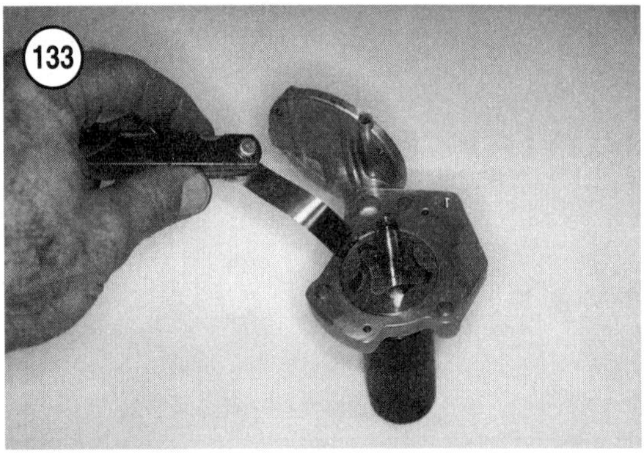
133

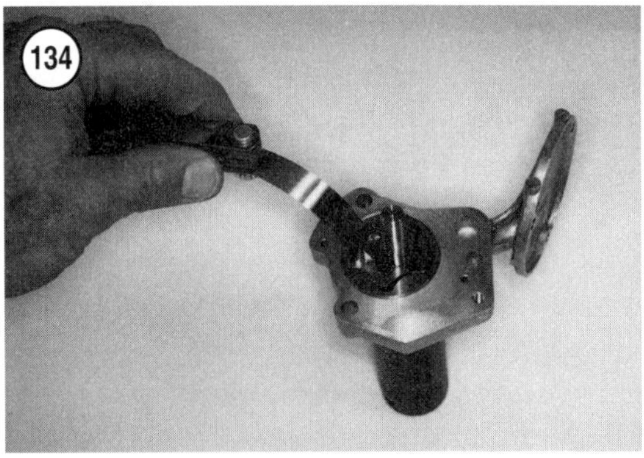
134

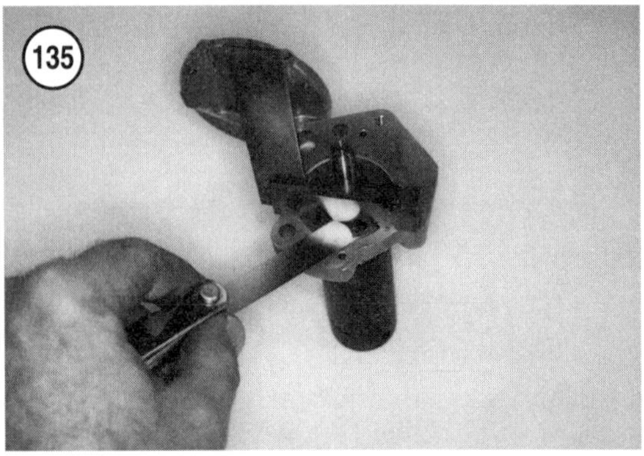
135

136

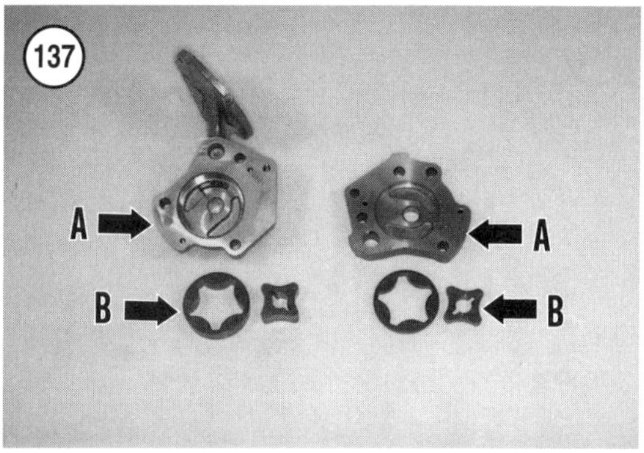

137

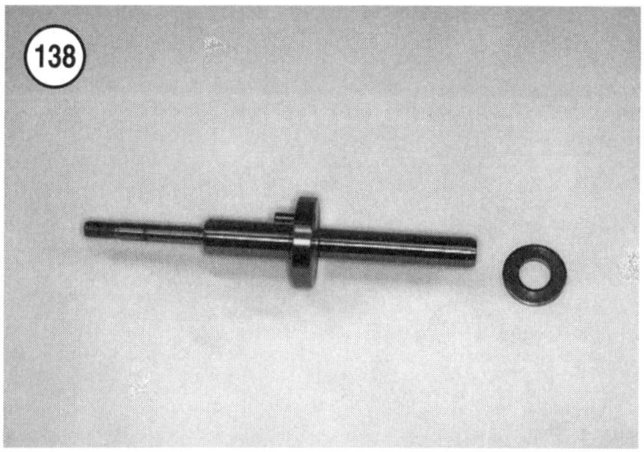
138

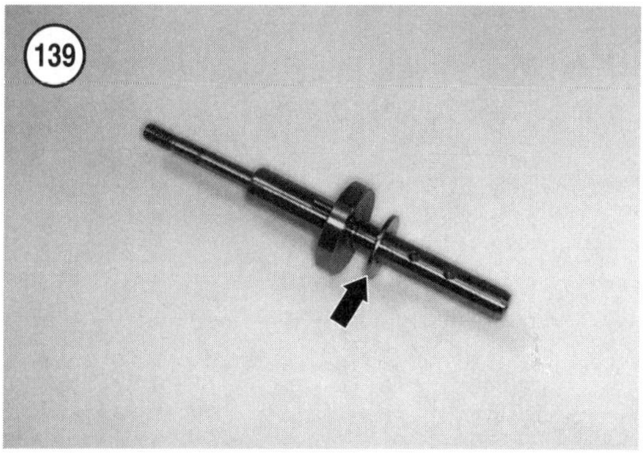
139

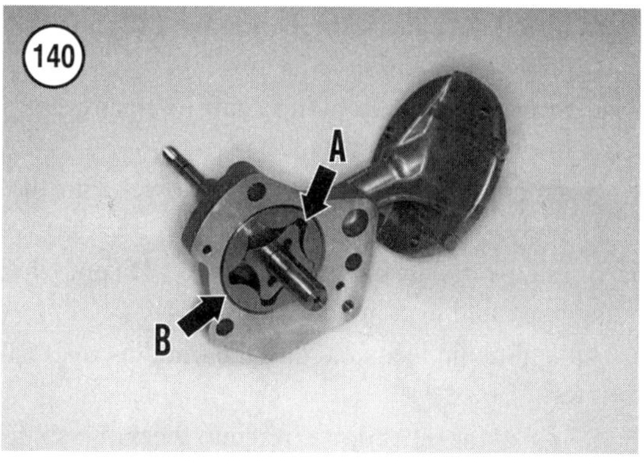

140

5. Remove the scavenge side inner rotor, outer rotor and dowel pin from the oil pump body. Keep these parts together as a set, do not intermix with feed rotors.

6. Withdraw the oil pump drive shaft (**Figure 136**) from the pump body. Do not lose the washer located between the pump body and the shaft shoulder.

7. Clean all parts in solvent and thoroughly dry.

8. Inspect the feed chamber cover, middle cover and the oil pump body for wear, cracks or damage (A, **Figure 137**). Check the inner wall for scuff marks.

9. Check the drive shaft bearing surface in the cover, middle cover and the oil pump body for wear. Insert the drive shaft into all three parts and rotate it and check for smooth operation.

10. Inspect the feed set and the scavenge set of rotors (B, **Figure 137**) for abrasion, wear, cracks or damage.

11. Inspect the drive shaft and washer (**Figure 138**) for wear or damage.

12. Install the dowel pins into the drive shaft and check for a tight fit. If loose, replace the damaged part(s).

Assembly/Installation

Refer to **Figure 123**.

1. Coat all parts of the pump with clean engine oil.

2. Make sure the washer is in place on the oil pump shaft, then install the shaft into the oil pump body (**Figure 139**). Push it in until it stops (**Figure 136**).

3. Assemble the scavenge side into the pump body as follows:

   a. Install the inner dowel pin into the pump shaft and center it.

   b. Install the inner rotor (A, **Figure 140**) and properly index it with the dowel pin.

c. Install the outer rotor (B, **Figure 140**) into the pump body and inner rotor.

d. Slowly rotate the pump shaft to ensure both rotors are moving freely.

4. If removed, install the locating dowel into the pump body.
5. Install the middle cover (A, **Figure 141**) onto the pump body and locating dowel.
6. Assemble the feed side into the middle cover as follows:

a. Install the outer dowel pin into the pump shaft and center it.

b. Install the inner rotor (B, **Figure 141**) and properly index it with the dowel pin.

c. Install the outer rotor (**Figure 142**) into the middle cover and inner rotor.

d. Slowly rotate the pump shaft to ensure both rotors are moving freely.

7. Install the feed chamber cover (**Figure 126**) onto the middle cover and dowel pin.
8. Install the cover screw and tighten to the torque specification listed in **Table 1**.
9. Install the pump intake screen (**Figure 143**) and screws. Tighten the screws securely.

NOTE
Do not use any gasket sealant when installing the pump onto the crankcase.

10. Prime the oil pump with clean engine oil (**Figure 144**). Add oil until it runs out the other opening.
11. Apply a light coat of clean engine oil to the mating surface of the oil pump and the right side crankcase. Install the oil pump (B, **Figure 124**) and bolts (A, **Figure 124**) and tighten the bolts to the torque specification listed in **Table 1**.
12. Assemble the crankcase halves as described in this chapter.

OIL SYSTEM ONE-WAY CHECK VALVE

The one-way check valve (**Figure 145**) is located under the flanged plug on the left side of the engine crankcase near the external oil pipes.

The check valve prevents oil in the tank from draining into the engine sump when the engine is not running. The valve consists of a check valve, spring and sealing washer and is not serviceable.

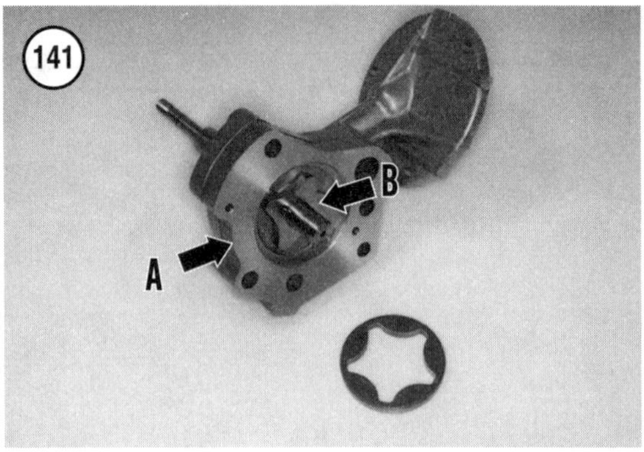

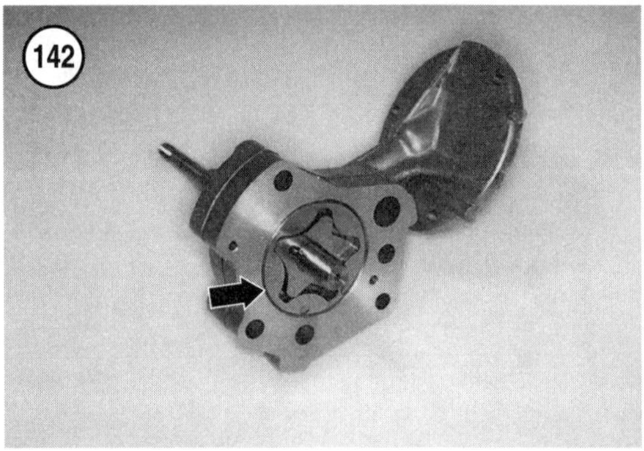

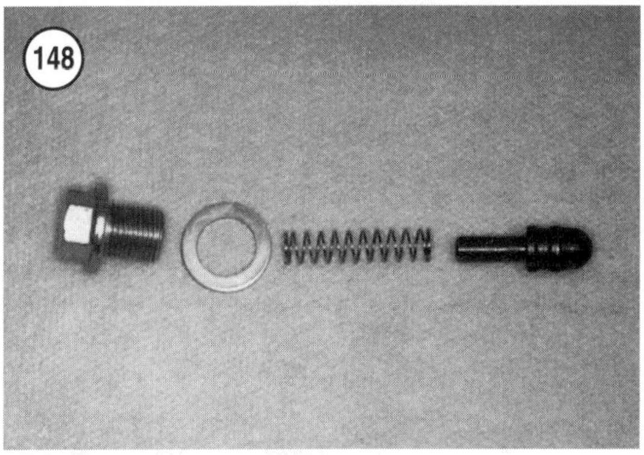

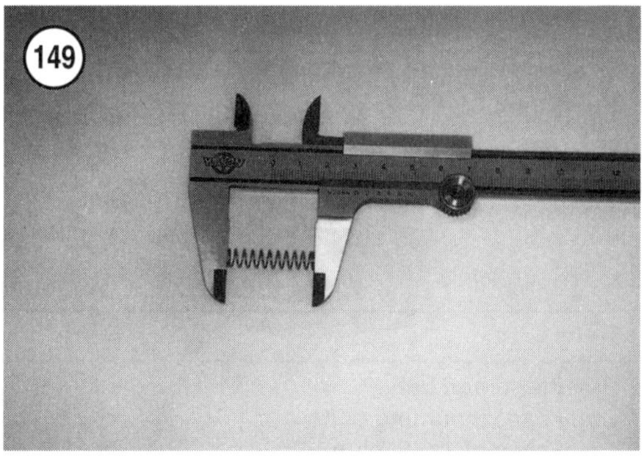

If engine oil drains from the oil tank when the engine is stopped, the check valve is probably leaking and should be cleaned or replaced.

NOTE
This procedure is shown with the engine removed from the frame to better illustrate the steps.

1. Remove the PVT system drive and driven pulleys and the inner cover as described in Chapter Eight.

NOTE
Place a shop cloth under the check valve as some residual oil will drain out.

2. Unscrew the plug and washer (**Figure 146**) and remove the one-way check valve and spring (**Figure 147**).
3. Clean the plunger, spring and plug in solvent and thoroughly dry (**Figure 148**).
4. Inspect the plunger for wear or damage and replace if necessary.
5. Measure the spring (**Figure 149**) and replace if it has sagged to less than the standard dimension listed in **Table 2**.
6. Install the spring and plunger into the plug.
7. Install a new gasket and install the plug into the cylinder block. Tighten the plug to the torque specification listed in **Table 1**.
8. If oil drained out during this procedure, top it off.

BREAK-IN PROCEDURE

If major lower end work was performed, break in the engine just as if it were new. The performance and service life of the engine depends greatly on a careful and sensible break-in.

For the first 5-10 hours of operation, use no more than 1/3 throttle, and vary the speed as much as possible within the 1/3 throttle limit. Avoid hard acceleration in addition to prolonged steady running at one speed, no matter how moderate.

After the initial 5-10 hours of operation, use progressively more throttle (with short bursts of speed) until the ATV has run for another 10-15 hours.

Table 1 ENGINE LOWER END TORQUE SPECIFICATIONS

Item	N•m	in.-lb.	ft.-lb.
Breather union bolt	9-15	80-132	-
Crankcase mounting bolts	19-21	-	14-15
Crankcase oil drain plug	19-23	–	14-17
Flywheel nut	80-99	–	58-72
Oil delivery pipe	25-34	–	18-25
Oil filter union bolt	50-59	–	36-43
Oil hose union bolt	9-15	80-132	–
Oil pressure blind plug	9-15	80-132	–
Oil pump			
Mounting bolts	7-9	62-80	–
Cover screw	3	26	–
One-way valve plug	19-26	–	14-19
Recoil starter housing bolts	7-9	62-80	–
Starter motor mounting bolts	7-9	62-80	–
Stator plate bolts	7-9	62-80	–
Water pump			
Impeller nut	7-9	62-80	–
Cover bolts	7-9	62-80	–

Table 2 ENGINE LOWER END SPECIFICATIONS

Item	New mm (in.)	Service limit mm (in.)
Connecting rod		
Piston pin bore diameter	23.007-23.020 (0.9058-0.9063)	–
Pistion pin end play clearance	0.007-0.026 (0.0003-0.0010)	0.05
Side play	0.1-0.65 (0.0039-0.0256)	0.80 (0.0315)
Bid end radial clearance	0.011-0.038 (0.004-0.0015)	0.0020 (0.0020)
Crankshaft runout limit	–	0.06 (0.0024)
One-way check valve spring	3.68 (1.450)	–
Oil pump (feed and scavenge)		
Pump end clearance	0.0254-0.0762 (0.001-0.003)	0.1016 (0.004)
Outer rotor-to-body clearance	0.0254-0.0762 (0.001-0.003)	0.1016 (0.004)
Inner rotor tip clearance	0.127 (0.005)	0.2032 (0.008)
Balance shaft end play	0.2-0.4 (0.008-0.016)	–
Crankshaft end play	0.2-0.4 (0.008-0.016)	–
Oil pump end play	0.2-0.4 (0.008-0.016)	–

CHAPTER SIX

FUEL SYSTEM

6

This chapter includes service procedures for all parts of the fuel system. Air filter service is covered in Chapter Three.

The fuel system consists of the fuel tank, fuel shutoff valve, fuel pump carburetor and air filter.

Carburetor specifications are covered in **Table 1**, located at the end of this chapter.

CARBURETOR OPERATION

Understanding the function of each of the carburetor components and their relation to one another aids in pinpointing carburetor trouble.

The carburetor's purpose is to supply and atomize fuel in correct proportions with air drawn into the engine through the air intake. At the primary throttle opening (idle), a small amount of fuel is siphoned through the pilot jet by the incoming air. As the throttle is opened further, the air stream begins to siphon fuel through the main jet and needle jet. A tapered needle is positioned in the needle jet and the effective flow capacity of the needle jet is increased as the needle is lifted.

At full throttle, the carburetor venturi is fully open and the needle is lifted far enough to permit the main jet to flow at full capacity.

The starting enrichment circuit is a starting jet system in which the choke lever opens a fuel enrichment valve rather than closing an air restricting butterfly. In the open position, the jet discharges a stream of fuel into the carburetor venturi to enrich the mixture when the engine is cold.

1

2

CARBURETOR

Removal/Installation

1. Place the vehicle on level ground and set the parking brake.
2. Remove the seat as described in Chapter Fifteen.
3. Remove the front fender as described in Chapter Fifteen.
4. Remove the clamping band, or tie-wrap, and remove the front portion of the PVT air exhaust duct (**Figure 1**).
5. Remove the air filter air box as described in this chapter.
6. Remove the two nuts and washers and two screws securing the carburetor mounting bracket (**Figure 2**) to the frame.
7. Mark all hoses prior to disconnecting them from the carburetor.
8. Disconnect the fuel supply hose (**Figure 3**) from the carburetor. Plug the end of the fuel supply hose.
9. Loosen the front clamp (**Figure 4**), slide the carburetor back and free it from the intake manifold on the cylinder head.
10. At the throttle cable midline adjuster on the left side, perform the following:
    a. Slide the rubber boots (A, **Figure 5**) off the adjuster.
    b. Loosen the locknut (B, **Figure 5**) and loosen the adjuster (C, **Figure 5**) to allow maximum slack in the cable.
11. Disconnect the throttle cable from the carburetor as follows:
    a. Remove the carburetor side cover mounting screws and remove the side cover and O-ring seal (**Figure 6**).

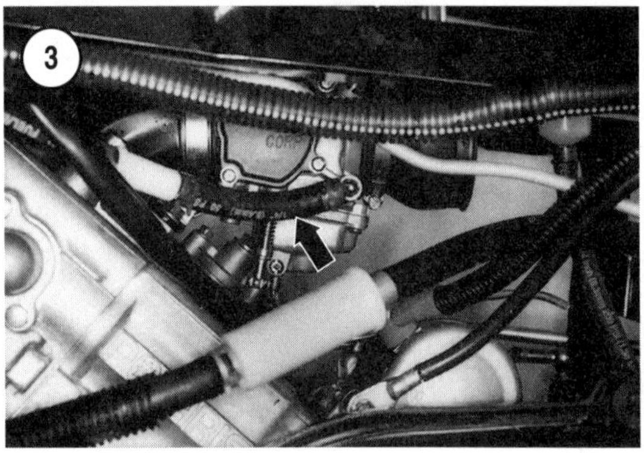

3

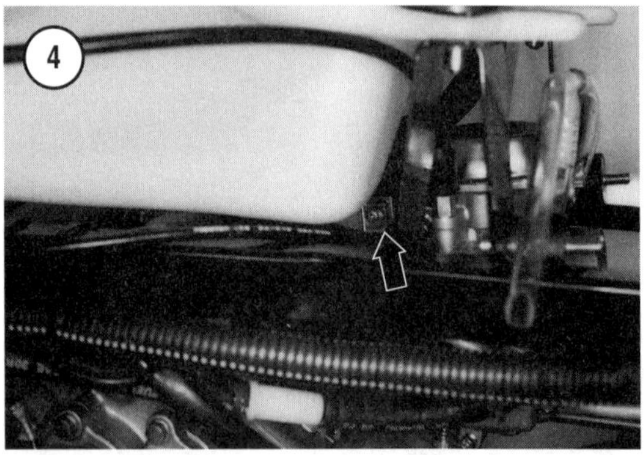

4

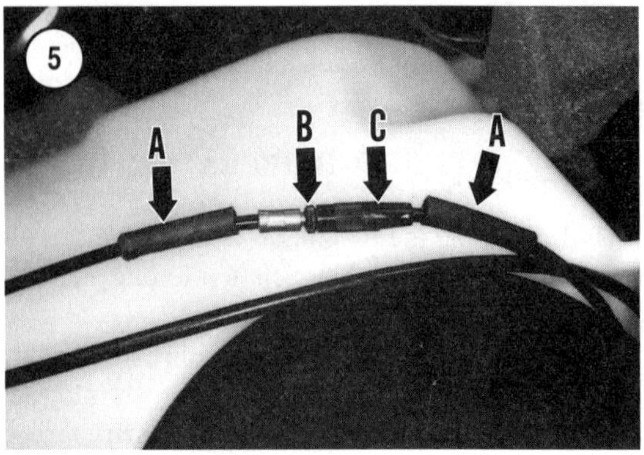

5

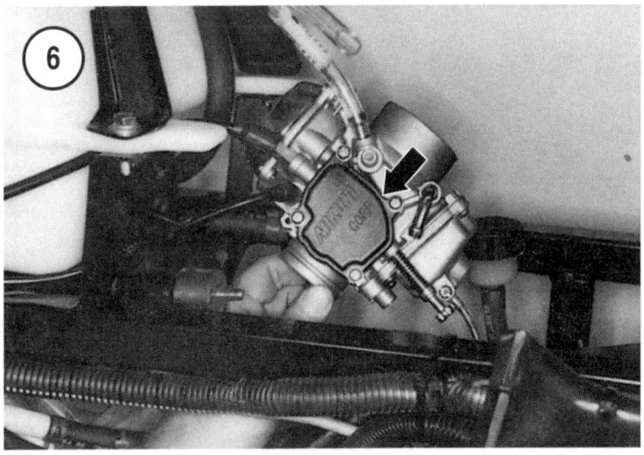

6

7

8

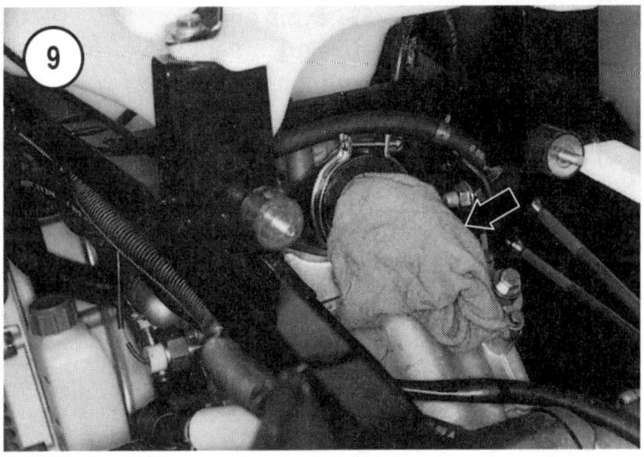

9

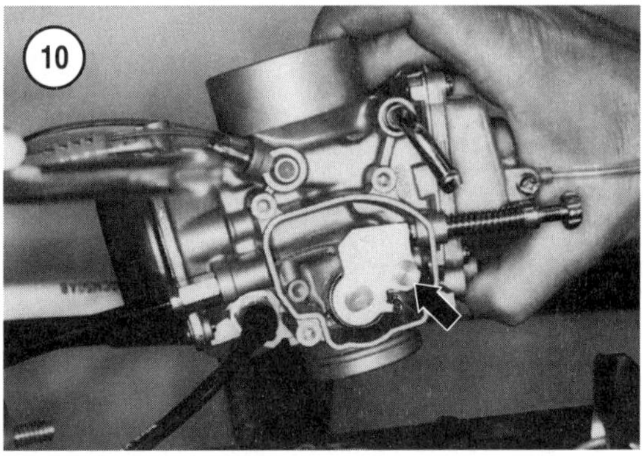

10

b. Disconnect the cable end from the throttle wheel (A, **Figure 7**).

c. Loosen and remove the throttle cable fitting (B, **Figure 7**), then withdraw the throttle cable from the throttle case.

12. Loosen, then remove the starting enrichment valve (choke) cable (**Figure 8**) from the carburetor.

13. Remove the carburetor from the engine and frame.

14. Place a clean lint-free shop cloth (**Figure 9**) or a plug into the intake manifold to prevent the entry of debris.

15. Install by reversing these removal steps, while noting the following:

a. Insert the throttle cable into the throttle case fitting (B, **Figure 7**) and attach the cable end to the lever (**Figure 10**).

b. Tighten the throttle cable fitting securely.

c. Make sure the O-ring seal is in place on the throttle case prior to installing the cover. Tighten the cover screws securely.

d. Insert the starting enrichment valve (choke) onto the carburetor (**Figure 8**) and tighten the retainer.

e. Operate the throttle lever and the starting enrichment (choke) control several times. Make sure the throttle lever moves smoothly at the carburetor with no binding and that the cable end does not pop out.

f. Adjust the throttle cable free play as described in Chapter Three.

Disassembly

Refer to **Figure 11**.

1. Remove the screws securing the cover (**Figure 12**).
2. Remove the cover and the spring (**Figure 13**).

(11)

MIKUNI CARBURETOR 34 MM

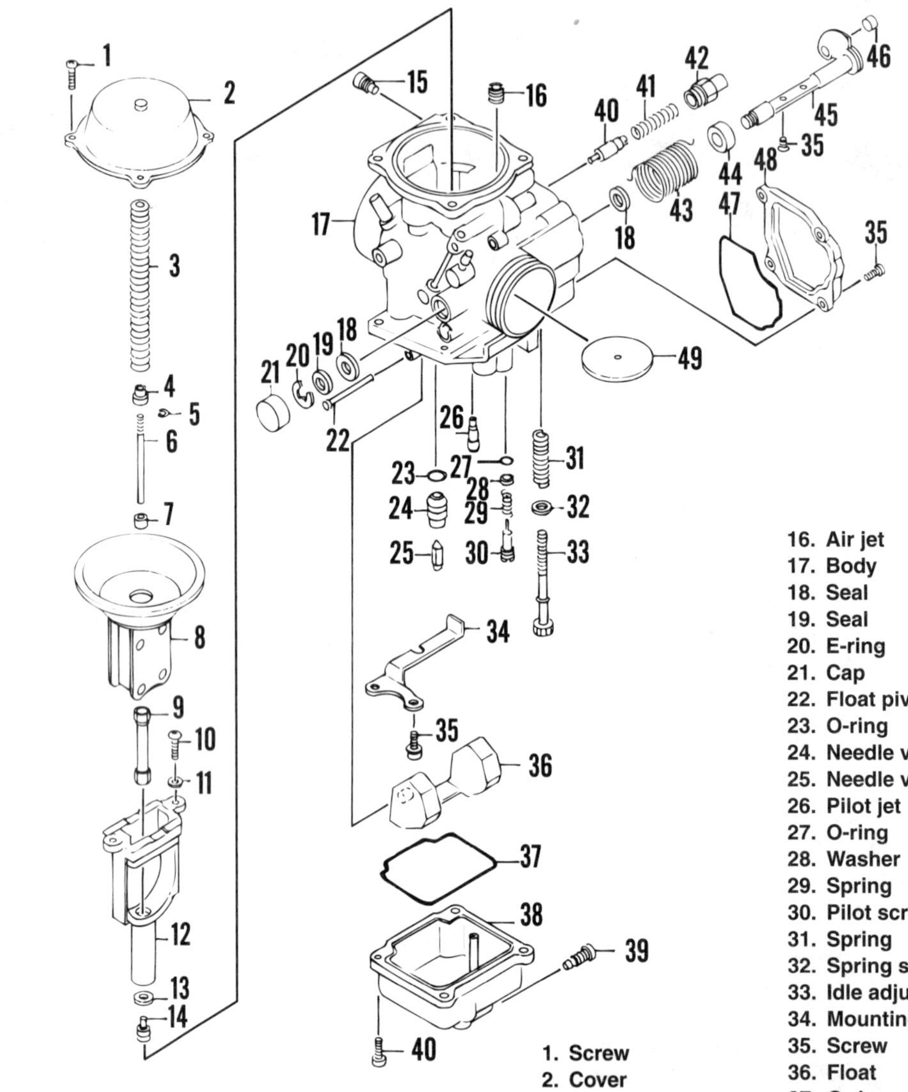

1. Screw
2. Cover
3. Spring
4. Upper ring
5. E-clip
6. Jet needle
7. Lower ring
8. Throttle valve/diaphragm
9. Needle jet
10. Screw
11. Washer
12. Jet block assembly
13. Spacer ring
14. Main jet
15. Air screw
16. Air jet
17. Body
18. Seal
19. Seal
20. E-ring
21. Cap
22. Float pivot pin
23. O-ring
24. Needle valve seat
25. Needle valve
26. Pilot jet
27. O-ring
28. Washer
29. Spring
30. Pilot screw
31. Spring
32. Spring seat
33. Idle adjust screw
34. Mounting plate
35. Screw
36. Float
37. O-ring gasket
38. Float bowl
39. Drain screw
40. Enrichment valve (choke) plunger
41. Screw
42. Guide holder
43. Spring
44. Ring
45. Throttle shaft
46. Throttle cable guide
47. O-ring gasket
48. Cover
49. Throttle plate

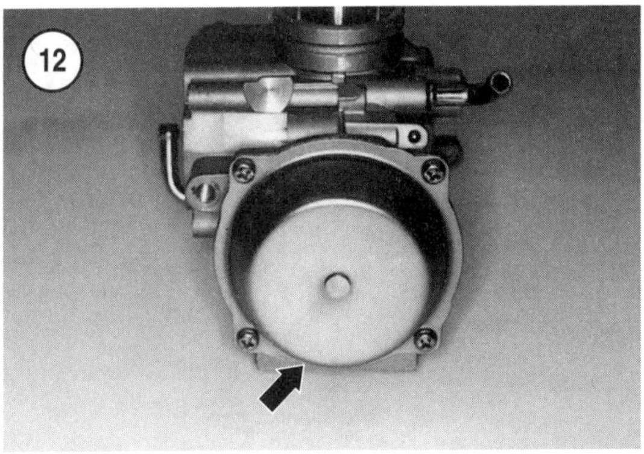

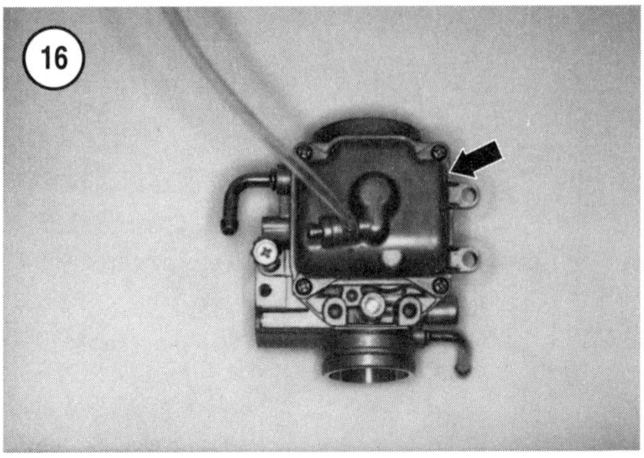

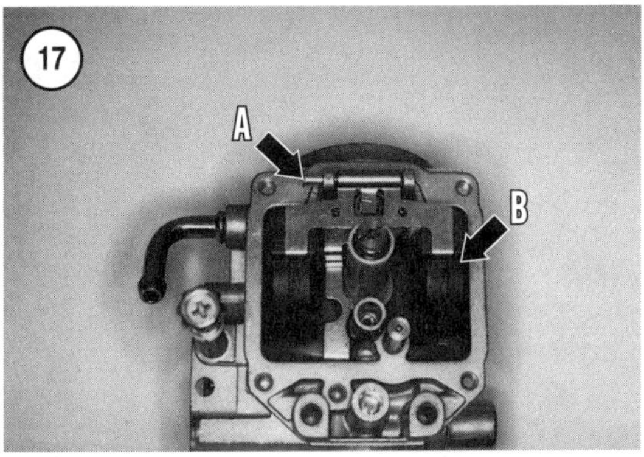

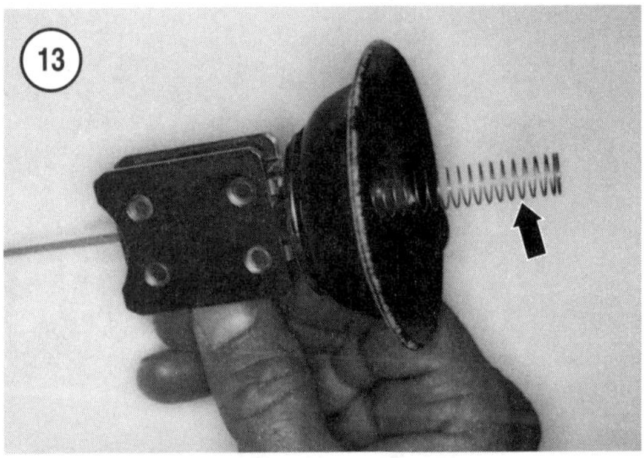

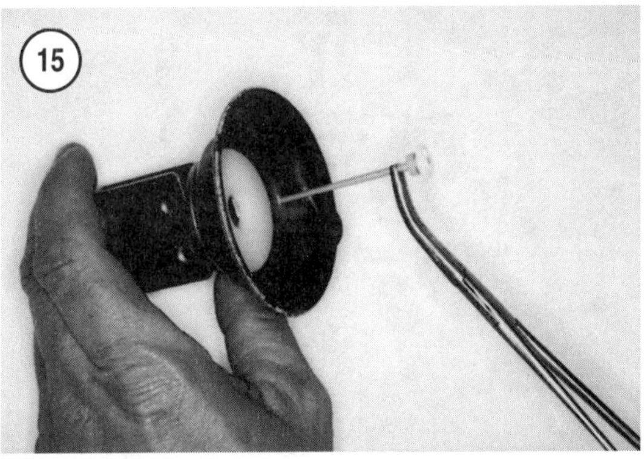

6

3. Carefully withdraw the throttle valve/diaphragm assembly (**Figure 14**).
4. To disassemble the throttle valve/diaphragm assembly, perform the following:
   a. Slowly push the jet needle up to dislodge the upper ring.
   b. Remove the upper ring, jet needle, E-ring and lower ring (**Figure 15**).
5. Remove the mounting screws and remove the float bowl and O-ring gasket (**Figure 16**).
6. Carefully tap out the float assembly pivot pin (A, **Figure 17**).
7. Pull straight up and remove the float assembly (B, **Figure 17**). Do not lose the needle valve attached to the float tang.
8. Remove the two screws and the mounting plate (**Figure 18**).
9. Pull straight up and remove the needle valve seat (**Figure 19**).
10. Unscrew and remove the pilot jet (**Figure 20**).
11. Unscrew and remove the main jet (**Figure 21**) and spacer ring (**Figure 22**).
12. Unscrew and remove the air jet (**Figure 23**).
13. Do not remove the pilot screw (**Figure 24**).

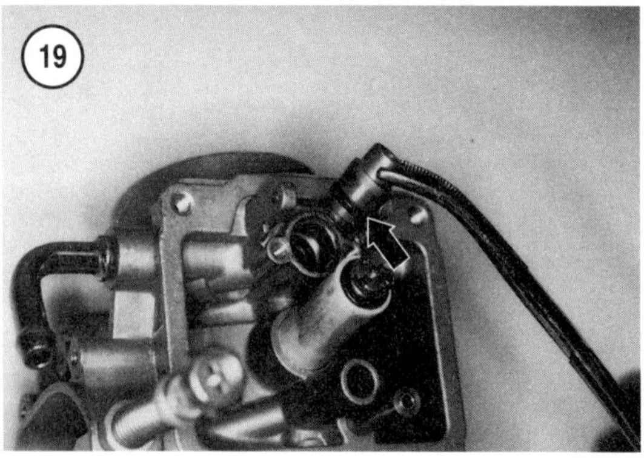

14. Turn the carburetor on its side and remove the needle jet (**Figure 25**) from the top of the carburetor.
15. If necessary, remove the screws and lockwashers (A, **Figure 26**) and carefully slide out the jet block assembly (B, **Figure 26**).
16. If necessary, unscrew and remove the throttle adjust screw, spring seat and spring (A, **Figure 27**).

NOTE
Further disassembly is not necessary or recommended. Do not remove the throttle shaft (B, ***Figure 27****) assembly. If these parts are damaged, replace the carburetor assembly, as these items are not available separately.*

17. Clean and inspect all parts as described under *Cleaning and Inspection* in this chapter.

Assembly

1. If removed, install the throttle adjust screw, spring seat and spring (B, **Figure 27**) and tighten securely.

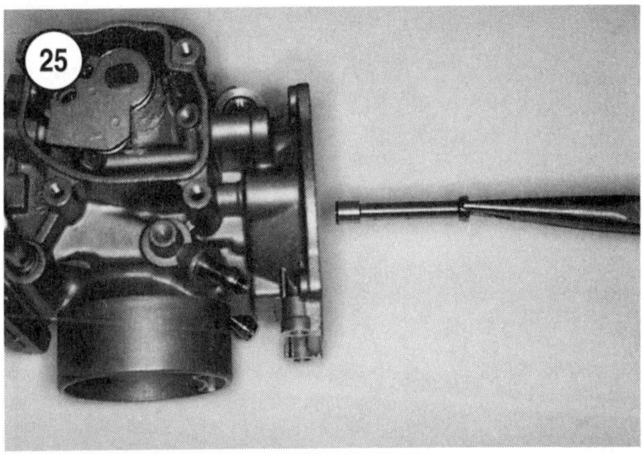

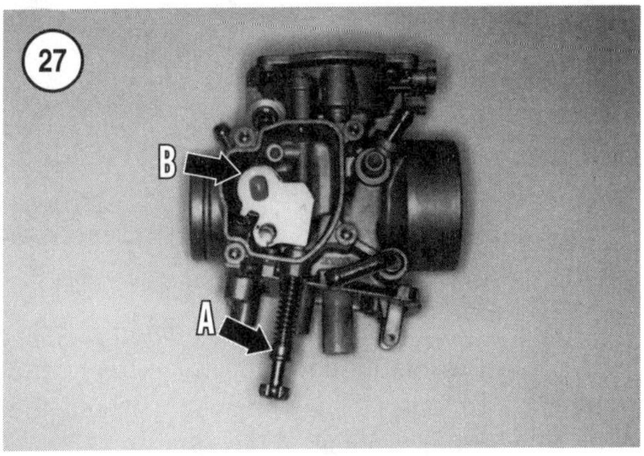

2. If removed, install the jet block assembly (B, **Figure 26**) and make sure it is seated correctly. Tighten the screws and washers securely.

3. Install the needle jet as follows:

   a. Correctly align the needle jet flat (A, **Figure 28**) with the flat (B, **Figure 28**) in the carburetor body.

   b. Insert the needle jet (**Figure 25**) into the top of the carburetor and into the post. Push it in until it bottoms.

   c. After installation, check that the needle jet flat is aligned with the flat in the carburetor body (**Figure 29**).

4. Install the air jet (**Figure 23**) and tighten securely.

5. Install the main jet spacer ring (**Figure 22**).

6. Make sure the needle jet is pushed all the way into the body, then install the main jet. Tighten the main jet securely (**Figure 21**).

7. Install the pilot jet (**Figure 30**) and tighten securely.

8. Make sure the O-ring is in place, then install the needle valve seat (**Figure 19**). Push it down until it bottoms.

9. Install the mounting plate (**Figure 18**) and tighten the two screws securely.
10. Install the needle valve (**Figure 31**) onto the float tang.
11. Install the float assembly (B, **Figure 17**) while aligning the needle valve with the needle valve seat.
12. Install the float pivot pin (A, **Figure 17**) and carefully tap it in until it is seated (**Figure 32**). Move the float up and down to ensure free movement of the needle valve within the seat.
13. Install the O-ring gasket (**Figure 33**) into the float bowl and install the float bowl (**Figure 16**). Tighten the screws securely.
14. To assemble the throttle valve/diaphragm assembly, perform the following:
   a. Install the E-clip (A, **Figure 34**) onto the jet needle in the correct location. Refer to **Table 1** for standard E-clip location.
   b. Install the lower ring (B, **Figure 34**) and the upper ring (**Figure 35**).
   c. Install the jet needle assembly into the throttle valve/diaphragm assembly (**Figure 15**).
15. Install the spring (**Figure 13**) into throttle valve/diaphragm assembly to hold the jet needle in place.
16. Install the throttle valve/diaphragm assembly (**Figure 36**) into the carburetor body. Make sure the outer perimeter of the diaphragm is seated correctly in the body groove (**Figure 14**).
17. Correctly align the diaphragm tab with the notch (**Figure 37**) in the carburetor body.
18. Install the cover (**Figure 12**) and the screws and tighten securely.
19. After the cover is in place, insert a finger into the carburetor body venturi and push up on the throttle valve assembly (**Figure 38**). The assembly must move up and return without any binding. If the throttle valve assembly does not move freely, the spring may be out of position within it and the cover. Correct this problem at this time.

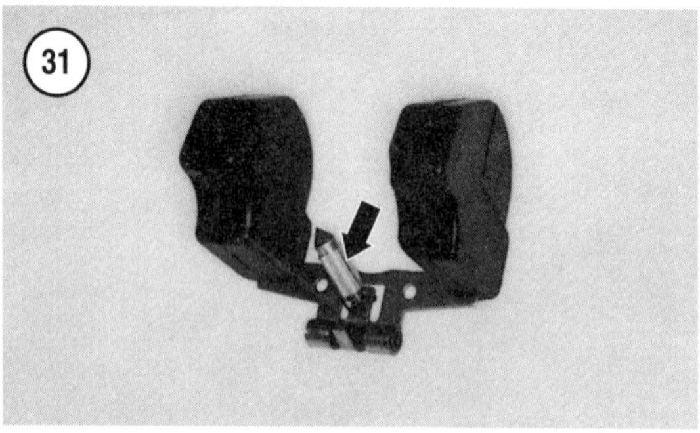

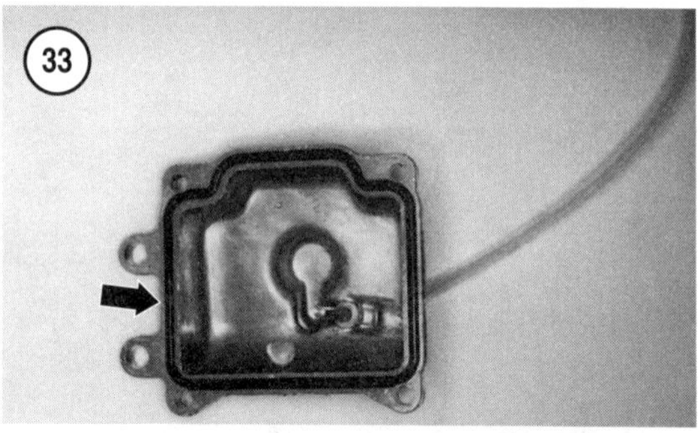

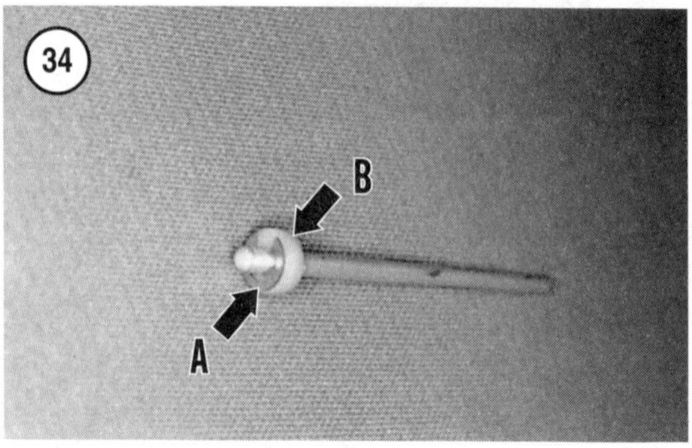

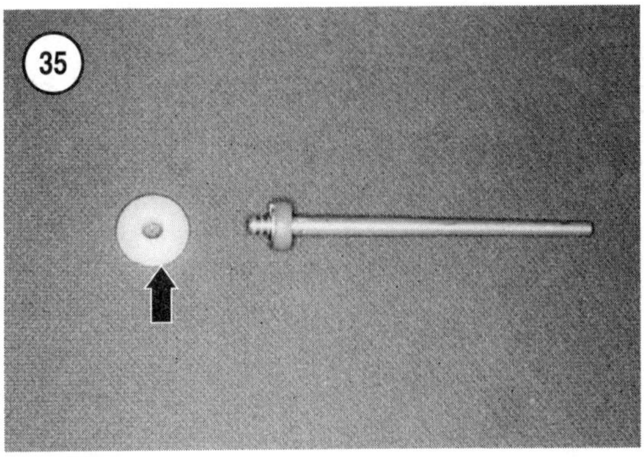

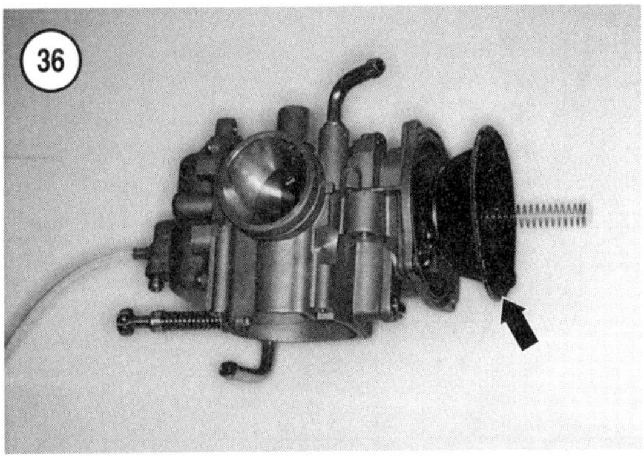

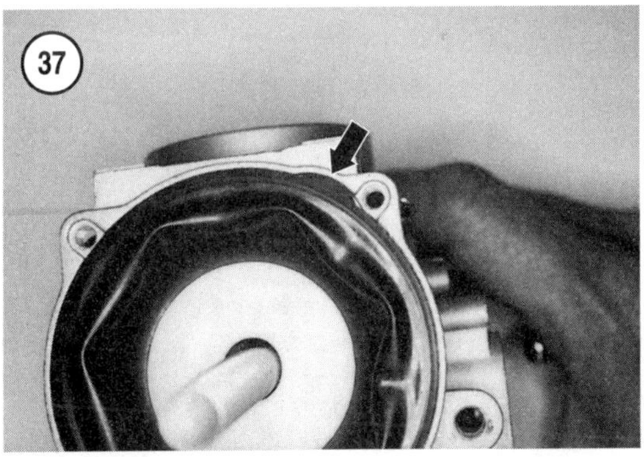

CARBURETOR CLEANING AND INSPECTION

CAUTION

The carburetor body is equipped with plastic parts that cannot be removed. Do not dip the carburetor body, O-rings, float assembly, needle valve or diaphragm and vacuum slide assembly in a carburetor cleaner or other harsh solution. Caustic carburetor solvent can damage these parts. Instead, clean the carburetor and related parts in a petroleum-based solvent, or Simple Green. Then thoroughly rinse in clean hot water.

1. Initially clean all parts in a mild petroleum-based cleaning solution. Then clean in hot soap and water and rinse with hot water. Thoroughly dry with low-pressure compressed air.

CAUTION

*If compressed air is not available, allow the parts to air-dry or use a clean lint-free cloth. Do **not** use a paper towel to dry carburetor parts, as small paper particles may plug openings in the carburetor housing or jets.*

2. Allow the carburetor to dry thoroughly before assembly and blow dry with compressed air. Blow out the jets with compressed air.

CAUTION

*Do **not** use wire or drill bits to clean jets, as minor gouges in the jet can alter the flow rate and change the air/fuel mixture.*

3. Inspect the float bowl O-ring gasket (**Figure 33**). Replace the O-ring if it is hard or starting to deteriorate.

6

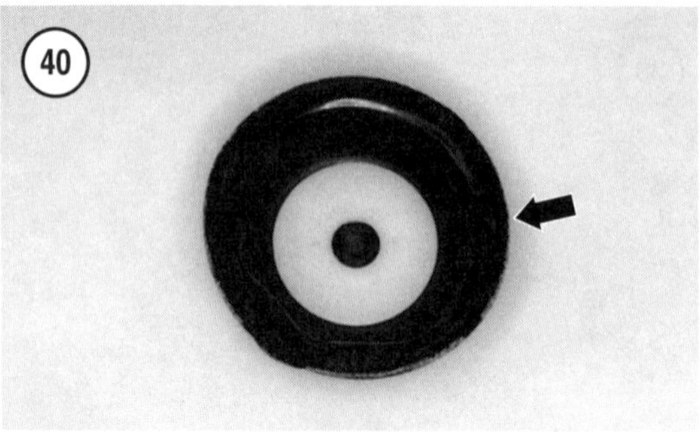

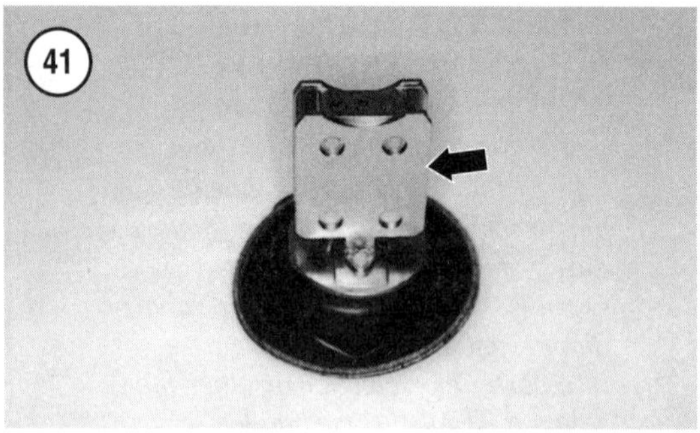

4. Make sure the drain screw (**Figure 39**) is in good condition and does not leak; replace the drain screw if necessary.
5. Inspect the throttle valve diaphragm (**Figure 40**) for cracks, deterioration or other damage. Check the sides of the throttle valve (**Figure 41**) for excessive wear.
6. Install the vacuum slide, or throttle valve, into the carburetor body and move it up and down in the bore. The vacuum slide, or throttle valve, should move smoothly with no binding or excessive play. If there is excessive play, replace the vacuum slide, or throttle valve, and/or jet block assembly.
7. Inspect the jet needle tapered end for steps, uneven wear or other damage. Replace if damaged.
8. Check the inlet valve needle seat O-ring seal (A, **Figure 42**) for hardness or deterioration, replace if necessary.
9. Inspect the inlet valve needle seat (B, **Figure 42**) for steps, uneven wear or other damage.
10. Insert the inlet valve needle into the seat and slowly move it back and forth and check for smooth operation. If either part is worn or damaged, replace the inlet valve assembly.
11. Inspect the needle valve (**Figure 43**) tapered end for steps, uneven wear or other damage.
12. Inspect all jets (**Figure 44**). Make sure all holes are open and none of them are either worn or damaged.

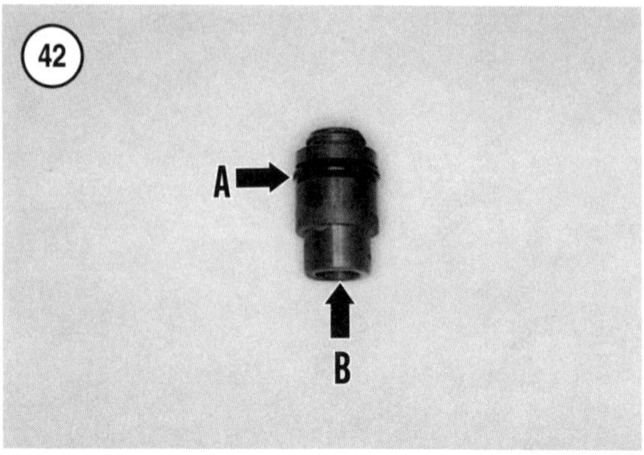

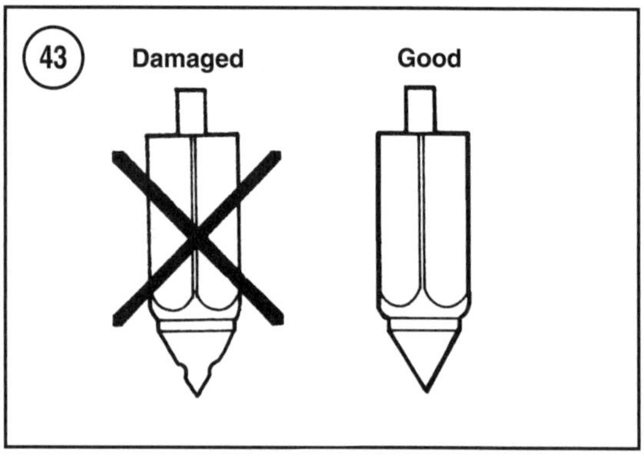

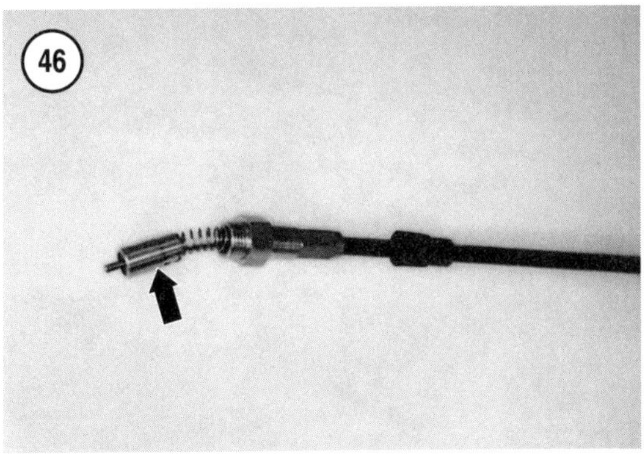
46

47

48

49

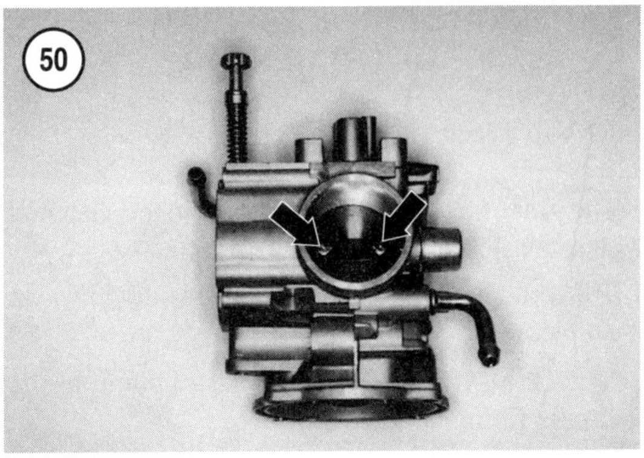
50

51

13. Inspect the float (**Figure 45**) for deterioration or damage. If the float is suspected of leakage, place it in a container of water and push it down. If the float sinks or if bubbles appear, this indicates a leak. Replace the float.
14. Inspect the starting enrichment (choke) valve plunger, spring and guide holder (**Figure 46**) for wear or damage.
15. Make sure all openings in the carburetor body are clear. Refer to **Figure 47**, **Figure 48** and **Figure 49**. Clean out if they are plugged in any way, then apply low-pressure compressed air to all openings.
16. Check the cover for cracks or damage; replace if necessary.
17. Make sure the throttle plate screws are tight (**Figure 50**).
18. Inspect the carburetor body (A, **Figure 51**) for internal or external damage. If damaged, replace the carburetor assembly, as the body cannot be replaced separately.
19. Move the throttle lever (B, **Figure 51**) back and forth from stop to stop and check for free movement. The throttle lever should move smoothly and return under spring tension. If it sticks in any position, replace the carburetor housing.

6

CARBURETOR TESTS AND ADJUSTMENTS

Inlet Valve Seat Inspection

The float valve sealing ability can be checked with a small hand-held pressure pump.

1. Turn the assembled carburetor upside down on the top cover.
2. Attach a small hand-held pressure pump to the fuel inlet fitting (**Figure 52**).
3. Apply 34.5 kPa (5 psi) of pressure to the inlet fitting.
4. The needle and seat should hold this pressure indefinitely.
5. If the needle and seat do no pass this test, replace both parts.
6. Remove the hand-held pressure pump.

Float Level Height Adjustment

The fuel inlet valve is controlled by the float to maintain a constant fuel level in the carburetor float bowl. Because the height of the fuel affects the air/fuel mixture throughout the engine's operating range, make sure the float position is correctly adjusted.

1. Remove the carburetor as described in this chapter.
2. Remove the mounting screws and remove the float bowl and O-ring gasket (**Figure 53**).
3. Hold the carburetor on its side so the tang in the middle of the float arm is just touching the fuel valve. Use a float level gauge, vernier caliper or small ruler (**Figure 54**) and measure the distance from the carburetor body gasket surface to the float. The correct distance is listed in **Table 1**.
4. If the float setting is incorrect, adjust as follows:
   a. Carefully bend the tang in the center of the float arm (**Figure 55**) with a small screwdriver to adjust the float level.
   b. Recheck the float level as described in Step 3. Repeat until the float level adjustment is correct.
5. Install the O-ring seal (**Figure 33**) into the float bowl and install the float bowl. Tighten the screws securely.
6. Install the carburetor as described in this chapter.

52

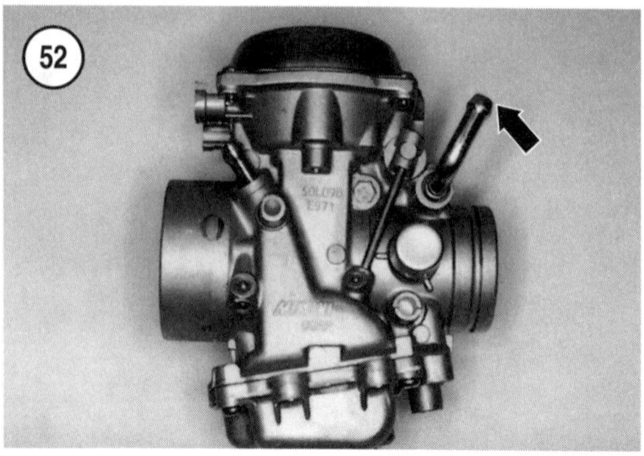

53

54

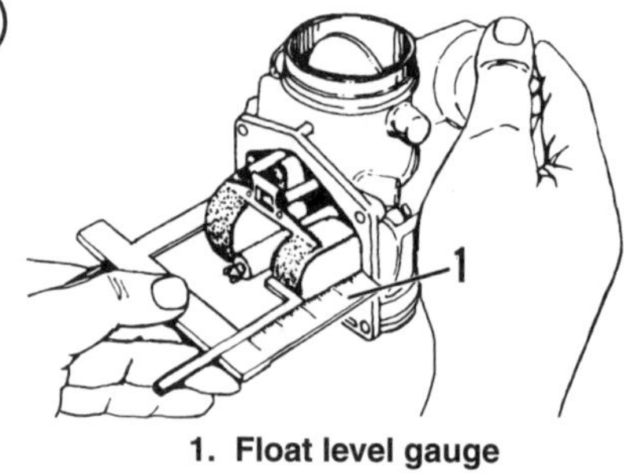

1. Float level gauge

55

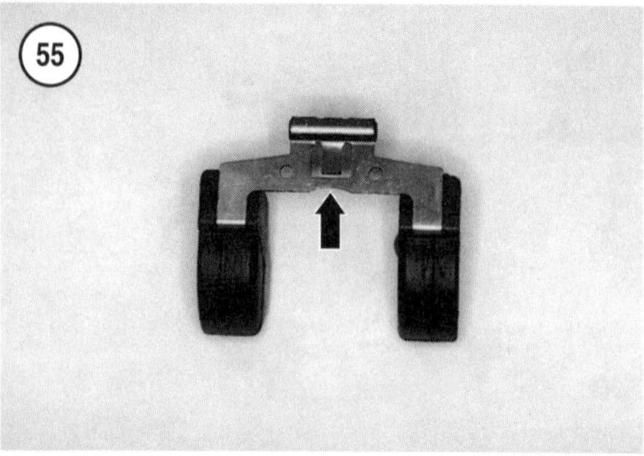

56

57

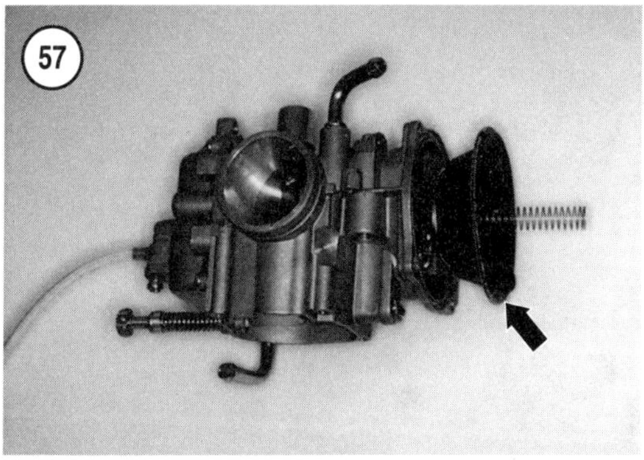

58

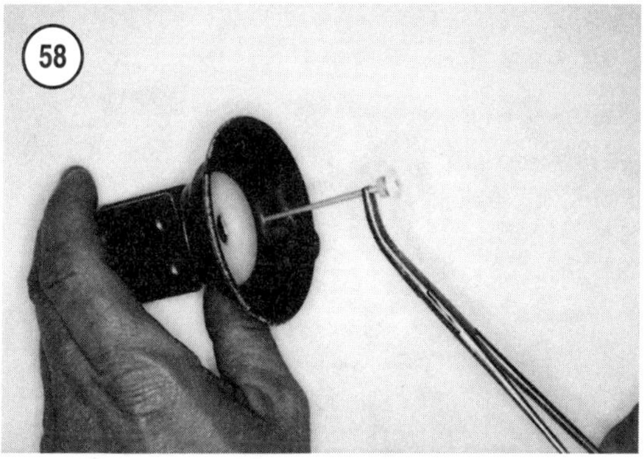

59

Jet Needle Adjustment

Adjust the position of the jet needle to affect the air/fuel mixture for medium throttle openings.

1. Remove the carburetor as described in this chapter.
2. Remove the screws securing the cover (**Figure 56**).
3. Remove the cover and the spring.
4. Carefully withdraw the throttle valve/diaphragm assembly (**Figure 57**).
5. To disassemble the throttle valve/diaphragm assembly, perform the following:
   a. Slowly push the jet needle up to dislodge the upper ring.
   b. Remove the upper ring, jet needle, E-ring and lower ring (**Figure 58**).
6. Remove the E-ring and lower ring from the jet needle.
7. Refer to **Table 1** for standard size jet needle and standard E-ring location from the top of the jet needle.

NOTE
Record the clip position prior to removal.

8. Raising the needle (lowering the E-ring) will enrichen the mixture during mid-throttle opening, while lowering the needle (raising the E-ring) will lean the mixture.
9. Install the jet needle, vacuum slide and diaphragm as described in this chapter.
10. Perform Steps 14-19 of *Carburetor Assembly* in this chapter.

Main Jet Replacement

The size of the main jet affects the air/fuel mixture during wide-open throttle operation. Different size main jets are available and can be installed to change the mixture for operation at high engine speeds.

The carburetor assembly must be removed and partially disassembled to remove the main jet.

1. Remove the carburetor as described in this chapter.
2. Remove the mounting screws and remove the float bowl (**Figure 53**) and O-ring gasket.
3. Unscrew and remove the main jet (**Figure 59**).
4. Do not remove the spacer ring under the main jet.
5. The size is stamped on the jet. The main jet size listed in **Table 1** is recommended for operation at ambient temperatures of 5-26° C (40-80° F) and at altitudes of 0-900 m (0-3000 ft.). A smaller size

6

main jet may be required for optimum performance at higher altitudes and at warmer temperatures. A larger main jet may be used at colder temperatures.
6. Install the main jet and reassemble the carburetor by reversing the disassembly procedure.

THROTTLE CABLE REPLACEMENT

1. Place the vehicle on level ground and set the parking brake.
2. Remove the seat as described in Chapter Fifteen.
3. Remove the front fender as described in Chapter Fifteen.
4. Disconnect the throttle cable from the carburetor as described under *Carburetor Removal/Installation* in this chapter.
5. Disconnect the throttle cable from the handlebar-mounted throttle lever as follows:
   a. Use a screwdriver to remove the throttle control cover (**Figure 60**).
   b. Detach the cable from the throttle arm (A, **Figure 61**). If the cable end can not be disconnected, remove the throttle arm nut, washer and lever, then disconnect the cable.
   c. Withdraw the cable from the throttle housing (B, **Figure 61**).
6. Disconnect the throttle cable from any clips or tie wraps securing the cable to the frame.
7. Mark the original path of the cable by attaching a piece of string to the cable before withdrawing it.
8. Make a note of the cable routing path through the frame, then remove it.
9. Lubricate the new cable as described in Chapter Three.
10. Attach the new cable to the string and pull in into the position of the original cable.
11. Reverse Steps 1-6 to install the new cable assembly.
12. Reattach the throttle cable to the carburetor as described under *Carburetor Removal/Installation* in this chapter.
13. Apply grease to the handlebar end of the cable and attach it to the throttle lever and housing.
14. Install the cover onto the throttle housing.
15. Adjust the cable free play as described in Chapter Three.
16. Operate the throttle lever and make sure the carburetor throttle linkage is operating correctly with no binding. If operation is incorrect or there is

binding, make sure the cable is attached correctly and there are no tight bends in the cable.
17. *Slowly* test ride the vehicle and make sure the throttle is operating correctly.

STARTING ENRICHMENT (CHOKE) CABLE

Removal/Installation

1. Place the vehicle on level ground and set the parking brake.

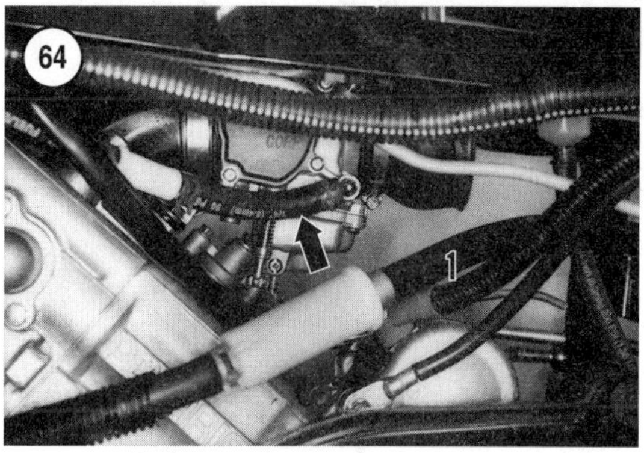

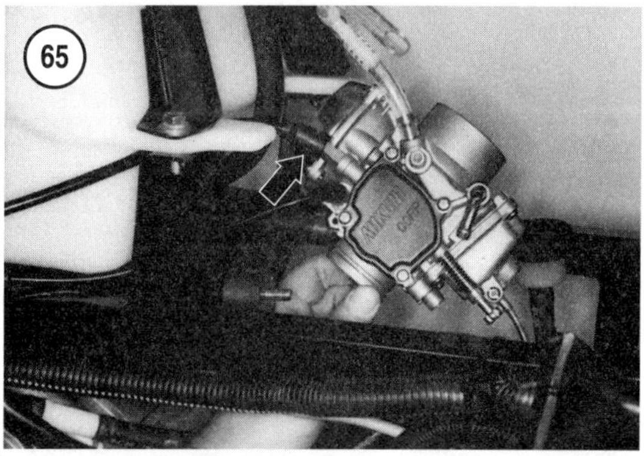

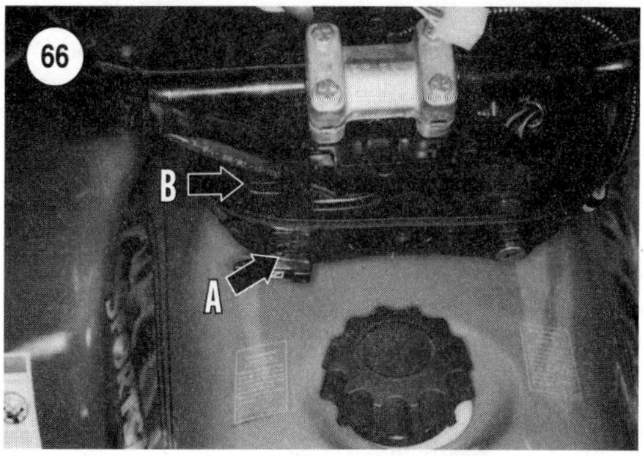

2. Remove the seat as described in Chapter Fifteen.

3. Remove the front fender as described in Chapter Fifteen.

4. Remove the clamping band, or tie-wrap, and remove the front portion of the PVT air exhaust duct (**Figure 62**).

5. Remove the air filter air box as described in this chapter.

6. Remove the two nuts and washers and two screws securing the carburetor mounting bracket (**Figure 63**) to the frame.

7. Mark all hoses prior to disconnecting them from the carburetor.

8. Disconnect the fuel supply hose (**Figure 64**) hose from the carburetor. Plug the end of the supply hose.

9. Loosen the front clamp, slide the carburetor back and free it from the intake manifold on the cylinder head.

10. Unscrew and disconnect the starting enrichment (choke) cable from the carburetor (**Figure 65**).

11A. On Xplorer models, perform the following:

a. Remove the top cover from the instrument panel cover.
b. Remove the two screws securing the instrument panel cover and remove the cover.
c. Unscrew the nut securing the toggle control knob to the instrument panel cover mounting bracket.
d. Carefully withdraw the toggle control knob and starting enrichment (choke) cable assembly from the instrument panel cover mounting bracket.

11B. On Sportsman models, perform the following:

a. Remove the headlight upper pod as described under *Handlebar Removal/Installation* in Chapter Twelve.
b. Unscrew the retaining ring (A, **Figure 66**) securing the toggle control knob to the headlight lower pod.
c. Carefully withdraw the toggle control knob and starting enrichment (choke) cable assembly (B, **Figure 66**) from the headlight lower pod.

12. Remove any clips holding the cable to the frame.

13. Make a note of the cable routing through the frame, then remove it.

14. Lubricate the new cable as described in Chapter Three.

15. Install by reversing these removal steps. Carefully insert the cable end into the carburetor and tighten securely.

6

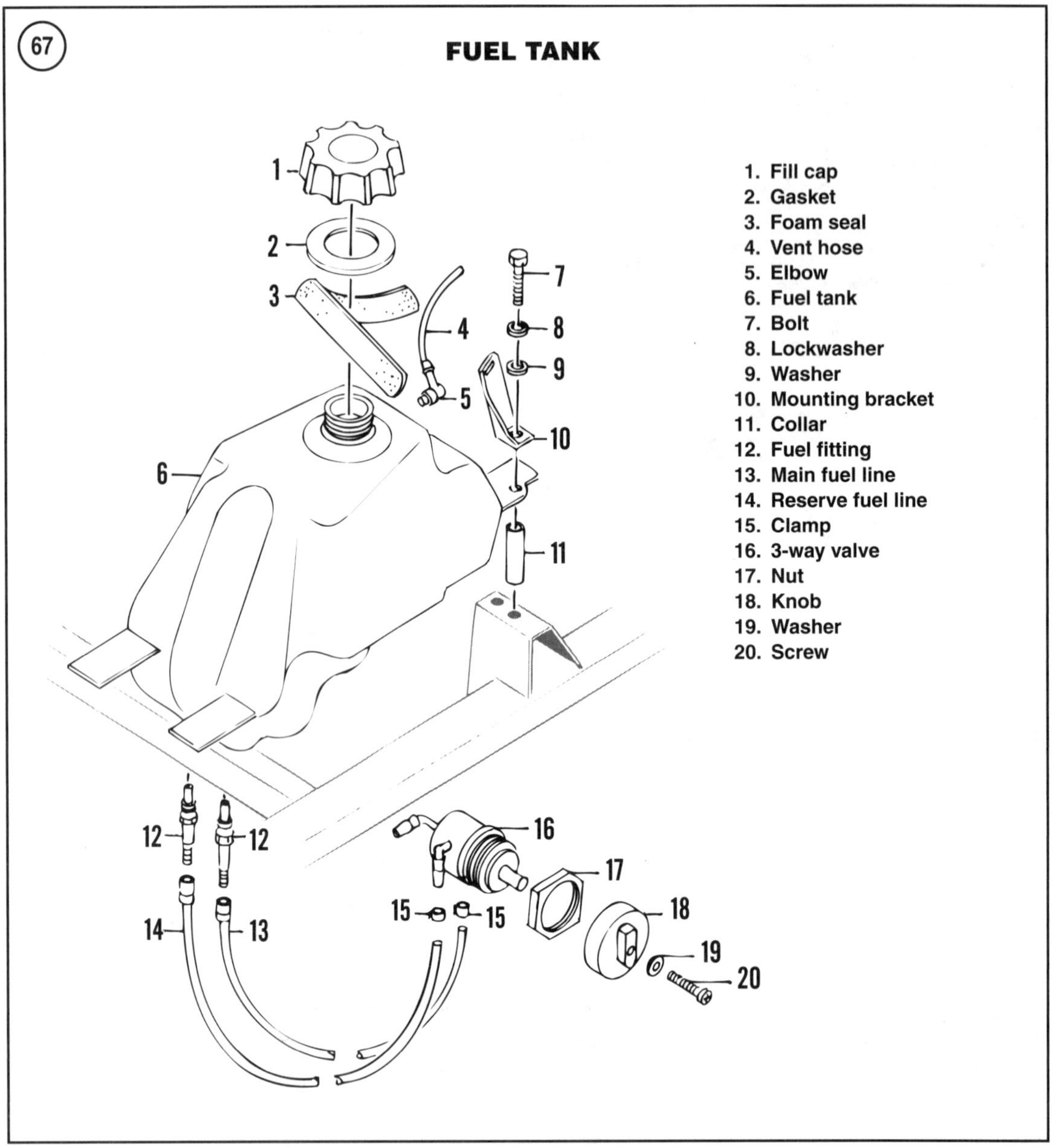

FUEL TANK

Removal/Installation

Refer to **Figure 67**.

WARNING

Some fuel may spill from the fuel tank hose when performing this procedure. Because gasoline is an extremely flammable and explosive petroleum, perform this procedure away from all open flames (including appliance pilot light) and sparks. Do not smoke or allow someone who is smoking in the work area as an explosion and fire may occur. Always work in a well-ventilated area. Wipe up any spills immediately.

1. Place the vehicle on level ground and set the parking brake.
2. Remove the seat as described in Chapter Fifteen.
3. Remove the front fender as described in Chapter Fifteen.

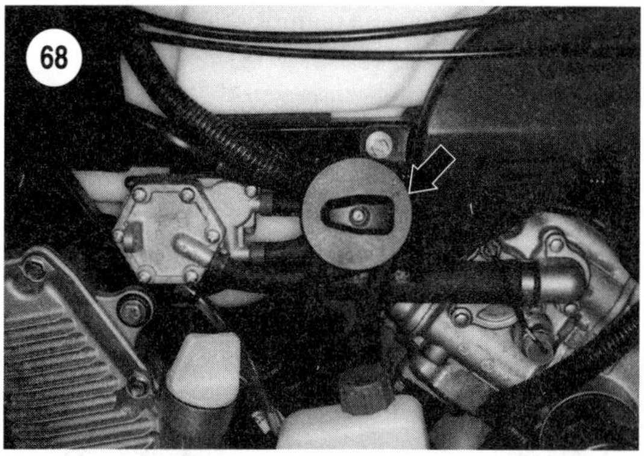

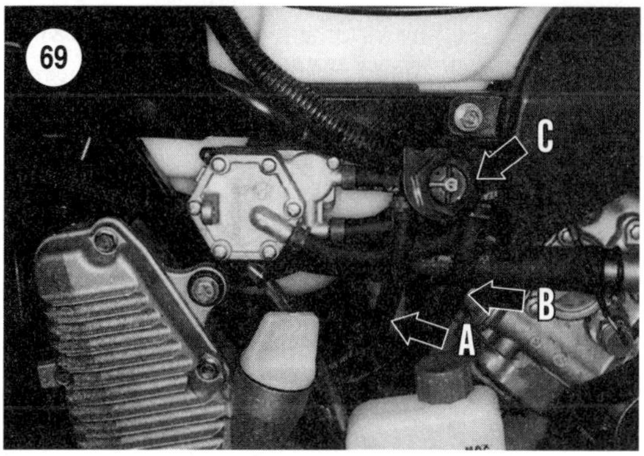

4. Disconnect the negative battery lead as described in Chapter Three.
5. Disconnect the vent hose from the top elbow fitting next to the fuel filler cap.
6. Disconnect the fuel lines from the shutoff valve as follows:
   a. Remove the screw securing the knob (**Figure 68**) to the fuel shutoff valve. Remove the knob.
   b. Disconnect the reserve fuel line (A, **Figure 69**) from the front fitting on the valve.
   c. Place the loose end into a sealable container suitable for gasoline storage.
   d. Open the fuel tank filler cap to allow the fuel to drain faster and drain the fuel tank. Plug the end to prevent fuel spillage.
   e. Disconnect the main fuel line (B, **Figure 69**) from the rear fitting on the valve. Plug the end to prevent fuel spillage.
7. Loosen the mounting bolt on each side securing the rear of the fuel tank mounting bracket and spacer to the frame.
8. Remove the clamping band, or tie-wrap, and remove the front portion of the PVT air exhaust duct.
9. Remove the air box inlet duct from the backside of the fuel tank.
10. Remove the mounting bolt, loosened in Step 7, on each side securing the rear of the fuel tank mounting bracket and spacer to the frame.
11. Carefully pull the fuel tank toward the rear and disengage the front locating tabs from the frame receptacles.
12. Pull the fuel tank straight up and remove the tank along with both fuel hoses attached to the bottom of the tank. Remove the fuel tank from the frame.
13. Inspect the tank for any damage or leaking.
14. Store the tank in a place where there is little chance for fire and where the tank will not be damaged.
15. Install by reversing these removal steps while noting the following:
   a. Check for fuel leakage after installation is completed.
   b. Tighten fuel tank mounting bolts securely.

FUEL SHUTOFF VALVE

Refer to **Figure 67.**

WARNING
Some fuel may spill from the fuel tank hose when performing this procedure. Because gasoline is an extremely flammable and explosive petroleum, perform this procedure away from all open flames (including appliance pilot light) and sparks. Do not smoke or allow someone who is smoking in the work area as an explosion and fire may occur. Always work in a well-ventilated area. Wipe up any spills immediately.

1. Place the vehicle on level ground and set the parking brake.
2. Remove the seat as described in Chapter Fifteen.
3. Remove the front fender as described in Chapter Fifteen.
4. Disconnect the battery negative lead as described in Chapter Three.
5. Remove the screw securing the knob (**Figure 68**) to the fuel shutoff valve. Remove the knob.
6. Disconnect the fuel lines from the shutoff valve as follows:
   a. Disconnect the reserve fuel line (A, **Figure 69**) from the front fitting on the valve.

b. Place the loose end into a seal able container suitable for gasoline storage.
c. Open the fuel tank filler cap to allow the fuel to drain faster and drain the fuel tank. Plug the line end to prevent fuel spillage
d. Disconnect the main fuel line (B, **Figure 69**) from the rear fitting on the valve. Plug the end of the line to prevent fuel spillage.

7. Remove the nut (C, **Figure 69**) securing the valve to the frame mount.
8. Partially pull the valve out from the frame mount and disconnect the vacuum hose from the fitting on the rear of the valve. Plug the hose end to prevent the entry of foreign matter.
9. Withdraw the valve from the frame mount.
10. Install by reversing these steps. Check for fuel leakage after installation is completed.

AIR FILTER AIR BOX

Removal/Installation

Refer to **Figure 70** for 1996-1998 models or **Figure 71** for 1999-and later models.

NOTE
This procedure is shown on a 2000 model. When differences occur between the various models, they are noted.

1. Place the vehicle on level ground and set the parking brake.
2. Remove the seat as described in Chapter Fifteen.
3. Remove the rear fender as described in Chapter Fifteen.
4. Loosen the carburetor inlet tube clamp (**Figure 72**) securing the air box to the carburetor.

5A. On 1996-1998 models, perform the following:
a. Remove the bolt and washer on each side securing the air box to the frame mounting brackets.
b. Loosen both hose clamps securing the engine breather hose and the oil tank breather hose and disconnect both hoses from the air box.
c. Release the air inlet duct from the foam pad at the rear of the fuel tank.

5B. On 1999 and later models, perform the following:
a. Remove the bolt and washer (**Figure 73**) on each side securing the air box to the frame.
b. Loosen both hose clamps securing the engine breather hose (**Figure 74**) and the oil tank breather hose (**Figure 75**) and disconnect both hoses from the air box.

6. Carefully lift the air box from the frame.
7. Cover the carburetor opening (**Figure 76**) to prevent the entry of debris.
8. Inspect the air box for fractures or heat damage (A, **Figure 77**).
9. Inspect all rubber carburetor inlet fitting (B, **Figure 77**) and hose clamps for damage. Replace any damaged parts.
10. Make sure the drainage tube (**Figure 78**) is clear and that the cap is secure. Clean out if necessary.
11. Install by reversing these removal steps while noting the following:
a. Make sure the carburetor-to-air box hose clamp is seated properly and tightened securely.
b. Service the air filter as described in Chapter Three.

FUEL PUMP

Testing

1. Remove the front fender as described in Chapter Fifteen.
2. Loosen the clamp, then disconnect the impulse hose (A, **Figure 79**) from the pump.
3. Check the impulse hose for signs of fuel leakage. The presence of fuel in the impulse hose indicates a broken diaphragm.
4. Attach a hand vacuum pump to the impulse port of the pump.
5. Apply a vacuum equal to 5 in. Hg (16.9 kPa) to the port and observe any leakage. The pump diaphragm should hold this amount of vacuum indefinitely.
6. Alternating pulses of pressure and vacuum at the impulse port of the pump should pump fuel.
7. If the pump is not operating correctly, it must be repaired or replaced.
8. If the pump is acceptable, reconnect the impulse hose and tighten the clamp securely.

(70)

AIR FILTER AIR BOX (1996-1998)

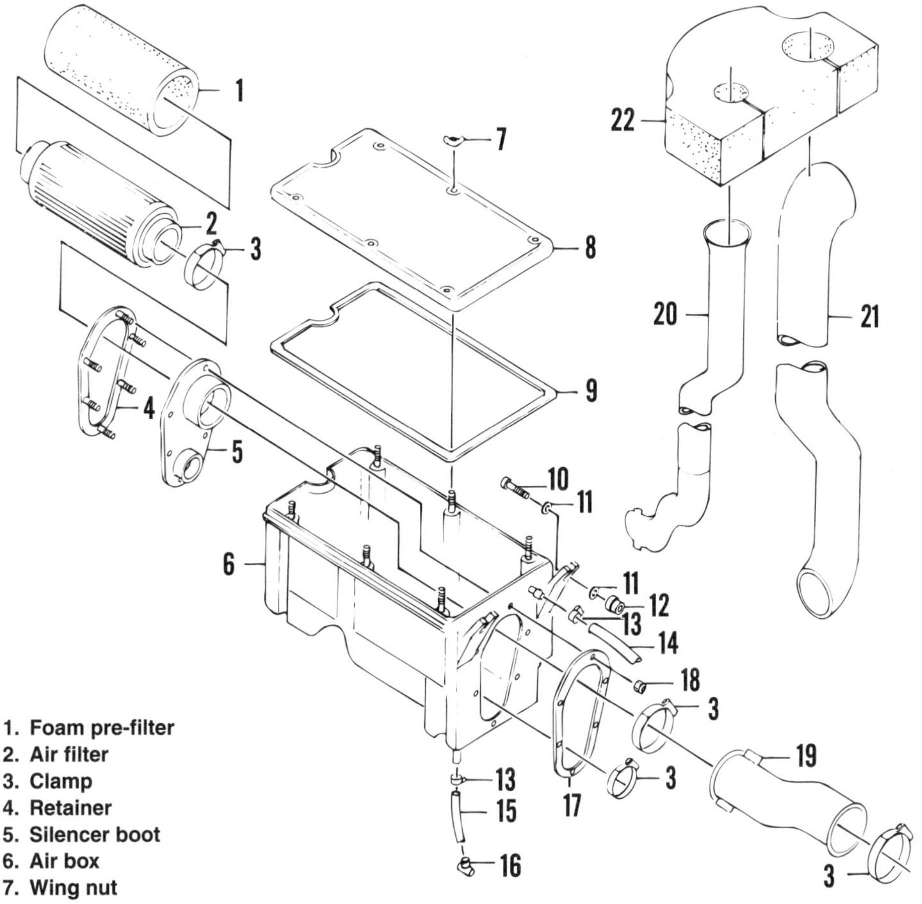

1. Foam pre-filter
2. Air filter
3. Clamp
4. Retainer
5. Silencer boot
6. Air box
7. Wing nut
8. Cover
9. Gasket
10. Screw
11. Washer
12. Special nut
13. Hose clamp
14. Hose
15. Drain tube
16. Cap
17. Retainer plate
18. Nut
19. Carburetor inlet tube
20. Air inlet duct
21. PVT air inlet duct
22. Foam pad

(71)

AIR FILTER AIR BOX (1999-ON)

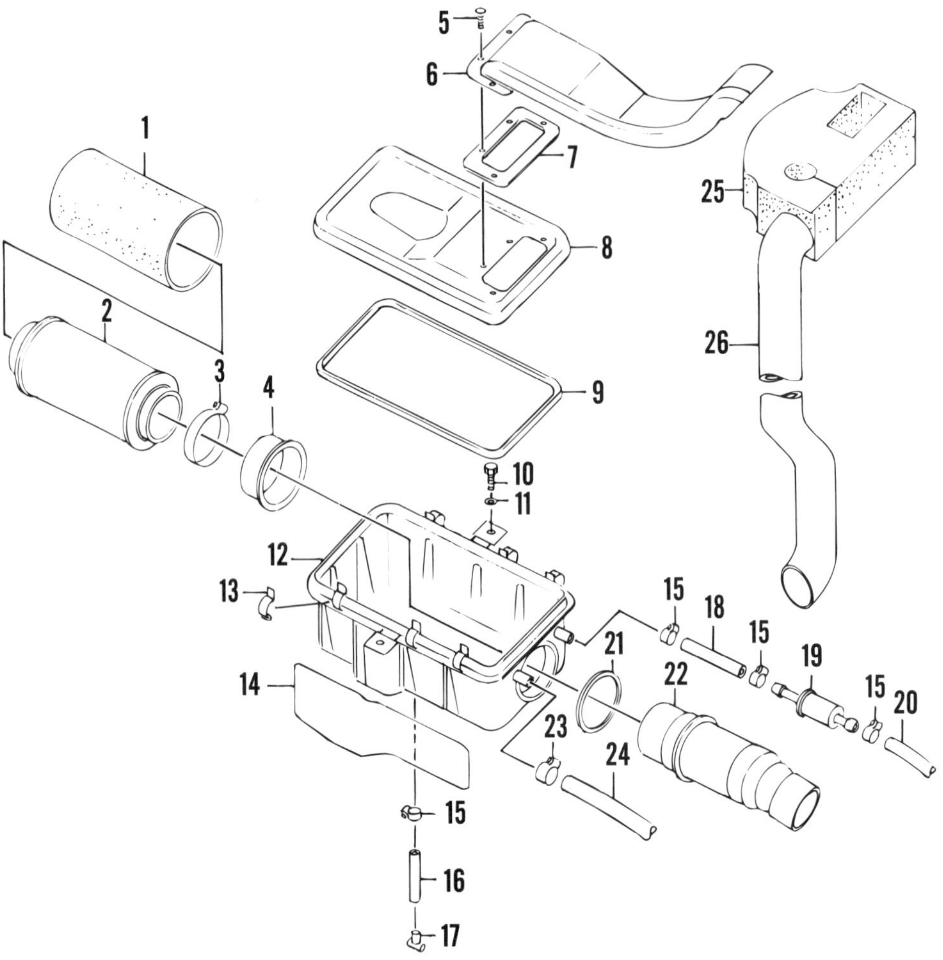

1. Foam pre-filter
2. Air filter
3. Clamp
4. Collar
5. Screw
6. Inlet duct
7. Gasket
8. Cover
9. Gasket
10. Bolt
11. Washer
12. Air box
13. Clip
14. Insulation
15. Clamp
16. Drain tube
17. Cap
18. Hose
19. Breather filter
20. Engine breather hose
21. Gasket
22. Carburetor inlet tube
23. Clamp
24. Oil tank breather hose
25. Foam pad
26. PVT air inlet duct

72

73

74

75

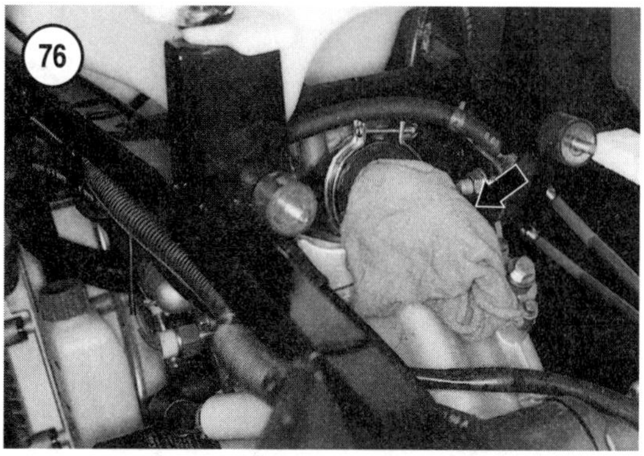
76

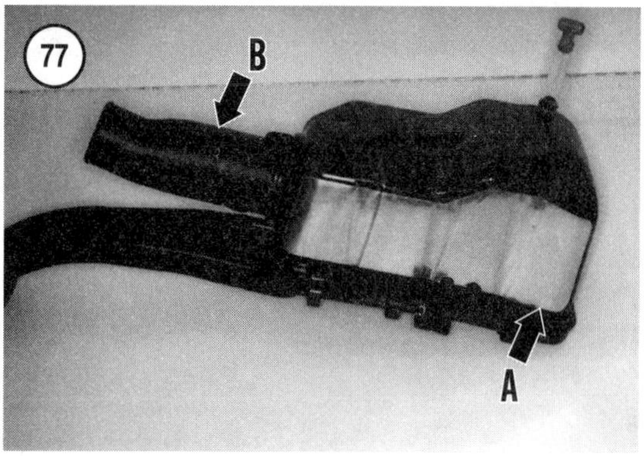

77

78

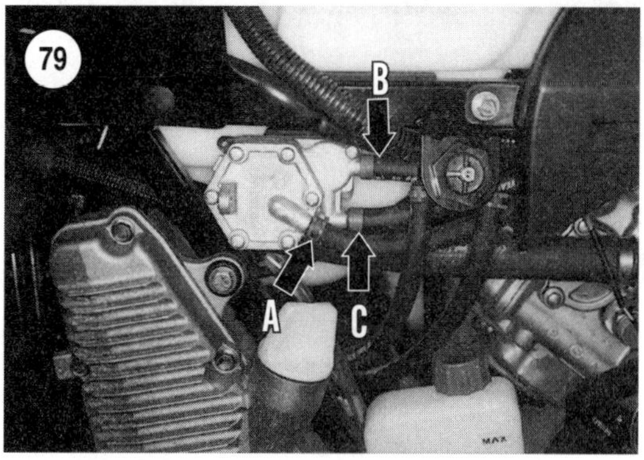

79

80

FUEL PUMP

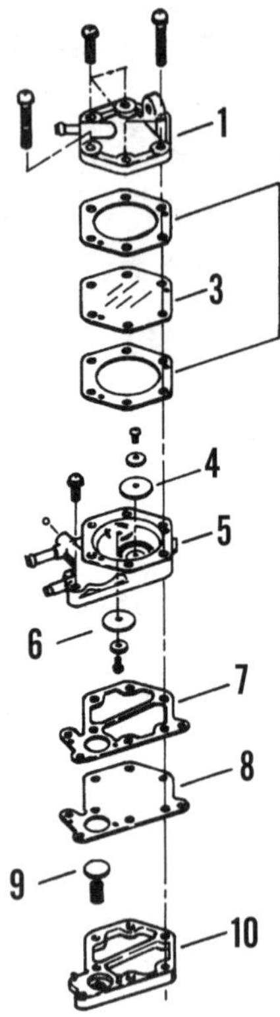

1. Cover
2. Gaskets
3. Diaphragm
4. Check valve
5. Pump body
6. Check valve
7. Gasket
8. Diaphragm
9. Pressure regulator
10. Cover

Removal/Installation

1. Remove the front fender as described in Chapter Fifteen.
2. Turn the shutoff valve to the OFF position.
3. Label each hose and fitting prior to disconnecting the hoses from the pump. The inlet hose is equipped with the inline fuel filter.
4. If still in place, loosen the clamp, then disconnect the impulse hose (A, **Figure 79**) from the pump.
5. Working on the backside of the fuel pump, remove the two nuts from the mounting screws securing the fuel pump to the frame rail.
6. Partially pull the fuel pump away from the frame rail.
7. Loosen the clamp, then disconnect the fuel inlet hose (B, **Figure 79**) from the pump.
8. Loosen the clamp, then detach the fuel outlet hose (C, **Figure 79**) from the pump.
9. Remove the fuel pump.

81

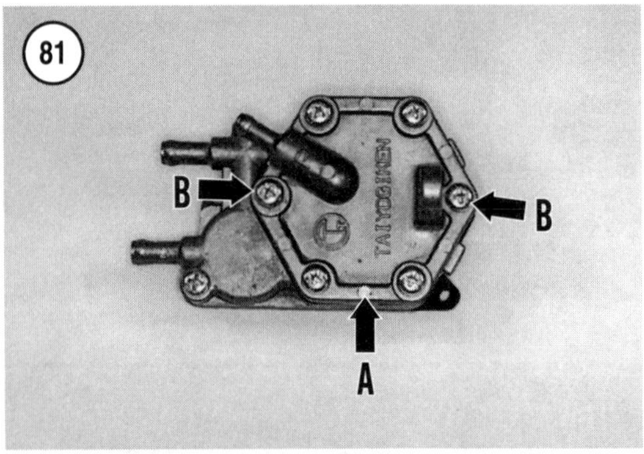

10. Install by reversing these removal steps while noting the following:

   a. Connect the hoses to the correct fittings on the fuel pump.
   b. Tighten the nuts securely.
   c. Check for fuel leakage after installation is completed.

Disassembly/Assembly

NOTE
Do not disassemble the pump until it has been determined whether new diaphragms, gaskets and valves are available. Contact a Polaris dealership.

Refer to **Figure 80**.

1. Remove the screws securing the diaphragm cover (A, **Figure 81**) and remove the cover. Note the location of the two longer screws (B, **Figure 81**).
2. Remove the diaphragm cover gasket, diaphragm and valve body gasket.
3. Remove the outlet check valve cover, diaphragm and gasket.
4. Clean all parts in soapy water and rinse in water. Carefully blow dry with low pressure compressed air.
5. Inspect the inlet and outlet check valves for cracks, warpage or damage.
6. Check the diaphragms for cracks, holes or swelling.
7. Check the sealing surfaces of the pump body and both covers.
8. Replace gaskets and diaphragms as complete sets.
9. Reassemble the pump in the reverse order of disassembly. Tighten all screws securely.

Table 1 CARBURETOR SPECIFICATIONS

Item	1996-1998	1999 and later
Carburetor		
Manufacturer	Mikuni CV	Mikuni CV
Type	BST 34	BTS 34
Main jet	142.5	155
Pilot jet	42.5	40
Pilot air jet	160	160
Jet needle and E-clip position	5D78-3	4HB41-3
Needle jet	P-1	Y-0
Throttle valve	100	Q-0
Pilot screw	–	2 5/8 turns out
1996-1997	1 1/2 turns out	
1998	2 turns out	
Float height	13.0 mm (0.51 in.)	13.0 mm (0.51 in.)
Idle speed	1100-1300 rpm	1000-1400 rpm

CHAPTER SEVEN

COOLING SYSTEMS

This chapter covers service procedures for the air (PVT) and liquid cooling systems. Cooling system specifications and capacity are in **Table 1** at the end of the chapter.

POLARIS VARIABLE TRANSMISSION (PVT) AIR COOLING SYSTEM

The Polaris Variable Transmission (PVT) assembly is air cooled. The air cooling system uses a centrifugal fan that is part of the drive pulley (**Figure 1**). Cooling air enters the system from the port in the left side of the crankcase, under the fuel tank. Air

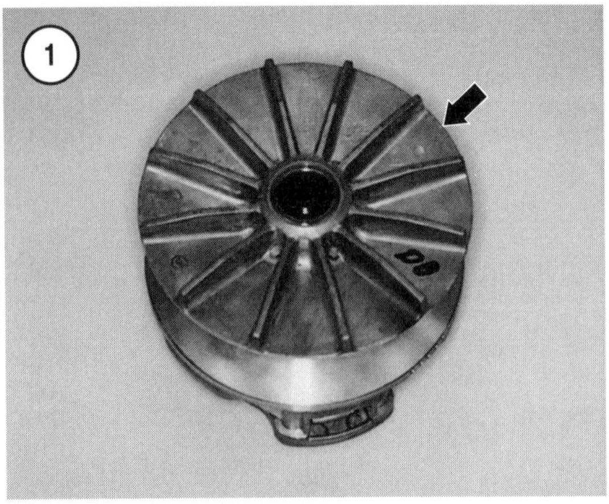

2

PVT COOLING SYSTEM

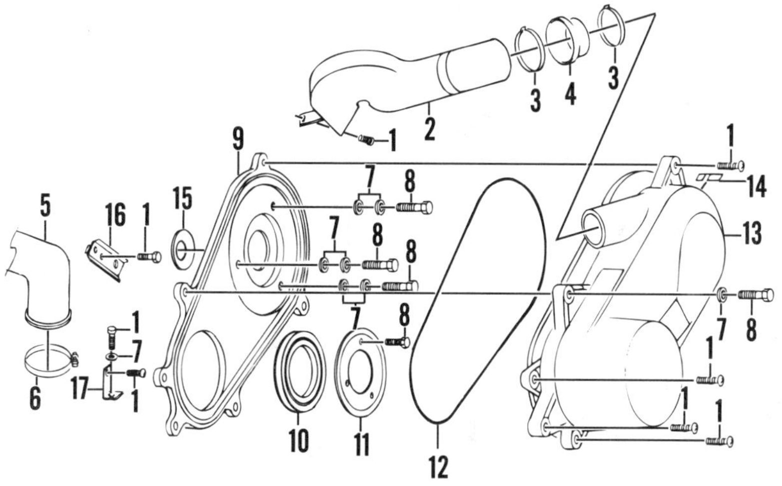

1. Screw
2. Outlet duct
3. Tie-wrap
4. Boot
5. Inlet duct
6. Hose clamp
7. Washer
8. Screw
9. Bolt
10. Front seal
11. Retainer
12. Seal
13. Outer cover
14. Clip
15. Seal
16. Bracket
17. Bracket

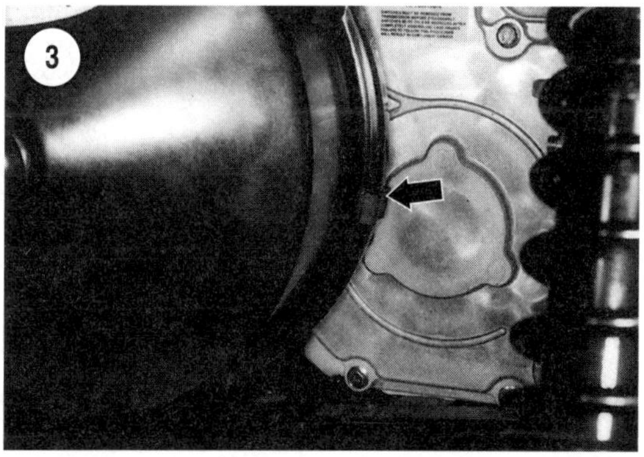

circulates around the primary drive pulley, belt and driven pulley to cool these components. The air then exits out thc outlet duct attached to the clutch cover.

For the system to operate properly, all covers, ducting, seals and hoses must be in place and properly attached. The air circulating around the PVT pulleys and belt must be dry. If water enters the PVT cooling system, shift the transmission to neutral, increase engine speed and allow the system to dry before proceeding.

Clutch Outer and Inner Cover Ducting

An obstruction in the ducting, missing parts or leaking connections can increase the operating temperature and shorten the life of the pulleys and the belt. Loose connections can also allow water to enter the system.

Clutch outer cover removal/installation

Refer to **Figure 2**:

1. Remove the front and rear fenders as described in Chapter Fifteen.
2. Remove the rear clip (**Figure 3**) from both covers.
3. To remove only the outlet duct, perform the following:
   a. Remove the front bolt (**Figure 4**) securing the air outlet duct to the frame.
   b. Remove the clamps or tie wraps (A, **Figure 5**) securing the air outlet duct to the outer cover and remove the air outlet duct (B, **Figure 5**).
4. Remove the front bolt and washer (**Figure 4**) securing the air outlet duct to the frame.
5. Remove the single top bolt and washer (**Figure 6**).

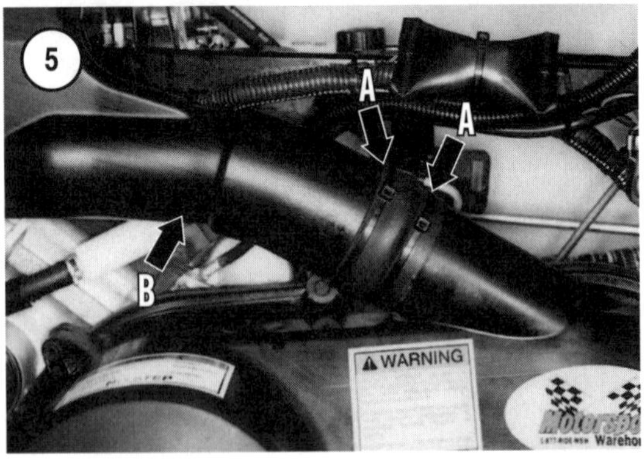

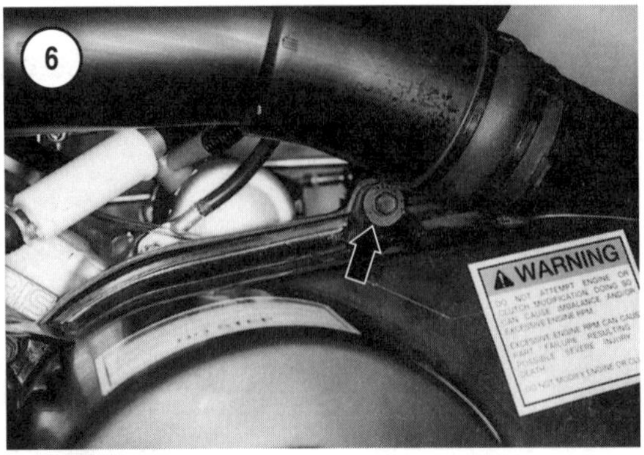

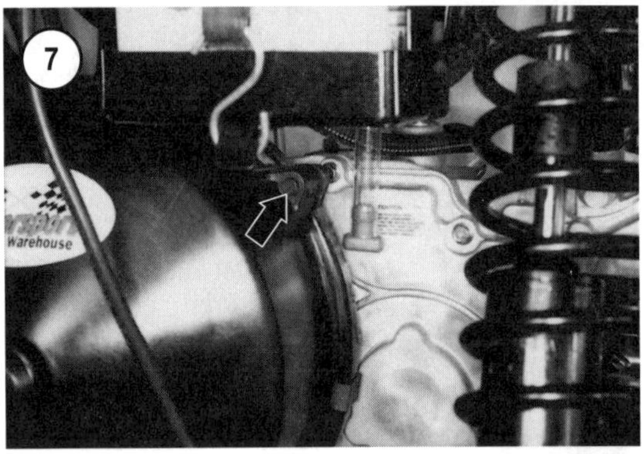

6. Remove single rear bolt and washer (**Figure 7**) and three front bolts and washers (**Figure 8**) securing the perimeter of the outer cover.

7. Remove the outer cover (**Figure 9**) assembly.

8. Inspect the outer cover (A, **Figure 10**) and outlet duct (B, **Figure 10**) for wear, cracks or damage. Replace if necessary.

9. Inspect the outer cover perimeter seal for hardness or deterioration; replace if necessary.

10. Install the outer cover onto the inner cover. Make sure it is seated correctly around the entire perimeter with no gaps.

11. Install the single rear bolt and washer (**Figure 7**) and three front bolts and washers (**Figure 8**) securing the outer cover. Tighten the bolts securely.

12. Install the single top bolt and washer (**Figure 6**) and tighten securely.

13. Install the front bolt and washer (**Figure 4**) securing the air outlet duct to the frame and tighten securely.

Clutch inner cover removal/installation

Refer to **Figure 2**.

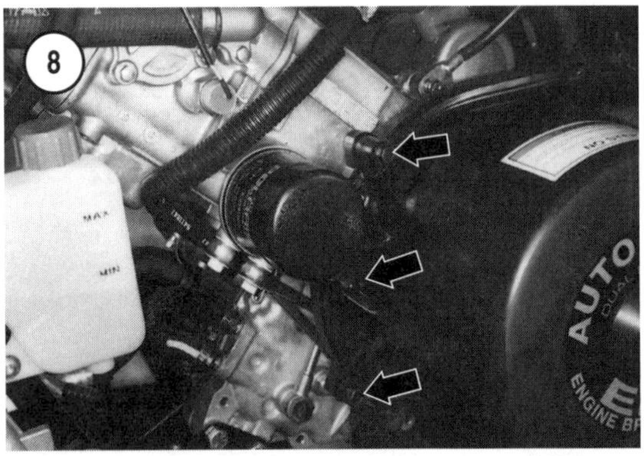

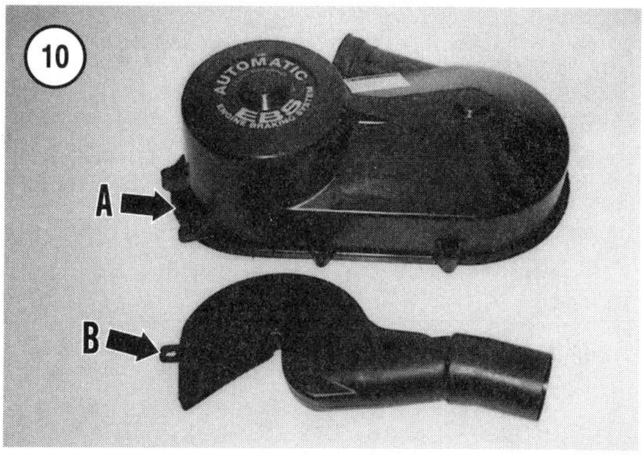

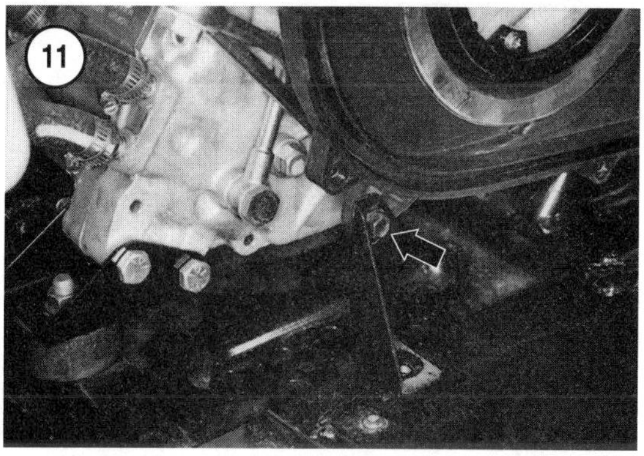

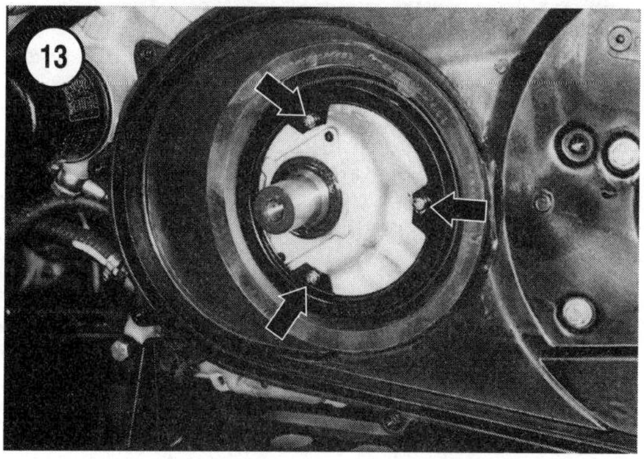

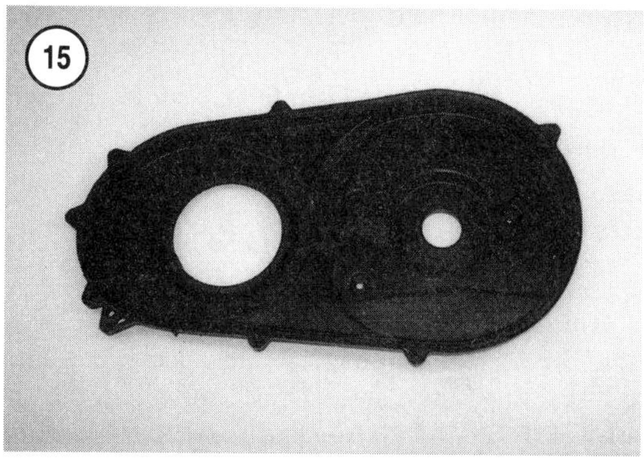

1. Remove the front and rear fenders as described in Chapter Fifteen.

2. Remove the clutch outer cover as previously described.

3. Remove the drive and driven pulleys as described in Chapter Eight.

4. Remove the front lower bolt (**Figure 11**) and the three rear screws, lockwashers and washers (**Figure 12**) securing the inner cover.

5. Remove the three screws (**Figure 13**) securing the front seal and retainer to the crankcase.

6. Pull the cover straight out from the engine being careful not to damage the rubber seal. Remove the clutch inner cover.

7. Inspect the front seal (**Figure 14**) and replace it if damaged. Install a new front seal with the marks facing toward the engine.

8. Inspect the inner cover (**Figure 15**) and inlet air ducts for wear, cracks or damage. Replace if necessary.

9. If removed, install the inlet air duct and tighten the clamp screws securely.

10. Make sure the seal (**Figure 16**) is in place on the transmission input shaft.

11. Install the inner cover onto the engine and guide the seal onto the crankcase flange (**Figure 17**). Ensure that the seal is seated around the entire perimeter (**Figure 18**) of the flange.

12. Install the three rear screws and washers (**Figure 12**) and tighten securely.

13. Install the front lower bolt (**Figure 11**). Tighten the bolt securely.

14. Make sure the inner cover seal (**Figure 19**) is in place around the entire perimeter.

15. Install the drive and driven pulleys as described in Chapter Eight.

16. Install the clutch outer cover as previously described.

17. Install the front and rear fenders as described in Chapter Fifteen.

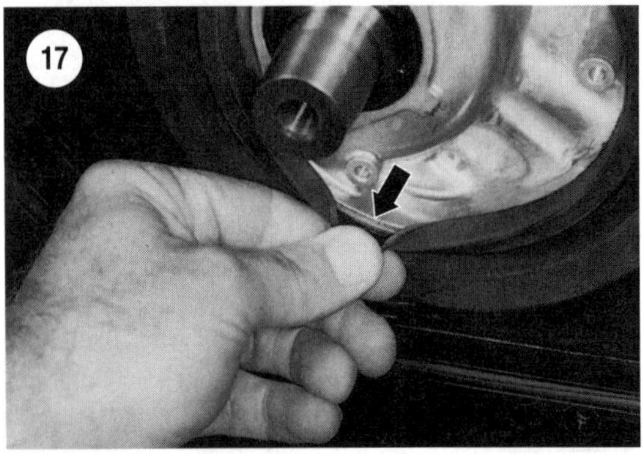

ENGINE COOLING SYSTEM

This section describes service to the engine liquid cooling system. Normal maintenance procedures are described in Chapter Three. Service to the engine gaskets, seals and coolant pump is described in Chapter Five.

A mixture of ethylene glycol antifreeze and distilled water circulated by the water pump maintains engine temperature. The coolant flows within the cooling passages inside the cylinder block, cylinder head and radiator as shown in **Figure 20**. The coolant pump is mounted on the right side of the engine crankcase. A thermostat is located in the cylinder head, under the outlet housing.

During normal engine operation, the coolant heats and expands. The radiator cap controls pressure caused by this expansion and excess pressure is released into the coolant reservoir. As the engine cools, the pressure decreases and coolant is drawn from the coolant reservoir back into the engine's cooling system. The radiator cap controls the amount of pressure maintained in the system, while it is warm.

SAFETY PRECAUTIONS

Keep certain safety precautions in mind to protect against injury and damage to the engine. For safety reasons, the cooling system must be cool before removing any part of the system, including the radiator cap.

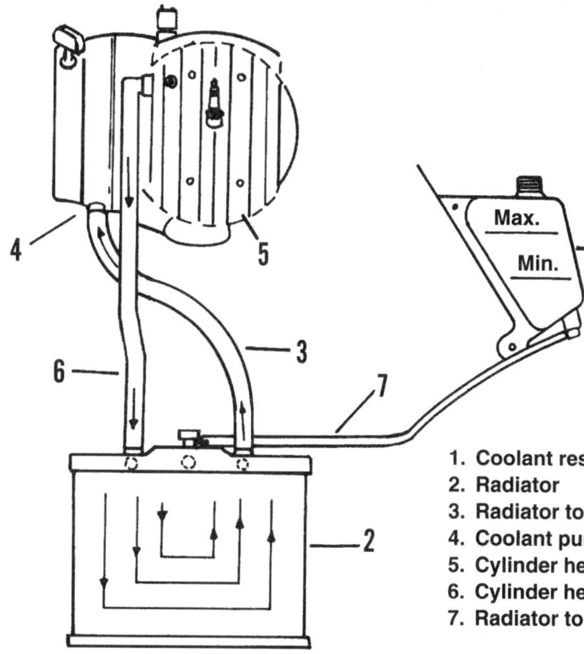

1. Coolant reservoir
2. Radiator
3. Radiator to coolant pump hose
4. Coolant pump
5. Cylinder head
6. Cylinder head to radiator hose
7. Radiator to coolant reservoir hose

21

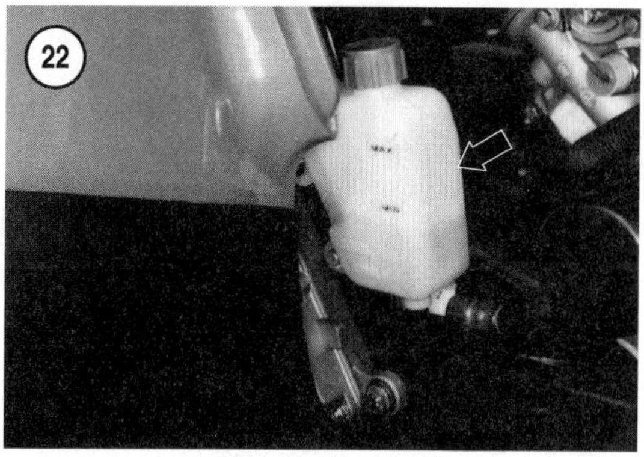
22

WARNING
*Do not remove the radiator cap (**Figure 21**, typical) when the engine is hot. The coolant is very hot and is under pressure. Severe scalding could result if the coolant comes in contact with exposed skin and clothing.*

To protect the engine cooling system, keep the system filled with the correct mixture of ethylene glycol antifreeze—formulated for use in aluminum engines—and distilled, or purified, water.

Maintain the coolant at the proper level as described in Chapter Three. The radiator must be full and the coolant level should always be between the minimum and maximum marks on the coolant reservoir (**Figure 22**). The system contains only a small amount of coolant and it is very important that it remains filled with the proper solution.

CAUTION
Drain and flush the cooling system at least every two years. Refill with a mixture of ethylene glycol antifreeze (formulated for aluminum engines) and purified water. Do not reuse the

old coolant, as it deteriorates with use. ***Do not*** *operate the cooling system with only purified water (even in climates where antifreeze protection is not required). This is important because the engine is all aluminum; it will not rust, but it will oxidize internally and have to be replaced. Refer to* ***Coolant Inspection and Change*** *in Chapter Three.*

WARNING
Antifreeze is a toxic waste material. Drain it into a suitable container and dispose of it according to local toxic waste regulations. Do not store coolant where it is accessible to children or pets.

HOSES AND HOSE CLAMPS

Hoses deteriorate with age and should be replaced periodically or whenever they show signs of cracking or leakage. Hot coolant from a cracked hose can injure the rider. Loss of coolant can also cause the engine to overheat, resulting in damage.

Whenever any component of the cooling system is removed, inspect the adjoining hose(s) and determine if replacement is necessary.

The small diameter coolant hoses are very stiff and are sometimes difficult to install onto the fittings of the various cooling system parts. Prior to installing the hoses, soak the ends in hot water to make them pliable and they will slide on much easier. Do not apply any type of lubricant to the inner surfaces of the hoses, as the hose may slip off even with the hose clamp in place.

Always use the screw adjusting type hose clamps. This type of clamp is superior in its holding ability and is easily released with a screwdriver.

1. Be sure the cooling system is cool before removing any coolant hose.
2. Always replace the hoses with Polaris replacement hoses since they are formed to a specific shape and of the correct length and inner diameter in order to fit correctly onto all components. This is necessary to help eliminate coolant leakage.
3. Loosen the hose clamps on the hose that is to be replaced. Slide the clamps from the component fittings.

CAUTION
Do not twist too hard, or the fittings may be damaged.

4. Twist the hose to release it from the fitting. If the hose is difficult to break loose, carefully insert a small screwdriver or pick tool between the fitting and hose. Carefully pry the hose from the fitting.
5. Examine the fittings for cracks or other damage. Repair or replace as necessary. If the fitting is in good condition, use a wire brush to clean off any hose residue that may have been transferred to the fitting. Wipe clean with a cloth.
6. Inspect the hose clamps; replace if necessary. The hose clamps are as important as the hoses. If they do not hold the hose in place tightly, there will be a coolant leak. For best results, always use the screw adjusting type hose clamps.
7. With the hose installed correctly on the each fitting, position the hose clamp back away from the end of the hose approximately 0.5 in. (12.7 mm). Make sure the hose clamps are still positioned over the fitting and tighten the clamps securely, but not too tight that the hose will be damaged.

ENGINE GASKETS/SEALS

A leaking gasket between the cylinder head and the cylinder block usually will allow coolant to leak into the cylinder. If a sufficient amount of coolant enters the cylinder, it will be difficult to crank the engine with the starter. White smoke (steam) may be observed at the muffler when the engine is running. Coolant in the cylinder may prevent the engine from starting or make starting difficult. Refer to Chapter Four and remove the cylinder head and install a new gasket.

A gasket is located between the coolant pump cover and pump body. Refer to *Coolant Pump* in this chapter and install a new gasket.

Coolant may leak into the crankcase. This mixture of coolant and oil can quickly cause serious damage. It is important to immediately disassemble and clean the engine, then install new seals to correct the leakage. Refer to Chapter Five to disassemble the engine and install new seals.

(23) RADIATOR ASSEMBLY (1996-1999 MODELS)

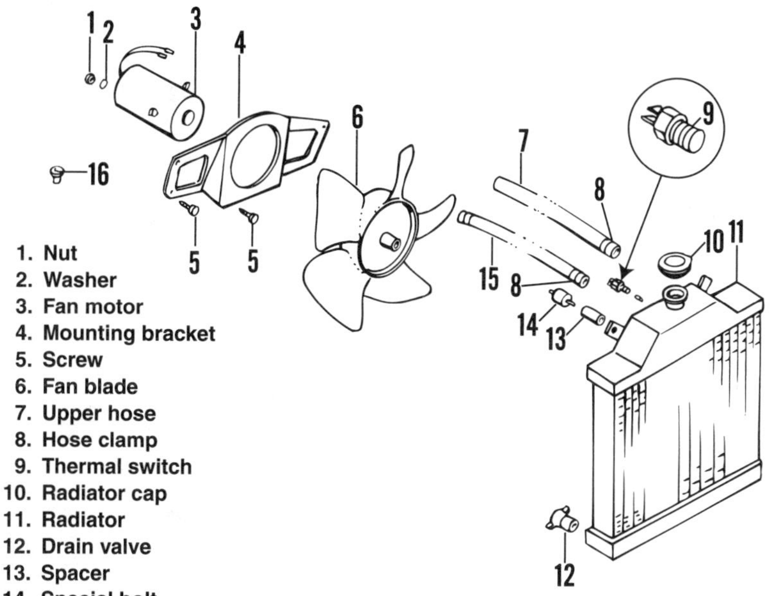

1. Nut
2. Washer
3. Fan motor
4. Mounting bracket
5. Screw
6. Fan blade
7. Upper hose
8. Hose clamp
9. Thermal switch
10. Radiator cap
11. Radiator
12. Drain valve
13. Spacer
14. Special bolt
15. Lower hose

COOLING SYSTEM INSPECTION

The cooling system is equipped with a coolant reservoir (**Figure 22**) and the coolant level can be checked without removing the radiator cap. Coolant is usually added to the coolant reservoir. If the cooling system requires frequent refilling, there is a leak in the system.

If the engine overheats, allow the engine to cool completely, then remove the radiator cap (**Figure 21**, typical) and check the fluid level in the radiator. The radiator should always be completely full. If the level of fluid in the radiator is low, refer to Chapter Three for filling and bleeding air from the system.

To pressure check the cooling system, refer to *Coolant Inspection* in Chapter Three.

RADIATOR

Removal/Installation (1996-1999 Models)

Refer to **Figure 23**.

1. Remove the front fender as described in Chapter Fifteen.
2. Remove the front skid plate, bumper and radiator shield as described in Chapter Fifteen.
3. Drain the cooling system as described in Chapter Three.
4. Disconnect the negative battery lead as described in Chapter Three.
5. Disconnect the electrical connector (A, **Figure 24**) from the temperature sensor switch on the top the radiator.

NOTE
Even though the cooling system has been drained, there will be some residual coolant remaining in the radiator and hoses. Place a drain pan under each hose as it is removed. Also have shop rag on hand to wipe up any spilled coolant.

6. Loosen the screws on both hose clamps (B, **Figure 24**) of both upper hoses. Move the clamps back onto the hoses and off of the radiator fittings.
7. Remove the bolts (**Figure 25**) securing the radiator to the frame. Account for the spacer (C, **Figure**

24) on each bolt between the back of the radiator and the frame.

8. Lift the radiator up and out of the two lower locating pin receptacles (**Figure 26**). Remove the radiator from the frame.
9. Inspect the radiator as described in this chapter.
10. Install by reversing these removal steps while noting the following:
   a. Replace all radiator hoses if they are starting to deteriorate or are damaged in any way as described in this chapter.
   b. Make sure the cooling fan and temperature sensor switch electrical connections are free of corrosion and are tight.
   c. Refill the cooling system with the recommended type and quantity of coolant as described in Chapter Three.

Removal/Installation (2000-On Models)

Refer to **Figure 27**.

1. Remove the front fender as described in Chapter Fifteen.
2. Remove the front skid plate, bumper and radiator shield as described in Chapter Fifteen.
3. Drain the cooling system as described in Chapter Three.
4. Disconnect the battery negative lead as described in Chapter Three.
5. Disconnect the electrical connector from the temperature sensor (A, **Figure 28**) and cooling fan (B, **Figure 28**) at the top the radiator.

NOTE

Even though the cooling system has been drained, there will some residual coolant remaining in the radiator and hoses. Place a drain pan under each hose as it is removed. Also have shop rags handy to wipe up any spilled coolant.

6. Loosen the screws on the hose clamps of both upper (A, **Figure 29**) and lower (B, **Figure 29**) hoses. Move the clamps back onto the hoses and off of the radiator fittings.
7. Remove the bolts (A, **Figure 30**) securing the radiator to the frame. Do not lose the spacer and collar (B, **Figure 30**) on each bolt between the back of the radiator and the frame.

8. Remove the bolts and self-locking nuts securing the frame extension (**Figure 31**) on each side. Move the extensions out of the way leaving the electrical harnesses (C, **Figure 30**) attached to them.
9. Lift the radiator up and out of the two lower locating pin receptacles located on the lower mounting bracket (**Figure 32**). Remove the radiator and cooling fan assembly from the frame.
10. Inspect the radiator as described in this chapter.
11. To remove the radiator filler neck fitting, perform the following:

(27)

RADIATOR ASSEMBLY (2000-ON)

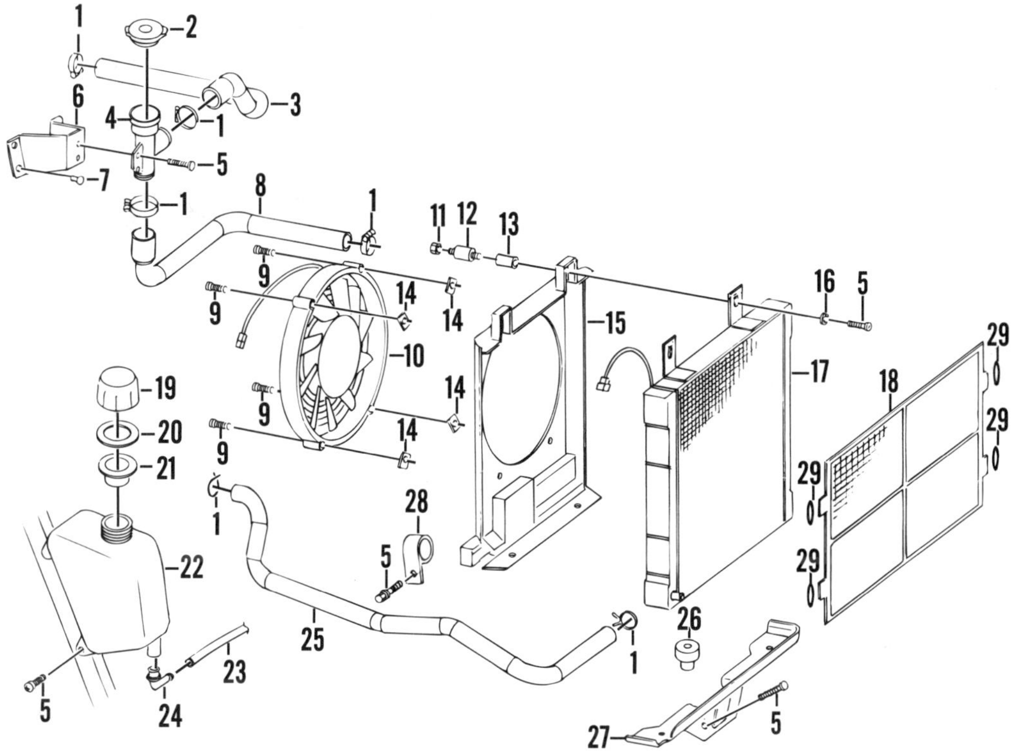

1. Hose clamp
2. Radiator cap
3. Engine hose
4. Filler neck
5. Screw
6. Mounting bracket
7. Screw
8. Upper hose
9. Screw
10. Fan assembly
11. Nut, self-locking
12. Rubber mount
13. Spacer
14. Special nut
15. Fan shroud
16. Washer
17. Radiator
18. Cover
19. Fill cap
20. Gasket
21. Cap plug
22. Reservoir
23. Hose
24. Elbow fitting
25. Lower hose
26. Rubber mount
27. Lower mounting bracket
28. Clamp
29. O-ring

a. Remove the bolts (A, **Figure 33**) securing the filler neck fitting to the mounting bracket.
b. Loosen the hose clamp and move the engine hose (B, **Figure 33**) off the fitting.
c. Pull the filler neck part way up to access the upper hose (C, **Figure 33**) and loosen the hose clamp. Move the upper hose off the fitting and remove the fitting.

12. Install by reversing these removal steps while noting the following:

a. Replace any radiator hose that is starting to deteriorate or is damaged in any way.
b. Make sure the cooling fan and temperature sensor switch electrical connections are free from corrosion and secure.
c. Refill the cooling system with the recommended type and quantity of coolant as described in Chapter Three.
d. Install new self-locking nuts onto the frame extension bolts and tighten securely.

Radiator Inspection (All Models)

1. If compressed air is available, use short spurts of air directed to the *backside* of the radiator core and blow out dirt and bugs.
2. Flush off the exterior of the radiator with a garden hose on low pressure. Spray both the front and the back to remove all debris. Carefully use a whisk broom or stiff paint brush to remove any stubborn dirt from the cooling fins.

CAUTION
Do not press too hard, or the cooling fins and tubes may be damaged and cause a leak.

3. Carefully straighten out any bent cooling fins with a broad-tipped screwdriver or putty knife.
4. Check for cracks or leakage (usually a moss green-colored residue) at both hose fittings and both side tank seams.
5. To prevent oxidation of the radiator, touch up any areas where the black paint is worn off. Use a good quality spray paint and apply several *light* coats of paint. Do not apply heavy coats, as this will cut down on the cooling efficiency of the radiator.
6. Check the tightness and for any sign of leakage at the temperature sensor switch; tighten if necessary.

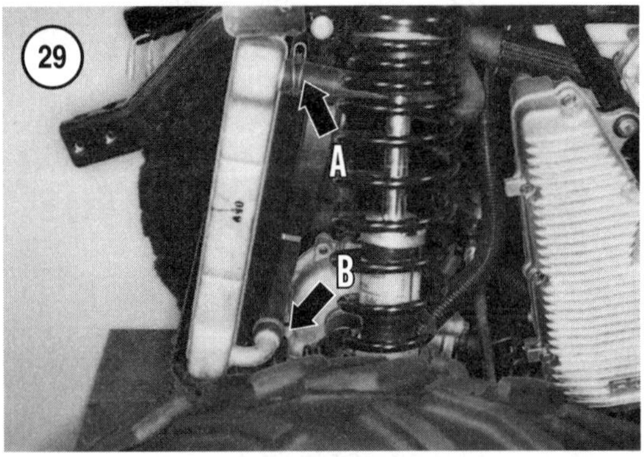

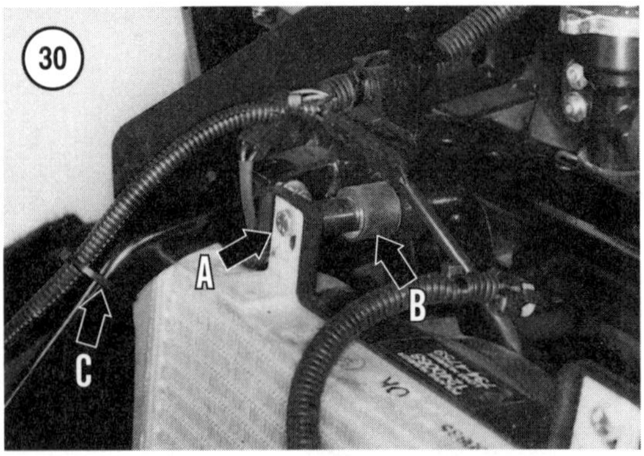

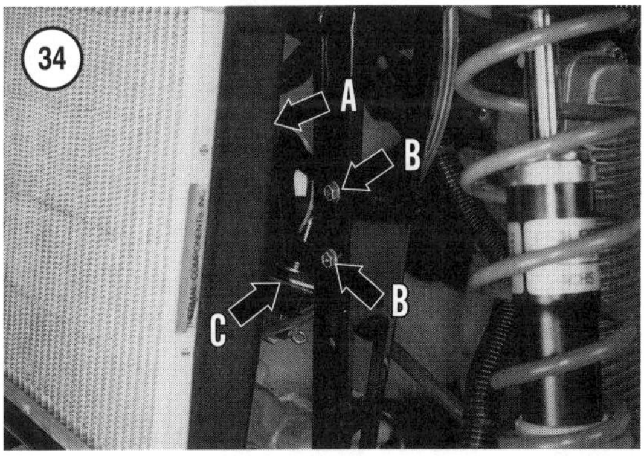

COOLING FAN

Removal/Installation (1996-1999 Models)

1. Remove the radiator (A, **Figure 34**) as described in this chapter.
2. Disconnect the electrical connector from the cooling fan.
3. Remove the two bolts (B, **Figure 34**) on each side securing the cooling fan bracket (C, **Figure 34**) to the frame.
4. Remove the cooling fan and bracket from the frame.
5. If necessary, remove the three screws, washers and nuts and separate the cooling fan motor from the bracket.
6. Install by reversing these removal steps.

Removal/Installation (2000-On Models)

1. Remove the radiator assembly as described in this chapter.
2. Disconnect the electrical connector from the temperature sensor (A, **Figure 28**) and cooling fan (B, **Figure 28**) at the top the radiator.
3. Remove the four screws securing the cooling fan assembly to the backside of the radiator.
4. Remove the cooling fan assembly from the radiator shroud.
5. Install by reversing these removal steps.

7

COOLANT PUMP

The engine must be removed from the frame and the crankcase must be separated to service the coolant pump shaft and seals. However, the outer cover and impeller can be removed for inspection without removing the engine.

Remove the oil pump as described in Chapter Four to service the shaft oil seal and the coolant pump mechanical seal. The coolant pump shaft is an extension of the oil pump drive shaft.

Removal/Installation

1. Drain the cooling system as described in Chapter Three.
2. Remove the front fender as described in Chapter Fifteen.
3. Place a drain pan under the coolant hose connections at the coolant pump. Some residual coolant may drain out.
4. Loosen the clamp on the upper coolant hose (A, **Figure 35**), detach the hose from the coolant pump outlet fitting.
5. Loosen both clamps and remove the coolant pump lower inlet hose (B, **Figure 35**) from the fitting.

NOTE
The remainder of the photographs are shown with the engine removed from the frame to better illustrate the steps.

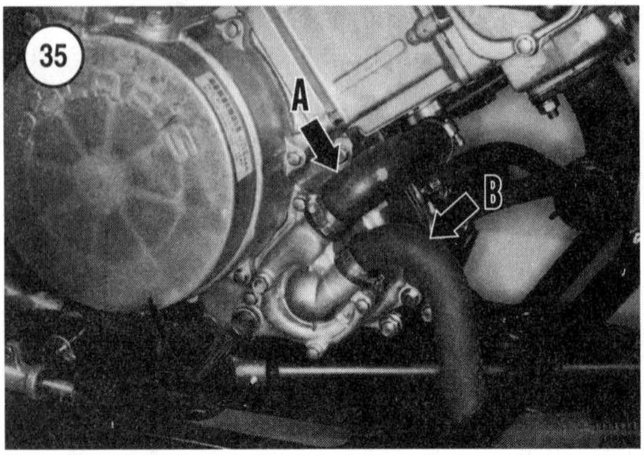

6. Remove the four bolts (**Figure 36**) securing the coolant pump cover.
7. Use a rubber mallet and tap the cover to loosen the gasket, then remove the cover.
8. Remove the nut (**Figure 37**) securing the impeller.
9. Remove the washer (A, **Figure 38**) from the shaft, then withdraw the impeller (B, **Figure 38**) from the shaft.
10. Remove the sealing washer (**Figure 39**) from the shaft.
11. If the mechanical seal (**Figure 40**) is leaking, remove the engine, separate the engine crankcase and replace the mechanical seal as described in Chapter Five.
12. Clean all parts in solvent and thoroughly dry.
13. Inspect the impeller (**Figure 41**) for damage; replace if necessary.
14. Clean all old gasket material from the back of the coolant pump cover (**Figure 42**) and the crankcase mating surface.
15. Install the sealing washer (**Figure 43**) onto the shaft and push it on until it bottoms.
16. Install the impeller (B, **Figure 38**) and washer (A, **Figure 38**).
17. Install a *new* self-locking nut (**Figure 37**) and tighten securely.
18. Install a new gasket and the cover. Tighten the four bolts (**Figure 36**) securely in a crisscross pattern.
19. Install the upper coolant hose (A, **Figure 35**) and the lower inlet hose (B, **Figure 35**) onto the cover fittings. Tighten the clamp screws securely.
20. Fill the cooling system with the correct mixture of antifreeze and purified water as described in Chapter Three.

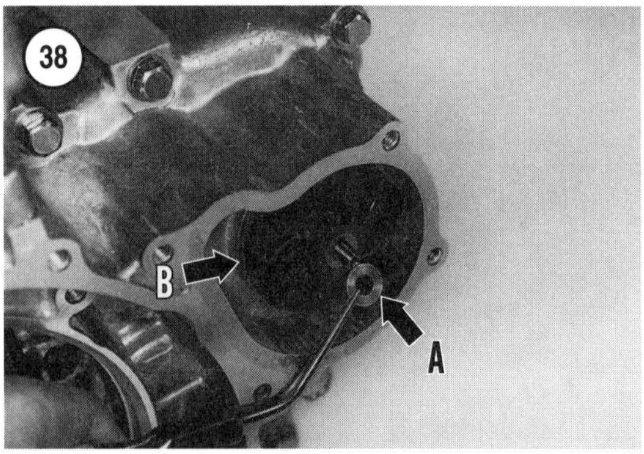

40

41

42

43

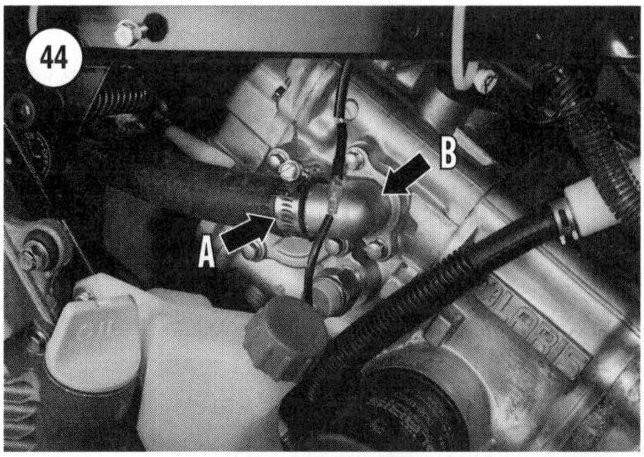

44

45

THERMOSTAT

Removal/Installation

The thermostat is located in the cylinder head under the coolant outlet housing.

1. Drain the cooling system as described in Chapter Three.
2. Place a shop cloth under the coolant hose connection at the thermostat cover. Some residual coolant may drain out.
3. Loosen the clamp on the coolant hose (A, **Figure 44**), detach the hose from the thermostat fitting.

NOTE

The following photographs are shown with the engine removed from the frame to better illustrate the steps.

4. Remove the two bolts securing the thermostat cover (B, **Figure 44**).
5. Use a rubber mallet and tap the cover to loosen the gasket, then remove the cover.
6. Withdraw the thermostat (A, **Figure 45**) from the cavity in the cylinder head.

7. Clean the surfaces of the cylinder head and the outlet housing.

8. Use a new seal and install the thermostat. The air bleed hole must be toward the top screw hole (B, **Figure 45**).

9. Apply a light coat of sealant to the thermostat cover and install the cover (B, **Figure 44**). Install the two bolts and tighten securely.

10. Install the coolant hose (A, **Figure 44**) onto the fitting and tighten the clamp securely.

NOTE

It is important to bleed all air from the cooling system when filling a system that was drained. The capacity of the cooling system is small, and air pockets will quickly result in overheating.

11. Fill and bleed the cooling system as described under *Coolant Change* in Chapter Three.

46

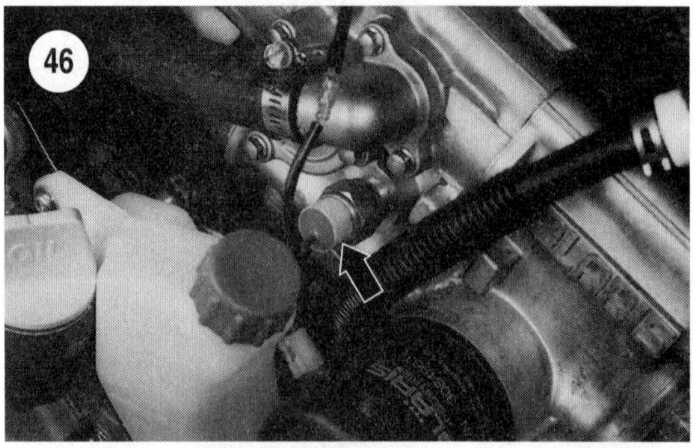

47

TEMPERATURE SENSORS

The liquid cooling system is equipped with two temperature sensors. The sensor located on the engine (**Figure 46**) controls the HOT indicator light. The other sensor, located on the top of the radiator (**Figure 47**), controls the operation of the electric cooling fan. Refer to **Table 1** for the on/off temperature specifications of these switches.

Table 1 COOLING SYSTEM SPECIFICATIONS

Item	Specification
Cooling fan	
1996	
Comes ON	85° C (185° F)
Goes OFF	74° C (165° F)
1997	
Comes ON	85° C (185° F)
Goes OFF	69° C (157° F)
1998-on	
Comes ON	85° C (185° F)
Goes OFF	74° C (165° F)
Temperature sensor	
Hot light comes ON	105° C (221° F)
System capacity	Approx. 2.16 L (2.25 U.S. qts.)
Radiator cap relief pressure	90 kPa (13 psi)

NOTE: Refer to the Supplement at the back of this manual for information unique to 2001-on models, including the Sportsman 400.

CHAPTER EIGHT

CLUTCH/DRIVE BELT SYSTEM

This chapter describes service procedures for the clutch and drive belt system. **Tables 1-5** at the end of the chapter list the drive system specifications.

The drive train includes the clutch/drive belt system, a transmission assembly and independent suspended rear shaft drive axles. The clutch/drive belt system is also called the Polaris Variable Transmission or PVT. The clutch/drive belt system consists of a drive pulley mounted on the left end of the engine crankshaft, a driven pulley mounted on the left end of the transmission input shaft and a belt connecting the two pulleys.

DRIVE UNIT

Torque is transferred from the engine crankshaft to the transmission by the Polaris Variable Transmission (PVT). The drive unit automatically changes the drive ratio to permit the machine to move from idle to maximum speed. Major components including the drive pulley assembly, driven pulley assembly and drive belt are shown in **Figure 1**.

The drive and driven pulleys function as two variable diameter pulleys that automatically vary the amount of reduction. Changes in the reduction ratio are achieved by moving the sides of the pulleys closer together or further apart. Changing the gap between the sides of the pulley causes the belt to move up or down in the pulley groove, changing the effective diameter of the pulley. These changes in pulley diameter adjust to correspond with the prevailing load and speed conditions as shown in **Figure 2**.

The shift sequence is determined by a combination of engine torque and engine speed. When the

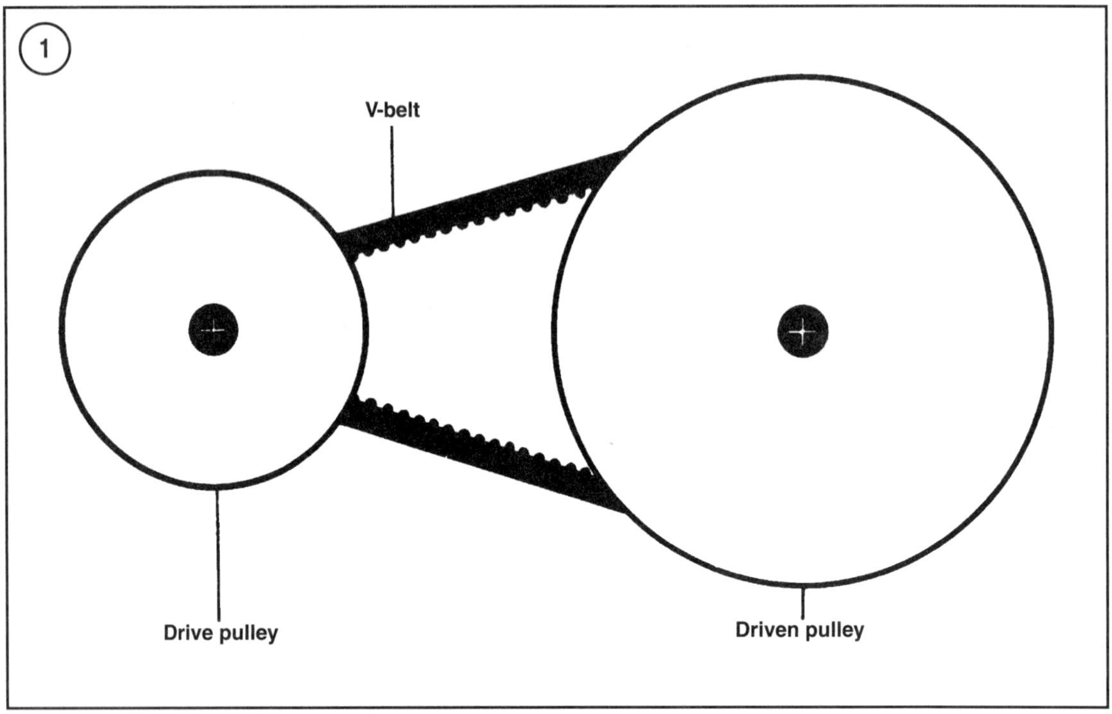

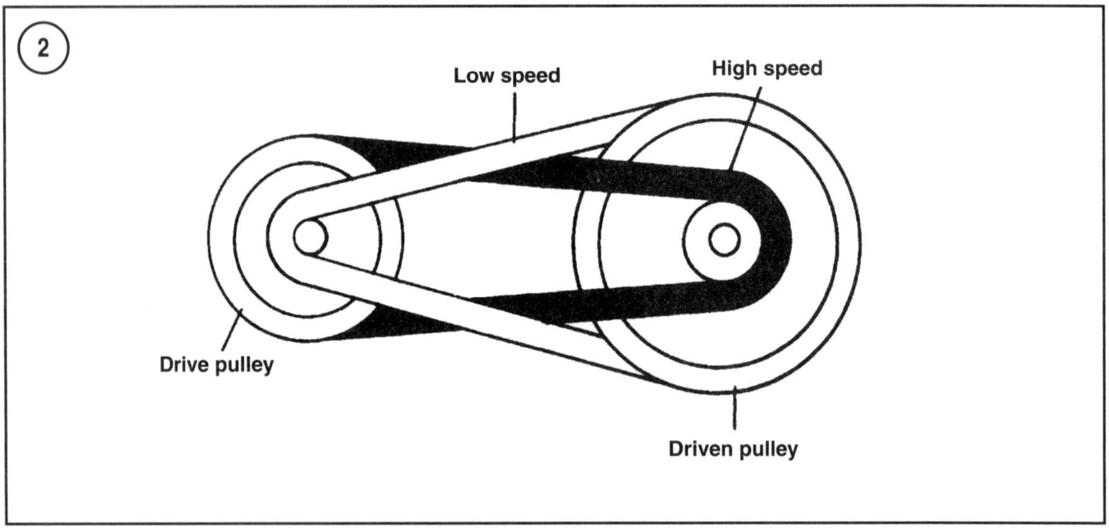

load resistance increases, such as when going uphill, the pulleys change the reduction ratio; engine speed will remain nearly the same, but the vehicle's speed will drop. When the load decreases, the pulleys automatically shift toward a higher ratio; engine speed remains the same but the vehicle's speed will increase.

The Engine Braking System (EBS) was incorporated into the clutch drive unit on all models produced since 1999. This system has a unique feature that allows engine braking to occur when the vehicle is coasting or going downhill. Engine braking occurs when the forward rotational speed of the one-way clutch within the drive clutch assembly exceeds the speed of the engine and the drive clutch. At this point the one-way clutch locks to the drive clutch shaft and becomes the driving clutch. Engine braking will continue until the drive clutch speed exceeds one-way clutch speed, or until the throttle is applied and engine speed reaches clutch engage-

3

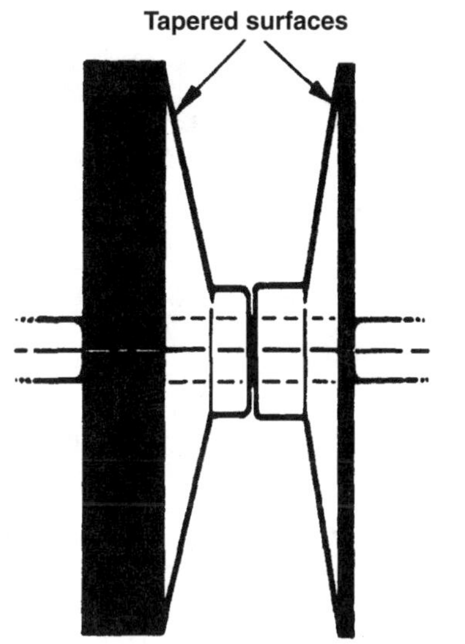

ment speed. When the engine is at idle speed and the vehicle is stopped, the one-way clutch freewheels on the drive clutch shaft.

DRIVE PULLEY

Fixed and Sliding Pulley Halves

The sides of the pulley are made of mild steel and the belt contact surfaces are precision machined to a smooth taper. The pulley is carefully balanced to prevent vibration. The tapered surfaces of both pulleys match the V-belt gripping surface (**Figure 3**).

The drive pulley assembly is mounted on the left end of the engine crankshaft. When the engine is at idle or stopped, the fixed and sliding halves of the pulley are held apart by the primary spring. At idle speed or when the engine is stopped, the groove should be wide enough for the V-belt to drop down between the sides of the pulley with no engagement. There is no engagement because the width of the belt is less than the space between the sides of the drive pulley.

When the engine speed is increased from idle, centrifugal force causes the weight levers mounted on the sliding half of the drive pulley to swing out. When the centrifugal force of the weights is sufficient to overcome the pressure of the primary spring, the sliding half of the pulley is moved closer to the fixed half. This movement narrows the groove between the pulley halves until the sides of the pulley grip the belt. The point at which the pulley grips the belt is called the engagement rpm. Engagement rpm will occur at approximately 1500 engine rpm. At low speed, the belt will be located at the low-speed position as shown in **Figure 2**.

As engine speed increases, centrifugal force causes the weights of the drive pulley to swing further out and force the sliding half of the pulley closer to the fixed half. As the groove of the drive pulley becomes narrower, the V-belt is forced upward in the groove toward the outer edge of the pulley. The V-belt is forced deeper into the groove of the driven pulley as indicated by the high-speed position of the belt in **Figure 2**.

Though not part of the drive pulley, it should be noted that the release (secondary) spring of the driven pulley forces the sides of the pulley together. Pressure against the sides of the driven pulley will force the sliding half away from the fixed side. Movement of the weight levers in the drive pulley will force the pulley halves together and the belt will move to the outer diameter of the drive pulley. At the same time the belt will force the sides of the driven pulley apart so that it can operate deeper in the groove.

Drive Pulley Spring

The drive pulley clutch release spring controls engagement speed. If a lighter spring is installed, or the weights are too heavy, the drive will up-shift too fast and the engine will not be able to reach its operating range of 6000 rpm. If a heavier spring is installed, the engine speed must be higher to overcome spring pressure and allow engagement. If the spring is too stiff or the weights too heavy, the drive will not be able to move high enough in the pulley groove to attain high gear. Refer to **Table 2** for the original spring installed on the specific model and year being worked on. **Table 3** lists specifications for identifying the different springs. Actual performance depends upon a combination of characteristics, but generally, the springs are listed in **Table 3** from the strongest at the top to the weakest at the bottom of the table.

8

Centrifugal Weight Levers

Weighted levers in the drive pulley react to engine speed and swing out. The weights attached to the movable sheave press against rollers on the spider to move the sliding half of the drive pulley. Centrifugal force causes the weights to swing out as the speed of the engine increases. Movement of the weighted levers and the sliding half of the pulley is opposed by the pressure of the primary spring. Until engine speed reaches the engagement rpm, the weights have not yet moved the sliding half of the pulley enough to engage the belt. The force exerted by the weighted levers is controlled by engine rpm. The faster the crankshaft rotates, the farther the weights pivot out. Movement of the sliding half of the drive pulley is controlled by the balance of the spring pressure along with the weight of the weighted levers. Refer to **Table 4** for the original weights installed in the specific model and year being worked on. Performance may be improved at higher altitudes by installing lighter weights as indicated in the table.

SPECIAL TOOLS

A series of special tools are required to adjust and service the drive and driven pulleys. These special tools (**Figure 4**) are manufactured by Victor Specialty Tools and are referred to as VST in the following service procedures. These tools are available from VST or through a Polaris dealership. Do not try to service either pulley assembly without the special tools, as the components will be damaged. If the necessary tools are not available, have the service performed by a Polaris dealership or a repair facility with the proper equipment.

DRIVEN PULLEY

Major components of the driven pulley assembly are the sliding sheave, fixed sheave, release spring and helix cam. Refer to **Figure 5** for 1996-1998 models or **Figure 6** for 1999-on models equipped with EBS. The pulley sheaves are made of mild steel. The belt surfaces are machined to a smooth tapered surface. The tapered surfaces of the pulley halves match the V-belt gripping surface.

The driven pulley assembly is mounted on the left end of the transmission input shaft. When the engine is stopped or at idle, the driven pulley assembly is held in its low speed position by tension from the secondary release spring.

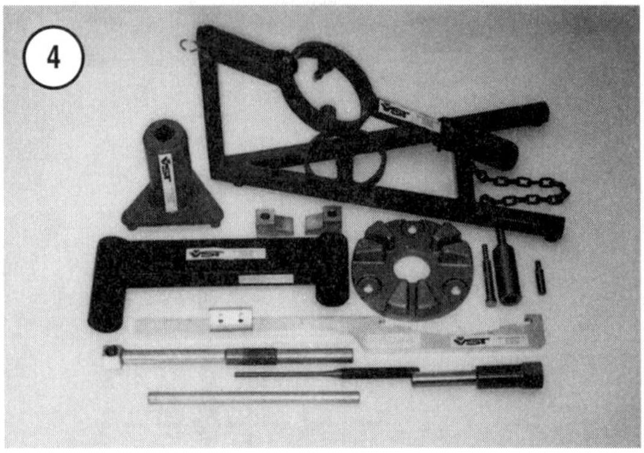

The driven pulley is a torque sensitive unit. If the ATV encounters an increased load condition, the cam helix forces the driven pulley to downshift by moving the driven pulley halves closer together. The speed of the vehicle will slow, but the engine will continue to run at a high rpm. By sensing load conditions and shifting accordingly, the engine can continue to operate in its peak power range.

Release Spring

The release spring located in the driven pulley assembly helps determine the shifting pattern. The spring is also used to keep the torque sensing helix cam in contact with the slider buttons. Spring tension can be changed by installing a different spring or by repositioning the end of the spring in holes drilled in the cam. The torque sensing cam angle will affect the shifting sequence under heavy load more than the release spring tension adjustment. Observe the following:

1. Increasing release spring tension will prevent the belt from moving to a higher speed position until the engine speed is increased. If the drive pulley moves to a faster ratio too soon, engine rpm will drop and the engine will begin to bog down. For peak efficiency, the engine should operate within its optimum peak power range. Increasing spring tension may prevent up-shifting too early. By not shifting up, the engine should continue to operate within its peak power range.
2. Decreasing secondary spring tension allows the belt to move to a higher speed position at a lower engine rpm. The engine will not operate as effi-

5

DRIVEN PULLEY (1996-1998 MODELS)

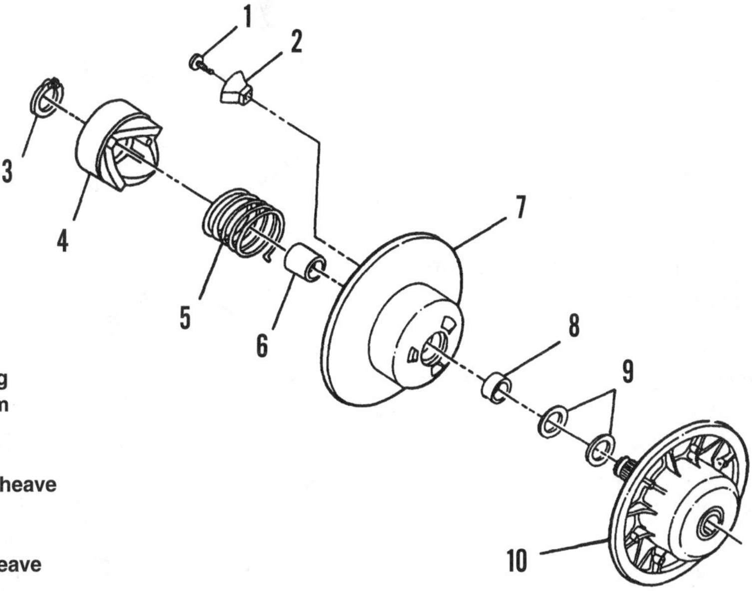

1. Screw
2. Ramp
3. Snap ring
4. Helix cam
5. Spring
6. Bushing
7. Sliding sheave
8. Bushing
9. Spacers
10. Fixed sheave

6

DRIVEN PULLEY (1999-ON MODELS WITH EBS)

1. Bolt
2. Washer
3. Domed washer
4. Circlip
5. Bushing
6. Washer
7. Fixed sheave
8. Bearing
9. Movable sheave
10. Roller
11. Torx screw
12. Washer
13. Bearing
14. Spring
15. Helix
16. Spacer
17. Circlip

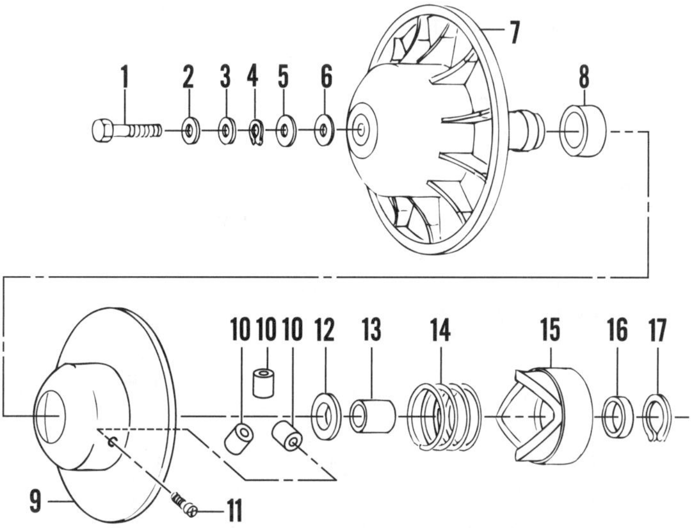

ciently if it is running faster than its peak power range. Decreasing spring tension allows adjustment so that the drive system will shift into a higher ratio sooner to match the engine power.

Torque Sensing Cam Angle

The drive pulley spring tension and the cam angle of the torque sensing helix cam work together to control how easily the driven pulley will shift to a faster speed ratio. Refer to **Table 4** for the original position of the spring ends for the specific model and year being worked on.

The helix cam pushes against the sliding sheave. If the cam angle is steep, the pulleys will shift to a faster speed ratio sooner and will not be as responsive to increases in load. Conversely, low cam angles will exert more side pressure and will slow shifts until the load is reduced and speeds are higher. Refer to **Table 4** for the standard helix angle.

DRIVE BELT

The drive belt transmits power from the drive pulley to the driven pulley. The belt provides a vital link in the operation and performance of the ATV. To ensure top performance, the drive pulley, drive belt and driven pulley must be matched to each other and to the vehicle model. The correct size drive belt must be installed, because belt width and length are critical to proper operation. Belt wear affects clutch operation and shifting characteristics. Since normal wear changes the width of the belt, it is important to check the belt frequently and adjust the 1996-1998 model clutch as described in this chapter. See **Table 1** for new drive belt specifications.

With general use, there is no specific mileage or time limit on belt life. Belt life is directly related to maintenance and the type of operation. The belt should be inspected at the intervals listed in Chapter Three. Early belt failure is abnormal and the cause should be determined to prevent subsequent damage. For proper belt cooling, it is important that all of the covers (**Figure 7**) are installed and all joints sealed as described in Chapter Seven.

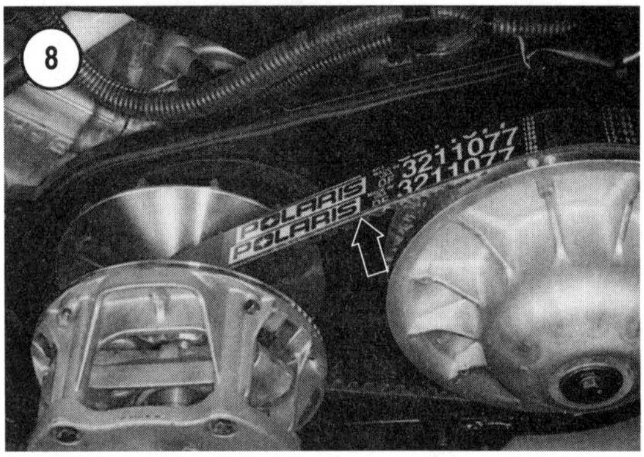

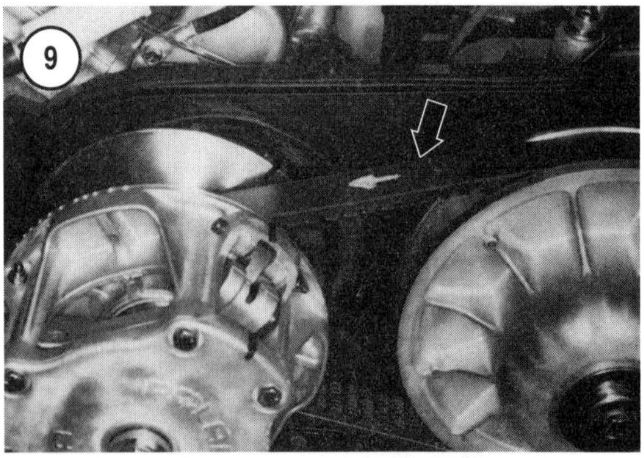

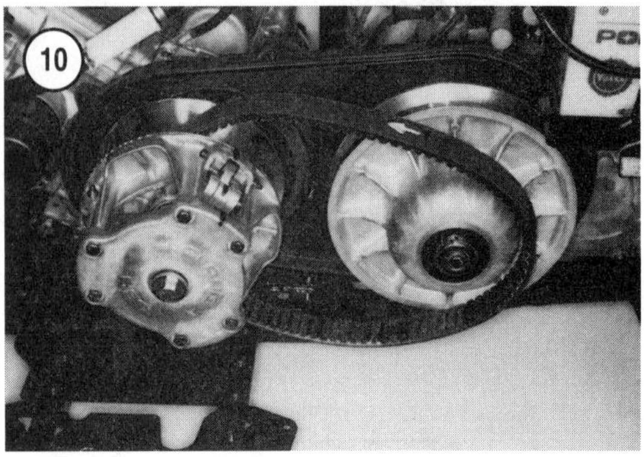

11

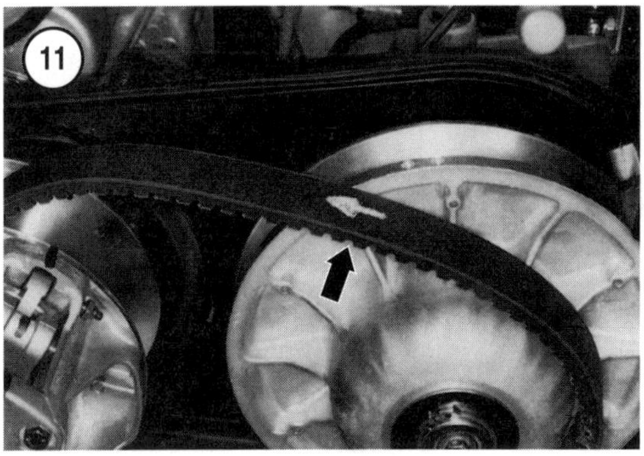

12

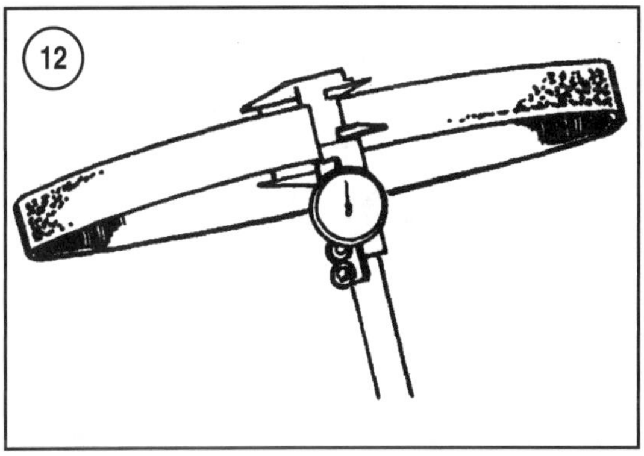

13

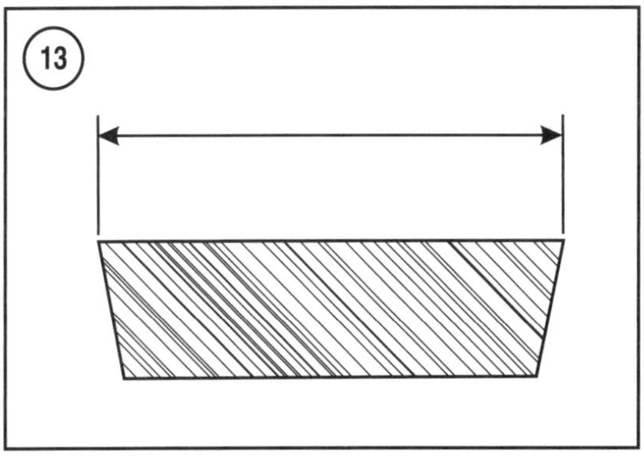

14

Removal/Installation

1. Remove the outer cover as described in Chapter Seven.
2. Check the drive belt for manufacturers markings (**Figure 8**) for reference during installation. If the belt is not marked, place an arrow on the belt facing forward. Reinstall the belt so it runs in the same direction as before removal.
3. Push against the inner sheave of the driven pulley (**Figure 9**) and rotate it clockwise to separate the pulley halves. Then roll the belt out of the pulleys (**Figure 10**).
4. Inspect the drive belt as described in this chapter.
5. Perform the drive belt alignment as described in this chapter.
6. Reverse Steps 1-3 and install the drive belt while noting the following:
   a. If installing the original belt, make sure to install it so that it runs in the same direction as before removal (**Figure 11**).
   b. If installing a new belt, install it so the belt identification marks (**Figure 8**) can be read while standing on the left side of the machine.

Inspection

Inspect the drive belt weekly or every 150 miles (240 km) of operation.

1. Remove the drive belt as described in this chapter.
2. Use a vernier caliper and measure the width (**Figure 12**) of the drive belt at its widest point (**Figure 13**). Replace the belt if the width is less than the wear limit listed in **Table 1**.
3. Visually inspect the belt for the following conditions:
   a. *Frayed edge*—This condition (**Figure 14**) indicates drive belt misalignment. Incorrect pulley alignment and loose engine mounting bolts can cause drive belt misalignment.
   b. *Worn narrow in one section*—This condition (**Figure 15**) is caused by excessive belt slippage probably due to excessive engine idle speed.
   c. *Belt disintegration*—This condition (**Figure 16**) is usually caused by severe belt wear or misalignment. Disintegration can also be caused by the use of an incorrect belt.

8

15

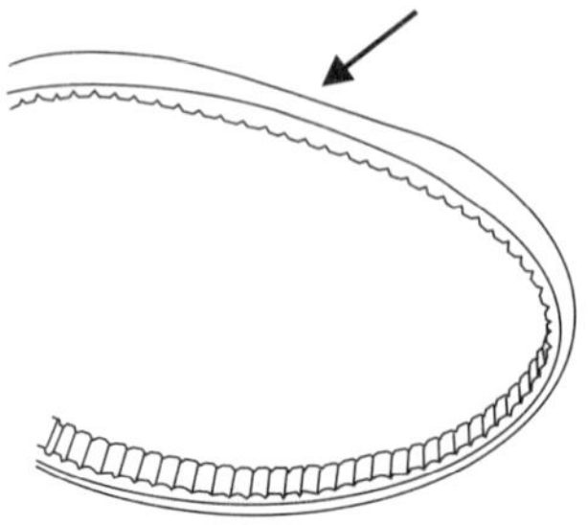

16

d. *Sheared cogs*—This condition (**Figure 17**) is usually caused by violent drive pulley engagement. This is an indication of a defective or improperly installed drive pulley.

4. Replace a worn or damaged belt immediately. It is a good idea to carry a spare belt on the vehicle at all times for an emergency.

17

Drive Belt Deflection (1996-1998 Models)

NOTE
The 1999-on models are equipped with the EBS system and the drive belt is always tight. On these models drive belt deflection is not adjustable.

Perform this procedure whenever a new drive belt is installed.

1. Check the drive belt alignment as described in this chapter.
2. Position a straight edge across the top of the drive belt as shown in **Figure 18**.
3. Compress the drive belt mid-way with a finger to remove belt slack; measure the belt defection from the top of the belt surface to the bottom of the straightedge. Belt deflection should be within the specification in **Table 1**.
4. If deflection is incorrect, disassemble the driven pulley as described in this chapter, then add or remove shims (**Figure 19**) as necessary. Observe the following.
   a. To decrease belt tension, remove shims.
   b. To increase belt tension, add additional shims.

18

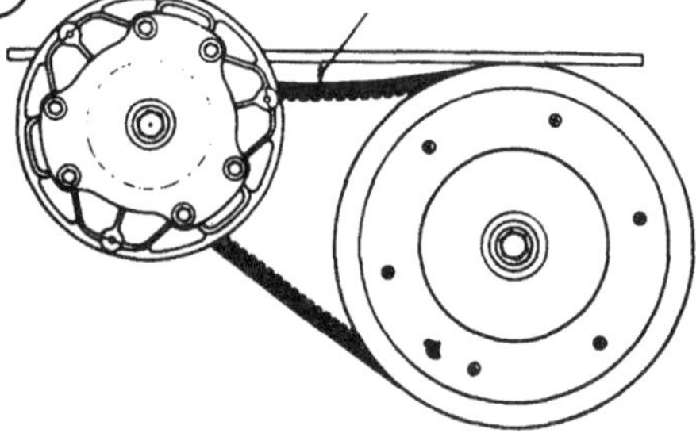

19

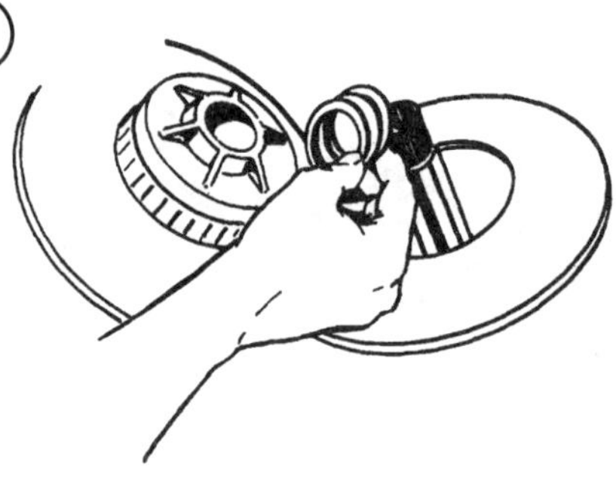

NOTE
*Always leave at least one shim (**Figure 19**) between the inner and outer sheaves of the driven pulley. If the de-*

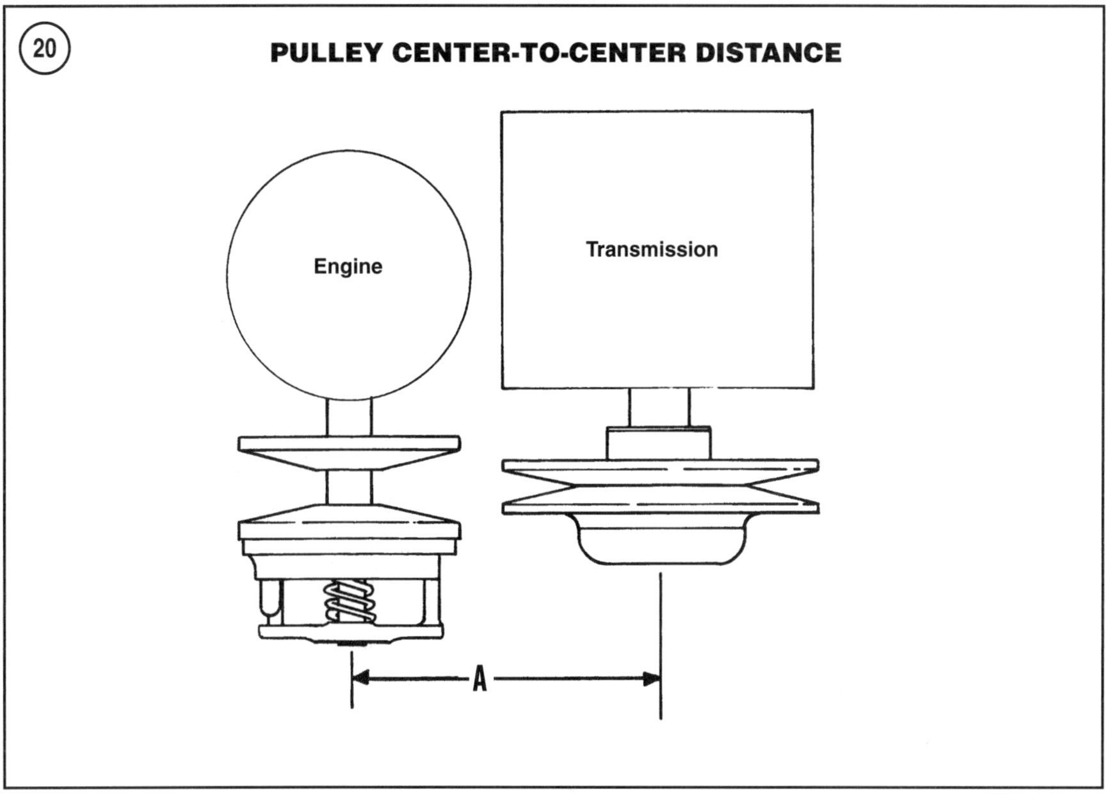

flection cannot be set correctly without removing the last shim, check the pulley center-to-center distance and the belt width.

c. After adjusting belt deflection, rotate the driven pulley to help seat the belt in the pulley grooves. Always recheck belt deflection after making any change.

Drive Belt Alignment (All Models)

The center-to-center distance (A, **Figure 20**) from the drive pulley to the driven pulley, alignment of the pulleys (**Figure 21**) and the offset of the pulleys (**Figure 22**) must be correctly maintained for good performance and long belt life. Refer to **Table 1** for the recommended pulley center-to-center distance.

Correct center-to-center distance ensures correct belt tension and reduction ratio. If the center-to-center distance (A, **Figure 20**) is too short, or the belt is too long, the shift ratio will be too short.

If the centers of the pulleys (A, **Figure 20**) are too far apart, or the belt is too short, the drive belt will be pulled down too deeply in the driven pulley groove too soon. The machine will not pull strongly because the pulleys are shifting too quickly towards the 1:1 ratio.

If the pulleys are not properly aligned (**Figure 21**) or if the pulley offset is incorrect (**Figure 22**), the belt will wear out prematurely.

1. Remove the drive belt as described in this chapter.

2. Measure the distance (A, **Figure 20**) between the pulley centers. If the distance is different from the specification listed in **Table 1**, check the engine and transmission mounting bolts. If loose, tighten the bolts and recheck pulley center-to-center distance.

3A. If a VST offset alignment bar (part No. 2870654) is available, check the pulley offset and alignment as follows:

a. Place the offset alignment bar across the drive and driven pulleys as shown in **Figure 23**.

b. Clutch alignment is correct when the bar fits easily over the drive pulley, contacts the rear edge of the driven pulley and has 3.2 mm (1/8

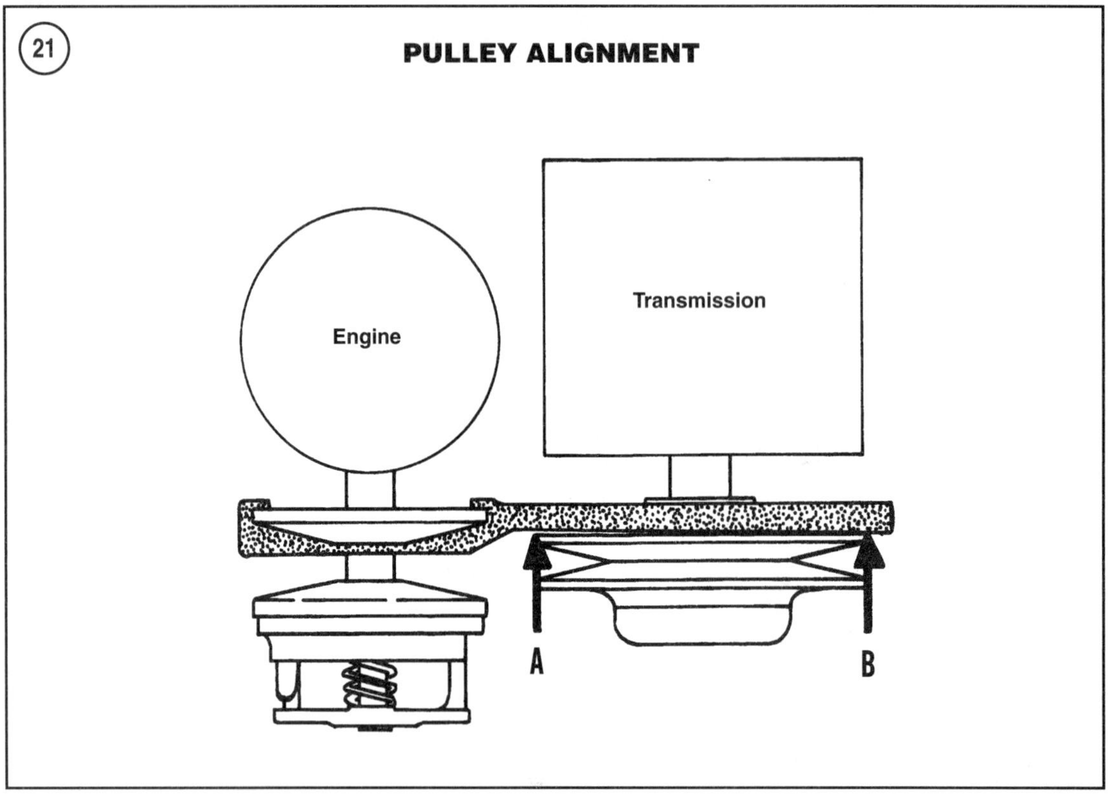
21
PULLEY ALIGNMENT
Engine
Transmission
A
B

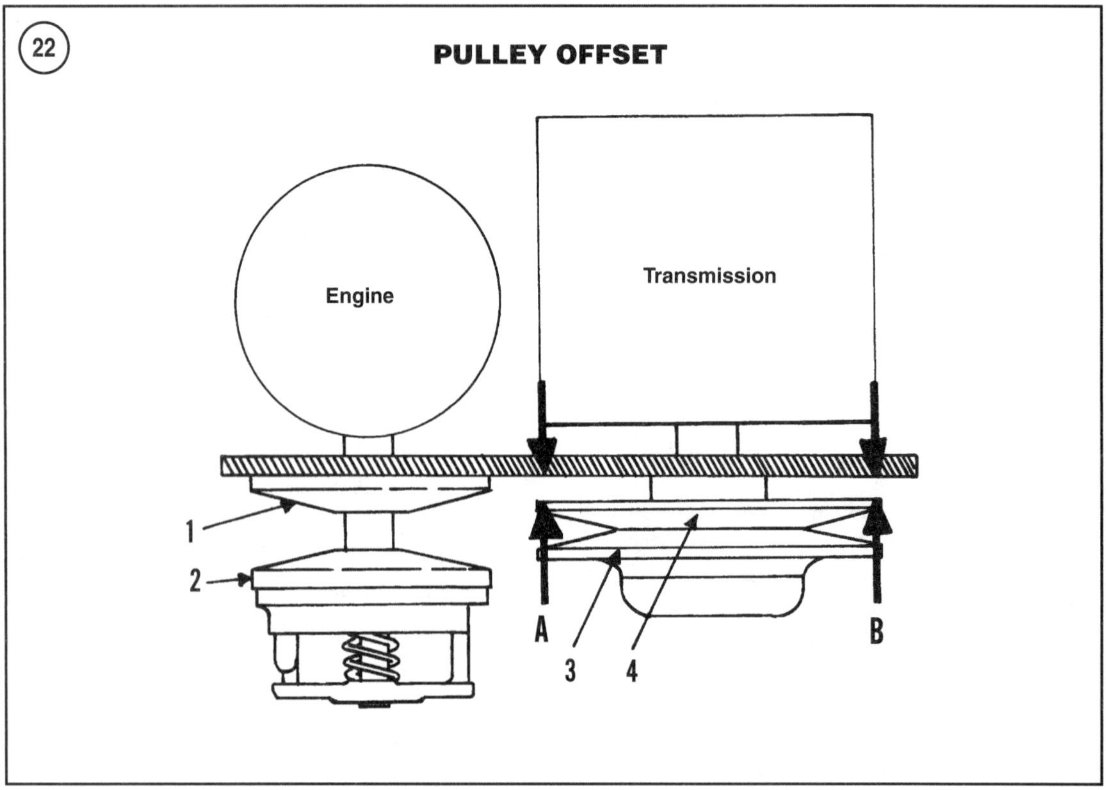
22
PULLEY OFFSET
Engine
Transmission
1
2
A
B
3
4

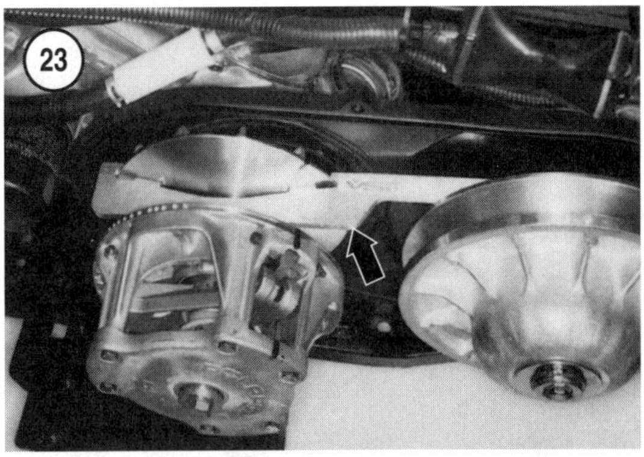

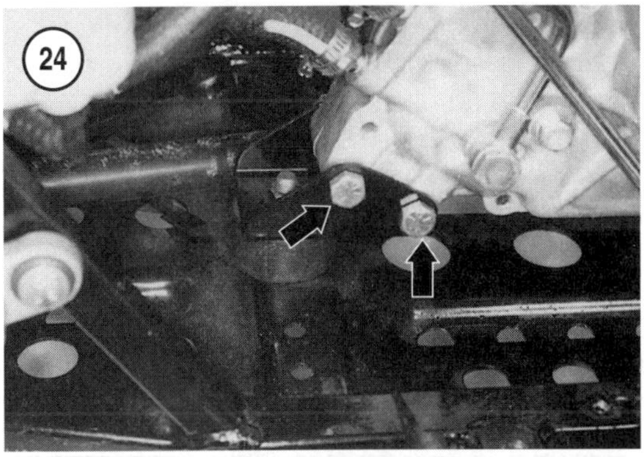

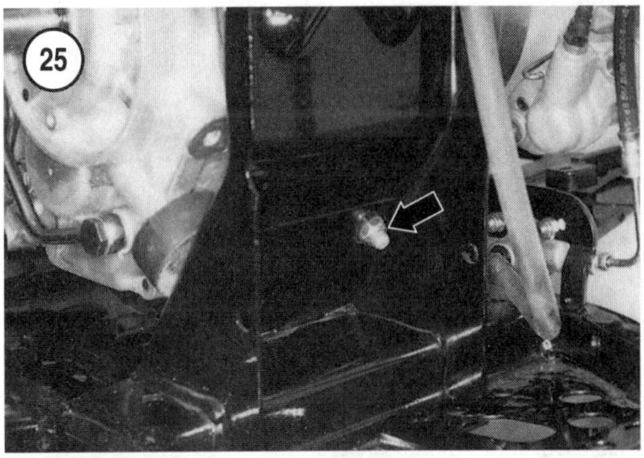

in.) clearance at the front edge of the driven pulley (A, **Figure 21**).

c. If alignment is incorrect, proceed to Step 4.

3B. If the VST alignment bar is not available, check the alignment as follows:

a. Place a straightedge across the drive pulley, making sure that it contacts the rim at both the front and rear of the pulley (**Figure 22**).

b. Measure the distance between the front and rear edges of the driven pulley and the straightedge.

c. The clearance between the front of the pulley (A, **Figure 22**) and the straightedge should be 3.2 mm (1/8 in.) more than at the rear of the pulley (B, **Figure 22**).

d. If alignment is incorrect, proceed to Step 4.

4. *Pulley Alignment*—If alignment is not correct, proceed as follows to change the alignment.

NOTE

*Make small corrections in the adjustment by adding or removing washers between the frame and the front, lower left engine mount. Add a washer to increase clearance at A, **Figure 21** or A, **Figure 22**. Follow the normal adjustment procedure for large corrections. Be sure that the bolts are tight before checking or changing the adjustment.*

a. Remove the drive and driven pulleys as described in this chapter.

b. Remove the inner clutch cover as described in Chapter Seven.

c. Loosen the bolts and self-locking nuts (**Figure 24**) securing the front engine mounts to the bracket.

NOTE

***Figure 25** shows the transmission assembly removed to better illustrate this step. Be sure to remove both self-locking nuts, as only one is shown in the illustration.*

d. Loosen the two self-locking nuts and frame support strap (**Figure 25**) securing the rear engine mount.

e. Loosen the self-locking nut and washer (**Figure 26**) securing the upper right side engine mount. On some models, the ground strap is also attached to this engine mount.

8

f. Adjust the position of the engine as necessary to align the pulleys correctly, then tighten the engine mount bolts.
g. Temporarily install the pulleys, then refer to Step 3A or 3B to recheck alignment before installing the inner cover.
h. Check the pulley offset using the VST offset alignment bar (part No. 2870654) as described in Step 5.

5. *Pulley Offset*—To check pulley offset, place the VST offset/alignment bar (part No. 2870654) across the drive and driven pulleys as shown in **Figure 23**. Offset is correct if the rear of the tool just contacts the rear of the driven pulley inner half (B, **Figure 21** and a 1.6-3.2 mm (1/16 to 1/8 in.) gap is present at the front of the pulley inner half (A, **Figure 21**). To adjust offset, remove the driven pulley assembly, and add or remove shims (**Figure 27**).
6. When the offset is correct and the pulleys are properly aligned, remove the pulleys and reinstall the inner cover as described in Chapter Seven.
7. Install the drive and driven pulleys as described in this chapter.
8. Install the drive belt and check deflection as described in this chapter.
9. Install the outer cover. Make sure that the cover seals properly.

DRIVE PULLEY

WARNING
The drive pulley is under spring pressure. Attempting to disassemble or reassemble the drive pulley without the use of the specified VST special tools may cause severe personal injury or death. If the necessary tools are not available, have the service performed by a Polaris dealership or other repair facility with the proper equipment.

Removal

The VST T-Handle Drive Clutch Puller (**Figure 28**) (part No. 2870506) and an air impact wrench are required to remove the drive pulley. If an air tool is not available, a strap wrench (**Figure 29**) can be used to hold the drive pulley during removal and installation.
1. Remove the drive belt as described in this chapter.

27

28

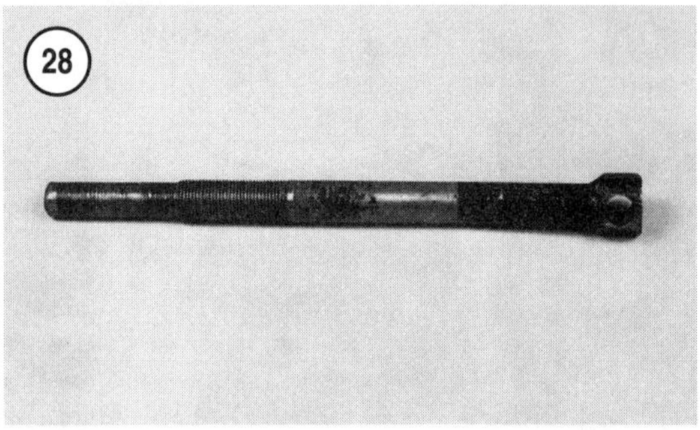

29

STRAP WRENCH

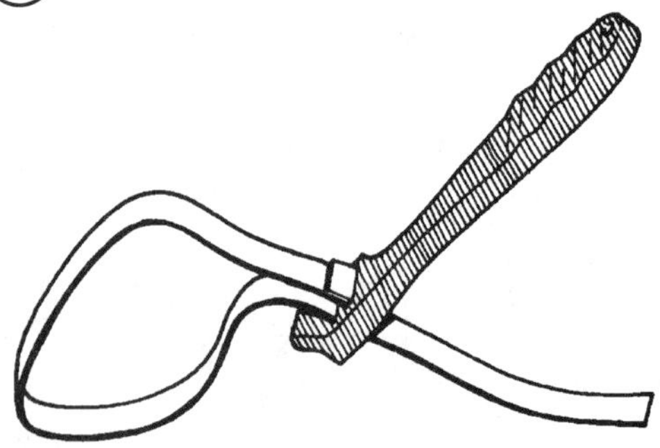

30

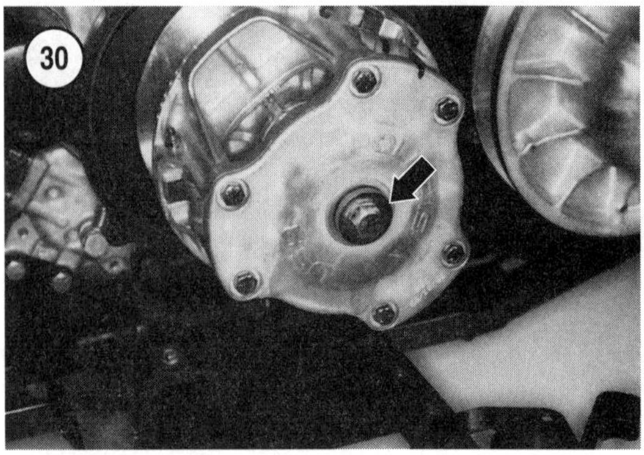

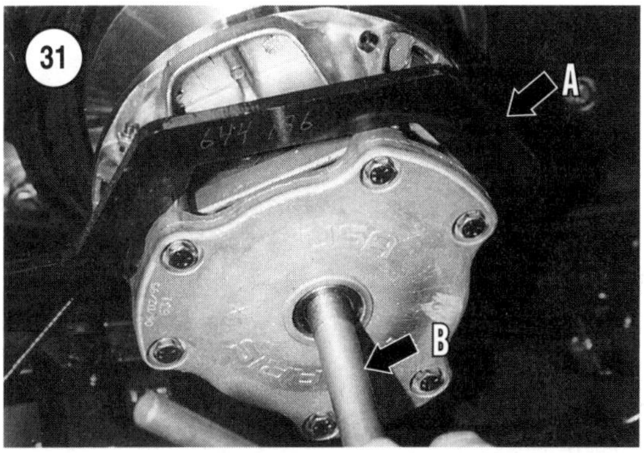

2. Secure the drive pulley with a strap wrench, then loosen and remove the bolt, lockwasher, thick washers and bushing (**Figure 30**).
3. Use the special clutch holding tool (A, **Figure 31**) or strap wrench to hold the drive pulley stationary during Step 4.
4. Install the special clutch puller (B, **Figure 31**) through the pulley. Tighten the puller screw to break the drive pulley loose from the taper on the crankshaft.

NOTE
If necessary, rap sharply on the head of the puller to break the drive pulley free from the crankshaft.

5. Pull the drive pulley (**Figure 32**) straight off the crankshaft, then remove the puller from the drive pulley.

Disassembly

Precise balance is critical to the operation of the drive pulley assembly and it is critical that the balance of the unit not be affected in any way. The manufacturer recommends that an authorized Polaris dealer perform all service work. If another repair facility is used, make sure they are properly equipped and experienced to service this type of equipment. Removing the assembly and having a repair facility perform the required service can save considerable expense.

Refer to **Figure 33** for 1996-1998 models and **Figure 34** for 1999-on models.

Inspect the drive pulley assembly before beginning any disassembly to determine if the components are in acceptable condition. Install a new complete drive clutch assembly (**Figure 35** and **Figure 36**) if any individual component is damaged. Never replace parts with similar used parts.

Two VST special tools are required to perform the following procedures: the VST drive clutch spider removal tool, part No. 2870341 (A, **Figure 37**) and the VST clutch holding fixture, part No. 2871358 (B). Do not attempt the disassembly/assembly procedure without these tools.

The following disassembly procedure is provided if the tools and expertise are available.

1. Before disassembling, use a felt-tip permanent marker to make an alignment mark across each clutch component (**Figure 38**). Refer to these marks during reassembly to ensure proper clutch alignment and balance.

WARNING
*The cover plate (A, **Figure 39**) is spring-loaded. To prevent it from flying off during removal, the cover plate must be removed as described in Step 2.*

2. Loosen the cover plate bolts (B, **Figure 39**) in small increments in a crisscross pattern until all spring tension is released. Remove the cover plate, bolts and washers.
3. Remove the spring (A, **Figure 40**).
4. Remove the spider (B, **Figure 40**) as follows:

CAUTION
*The spider (B, **Figure 40**) is secured tightly onto the fixed sheave with locking compound. To prevent primary sheave damage, make sure the fixed sheave is held securely when loosening the spider assembly as described in this procedure.*

8

33

DRIVE PULLEY (1996-1998)

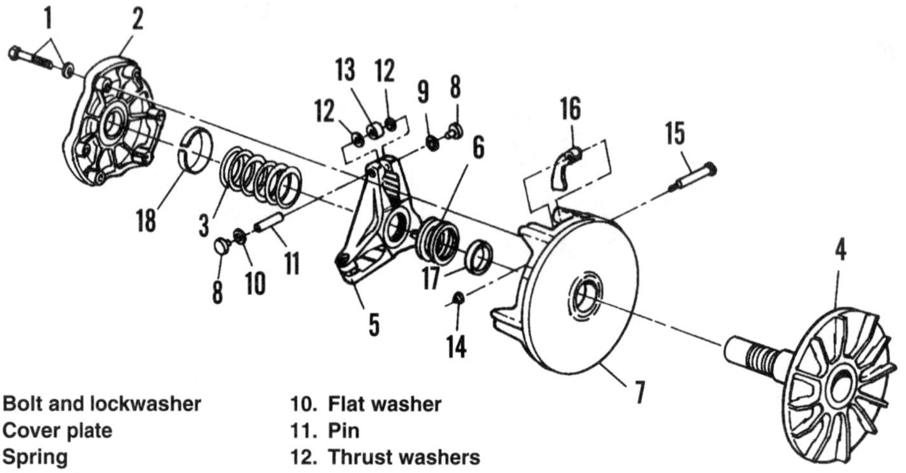

1. Bolt and lockwasher
2. Cover plate
3. Spring
4. Fixed sheave
5. Spider
6. Spacer washers
7. Sliding sheave
8. Button
9. O-ring
10. Flat washer
11. Pin
12. Thrust washers
13. Roller
14. Nut
15. Pivot bolts
16. Weights
17. Bushing
18. Cover bushing

34

DRIVE PULLEY (1999-ON MODELS WITH EBS)

1. Screw
2. Washer
3. Cover
4. Spring
5. Spider
6. Button
7. Thrust washer
8. Roller
9. Thrust washer
10. Pivot bolt
11. Weight
12. Nut
13. Pin
14. Button
15. Spacer sleeve
16. Outer washer
17. One-way drive clutch
18. Inner washer
19. Fixed sheave

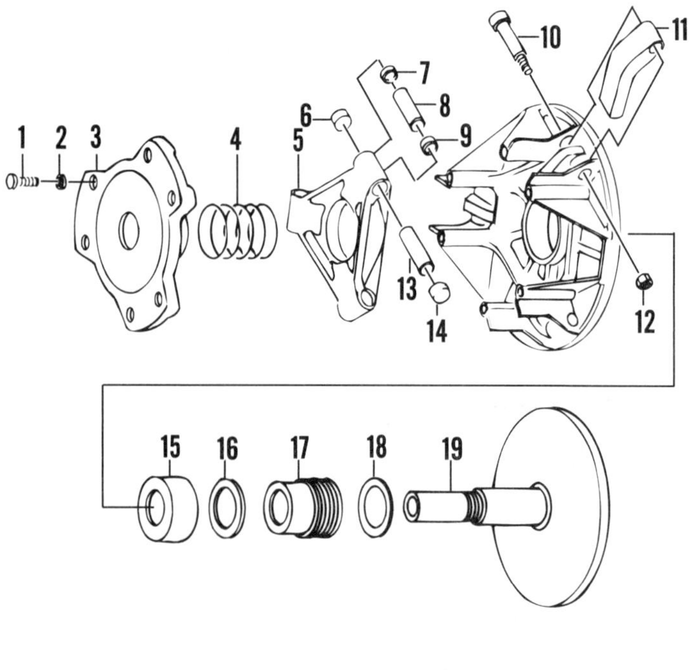

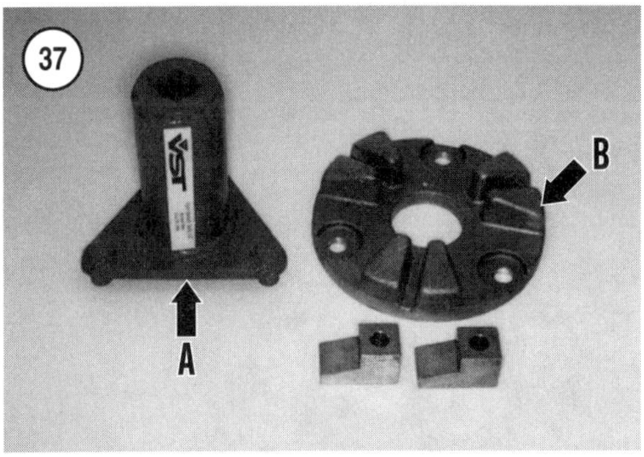

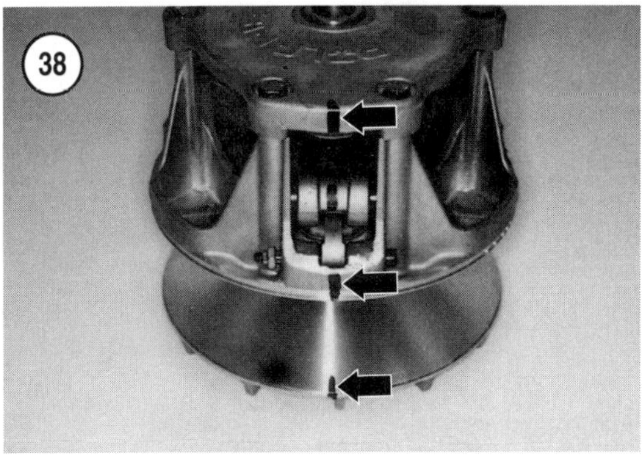

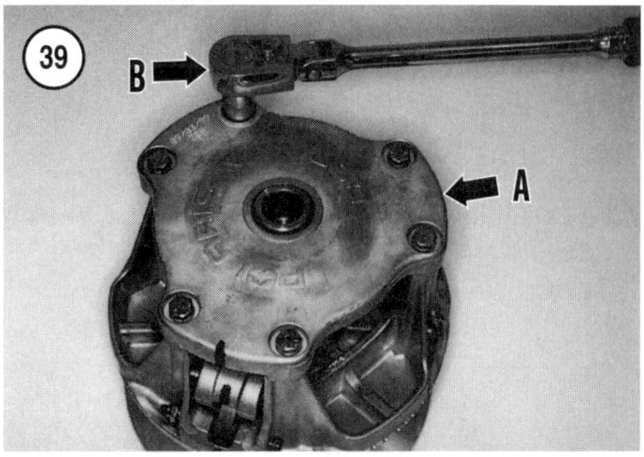

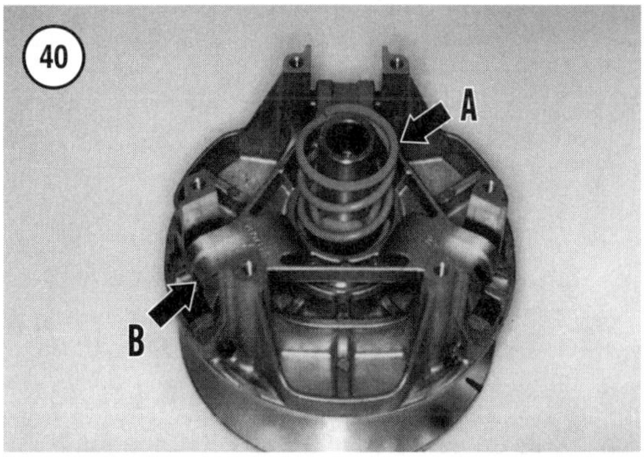

a. Securely bolt the VST clutch holding fixture onto a workbench (**Figure 41**) or stand.

b. Position the fixed sheave over the clutch holder and secure the sheave assembly with the holding tabs (**Figure 42**). Tighten the tab bolts securely.

c. On 1999-on models, unscrew (**Figure 43**) and remove the spacer sleeve and outer washer (A, **Figure 44**).

d. Install the VST drive clutch spider removal and installation tool (A, **Figure 45**) onto the

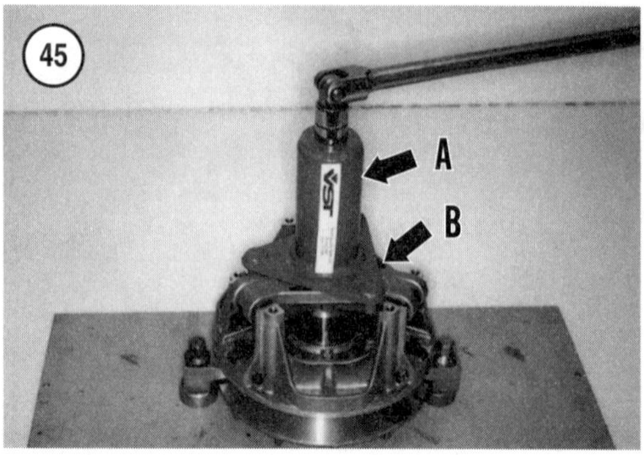

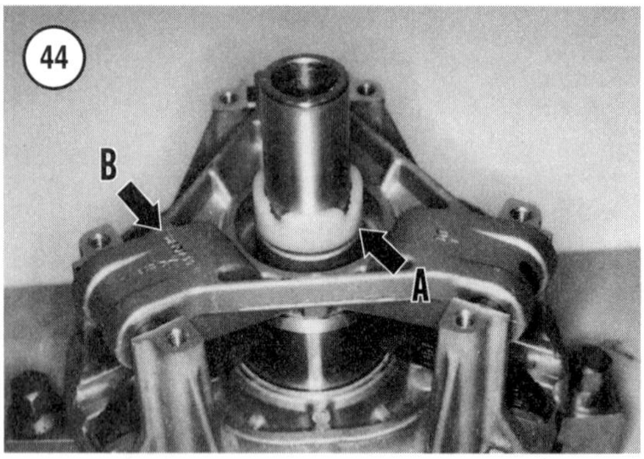

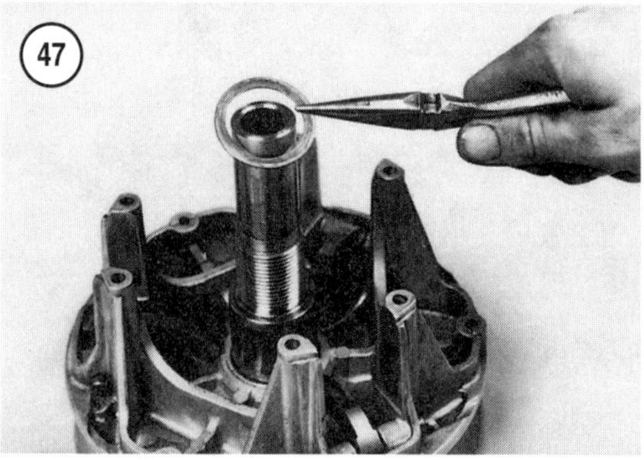

spider and position the tool posts up against the three legs of the spider (**Figure 46**).

e. Loosen the spider (B, **Figure 45**), counterclockwise, with the VST spider removal tool (A, **Figure 45**).
f. Remove the spider (B, **Figure 44**).
g. On 1996-1998 models, remove the spacer washers (**Figure 47**). The same number and thickness of spacer washers must be reinstalled.

5. Remove the movable sheave assembly (**Figure 48**) from the fixed sheave.

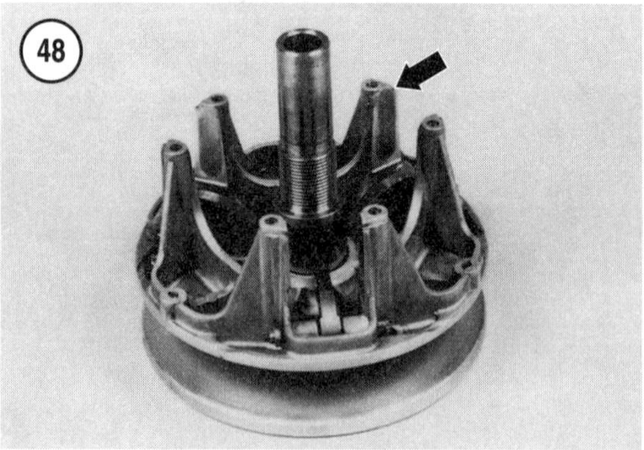

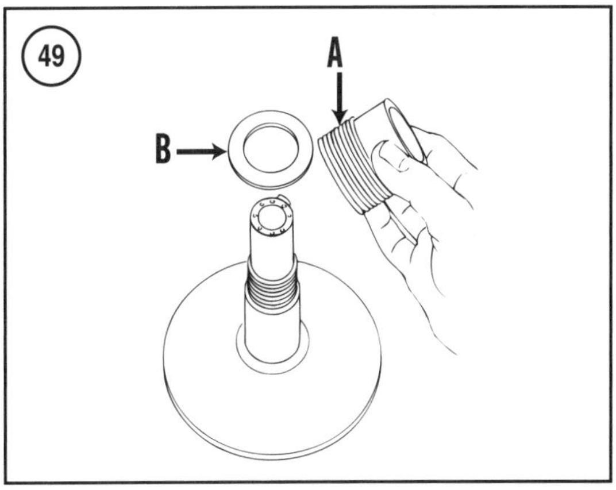

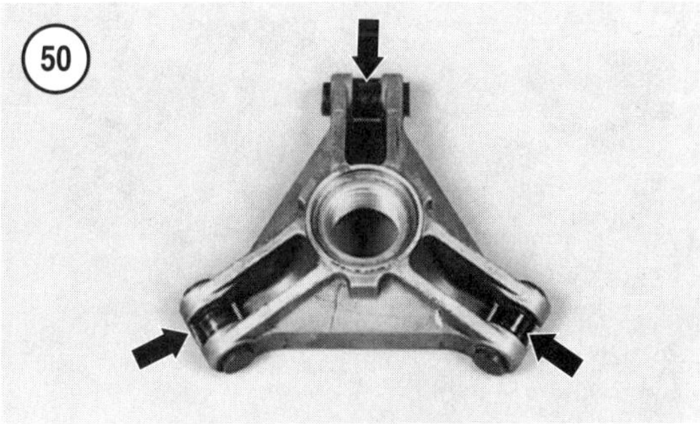

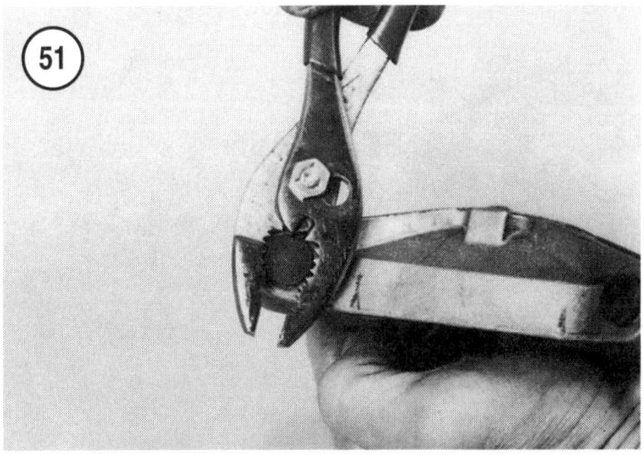

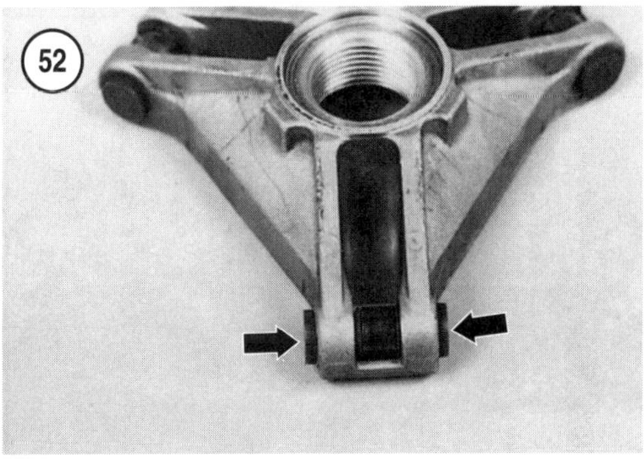

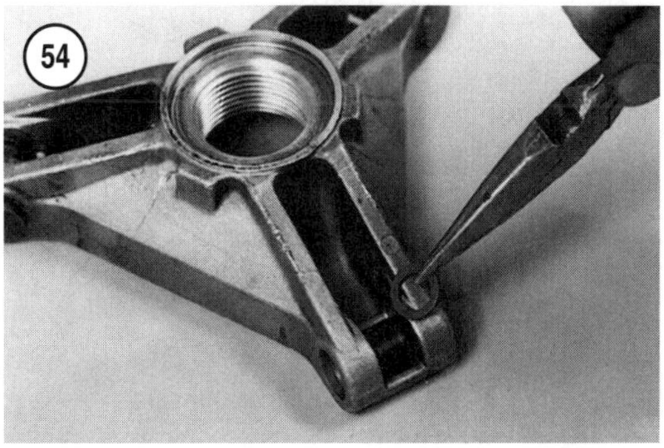

6. On 1999-on models, remove the EBS one-way drive clutch (A, **Figure 49**) and inner washer (B, **Figure 49**) from the fixed sheave.

7. Disassemble the spider roller assembly (**Figure 50**) as follows:

   a. Using pliers (**Figure 51**), remove the two buttons (**Figure 52**) from the one spider arm.
   b. Support the spider arm with a socket or similar tool and drive the pin out of the spider (**Figure 53**) with a VST Roller Pin special tool (part No. 2870910).
   c. Remove the two thrust washers (**Figure 54**) and the roller (**Figure 55**).
   d. Store the roller and bushing assembly as a set until inspection and reassembly. Do not intermix these parts.
   e. Repeat substeps a-d for the two remaining roller assemblies.

8. Remove the sliding weights (**Figure 56**) from the sliding sheave as follows:

   a. Remove the sliding weight mounting nut (A, **Figure 57**) and the Allen bolt (B, **Figure 57**).
   b. Remove the sliding weight (**Figure 58**).
   c. Repeat substeps a and substep b for the two remaining weight assemblies.

8

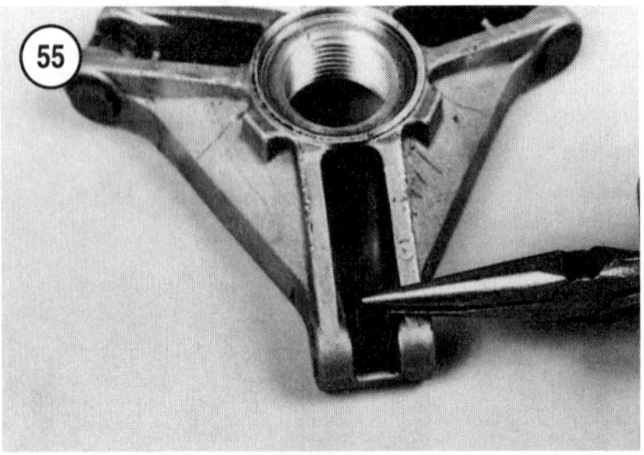

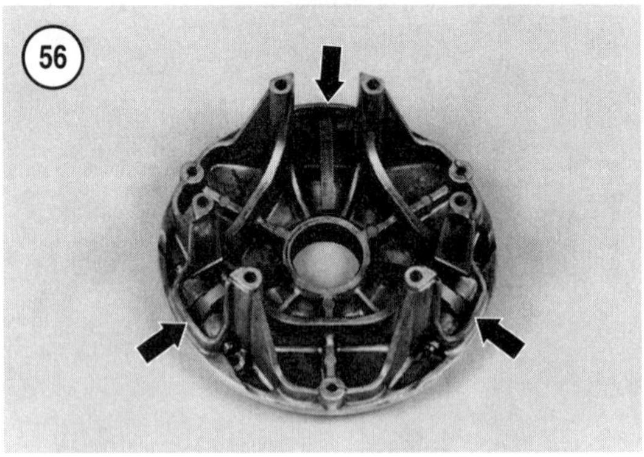

Inspection

NOTE
When cleaning parts in Step 1 of Inspection, do not remove the alignment marks made in Step 1 of Disassembly.

1. Thoroughly clean all parts in solvent and dry with compressed air.
2. Remove all threadlocking compound from the threads.
3. Check the sliding and fixed sheaves, spider and cover plate for cracks or damage.
4. Check the sheave drive belt surfaces (A, **Figure 59**) for rubber or corrosion buildup. For proper operation, the surfaces must be *clean*. Remove debris with fine-grade steel wool. Clean with a piece of lint-free cloth.
5. Check the fixed sheave for stripped or damage threads (B, **Figure 59**). If a machine shop cannot repair the damaged threads, replace the fixed sheave.
6. On 1999-on models, perform the following:
   a. Measure the outside diameter of the fixed sheave where the EBS one-way clutch makes contact (**Figure 60**). Refer to the specification listed in **Table 1** and replace if necessary.

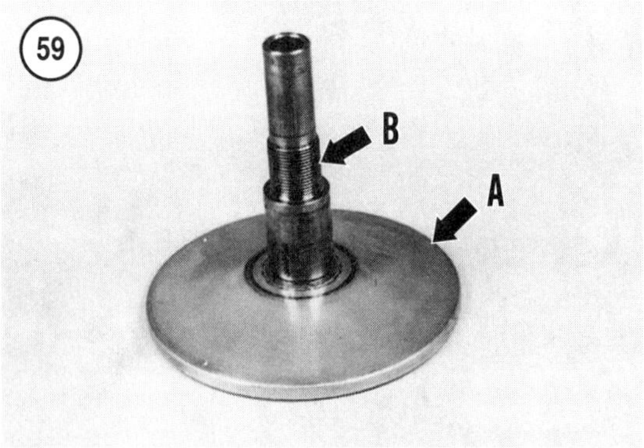

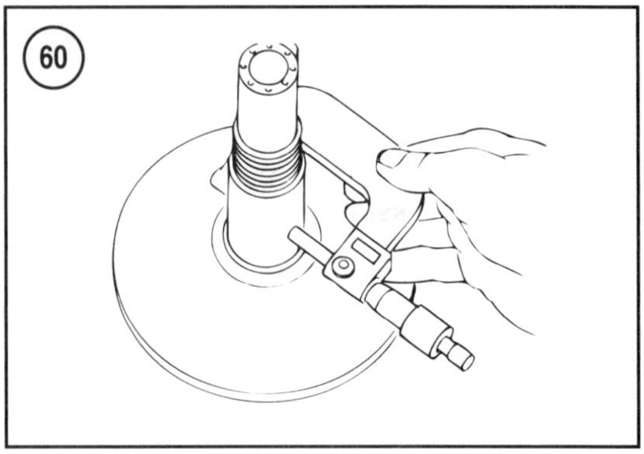

61

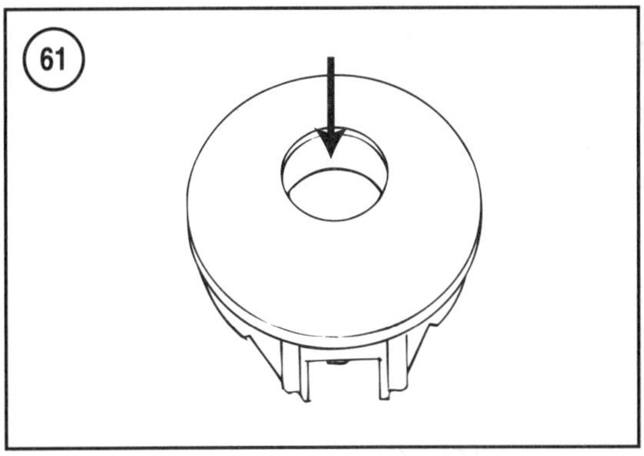

62

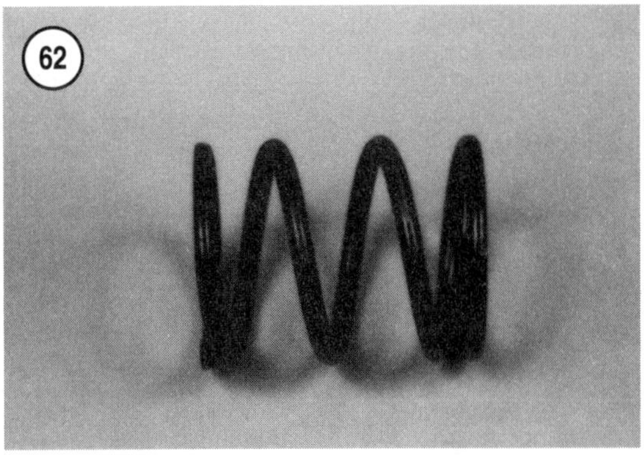

63

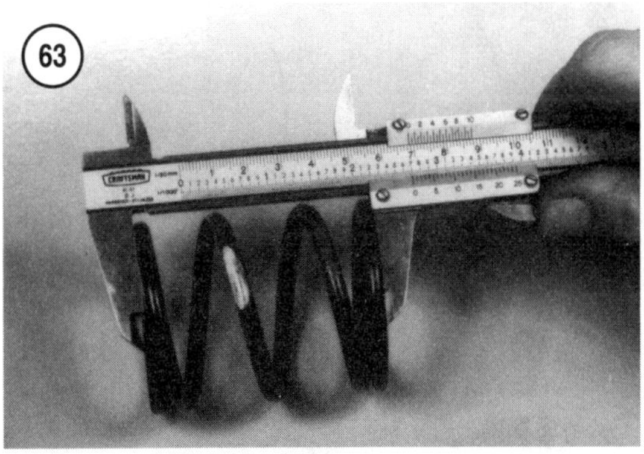

64

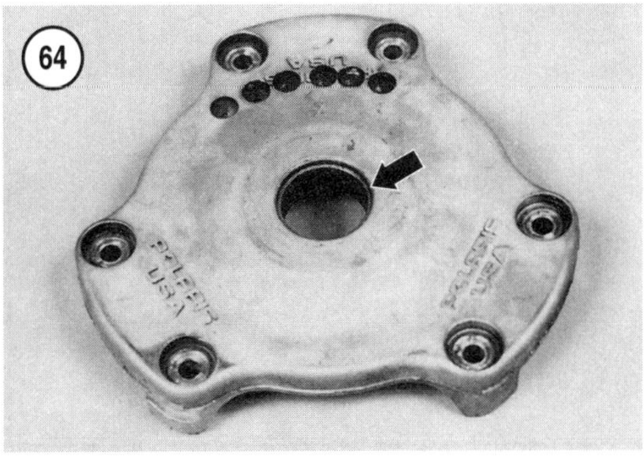

65

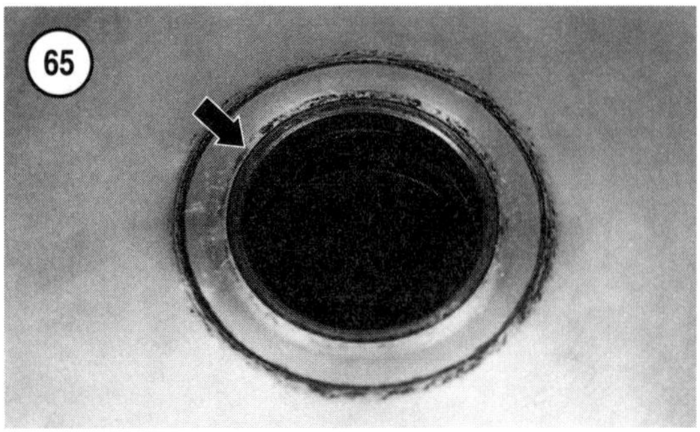

66

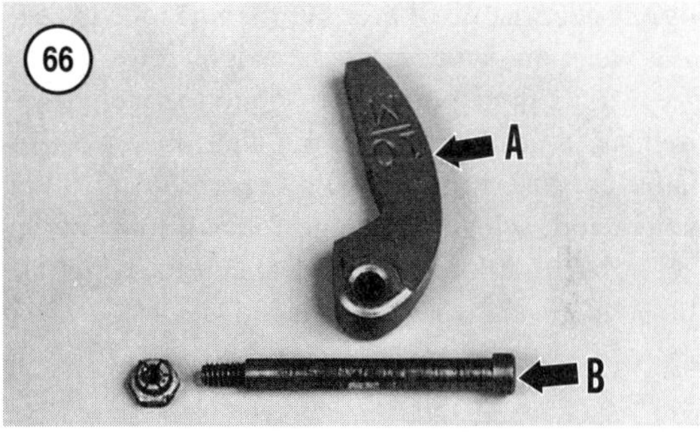

b. Measure the thickness of the inner washer (B, **Figure 49**). Refer to specification listed in **Table 1** and replace if necessary.

c. Inspect the Teflon coating on the sliding sheave bushing (**Figure 61**). The bushing is coated with Teflon and a new bushing should be installed if more brass is showing than Teflon. Do not remove the old bushing unless replacement is necessary.

7. Check the spring (**Figure 62**) for cracks or distortion. If the spring appears good, measure the free length with a vernier caliper (**Figure 63**). Replace the spring if its free length is less than the free length limit listed in **Table 3**. Replace the spring with the same color code and wire diameter.

8. Inspect the cover plate bushing (**Figure 64**) for wear or cracks. Inspect the Teflon coating and install a new bushing if more brass is visible than Teflon. Do not remove the old bushing unless replacement is necessary.

9. On 1996-1998 models, inspect the sliding sheave bushing (**Figure 65**) for wear or cracks. Inspect the Teflon coating and install a new bushing if more brass is visible than Teflon. Do not remove the old bushing unless replacement is necessary.

10. Check the complete surface of the cam weights (A, **Figure 66**) for cracks, chips or scor-

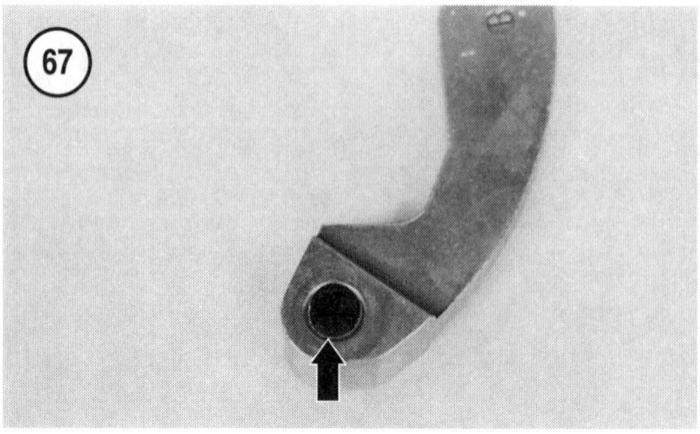

ing. Inspect the pivot area (**Figure 67**) for excessive wear or damage. Each weight must rotate freely at its pivot point. Damage to the weights is often an indication that the pin and roller are also damaged. Insert the bolt (B, **Figure 66**) into the weight and swing it back and forth. It must move freely, but also not too loose. Replace the weight if the pivot area is worn or damaged.

WARNING

*Refer to **Figure 68** for the shape and gram weight of the drive pulley weights. It is important that all three weights are exactly the same. Do not change the shape of the weights without a thorough understanding of PVT operation. Components of the drive and driven pulleys must be carefully matched for proper operation. Before changing the weights in the drive pulley, consult with a Polaris dealership.*

11. Install new weights as a set if any are damaged. Weights are marked to indicate their original size and **Table 4** lists original application. It may be necessary to install lighter weights when operating at higher altitudes, as indicated in **Table 4**.

NOTE

If the outer roller surface is worn unevenly, the roller may have seized onto the bushing. If this condition is noted, check both parts for damage.

12. Check the spider buttons (**Figure 69**) for excessive wear or damage. Then check the spider button contact surface on the sliding sheave for galling or excessive wear. Replace the spider buttons as a set.

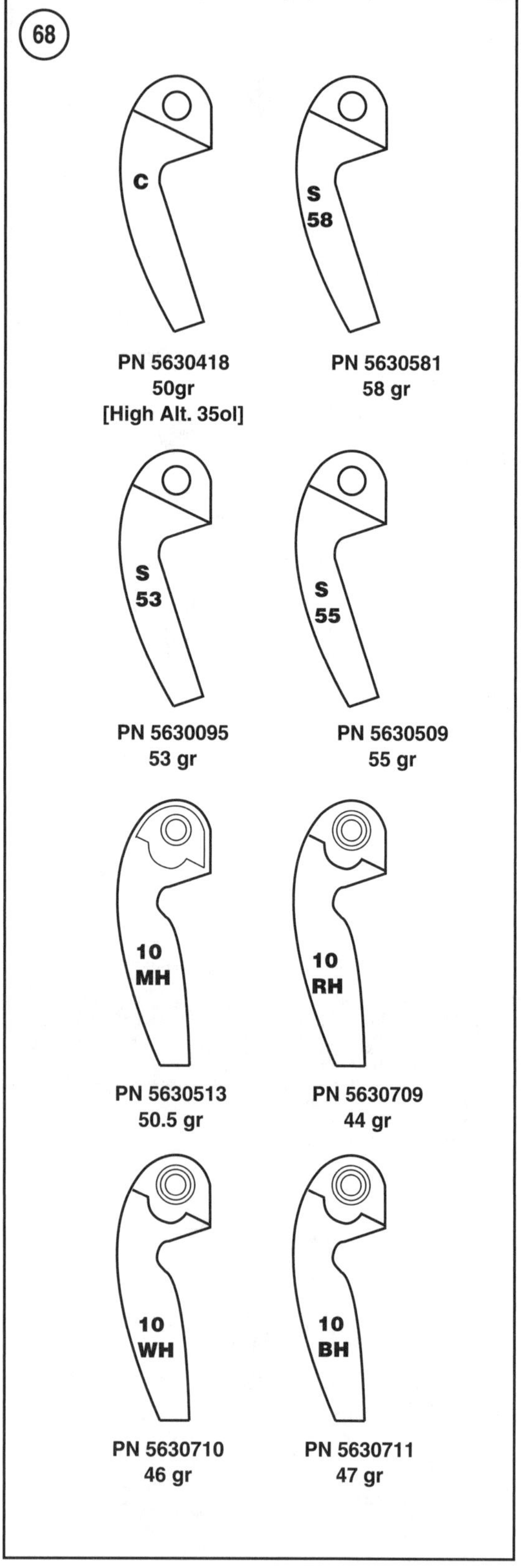

69

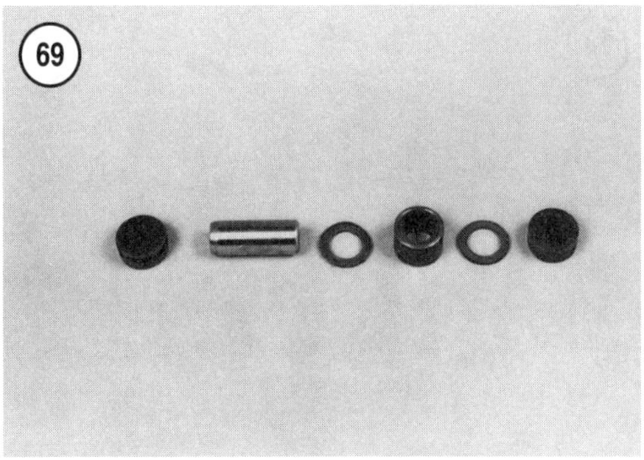

70

71

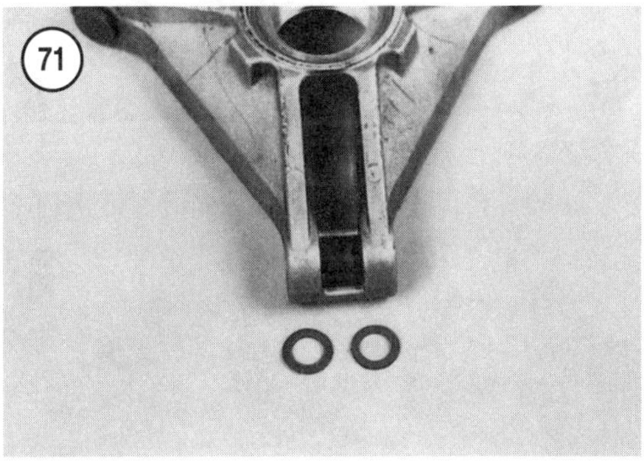

72

Assembly

Refer to **Figure 33** for 1996-1998 models or **Figure 34** for 1999-on models with EBS.

WARNING
*Precise balance is critical to the operation safety of the drive pulley. Refer to the alignment marks made in **Figure 70** for this procedure.*

CAUTION
The drive pulley must be assembled dry. Do not apply any lubricate to any component.

1. Install the weights (**Figure 58**) as follows:

NOTE
*The three Allen bolts used to secure the cam weights must be installed so that each head faces to the right of its weight as shown in B, **Figure 57**.*

a. Fit each weight (**Figure 56**) into the sliding sheave and slide the Allen bolt (B, **Figure 57**) through the weight.
b. Apply ThreeBond TB1342, Loctite No 242 or an equivalent to the threads of *new* locknuts and install the locknuts (A, **Figure 57**). Tighten the locknut until it bottoms against the aluminum sliding sheave tower; do not overtighten the locknut.

NOTE
If a weight does not pivot smoothly, the locknut is too tight.

c. Pivot the weight back and forth and check for free movement of the weight. It must pivot smoothly.
d. Repeat for each weight assembly.

2. Assemble the spider roller assembly (**Figure 69**) as follows:
a. Place a bushing into the middle of the tower (**Figure 55**).
b. Insert a washer (**Figure 54**) on both sides of the bushing (**Figure 71**).
c. Install the pin as follows. Place the spider over a socket or suitable tool and drive the pin through the bushing and washers (**Figure 72**). Maintain the same amount of clearance on both sides of the pin.

8

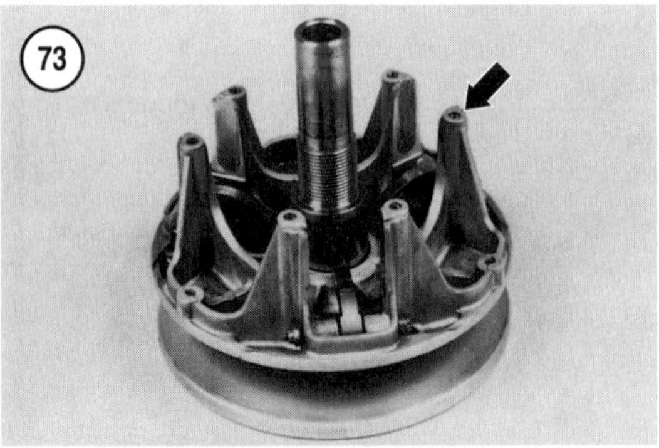

d. Install the guide buttons (**Figure 52**) and tap them into the spider with a soft-faced hammer.
e. Repeat for each roller assembly.

3. On 1999-on models, install the inner washer (B, **Figure 49**) and the EBS one-way drive clutch (A, **Figure 49**) onto the fixed sheave.
4. Install the sliding sheave over the fixed sheave (**Figure 73**).

NOTE
As noted during disassembly, the same number and thickness of spacer washer(s) must be reinstalled.

5. On 1996-1998 models, install the spacer washer(s) over the fixed sheave shaft (**Figure 47**).
6. Apply ThreeBond TB1342, Loctite No 242 or equivalent to the threaded portion of the fixed sheave.
7. Install the spider (**Figure 74**) over the fixed sheave shaft, making sure to align the marks made on the spider and sliding sheave (**Figure 70**).
8. Correctly tighten the spider (**Figure 74**) as follows:
   a. If removed, bolt the VST clutch holding fixture onto a workbench (**Figure 41**) or stand so that the holding fixture is secure.
   b. Position the fixed sheave (A, **Figure 75**) over the clutch holder and secure the sheave assembly with the holding tabs (B, **Figure 75**). Tighten the tab bolts securely.
   c. Install the VST drive clutch spider removal and installation tool (A, **Figure 76**) onto the spider and position the tool posts up against the three legs of the spider.
   d. Tighten the spider (B, **Figure 76**), clockwise, with the VST spider removal tool (A, **Figure 76**). Tighten to the torque specification listed in **Table 5**.

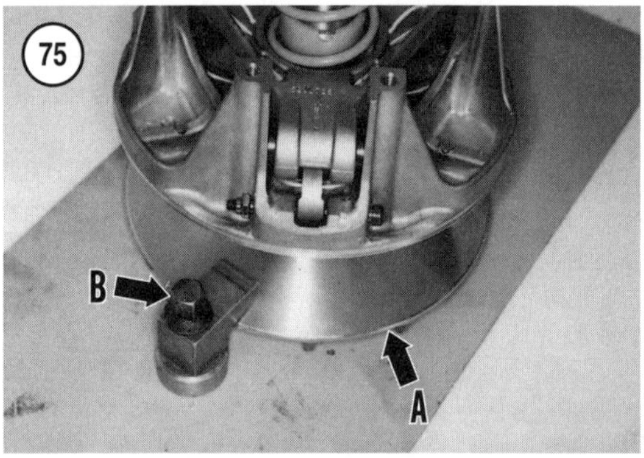

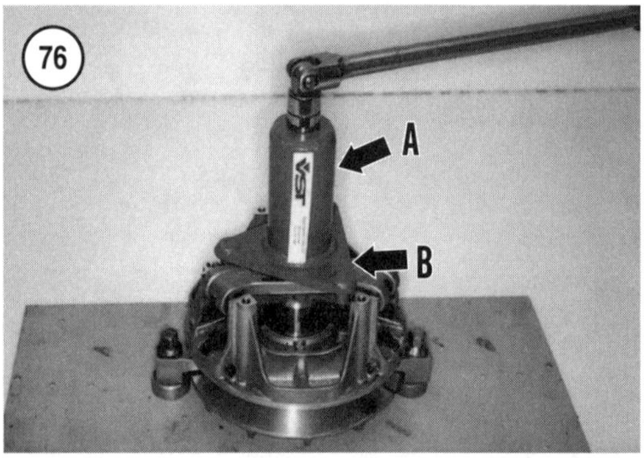

78

79

80

81

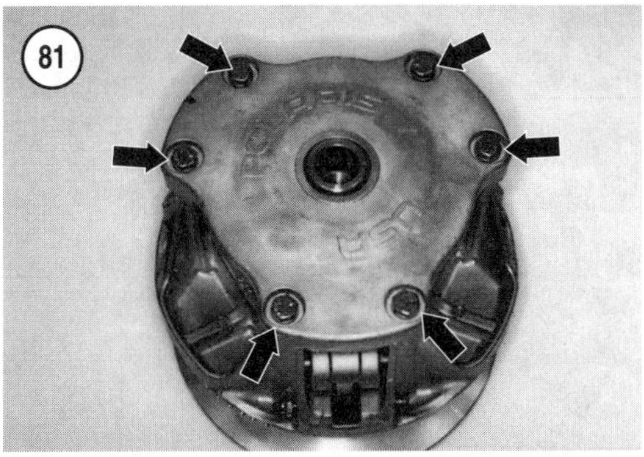

82

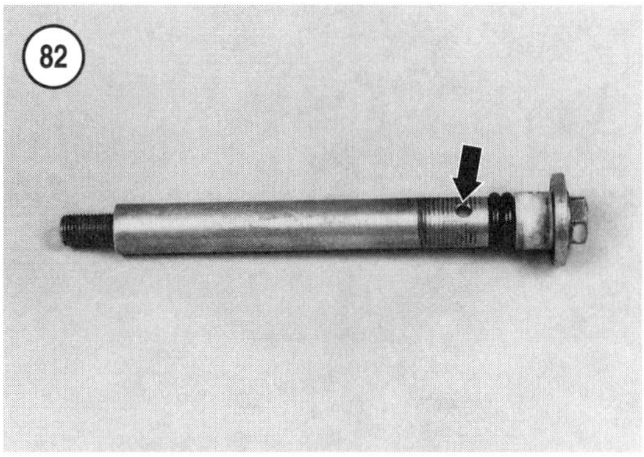

e. On 1999-on models, install the outer washer and spacer sleeve (**Figure 77**). Tighten the spacer sleeve securely.

NOTE

After tightening the spider, move the sliding sheave up and down by hand. The sheave should slide freely without any signs of binding. If any binding is noted, the cam weight Allen bolts and nuts may be too tight. Loosen, then retighten the bolts and nuts, then recheck for free movement.

9. Place the cover plate (**Figure 78**) over the fixed sheave shaft without the spring and check plate movement along the shaft. If binding is noted during plate movement, the fixed sheave shaft is out of round. Repair the shaft with a fine file until the plate moves freely. Remove the cover plate.

10. Install the spring (**Figure 79**).

11. Align the mark made on the cover plate with the mark on the spider and sliding sheave and install the cover plate.

12. Apply ThreeBond TB1342, Loctite No. 242 or equivalent to the threads on the cover plate bolts. Install the bolts and washers (**Figure 80**).

13. Tighten the bolts (**Figure 81**) evenly in a crisscross pattern to the torque specification listed in **Table 5**.

Drive Pulley Bolt Inspection

Inspect the drive pulley bolt (**Figure 82**) every time it is removed.

1. Remove any washers, spacers or O-rings from the bolt.

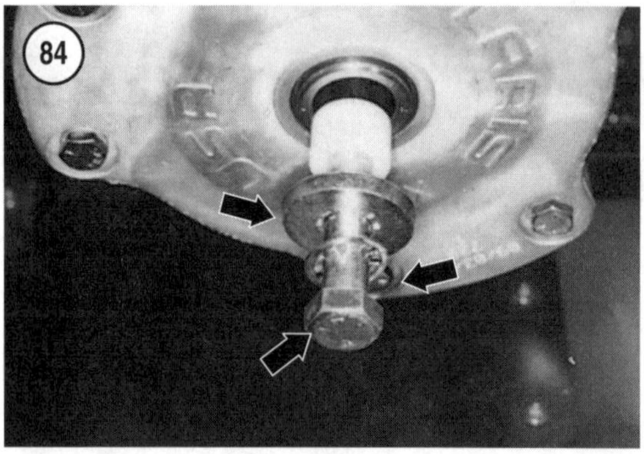

2. Check the components for excessive wear or damage.

3. Check the bolt for cracks, bending or other damage. Check for worn or deformed threads. Clean the thread with an appropriate size die and clean the belt off.

4. Check the hex head for rounding at the corners.

Installation

CAUTION
Do not apply antiseize lubricant or any other lubricant onto the crankshaft taper when installing the drive pulley assembly.

1. Clean the crankshaft taper with an aerosol parts cleaner.

2. Slide the drive pulley (**Figure 83**) onto the crankshaft. Push it on until it bottoms.

3. Install the bushing, thick washer and lockwasher onto the bolt, then install the bolt (**Figure 84**) and hand tighten.

4. Secure the drive pulley as follows:
   a. Secure the end of a tie-down onto one of the legs of the drive pulley (**Figure 85**). Make sure the end is snug against the leg.
   b. Tightly wrap the tie-down around the drive pulley *counterclockwise* 2-3 times (A, **Figure 86**) and secure the other end of the tie-down to the chassis.
   c. Tighten the bolt (B, **Figure 86**) to the torque specification listed in **Table 5**.

5. Install the drive belt as described in this chapter.

6. Check the outer cover seals, then install the outer cover as described in Chapter Seven.

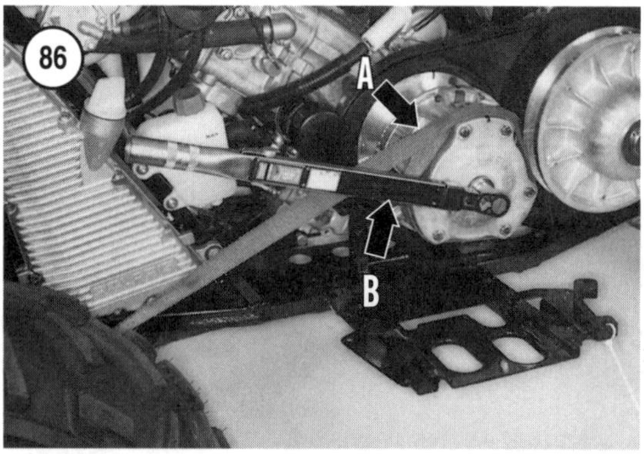

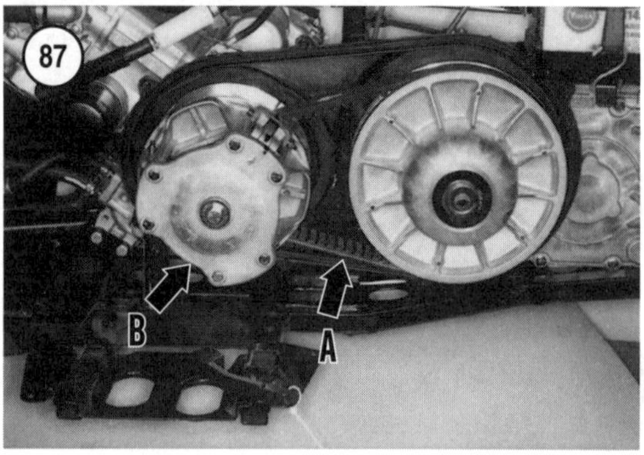

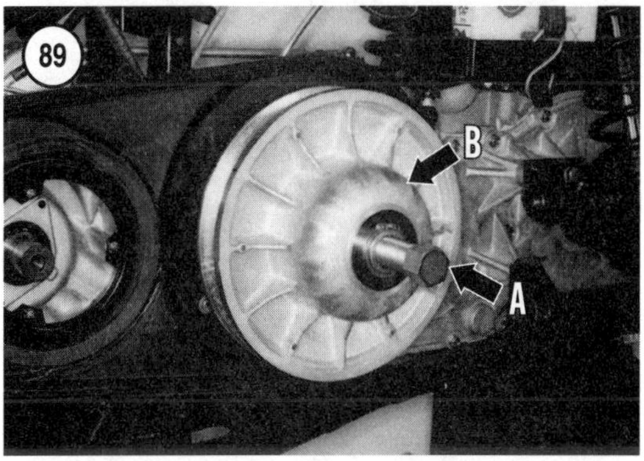

DRIVEN PULLEY

The driven pulley is mounted onto the left side of the transmission input shaft.

Removal (All Models)

1. Remove the drive belt (A, **Figure 87**) as described in this chapter.

NOTE
*This procedure is shown with the drive pulley (B, **Figure 87**) removed to better illustrate the steps. It is not necessary to remove the drive pulley prior to removing the driven pulley.*

2. Loosen and remove the driven pulley mounting bolt, lockwasher and domed washer (**Figure 88**).
3. Install the VST Driven Clutch Puller (part No. 2870913) (A, **Figure 89**) onto the driven pulley. Tighten the pulley and loosen the pulley from the transmission input shaft. If necessary, tap on the end of the puller to loosen the pulley.
4. Slide the driven pulley (B, **Figure 89**) straight off from the transmission input shaft splines.

5A. On 1996-1998 models, remove the shim(s) (**Figure 90**) and on some models, the bushing from the transmission shaft.

5B. On 1999-on models, remove the washer (**Figure 91**) and shim(s) (**Figure 92**).

NOTE
The shim(s) installed behind the driven pulley are used to adjust the pulley offset. Do not remove the shim(s) unless required for other service. Be sure to install the same num-

8

ber of shim(s) prior to installing the driven pulley.

Installation (All Models)

NOTE
Make sure the same number of shim(s), as noted during removal, are in place on the transmission input shaft.

1A. On 1996-1998 models, install the shim(s) (**Figure 90**) and on some models, the bushing onto the transmission shaft.
1B. On 1999-on models, install the shim(s) (**Figure 92**) and washer (**Figure 91**) onto the transmission shaft.
2. Clean the splines on the transmission input shaft and apply a light film of low-temperature grease to the splines.
3. Align the master splines of the pulley assembly with the input shaft and slide the driven pulley onto the shaft. Push it on until it bottoms.
4. Position the domed washer (A, **Figure 93**) as shown so it can accept the smaller lockwasher (B, **Figure 93**).
5. Install the mounting bolt (**Figure 88**) and tighten to the torque specification listed in **Table 5**.
6. Check the pulley offset as described in this chapter.
7. Install the drive belt (A, **Figure 87**) as described in this chapter.
8. Check the drive belt deflection as described in this chapter.
9. Check the outer cover seals, then install as described in Chapter Three.

Disassembly (1996-1998 Models)

Refer to **Figure 94**.

WARNING
The driven pulley is under spring pressure. Attempting to disassemble or reassemble the driven pulley without the use of the specified VST special tools may cause personal injury. If the necessary tools are not available, have the service performed by a Polaris dealership or repair facility with the proper equipment.

93

NOTE
Inspect the drive pulley assembly before beginning to disassemble it to determine if any of the major components requires replacement. Install a new complete drive clutch assembly if the cover, fixed sheave, spider or movable sheave is damaged. Never replace parts with used parts from another assembly.

1. Before disassembling the driven pulley, locate the end of the spring in one of the two holes in helix cam. Mark the hole for identification of original setting.

WARNING
Wear eye protection and hold the helix cam securely when removing the snap ring in Step 2.

2. Set the driven pulley on the workbench with the fixed sheave facing down, push the helix cam (A, **Figure 95**) down and remove the snap ring (B, **Figure 95**). Slowly release the helix, allowing it to come up and turn.
3. Carefully remove the helix cam from the spring, but leave the spring located in the moveable sheave.
4. Note and mark the location of the end of the spring in the movable sheave, then remove the spring. The suggested initial setting for a new spring is listed in **Table 4**.

NOTE
The spacer washers located between the movable and fixed sheaves are used to adjust belt deflection. Do not lose or damage these spacer washers. At least one spacer must always be located between the sheaves.

94

DRIVEN PULLEY (1996-1998 MODELS)

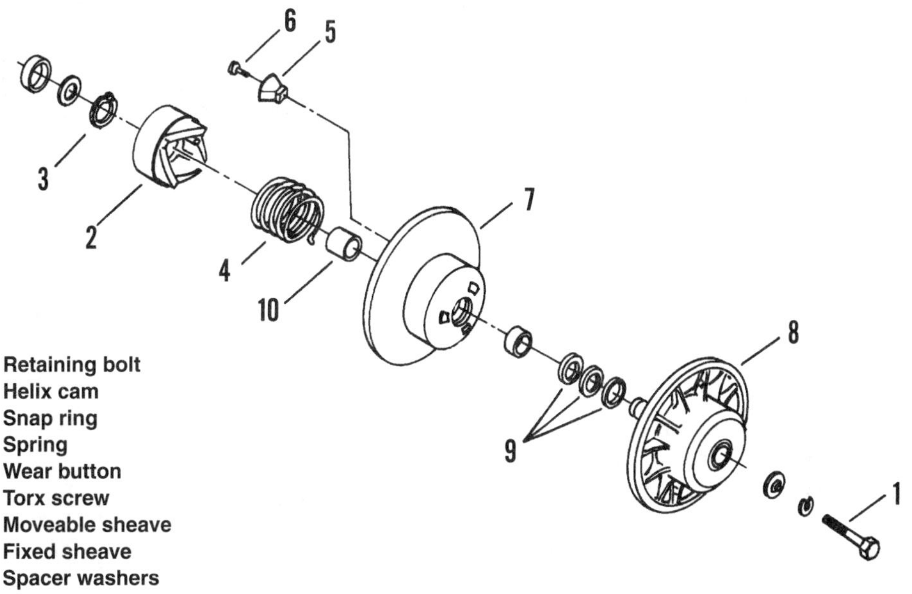

1. Retaining bolt
2. Helix cam
3. Snap ring
4. Spring
5. Wear button
6. Torx screw
7. Moveable sheave
8. Fixed sheave
9. Spacer washers
10. Bushing

95

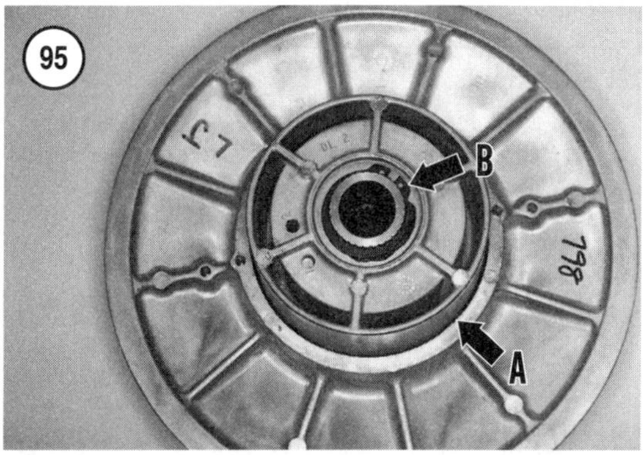

96

5. Slide the movable sheave from the fixed sheave (**Figure 96**).

6. Inspect all parts as described in this chapter.

Assembly (1996-1998 Models)

1. Place the fixed sheave on the workbench so the belt surface faces up.

2. Install the same number of spacer washers that were removed onto the shaft. The spacer washers are used to adjust belt deflection and several may be installed, but there must always be at least one spacer between the sheaves.

3. Install the movable sheave onto the fixed sheave so the belt surfaces face each other.

NOTE

The positioning of the ends of the spring will determine the shifting pattern. The greatest amount of spring tension will cause the engine rpm to be higher during up-shift and will cause the unit to downshift sooner when the load is increased, such as going up a hill. Less spring tension *will up-shift faster and downshift slower. The actual position of the spring ends may be different from those listed in **Table 4** to suit operator preference. This is especially true for a spring that has been in service for some time. The spring tension should also be increased for operation at high altitudes.*

4. Install the spring with one end in the correct hole (**Figure 97**).
5. Install the helix cam with the end of the spring in the hole marked during disassembly. Refer to **Table 4** to determine which of the two holes was used on original assembly.
6. Install the helix cam and preload the spring approximately 1/3 turn as follows:
   a. Align the master splines of the helix and the shaft and push the helix cam partly onto the spline.
   b. Twist the movable sheave (**Figure 98**) *counterclockwise* approximately 1/3 turn (120°). The location of the cam surfaces on the helix and the buttons will determine actual position.
   c. Push the helix cam (A, **Figure 95**) down onto splines against spring pressure, then install the snap ring (B, **Figure 95**).
   d. Make sure the snap ring is correctly seated in the pulley shaft groove.

Disassembly (1999-On Models)

Refer to **Figure 99**.

The VST Clutch Compression Tool (A, **Figure 100**) (part No. 8700220) is required to disassemble the driven pulley.

WARNING
The driven pulley is under spring pressure. Attempting to disassemble or reassemble the driven pulley without the use of the specified VST special tools may cause personal injury. If the necessary tools are not available, have the service performed by a Polaris dealership or repair facility with the proper equipment.

WARNING
Wear eye protection when removing the snap rings in this procedure.

97

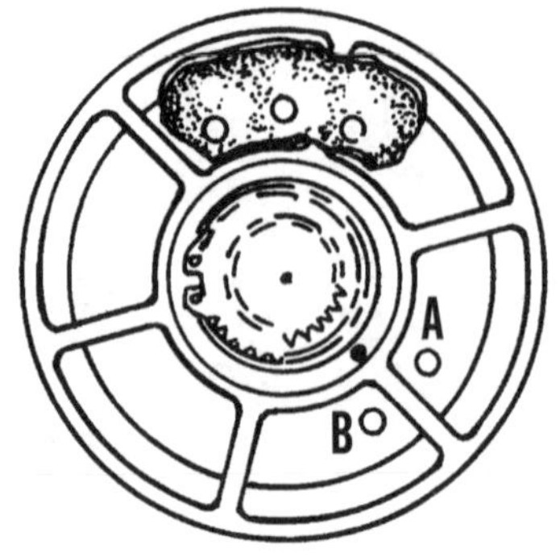

98

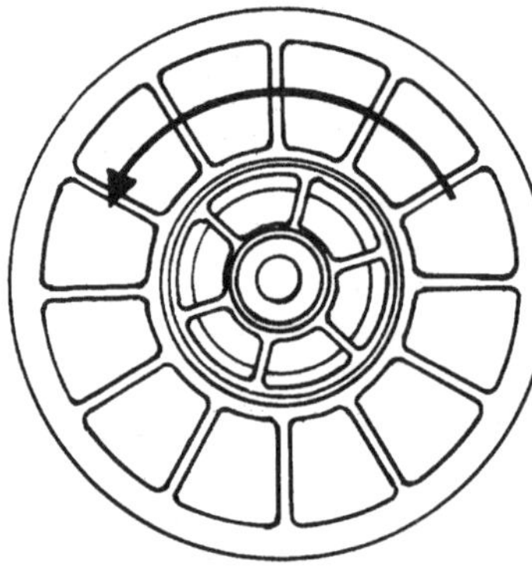

1/3 turn

NOTE
*Inspect the driven pulley assembly before beginning to disassemble it to determine if any of the major components require replacement (**Figure 101**). Install a new complete driven clutch assembly if the cover, fixed sheave, spider or movable sheave is damaged. Never replace parts with used parts from another assembly.*

1. Before disassembling, use a felt tip permanent marker to make an alignment mark across both clutch components. Use these marks during re-assembly to ensure proper clutch alignment and balance.
2. Set the driven pulley in the VST tool with the fixed sheave facing up (B, **Figure 100**).
3. Close and center the VST special tool on the fixed sheave and compress the spring. Lock the tool handle down with the chain restraint (C, **Figure 100**).
4. Remove the circlip (**Figure 102**).

99

DRIVEN PULLEY (1999-ON WITH EBS)

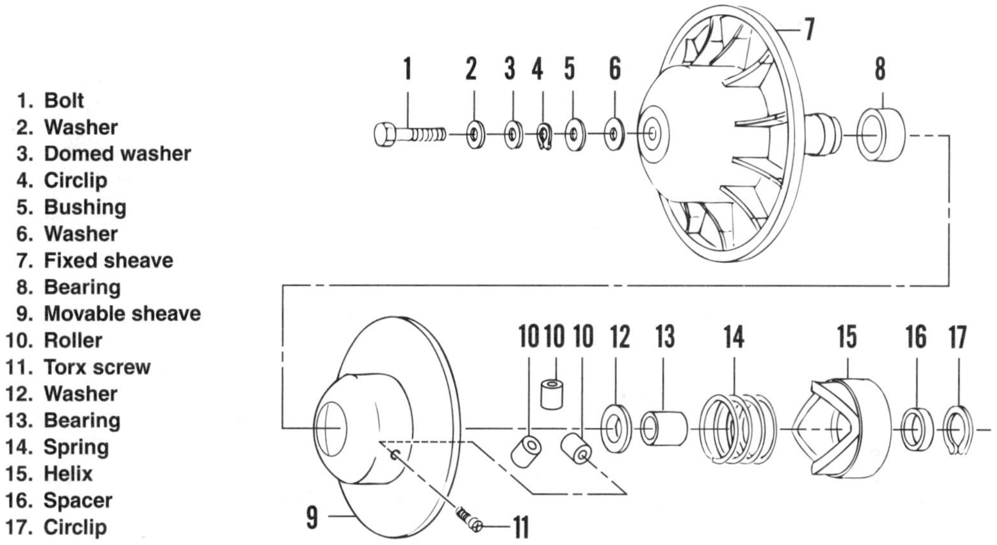

100

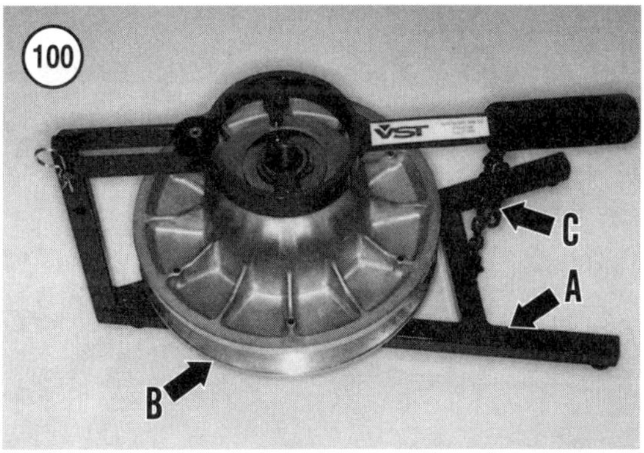

102

101

5. Push down on the VST special tool and unlock the tool handle from the chain restraint. Open the special tool.

6. Remove the bushing and washer (**Figure 103**).

7. Turn the driven pulley over and set it into the VST tool with the movable sheave facing up (A, **Figure 104**).

8. Close and center the VST special tool on the movable sheave and compress the spring. Lock the tool handle down with the chain restraint (B, **Figure 104**).

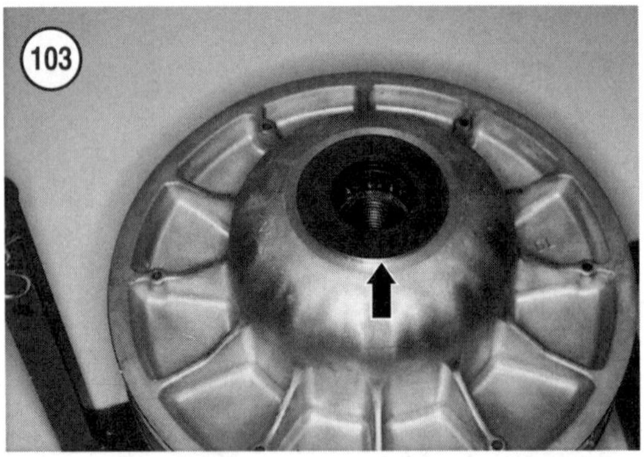
103

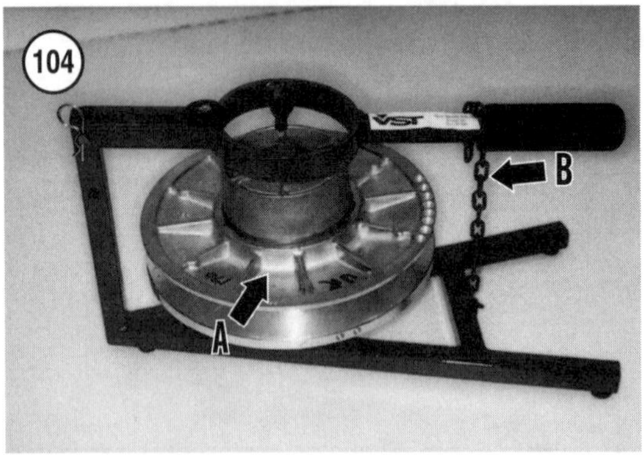

104

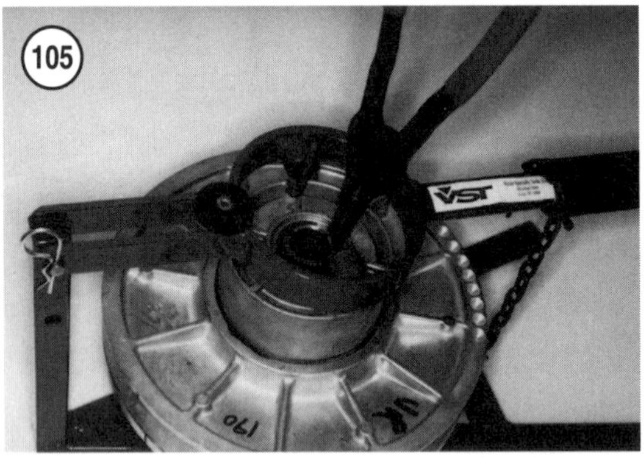

105

9. Remove the circlip and spacer (**Figure 105**).

10. Push down on the VST special tool and unlock the tool handle from the chain restraint. Slowly open the special tool.

11. Remove the helix (A, **Figure 106**) and spring (B, **Figure 106**).

12. Remove the washer (**Figure 107**) from the shaft.

13. Remove the movable sheave (**Figure 108**) and the fixed sheave (**Figure 109**) from the special tool.

14. Remove the shaft (A, **Figure 110**) from fixed sheave.

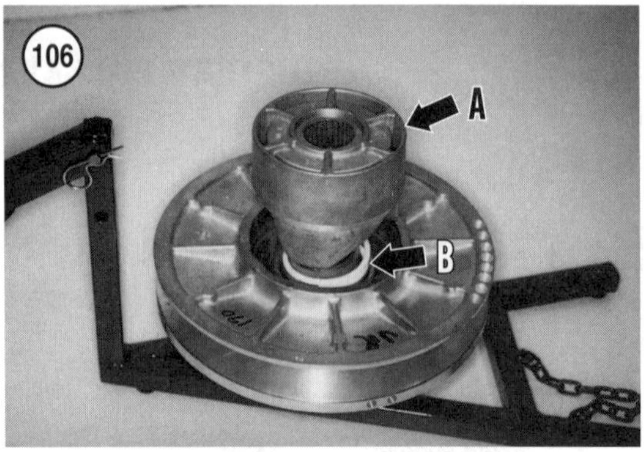

106

107

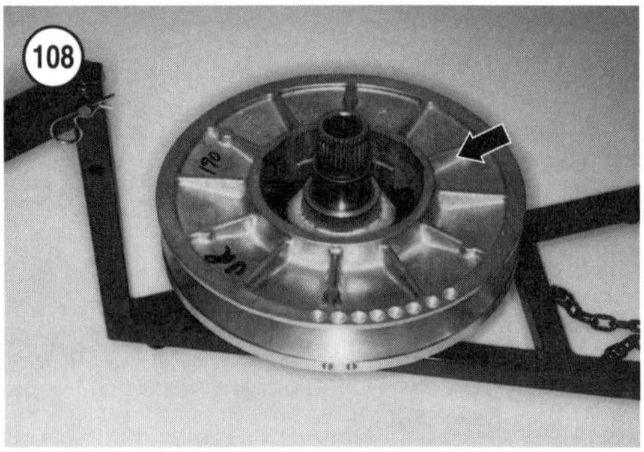
108

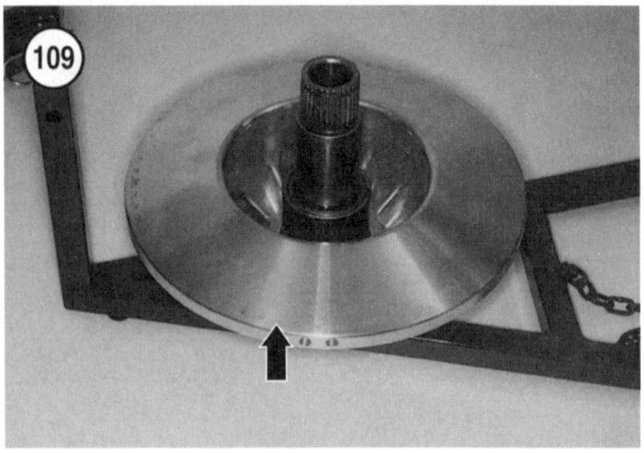
109

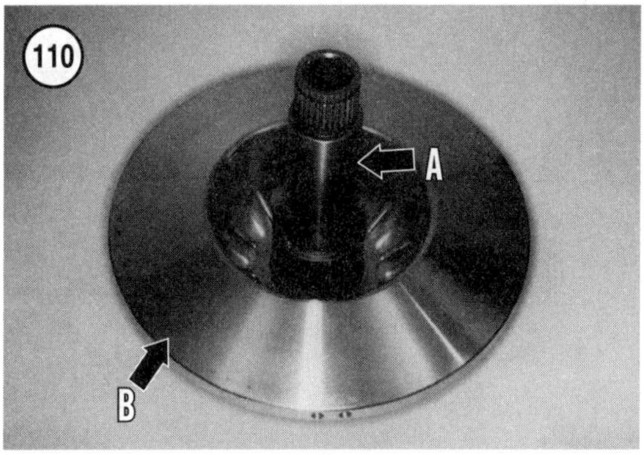

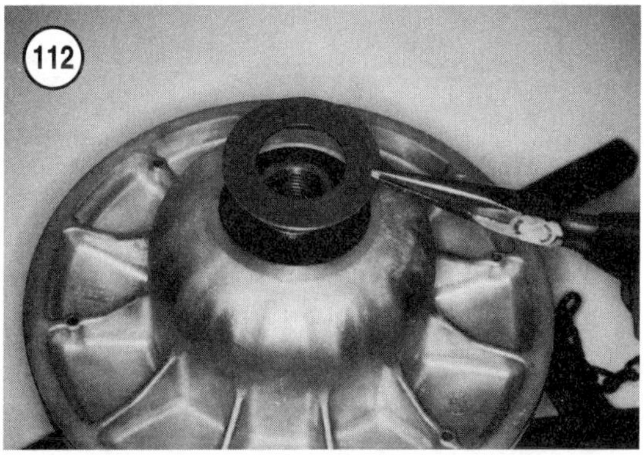

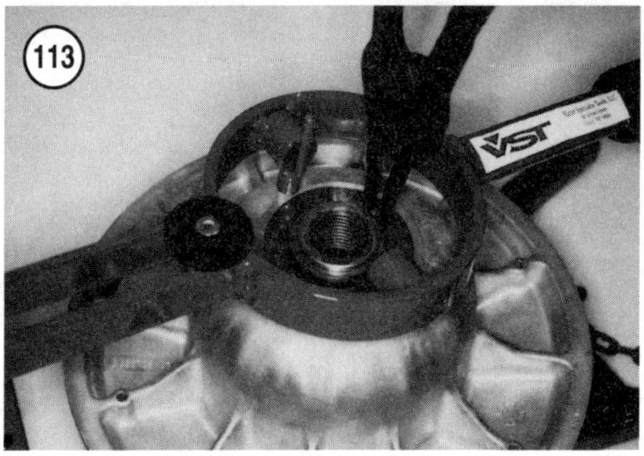

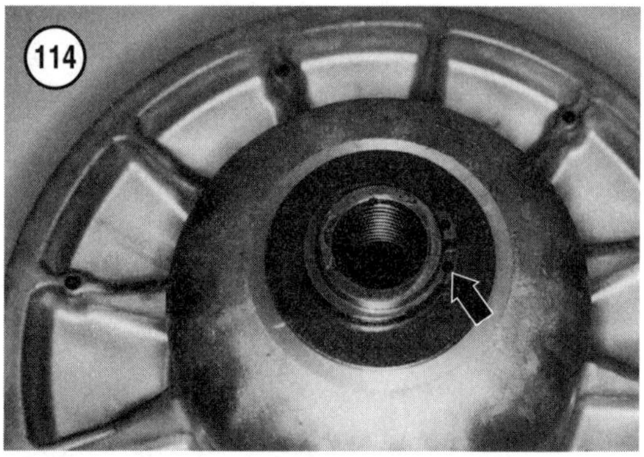

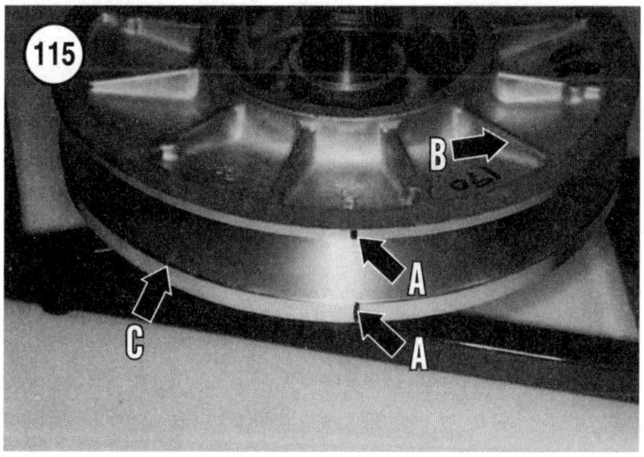

15. Inspect all parts as described in this chapter.

Assembly (1999 and Later Models)

1. Install the shaft (A, **Figure 110**) into fixed sheave. Push it down until it bottoms.
2. Turn the fixed sheave and shaft over and install it onto the special VST tool.
3. Install the washer (**Figure 111**) and bushing (**Figure 112**).
4. Close and center the VST special tool on the fixed sheave to hold all parts in place.
5. Install the circlip (**Figure 113**) into the shaft groove. Make sure the circlip is correctly seated in the shaft groove (**Figure 114**).
6. Turn the fixed sheave over and install it onto the speed control. Align the index marks made during disassembly (A, **Figure 115**) and install the movable sheave (B, **Figure 115**) onto the fixed sheave (C, **Figure 115**) so the belt surfaces face each other.
7. Install the washer (**Figure 116**) onto the shaft.
8. Install the spring (**Figure 117**).
9. Align the master splines of the helix (A, **Figure 118**) and the shaft master spline (B, **Figure 118**) and

116

117

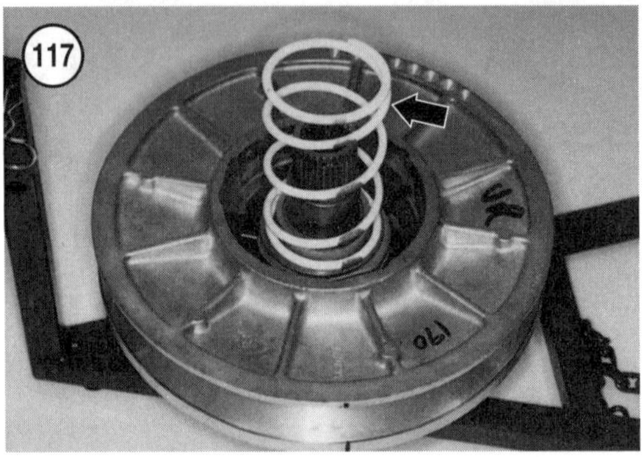

118

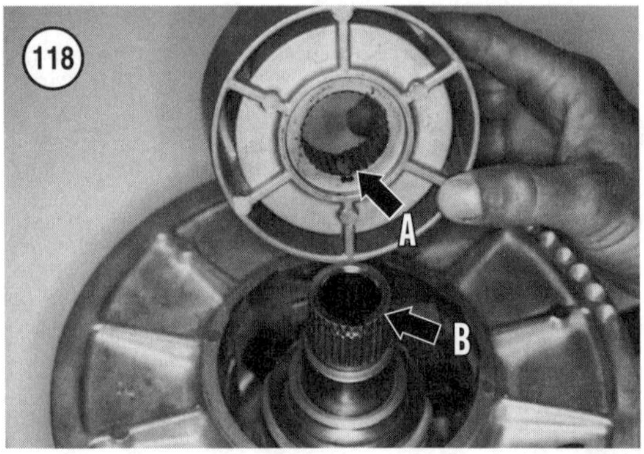

119

push the helix cam partly onto the spline (**Figure 119**).

10. Close and center the VST special tool (A, **Figure 120**) on the helix and compress the spring until the circlip groove on the shaft is visible. Lock the tool handle down with the chain restraint.

11. Install the spacer (B, **Figure 120**) and the circlip (**Figure 121**).

12. Push down on the VST special tool and unlock the tool handle from the chain restraint. Slowly open the special tool.

13. Make sure the circlip is correctly seated in the shaft groove (**Figure 122**).

Inspection (All Models)

1. Thoroughly clean all parts in solvent and dry with compressed air.

2. Check both sheaves of each pulley for cracks or damage.

3. Check the drive belt surfaces of the pulley halves (B, **Figure 110**, typical) for rubber or corrosion buildup. For proper operation, the surfaces must be

120

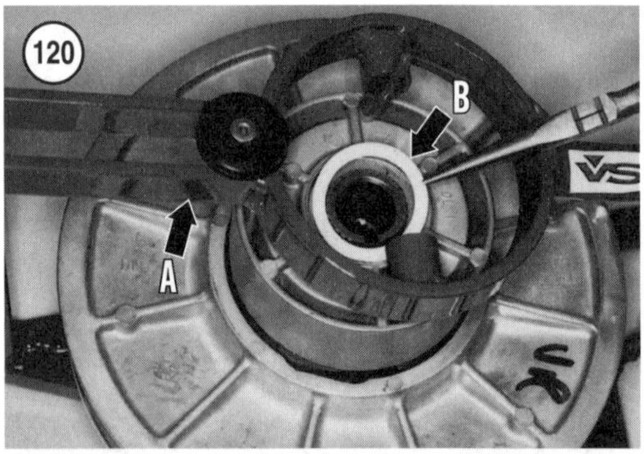

121

122

125

123

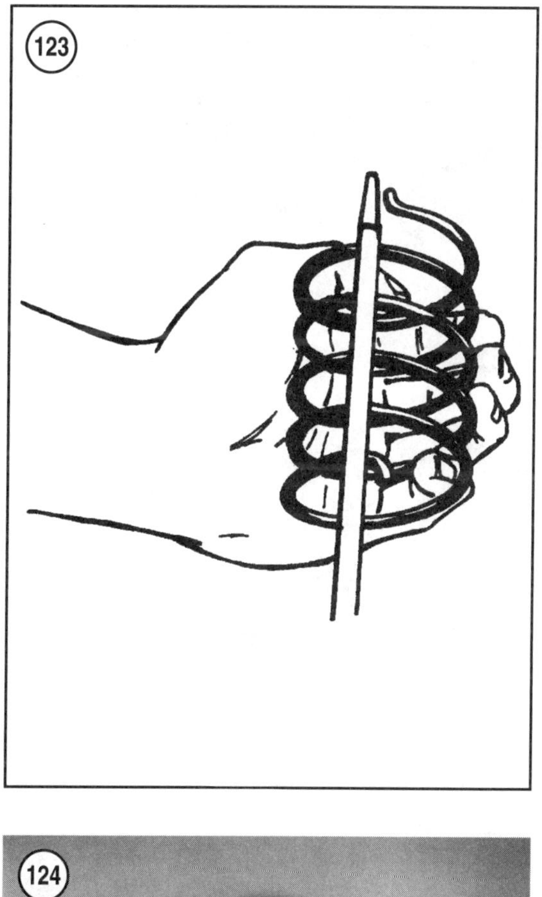

124

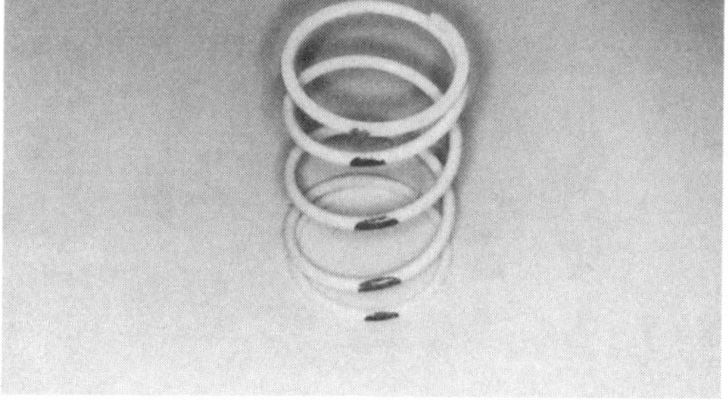

clean. Remove debris with a fine-grade steel wool. Clean with a piece of lint-free cloth.

NOTE
On 1996-1998 models, the constant twisting action will eventually weaken the driven pulley spring. A weak spring will allow the driven pulley to open quicker than specified. This condition can be noticed when riding up steep grades or with a heavy load; the vehicle will be slower and have much less pulling power than normal. It is difficult to gauge spring wear, therefore, consider replacing the spring during driven pulley service.

4A. On 1996-1998 models, check the spring for cracks or distortion. Check the alignment of the ends of the spring as shown in **Figure 123**. The ends of the spring are aligned when new. If the ends are no longer aligned, or the spring has sagged, replace the spring.

4B. On 1999-on models, check the spring for cracks or distortion (**Figure 124**). Replace the spring if it has sagged.

5. Inspect the wear buttons (**Figure 125**, typical) for wear or damage. The wear buttons provide a sliding surface between the helix cam and the movable sheave. The buttons rub against aluminum and wear is usually minimal. If necessary, remove the Torx screws (**Figure 126**) and remove the wear buttons from the backside of the movable sheave.

6. Check the cam ramps on the helix cam (**Figure 127**) for scoring, gouging or other signs of damage. Smooth the ramp area with No. 400 wet or dry sandpaper. If the ramp area is severely damaged, replace the helix cam.

8

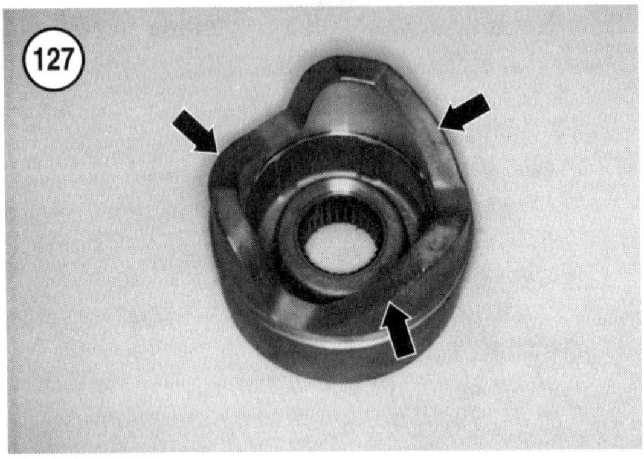

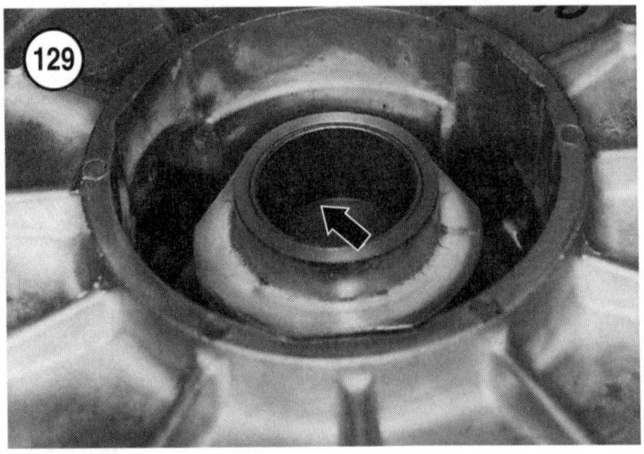

7. Inspect both bushings in the movable sheave. Refer to **Figure 128** and **Figure 129**. The bushing is coated with Teflon and a new bushing must be installed if more brass is showing than Teflon. Do not remove the bushing(s) unless replacement is necessary.
8. Inspect the bushing contact areas of the fixed pulley sheave for wear, nicks or scratches.
9. Inspect the shaft (**Figure 130**) for wear or damage. Check the external splines (A, **Figure 131**), internal splines (**Figure 132**) and circlip grooves (B, **Figure 131**) for wear. Repair or replace the shaft.
10. On 1999-on models, inspect the roller bearing (**Figure 133**) in the fixed sheave for wear or damage. Replace if necessary.
11. Inspect the inner splines of the helix (**Figure 127**) for wear or damage. Replace, if necessary.

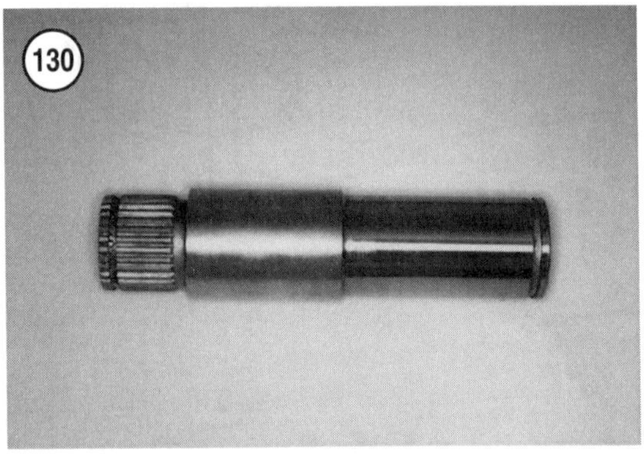

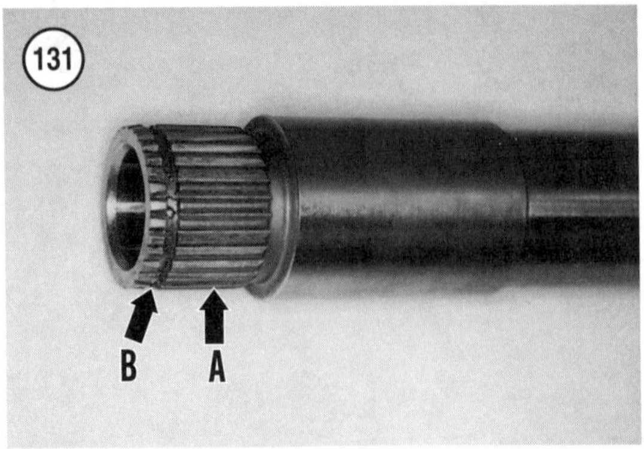

CLUTCH OUTER AND INNER COVER (ALL MODELS)

The clutch outer and inner covers are an important component of the Polaris Variable Transmis-

sion cooling system. The belt and other drive components can be quickly damaged by heat generated by normal operation if they are not properly cooled. Slippage caused by mud, water or oil entering the system can also quickly damage the drive system components. Refer to Chapter Seven for clutch outer and inner covers and additional service to the cooling system not covered in this chapter.

8

Table 1 DRIVE BELT AND PULLEY SPECIFICATIONS

Item	mm	in.
Belt deflection (non-EBS models)	29-32	1.14-1.26
Belt width		
New	29.8-30.2	1.174-1.188
Wear limit	28.6	1.125
Pulley center-to-center distance	252.7-256.5	9.95-10.10
Fixed sheave diameter (EBS models*)		
New	34.9123-34.925	1.3745-1.375
Wear limit	34.8742	1.3730
Inner washer thickness (EBS models)		
New	0.76	0.30
Wear limit	0.64	0.25

* See text in chapter

Table 2 OPERATING RPM AND DRIVE SPRING SPECIFICATIONS

Model year	Operating RPM	Drive pulley spring color and part No.
All years	5800-6200	Blue/green (part No.7041157)

Table 3 DRIVE PULLEY SPRING SPECIFICATIONS

	Wire diameter		Free length		
Color	mm	in.	mm	in.	Part No.
Blue/gold	5.26	0.207	85.9-92.2	3.38-3.63	7041080
Gold	5.26	0.207	79.5-85.9	3.13-3.38	7041148
Silver	5.28	0.208	76.2-82.6	3.00-3.25	7041062
Red	4.88	0.192	92.7-99.1	3.65-3.90	7041083
Red/white	4.88	0.192	88.1-94.5	3.47-3.72	7041150
Brown	5.08	0.200	74.7-81.0	2.94-3.19	7041061
Orange	4.98	0.196	82.6-88.9	3.25-3.50	7041060
Pink	4.50	0.177	116.1-122.4	4.57-4.82	7041065
Yellow	4.88	0.192	71.1-77.5	2.80-3.05	7041102
Green	4.05	0.159	74.4-80.8	2.93-3.18	7041168
Purple	4.27	0.168	107.9-114.3	4.25-4.50	7041063
White	4.05	0.159	71.1-77.5	2.80-3.05	7041032
Plain	3.99	0.157	108.2-114.6	4.26-4.51	7041021
Blue/green	4.05	0.159	61.0-67.6	2.40-2.66	7041157
Black	3.56	0.140	104.8-111.1	4.13-4.38	7041022

Table 4 SHIFT WEIGHTS AND DRIVEN PULLEY SPECIFICATIONS

	Shift weights I.D. mark/weight		Driven pulley*	
Model	Original production	Above 6000 ft	Helix angle	Spring position
1996	10WH 50 grams	10MW 44 grams	40°	2-2
1997	10MH 50 grams	10MW 44 grams	Compound	2-2
1998-on	10MH 50 grams	10WH 50 grams	Compound	2-2

* The first number of spring position is the recommended position of the spring in the movable sheave and the second number is the hole location in the helix cam.

Table 5 TIGHTENING TORQUE SPECIFICATIONS

Item	N•m	in.-lb.	ft.-lb.
Clutch inner cover bolts	16	–	12
Cover plate bolts	17	–	13
Drive clutch spider			
Non-EBS models	271	–	200
EBS models	250	–	185
Drive pulley bolt	54	–	40
Driven pulley bolt	23	–	17

NOTE: Refer to the Supplement at the back of this manual for information unique to 2001-on models, including the Sportsman 400.

CHAPTER NINE

TRANSMISSION

The transmission includes the high, low and reverse gears, as well as the center drive shaft and output gear that drives the rear axles. The rear axles are attached directly to the output gear in the transmission case.

WARNING
The majority of the procedures in this chapter specify the removal of the rear rack and rear fender. After the rear fender is removed, the rear rack support ends are exposed on each side and present a dangerous protrusion during additional component removal and installation. Wrap several brightly colored shop cloths around each end to prevent running into them.

Refer to **Table 1** for tightening torque specifications and **Table 2** for transmission specifications.

Transmission Service Notes

1. As each part is removed from the shaft, set it in the exact order of removal and in the same position from which it was removed. Store the transmission gears, washers and circlips in a divided container, such as a restaurant-size egg carton (**Figure 1**), to help maintain the correct alignment and position.
2. The circlips are a tight fit on the transmission shafts. It is recommended that all circlips be replaced during reassembly.
3. To avoid bending and twisting the new circlips when installing them, use the following installation

technique: Open the new circlip with a pair of circlip pliers while holding the back of the circlip with a pair of pliers (**Figure 2**). Then slide the circlip down the shaft and seat it into its correct transmission groove. This technique can also be used to remove the circlips from a shaft once they are free from their grooves.

TRANSMISSION

Removal/Installation

1. Place the ATV on a level surface and set the parking brake. Block the front wheels to keep it from rolling in either direction.
2. Remove the seat, the front and rear fenders as described in Chapter Fifteen.
3. Remove the carburetor as described in Chapter Six.
4. Remove the air filter air box as described in Chapter Six.
5. Remove the exhaust pipe and muffler as described in Chapter Four.
6. Drain the transmission oil as described in Chapter Three.

CAUTION
Do not lose or damage the spacer washers located behind the driven pulley. These spacers are used to adjust the pulley offset and must be reinstalled.

7. Remove the outer cover, drive belt, drive pulley, driven pulley and inner cover as described in Chapter Eight.
8. On 1996-1998 models, disconnect the speedometer cable from the left side of the transmission case cover.
9. Loosen the rear wheel lug nuts on both rear wheels.
10. Raise the vehicle and support it on wooden blocks under the footrest and frame with the rear wheels off the ground.
11. Remove both rear wheels as described in Chapter Thirteen.
12. Remove the transmission output shaft brake caliper and brake disc (**Figure 3**) as described in Chapter Fourteen. It is not necessary to disconnect the brake lines from the caliper. Move the caliper

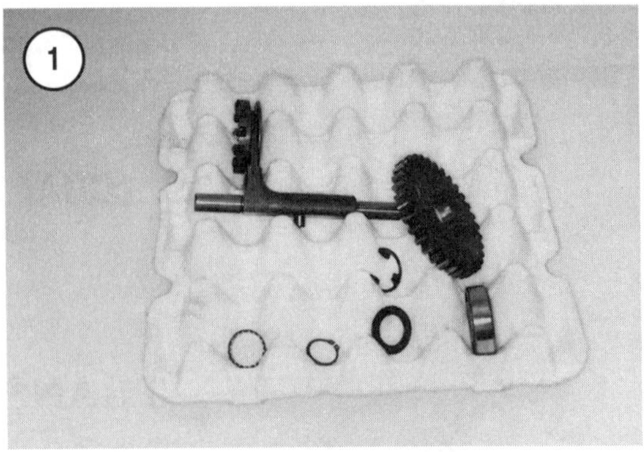

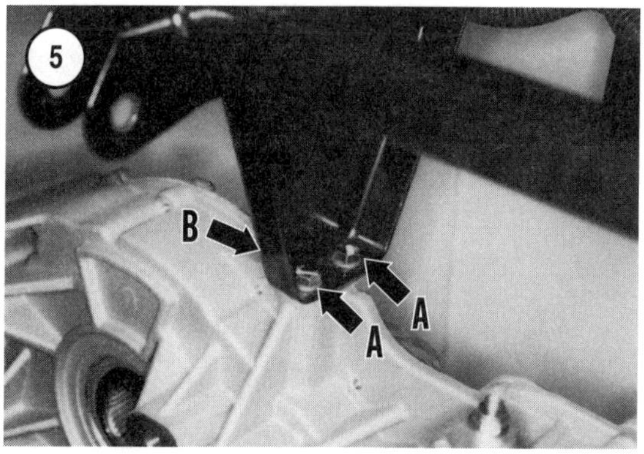

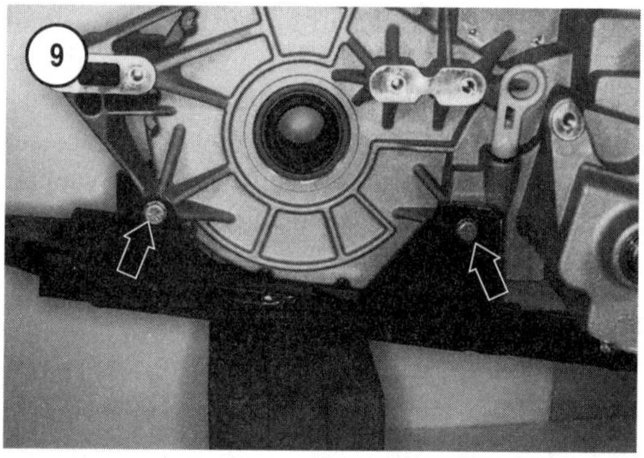

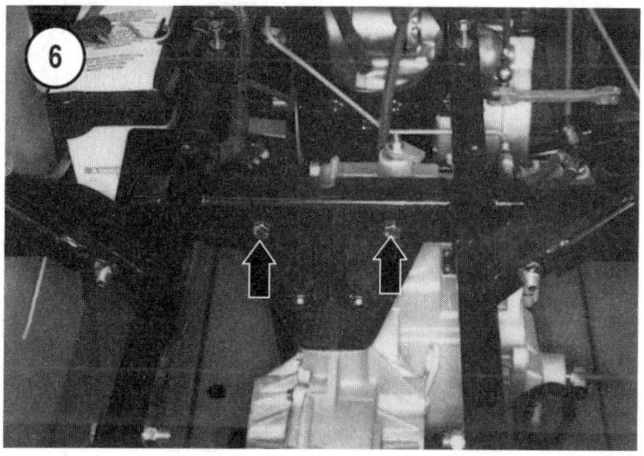

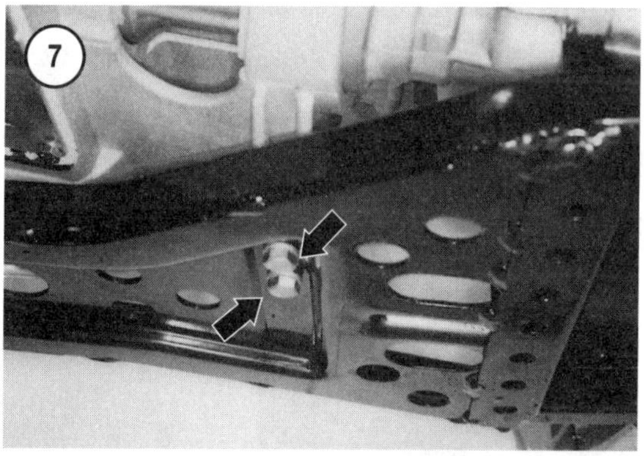

out of the way and support it to the frame with a piece of wire.

13. On 1999-on models, disconnect the electrical connectors from the gear position switches (**Figure 4**).

14. Mark the location of the shift rods in relation to the transmission bell cranks. Remove the nut securing each shift rod end to the transmission bell cranks. Pull straight up and release the shift rod end from both bell cranks. Move the shift rods out of the way.

15. Remove the following rear suspension components as described in Chapter Thirteen:

a. Both shock absorbers.

b. Both upper and lower control arms and rear axle bearing carriers.

c. Both drive axles.

d. Stabilizer support.

16. Remove the two lower bolts (A, **Figure 5**) and two upper bolts (**Figure 6**) securing the transmission upper front support bracket (B, **Figure 5**). Remove the bracket.

17. Remove the two lower bolts (**Figure 7**) and single lower bolt (**Figure 8**) securing the transmission to the frame.

18. Remove the two bolts (**Figure 9**) on each side, securing the transmission to the frame rear mounting brackets.

19. Carefully pull the transmission back and disengage the front output shaft from the front propeller shaft (**Figure 10**).

20. Lift up and remove the transmission from the right side of the frame.

21. Inspect the transmission frame mounting bolt holes (**Figure 11**, typical) for elongation and cracks. Repair or replace as necessary.

22. Install by reversing these removal steps while noting the following:

a. Apply a coat of antiseize to the front output shaft splines (**Figure 12**) prior to installation into the front propeller shaft (**Figure 10**).
b. Tighten the transmission mounting bolts securely in the following order: front support bracket, front support bracket upper and lower bolts, transmission lower mounting bolts, lower left and right transmission frame mounting bolts.
c. Refill the transmission oil as described in Chapter Three.
d. Adjust the shift rod as described in this chapter.

10

11

12

Transmission Case Disassembly

Refer to **Figure 13**.

1. If not already drained, remove the dipstick and drain the oil from the transmission.
2. Remove the drain plug and washer (**Figure 14**) from the base of the right case half.
3. Shift the transmission into NEUTRAL.
4. On 1999-on models, perform the following:
   a. Mark the front gear indicator switch with a F (front) (A, **Figure 15**). The switches are different and must be reinstalled in the correct location.
   b. Remove the mounting screws and remove both gear indicator switches (A and B, **Figure 15**) from the top of the transmission case.
5. Set the transmission on wooden blocks with the left side facing up.

6A. On 1996 models, remove the perimeter bolts, washers and self-locking nuts securing the transmission cover to the case. Make sure to remove the two center bolts. Discard the self-locking nuts, as they cannot be re-used.

NOTE

*On 1997-on models, the bolts securing the cover are unique since the underside of the bolt head flange is serrated (**Figure 16**). While loosening these bolts, it will feel like the bolt is stripped within the bolt hole in the transmission case. This is not the case and there is no threadlocking compound on the bolt threads.*

6B. On 1997-on models, remove the perimeter bolts securing the transmission cover (A, **Figure 17**) to the case. Make sure to remove the two center bolts (B, **Figure 17**).

CAUTION

***Do not pry** the cover away from the transmission case. The cover is very long and is relatively thin. If prying to release it, there is a very good chance the cover will crack and have to be replaced (it can be replaced separately). The sealing surface between the two parts is large and the*

(13)

TRANSMISSION CASE

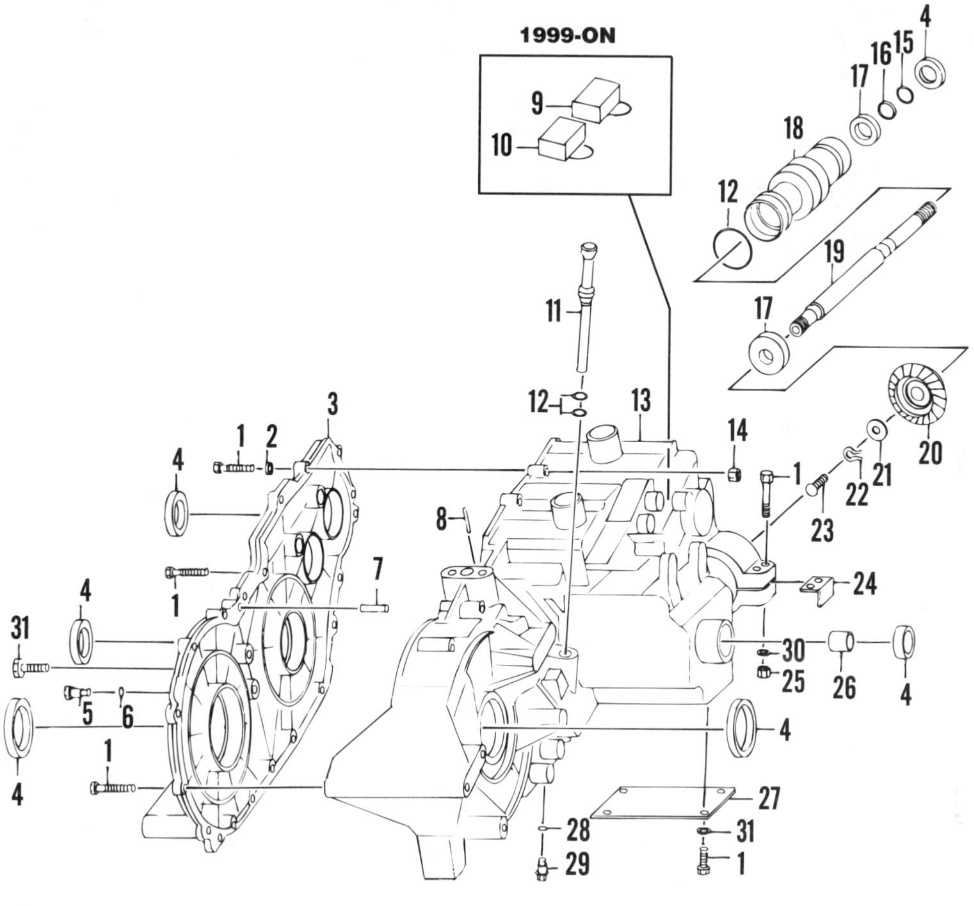

1. Bolt
2. Washer (1996 models)
3. Cover
4. Oil seal
5. Bolt
6. Washer (1996 models)
7. Dowel pin
8. Vent tube fitting
9. Front switch (two position) (1999-on)
10. Rear switch (three position) (1999-on)
11. Dipstick
12. O-rings
13. Transmission case
14. Nuts (self-locking) (1996 models)
15. Circlip
16. Shim
17. Bearing
18. Front output housing
19. Front output shaft
20. Front output shaft ring gear
21. Washer
22. Lockwasher
23. Bolt
24. Plate (models so equipped)
25. Nut
26. Bushing
27. Bottom access cover
28. Washer
29. Drain plug
30. Washer
31. Washer

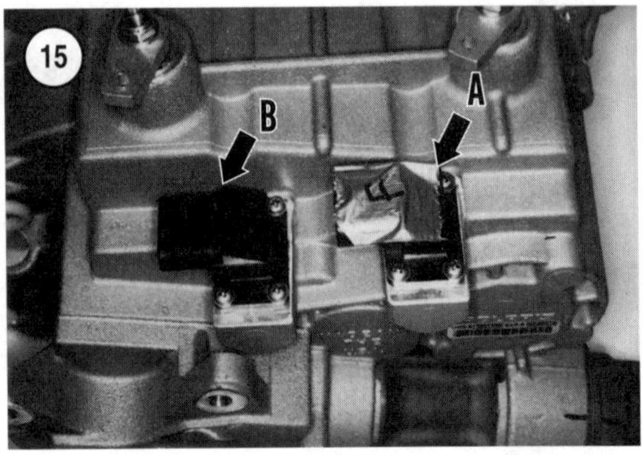

sealing compound has a tendancy to hold the parts together.

7. There are four projections around the perimeter of the cover. Refer to **Figures 18-21**. These projections *must be used* to aid in loosening the cover from the transmission case.

CAUTION

***Do not** use any other method of loosening the cover from the transmission case as the cover will be damaged. This is a time-consuming task and it must be carried out as indicated in Step 8.*

8. Use a plastic or soft-faced mallet and wooden or plastic dowel to carefully tap on the four projections around the perimeter of the cover (**Figure 22**) in a crisscross pattern. Continue to work around the cover until the tapping sound becomes dull. The dull sound indicates that the cover is starting to separate. Try to insert a fingernail between the mating surfaces around the entire perimeter. If a fingernail can be inserted this indicates separation has started. Continue to tap around the perimeter in a crisscross pattern until the cover has separated from the case and the three locating dowels.

9. Also, carefully tap in the areas where the shaft bearings are located (**Figure 23**) to loosen the outer races from the cover.

10. Carefully pull the cover straight up and off the transmission case and shafts. Remove the cover, do not lose the three locating dowels. Refer to **Figures 24-26**.

NOTE

The bottom access cover had a sealant applied to it during assembly and

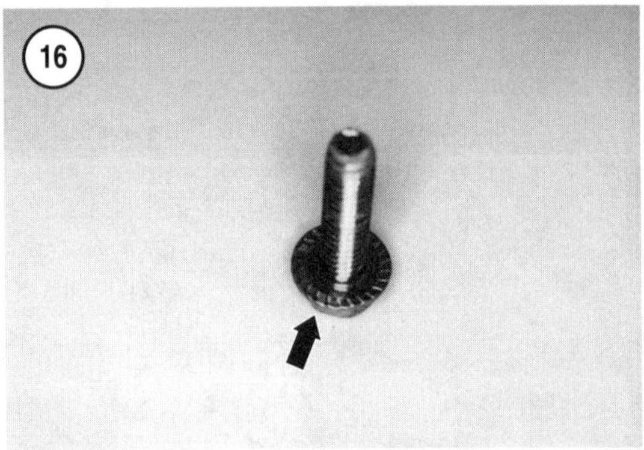

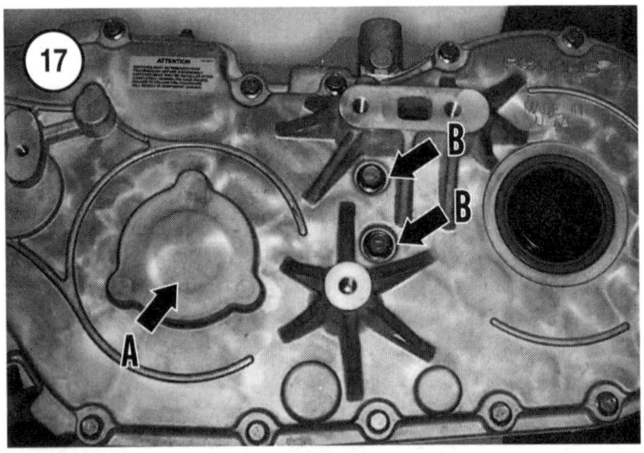

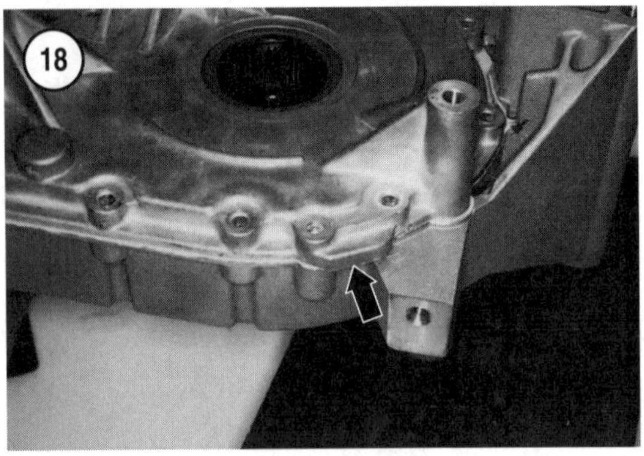

19

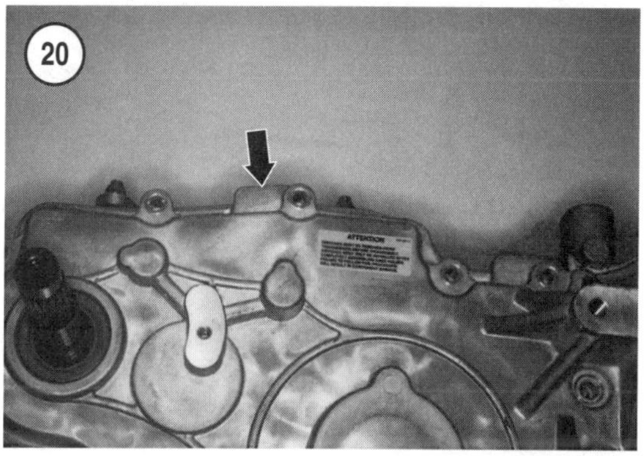
20

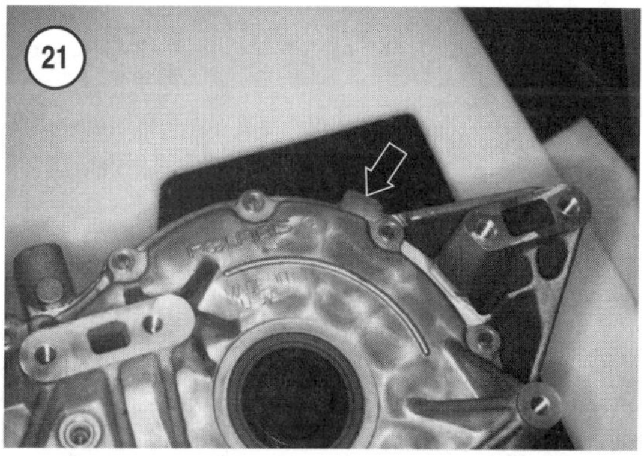
21

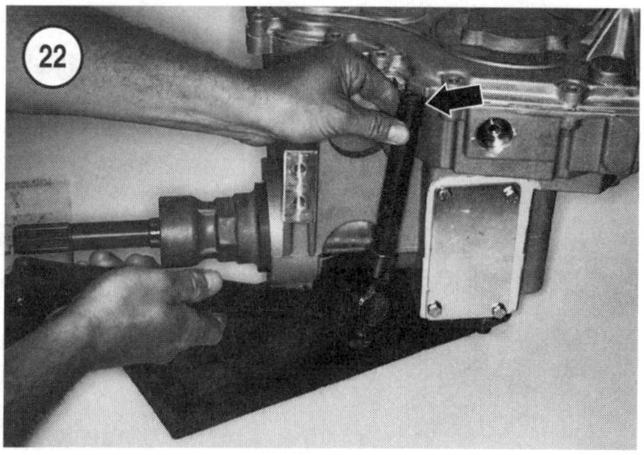
22

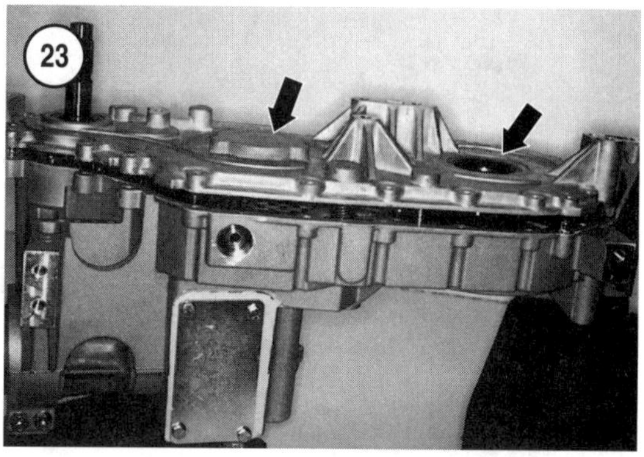
23

24

25

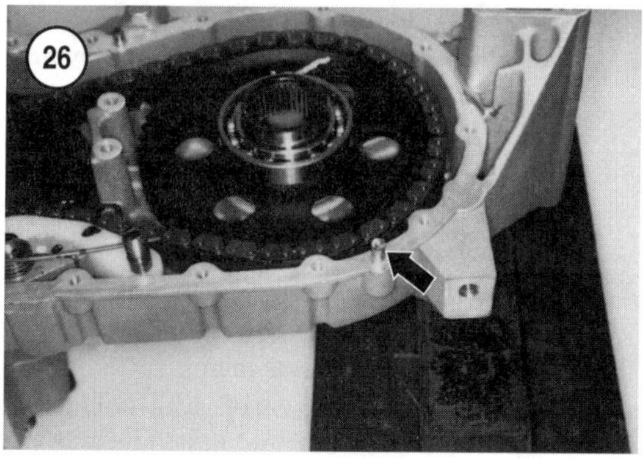
26

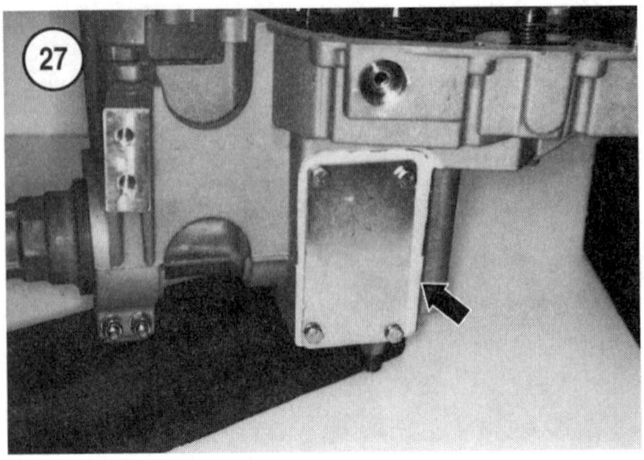

is difficult to loosen from the bottom of the transmission case.

11. Remove the screws and lockwashers securing the bottom access cover (**Figure 27**). Tap around the perimeter of the cover to break the sealant loose, then remove the cover.

12. Prior to removing the chain tensioner cam, note if the tensioner is fully extended. If the tensioner cam is fully extended, the drive chain has stretched to its service limit and must be replaced. Also replace the tensioner shoe.

NOTE
*Looking directly at the drive chain and transmission gears, the output sprocket drive chain travels counterclockwise on the two gears, as shown in **Figure 28**.*

13. Remove the chain tensioner assembly as follows:
   a. Carefully unhook the torsion spring from the rear dowel pin (A, **Figure 29**) and remove the torsion spring from the front dowel pin (B, **Figure 29**).
   b. Remove the front dowel pin and tensioner lock cam (**Figure 30**).
   c. Withdraw the rear dowel pin and remove the chain tensioner shoe as an assembly (**Figure 31**).
   d. On models so equipped, remove the two spacers located between the base of the tensioner and the transmission case.

14. Use a permanent marking pen and mark one or two of the chain link plates (**Figure 32**) indicating the surface of the chain that is facing out. This will indicate the rotational direction of the drive chain. If the existing drive chain is going to be reinstalled it

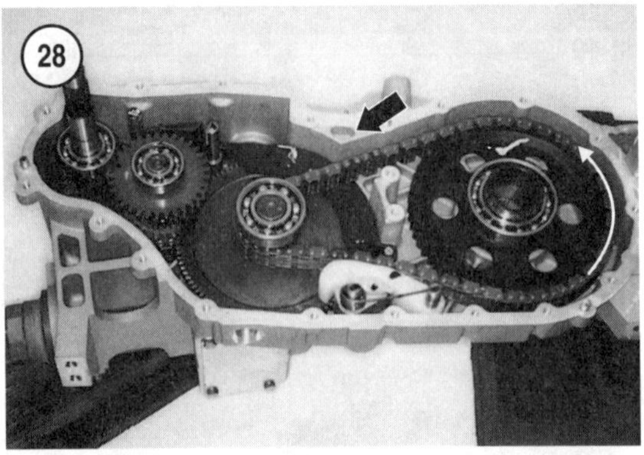

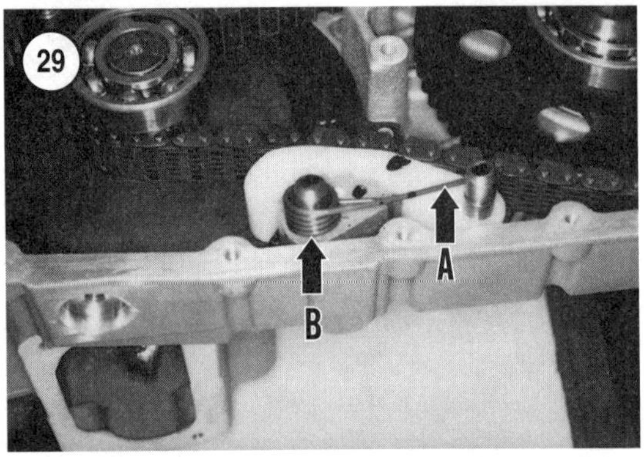

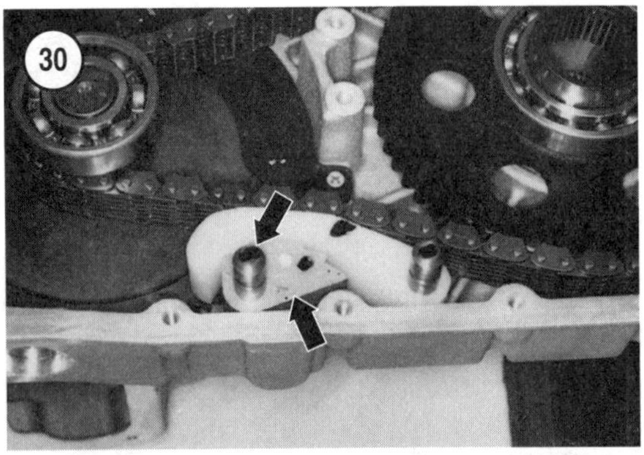

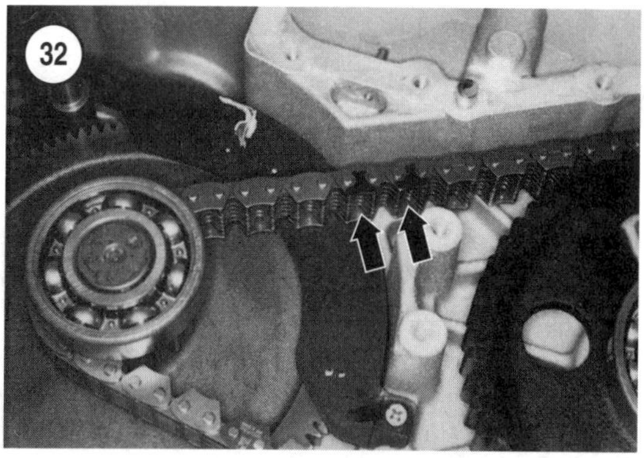

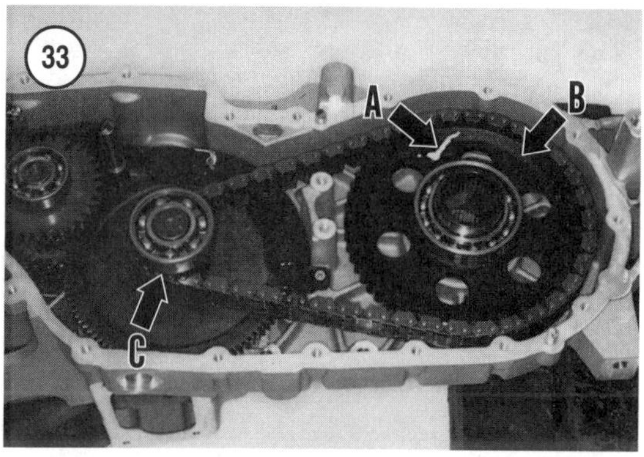

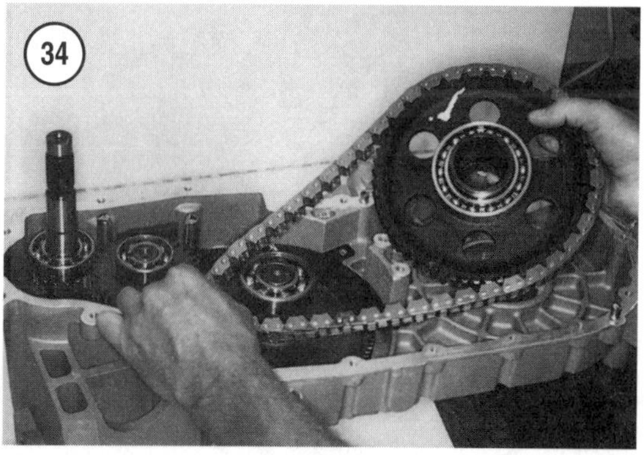

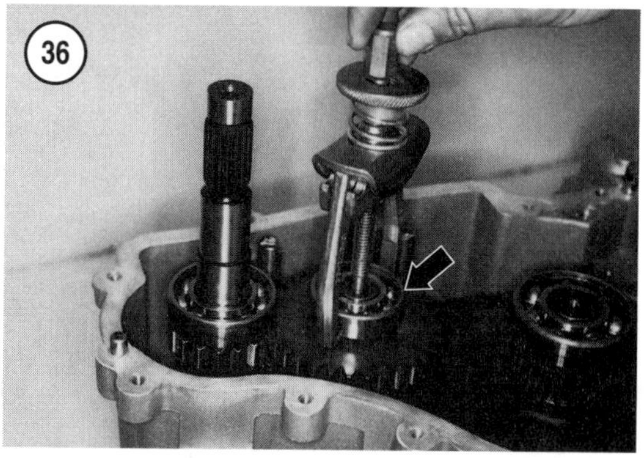

must be installed with the marked links facing up so it will travel in the same direction. A new drive chain can be installed facing in either direction.

15. Make a paint mark (A, **Figure 33**) on the outer surface of the output gear, indicating the left side of the gear. The gear must be positioned in the same direction during installation.

NOTE
The following step is difficult if working on a transmission with a new chain that has not yet stretched. A tight chain makes it difficult to withdraw the output shaft right side bearing out of the transmission case receptacle.

16. Carefully pull the output gear and bearing assembly (B, **Figure 33**) straight up and out of the transmission case.

17. Disengage the chain from the center drive shaft (C, **Figure 33**) and remove the output gear and chain (**Figure 34**).

18. Remove the screws and the oil deflector (**Figure 35**).

19. Use a two- or three-jaw puller and remove the bearing (**Figure 36**) from the output shaft.

20. On 2000 models, remove the circlip (A, **Figure 37**) and washer (B, **Figure 37**) securing the low gear.

21. Wiggle the low gear (A, **Figure 38**) on the shaft and withdraw the needle bearing (B, **Figure 38**) out of the low gear. Remove the needle bearing from the shaft.

22. Move the low gear (**Figure 39**) to one side and remove it from the shaft.

23A. On 1996-1999 models, slide off the thrust washer.

23B. On 2000 models, remove the retaining ring (**Figure 40**).

24. Withdraw the low gear shift fork (A, **Figure 41**) and low gear engagement dog (B, **Figure 41**) from the transmission case.

NOTE

*Make sure the drain plug and washer (**Figure 14**) were removed in Step 2. If not, remove them at this time since the center drive shaft and gear cannot be removed while they are in place.*

25. Use a plastic mallet and tap on the right end of the center drive shaft and withdraw the center shaft and output gear assembly (**Figure 42**) from the transmission case.

26. Place a 1/2 inch wrench on the front high/low range shift fork shaft nut and rotate the shift shaft arm to release it from the high/low range shift fork (**Figure 43**).

CAUTION

Do not try to remove only one shaft at a time. The two shafts are held together with a common silent chain and must be removed as an assembly.

27. Remove the high/low/reverse shaft assembly, the input shaft assembly, the silent chain and high/low gearshift fork from the transmission case as an assembly (**Figure 44**).

28. If necessary, perform the following:
  a. Remove the screws and lockwashers securing the pinion gear retaining plate (A, **Figure 45**).
  b. Withdraw the pinion gear assembly (B, **Figure 45**) from the transmission case half.

29. Inspect all parts as described in this chapter.

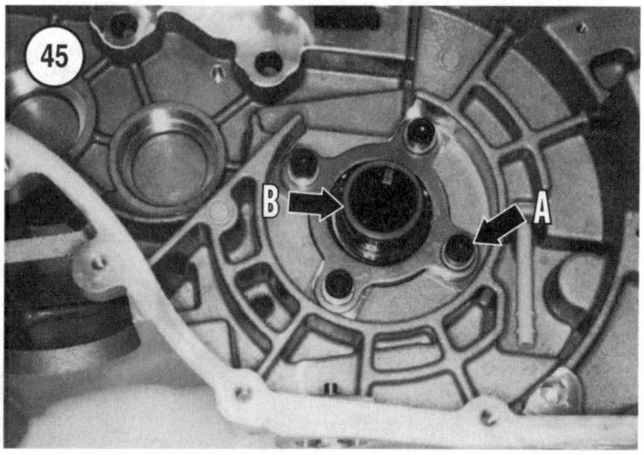

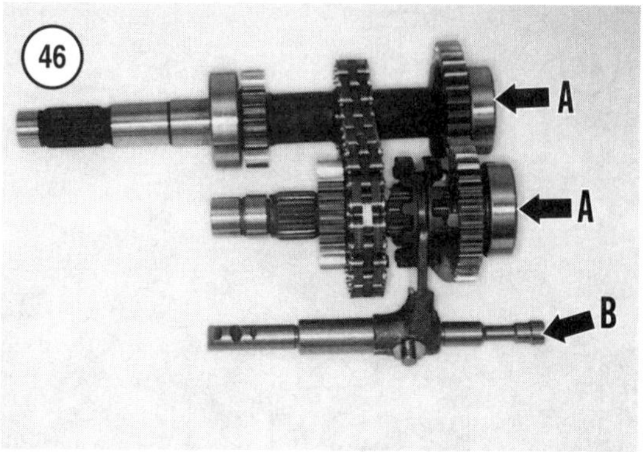

Transmission Case Assembly

Refer to **Figure 13**.

1. Install new oil seals in the transmission case as described in this chapter.
2. Apply clean transmission oil to all sliding parts, to the bearings and to the bearing receptacles in the transmission case.
3. If removed, perform the following:
   a. Install the pinion gear assembly (B, **Figure 45**) into the transmission case.
   b. Install the pinion gear retaining plate (A, **Figure 45**).
   c. Apply a light coat of ThreeBond TB1342, Loctite 242, or equivalent threadlocking compound to the screw threads prior to installation.
   d. Install the lockwashers and screws and tighten the screws to the torque specification listed in **Table 1**.
4. If the two shafts have been separated from each other, correctly assemble the input shaft and high/low/reverse shaft and the silent chain (A, **Figure 46**).
5. Correctly install the high/reverse shift fork onto the high/reverse gear engagement dog on the shaft (B, **Figure 46**).
6. Correctly position the assembled shafts, silent chain and shift fork into the transmission case (**Figure 47**). Correctly locate the shift fork pin into the high/reverse shift shaft fingers and spring (**Figure 48**).
7. Align the shafts with the bearings in the case and press the shafts into place. Carefully tap on the shaft ends (**Figure 49**) with a soft-faced mallet to ensure the shafts and shift fork shaft are completely seated in the transmission case bearings.

9

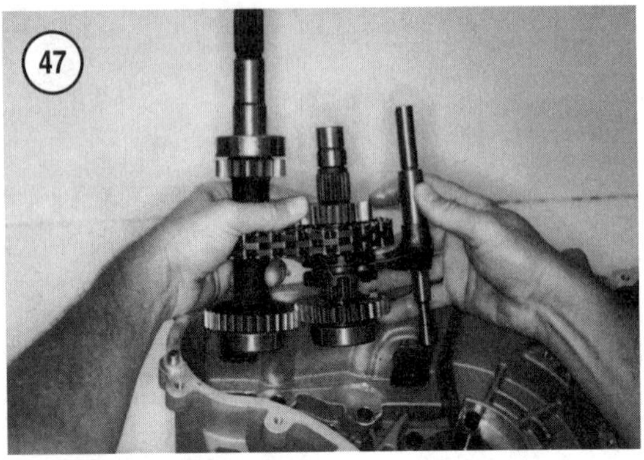

8. Check that the shift fork is still correctly engaged with the engagement dog and the shift shaft (**Figure 43**).
9. Tap on the end of the shift fork to make sure it is completely seated in the transmission case receptacle (**Figure 50**). Check that the shift fork is still correctly engaged with the engagement dog.
10. Shift the high/low/reverse gear shaft into NEUTRAL. If not located in the neutral position, the interlock mechanism will prevent the installation of the low gearshift fork.
11. Rotate the input shaft to make sure the shafts are seated correctly and there is no binding.
12. Install the center drive shaft assembly into the transmission case (**Figure 51**).
13. Align the shaft with the bearing in the case and press the shaft into place while correctly meshing it with the mating gear (A, **Figure 52**) on the high/low/reverse shaft. Carefully tap on the shaft end (B, **Figure 52**) with a soft-faced mallet to ensure the shaft is completely seated in the transmission case bearing.
14. Rotate the center shaft to make sure the shaft is seated correctly and there is no binding.
15. Correctly position the low gear engagement dog with the dogs facing out (A, **Figure 53**) and install it onto the low gearshift fork (B, **Figure 53**).
16. Install the assembly (**Figure 54**) into the transmission case.
17. Slide the low gear engagement dog onto the splines of the high/low/reverse shaft (**Figure 55**) and guide the low gearshift fork into position.
18. Correctly locate the low gearshift fork pin into the low shift shaft fingers (**Figure 56**).
19. Tap on the end of the low gearshift fork to make sure it is completely seated in the transmission case receptacle. Check that the shift fork is still correctly engaged with the engagement dog.

52

56

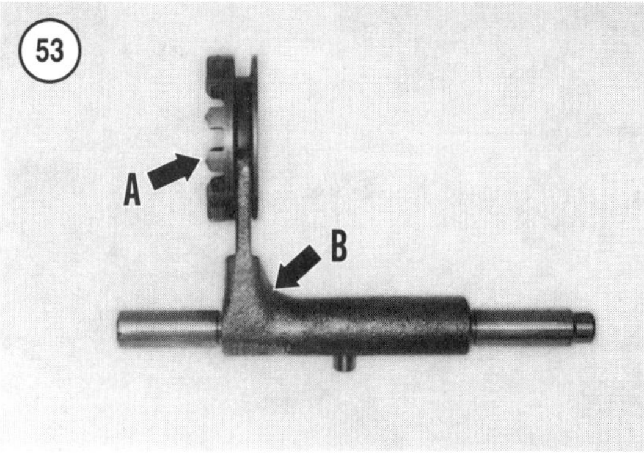

53

57

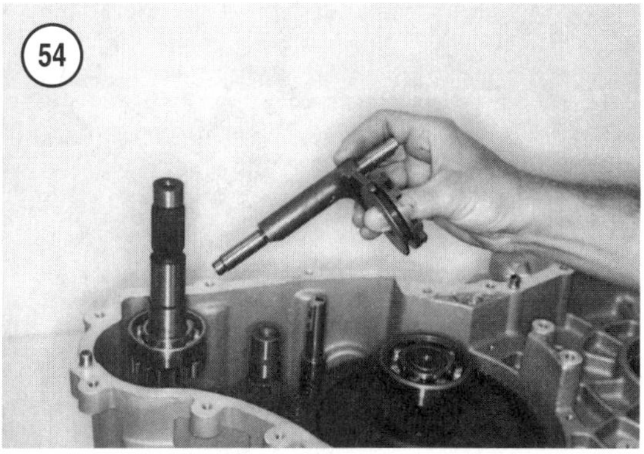
54

55

20A. On 1996-1999 models, slide the thrust washer onto the high/low/reverse shaft.

20B. On 2000 models, install the retaining ring (**Figure 57**) onto the high/low/reverse shaft. Make sure the ring is correctly seated in the shaft (**Figure 40**).

NOTE
Do not install the needle bearing at this time. It must be installed after the low gear is installed onto the shaft.

21. Position the low gear with the shift dogs facing down (**Figure 58**) and install the low gear past the input shaft bearing and onto the high/low/reverse shaft.

22. Center the low gear (A, **Figure 38**) on the shaft.

23. Apply clean gearcase lubricant to the needle bearing and insert the bearing into the low gear (B, **Figure 38**). Push it in until it bottoms.

24. Install the inner washer (**Figure 59**) onto the high/low/reverse shaft.

25. On 2000 models, install the circlip (**Figure 60**) onto the shaft. Make sure the circlip is correctly seated within the shaft groove (A, **Figure 37**).

26. Install the bearing onto the high/low/reverse shaft as follows:

   a. Heat the bearing on a hot plate to aid in installation.
   b. Install the bearing onto the shaft. Tap on the inner race of the bearing and install the bearing until it bottoms on the washer or circlip (**Figure 61**).

27. Apply ThreeBond No. 1342, or equivalent, threadlocking compound to the screw threads prior to installation. Install the oil deflector (**Figure 62**). Do not overtighten the screws, as the mounting hole surrounding area may crack.

NOTE
If a new drive chain is being installed, it can be installed running in either direction.

NOTE
*Looking directly at the drive chain and gears, the drive chain travels counterclockwise on the two gears (**Figure 63**).*

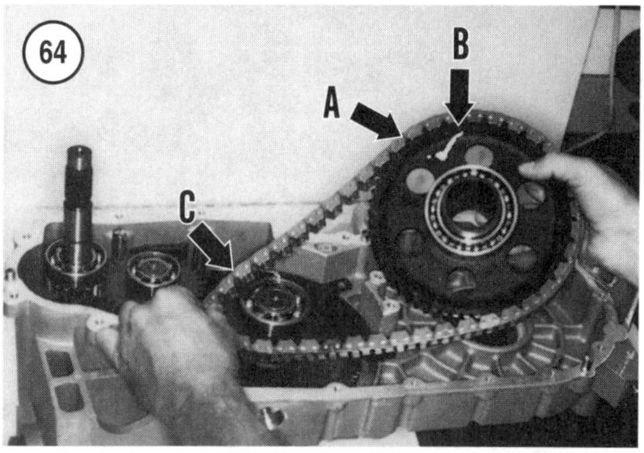

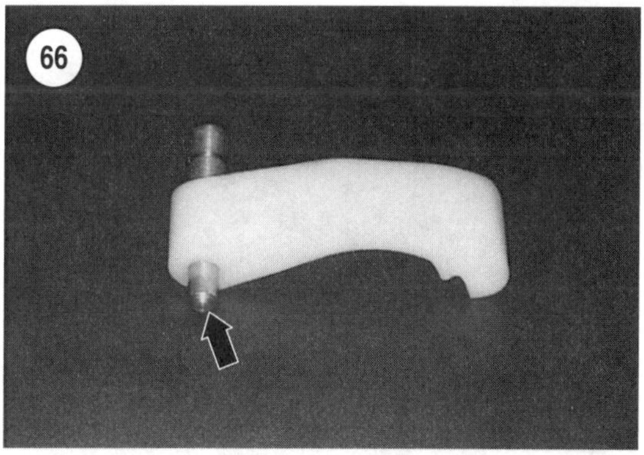

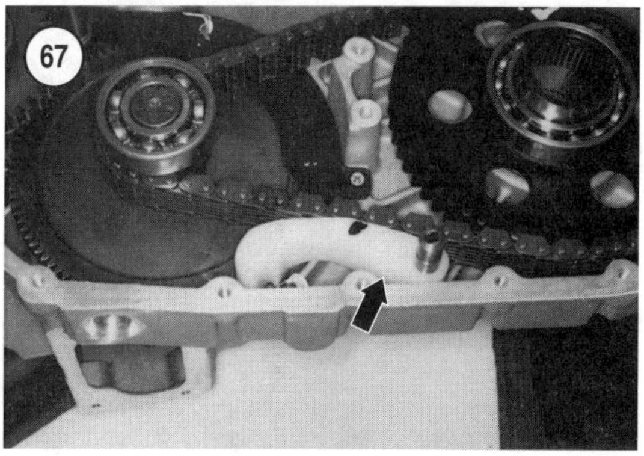

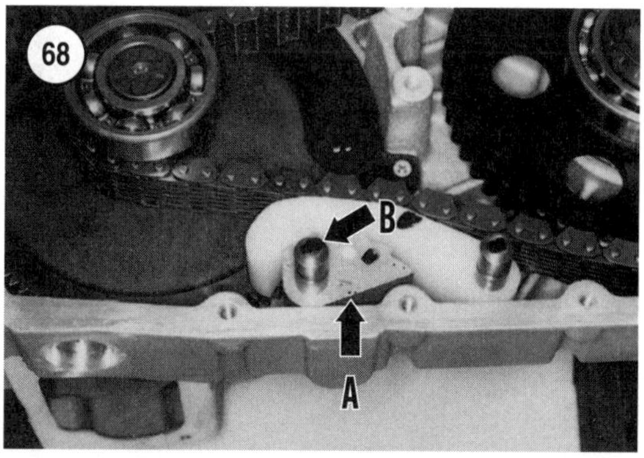

28. Position the output gear with the paint mark made in *Disassembly* Step 15, facing up (A, **Figure 64**).

29. If installing the existing drive chain, refer to the rotational marks (**Figure 32**) made in *Removal* Step 14 and install the drive chain (A, **Figure 64**) onto the output gear (B) so it travels in the same direction.

30. Install the drive chain onto the center drive shaft gear (C, **Figure 64**) and install the output gear bearing into the right case receptacle.

31. Tap on the end of the output gear (**Figure 65**) to make sure it is completely seated in the transmission case bearing receptacle.

32. Rotate the output gear and chain to make sure the output gear is seated correctly and there is no binding.

33. To install the drive chain tensioner, perform the following:

a. On models so equipped, install the two spacers onto the transmission case and align the holes with the transmission case holes. This is necessary for dowel pin installation in the following substeps.

b. Install the rear dowel pin into the chain tensioner shoe (**Figure 66**).

c. Install the rear dowel pin and the chain tensioner shoe as an assembly (**Figure 67**). Push the dowel pin in until it bottoms.

d. Press the tensioner shoe against the chain and install the front dowel pin and tensioner lock cam (A, **Figure 68**). Push the dowel pin in until it bottoms (B).

e. Install the tensioner spring onto the front dowel pin (B) and hook it onto the lock cam as shown in **Figure 69**.

f. Move the end of the spring around and place it on the inner surface of the rear dowel pin. Correctly position the spring into the rear

9

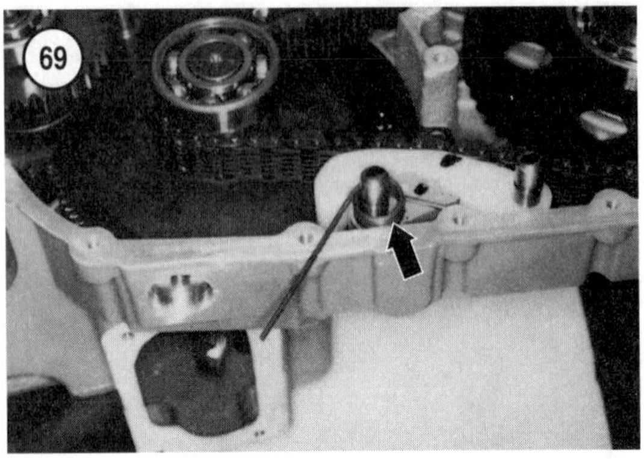

dowel pin groove (**Figure 70**). The spring must be located as shown to apply pressure against the tensioner lock cam and shoe.

g. Check that the tensioner cam has pressed the tensioner shoe up against the drive chain (**Figure 71**).

34. Rotate the bearings on the end of the shafts and apply clean transmission gearcase lubricant to the bearings and to the outer races. Refer to **Figure 72** and **Figure 73**. Make sure the bearings rotate freely.

35. Clean the sealing surfaces of the transmission case and cover with an aerosol parts cleaner.

36. Apply an even coating of Loctite 515 or 518 gasket sealant, or equivalent, to the sealing surface of the transmission case. Also apply sealant to the two raised posts (**Figure 74**) for the two center bolts.

37. If removed, install the three locating dowels (**Figures 75-77**) onto the transmission case.

38. Thoroughly lubricate the transmission bearing receptacles in the cover. This will make installing the bearing outer races into the cover easier.

CAUTION

When properly aligned, the cover will slide over the input shaft, center drive shaft and the bearings and will seat against the transmission case. If the cover will not fit together completely, do not attempt to pull the cover together against the case with the case bolts. Remove the cover and investigate the cause of the interference. Check that the gears and shift forks are properly installed. The transmission cover and case are sold separately; they are not a matched set, but are still very expensive. Do not risk

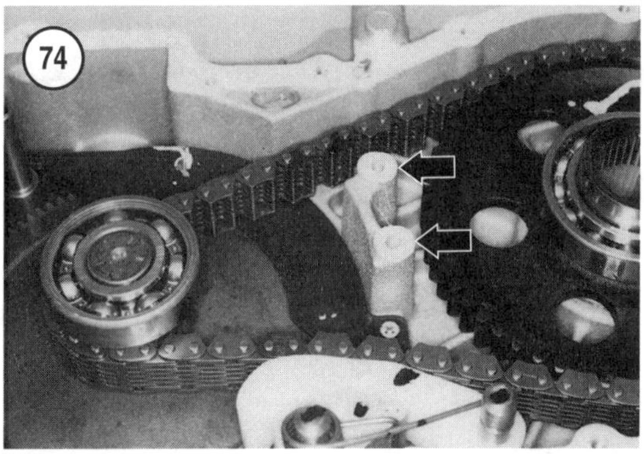

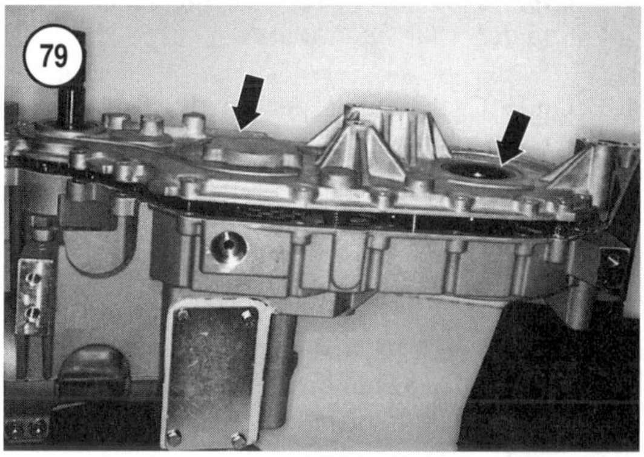

damage by trying to force the two parts together.

39. Install and slowly lower the cover onto the input shaft, center drive shaft and onto the bearings until the cover is parallel to the case around the entire perimeter (**Figure 78**). Slowly press the case half down onto the bearings until both case halves are seated against each other around the entire perimeter. If necessary, use a plastic or soft-faced mallet and tap the cover into place in the areas of the shaft bearings (**Figure 79**).

CAUTION
*There are two different size case bolts. The two center bolts are 5/16 in. and the remaining perimeter bolts are 1/4 in. bolts. Be sure to refer to the correct torque specification listed in **Table 1**.*

40A. On 1996 models, perform the following:

a. Install the perimeter 1/4 in. bolts, washers and new self-locking nuts.
b. Install the two center 5/16 in. bolts and washers securing the transmission case halves together.

9

c. Tighten the two center 5/16 in. bolts first, then the perimeter bolts and nuts in three steps in a crisscross pattern to the torque specification listed in **Table 1**.

NOTE
*On 1997-on models, the bolts securing the cover are unique since the underside of the bolt head flange is serrated (**Figure 80**). While tightening these bolts it will feel like the bolt is stripping the bolt hole in the transmission case. This is not the case. Do **not** apply any threadlocking compound to the bolt threads.*

40B. On 1997-on models, perform the following:

a. Install the perimeter 1/4 in. bolts (A, **Figure 81**) and the two center 5/16 in. bolts (B, **Figure 81**) securing the transmission case halves together.
b. Tighten the two center 5/16 in. bolts (B, **Figure 81**) first, then the perimeter bolts (A, **Figure 81**) in three steps in a crisscross pattern to the torque specification listed in **Table 1**.

41. At this point, check the transmission operation. Rotate the shafts by hand and check for smooth operation. The shafts should not have end play, but should also not bind.
42. Clean the sealing surfaces of the transmission case and the inside surface of the bottom access plate with an aerosol parts cleaner.
43. Apply an even coat of ThreeBond 1215 or equivalent gasket sealant to the sealing surface of the transmission case (**Figure 82**).
44. Install the bottom access plate, bolts and lockwashers (**Figure 83**). Tighten the bolts to the torque specification listed in **Table 1**.

CAUTION
*The internal contacts of both switches are different (**Figure 84**) and they must be reinstalled in the correct location on the transmission case. If installed incorrectly, the switches will be damaged.*

45. On 1999-on models, perform the following:

a. Refer to the F mark made in *Disassembly* Step 4. Install the front gear indicator switch with a F (front) (A, **Figure 85**) in the front receptacle. Install the screws and tighten securely.
b. Install the rear gear indicator switch (B, **Figure 85**) in the rear receptacle. Install the screws and tighten securely.

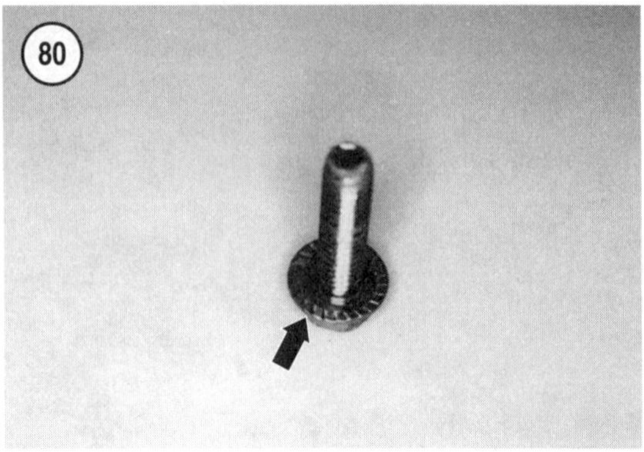

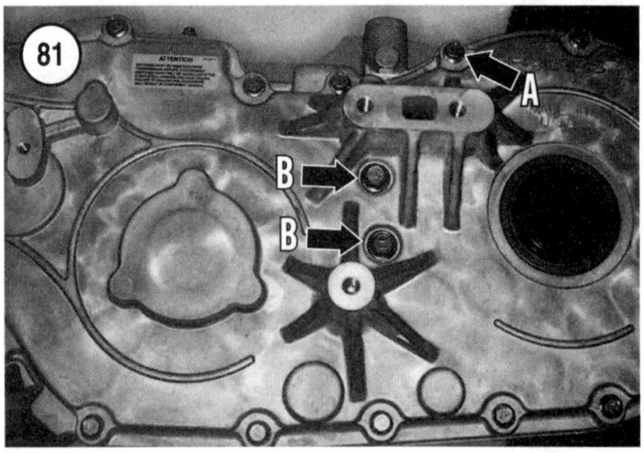

46. Install the drain plug and washer (**Figure 86**) into the base of the right case half. Tighten to the torque specification listed in **Table 1**

47. Install new oil seals as described in Chapter One.

83

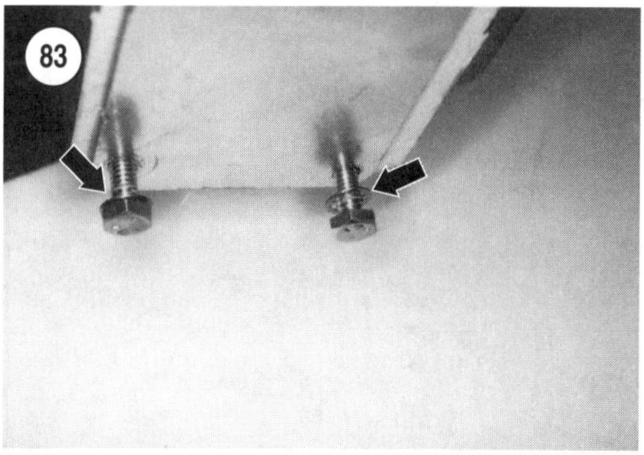

84

85

86

Transmission Shafts

Disassembly

Refer to **Figure 87**.

1. To separate the input shaft from the high/low/reverse shaft, perform the following:
   a. Carefully twist the shafts (**Figure 88**) disengaging the silent chain from the gear sprocket on the high/low/reverse shaft.
   b. Slide the high/low/reverse shaft out of the chain (**Figure 89**) and remove it.
   c. Remove the silent chain from the input shaft gear sprocket (**Figure 90**).
2. The input shaft cannot be disassembled with the exception of the bearings. If the bearings (A, **Figure 91**) are defective, replace them as described in Chapter One.
3. To disassemble the high/low/reverse shaft (**Figure 92**), perform the following:
   a. Use a two- or three-jaw puller to remove the bearing (A) from the right end of the shaft.
   b. Remove the circlip and slide off the thrust washer.
   c. Slide off the high gear (B), needle bearing and washer.
   d. Slide off the high/reverse engagement dog (C).
   e. Remove the circlip and slide off the washer.
   f. Slide off the reverse gear (D), needle bearing and washer.
4. To disassemble the center drive shaft, slide off the output gear (**Figure 93**). If necessary, use a two- or three-jaw puller to remove the bearing (**Figure 94**) from the left end of the shaft.
5. Inspect the shaft components as described under *Transmission Inspection* in this chapter.

Assembly

1. If removed, install the bearing (**Figure 94**) onto the left end of the center drive shaft. Install the output gear (**Figure 93**) onto the shaft.
2. To assemble the high/low/reverse shaft (**Figure 92**), perform the following:
   a. Slide on the washer and the needle bearing.
   b. Position the reverse gear with the gear dogs side going on last and slide the gear (D) onto the shaft and onto the needle bearing.

(87)

TRANSMISSION

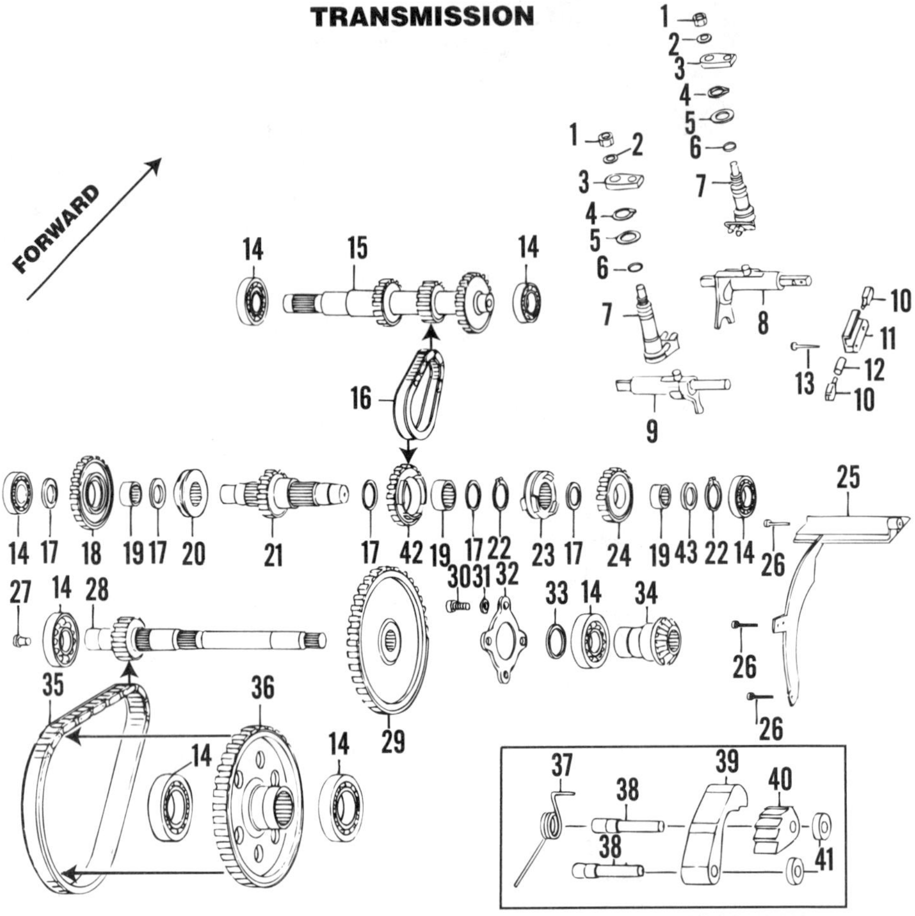

1. Nut
2. Washer
3. Bell crank
4. Circlip
5. Washer
6. O-ring
7. Shift fork
8. Shift fork (low gear)
9. Shift fork (high/reverse)
10. Pin
11. Interlock bracket
12. Spring
13. Screw
14. Bearing
15. Input shaft
16. Silent chain
17. Washer
18. Low gear (33 teeth)
19. Needle bearing
20. Low gear engagement dog
21. High/low/reverse shaft
22. Circlip
23. High/reverse engagement dog
24. High gear (30 teeth)
25. Oil deflector
26. Screw
27. Pin
28. Center drive shaft
29. Output gear (100 teeth)
30. Screw
31. Washer
32. Bearing retainer
33. Circlip
34. Pinion gear (16 teeth)
35. Drive chain
36. Output gear
37. Torsion spring
38. Dowel pin
39. Tensioner shoe
40. Tensioner lock cam
41. Spacer (models so equipped)
42. Reverse gear (24 teeth)
43. Thrust washer

88

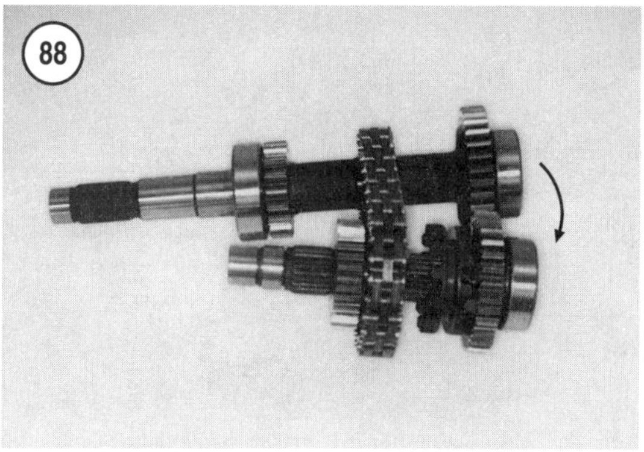

92

89

93

90

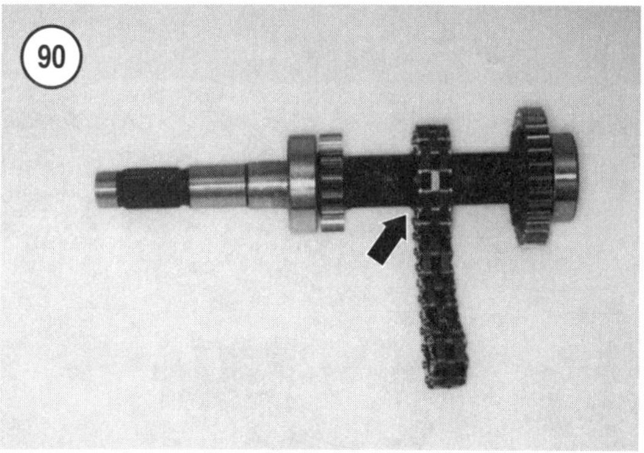

91

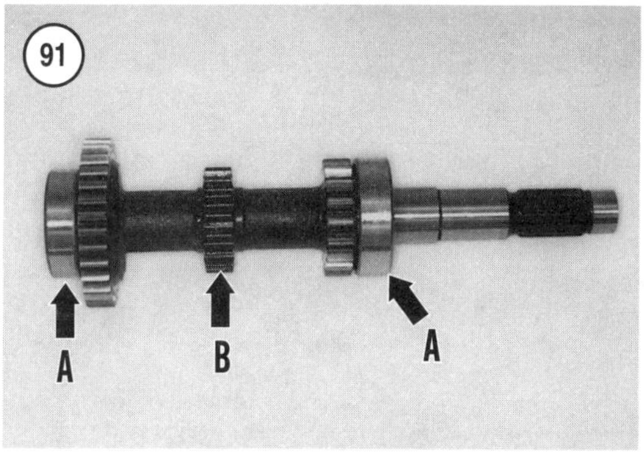

c. Slide on the washer and install the new circlip. Make sure the circlip is correctly seated in the shaft groove.

d. Slide on the high/reverse engagement dog (C).

e. Slide on the washer and the needle bearing.

f. Position the high gear with the gear dogs side going on first and slide the gear (B) onto the shaft and onto the needle bearing.

g. Slide on the washer and install the new circlip. Make sure the circlip is correctly seated in the shaft groove.

h. Heat the bearing on a hot plate to aid in installation.

i. Install the bearing (A) onto the shaft. Tap on the inner race of the bearing and install the bearing until it bottoms on the shaft shoulder (**Figure 95**).

3. To assemble the silent chain and input shaft onto the high/low/reverse shaft, perform the following:

a. Install the silent chain onto the gear sprocket on the input shaft (**Figure 90**).

b. Insert the high/low/reverse shaft (**Figure 89**) through the silent chain and mesh the chain onto the gear sprocket.
c. Carefully twist the shafts while engaging the silent chain and meshing the two gears (**Figure 88**).
d. Hold onto both shafts and slowly rotate them to make sure the gears and silent chain are properly meshed.

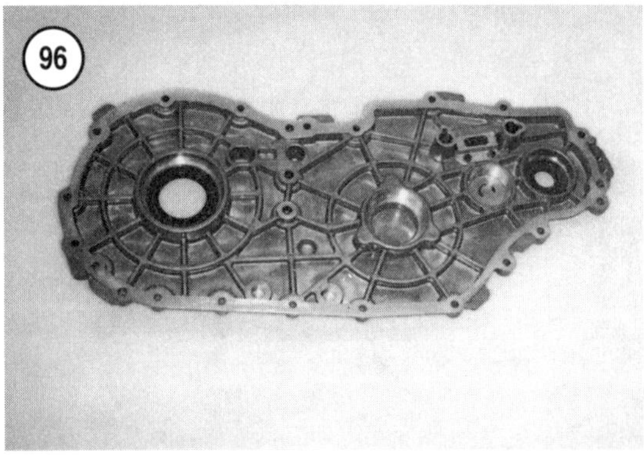

TRANSMISSION INSPECTION

Transmission Case

1. Clean the transmission case and cover inside and out with cleaning solvent. Thoroughly dry with compressed air.
2. Using a scraper, *carefully* remove any remaining sealer residue from both case and cover gasket sealing surfaces.
3. Thoroughly check the gasket sealing surface of both parts. Check for gouges or nicks that may lead to an oil leak.
4. Inspect the case and cover (**Figure 96**) for cracks and fractures, especially in the lower areas where they are vulnerable to rock damage. Check the areas around the stiffening ribs, around bearing bosses and threaded holes for damage. If damage is found, have it repaired by a shop specializing in the repair of precision aluminum castings or replace the damaged case and/or cover.
5. Check the mounting threaded holes for thread damage, dirt or oil buildup. Refer to **Figures 97-100**, typical. If necessary, clean or repair the threads with a suitable size metric tap. Coat the tap threads with kerosene or an aluminum tap fluid before use.

99

100

101

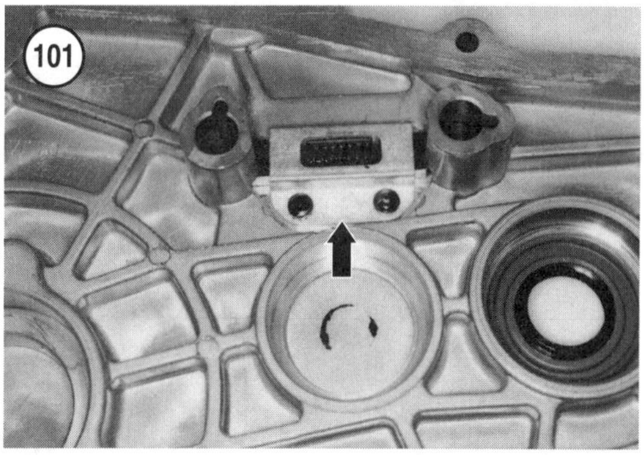

102

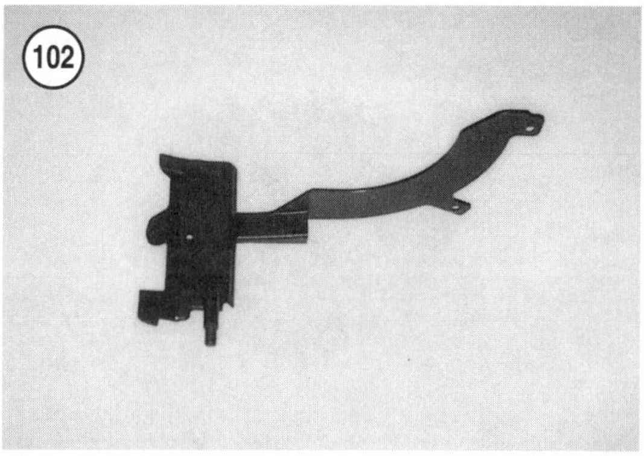

103

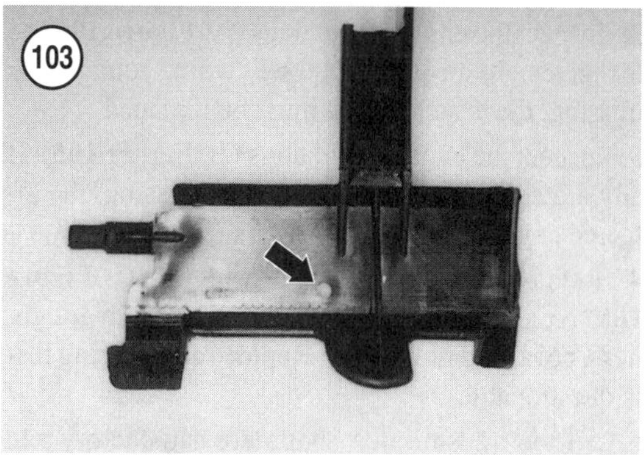

104

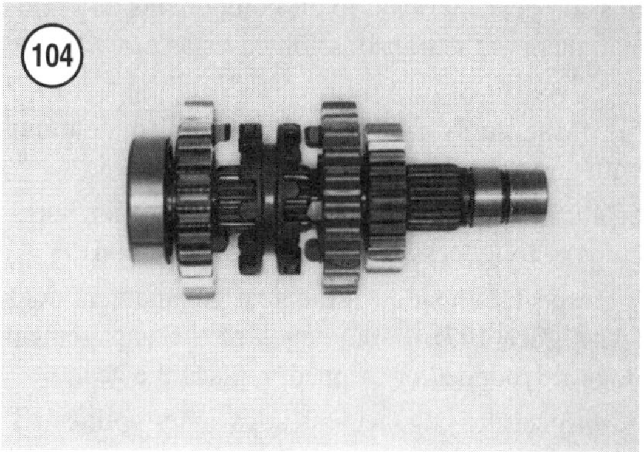

9

6. On 1999-on models, if necessary, remove the screws securing the interlock bracket (**Figure 101**). Remove the bracket, two pins and the spring.

7. Inspect the oil deflector (**Figure 102**) for hardness or damage. Make sure the oil hole (**Figure 103**) is open. Clean out if necessary.

Gear Shafts and Shift Forks

Clean and inspect the shaft assemblies prior to disassembling them. Place the assembled shaft into a large can or plastic bucket and thoroughly clean with a petroleum-based solvent such as kerosene and a stiff brush. Dry with compressed air or let it sit on rags to drip dry. Repeat for the other shaft assemblies.

1. After cleaning, visually inspect the components of each assembly (**Figure 104**) for excessive wear. Any burrs, pitting or roughness on the teeth of a gear will cause wear on the mating gear. Minor roughness can be cleaned up with an oilstone, but there is little point in attempting to remove deep scars.

2. Inspect the engagement dogs (A, **Figure 105**) on the gears. If any are chipped, worn, rounded or missing, the affected gear must be replaced.

3. Inspect the engagement dogs (B, **Figure 105**). If any are chipped, worn, rounded or missing, the affected engagement dog must be replaced.

4. Rotate the transmission bearing(s) (C, **Figure 105**) on all three shafts by hand. Check for roughness, noise and radial play. Replace any bearing that is questionable.

5A. If the transmission shafts are satisfactory and are not going to be disassembled, apply clean transmission gear lubricant to all components and reinstall them in the transmission cases as described in this chapter.

5B. If the shafts have been disassembled, continue with this procedure.

6. Clean and carefully inspect all gears for burrs, chips or roughness on the teeth (**Figure 106**).

7. Inspect both sides of the gear engagement dogs (A, **Figure 107**). If the edges of the engagement dogs are rounded or chipped, replace the gear.

8. Inspect the engagement dogs inner splines (B, **Figure 107**) for wear or damage. If any of the splines are damaged, replace the engagement dog(s).

9. Check the needle bearings for severe wear, cracks or other damage. Install the needle bearing into the gear (**Figure 108**) and rotate it inside the gear. It must rotate freely. Replace as necessary.

10. Inspect the input shaft as follows:
   a. Inspect the splines (**Figure 109**) for wear or damage.
   b. Inspect the bearings (A, **Figure 91**). They must turn smoothly; if necessary, replace them as described in Chapter One.
   c. Inspect the silent chain gear sprockets (B, **Figure 91**) for wear or damage. If damaged, replace the shaft as well as the silent chain.

NOTE
There are no service limit specifications for the silent and drive chains.

11. Inspect the high/low/reverse gear shaft as follows:
   a. Check the circlip grooves in the shaft for cracks or damage. The groove should be square to prevent the circlip from coming out.

105

106

107
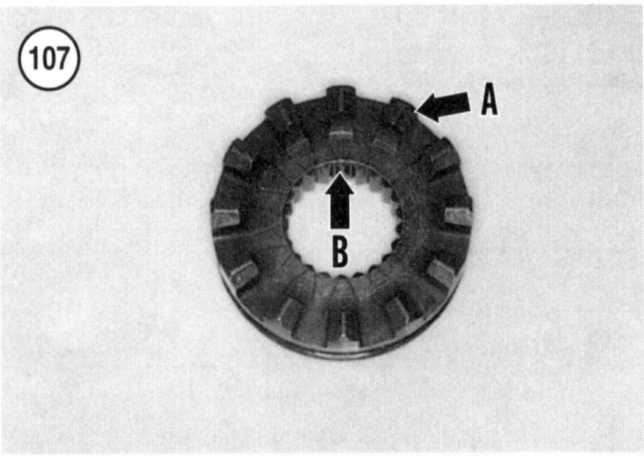

108

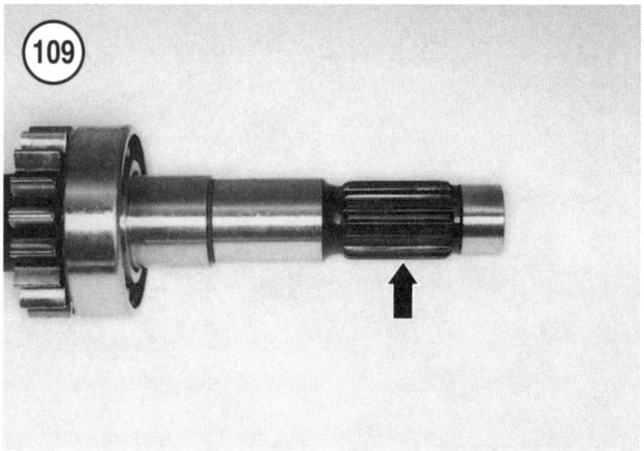

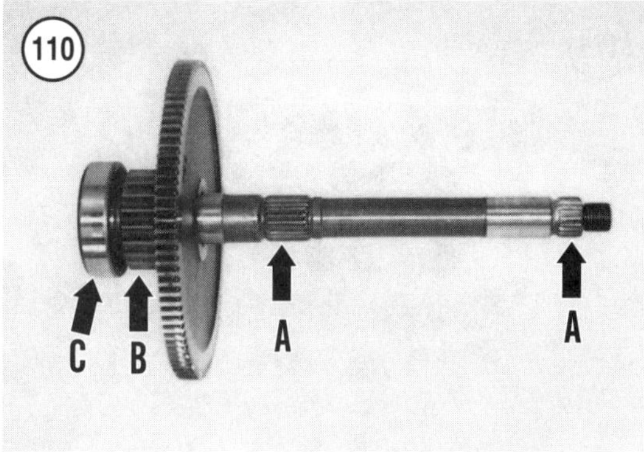

b. Make sure that the shaft splines are not damaged and there are no signs of cracks, galling or fatigue.

c. Inspect the silent chain gear sprockets (D, **Figure 105**) for wear or damage. If damaged, replace the shaft as well as the silent chain.

12. Inspect the center drive shaft as follows:

a. Make sure that the shaft splines (A, **Figure 110**) are not damaged and there are no signs of cracks, galling or fatigue.

b. Inspect the drive chain gear sprockets (B, **Figure 110**) for wear or damage. If damaged, replace the shaft as well as the silent chain.

c. Inspect the bearing (C, **Figure 110**). It must turn smoothly. If necessary, replace it as described in Chapter One.

d. Inspect the gear (**Figure 111**). Any burrs, pitting or roughness on the teeth of a gear will cause wear on the mating gear.

13. Inspect the output gear as follows:

a. Make sure that both inner splines (**Figure 112**) are not damaged and there are no signs of cracks, galling or fatigue. If the splines are damaged, check the outer splines on the drive axles as described in Chapter Thirteen.

b. Inspect the bearing (A, **Figure 113**) on each side of the output gear. They must turn smoothly, if necessary, replace them as described in Chapter One.

c. Inspect the gear (B, **Figure 113**). Any burrs, pitting or roughness on the teeth of a gear will cause wear on the mating gear.

14. Inspect the silent chain (**Figure 114**) and drive chain (**Figure 115**) for wear or damage. Replace as necessary.

15. Inspect the shift fork as follows:

a. Check the shift fork fingers for wear or damage (**Figure 116**).
b. Check the shift fork guide pin (A, **Figure 117**) for severe wear or roughness.
c. Inspect the portion of the shaft where they ride in the case and cover (B, **Figure 117**). Install the shift fork into the case and cover. Check for smooth operation.
d. Replace the shift shaft(s) as necessary.

SHIFT SHAFTS

Removal/Inspection/Installation

1. Disassemble the transmission as described in this chapter.

NOTE
The bell cranks are unique and must be installed in the correct location in the transmission case. All of the mounting components are identical to both bell cranks.

2. Mark the bell cranks with an F (front) and R (rear) as shown in **Figure 118**.
3. Remove the nut and washer (A, **Figure 119**) securing the shift shaft bell crank.
4. Mark the bell crank and the end of the shift shaft with a punch so the bell crank will be installed in the correct position during assembly. Remove the bell crank (B, **Figure 119**).
5. Remove the circlip and washer securing the shift shaft into the transmission case.
6. Withdraw the shift shaft (**Figure 120**) from the interior of the transmission case.
7. If necessary, repeat for the other shift shaft.
8. Check each shift shaft for wear or damage.
9. Remove the O-ring seals and install new ones.
10. Check the washer and circlip for wear or damage. Replace them as necessary.
11. Check the spring retainer for cracks or damage. If damaged, replace the shift shaft as the spring retainer is not replaceable.
12. Install by reversing these removal steps while noting the following:
   a. Apply clean transmission oil to the new O-ring seals prior to installing the shift shaft into the transmission case.

(114)

(115)

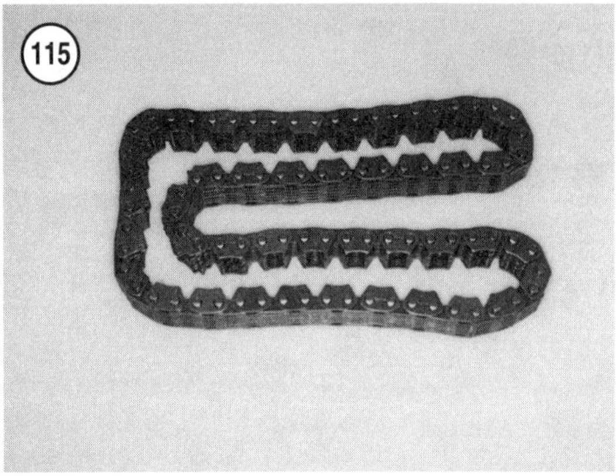

(116)

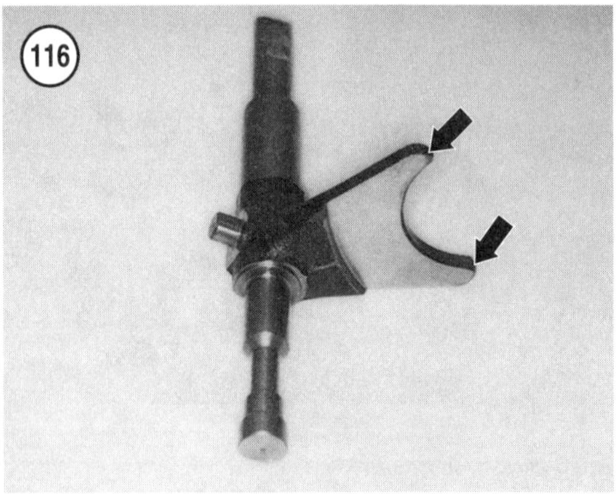

   b. Refer to the marks made in Step 2 and correctly install the shift shaft into the correct receptacle in the transmission case.
   c. Refer to the marks made in Step 4 and correctly align the bell crank with the shift shaft.
   d. Tighten the nut securely. Move the shift shaft back and forth and check for smooth operation.
   e. Repeat for the other shift shaft.

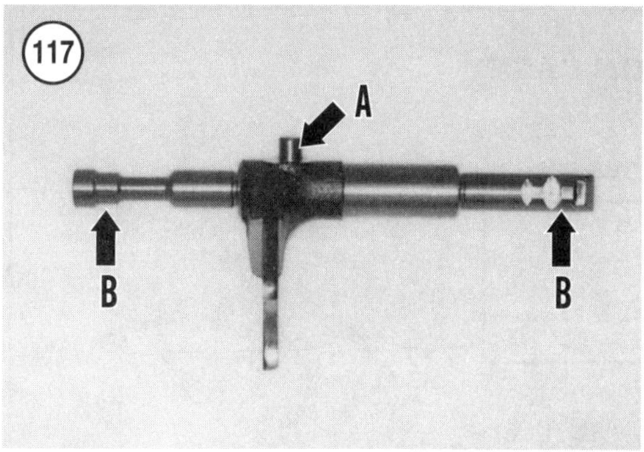

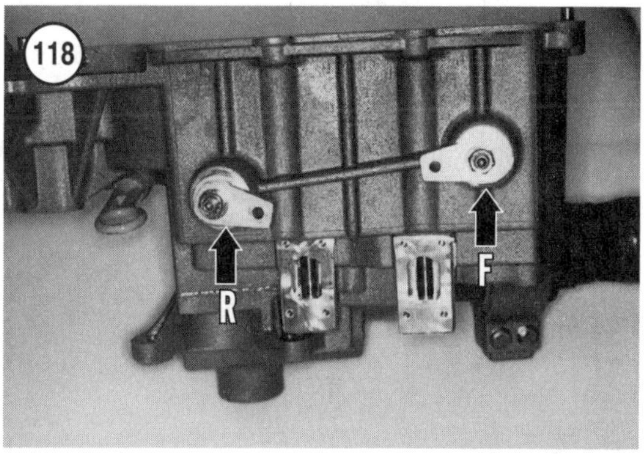

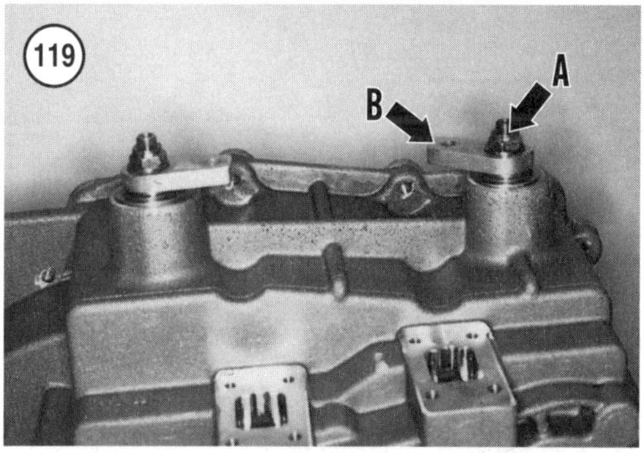

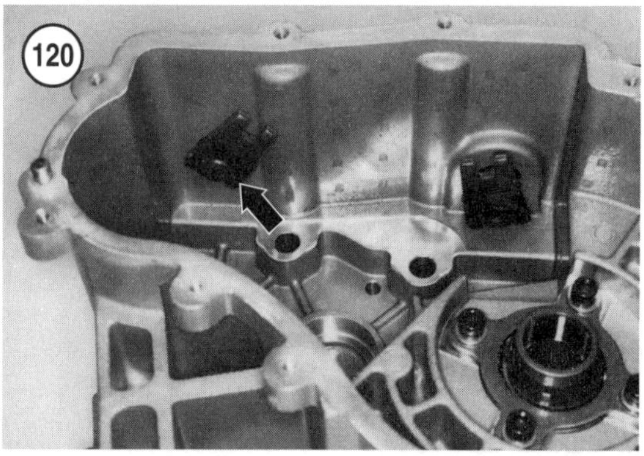

FRONT OUTPUT SHAFT

Do not remove the front output shaft assembly unless necessary. If removed, special tools are necessary during installation and two inspection and adjustment procedures are required to check *Output Shaft End Play* and *Output Shaft Gear Backlash*.

It is recommended that both of these procedures be performed by a Polaris dealership due to the special tools and expertise required.

Removal

Refer to **Figure 121**.

1. Remove all transmission components from the case as previously described in this chapter.
2. Remove the screws and lockwashers securing the pinion gear retaining plate (A, **Figure 122**).
3. Withdraw the pinion gear assembly (B, **Figure 122**) from the transmission case half.
4. Use a permanent marking pen to make an alignment mark between the front output housing and the transmission case (**Figure 123**). This will ensure correct alignment during installation.
5. Loosen the output housing pinch bolts (**Figure 124**).

CAUTION
Do not try to completely unscrew the front output housing in substep c.

6. Use the VST 2 1/8 inch wrench (part No. 2871701) (A, **Figure 125**) to partially unscrew the front output housing from the transmission case until the O-ring is exposed by 13 mm (0.5 in.).

NOTE
The bottom access cover had a sealant applied to it during assembly, and is difficult to loosen from the bottom of the transmission case.

7. Remove the bolts and lockwashers securing the bottom access cover (**Figure 126**). Tap around the perimeter of the cover to break the sealant loose, then remove the cover.
8. Secure the front output ring gear (A, **Figure 127**) or shaft with a strap wrench.
9. Straighten the lock washer tab away from the bolt head.

121

TRANSMISSION CASE

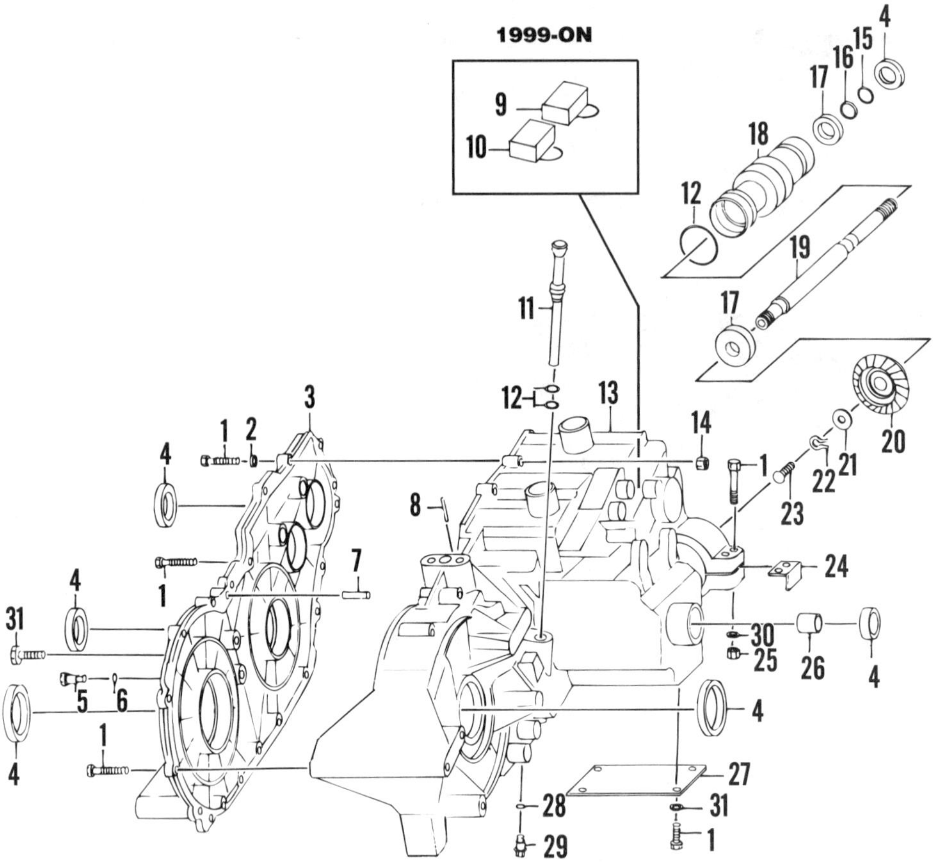

1. Bolt
2. Washer (1996 models)
3. Cover
4. Oil seal
5. Bolt
6. Washer (1996 models)
7. Dowel pin
8. Vent tube fitting
9. Front switch (two position) (1999-on)
10. Rear switch (three position) (1999-on)
11. Dipstick
12. O-rings
13. Transmission case
14. Nuts (self-locking) (1996 models)
15. Circlip
16. Shim
17. Bearing
18. Front output housing
19. Front output shaft
20. Front output shaft ring gear
21. Washer
22. Lockwasher
23. Bolt
24. Plate (models so equipped)
25. Nut
26. Bushing
27. Bottom access cover
28. Washer
29. Drain plug
30. Washer
31. Washer

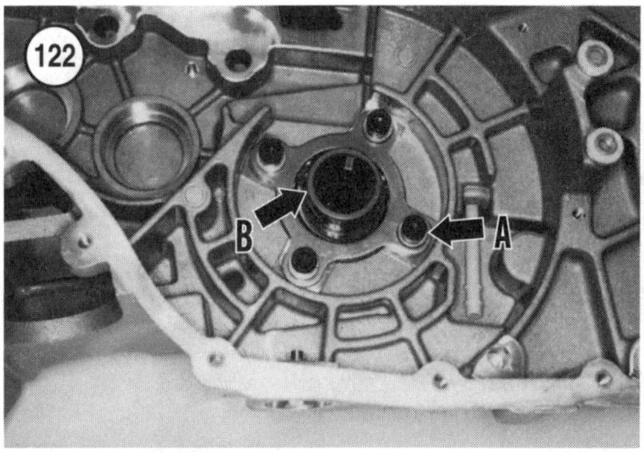

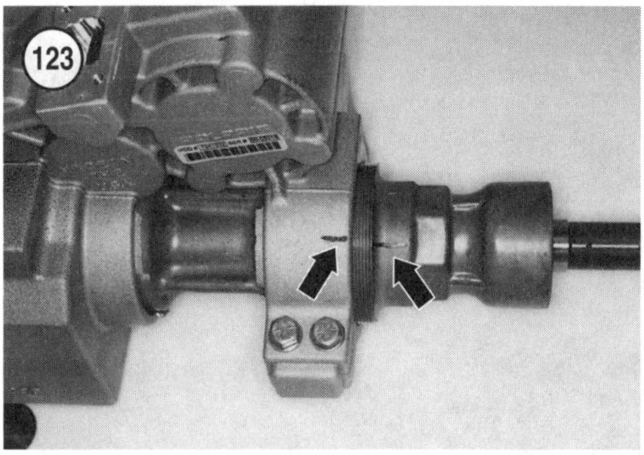

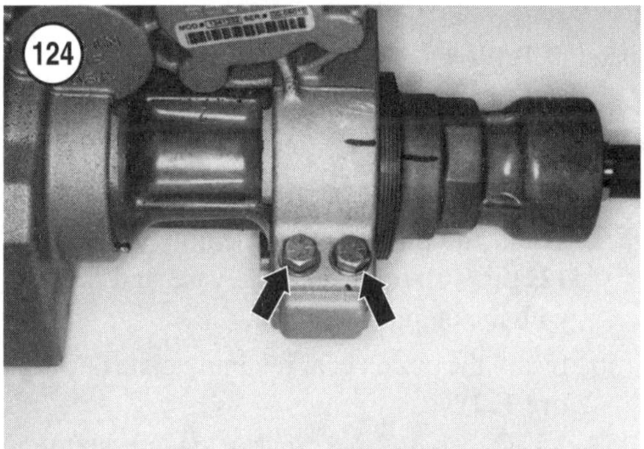

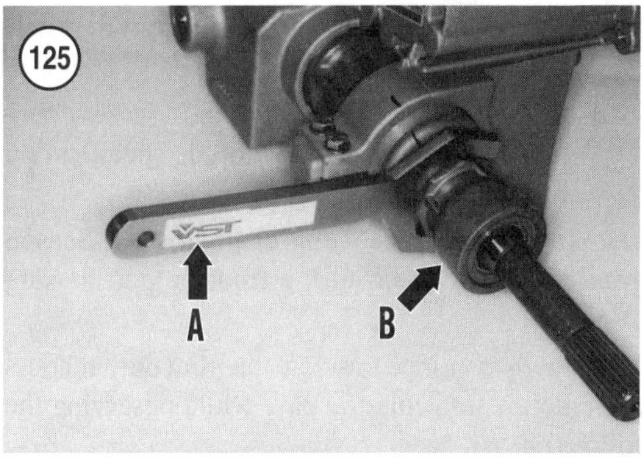

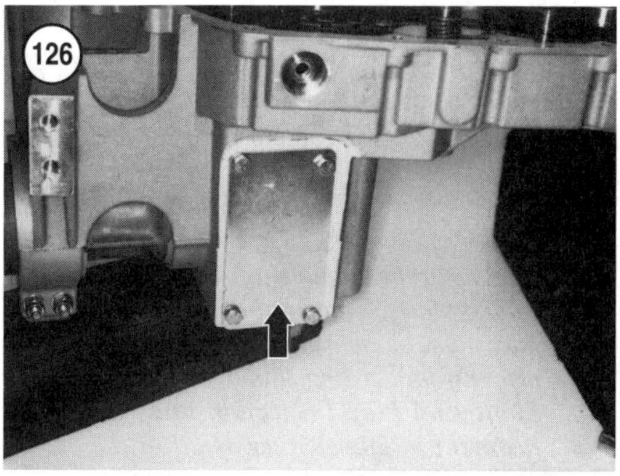

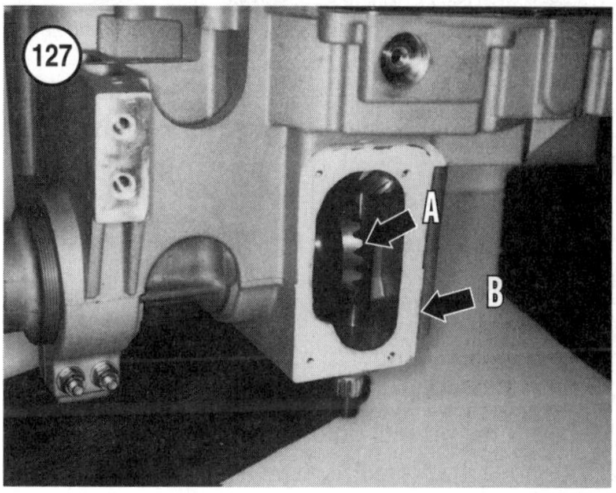

10. Loosen and remove the bolt, lock washer and flat washer securing the front output ring gear to the output shaft.

11. Remove the front output ring gear (A, **Figure 127**) from the bottom access area.

12. Unscrew the front output housing (B, **Figure 125**) and remove it from the transmission case. After removal, protect the threads from damage with duct or electrical tape.

13. If necessary, use a brass hammer or press to withdraw the front output shaft, bearing, then the circlip, shims and oil seal out of the transmission end of the front output housing. The inner bearing will remain on the shaft.

14. Slide the oil seal off the shaft.

15. Remove the circlip and shims from the shaft. Record the number and thickness of the shims as the same number and thickness must be reinstalled if the existing components are going to be reinstalled. Remove the outer bearing from the shaft.

9

Installation

1. Install the shaft and inner bearing into the transmission end of the front output housing. Push it in until it stops.

NOTE

If either front output shaft or housing was replaced, the output shaft end play must be measured and adjusted prior to proceeding. Refer to ***Output Shaft End Play Inspection and Adjustment*** *in this chapter. If all of the original components are going to be installed, end play measurement is not necessary providing the same number and thickness shims are reinstalled.*

2. Turn the front output housing over and install the outer bearing onto the shaft. Push it in until it is fully seated in the housing.
3. Install the same number and thickness of shims that were removed onto the shaft.
4. Install the circlip onto the shaft. It may be necessary to tap the circlip into place. Make sure it is correctly seated in the shaft groove.
5. Install the oil seal onto the shaft.
6. Remove the protective tape from the front output housing threads. Apply a liberal coat of antiseize compound to the threads.

CAUTION

Do not crossthread the front output housing into the transmission case.

7. Slowly screw the front output housing onto the transmission case by hand.
8. Use the VST 2 1/8 inch wrench (part No. 2871701) (A, **Figure 125**) and screw the front output housing in until the O-ring seal is 8 mm (0.31 in.) from the transmission housing, then stop.
9. Position the front output ring gear with the shoulder side facing the shaft. Install the gear into the bottom access area and onto the shaft splines and push it on until it bottoms.
10. Apply ThreeBond No. 1342, or equivalent, threadlocking compound to the bolt threads prior to installation.
11. Install the flat washer, new lockwasher and bolt onto the shaft end.
12. Secure the front output ring gear or shaft with a strap wrench.

128

129

13. Tighten the bolt to the torque specification listed in **Table 1**.
14. Bend one side of the new lockwasher up against one of the flats on the bolt.
15. Install the pinion gear assembly as follows:
    a. Install the pinion gear assembly (B, **Figure 122**) into the transmission case and mesh it with the output shaft gear.
    b. Install the pinion gear retaining plate (A, **Figure 122**).
    c. Apply a light coat of ThreeBond TB1342, Loctite 242, or equivalent threadlocking compound to the screw threads prior to installation.
    d. Install the lockwashers and screws and tighten the screws to the torque specification listed in **Table 1**.
16. Apply a liberal coating of Polaris All-Season grease, or equivalent, to the front output housing O-ring.
17. Slowly continue to screw the front output housing onto the transmission case while observing the following:

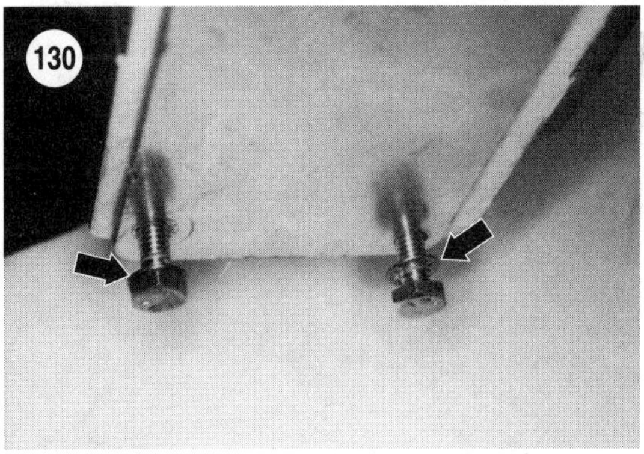

130

131

a. Ensure that the O-ring enters the transmission case without damage.

b. Slowly rotate the pinion gear assembly (**Figure 128**) back and forth to ensure the gears mesh properly without damage.

c. Have an assistant slowly rotate the front output shaft while screwing the front output housing onto the transmission case. As gear backlash is reduced to zero, the shaft will begin to bind. At this point stop screwing in and back the front output housing out of the transmission case by 1/4 of a turn.

d. If none of the internal components were replaced, the alignment mark made in *Removal* Step 2, between the front output housing and the transmission case (**Figure 123**) should now be aligned.

e. Measure the output gear backlash as described under *Output Shaft Gear Backlash Inspection and Adjustment* in this chapter.

18. Clean the sealing surfaces of the transmission case (B, **Figure 127**) and the inside surface of the bottom access plate with an aerosol parts cleaner.

19. Apply an even coat of ThreeBond 1215, or equivalent, gasket sealant to the sealing surface of the transmission case (**Figure 129**).

20. Install the bottom access plate, bolts and lockwashers (**Figure 130**). Tighten the screws to the torque specification listed in **Table 1**.

21. Install a new front seal into the output housing. Press it in until it is flush with the housing.

22. Tighten the output housing pinch bolts (**Figure 131**) securely.

Output Shaft End Play Inspection and Adjustment

This procedure requires the use of a dial indicator and stand. It is recommended that a Polaris dealership perform this procedure due to the special tools and expertise required.

1. Install the shaft and inner bearing into the transmission end of the front output housing. Push it in until it stops.

2. Turn the front output housing over and install the outer bearing onto the shaft. Push it in until it is fully seated in the housing.

NOTE

Do not install the original shims between the shaft and the circlip at this time.

3. Install the circlip onto the shaft. It may be necessary to tap the circlip into place. Make sure it is correctly seated in the shaft groove.

4. Install the housing in a vise with soft jaws so it is secure. Do not overtighten as the housing may be damaged.

5. Set up a dial indicator so it touches the end of the output shaft.

6. Push the output shaft all the way into the housing and zero the dial indicator.

7. Slowly pull the output shaft out from the housing and note the reading *without* any shims.

8. Measure the thickness of the existing shims and note the dimension.

9. To calculate correct end play, subtract the total shim thickness measured in Step 8, from the end play measured in Step 7. Add or subtract shims to achieve the end play specification listed in **Table 2**. Replacement shims are available from Polaris dealerships in five different thickness.

9

10. Remove the circlip and install the new set of shims.
11. Install the circlip onto the shaft. It may be necessary to tap the circlip into place. Make sure it is correctly seated in the shaft groove.
12. Repeat Steps 5-7 and note the end play reading. If the end play is still not within the specified dimension, add or subtract shims until it is correct.
13. Remove the housing from the vise.

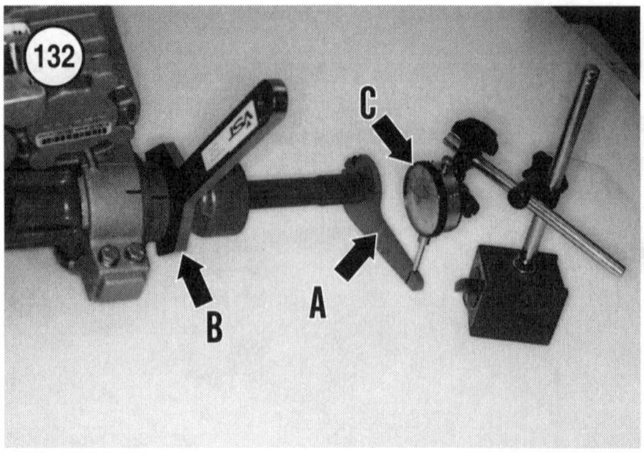

Output Shaft Gear Backlash Inspection and Adjustment

This procedure requires the use of the VST Backlash setting tool (part No. 2871695), a dial indicator and stand. It is recommended that a Polaris dealership perform this procedure due to the special tools and expertise required.

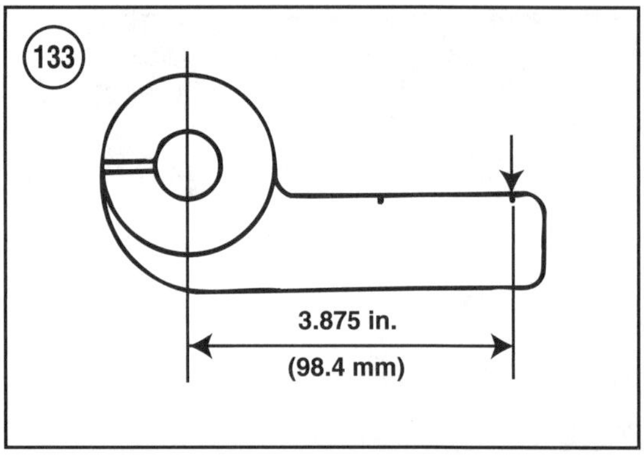

1. Secure the center drive shaft so the pinion gear is stationary. The shaft must not rotate during this procedure, or the backlash readings will be incorrect.
2. If necessary, loosen the pinch bolts (**Figure 124**).
3. If installed, remove the front output housing seal from the end of the housing.
4. Install the VST special tool onto the output shaft splines as shown in A, **Figure 132**. Using the VST 2 1/8 inch wrench (B), rotate the output housing and push the tool down toward the work surface until it stops. For best results install the special tool so that when the shaft stops rotating, the tool is almost flat against the work surface.

5. Position the dial indicator (C, **Figure 132**) at the outer mark on the special tool (**Figure 133**) and at a 90° angle to the tool surface (**Figure 134**). Zero the dial indicator.
6. Rotate the output housing in the opposite direction of Step 3 so the special tool will push up on the dial indicator. Rotate the housing until it stops, then compare the dial indicator reading to the backlash specification in **Table 2**.

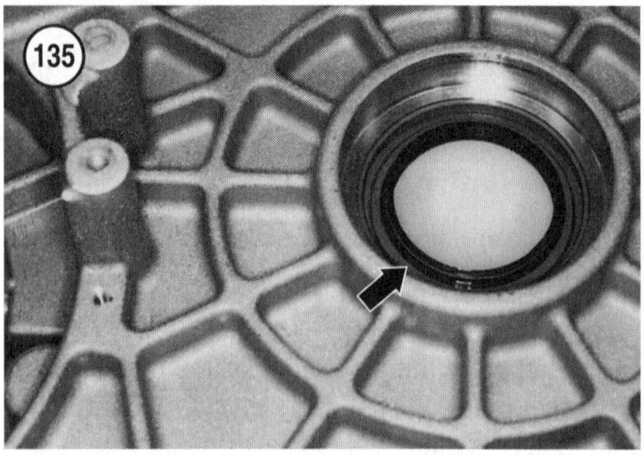

NOTE

Backlash is achieved by screwing the front output housing in or out of the transmission case. This moves the front output shaft ring gear in or out of contact with the center drive shaft pinion gear.

7. To adjust the backlash, perform the following:

136

137

138

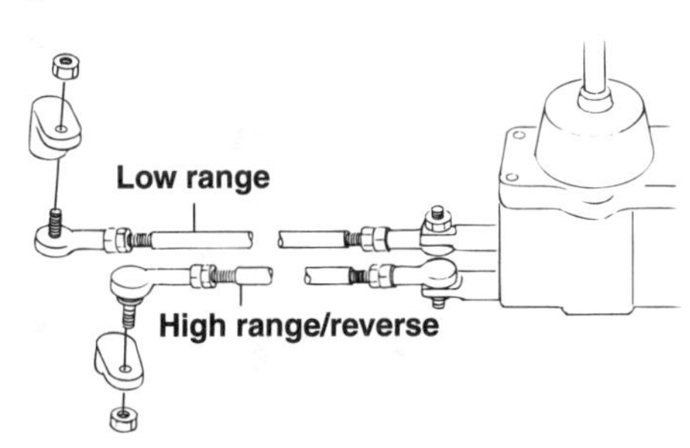

a. To *reduce backlash*, use the VST 2 1/8 in. wrench to rotate the housing *clockwise* as viewed from the front of the housing.

b. To *increase backlash*, use the VST 2 1/8 in. wrench to rotate the housing *counterclockwise* as viewed from the front of the housing.

8. Repeat Steps 4-6 and recheck backlash. If still not within specification, repeat Step 7 until correct.

9. Tighten the pinch bolts (**Figure 131**) securely.

10. Recheck backlash and readjust if necessary.

11. Remove both special tools from the output shaft.

TRANSMISSION GEARCASE OIL SEAL INSPECTION AND REPLACEMENT

NOTE
It is recommended that the oil seals be replaced every time the transmission is disassembled.

Inspect the oil seals in the transmission case (**Figure 135**, typical) and cover. Refer to **Figure 136** and **Figure 137**. Check for nicks, hardness or deterioration. Replace the oil seals as described in Chapter One.

SHIFT SELECTOR LINKAGE

Adjust the shift linkage as the first step to correct transmission or shifting problems.

Shift linkage adjustment is necessary when the following symptoms are evident:

1. Whenever the transmission has been removed and installed.
2. The All-Wheel Drive light will not illuminate.
3. Noise on deceleration.
4. Inability to engage any gear.
5. Excessive gear clash when shifting.
6. Shift selector moving out of range.

Always check the adjustment of both control rods at the same time. The adjustment of one rod can prevent proper adjustment of the other rod.

The high range/reverse rod is located on the outer selector slide and the low range rod is located on the inner selector slide as shown in **Figure 138**.

Checking and Preliminary Adjustment

1. Remove the seat and rear fender as described in Chapter Fifteen.

2. Before adjusting the shift control rods, check for wear or improper installation as follows:

   a. Check each shift control rod where it attaches to the gear selector slides for looseness (**Figure 139**). Make sure the nut is tight and that rod ends are not worn.

9

b. Check to be sure that each shift control rod is attached correctly to the bell crank on top of the transmission (A, **Figure 140**) and to the shift arm pivot plate (B, **Figure 140**) and that the nuts are tight.

c. Verify that the gear selector lever mounting plate bolts are tight. Refer to A, **Figure 141** and **Figure 142**.

d. Lubricate the rod ends with a light aerosol lubricant or grease.

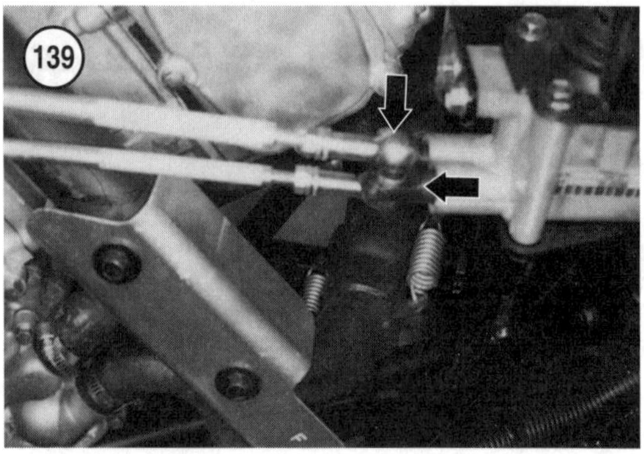

Adjusting

1. Perform *Checking and Preliminary Adjustment* as previously described.
2. Shift the transmission into NEUTRAL.
3. Loosen both jam nuts (**Figure 143**) on the ends of both rods.
4. Note the orientation of the rod ends at the shift lever as follows:

   a. High/reverse shift rod (outside rod) is mounted above the bell crank (B, **Figure 141**).

   b. Low range shift rod (inside rod) is mounted below the bell crank (C, **Figure 141**).

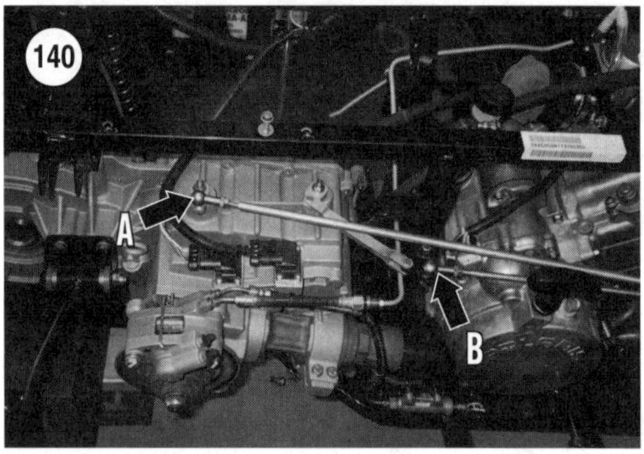

5. Remove the nuts and disconnect the shift rods from the transmission bell crank on top of the transmission (A, **Figure 140**) and on the shift arm pivot plate (B, **Figure 140**).
6. Place the gear selector in the NEUTRAL position. Make sure the transmission bell cranks are engaged in the neutral detents. Move the bell cranks if necessary.
7. Make sure the shift rods are secured correctly to the gear selector slides (B, C, **Figure 141**).

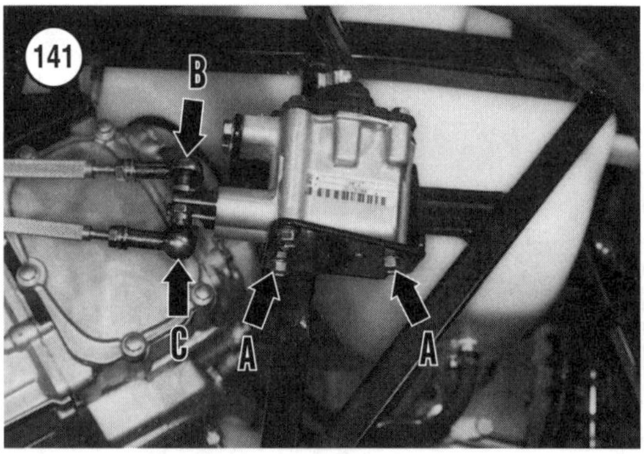

8. Rotate the inside low range shift rod in either direction until the rod end is exactly centered over the mounting hole in the transmission bell crank. Install the rod end onto the bell crank and install the nut (**Figure 144**). Tighten the nut to the torque specification listed in **Table 1**.
9. Make a longitudinal mark on the control rod (**Figure 145**) so the revolutions can be easily counted in the following steps.
10. Rotate the shift rod *clockwise* until resistance is felt, counting the revolutions as the rod is turned. Note the number of revolutions.
11. Rotate the shift rod *counterclockwise* until the same resistance is felt, counting the revolutions as the rod is turned. Note the number of revolutions.

143
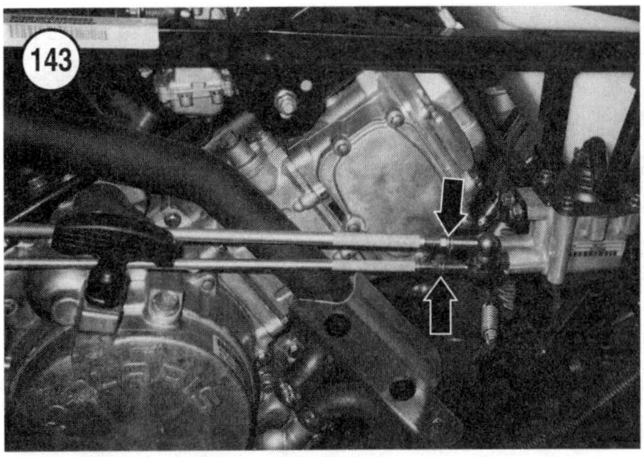

144

145
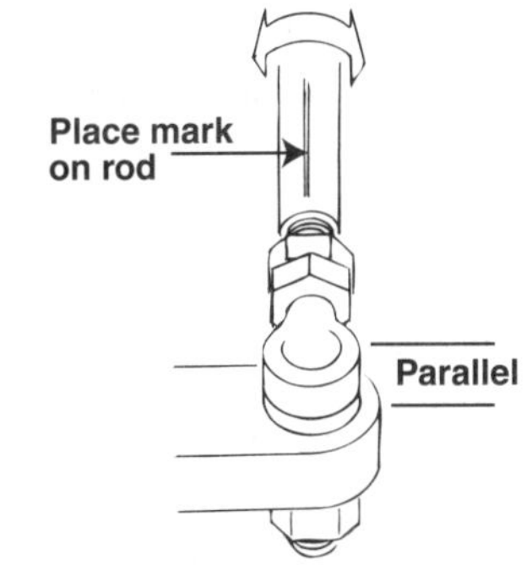

146

12. Once again, rotate the shift rod *clockwise* one-half of the revolutions counted in Step 11. The shift rod is now properly adjusted to the midway point.

13. Secure the shift rod to prevent if from turning. Also hold the rod end so it is parallel to the mounting surface (**Figure 145**) and securely tighten the jam nut at each end. The top surface of the rod ends must be parallel to each other. Binding can occur if the rod ends are not straight. Check by rotating the control rod. The rod should rotate freely 1/4 turn without binding.

14. Repeat Steps 8-13 for the high/reverse shift rod on the shift arm pivot plate (**Figure 146**).

Shift Selector Removal/Installation

1. Remove the fuel tank as described in Chapter Eight.
2. Remove the front fender as described in Chapter Fifteen.
3. On 1996-1998 models, perform the following:
   a. Remove any cable ties securing the wiring harness to the frame.
   b. Disconnect the electrical wires from the terminal board located on the frame panel adjacent to the steering shaft.
   c. Note the routing of the wiring harness and pull it through the gearshift selector side of the frame.
5. Note the orientation of the rod ends at the shift lever as follows:
   a. High/reverse shift rod (outside rod) is mounted above the bell crank (B, **Figure 141**).
   b. Low range shift rod (inside rod) is mounted below the bell crank (C, **Figure 141**).
6. Remove the nuts securing the shift rods to the selector slides (A, **Figure 147**).
7. Remove the bolts securing the shift selector (B, **Figure 147**) to the frame mount.
8. Lift the shift selector out of the mounting bracket and out of the frame.
9. Installation is the reverse of removal while noting the following:
   a. Install new mounting bolts and tighten them securely.
   b. On 1996-1998 models, reconnect the electrical wires to the correct location on the terminal board.

9

Boot Replacement

Replace the rubber boot whenever a tear or hole is found or if the rubber has started to deteriorate. If the boot is damaged, it will allow moisture to enter the shift selector body and result in internal damage and shifting problems.

1. Remove the cap from the shift knob.
2. Remove the Torx screw securing the shift knob to the shift selector rod. Remove the shift knob.

3A. On 1996-1999 models, perform the following:
   a. Remove the upper and lower clamps securing the rubber boot to the shift select rod and cover.
   b. Slide the rubber boot up and off the shift selector rod.

3B. On 2000 models, perform the following:
   a. Remove the wire strap securing the rubber boot to the shift select rod and cover. Discard the wire strap.
   b. Remove the four screws securing the rubber boot/cover to the lever body.
   c. Slide the rubber boot/cover up and off the shift selector rod.

4. Clean off any rust or corrosion from the shift selector rod where the boot attaches.

5A. On 1996-1999 models, perform the following:
   a. Set the rubber boot next to the cover and note the location of the upper clamping area of the boot.
   b. Mark this area with a permanent marking pen, then apply RTV silicone to the rod in this area. This ensures a watertight seal when the boot is installed.
   c. Slide the new rubber boot onto the shift selector rod and into position on the cover. If necessary, apply a light coat of RTV silicone around the top of the boot and rod.
   d. Install the lower clamp and tighten it securely.
   e. Install the upper clamp and tighten it securely.

5B. On 2000 models, perform the following:
   a. Apply a light coat of ThreeBond 1215 gasket sealer to the body mating surface.
   b. Slide the rubber boot/cover down onto the shift selector rod.
   c. Install the screws. Tighten the screws a few turns at a time in a crisscross pattern to the torque specification listed in **Table 1**.
   d. Install a new wire strap securing the rubber boot to the shift select rod and cover.

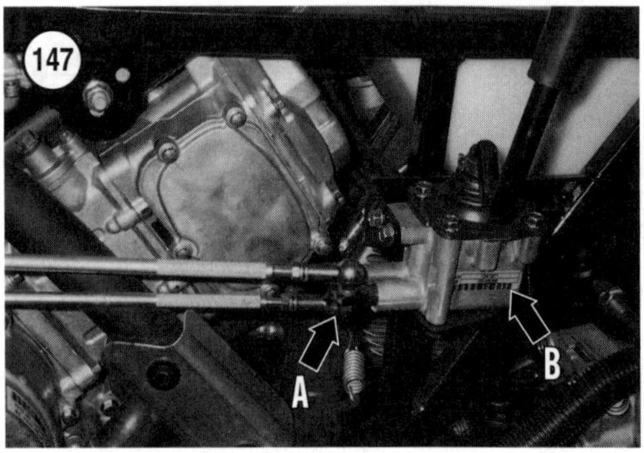

6. Install the shift knob onto the shift selector rod and push it down until it bottoms.
7. Install the Torx screw and tighten securely.
8. Install the cap onto the shift knob.

Gearshift Selector (1996-1999 Models)

Disassembly

Refer to **Figure 148**.

1. Remove the gearshift selector as described in this chapter.
2. Remove the cap from the shift knob.
3. Remove the Torx screw securing the shift knob to the shift selector rod. Remove the shift knob.
4. Place the gearshift selector body in a vise with soft jaws.

NOTE

On 1996-1998 models, the cover is under spring pressure and must be held in place while loosening the cover screws. The 1999 model is not equipped with this spring.

5. While holding onto the cover, loosen the cover screws a few turns at a time in a crisscross pattern. Remove all screws.

6A. On 1996-1998 models, perform the following:
   a. Carefully pull the cover/shift selector rod assembly *straight up* and off the body to avoid damage to the internal gear selector switch.
   b. Carefully remove the internal gear selector switch straight up and out of the body.

6B. On 1999 models, remove the cover/shift selector rod assembly from the body.

7. Withdraw the white plastic bearing cup and springs from the body.

148

SHIFT LINKAGE (1996-1999)

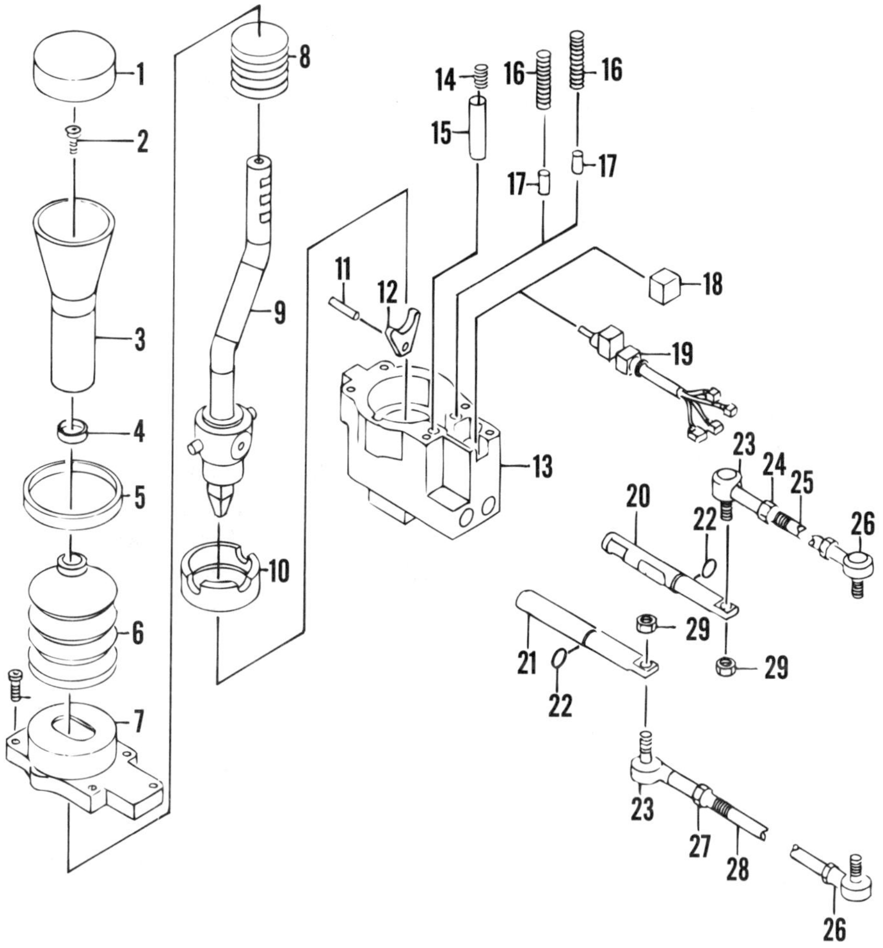

1. Cap
2. Torx screw
3. Knob
4. Clamp, small
5. Clamp, large
6. Boot
7. Cover
8. Spring (1996-1998)
9. Shift select rod
10. Bearing cup
11. Interlock pin
12. Interlock butterfly
13. Body
14. Spring
15. Stop pin
16. Detent spring
17. Detent pin
18. Pad (models so equipped)
19. Switch (1996-1998)
20. High/reverse range selector slide
21. Low range selector slide
22. O-ring
23. Rod end (right-hand threads)
24. Locknut (right-hand threads)
25. Shift rod (high/reverse range)
26. Rod end (left-hand threads)
27. Locknut (right-hand threads)
28. Shift rod (low range)
29. Nut

NOTE
In Step 8, do not turn the body upside down to drain the oil as the detent bullets and stop pin may fall out.

8. Remove the body from the vise, tilt it side ways over a pan and drain out the oil.
9. Check for signs of moisture within the body. If moisture is present, replace the rubber boot as previously described.
10. Turn the body upside down over another pan on the work surface. Tap the body onto the pan to dislodge the stop pin, spring and two detent springs and pins. Make sure to remove both detent springs and pins and the stop pin and spring.

NOTE
The left side low range selector slide has two notches. The right side high/reverse selector slide has three notches. The selector slides must be reinstalled into the correct receptacle in the body.

11. Hold the interlock butterfly out of the way and withdraw the two selector slides.
12. Remove the interlock pin and the interlock butterfly.
13. Inspect all parts as described in this chapter.

Assembly

Refer to **Figure 148**.

1. Install the interlock butterfly and pin.
2. Coat each selector slide O-ring with clean engine oil.
3. Carefully install the left side low range selector slide (two notches) into the correct receptacle in the body and index it into the interlock butterfly. Do not damage the O-ring during installation.
4. Carefully install the right side low range selector slide (three notches) into the correct receptacle in the body and index it into the interlock butterfly. Do not damage the O-ring during installation.
5. Install the spring and stop pin into the body.
6. Install the two detent springs and detents into the body.
7. Install the white plastic bearing cup and springs into the body.
8. Place the gearshift selector body in a vise with soft jaws. Locate the body so it is level.

CAUTION
Do not add more oil than specified as this could cause the gearshift selector to hydrolock while shifting.

9. Add Polaris 10W-40 All-Season Synthetic motor oil to the body until the lower half of the selector slides are covered.

NOTE
On 1996-1998 models, the cover is spring loaded and must be carefully pushed down while tightening the cover screws.

NOTE
The switch must be installed correctly otherwise the all wheel drive (AWD) will not function.

10. On 1996-1998 models, carefully install the internal gear selector switch straight down into the body with the hook facing down toward the shift selector slides. The hook must be installed correctly as it prevents the switch from moving out of place within the body.
11. Thoroughly clean the mating surface of the body and cover with Loctite Primer T, or equivalent. Apply a light coat of ThreeBond 1215 gasket sealer to the body mating surface.
12. Move the selector slides to the NEUTRAL position.

13A. On 1996-1998 models, perform the following:
   a. Carefully install the cover/shift selector rod assembly onto the body. The tab end of the selector switch must be positioned in the hole of the striker portion of the shift selector rod or the switch will be damaged.
   b. Install the five screws in the cover. Carefully press down on the cover to compress the spring and screw in the five screws. Tighten the screws a few turns at a time in a crisscross pattern to the torque specification listed in **Table 1**.

13B. On 1999 models, carefully install the cover/shift selector rod assembly onto the body and install the five screws. Tighten the screws a few turns at a time in a crisscross pattern to the torque specification listed in **Table 1**.

14. Install the shift knob and Torx screw. Tighten the screw securely.
15. Install the cap onto the shift knob.

16. Remove the gearshift selector body from the vise and install it in the frame as described in this chapter.

Gearshift Selector (2000 Models)

Disassembly

Refer to **Figure 149**.

1. Remove the gearshift selector as described in this chapter.
2. Place the gearshift selector body in a vise with soft jaws.
3. Remove the cap from the shift knob.
4. Remove the Torx screw securing the shift knob to the shift selector rod. Remove the shift knob.
5. Remove the wire strap securing the rubber boot to the shift select rod and cover. Discard the wire strap.
6. Remove the four screws securing the rubber boot/cover to the lever body.
7. Slide the rubber boot/cover up and off the shift selector rod.
8. Carefully pull the shift selector rod assembly *straight up* and off the body to avoid damage to the selector slides.

NOTE

In Step 9, do not turn the body upside down to drain the oil as the detent bullets and stop pin may fall out.

9. Remove the body from the vise, tilt it sideways over a pan and drain out the oil.
10. Check for signs of moisture within the body. If moisture is present, replace the rubber boot as previously described.
11. Turn the body upside down over another pan on the work surface. Tap the body onto the pan to dislodge the stop pin, centering spring and two detent springs and pins. Make sure to remove both detent springs and pins and the stop pin and spring.

NOTE

The left side low range selector slide has two notches. The right side high/reverse selector slide has three notches. The selector slides must be reinstalled into the correct receptacle in the body.

12. Withdraw both selector slides from the body.
13. Inspect all parts as described in this chapter.

Assembly

Refer to **Figure 149**.

1. Coat each selector slide O-ring with clean engine oil.
2. Carefully install the left side low range selector slide (two notches) into the correct receptacle in the body and index it into the interlock butterfly. Do not damage the O-ring during installation.
3. Carefully install the right side low range selector slide (three notches) into the correct receptacle in the body. Do not damage the O-ring during installation.
4. Install the spring and stop pin into the body.
5. Install the two detent springs and detents into the body.
6. Place the gearshift selector body in a vise with soft jaws. Locate the body so it is level.

CAUTION

Do not add more oil than specified, as this could cause the gearshift selector to hydrolock while shifting.

7. Add Polaris 10W-40 All-Season Synthetic motor oil to the body until the lower half of the selector slides are covered.
8. Move the selector slides to the NEUTRAL position.
9. Carefully install the shift selector rod assembly *straight down* into the body and index the end into the selector slides.
10. Apply a light coat of ThreeBond 1215 gasket sealer to the body mating surface.
11. Slide the rubber boot/cover down onto the shift selector rod.
12. Install the screws. Tighten the screws a few turns at a time in a crisscross pattern to the torque specification listed in **Table 1**.
13. Install a new wire strap securing the rubber boot to the shift select rod and cover.
14. Install the shift knob and Torx screw. Tighten the screw securely.
15. Install the cap onto the shift knob.
16. Remove the gearshift selector body from the vise and install it in the frame as described in this chapter.

(149)

SHIFT LINKAGE (2000)

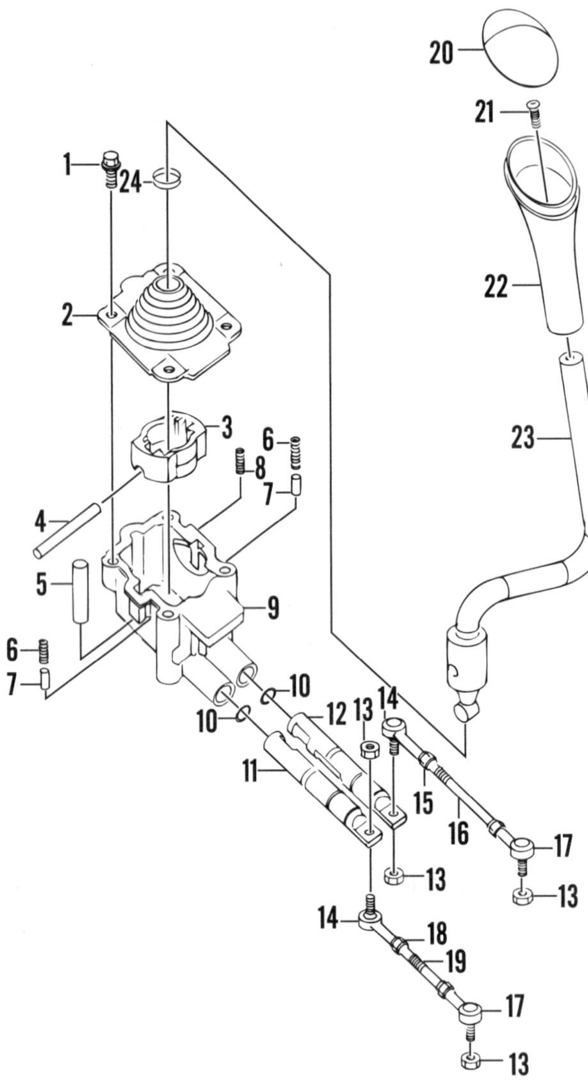

1. Bolt
2. Rubber boot/cover
3. Plastic sphere
4. Groove pin
5. Stop pin
6. Spring
7. Detent bullet
8. Spring
9. Body
10. O-ring
11. Low range selector slide
12. High/reverse range selector slide
13. Nut
14. Rod end (right-hand threads)
15. Locknut (right-hand threads)
16. Shift rod (high/reverse range)
17. Rod end (left-hand threads)
18. Locknut (right-hand threads)
19. Shift rod (low range)
20. Cap
21. Torx screw
22. Knob
23. Shift select rod

Inspection (All Models)

1. Inspect the selector slide O-ring seals for damage and hardness. Replace as a set, if necessary.

2. If moisture was evident when the oil was drained, clean the body and cover with cleaning solvent or penetrating oil. Thoroughly dry with compressed air.

3. Clean all parts in solvent and dry with compressed air.

4. Inspect the receptacles in the body for the stop pin and detent pins for wear or damage.

5. Check all parts for wear or damage and replace as necessary.

Table 1 TRANSMISSION AND SHIFT LINKAGE TORQUE SPECIFICATIONS

Item	N•m	in.-lb.	ft.-lb.
Transmission case cover bolts			
1/4 inch bolts	11	97	–
5/16 inch bolts	23-28	–	17-21
Transmission drain plug	19	–	14
Front output ring gear bolt	23-28	–	17-21
Pinion gear retaining plate screws	11-14	97-124	–
Bottom access plate screws	11-14	97-124	–
Bell crank nut	17	–	13
Shift rod-to-bell crank nut	3.5	31	–
Gearshift selector cover screws	17	–	13

Table 2 TRANSMISSION SPECIFICATIONS

	mm	in.
Output shaft gear backlash	0.20-0.36	0.008-0.014
Output shaft end play	0.00-0.075	0.000-0.003

CHAPTER TEN

FRONT DRIVE SYSTEM

The front drive system permits the vehicle to be driven by the rear wheels as long as the front wheels rotate faster than the front drive axles. If the rotational speed of the front wheels slows to less than the speed of the rear drive axles, the front wheel hubs engage. Each front hub has an electrical engagement control and is referred to as a Hillard clutch.

Tables 1-3 provide tire and drive train specifications at the end of this chapter.

NOTE
Tire size is very important for proper operation on all models. If the tire size is changed, the engagement of the front drive may be erratic and could result in dangerous control problems. Refer to ***Table 1*** *for original equipment tire size and for proper tire inflation.*

FRONT HUB AND HILLARD CLUTCH

Removal

Refer to **Figure 1**.

1. Place the ATV on a level surface.
2. Raise and secure the vehicle so that all wheels are off the ground.

1

FRONT HUB

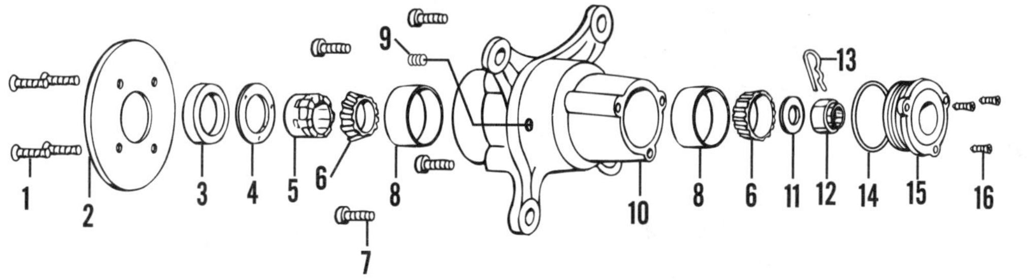

1. Bolt
2. Brake rotor
3. Oil seal
4. Armature plate
5. Front hub clutch
6. Bearing
7. Screw
8. Bearing outer race
9. Screw
10. Front hub
11. Washer
12. Castellated nut
13. Cotter pin
14. Retaining spring
15. Hub cap
16. Torx screws

2

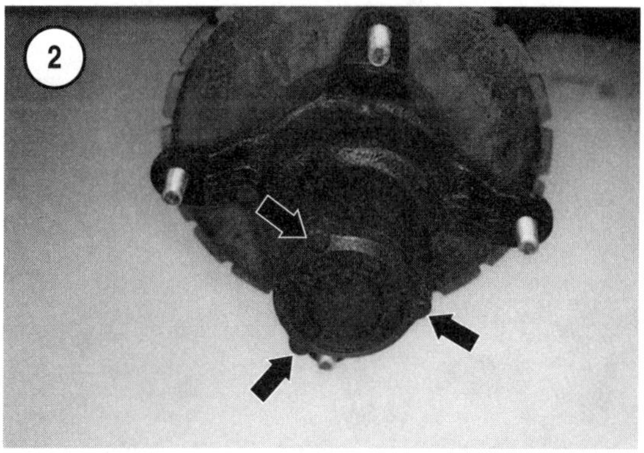

4

3

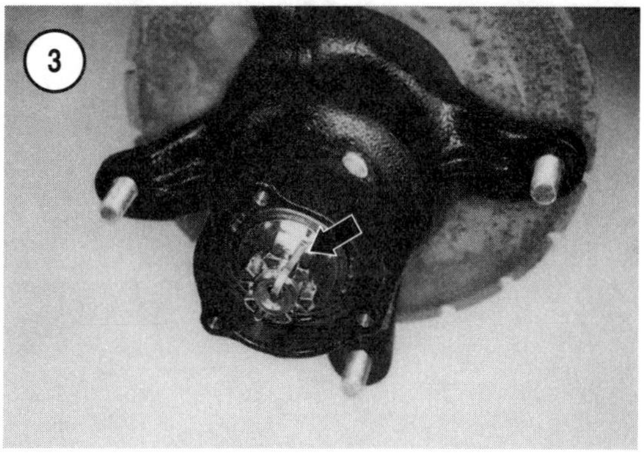

3. Remove the front wheels as described in Chapter Twelve.

4. Remove the front brake calipers as described in Chapter Fourteen.

5. Place a drain pan under the front hub.

6. Remove the three T-25 Torx bolts (**Figure 2**) securing the hub cap and carefully remove the hub cap.

7. Remove the cotter pin (**Figure 3**) from the axle nut. Discard the cotter pin.

8. Remove the axle nut and washer (**Figure 4**).

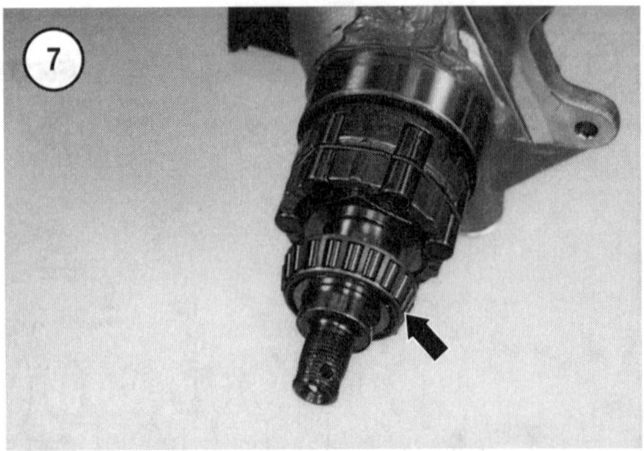

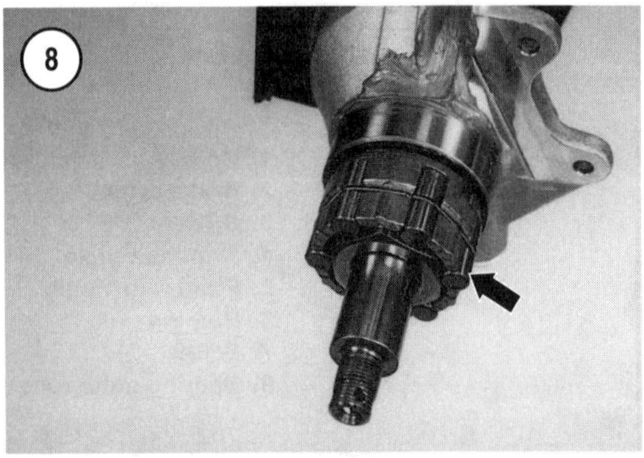

9. Carefully slide the wheel hub and brake rotor off the front axle (**Figure 5**).

10. Remove the outer bearing (**Figure 6**) from the wheel hub.

11. Remove the inner bearing (**Figure 7**) from the front axle.

12. Remove the Hillard clutch assembly (**Figure 8**).

NOTE
Do not mix parts of one Hillard clutch assembly with similar parts from another clutch assembly.

13. Remove the spacer (**Figure 9**).

14. Note the location of the armature plate (**Figure 10**), then remove it. The plate must be reinstalled in the same position during assembly.

15. Inspect the front hub components as described in the following procedure.

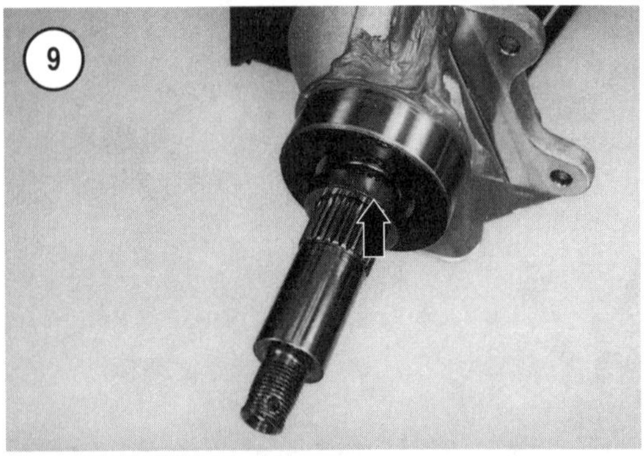

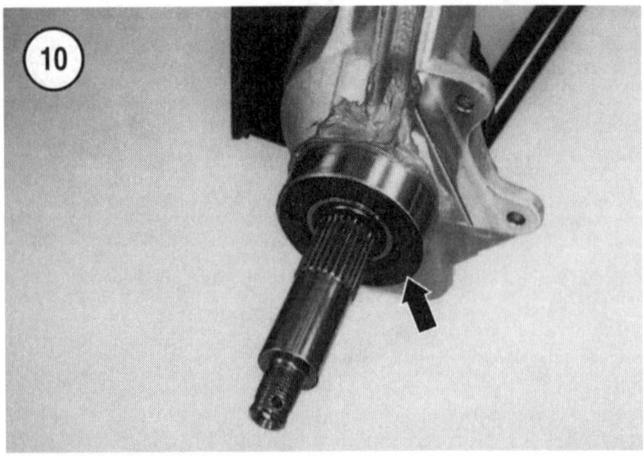

Inspection

Refer to **Figure 11**.

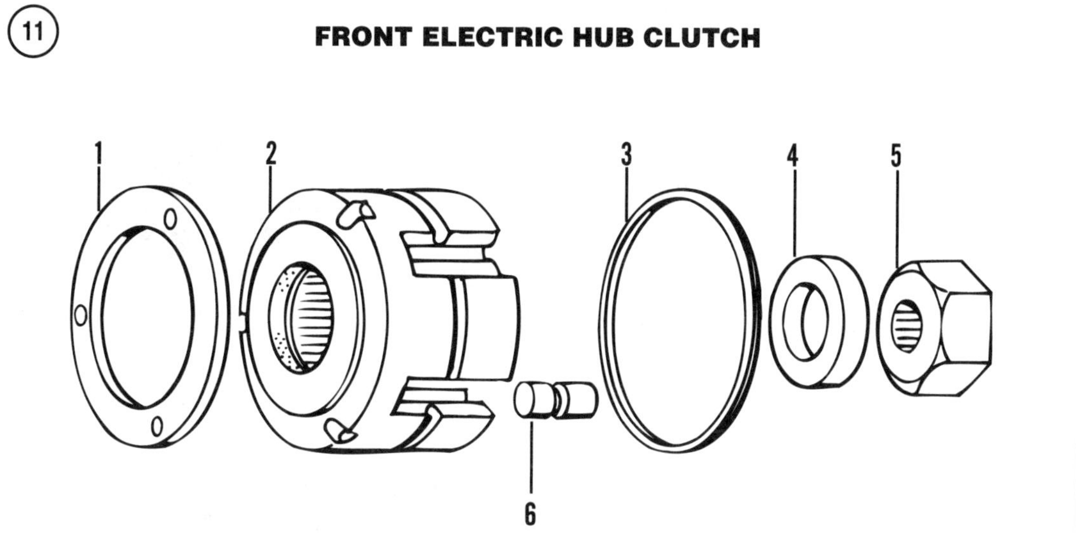

1. Armature plate
2. Roller cage
3. Retaining spring
4. Spacer
5. Cam
6. Roller

NOTE

The roller cage and rollers can usually be cleaned and inspected without removing the retaining spring and rollers. If the rollers are removed, do not stretch the retaining spring farther than necessary to remove one roller at a time. If the retaining spring is removed from the cage, it has been stretched too far and must be replaced.

1. Thoroughly clean the roller cage and roller assembly (**Figure 12**) in solvent and dry with low-pressure compressed air.
2. Inspect the inner splines (**Figure 13**) for wear or damage.
3. Inspect the roller cage and the rollers (A, **Figure 14**). Make sure the rollers move freely within the sliding surfaces of the roller cage. Small burrs can sometimes be removed using fine emery cloth or a small file, but be sure all of the parts are thoroughly clean before assembling.
4. Inspect the retaining spring (B, **Figure 14**) for irregular gaps without removing it. Install a new spring if the gaps are not even and whenever the old

spring has been removed. Cut the old spring and remove it.

WARNING
*Do **not** install an older model retaining spring. The older model retaining spring looks similar to the new design, but it is not strong enough to hold the rollers in position. Use only a new retaining spring, part No. 3250032. Using the older design retaining spring can allow the hubs to engage at high speed, which will result in severe vehicle instability.*

5. Install the *new* retaining spring using a special tool and the following procedure:
   a. Apply a light coat of grease to the rollers and install the rollers in the roller cage.
   b. Position the special tapered tool (part No. 2870888) against the end of the roller cage.
   c. Hook the ends of the retaining spring together and install it onto the special tool. Carefully and evenly roll the retaining spring off of the special tool and onto the roller cage and into the groove holding the rollers in place.

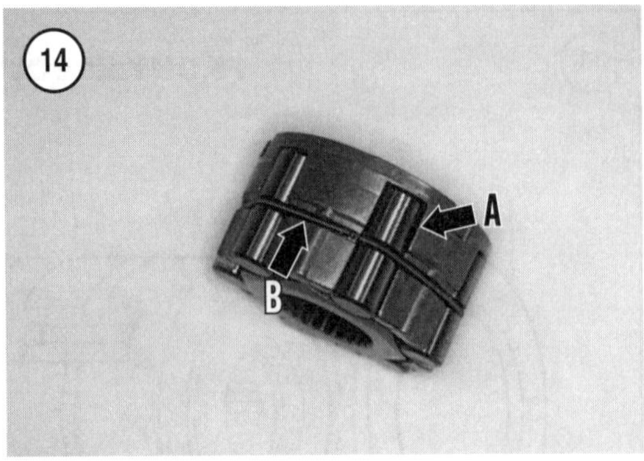

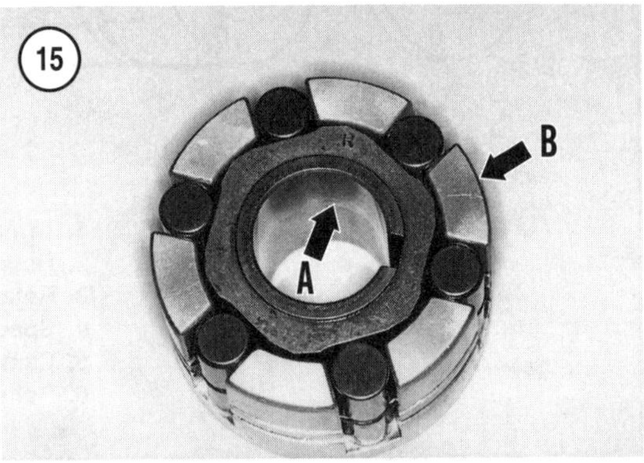

Hillard Clutch Testing

Prior to installing the clutch assembly in the front hub, assemble and test the cam and roller cage to simulate engagement and disengagement.

1. Apply a light coat of the specified lubricant to the inner surface of the roller cage, to the rollers and to the outer surface of the cam.
2. Insert the cam (A, **Figure 15**) into the roller cage (B, **Figure 15**).
3. To simulate clutch engagement, hold onto the roller cage and rotate the cam within the roller cage.
4. When the cam is rotated and the cam shoulders contact the rollers, the rollers should move out and increase the spring tension on the rollers.
5. Retain a hold on the cam while releasing the roller cage to simulate disengagement.
6. When the roller cage rotates, the cam shoulders move away from the rollers, the rollers should move back into the neutral position in the roller cage because of spring tension.
7. If the clutch does not operate correctly, check the following:

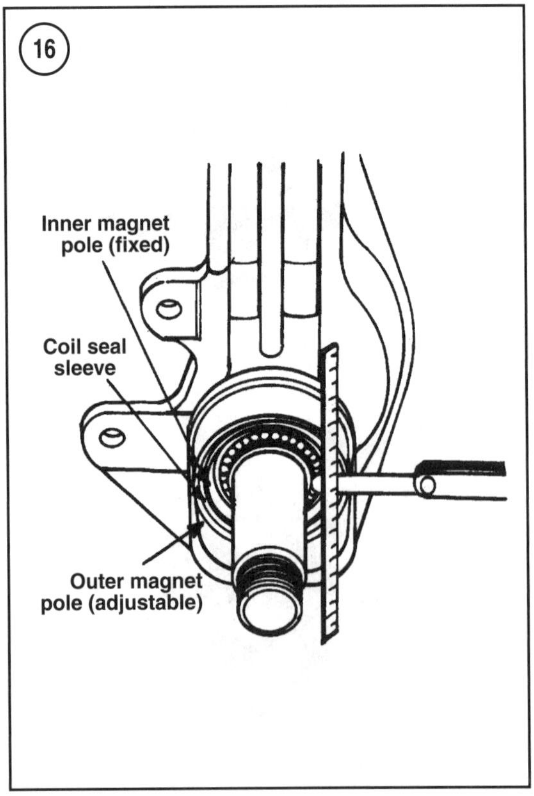

17
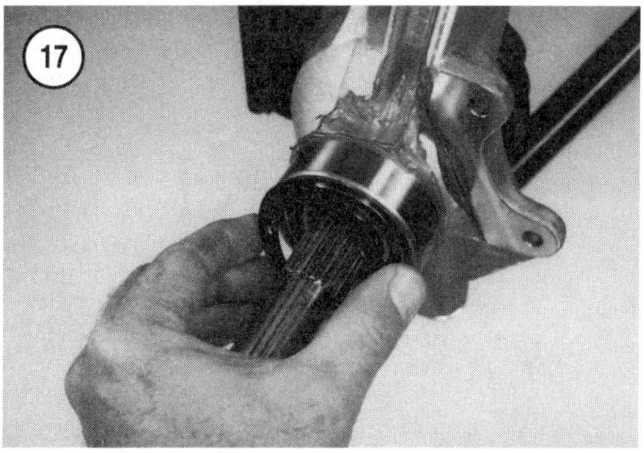

18

19
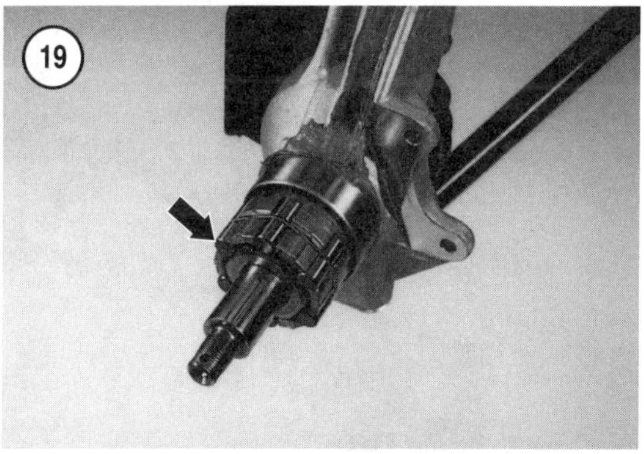

20
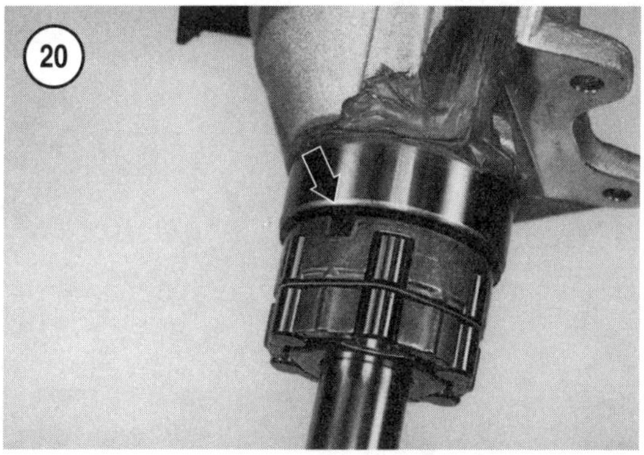

a. Roller-to-roller cage sliding surface roughness or interference.
b. Roller cage-to-cam mating surface, including the cam shoulder and cage-to-cam mating surfaces for roughness or interference.
c. Retainer spring tension that is insufficient to pull the rollers back into the roller cage in the neutral position.

Installation

Improper installation and adjustment of the Hillard clutch can result in a dangerous lack of vehicle control. The drive clutches must be correctly installed for the front drive to function properly.

NOTE
The cam on some models is marked L or R and must be installed on the correct side. If the cam is not marked, the cam can be installed on either side.

1. Test the operation of the Hillard clutch prior to installing it on the front axle.
2. Use a depth gauge or a straightedge and feeler gauge to measure the distance from the outer pole (seal sleeve) to the inner pole as shown in **Figure 16**. Measure the pole gap in at least three locations and compare with the specification in **Table 2**.
3. If the pole gap measured is incorrect, move the outer magnet pole by tapping the seal sleeve.
4. Install the armature plate (**Figure 17**) into the same location as noted in *Removal* Step 14 (**Figure 10**).
5. Install the spacer (**Figure 9**) and push it on until it stops against the axle bearing.
6. Apply the recommended lubricant to the Hillard clutch assembly.
7. Position the Hillard clutch as shown in **Figure 18** and install it. Push it on until it stops (**Figure 19**).
8. Be sure the tabs of the armature plate are engaged with the holes in the roller cage, as shown in **Figure 20**.
9. Install the inner bearing (**Figure 21**).
10. Coat the wheel hub seal (**Figure 22**) with grease, then install the wheel hub over the clutch and onto the front axle (**Figure 23**). Be careful not to damage the seal.
11. Install the outer bearing (**Figure 24**) and press it into the front hub until it is correctly seated in the hub outer race (**Figure 25**).

10

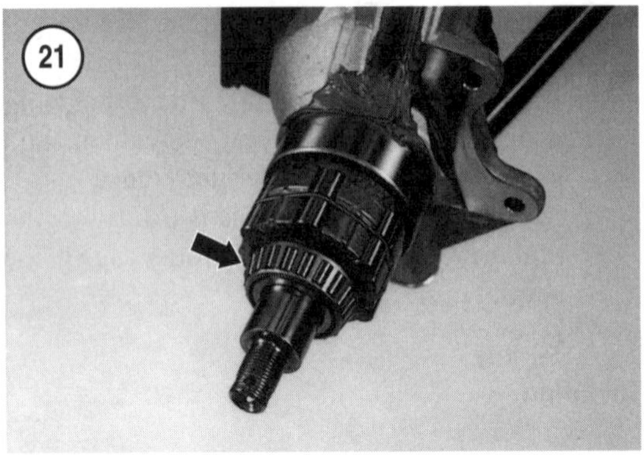

12. Install the washer and hub nut (**Figure 26**).
13. Install and tighten the hub nut as follows:
    a. Install the nut (**Figure 27**) and tighten to the first-stage torque in **Table 3**.
    b. Rotate the wheel hub several revolutions by rotating the rear wheel.
    c. Loosen, then retighten the axle nut to the second-stage torque specification in **Table 3**.

NOTE
If the cotter pin hole does not align properly, slightly tighten the nut until alignment is reached. Never loosen the nut, but never tighten beyond 16 N•m (144 in.-lb.).

    d. Install a new cotter pin and bend the ends over completely (**Figure 28**).
14. Inspect the hubcap O-ring seals (**Figure 29**) for nicks, cuts and deterioration. Replace as necessary. Apply a light coating of grease to the O-rings.
15. Install the hubcap and the three T-25 Torx bolts (**Figure 2**). Tighten the Torx bolts securely.
16. Install the front brake caliper as described in Chapter Fourteen.
17. Refill the front hub with the specified lubricant as described under *Front Hub Oil Change* in Chapter Three.
18. Install the front wheels as described in Chapter Twelve.

Front Hub Seal Replacement

NOTE
The four bolts are installed with threadlocking compound and may be difficult to loosen. Use an impact driver and appropriate size socket to loosen the bolts.

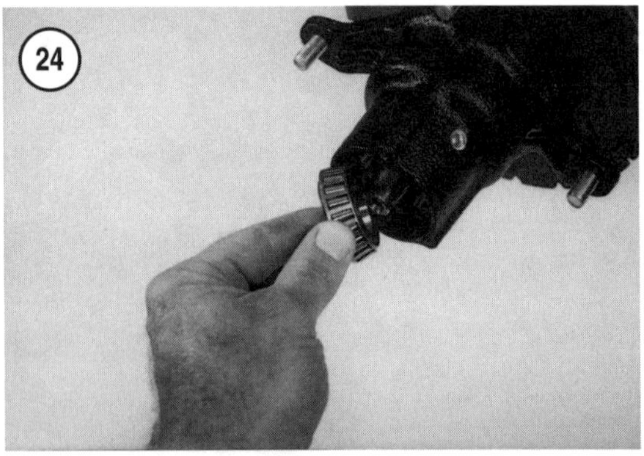

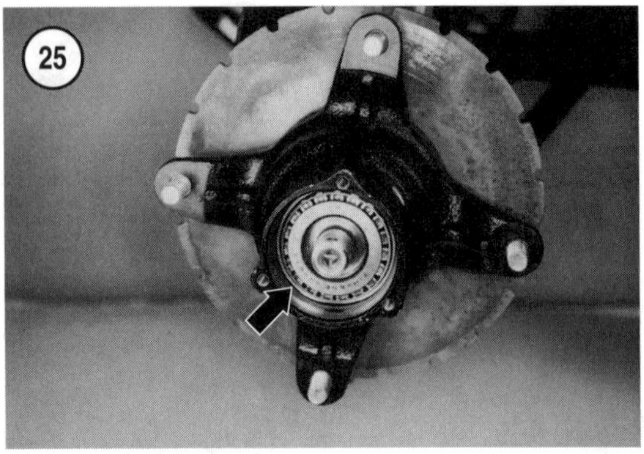

26

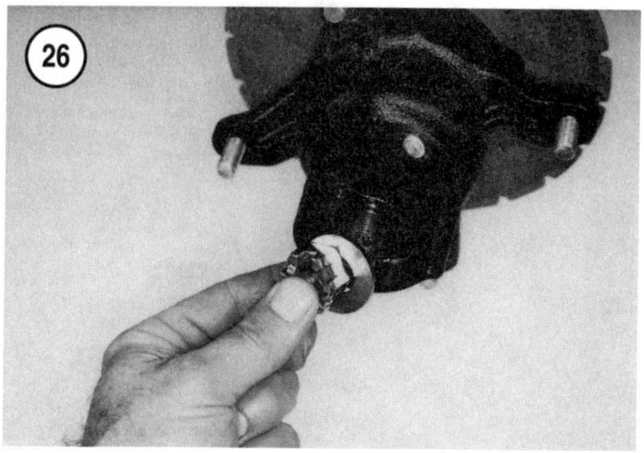

27

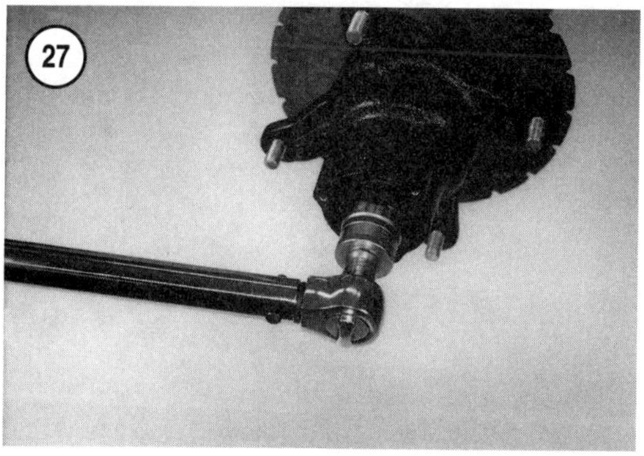

28

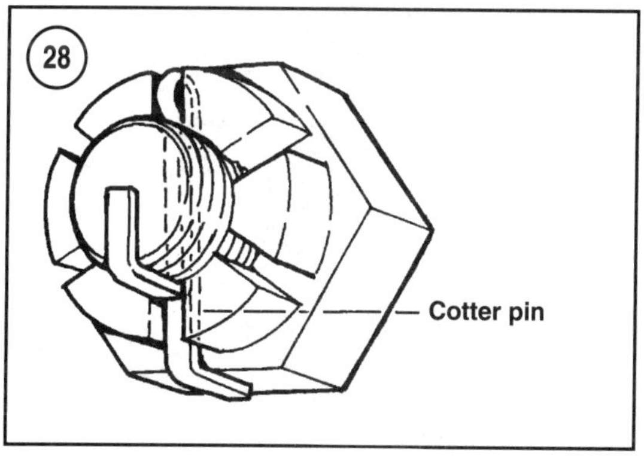

29

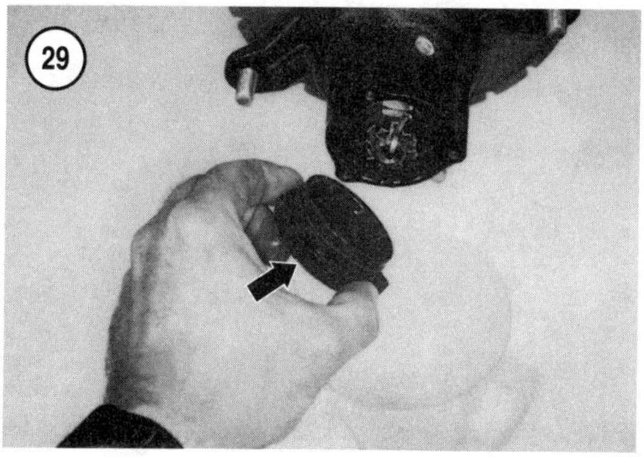

30

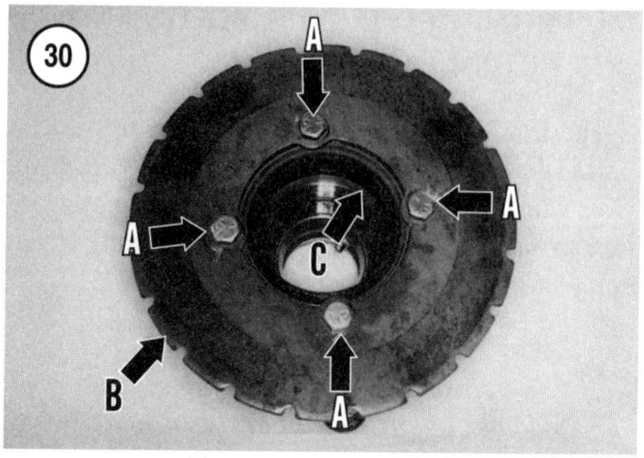

31

1. Remove the four hex bolts (A, **Figure 30**) securing the brake rotor to the hub. Remove the brake rotor (B, **Figure 30**). Discard the hex bolts.

2. Pry the seal (C, **Figure 30**) out of the hub with a wide-blade screwdriver.

3. Thoroughly clean the seal-seating surface of the front hub.

4. Apply a light coat of oil to the seal-seating surface of the front hub and to the outer surface of the seal.

5. Position the new seal with the spring-loaded lip toward the hub.

6. Carefully press the new seal into the front hub until it is flush with the rotor disc mounting surface (**Figure 31**).

7. Install the brake rotor onto the front hub and align the mounting holes.

8. Install *new* hex bolts with the pre-applied threadlocking compound. Tighten to the torque specification listed in **Table 3**.

FRONT DRIVE AXLE, BOOTS AND CV (CONSTANT VELOCITY) JOINTS

The front drive axles connect to the front drive unit. The Hillard drive clutches are located in the front wheel hubs. Service to the axles is usually limited to installing new seal boots or installing the complete shaft and universal joints.

NOTE

To reinstall the original equipment clamps on the CV joint rubber boots, a special Polaris tool is required. For ear-type clamps, use part No. 8700225 or for earless type clamp, use part No. 8700226. A screw clamp of exactly the same size may be substituted.

Removal

1. Place the vehicle on level ground and set the parking brake. Block the rear wheel so the vehicle will not roll in either direction.
2. Remove the front fender as described in Chapter Fifteen.
3. Raise the front of the vehicle up to gain working room under the front strut. Secure the vehicle in this position so it will not shift or fall while working on it.
4. Remove the front caliper as described in Chapter Fourteen.
5. Remove the front hub as described in Chapter Ten.
6. Disconnect the front wheel drive coil electrical connector (**Figure 32**).
7. Disconnect the front suspension arm from the front strut as described in Chapter Twelve.
8. Disconnect the outboard end of the tie rod (**Figure 33**) from the front strut as described in Chapter Twelve.
9. Move the front strut out from the drive axle to loosen the outer bearing from the strut (**Figure 34**), then slide the outer bearing off the axle.
10. Move the front strut farther out and withdraw the drive axle from it.
11. Slide the outer bearing back onto the drive axle.

NOTE

The rubber boot can be replaced with the drive axle still attached to the front drive eccentric shaft, or front

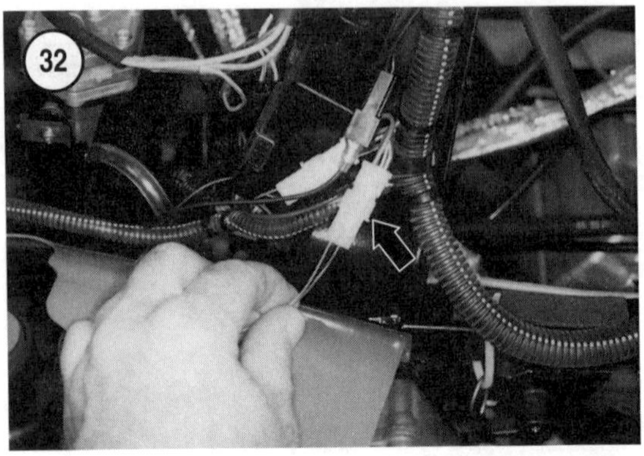

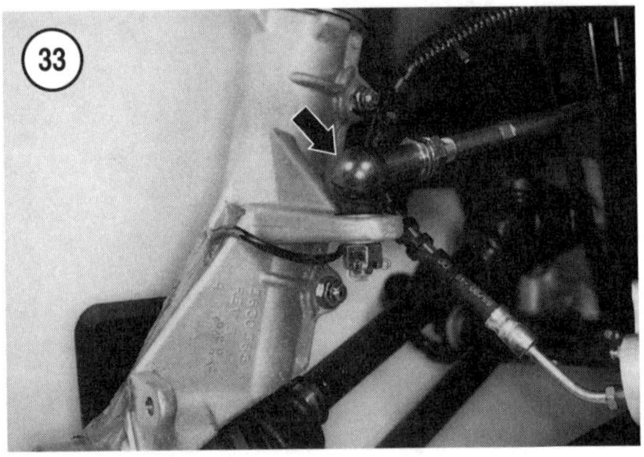

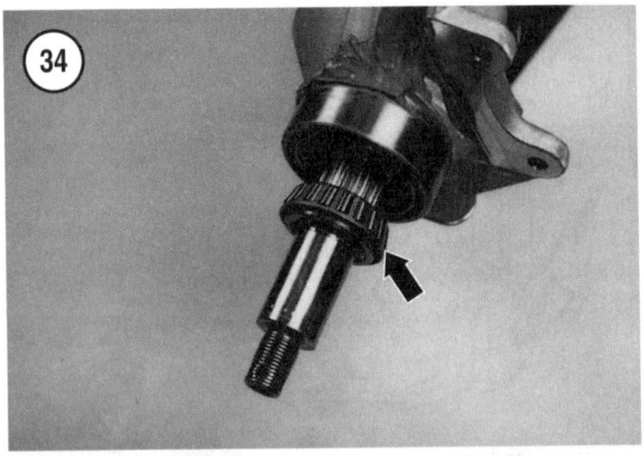

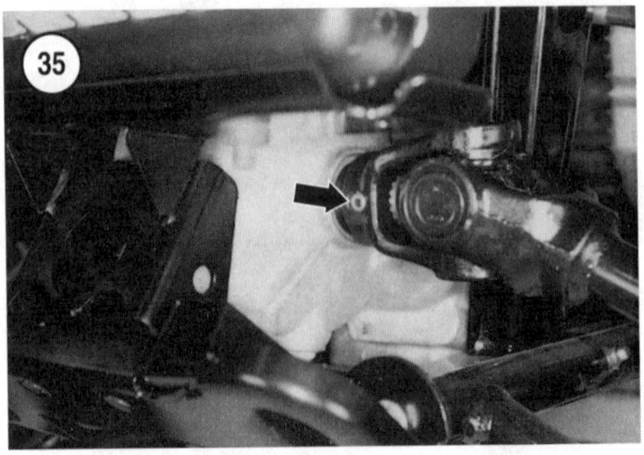

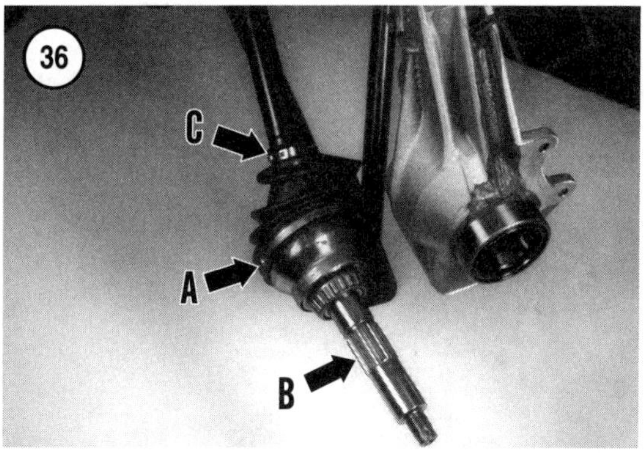

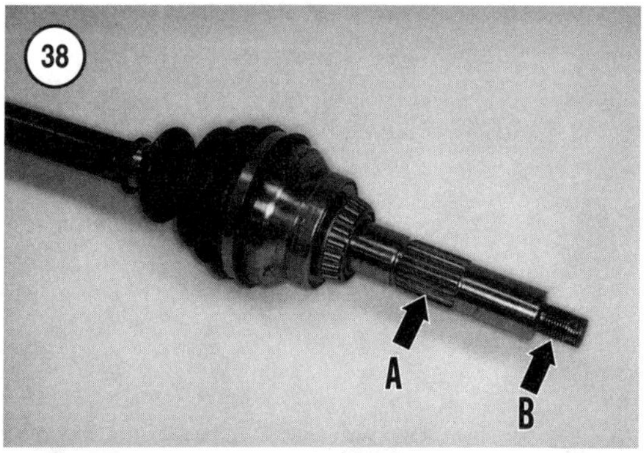

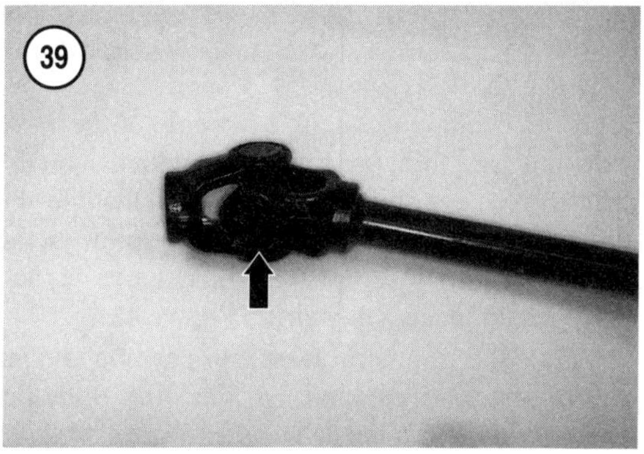

drive unit. If necessary, remove the drive axle and perform the procedure at a workbench.

NOTE
If only replacing the rubber boot(s), proceed to Step 13.

12. To remove the drive axle, remove the roll pin (**Figure 35**). Slide the drive axle and inner universal joint off the spline on the front drive eccentric shaft.

13. To remove the CV joint boot, perform the following:
   a. Remove the large clamp (A, **Figure 36**) securing the rubber boot to the front spindle portion of the CV joint. Slide the boot off the CV joint.
   b. Withdraw the front spindle portion (B, **Figure 36**) of the CV joint from the front drive axle. If necessary, use a plastic mallet and tap on the inner surface of the front spindle to separate it from the circlip on the end of the drive axle.
   c. Remove the small clamp (C, **Figure 36**) securing the rubber boot to the drive axle and slide the rubber boot off the drive axle.

Inspection/Lubrication

1. Check the drive axle for damage (**Figure 37**).
2. Inspect the front spindle splines (A, **Figure 38**) for wear or damage. Minor damage can be cleaned up with a fine-cut file, but if damage is severe, replace the damaged parts.
3. Inspect the spindle nut threads (B, **Figure 38**) for damage.
4. Inspect the universal joint (**Figure 39**) for wear or damage.
5. Check the rubber boot (**Figure 40**) for hardness, tears or damage. Replace if necessary.
6. If the rubber boot was removed, perform the following:
   a. Inspect the splines on both the front spindle and front axle for wear or damage. Minor damaged can be cleaned up with a fine-cut file, but if damage is severe, replace the damaged parts.
   b. Make sure the circlip is secured onto the drive axle. If loose, install a new circlip

and make sure it is correctly seated in the axle groove.

c. Clean the areas of the drive shaft and CV joint where the boot is attached.

d. Inspect the grease on the CV joint for contamination. If the boot has been damaged or if the CV joint is worn, the grease will be contaminated. Clean the CV joint using Polaris special cleaner (part No. 2870770).

e. After the CV joint is thoroughly clean, assemble the joint using Polaris special grease (part No. 3260110).

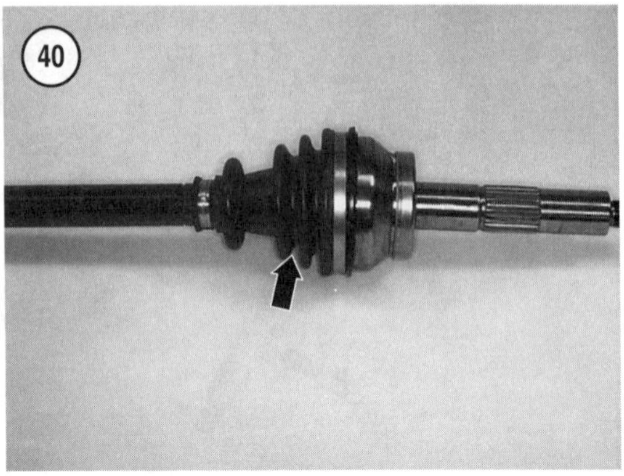
40

Installation

1. If the CV joint boot was removed, perform the following:

a. Lubricate the CV joint using Polaris grease (part No. 3260110).

b. Remove all grease from the CV boot clamps to the spindle and drive axle.

c. Carefully slide the small end of the boot (C, **Figure 36**) over the splines of the drive axle. Do not damage the inner surface of the boot as it passes over the splines.

d. Make sure the circlip is in place on the end of the drive axle.

e. Slide the front spindle (B, **Figure 36**) onto the drive axle. It may be necessary to tap on the end of the drive axle with a plastic mallet to force the spindle past the circlip.

f. After the front spindle is installed, pull back on it to make sure it is secured in place on the drive axle. If the front spindle slides off, it was not installed correctly.

g. Slide the large end of the rubber boot into the place on the front spindle.

CAUTION

Install both clamps on the boot. Make sure that clamps are tight, but not too tight that they cut the rubber boot under the clamp.

h. Install the large clamp (A, **Figure 36**) onto the large end of the front spindle and tighten securely.

i. Install the small clamp (C, **Figure 36**) onto the small end of the drive axle and tighten securely.

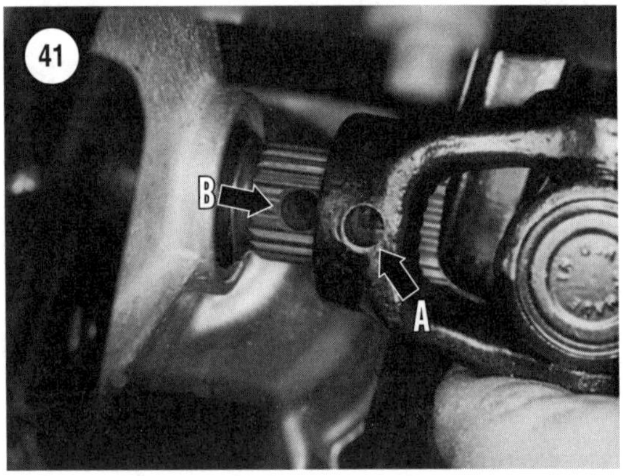

41

42

2. If removed, align the roll pin hole of the drive axle universal joint (A, **Figure 41**) with that on the front drive unit spline (B, **Figure 41**). Slide the drive axle and universal joint onto the spline on the front drive unit. Install the roll pin (**Figure 42**) and drive it into place with a drift (**Figure 43**).

3. Move the front strut back into position and insert the front spindle through the strut. Slide the outer bearing onto the drive axle (**Figure 34**).

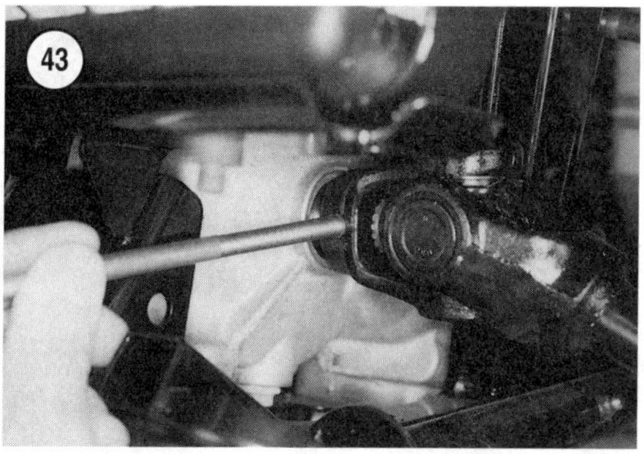

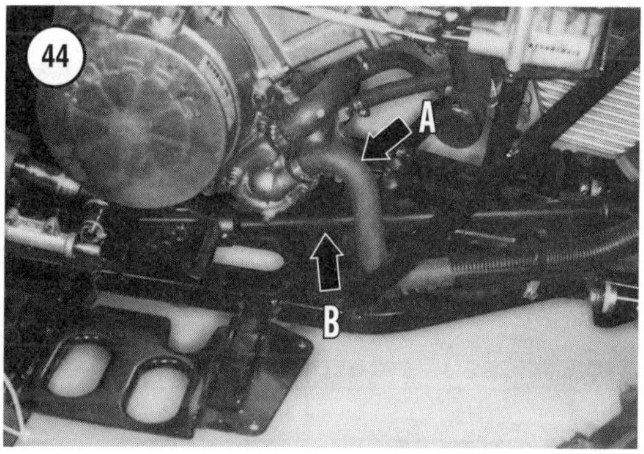

4. Connect the outboard end of the tie rod (**Figure 33**) onto the front strut as described in Chapter Twelve.

5. Connect the front suspension arm onto the front strut as described in Chapter Twelve.

6. Connect the front wheel drive coil electrical connector (**Figure 32**).

7. Install the front hub as described in Chapter Nine.

8. Install the front caliper as described in Chapter Fourteen.

9. Install the front fender as described in Chapter Fifteen.

FRONT DRIVE SHAFT

Removal/Installation

1. Remove the front fender as described in Chapter Fifteen.
2. Drain the cooling system as described in Chapter Three.
3. Loosen the clamp and remove coolant pump lower inlet hose (A, **Figure 44**).
4. Use a drift punch and drive the roll pin (A, **Figure 45**) out of the drive shaft front universal joint and front drive unit shaft.
5. Slide the drive shaft (B, **Figure 44**) toward the rear onto the transmission front output shaft until the front universal joint clears the front drive unit shaft.
6. Pull the drive shaft forward and disengage it from the transmission front output shaft and remove the drive shaft (B, **Figure 45**) from the frame.
7. Install by reversing these removal steps.

10

FRONT DRIVE UNIT

NOTE
There are two different front drive units used among the different years. The only difference is with the external appearance of the housing. The internal components are almost identical. The older unit was used from 1996 through September 13, 1998. After September 14, 1998 the new unit was installed on all models covered in this manual.

Removal/Installation

NOTE
This procedure is shown on a 2000 model unit.

1. Remove both front drive axles as described in this chapter.
2. Remove the front drive shaft as described in this chapter.

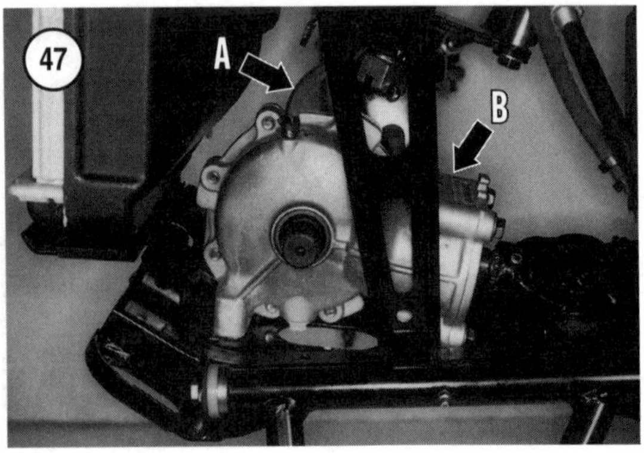

3. Remove the four bolts (**Figure 46**) securing the front drive unit to the frame.
4. Disconnect the vent line (A, **Figure 47**).
5. Remove the front drive unit (B, **Figure 47**) from the frame.
6. Install by reversing these removal steps. Tighten the mounting bolts securely.

Inspection

It is recommended that the front drive unit inspection and overhaul be entrusted to a Polaris dealership. The cost of the required tools will most likely outweigh the cost of the repairs or replacement.

Table 1 TIRE SIZE AND INFLATION PRESSURE (COLD)*

Model	Size	kPa	PSI
Front wheels	25 × 8 × 12	34.5	5
Rear wheels			
1996	25 × 12 × 10	34.5	5
1997-on	22 × 11 × 10	34.5	5

*Tire pressure for original equipment tires. Aftermarket tires may require different inflation pressure.

Table 2 FRONT WHEEL DRIVE HUB SPECIFICATIONS

Item	Specification
Front hub retainer spring	Part No. 3250032
Wire diameter	0.40 mm (0.016 in.)
Spring free length inside hooks	168 mm (6.61 in.)
Pole gap	0-0.025 mm (0-0.001 in.)

Table 3 TORQUE SPECIFICATIONS

Item	N•m	in.-lb.	ft.-lb.
Front hub castellated nut[1]			
First stage	18.6	165	–
Second stage	14.0	124	–
Front brake rotor hex bolts[2]	24	–	18

1. See text in this chapter for torque procedure.
2. New bolts with pre-applied thread locking compound.

NOTE: Refer to the Supplement at the back of this manual for information unique to 2001-on models, including the Sportsman 400.

CHAPTER ELEVEN

ELECTRICAL SYSTEM

11

This chapter contains service and test procedures for all electrical and ignition components. ATVs are often exposed to moisture during operation, so it is important to keep all electrical connections firmly attached. Also, apply dielectric grease (available from a Polaris dealerships or automotive parts stores) to all electrical connectors before they are reconnected. Dielectric grease helps seal out moisture and helps prevent corrosion of the electrical connector terminals.

Service information relating to the battery, spark plug and ignition timing are covered in Chapter Three.

The electrical system includes the following systems:

1. Charging system.
2. Ignition system.
3. Starting system.
4. Lighting system.
5. Other electrical systems and components.

Table 1 and **Table 2** are at the end of this chapter.

BASIC INFORMATION

Electrical Component Resistance Testing

Because the resistance of a component varies with temperature, perform the resistance tests with the component at room temperature (68° F [20° C]).

The specifications provided in this manual are based on tests performed at this temperature.

NOTE
When using an analog ohmmeter, always touch the test leads, then calibrate the meter to zero.

Electrical Component Replacement

Most ATV dealerships and parts suppliers will not accept returns on electrical parts. Avoid purchasing parts unless the cause of the malfunction has been determined. If a thorough diagnosis has not located the exact cause of the electrical system malfunction, have a Polaris dealership determine the possible cause.

Electrical Connector Location

The location of electrical connectors varies with the different years. Also, if the vehicle has been worked on by someone else, they may have positioned the connector differently than the original location. The photographs shown in this chapter may differ from the vehicle being worked on. Always compare the connector's wire colors to those listed in the procedures and the wiring diagrams at the end of this manual to make sure the correct electrical connector is being worked on. Also, follow the wire from the specific component to where it connects to the harness or to another electrical component.

NEGATIVE BATTERY TERMINAL

Some of the component replacement procedures and some of the test procedures in this chapter require disconnecting the negative cable from the battery as a safety precaution.

NOTE
The battery can be removed with the rear fender in place by removing the rear wheel but the working room is very limited. Remove whatever component is most convenient.

1A. Remove the rear fender as described in Chapter Fifteen.
1B. Remove the left rear wheel as described in Chapter Thirteen.

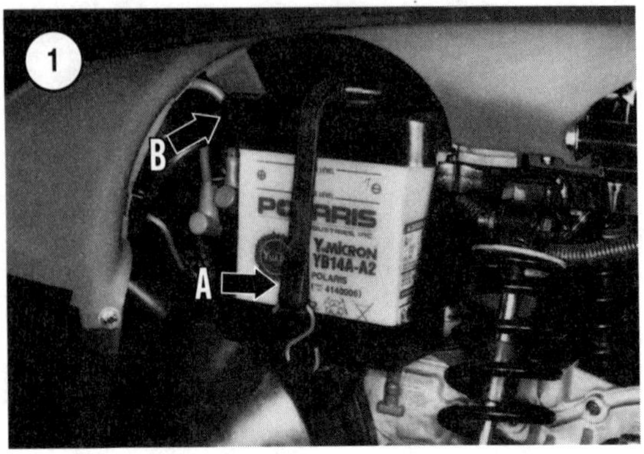

2. Use a stiff whiskbroom or brush to thoroughly clean off any dirt or debris from the top of the battery cover prior to removing any parts or connectors.
3. Unhook and remove the battery hold down strap (A, **Figure 1**).
4. Remove the battery cover (B, **Figure 1**).
5. Disconnect the negative battery cable from the battery. Move and secure the cable away from the battery to prevent accidental contact with the battery post.

CHARGING SYSTEM

The charging system consists of the battery, alternator, circuit breaker and a voltage regulator/rectifier. Refer to **Figure 2-Figure 4** or the wiring diagrams at the back of the manual. Alternating current generated by the alternator is rectified to direct current. The voltage regulator maintains the voltage to the battery and additional electrical loads at a constant voltage regardless of variations in engine speed and load.

Charging System Output Test

If charging system trouble is suspected, clean and test the battery as described under *Battery Testing* in Chapter Three. Make sure all electrical connectors in the charging system are secure, making good contact and free of corrosion. To test the system, proceed as follows:

1. If the electrical system appears to be dead, check the battery cable connections and the main circuit breaker that is located adjacent to the battery. If the main circuit breaker is good, proceed to the next step.

2

CHARGING SYSTEM (1996-1997)

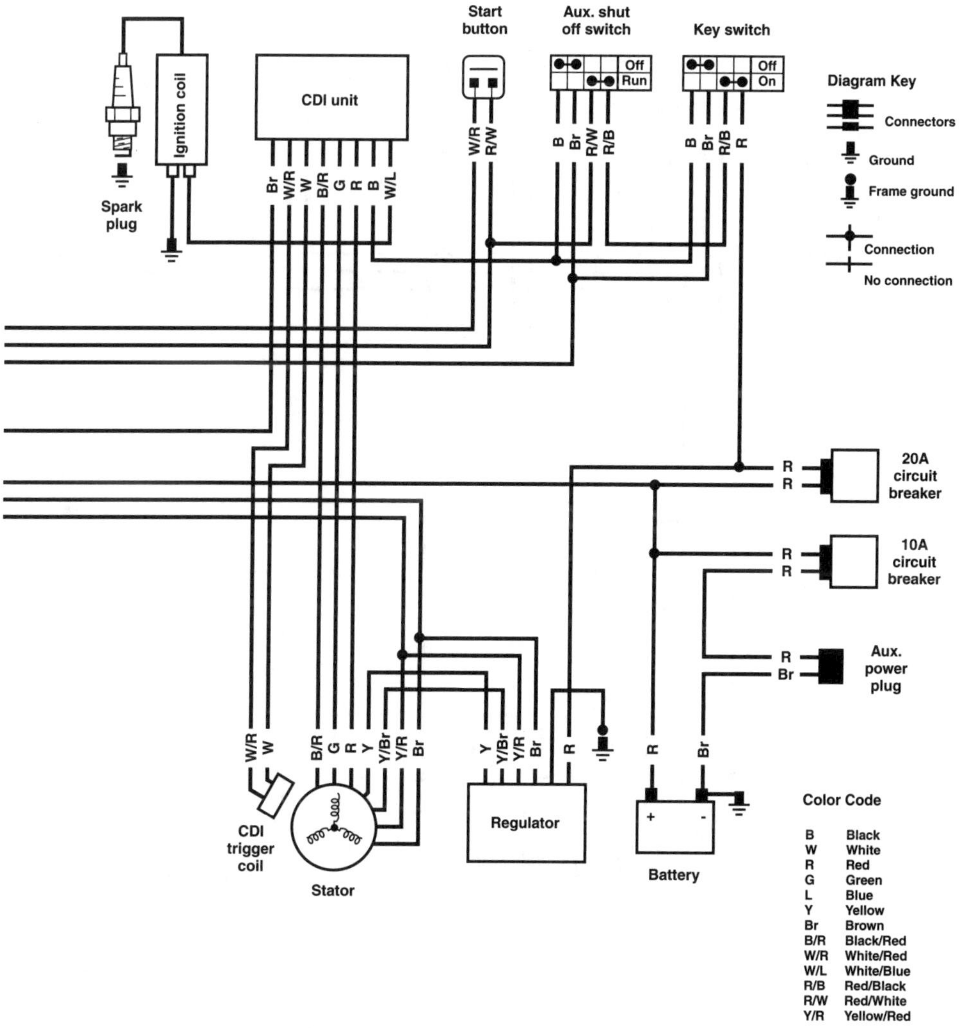

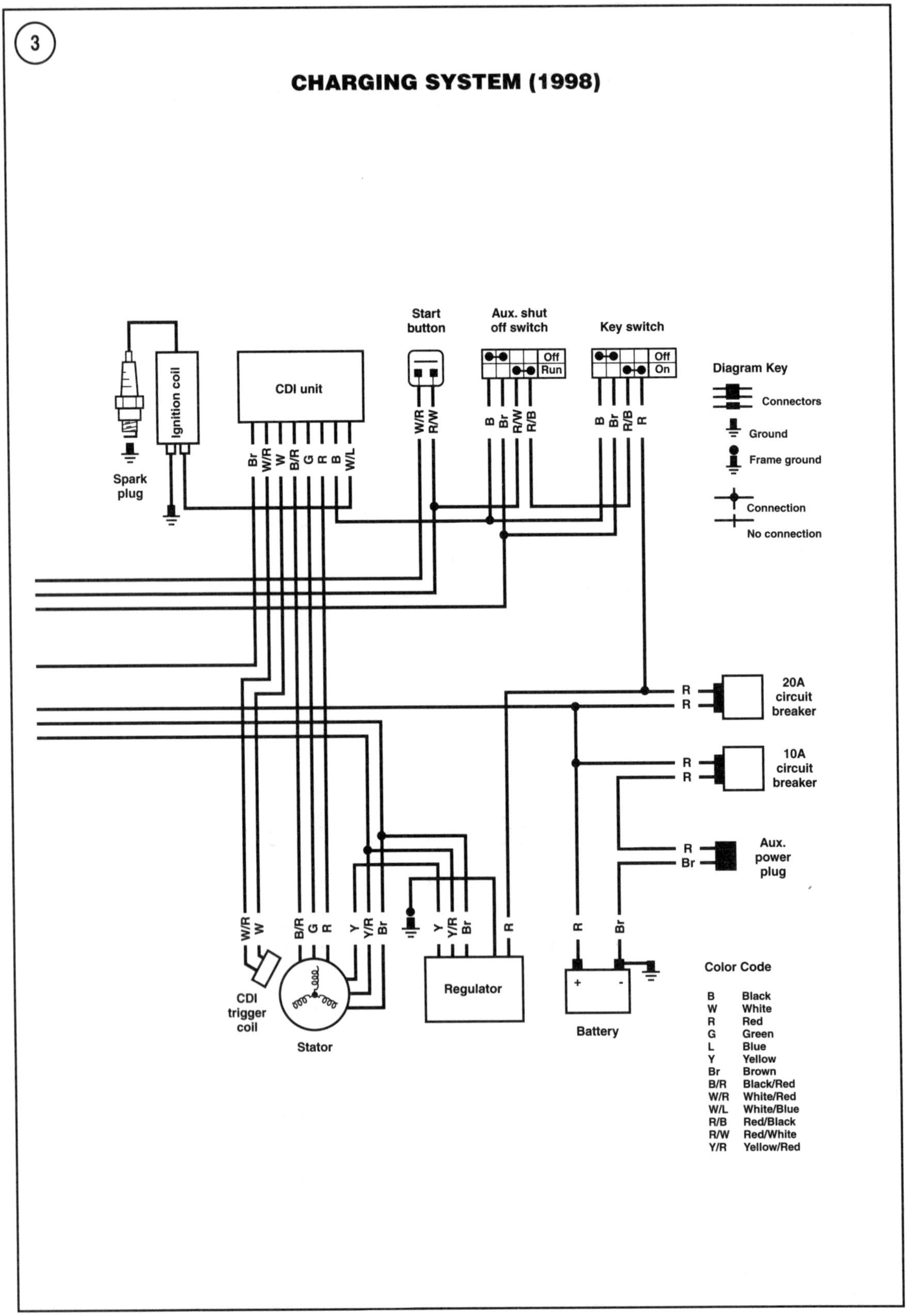
3
CHARGING SYSTEM (1998)
Start button
Aux. shut off switch
Key switch
Off
Run
Off
On
Ignition coil
CDI unit
Spark plug
Br W/R W B/R G R B W/L
W/R R/W
B Br R/W R/B
B Br R/B R
Diagram Key
Connectors
Ground
Frame ground
Connection
No connection
R
R
20A circuit breaker
R
R
10A circuit breaker
R
Br
Aux. power plug
W/R W B/R G R Y Y/R Br
Y Y/R Br R
R Br
CDI trigger coil
Stator
Regulator
Battery
Color Code
B Black
W White
R Red
G Green
L Blue
Y Yellow
Br Brown
B/R Black/Red
W/R White/Red
W/L White/Blue
R/B Red/Black
R/W Red/White
Y/R Yellow/Red

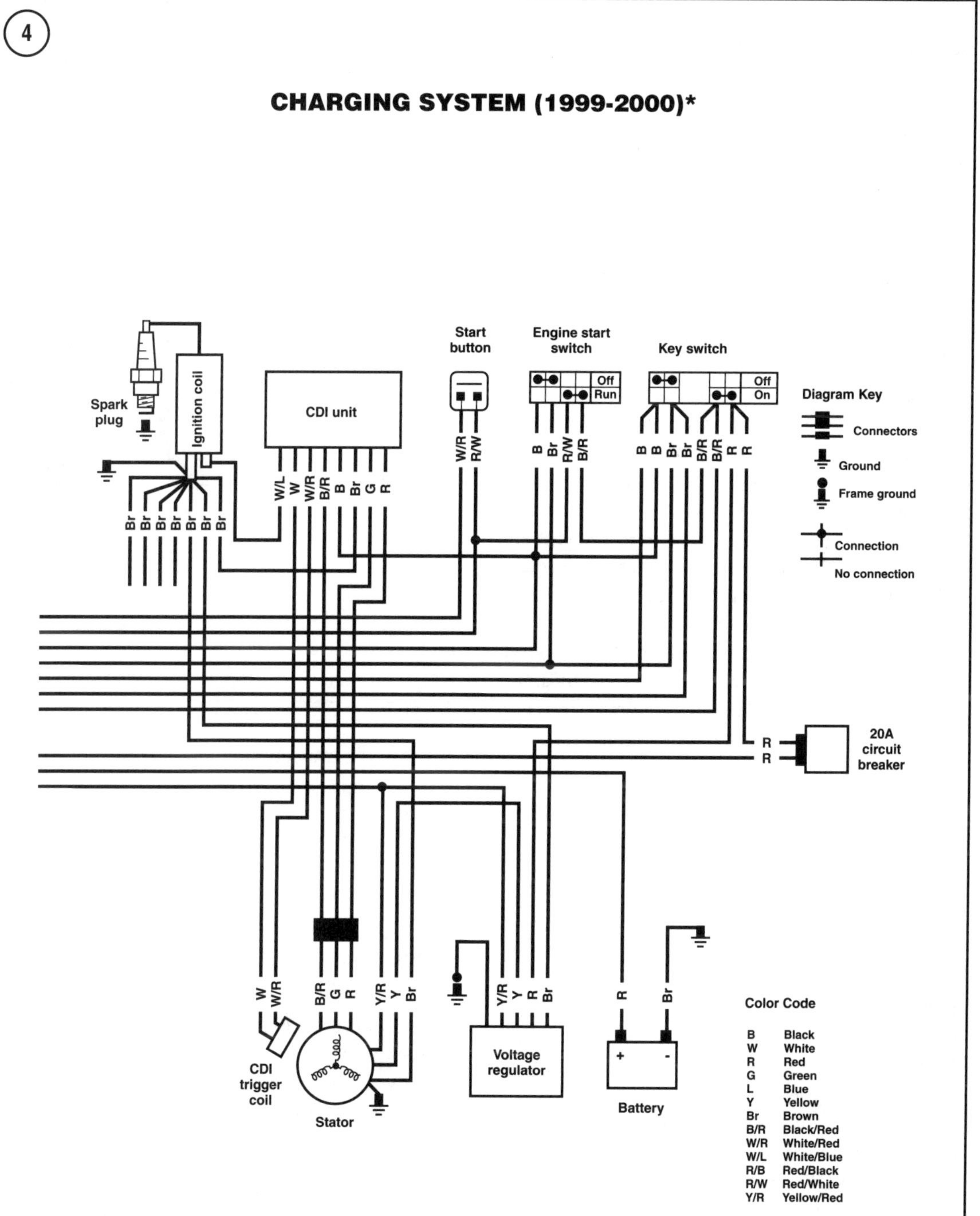

*Refer to the wiring diagram at the end of the manual for 2001-on models.

2. Test the battery specific gravity as described under *Battery Testing* in Chapter Three. Charge or replace the battery as required.
3. Connect a 0-20 DC voltmeter to the battery terminals. Connect an inductive tachometer to the spark plug following the manufacturer's instructions.
4. Start the engine and increase engine speed to 4000 rpm. Read the voltage indicated on the voltmeter. It should be between 13-14.6 volts. Note the following:
   a. Charging voltage correct: The charging system is operating properly.
   b. Charging voltage incorrect: Test the stator charge coils as described under *Alternator Stator* in this chapter. Replace the stator coils if they are defective. If the charging coils are good, perform Step 5.
5. Check the charging system wiring harness and connectors for dirty or loose-fitting terminals; clean and repair them as required. If the wiring harness and connectors are acceptable and no problem has been found after performing the previous tests, consider the regulator/rectifier to be defective by a process of elimination. Install a regulator/rectifier unit that is known to be in working order, then retest the charging system.

Charging System Amperage Test

This test determines when the charging system overcomes all electrical system loads and begins to charge the battery.

1. Place the vehicle on level ground and set the parking brake.
2. Test the battery specific gravity as described under *Battery Testing* in Chapter Three. Charge or replace the battery as required.
3. Disconnect the negative battery cable as described in this chapter.
4. Connect a DC ammeter in series with the negative battery terminal and the disconnected negative cable (**Figure 5**).
5. Connect an inductive tachometer to the spark plug following the manufacturer's instructions.
6. Turn both the key switch and the auxiliary shutoff switch to the ON position.
7. The ammeter should read negative amps (battery discharge). Reverse the ammeter test leads if the ammeter reads positive.

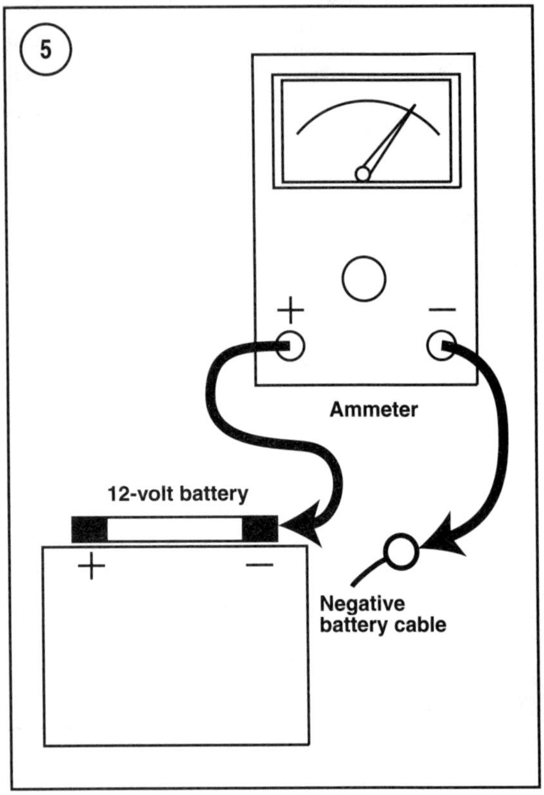

8. Shift the transmission into neutral.

CAUTION
Do not start the engine with the electric starter as the ammeter will be damaged.

9. Start the engine with the *recoil starter* and slowly increase engine speed.
10. Observe the ammeter and tachometer and note the engine speed when the ammeter reverses and the battery starts to charge. This should occur at approximately 1500 rpm.
11. Turn the headlight ON and apply the brake to turn the brake light ON.
12. Once again slowly increase engine speed.
13. Observe the ammeter and tachometer and note the engine speed when the ammeter reverses and the battery starts to charge. This should occur at approximately 3000 rpm.
14. If the charge system fails either of these tests, check the resistance of the charging coils, described under *Battery Charge Coils Testing* in this chapter.

6

7
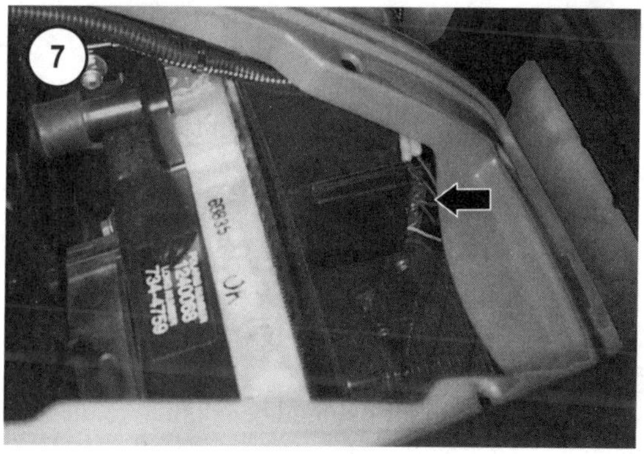

ALTERNATOR STATOR

Procedures for removing and installing the alternator rotor are covered in Chapter Five.

Exciter Coils Testing

1. Place the vehicle on level ground and set the parking brake.
2. Remove the seat and front fender as described in Chapter Fifteen.
3. Follow the electrical harness from the alternator to the location where it connects to the CDI unit (**Figure 6**).
4. Disconnect the three-pin electrical connector from the CDI.
5. Connect an ohmmeter between the following wires in the three-pin stator connector and compare the resistance to the specification in **Table 1**.
   a. The red and green terminals.
   b. The black/red and green terminals.
6. Replace the stator assembly if the resistance is not as specified.
7. Apply dielectric grease to the electrical connector and reconnect it.

Battery Charge Coils Testing

1. Place the vehicle on level ground and set the parking brake.
2. Remove the front fender cover as described in Chapter Fifteen.
3. Follow the electrical harness from the alternator to the location where it connects to the voltage regulator.
4. Disconnect the two individual yellow and the yellow/red electrical connectors from the voltage regulator (**Figure 7**).
5. Connect an ohmmeter to the wires indicated in **Table 1** and note the resistance.
6. Replace the stator assembly if the resistance is not as specified.
7. Apply dielectric grease to the electrical connectors and reconnect them.

Alternator Output Test

1. Place the vehicle on level ground and set the parking brake.
2. Remove the front fender front cover as described in Chapter Fifteen.
3. Follow the electrical harness from the alternator to the location where it connects to the voltage regulator.
4. Disconnect the two individual yellow and the yellow/red electrical connectors from the voltage regulator (**Figure 7**).
5. Connect an AC ammeter to the yellow and the yellow/red stator wires leading from the alternator.
6. Shift the transmission into neutral.

CAUTION
Do not start the engine with the electric starter, as the ammeter will be damaged.

CAUTION
Do not conduct this test for longer than 10-15 seconds, as the alternator windings may overheat.

7. Start the engine with the *recoil starter* and let idle.

8. The specified amperage is listed in **Table 1**. Replace the stator assembly if the amperage is not as specified.
9. Apply dielectric grease to the electrical connectors prior to reconnecting to help seal out moisture.

VOLTAGE REGULATOR/RECTIFIER

Testing

Service specifications are not available for testing the voltage regulator/rectifier. To determine if the voltage regulator is defective, proceed as follows.
1. Test the condition of the battery as described under *Battery Testing* in Chapter Three.
2. Perform the charging system output test as described in this chapter.
3. If the charging system output is less than specified, check the resistance of the charging coils as described in this chapter.
4. Before replacing the voltage regulator, check all electrical connections within the charging system. If all other possible sources of problems are eliminated, assume that the voltage regulator is defective by a process of elimination.

Removal/Installation

1. Place the vehicle on level ground and set the parking brake.
2. Remove the seat and front fender as described in Chapter Fifteen.
3. Disconnect the negative battery cable as described in this chapter.
4. Disconnect the two-pin and the two individual electrical connectors (A, **Figure 8**) from the voltage regulator/rectifier unit.
5. Remove the three mounting screws and remove the voltage regulator/rectifier unit (B, **Figure 8**) from the radiator upper shield. Do not lose the heat sink located between the unit and the shield.
6. Install by reversing these removal steps while noting the following:
   a. Be sure to install the heat sink between the unit and the shield.
   b. Apply dielectric grease to the electrical connectors prior to reconnecting them.
   c. Make sure all electrical connectors are clean, free of corrosion and secure.

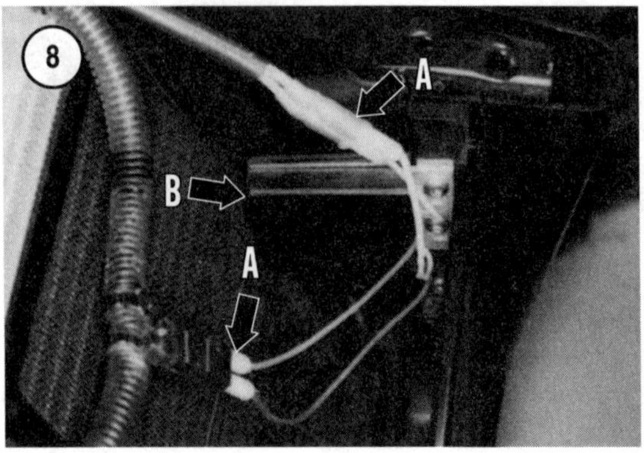

CAPACITOR DISCHARGE IGNITION

All models are equipped with a capacitor discharge ignition (CDI) system. Refer to **Figure 9-Figure 11** or the wiring diagram at the end of the manual. This solid-state system uses no contact breaker points or other moving parts.

CDI Precautions

Certain precautions should be taken to reduce the chance of damaging the capacitor discharge ignition system. Damage to the solid-state components of the system may occur if the following precautions are not observed.
1. Never disconnect any electrical connection while the engine is running.
2. Apply dielectric grease to all electrical connectors before connecting to help seal out moisture.
3. Make sure all electrical connections are clean, free of corrosion and secure.

CDI Troubleshooting

Refer to Chapter Two.

CDI Unit Testing

Service specifications for testing the CDI unit are not available.

CDI Unit Replacement

1. Place the vehicle on level ground and set the parking brake.

9

IGNITION SYSTEM (1996-1997)

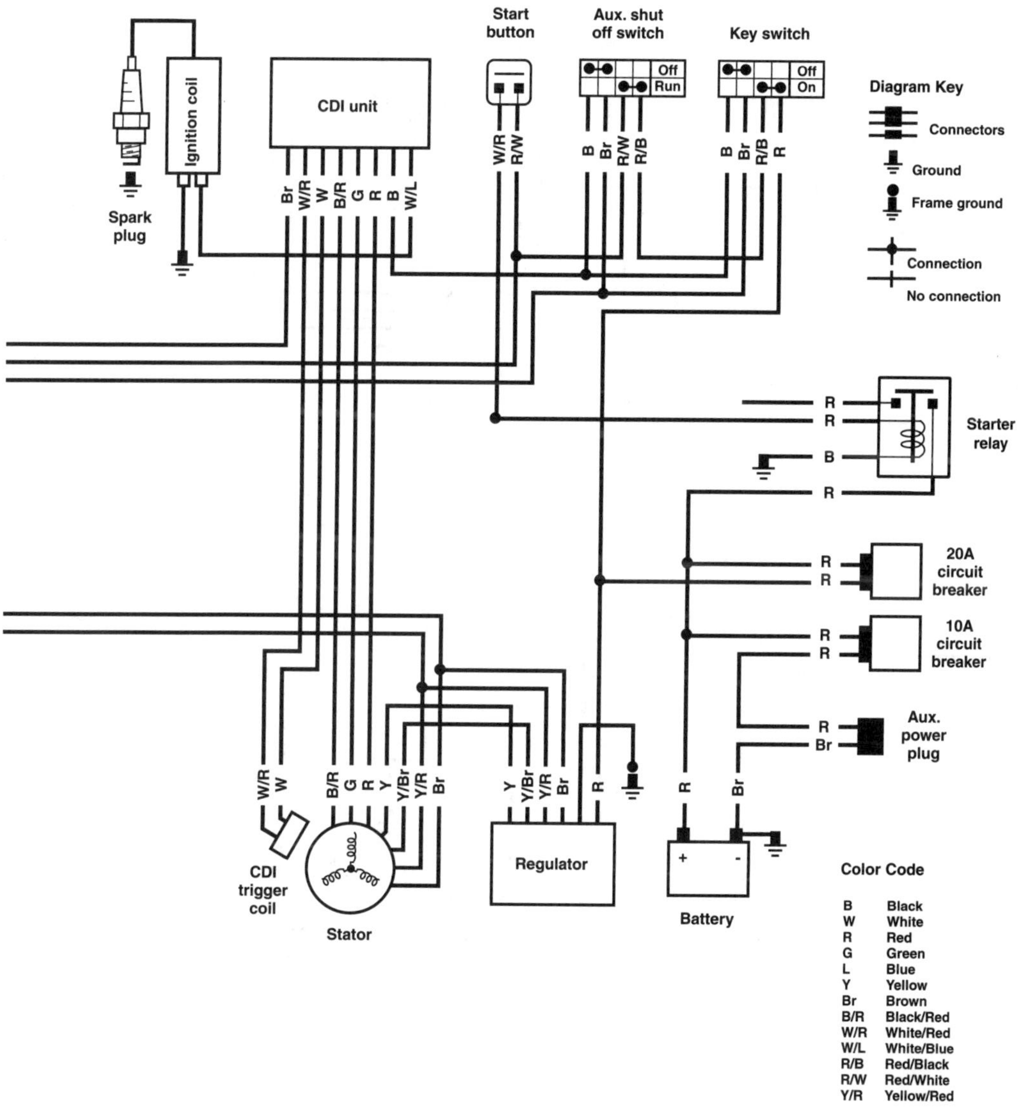

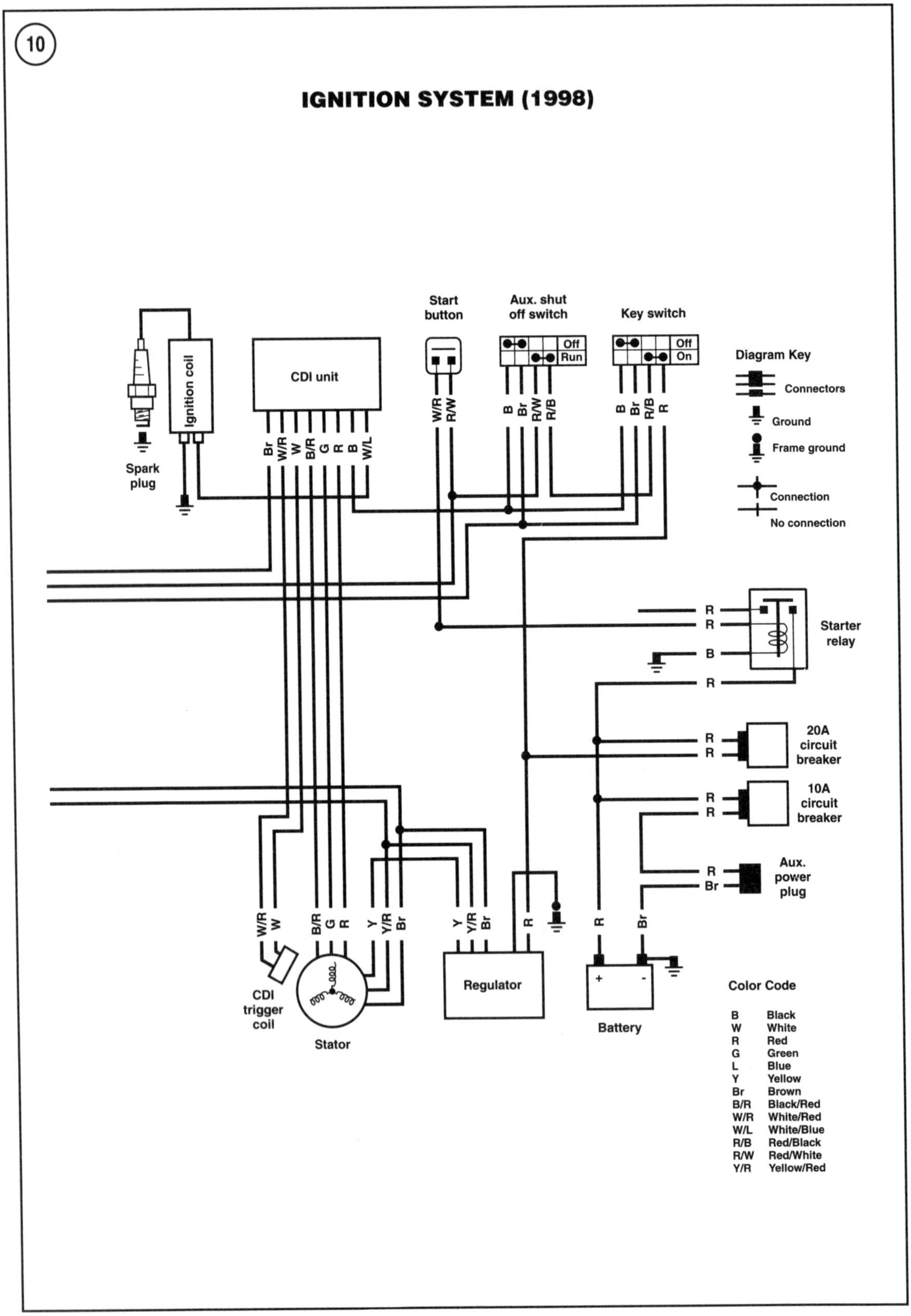
10
IGNITION SYSTEM (1998)
Start button
Aux. shut off switch
Key switch
Off
Run
Off
On
Diagram Key
Connectors
Ground
Frame ground
Connection
No connection
Spark plug
Ignition coil
CDI unit
Br W/R W B/R G R B W/L
W/R R/W
B Br R/W R/B
B Br R/B R
Starter relay
20A circuit breaker
10A circuit breaker
Aux. power plug
W/R W B/R G R Y Y/R Br
Y Y/R Br
R R Br
CDI trigger coil
Stator
Regulator
Battery
Color Code
B Black
W White
R Red
G Green
L Blue
Y Yellow
Br Brown
B/R Black/Red
W/R White/Red
W/L White/Blue
R/B Red/Black
R/W Red/White
Y/R Yellow/Red

11

IGNITION SYSTEM (1999-2000)*

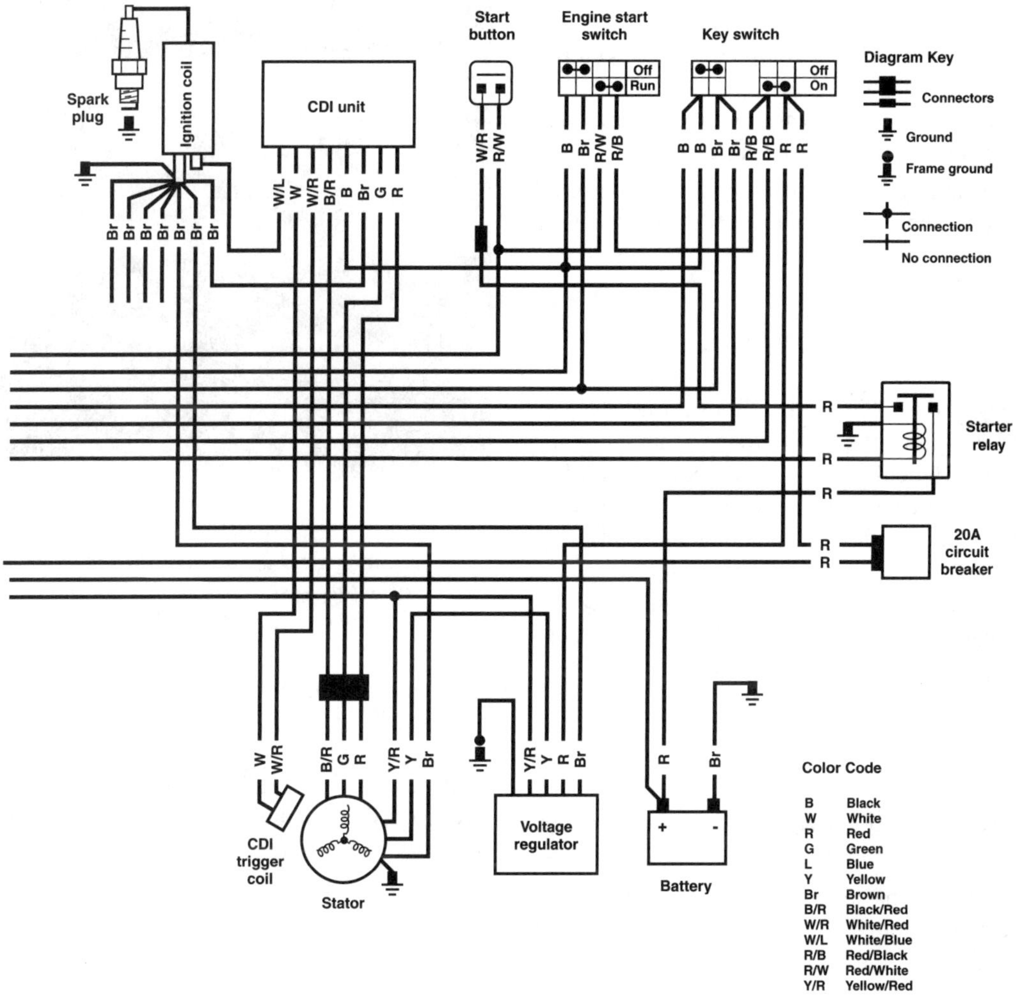

*Refer to the wiring diagram at the end of the manual for 2001-on models.

2. Remove the seat and front fender as described in Chapter Fifteen.

3. Disconnect the negative battery cable as described in this chapter.

4. Remove the CDI unit mounting strap screw (A, **Figure 12**). Remove the CDI unit (B, **Figure 12**) from the frame.

5. Disconnect the multi-pin and individual electrical connectors (C, **Figure 12**) from the CDI unit and remove the unit.

6. Install by reversing these steps while noting the following:

   a. Apply dielectric grease to the electrical connectors prior to reconnecting them.
   b. Make sure all electrical connectors are free of corrosion and are completely coupled to each other.

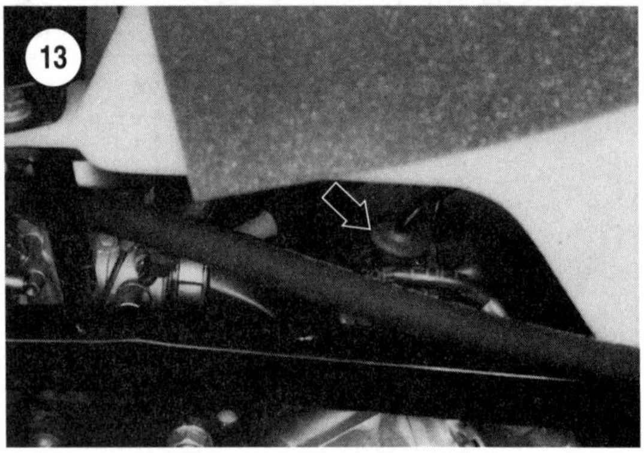

IGNITION COIL

The ignition coil is a form of transformer that develops the high voltage required to jump the spark plug gap. The only maintenance required consists of making sure the electrical connections are clean and tight and that the coil is mounted securely.

Resistance tests for the coil's windings are described in Chapter Two. If the condition of the system is doubtful, the following quick check may help identify if the ignition coil is delivering a spark.

Performance Test

1. Remove the left side cover as described in Chapter Fifteen.

2. Disconnect the spark plug wire and remove the spark plug (**Figure 13**) as described in Chapter Three.

NOTE
Make sure to use a known-good spark plug for this test. If the test is conducted with a damaged spark plug, the test results will be incorrect.

3. Insert the spark plug into its cap and touch the spark plug base against the cylinder head or chassis to ground it (**Figure 14**). Position the spark plug so the electrode is visible.

WARNING
If the engine is flooded, do not perform this test. Fuel ejected through the spark plug hole may be ignited.

4. Turn the ignition ON and crank the engine with the electric or recoil starter while observing the spark plug electrodes. A crisp blue spark should be evident across the spark plug electrode. If there is strong sunlight on the plug, shade the plug in order to see the spark better.

WARNING
*If necessary, hold onto the spark plug wire with a pair of insulated pliers. Do **not** hold the spark plug, wire or connector, or a serious electrical shock may result.*

5. If a crisp blue spark occurs, the ignition coil is good.

6. If there is no spark at the test plug, check the auxiliary shut off switch and safety switches. Additional tests of the ignition exciter, pulser and high-tension coils are described in Chapter Two.

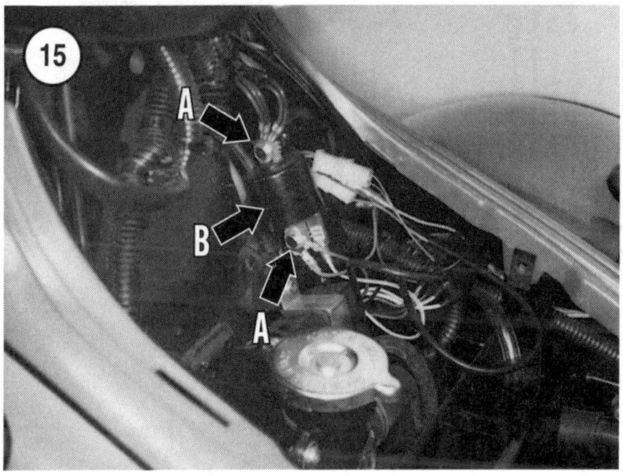

Removal/Installation

1. Place the vehicle on level ground and set the parking brake.
2. Remove the front fender cover as described in Chapter Fifteen.
3. Disconnect the negative battery cable as described in this chapter.
4. Disconnect the connectors from the ignition coil (A, **Figure 15**).
5. Disconnect the spark plug cap secondary lead from the spark plug.
6. Remove bolts, washers and nuts securing the ignition coil (B, **Figure 15**) to the frame.
7. Install by reversing these steps while noting the following:
   a. Apply dielectric grease to the electrical connectors prior to reconnecting them.
   b. Make sure all electrical connectors are free of corrosion and secure.

IGNITION STATOR COILS

The ignition exciter and trigger coils are located under the flywheel and are part of the stator assembly. Removal and installation of the stator plate assembly is covered under *Flywheel and Stator Plate Removal/Installation* in Chapter Five.

ELECTRIC STARTING SYSTEM

The starting system consists of the starter motor, starter gears, solenoid and the handlebar-mounted starter button.

An electrical diagram of the starting system is shown in **Figure 16** and **Figure 17** for 1996-2000 models. Refer to the wiring diagrams at the end of the manual for 2001-on models. When the starter button is pressed, it engages the starter solenoid that completes the circuit allowing electricity to flow from the battery to the starter motor.

CAUTION
Do not operate the starter for more than five seconds at a time. Let it rest approximately ten seconds, then use it again.

Troubleshooting

Refer to Chapter Two.

11

Starter Removal/Installation

1. Place the vehicle on level ground and set the parking brake.
2. Remove the seat and front fender as described in Chapter Fifteen.
3. Disconnect the negative battery cable as described in this chapter.
4. Remove the clutch assembly as described in Chapter Eight.
5. Pull back the rubber boot (A, **Figure 18**) from the electrical connector.
6. Remove the nut (B, **Figure 18**) and disconnect the starter cable.
7. Remove mounting bolt (C, **Figure 18**) and detach the ground cable from the starter.
8. Remove the remaining bolt (D, **Figure 18**) securing the starter to the crankcase.
9. Pull the starter toward the left side and remove it from the engine.

16

STARTING SYSTEM (1996-1998)

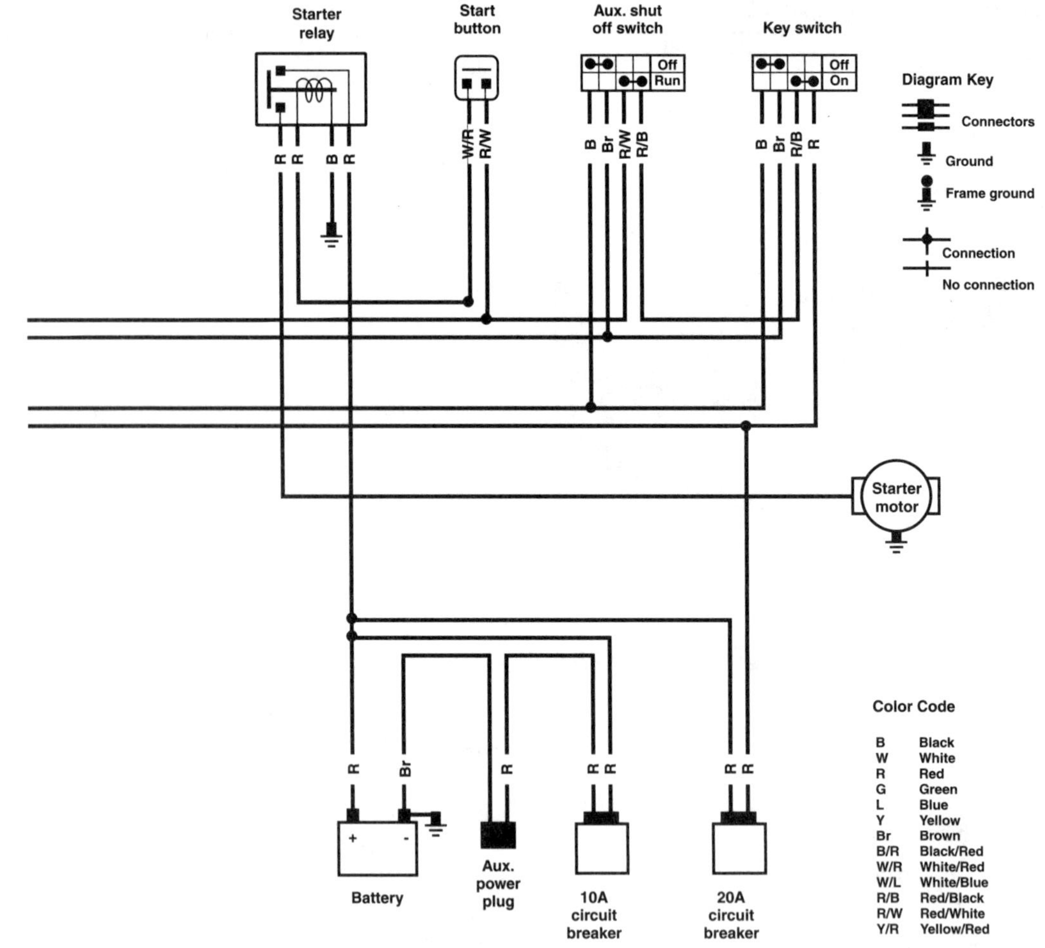

(17)

STARTING SYSTEM (1999-2000)*

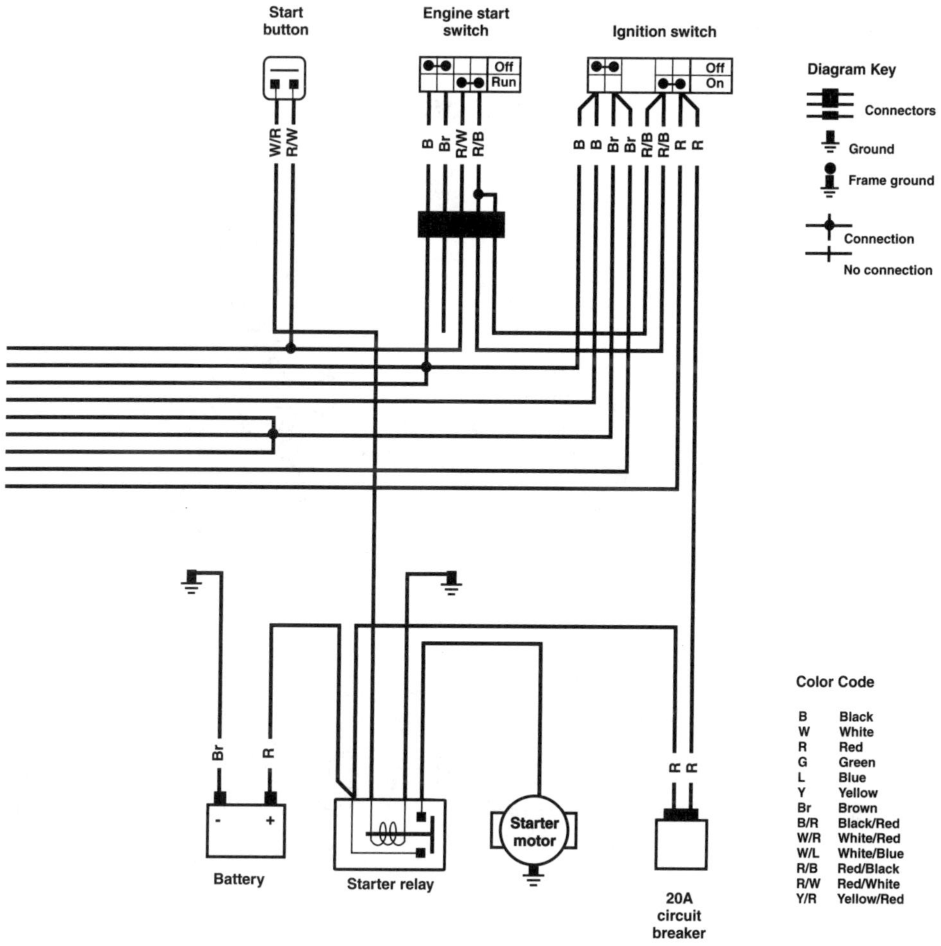

*Refer to the wiring diagram at the end of the manual for 2001-on models.

18

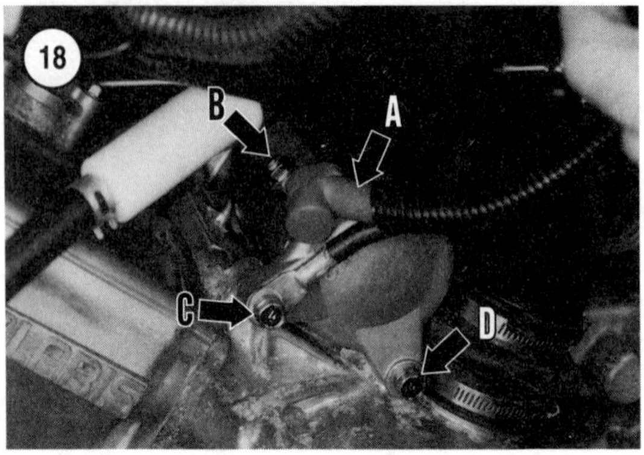

19

20

STARTER MOTOR

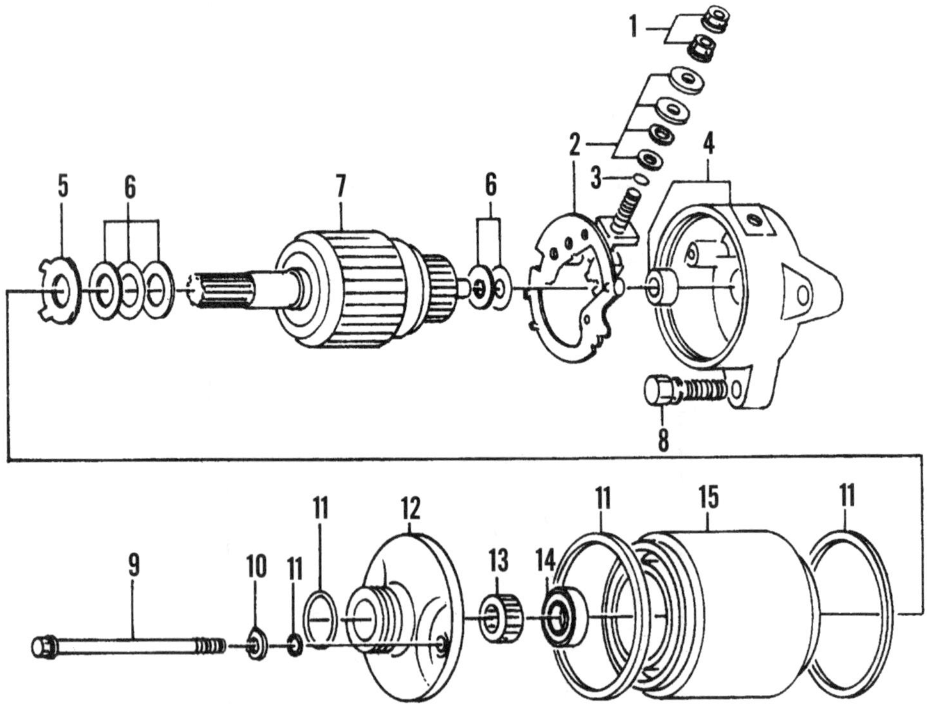

1. Nuts
2. Insulated brush assembly
3. O-ring
4. Rear cover
5. Washer
6. Shims
7. Armature
8. Bolt
9. Long bolts
10. Special washer
11. O-ring
12. Front cover
13. Bearing
14. Seal
15. Housing

21

25

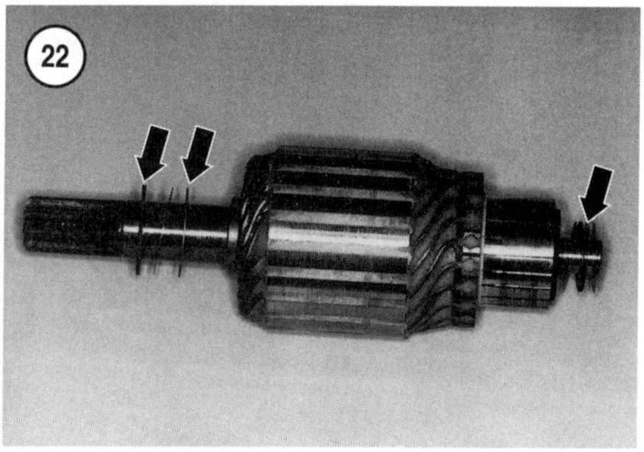
22

23

24

10. Install by reversing these removal steps while noting the following:.
   a. Install and lubricate the O-ring (**Figure 19**) before installing.
   b. Connect the ground cable under the mounting bolt (C, **Figure 18**).
   c. Make sure the electrical connector is free of corrosion and secure.

Disassembly

Refer to **Figure 20**.

1. If not already marked, make an alignment mark across both end covers and the armature housing for reference during re-assembly.

2. Remove the two long throughbolts (**Figure 21**), special washers and O-rings.

NOTE

*In Step 3 and Step 4, record the thickness and number of shims (**Figure 22**) installed on each end of the shaft as they are removed. Be sure to install these shims in their same position when reassembling the starter. The number of shims used in each starter varies. The starter being worked on may use a different number of shims from that shown in the photographs.*

3. Remove the rear cover (**Figure 23**) and shims (Figure 24).
4. Slide the front cover (A, **Figure 25**) from the armature. Remove the shim(s) (B, **Figure 25**).

NOTE

*Before removing the nuts and washers, record their order (**Figure 26**). They must be reinstalled in the same*

26

27

order to insulate the positive brush plate assembly from the case.

5. Remove the nut, washers, insulators (**Figure 26**) and O-ring (**Figure 27**).

6. Carefully remove the brush plate assembly (**Figure 28**) from the case.

7. Slide the armature from the housing (**Figure 29**).

8. Clean all grease, dirt and carbon from the armature, case and end covers.

CAUTION
Do not immerse any of the wire windings in solvent, because most solvents will damage the insulation. Wipe the windings with a cloth lightly moistened with solvent, then allow the solvent to dry thoroughly.

Inspection

1. Pull the spring away from each brush and pull the brushes (**Figure 30**) from their guides.

28

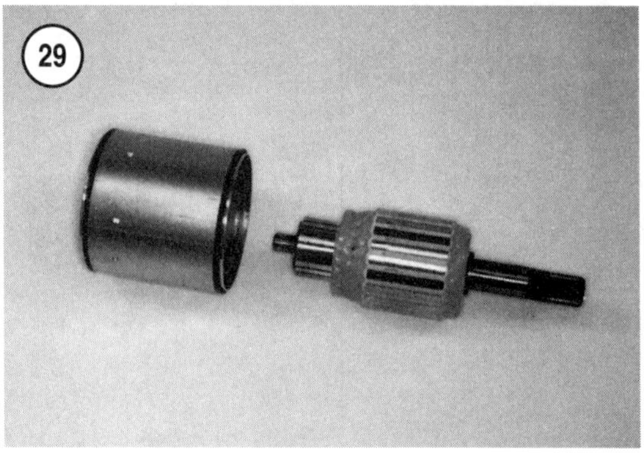
29

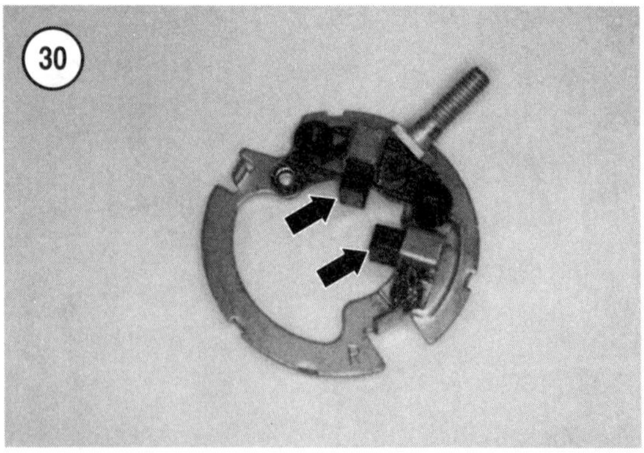
30

31

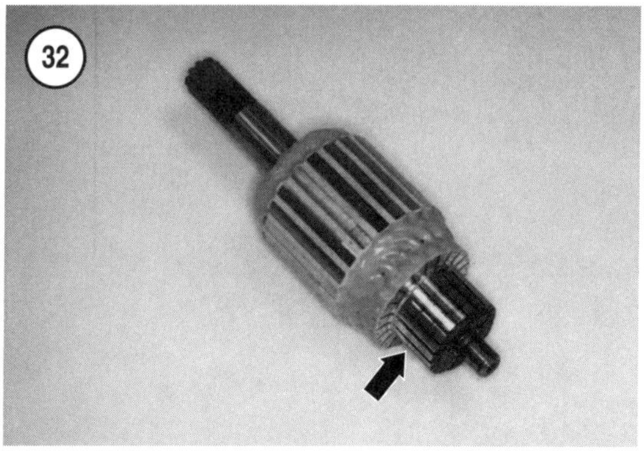
32

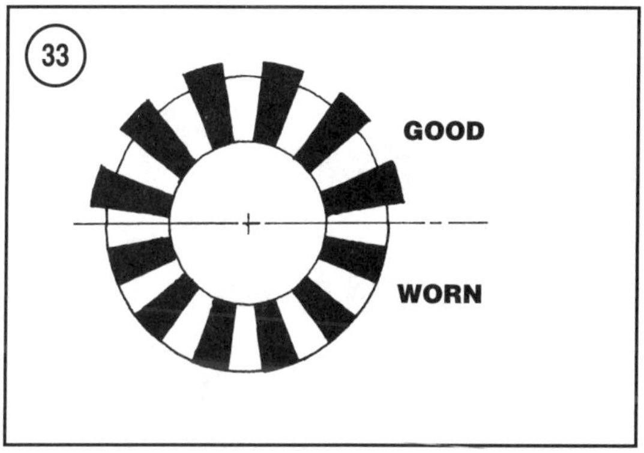

33

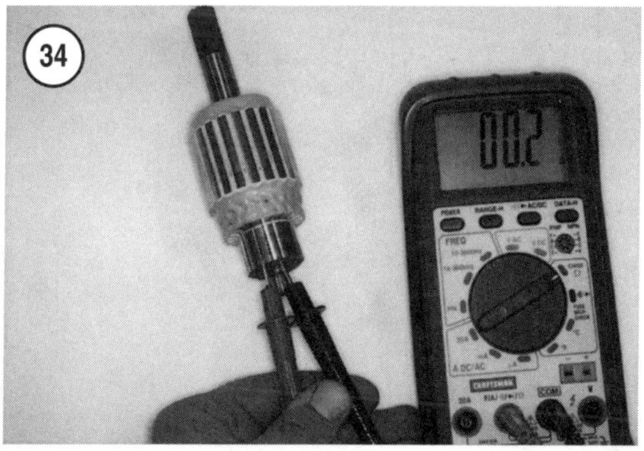
34

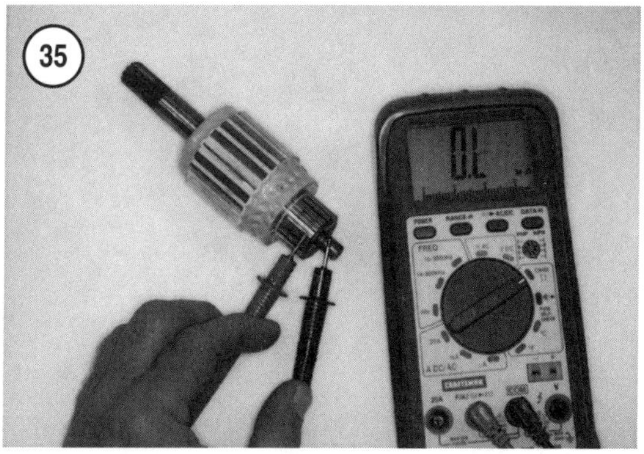
35

36

2. Measure the length of each brush (**Figure 31**). If the length is equal to or less than the limit in **Table 1**, replace the brushes as a set.

3. Inspect the brush springs for damage or weakness. Replace the springs if necessary.

4. Inspect the commutator (**Figure 32**). The mica should be below the surface of the copper commutator segments (**Figure 33**). If the commutator segments are worn to the same level as the mica insulation, have the commutator serviced by a dealer or electrical repair shop.

5. Inspect the commutator copper segments for discoloration. If the commutator segments are rough, discolored or worn, have the commutator serviced at a Polaris dealership or electrical repair shop.

6. Use an ohmmeter to perform the following:

   a. Check for continuity between the commutator bars (**Figure 34**); there should be continuity between pairs of bars.

   b. Check for continuity between the commutator bars and the shaft (**Figure 35**); there should be no continuity (infinite resistance).

   c. If the unit fails either of these tests, the starter assembly must be replaced. The armature cannot be replaced individually.

7. Inspect the bearing and seal (**Figure 36**) in the front cover for wear or damage.

8. Inspect the bushing (**Figure 37**) in the rear cover for wear or damage.

9. Inspect the starter housing (A, **Figure 38**) for cracks or other damage.

10. Inspect inside the starter housing for loose, chipped or damaged magnets (B, **Figure 38**).

11. Inspect the starter housing O-rings (**Figure 39**) for deterioration, flat spots or other damage. Replace them as required.

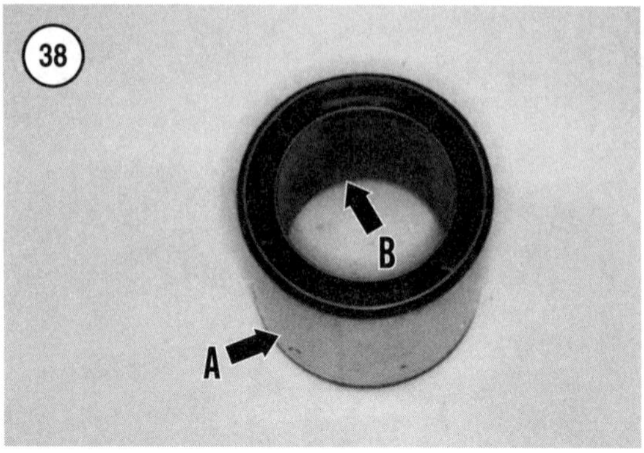

Assembly

1. If removed, install the brushes into their holders and secure the brushes (**Figure 30**) with the springs.
2. Assemble the brushes and brush plate into the end cover. Align the locating tab with the end cover (**Figure 40**) and push the plate into place (**Figure 41**).
3. Temporarily cover the threads of the terminal stud with electrical tape to avoid damaging the O-ring (**Figure 27**) during installation. Remove the tape after the O-ring is installed.
4. Install the insulators, washers and nut (**Figure 26**) in the reverse order of removal. Tighten the nut securely.
5. Install the shims (**Figure 42**) onto the armature shaft.

NOTE

Lubricate the end bushing with a silicone (non-petroleum) grease before installing the end cover.

6. Compress the brushes against their springs, slide the brush plate and rear cover (**Figure 43**) over the commutator, then release the brushes.

NOTE

*Before installing the end frame, lubricate the large O-rings (A, **Figure 44**) with clean engine oil. Make sure that the O-rings are not twisted when installing the end covers.*

7. Insert the armature and rear cover assembly (B, **Figure 44**) into the housing, aligning the mark on the rear cover with the matching mark on the housing (**Figure 45**). The tab on the brush plate must also align with the notch in the brush end frame.

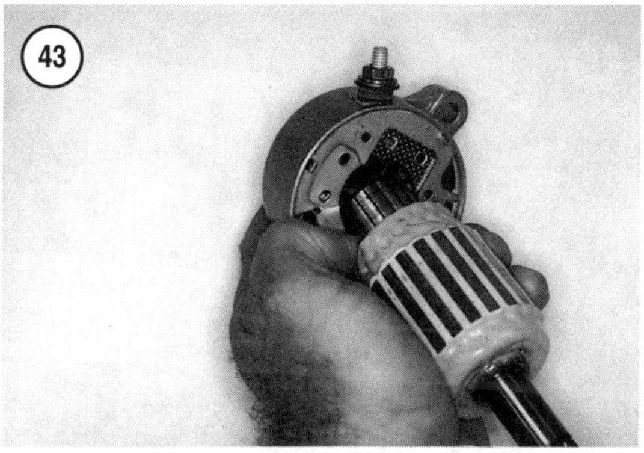

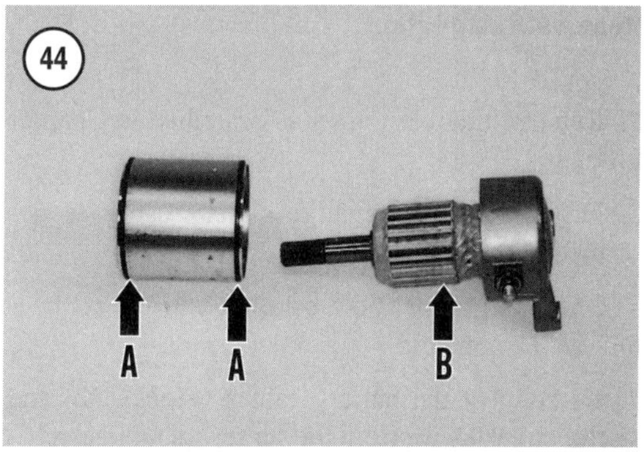

8. Install the shim(s) (A, **Figure 46**) onto the armature shaft.

NOTE

Lubricate the end bearing with silicone (non-petroleum) grease before installing the end cover. Lubricate the large O-ring sealing the case before installing it. Make sure that the O-ring is not twisted when installing the end cover.

9. Install the front cover (B, **Figure 46**) onto the armature, aligning the marks on the front cover with the housing (**Figure 47**).

NOTE

*Make sure the O-rings (A, **Figure 48**) and special washers (B) are installed on the long throughbolts (C) before installing.*

10. Hold both covers, align the marks (**Figure 47**) and install the throughbolts (**Figure 21**). If the bolts will not pass through the starter motor, the end cov-

ers and/or brush plate are installed incorrectly. Tighten the bolts securely.

STARTER DRIVE GEARS

The electric starter operates through a set of reduction gears and an overrunning clutch. The starter pinion at the end of the armature shaft meshes with the larger gear. The larger starter drive gear engages the overrunning clutch, which drives the smaller of the two gears. The smaller drive gear engages the flywheel ring gear to start the engine.

The starter drive gears (**Figure 49**) are located between a bearing in the crankcase and a bearing in the recoil starter housing. The starter drive gear and starter clutch assembly can be removed after removing the recoil starter as described in Chapter Five.

When installing, be sure to lubricate and install the thrust washers (**Figure 50**).

STARTER SOLENOID

The starter solenoid is mounted in front of the battery on the left side.

Starter Solenoid Resistance Test

Test the starter solenoid with an ohmmeter as follows.

1. Remove the rear fender as described in Chapter Fifteen.
2. Turn the key or ignition switch off.
3. Remove the screw and washer and disconnect the connector (**Figure 51**) of the small white/red wire attached to the starter solenoid.
4. Switch the ohmmeter to R × 1 and connect one lead to the small red wire attached to the solenoid and ground the other ohmmeter lead to the frame.
5. The specified resistance is listed in **Table 1**.
6. Replace the starter solenoid if the resistance reading exceeds the specified resistance.
7. Apply dielectric grease to the electrical connector prior to reconnecting it.
8. Make sure the electrical connectors are free of corrosion and are securely coupled together.

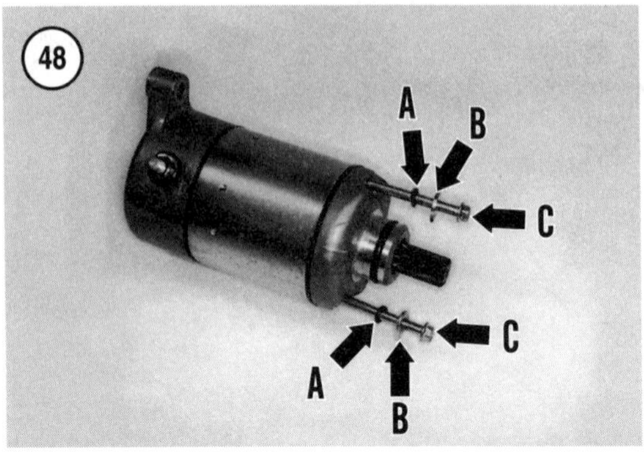

Removal/Installation

1. Remove the rear fender as described in Chapter Fifteen.
2. Disconnect the negative battery cable as described in this chapter.
3. Move the rubber boot off the electrical connectors on the solenoid.
4. Disconnect the battery cables (**Figure 52**) and starter control wire from the starter solenoid electrical connectors.
5. Remove the nuts and lockwashers securing the solenoid to the threaded studs on the battery case.
6. Install by reversing these removal steps while noting the following:
   a. Attach both starter cables to the solenoid and tighten the nuts securely.
   b. Make sure the electrical connector is free of corrosion.
   c. Make sure the rubber boots are properly installed to seal out moisture.

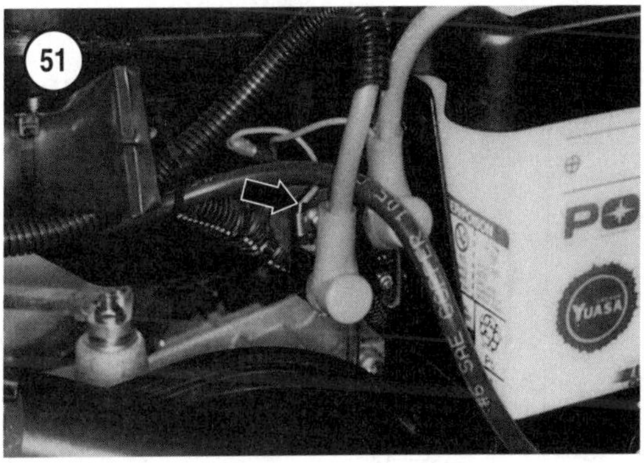

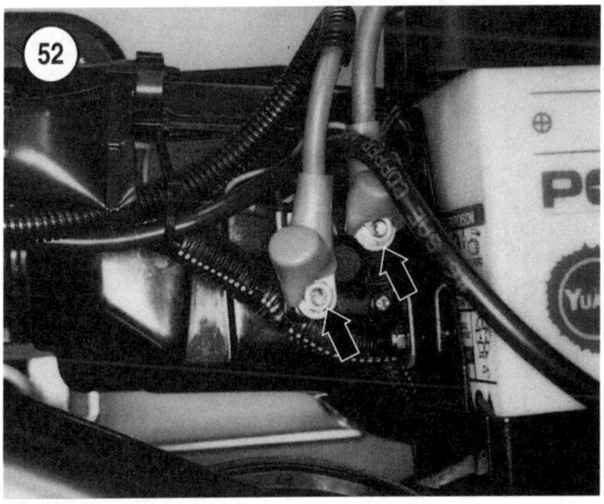

LIGHTING SYSTEM

The lighting system consists of a single handlebar mounted high-beam headlight, two grille-mounted low-beam headlights, a taillight/brake light and indicator lights. **Table 2** lists replacement bulbs for some of these components.

Always use the correct wattage bulb. The use of a larger wattage bulb will give a dim light and a smaller wattage bulb will burn out prematurely.

High-Beam Headlight (Sportsman Models)

NOTE
The 1997 Xplorer model is not equipped with a high-beam headlight. It is equipped with only two grille mounted low-beam headlights.

Bulb replacement

Refer to **Figure 53**.

1. Remove the front fender cover as described in Chapter Fifteen.
2. Remove the headlight upper pod as follows:
   a. Remove the front screws securing the upper pod to the lower pod (**Figure 54**).
   b. Remove the three rear screws securing the upper pod to the lower pod (**Figure 55**).
   c. Lift the upper pod up and partially off the lower pod.
   d. Disconnect the electrical connector from the headlight bulb/socket assembly (**Figure 56**).
   e. Disconnect the individual electrical connectors from the DC outlet (**Figure 57**).
   f. Disconnect all electrical connectors from the indicator lights and speedometer (**Figure 58**).
   g. On 1996-1998 models, disconnect the speedometer cable from the speedometer housing.
   h. Remove the upper pod.
3. Remove the rubber cover (**Figure 59**) from the backside of the headlight case.
4. Twist the bulb/socket assembly counterclockwise until the locking tabs align with the headlight cases notches.
5. Pull straight back and remove the bulb/socket assembly (**Figure 60**) from the backside of the headlight case.
6. Remove the old bulb. Install a new bulb into the socket until it snaps into place.
7. Install the bulb/socket assembly into the backside of the headlight case. Push it in and twist it clockwise until it stops and is seated correctly.
8. Install the rubber cover (**Figure 59**) onto the backside of the headlight case. Push it on until it is completely seated.
9. Install the headlight upper pod as follows:
   a. Move the upper pod into position.
   b. On 1996-1998 models, connect the speedometer cable onto the speedometer housing.

(53)

HEADLIGHT AND POD (SPORTSMAN)

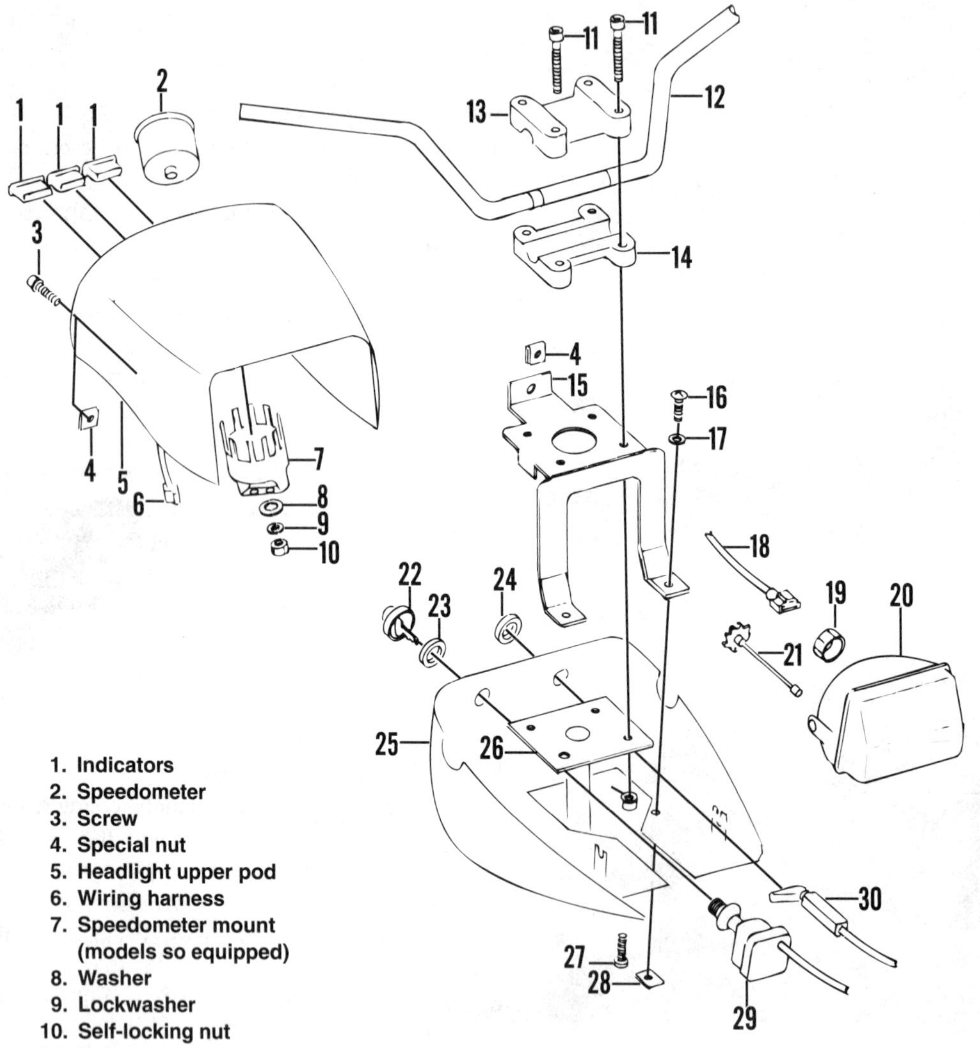

1. Indicators
2. Speedometer
3. Screw
4. Special nut
5. Headlight upper pod
6. Wiring harness
7. Speedometer mount (models so equipped)
8. Washer
9. Lockwasher
10. Self-locking nut
11. Bolt
12. Handlebar
13. Upper holder
14. Lower holder
15. Pod mounting bracket
16. Screw
17. Washer
18. Headlight wire harness
19. Cover
20. High-beam headlight
21. Adjuster
22. Ignition key
23. Lock ring
24. Lock ring
25. Headlight lower pod
26. Steering shaft
27. Screw
28. Special nut
29. Key or ignition switch
30. Enrichment (choke) knob

54

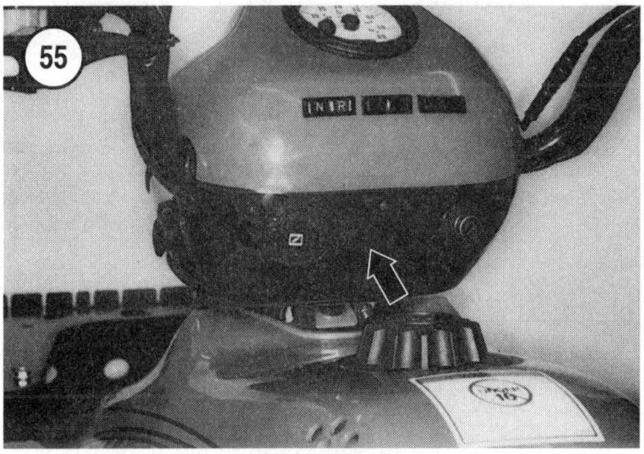
55

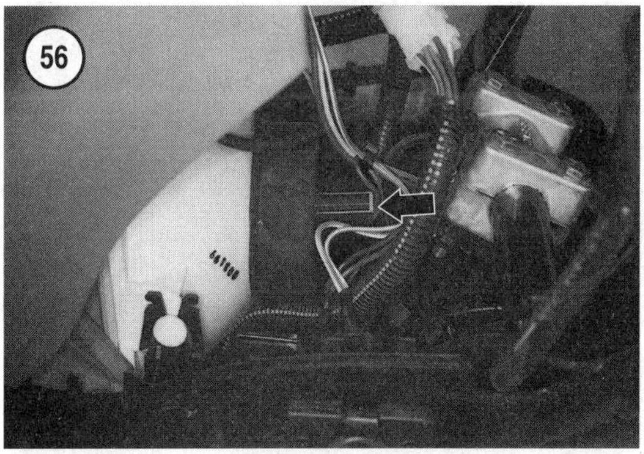
56

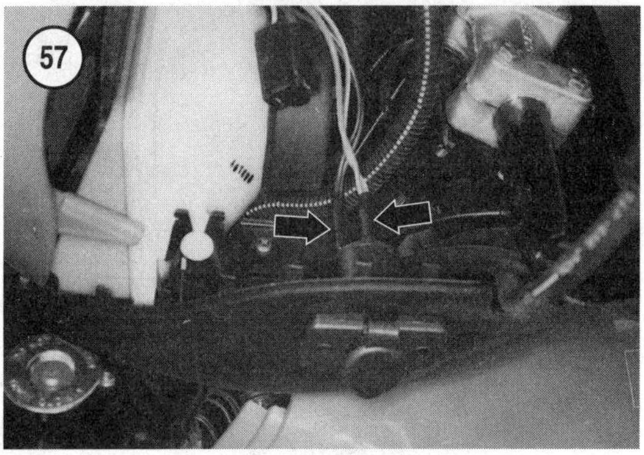
57

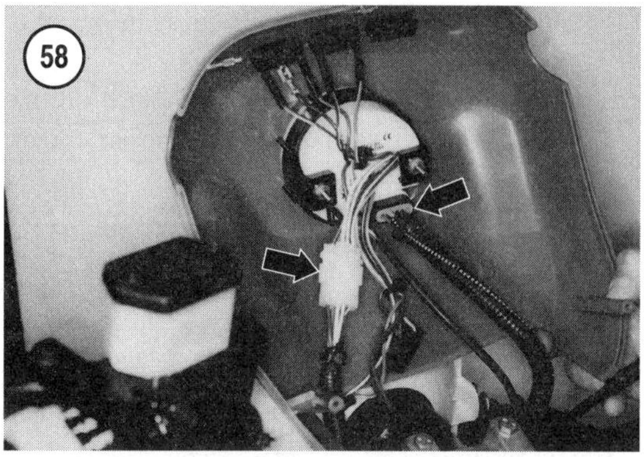
58

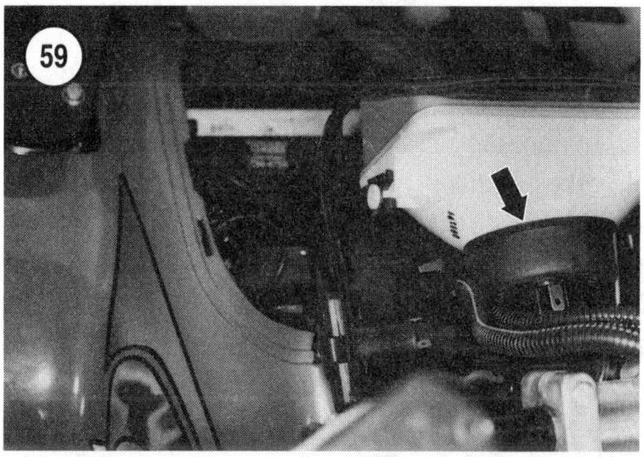
59

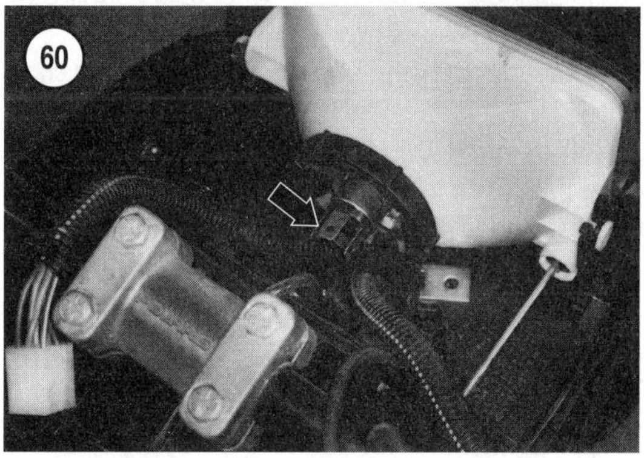
60

c. Connect the electrical connectors to the indicator lights and speedometer (**Figure 58**).

d. Connect the individual electrical connectors onto the DC outlet (**Figure 57**).

e. Move the upper pod partially down onto the lower pod and connect the electrical connector onto the headlight bulb/socket assembly (**Figure 56**).

f. Make sure the three metal push-on special nuts are in place on the upper pod mounting tabs (**Figure 61**). The nuts must be aligned with the holes in the mounting tabs.

g. Move the upper pod down into place on the lower pod and partially install the three rear screws.

h. Install the front screws securing the upper pod to the lower pod (**Figure 54**).

i. Tighten the front and rear screws securely. Do not overtighten, as the mounting tabs and posts may fracture.

10. Install the front fender front cover as described in Chapter Fifteen.

High-beam headlight adjustment

The headlight can only be adjusted vertically.

1. To raise the headlight beam, turn the adjust knob (**Figure 62**) *counterclockwise*.
2. To lower the headlight beam, turn the adjust knob (**Figure 62**) *clockwise*.

High-beam headlight case removal/installation

Refer to **Figure 53**.

1. Disconnect the electrical connector from the headlight bulb/socket assembly (**Figure 56**) from the headlight case as previously described.
2. Remove the O-ring from the locking tab on each side.
3. Lift up on the headlight case and disengage the pivot post from the locking tabs (A, **Figure 63**) on the lower pod.
4. Lift up and disengage the headlight adjuster (B, **Figure 63**) from the mounting bracket on the lower pod.
5. Remove the headlight case (C, **Figure 63**).
6. Install by reversing these removal steps. Adjust the headlight as previously described.

Grille-Mounted Low-Beam Headlight Bulb Replacement (All Models)

1. Disconnect the wiring harness (**Figure 64**) from the bulb/socket assembly.
2. Twist the bulb/socket assembly (**Figure 65**) until the locking tabs align with the headlight case notches. Remove the bulb/socket assembly.
3. Pull the bulb (**Figure 66**) straight out of the socket assembly.
4. Install a new bulb and press it in until it stops.

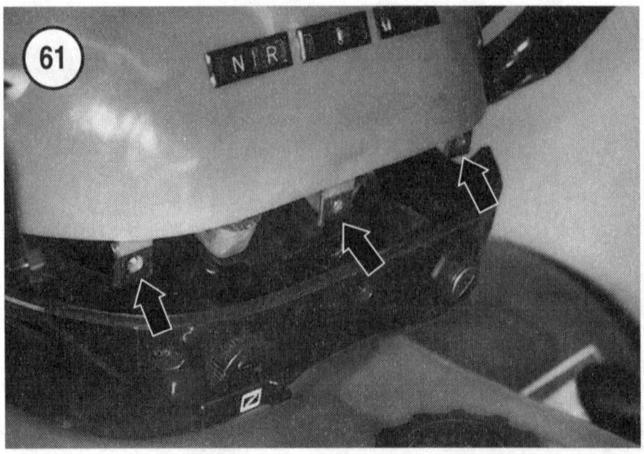

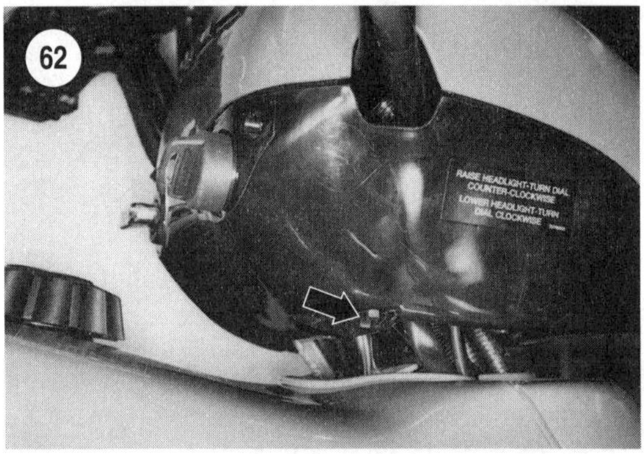

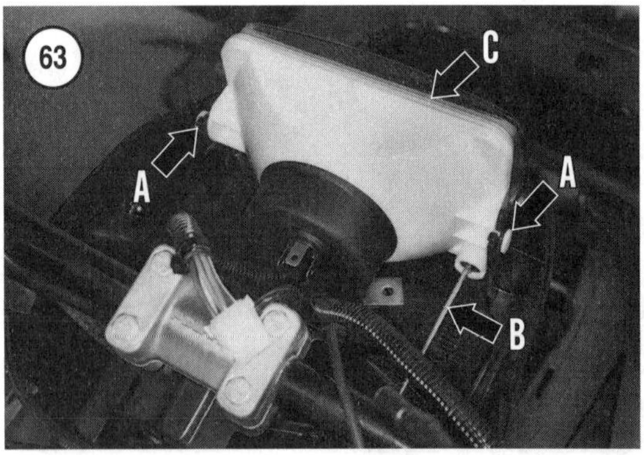

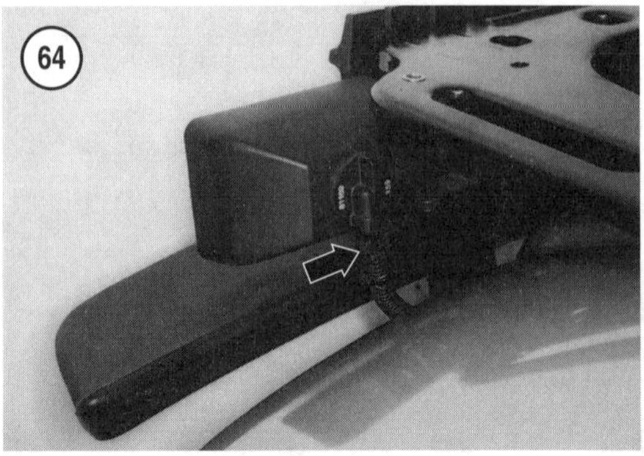

65

66

67

68

69

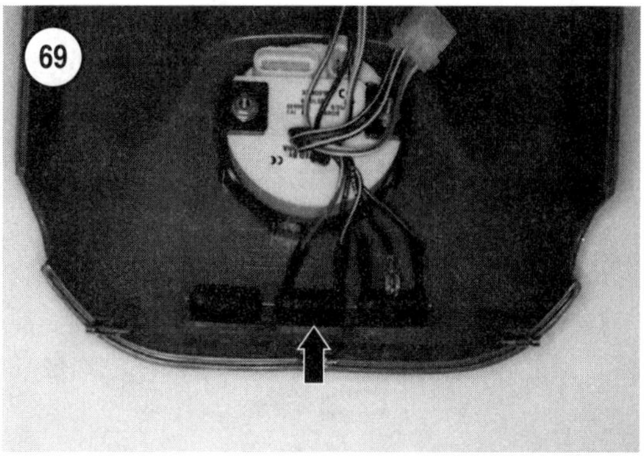

5. Install the bulb/socket assembly and turn it until the locking tabs are locked in place.

6. Connect the wiring harness into the bulb/socket assembly.

Taillight/Brake Light Bulb and Lens Replacement

1. Remove the two screws (**Figure 67**) securing the lens. Remove the lens.

2. Remove the bulb (**Figure 68**) from the socket and install a new bulb.

3. Wash the lens in mild detergent and thoroughly dry it before installing.

4. Install the screws securing the lens to the housing and tighten securely, but do not overtighten the screw, as the lens may crack

5. Make sure the rubber gasket seal is seated all the way around the lens when assembling.

Indicator Lamp Replacement

1. Remove the headlight upper pod as described under *High-Beam Headlight (Sportsman Models), Bulb Replacement* in this chapter.

2. Disconnect the electrical connectors from the backside of the indicator lamp.

3. Release the locking tabs and remove the indicator lamp (**Figure 69**) from the headlight upper pod.

4. Install the headlight upper pod.

70

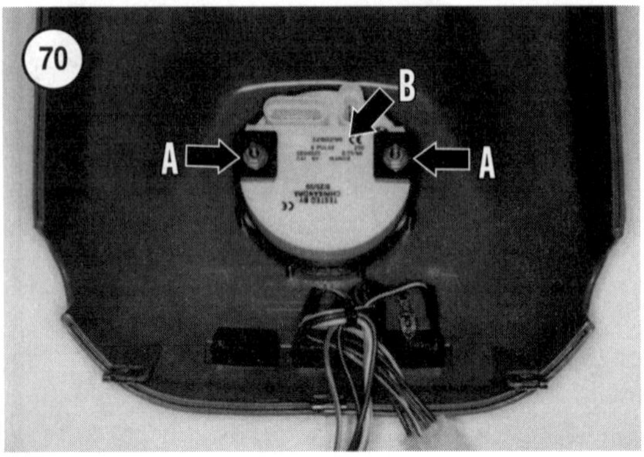

71

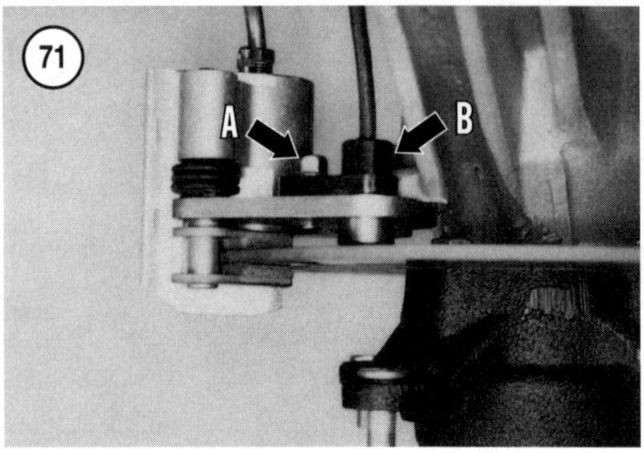

ELECTRICAL COMPONENTS

Speedometer (Sportsman Models) Removal/Installation

1. Remove the headlight upper pod as described under *High-Beam Headlight (Sportsman Models), Bulb Replacement* in this chapter.
2. Remove the nuts, lockwashers and washers (A, **Figure 70**) securing the speedometer housing to the headlight upper pod.
3. Withdraw the speedometer housing (B, **Figure 70**) out through the front of the headlight pod.
4. Install the speedometer housing in through the front of the headlight pod.
5. Install washers, lockwashers and nuts securing the speedometer housing. Tighten the nuts securely.
6. Install the headlight upper pod.

Speed Sensor (1999-On Sportsman Models) Removal/Installation

1. Remove the right side front wheel as described in Chapter Twelve.
2. Remove the front fender as described in Chapter Fifteen.
3. Remove the bolt and washer (A, **Figure 71**) securing the speed sensor to the caliper mounting bracket.
4. Remove the speed sensor (B, **Figure 71**) from the bracket.
5. Follow the speed sensor electrical wires from the sensor up to the headlight lower pod. Remove the wires from the headlight lower pod.
6. Install by reversing these removal steps. Tighten the bolt securely.

72

STARTER SWITCH

Position \ Color	Red/White	White/Red
FREE		
PUSHED	●———	———●

73

KEY SWITCH OR IGNITION SWITCH

	Black	Brown	Black/ Red	Red
OFF	●———	———●		
ON			●———	———●

74

HEADLIGHT SWITCH

Position \ Color	Red/white	Green	Yellow
OFF			
LO	●———	———●	
HI	●———	——————	———●

75 SHUTOFF SWITCH

	Black	Brown	Red/ White	Black/ Red
OFF	●	●		
RUN			●	●

76 ALL-WHEEL DRIVE SWITCH

BUTTON	Gray/ White	Gray	AWD LAMP
OUT (OFF)			
IN (ON)	●	●	
IN (ON)	●		●

77 ELECTRONIC THROTTLE CONTROL (1996-1998)

Color / Position	Red/White	White
NORMAL		
FAULT	●	●

78 ELECTRONIC THROTTLE CONTROL (1999-ON)

Color / Position	Black	Brown
NORMAL		
FAULT	●	●

79 TRANSMISSION SWITCH (1996-1998)

Color / Position	Red/ White	Gray/ White	Green/ White	Purple
FWD	●	●		
N	●		●	

80 TRANSMISSION FRONT SWITCH (1999-ON)

Color / Position	Gray/ White	Green/ White	White
NEUTRAL		●	●
LOW	●		●

SWITCHES

Testing

Test switches for continuity using an ohmmeter (see Chapter One) or a self-powered test light at the switch connector plug. Operate the switch in each of its operating positions and compare the results with the switch operating diagram. For example, **Figure 72** (starter switch) shows which terminals should have continuity when the switch is in a given position.

When the starter switch is pushed, there should be continuity between the white/red and red/white terminals. The line on the continuity diagram indicates this. An ohmmeter connected between these two terminals should indicate little or no resistance, or a test light should light. When the starter switch is free, there should be no continuity between the same terminals. Refer to **Figures 72-83** for switch continuity diagrams.

When testing the switches, note the following:

1. Check the battery as described under *Battery Testing* in Chapter Three; if necessary, charge or replace the battery.

2. Disconnect the negative battery cable (see this chapter) before checking the continuity of any switch.
3. Detach all connectors located between the switch and the electrical circuit.

CAUTION
Do not attempt to start the engine with the battery disconnected.

4. When separating two connectors, pull on the connector housings but not the wires.
5. After locating a defective circuit, check the connectors to make sure they are clean and properly connected. Check all wires going into a connector housing to make sure each wire is positioned properly and that the wire end is not loose.
6. To reconnect connectors properly, push them together until they click or snap into place.
7. If the switch or button does not perform properly, replace it.

Right Handlebar Switch Housing Replacement

The right handlebar contains the all-wheel drive switch and the electronic throttle control switch.

NOTE
The switches mounted in the right handlebar switch housing (A, ***Figure 84****) are not available separately. If one switch is damaged, replace the entire switch housing.*

1. Disconnect the negative battery cable as described in this chapter.
2. Remove the front fender as described in Chapter Fifteen.

3A. On Xplorer models, perform the following:

a. Remove the top cover from the instrument panel cover.
b. Remove the two screws securing the instrument panel cover and remove the cover.

3B. On Sportsman models, remove the headlight upper pod as described under *High-Beam Headlight (Sportsman Models), Bulb Replacement* in Chapter Eleven.

4. Remove the tie wraps securing the switch wiring harness to the handlebar and frame.
5. Follow the right switch electrical wires from the switch down through the headlight lower pod (**Fig-**

(81) **TRANSMISSION REAR SWITCH (1999-ON)**

Position \ Color	Red/White	Purple	Gray/White	White
REVERSE	●	●		
NEUTRAL	●	—	—	●
HIGH	●	—	●	

(82) **OVERRIDE SWITCH (1996-1998)**

Position \ Color	Purple	Gray/White	Green
FREE	●	—	●
PUSHED	●	●	

(83) **OVERRIDE SWITCH (1999-ON)**

Position \ Color	Purple	Gray/White	Grey/Orange
FREE	●	—	●
PUSHED	●	●	

(84)

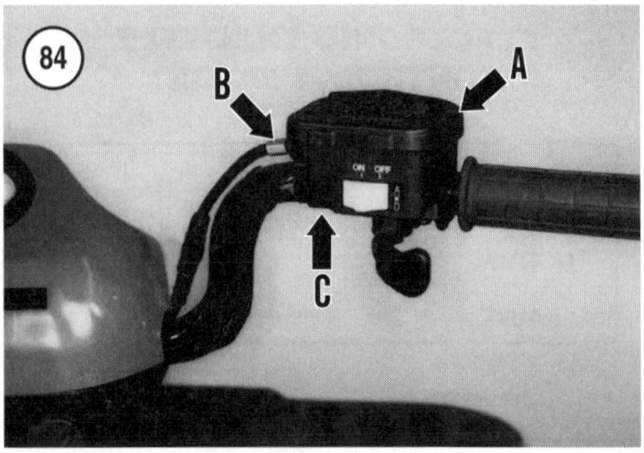

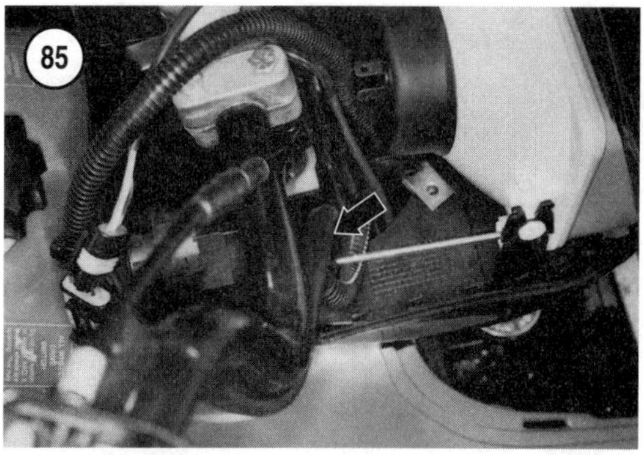

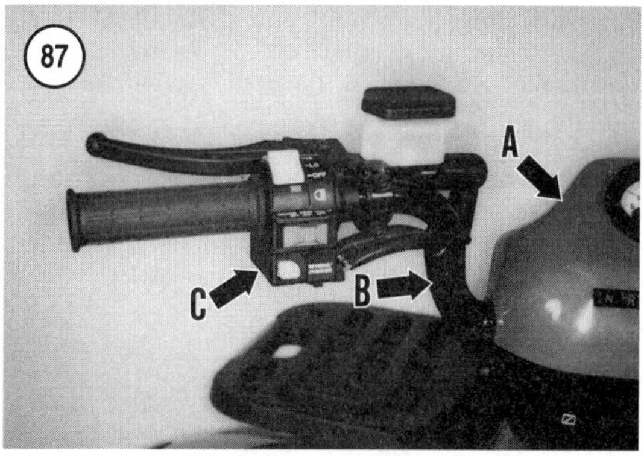

ure 85) to where they connect to the main harness. Disconnect all electrical connectors.

6. Detach the throttle control cable (B, **Figure 84**) from the switch assembly as described in Chapter Six.

7. Remove the screws and clamp and remove the switch and throttle control assembly (C, **Figure 84**).

8. Install by reversing these steps while noting the following:

   a. Make sure the electrical connector is free of corrosion.

   b. Make sure all of the electrical connectors are secure.

   c. Adjust the throttle cable as described in Chapter Three.

Left Handlebar Switch Housing Replacement

The left handlebar switch housing contains the headlight switch, override switch, auxiliary shut off switch, and starter switch.

NOTE
The switches mounted in the left handlebar switch housing are not available separately. If one switch is damaged, replace the switch housing.

1. Disconnect the negative battery cable as described in this chapter.

2. Remove the front fender (A, **Figure 86**) as described in Chapter Fifteen.

3A. On Xplorer models, perform the following:

   a. Remove the top cover from the instrument panel cover.

   b. Remove the two screws securing the instrument panel cover and remove the cover.

3B. On Sportsman models, remove the headlight upper pod (A, **Figure 87**) as described under *High-Beam Headlight (Sportsman Models), Bulb Replacement* in Chapter Eleven.

4. Remove all tie wraps, securing the switch wiring harness (B, **Figure 87**) to the handlebar and frame.

5. Follow the right switch electrical wires from the switch down through the headlight lower pod (B, **Figure 86**) to where they connect to the main harness. Disconnect the electrical connectors.

6. Follow the left switch electrical wires from the switch to where they connect to the main harness. Disconnect all electrical connectors.

7. Remove the trim cap and set screw securing the switch to the handlebar and remove the switch (C, **Figure 87**).

8. Install by reversing these steps while noting the following:

   a. Make sure the electrical connector is free of corrosion.

   b. Make sure all of the electrical connectors are secure.

Key Switch, or Ignition Switch Replacement

Xplorer models

The switch is mounted on the instrument panel bracket on Xplorer models.

1. Disconnect the negative battery cable as described in this chapter.
2. Remove the top cover from the instrument panel cover.
3. Remove the two instrument panel screws and remove the cover.
4. Unscrew the nut securing the switch to the instrument panel cover mounting bracket. Remove the switch through the backside of the mounting bracket.
5. Disconnect the key switch electrical connector from the switch.
6. Install by reversing these steps while noting the following:
   a. Make sure the electrical connectors are free of corrosion.
   b. Make sure all of the electrical connectors are on tight.

Sportsman models

The switch is mounted in the headlight pod on Sportsman models.

1. Disconnect the negative battery lead as described in this chapter.
2. Remove the headlight upper pod as described under *High-Beam Headlight (Sportsman Models), Bulb Replacement* in this chapter.
3. Unscrew the nut (A, **Figure 88**) securing the switch to the lower pod. Remove the switch (B, **Figure 88**) through the backside of the headlight lower pod.
4. Disconnect the key switch electrical connector from the switch.
5. Install by reversing these steps while noting the following:
   a. Make sure the electrical connectors are free of corrosion.
   b. Make sure all of the electrical connectors are on tight.

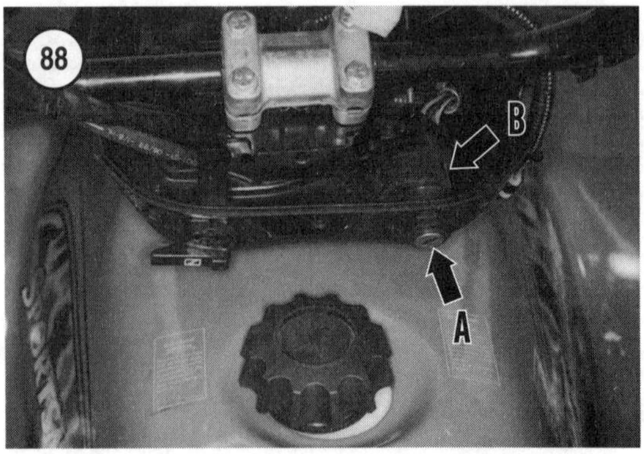

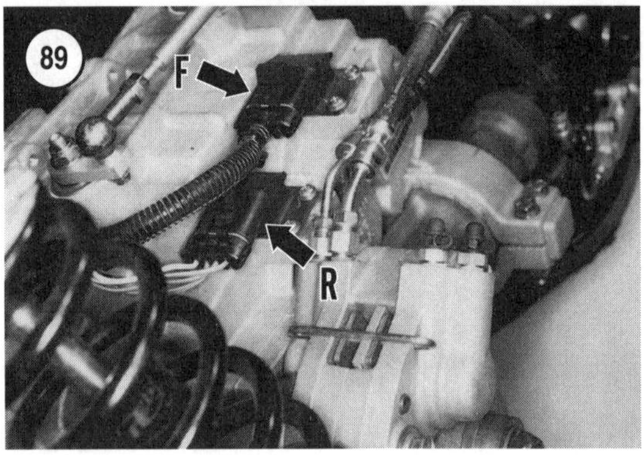

Transmission (Forward/Neutral/Reverse) Switch (1996-1998)

The transmission switch is mounted in the shifter selector housing. Refer to Chapter Nine for service.

Transmission (Forward/Neutral/Reverse) Switches (1999-On)

1. Disconnect the negative battery cable as described in this chapter.
2. Remove the rear fender as described in Chapter Fifteen.
3. Shift the transmission into NEUTRAL.
4. Mark the front gear indicator switch with an F (front) (F, **Figure 89**) and the rear with an R (rear) (R, **Figure 89**). The switches are different and must be reinstalled in the correct location.
5. Disconnect the electrical connectors from both switches.
6. Remove the mounting screws and remove both gear indicator switches from the top of the transmission case.

90

7. Install by reversing these steps while noting the following:

CAUTION

*The internal contacts of both switches are different (**Figure 90**) and they must be reinstalled in the correct location on the transmission case. If installed incorrectly, the switches will be damaged.*

a. Refer to the F mark made in *Disassembly* Step 4. Install the front gear indicator switch with an F (front) (F, **Figure 89**) in the front receptacle. Install the screws and tighten securely.
b. Install the rear gear indicator switch (R, **Figure 89**) in the rear receptacle. Install the screws and tighten securely.
c. Make sure the electrical connectors are free of corrosion.
d. Make sure all of the electrical connectors are secure.

WIRING DIAGRAMS

Wiring diagrams for all models are located at the end of this book.

Table 1 ELECTRICAL SYSTEM SPECIFICATIONS

Item	Specification
Alternator output	
1996-1997	200 watts
1998-on	250 watts
Between yellow and yellow/red	7 amps
Alternator stator coils	
Exciter coils (1996-1998)	
Between red and green	3.2 ohms
Between black/red and green	446 ohms
Exciter coils (1999-on)	
Between red and green	1.6 ohms
Between black/red and green	446 ohms
Trigger coil	
Between white and white/red	97 ohms
Charge coil (1996-1998)	
Yellow to yellow/brown	0.17 ohms
Yellow/red to yellow/brown	0.17 ohms
Charge coil (1999-on)	
Yellow to yellow/red	0.13 ohms
Yellow to ground	infinity
Bush length minimum	0.8 mm (0.031 in.)
Ignition coil	
Primary resistance	0.3 ohms
Secondary resistance	6300 ohms
Spark plug cap resistance	5000 ohms
Starter solenoid resistance	3.4 ohms

Table 2 REPLACEMENT BULBS

Item	Specification
High-beam headlights	12 volt, 60/60 watt Halogen
Low-beam grill mounted lights	
1996	12 volt, 37.5 watt (2)
1997	12 volt, 35 watt (2)
1998-on	12 volt, 27 watt (2)
Taillight	12 volt, 8.26 watt
Brake light	12 volt, 6.9 watt
Indicator lights	
1996	12 volt, 1.25 watt
1997-on	12 volt, 1.0 watt

NOTE: Refer to the Supplement at the back of this manual for information unique to 2001-on models, including the Sportsman 400.

CHAPTER TWELVE

FRONT SUSPENSION AND STEERING

This chapter describes repair and maintenance of the front wheels, front strut, front suspension A-arms and steering components. Front hub service is covered in Chapter Ten.

The front suspension consists of two lower A-arms and struts and springs. A ball joint (**Figure 1**) connects the lower A-arm to the front strut on all models. The lower portion of the front strut is an aluminum casting. Two tie rods that are attached to the steering shaft and front strut arms control the steering.

Tables 1-3 are located at the end of this chapter.

FRONT WHEEL

Removal/Installation

1. Place the vehicle on level ground and set the parking brake. Block the rear wheel so the vehicle will not roll in either direction.
2. Mark the front tires with an L (left side) or R (right side) so that they will be installed onto the same side of the vehicle from which they were removed. If the tire is to be removed from the rim, also mark the tire with an arrow indicating the direction of rotation when traveling forward.

3. Loosen but do not remove the four lug nuts (**Figure 2**) securing the wheel to the front hub.
4. Raise the front of the vehicle with a small hydraulic or scissor jack. Place the jack under the frame with a piece of wood between the jack and the frame.
5. Place jacks under the frame to support the vehicle securely with the front wheels off the ground.
6. Remove the wheel lug nuts and remove the front wheel.
7. Clean the lug nuts using solvent and dry thoroughly.
8. Inspect the wheel for cracks, bending or other damage. If damage is severe, replace the wheel as described under *Tires and Wheels* in this chapter.
9. Install the four lug nuts (**Figure 2**). Finger-tighten the lug nuts until the wheel is positioned squarely against the front hub.

WARNING
Always tighten the lug nuts to the correct torque specification, or the nuts may work loose.

10. Use a torque wrench and tighten the four lug nuts in a crisscross pattern to the torque specification listed in **Table 2**.
11. After the wheel is installed, rotate it and apply the front brake several times to make sure that the wheel rotates freely and that the brake is operating correctly.
12. Lower the front of the vehicle to the ground and recheck the torque of the lug nuts.

FRONT HUB

Front hub service is covered in Chapter Ten along with the front drive system.

FRONT STRUT CARTRIDGE AND SPRING

The following Polaris special tools are required:
1. Spring compressor for right side strut spring (part No. 2871574).
2. Spring compressor for left side strut spring (part No. 2871573).
3. An aftermarket coil spring compressor can be used for both strut springs. The Performance Tool MacPherson Strut Coil Spring Compressor (part No. W80555) (**Figure 3**) is used in the following procedure.

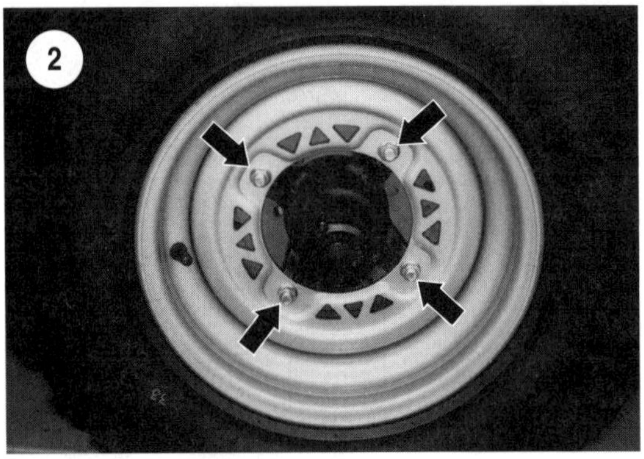

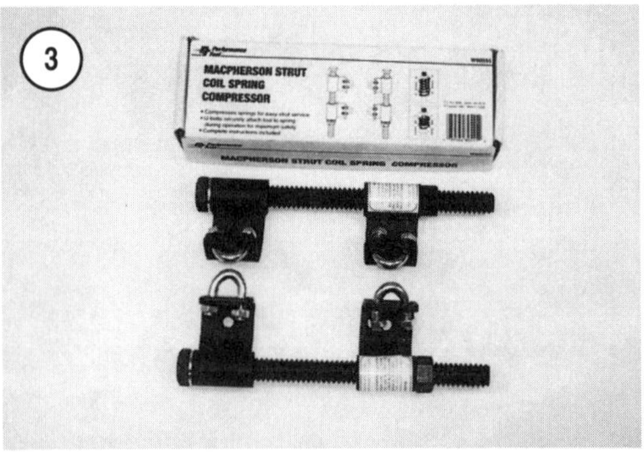

Removal

Refer to **Figure 4**.

The spring is installed on the hydraulically damped strut cartridge. The strut unit is sealed and cannot be disassembled. Service is limited to removal and replacement of the damper unit, spring and mounting bushings.

This procedure is for the complete disassembly of the front strut assembly. If only a portion of the front strut requires service, perform only those steps relating to that service.

(4)

FRONT STRUT

1. Nut
2. Washer
3. Rubber spacer
4. Upper ball pivot
5. Nut
6. Lower ball pivot
7. Upper spring seat
8. Spring
9. Strut
10. Lower spring seat
11. Clamp
12. Wire retainer
13. Roller bearing
14. Outer race
15. Sleeve seal
16. Magnetic coil
17. Grease fitting
18. Bolt
19. Seal
20. Lockwasher
21. Strut support/spindle

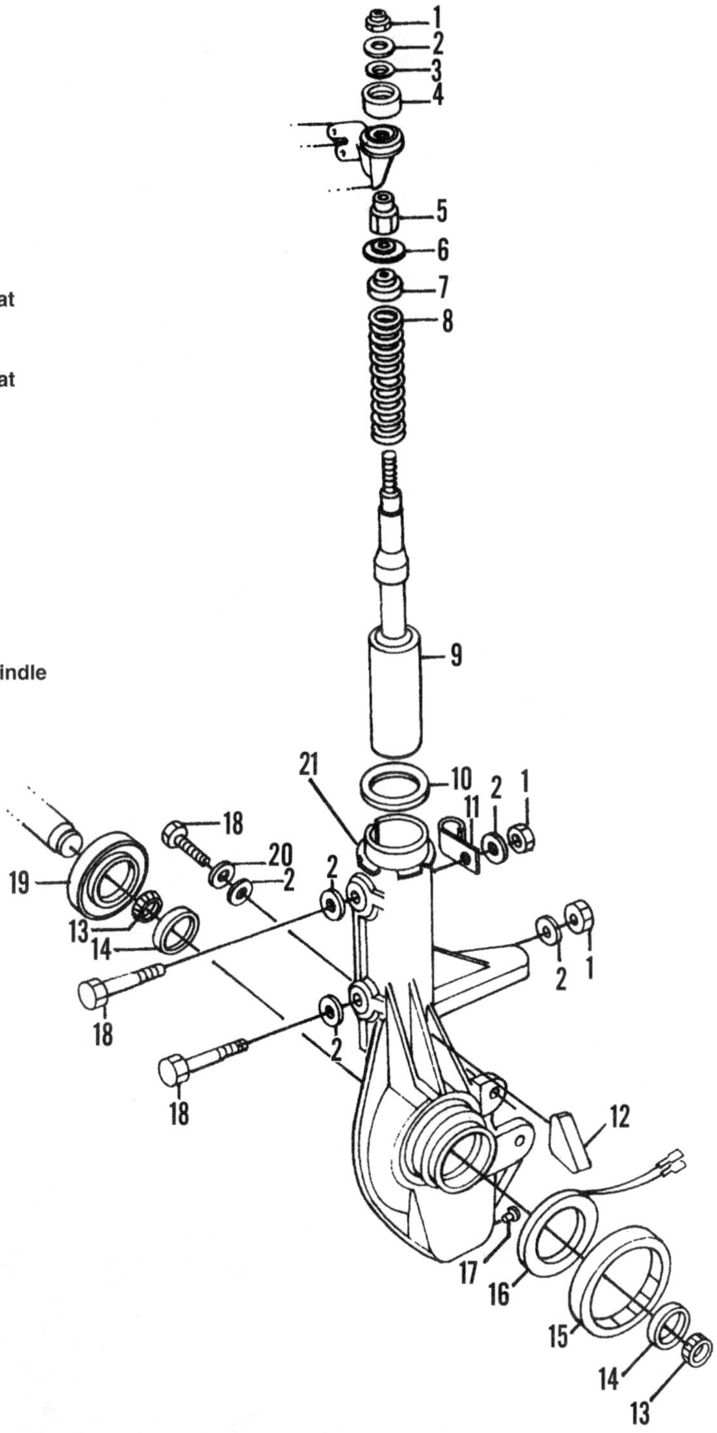

1. Place the vehicle on level ground and set the parking brake. Block the rear wheel so the vehicle will not roll in either direction.
2. Raise the front of the vehicle up to gain working room under the front strut. Secure the vehicle in this position so it will not shift or fall while working on it.
3. Remove the front wheel as described in this chapter.
4. Remove the front fender as described in Chapter Fifteen.
5. Secure the upper end of the strut with a socket (A, **Figure 5**) and loosen the nut with a wrench (B, **Figure 5**).
6. Hold onto the lower end of the front strut, as it will lower when the nut is removed.
7. Remove the nut (**Figure 6**) and lower the front strut assembly out of the frame.
8. Remove the upper ball pivot (**Figure 7**).

WARNING

Do not remove the spring without a spring compressor. The spring is under considerable pressure and may fly off and cause injury.

9. Attach the spring compressor tool onto the spring (**Figure 8**) following the manufacturer's instructions. Compress the spring until there is no spring pressure on the upper spring seat.

CAUTION

The self-locking nut used at the top of the strut must be discarded every time it is removed. Once removed it has lost its locking ability and a new nut must be installed.

10. Prior to removing the self-locking nut in Step 11, measure the distance from the top of the strut

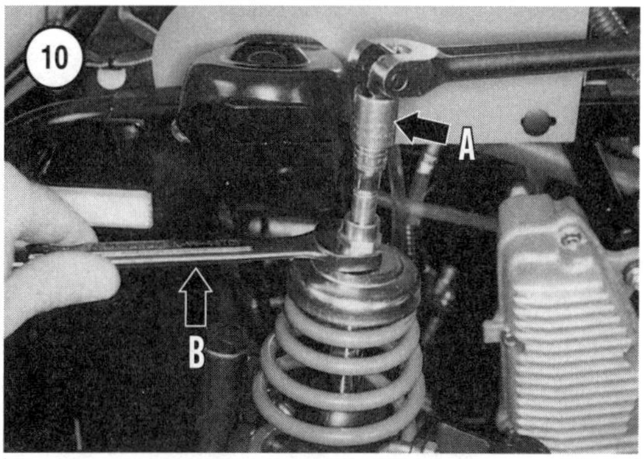

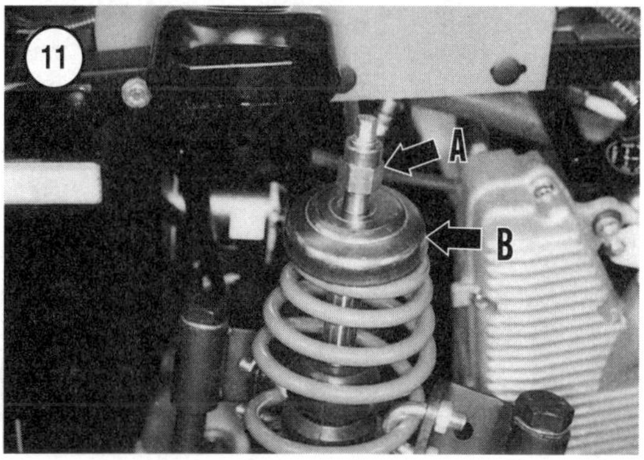

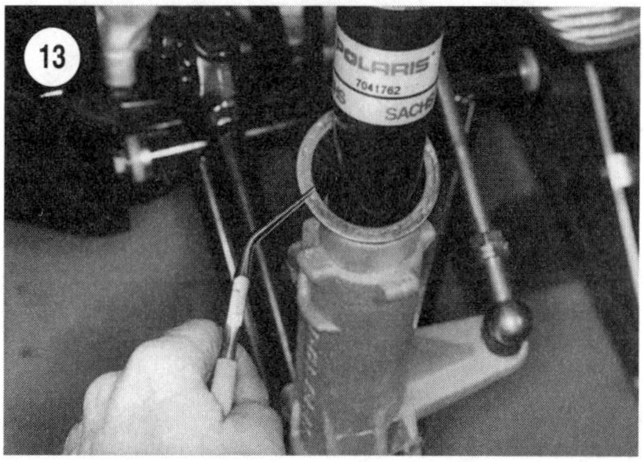

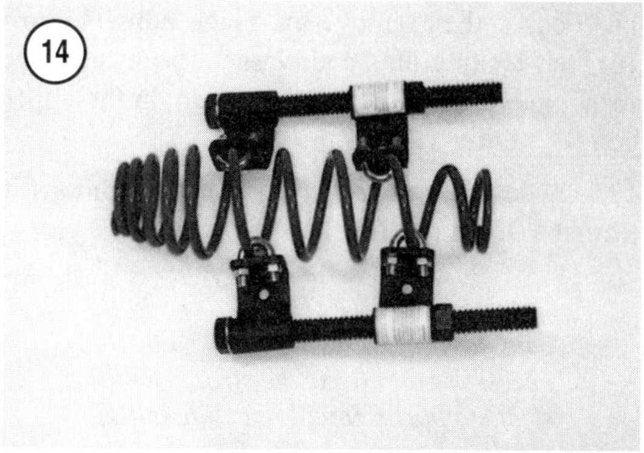

damper rod to the top the nut (**Figure 9**). Record this dimension. There is no standard dimension for the location of this nut, but the nut should be at the same location on both sides of the vehicle.

11. Secure the upper end of the strut with a socket (A, **Figure 10**) and loosen the self-locking nut with a 3/8 in. wrench (B, **Figure 10**).

12. Remove the self-locking nut (A, **Figure 11**) and the lower ball pivot and upper spring seat (B, **Figure 11**). Discard the self-locking nut, as it cannot be reused.

13. Remove the spring and spring compressor assembly (**Figure 12**) up and off the strut.

14. Remove the lower spring seat (**Figure 13**) from the strut.

15. If the spring is going to be replaced, slowly and carefully loosen, and remove the spring compressor (**Figure 14**) from the spring and remove the tool.

NOTE

The strut cartridge location within the strut support may vary. Make sure to perform Step 16 to ensure the correct location of the strut during assembly.

16. Scribe a line on the existing strut cartridge level with the top surface of the support strut (A, **Figure 15**). This acts as a reference line for reinstallation of the old strut or for the new strut into the strut support.

CAUTION

The self-locking nuts used on the clamping bolts must be discarded every time they are removed. Once removed, they have lost their locking ability and a new nut must be installed.

17. Loosen then remove the pinch bolts (**Figure 16**), self-locking nuts and washers from the front strut. Note the location of the clamp on the upper bolt (B, **Figure 15**).

18A. Slide the strut (**Figure 17**) up to withdraw it from the strut support.

NOTE

One of the following steps may be necessary to release the strut from the strut support if it will not slide out after the clamping bolts and nuts have been removed.

18B. Apply a liberal amount of penetrating oil between the strut cartridge and the strut support. Let the oil work about 15-20 minutes. Using a soft-faced mallet, carefully tap around the strut support where the cartridge is located. Withdraw the strut from the strut support.

CAUTION

Do not spread the strut support joint in the areas of the bolt hole bosses. Also do not spread the joint any farther than necessary, as the aluminum casting will crack and must be replaced. When using this method, spread the joint very slowly to avoid damaging the strut support.

18C. Carefully spread the front strut joint with an aluminum or brass tool sufficiently to release the strut. Withdraw the strut from the strut support.

18D. If the previous methods were unsuccessful, perform the following:

a. Tap both upper bolt mounting bosses with a 3/8 in. tap.
b. Screw a 3/8 in. bolt part way into each upper mounting boss.
c. Place a thick steel washer into the joint below the bolts. Do not align the washer bolt hole, the bolt is to contact the washer, not go through it.
d. Slowly tighten the bolts onto the washers to spread the joint sufficiently to release the strut. Withdraw the strut from the strut support.
e. Remove the bolts and washers.

15

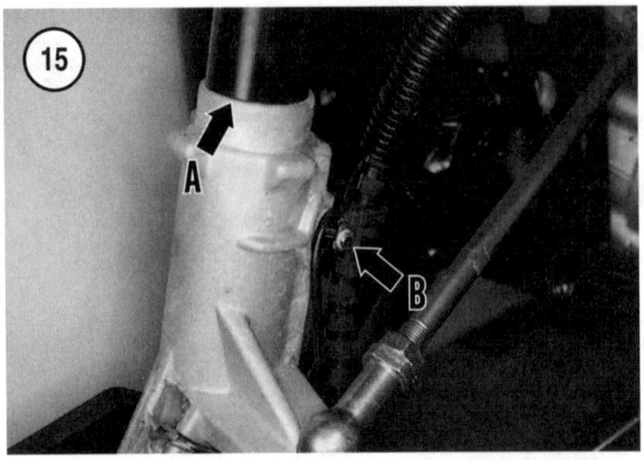

16

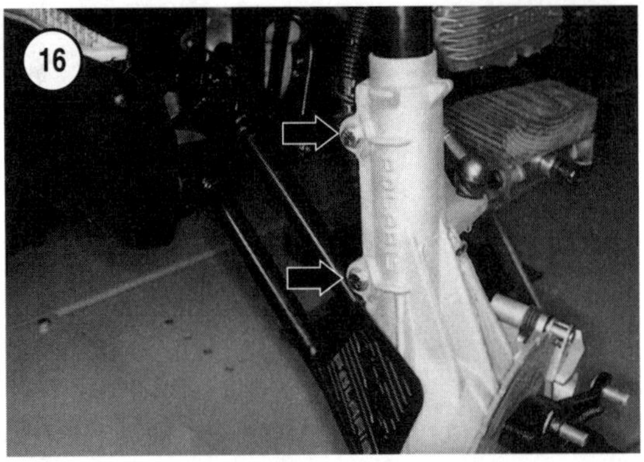

17

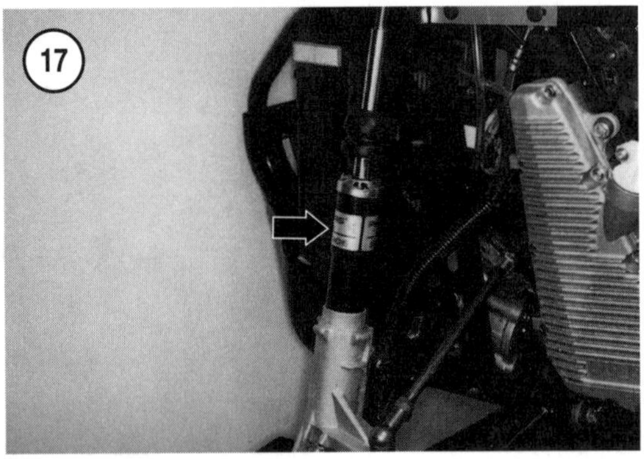

Inspection

1. Inspect the spring for distortion, cracks, or other damage. If one spring is damaged, replace both springs.
2. Inspect the strut for oil leaks (A, **Figure 18**).
3. Check the rubber bumper (B, **Figure 18**) for deterioration or hardness. Replace if necessary.
4. Check the upper spring seat for wear or damage.
5. Clean the strut receptacle in the strut support (**Figure 19**) with solvent and dry. Clean any corro-

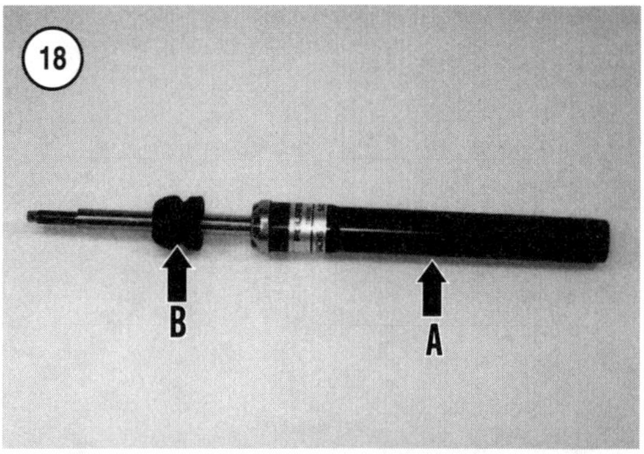

18

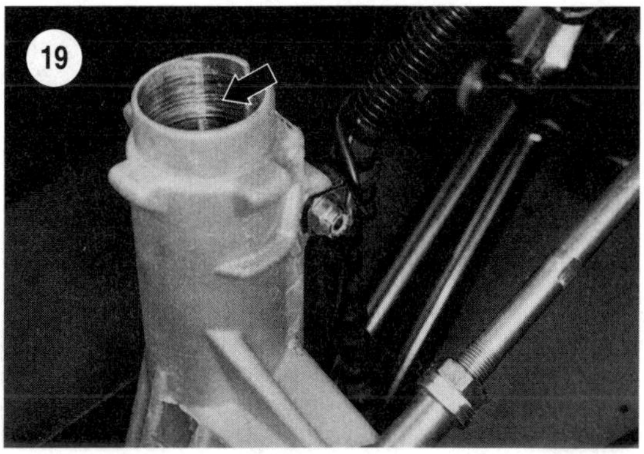

19

20

sion or burrs from the inner surface that would make installation of the strut difficult.

Installation

Refer to **Figure 4**.

NOTE

If installing a new strut, transfer the scribe line made in Removal Step 15 onto the new shock body. This will ensure the correct installed location of the strut within the strut support.

1. Slide the strut down into the strut support. Push the strut into the correct location within the strut support (A, **Figure 15**). Refer to the scribe line made in *Removal* Step 16.
2. Install the pinch bolts (**Figure 16**), washers and *new* self-locking nuts. Note the location of the clamp on the upper bolt (B, **Figure 15**).
3. Verify the location of the strut in the strut support, readjust if necessary, and then tighten the nuts to the torque specification listed in **Table 2**.
4. Slide the lower spring seat over the strut and into position on the strut support (**Figure 13**).
5. If the spring was replaced, install the spring compressor on the spring (**Figure 14**). Slowly and carefully tighten the spring compressor until the spring is compressed sufficiently for installation.
6. Install the compressed spring over the strut and set it on the lower spring seat (**Figure 12**).
7. Install the upper spring seat (B, **Figure 11**) and lower ball pivot onto the spring.
8. Install the *new* self-locking nut (A, **Figure 11**).
9. Tighten the self-locking nut onto the strut damper rod to the same location noted in Step 10 of *Removal*. Secure the upper end of the strut with a socket (A, **Figure 10**). Securely tighten the new self-locking nut with a 3/8 in. wrench (B, **Figure 10**).
10. Slowly and carefully loosen the spring compressor. Make sure the spring (**Figure 20**) is seated correctly in both the upper and lower spring seats, then remove the tool (**Figure 8**) from the spring.
11. Install the upper ball pivot and washer (**Figure 7**) onto the frame.
12. Raise the strut assembly up and insert the upper end of the strut through the frame opening and the upper pivot ball and washer.
13. Install the nut (**Figure 6**) and tighten it securely to hold the assembly in place.

NOTE

Position the crows foot wrench at a 90° angle to the torque wrench so that the torque specification does not have to be recalculated.

14. Secure the upper end of the strut with a wrench (A, **Figure 21**) and tighten the nut with a crows foot wrench (B, **Figure 21**) to the torque specification listed in **Table 2**.

15. Install the front fender as described in Chapter Fifteen.
16. Install the front wheel as described in this chapter.
17. Lower the front of the vehicle.
18. Push down on the front of the vehicle several times to make sure the front suspension is operating correctly.

FRONT STRUT/SPINDLE

Removal/Installation

The threads of the tie rod ends and ball joints are easily damaged during tie rod removal. If it is difficult to remove the studs of the tie rods or ball joints, have a Polaris dealership perform this operation.

1. Place the vehicle on level ground and set the parking brake. Block the rear wheel so the vehicle will not roll in either direction.
2. Raise the front of the vehicle up to gain working room under the support strut. Secure the vehicle in this position so it will not shift or fall while working on it.
3. Remove the front caliper as described in Chapter Fourteen.
4. Remove the front hub as described in Chapter Ten.
5. Disconnect the front wheel drive coil electrical connector (**Figure 22**).
6. Disconnect the front suspension arm from the front strut as described in this chapter.

CAUTION
Do not hammer on the threaded stud of the tie rod ball joint when trying to remove it. Doing so will damage the threads and requires installation of a new tie rod end or complete tie rod assembly.

7. Disconnect the outboard end of the tie rod (**Figure 23**) from the front strut as described in this chapter.
8. Move the front strut out from the drive axle to loosen the outer bearing from the strut (**Figure 24**), then slide the outer bearing off the axle.
9. Move the front strut farther out and withdraw the drive axle from it.
10. Slide the outer bearing back onto the drive axle to avoid misplacing it.

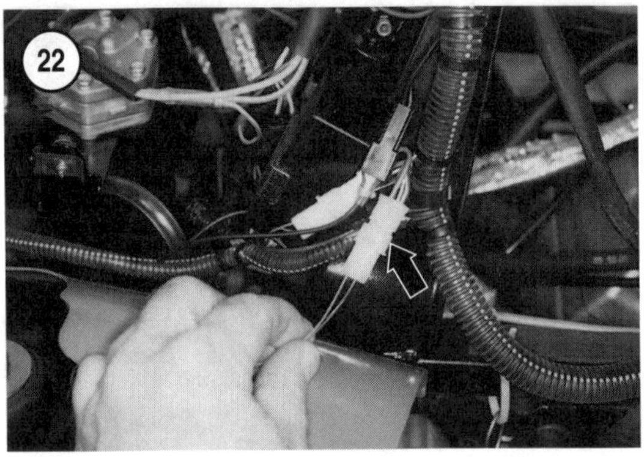

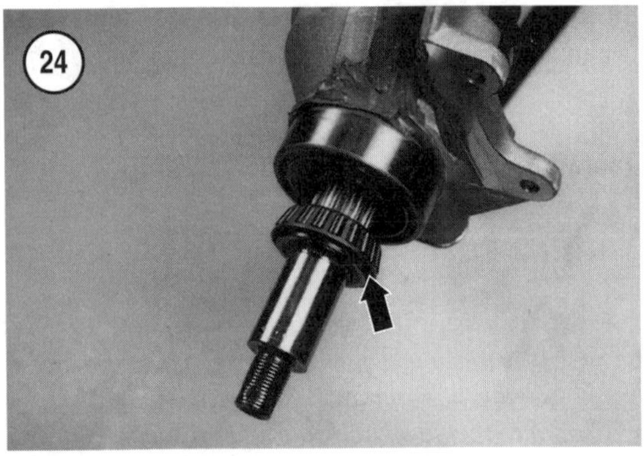

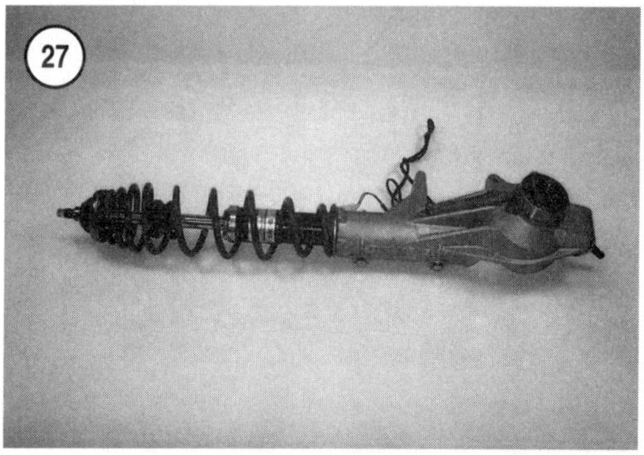

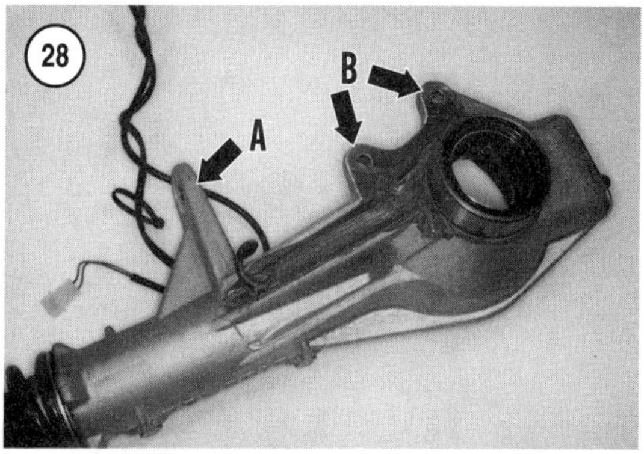

11. Raise the drive axle and secure it to the frame with wire or a bungee cord.
12. Secure the upper end of the strut with a socket (A, **Figure 25**) and loosen the nut with a wrench (B, **Figure 25**).
13. Hold onto the lower end of the strut support, as it will lower when the nut is removed.
14. Remove the nut (**Figure 26**) and lower the strut assembly out of the frame. Install the nut onto the top of the strut to avoid misplacing it.
15. Install by reversing these removal steps. Tighten the fasteners to the torque specification listed in **Table 2**.

Inspection

1. Clean the strut assembly in solvent and dry.
2. Inspect the strut support for cracks or damage (**Figure 27**).
3. Check the tie rod end mounting boss (A, **Figure 28**) and the front brake caliper mounting bosses (B, **Figure 28**) for cracks or damage.
4. Inspect the drive axle bearing outer races as described in the following procedure.

12

Bearing Inspection and Replacement

1. Thoroughly clean bearing outer races (**Figure 29**) within the strut support with solvent and dry with compressed air.
2. Inspect both outer races for evidence of wear, pitting or excessive heat (bluish tint). Refer to **Figure 29** and A, **Figure 30**.
3. Remove the bearings from the drive axle, clean with solvent and dry with low-pressure compressed air. Do not allow the inner race to spin while applying the compressed air.

4. Inspect the bearings (**Figure 31**) for evidence of wear, pitting or excessive heat (bluish tint).
5. If either the outer race or the bearing requires replacement, replace both as a set.
6. Inspect the seal (B, **Figure 30**) for leakage or damage.
7. If the seal and/or the bearings require replacement, refer this work to a Polaris dealership, as special tools and a press are required.
8. If the bearings are good, pack the bearing with Polaris All-Season Grease, or NLGI No. 2 equivalent.

30

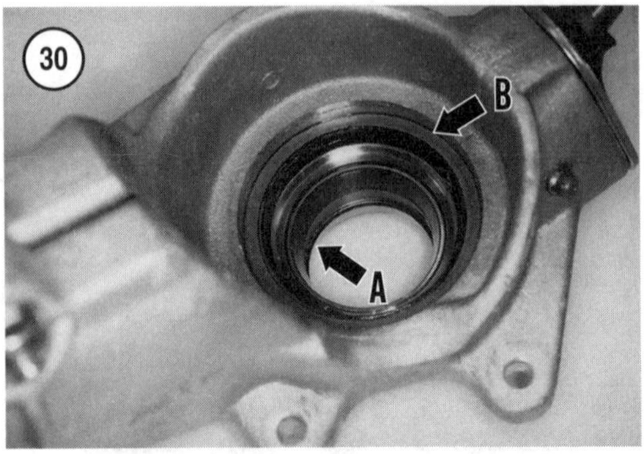

31

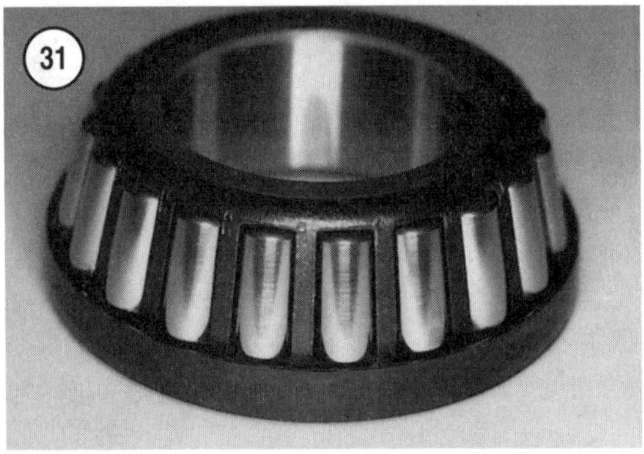

Ball Joint Inspection/Replacement

A ball joint connects the bottom of the strut assembly to the control arm. Only remove the ball joint assembly if replacement is necessary.

1. Inspect the ball joint rubber boot. The swivel joint is packed with grease. If the rubber boot or ball joint is damaged, replace the ball joint as follows.
2. Remove the strut assembly as described in this chapter.
3. Place the strut support, upside down, in a vise with soft jaws.

NOTE
It may be necessary to heat the front strut to soften the threadlocking compound. Heat the area with an industrial grade heat gun—do not apply direct heat from any type of torch.

4. Use an impact driver with the correct size Allen bit. Loosen both mounting bolts (**Figure 32**) securing the ball joint mounting bracket to the base of the front strut.
5. Remove the rubber boot (**Figure 33**).
6. Remove the bolts, the mounting bracket and the ball joint (**Figure 34**) from the front strut.
7. Clean the ball joint pocket in the front strut and the mounting bolt holes. Thoroughly clean out all threadlocking residue in the bolt holes.
8. Inspect the threaded holes and clean out with an appropriate size tap if necessary.
9. Install a new ball joint into the mounting plate and install the plate onto the base of the front strut.
10. Apply ThreeBond TB1342, Loctite 242, or equivalent threadlocking compound, to the bolt threads prior to installation.
11. Install the bolts and tighten to the torque specification listed in **Table 2**.

32

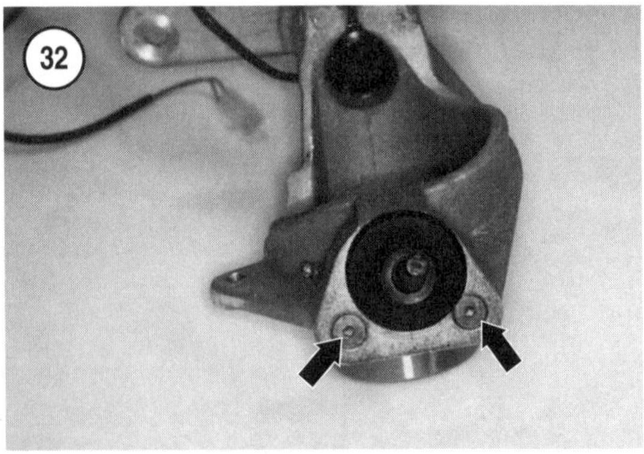

33

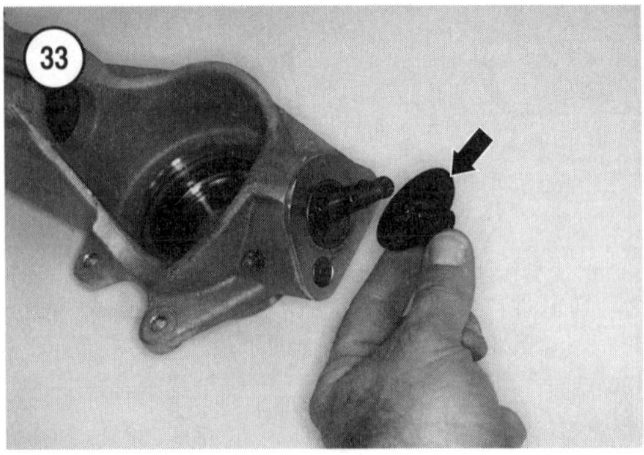

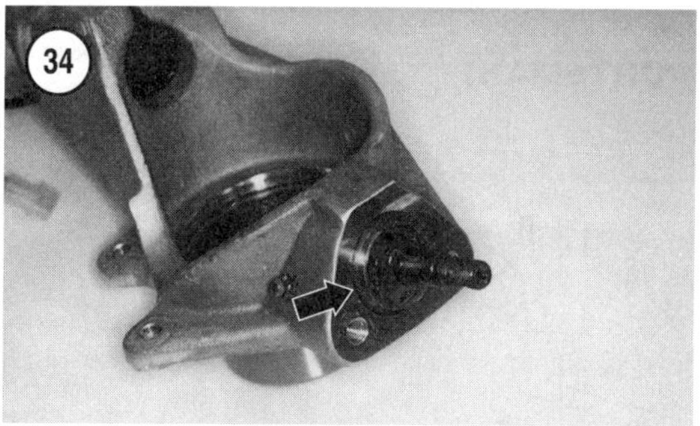

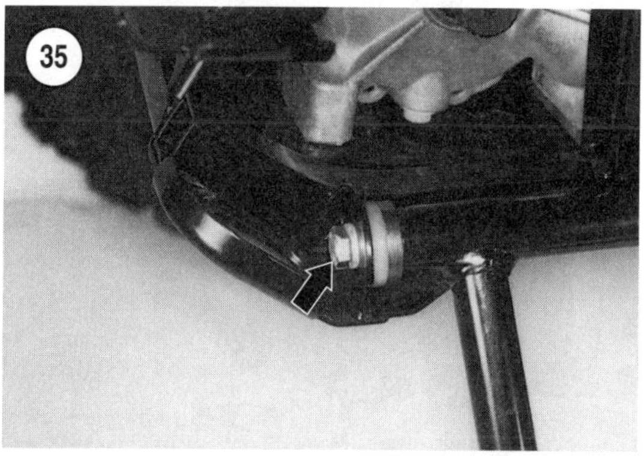

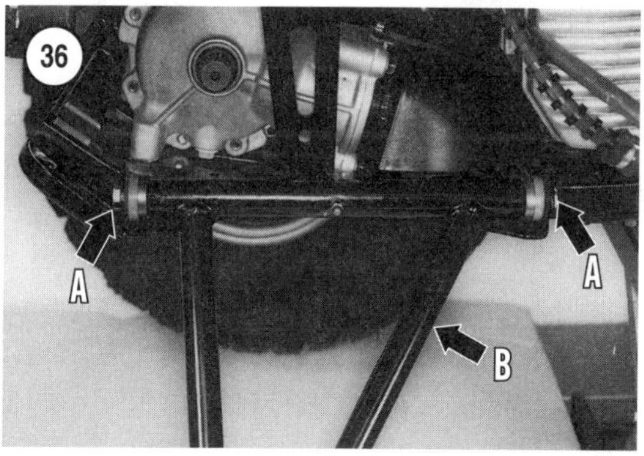

12. Install the rubber boot and press it on until it is correctly seated.

CONTROL ARM

Removal

1. Block the front of the vehicle up to gain working room under the control arm. Secure the vehicle in this position so it will not shift or fall.
2. Remove the front wheel as described in this chapter.
3. Remove the front strut as described in this chapter.
4. Remove the front drive axle as described in Chapter Ten.
5. Alternating from side to side, loosen the bolts (**Figure 35**) securing the control arm to the frame mounting brackets. Hold onto the control arm and remove both bolts and washers (A, **Figure 36**).
6. Hold onto both ends of the control arm assembly (B, **Figure 36**) and remove it from the frame.

Inspection

NOTE
There are no service specifications for any of these components. If a part is worn or damaged, replace it. If one of the long bushings requires replacement, replace both at the same time.

1. Remove the long bushing and flat bushing from each end of the control arm.
2. Withdraw the shaft from the control arm.
3. Clean parts in solvent and dry them with compressed air.
4. Inspect the control arm for cracks, fractures and dents. If damage is severe, replace the control arm. Never try to straighten a damaged or dented control arm.
5. Inspect each bushing for severe wear or damage. Replace rusted or otherwise damaged parts.
6. Inspect the mounting bolts for bending or other damage. Replace damaged bolts.
7. Inspect the mounting bracket on the frame for damage. If repair is required, consult a competent welder who is familiar with this type of repair.
8. Apply a heavy coat of grease to the shaft and insert it into the control arm. Wipe off excessive grease from the end of the control arm after the shaft has been installed.
9. Install the flat and long bushing into each end of the control arm.

Installation

1. Hold onto both ends of the control arm assembly and position it into the frame between the mounting brackets.
2. Hold the assembly in place (B, **Figure 36**) and install the bolt and washer onto each end (A, **Figure 36**).

37

HANDLEBAR (SPORTSMAN)

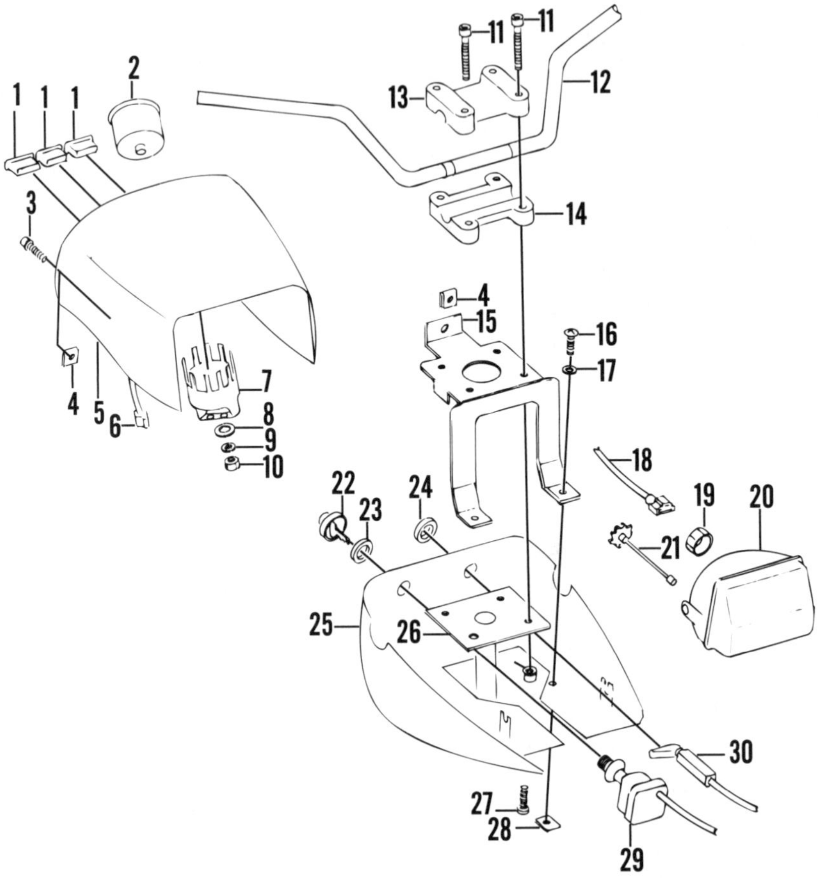

1. Indicators
2. Speedometer
3. Screw
4. Special nut
5. Headlight upper pod
6. Wiring harness
7. Speedometer mount (models so equipped)
8. Washer
9. Lockwasher
10. Self-locking nut
11. Bolt
12. Handlebar
13. Upper holder
14. Lower holder
15. Pod mounting bracket
16. Screw
17. Washer
18. Headlight
19. Cover
20. High-beam headlight
21. Adjuster
22. Ignition key
23. Lock ring
24. Lock ring
25. Headlight lower pod
26. Steering shaft
27. Screw
28. Special nut
29. Key or ignition switch
30. Enrichment (choke) knob

38 **HANDLEBAR (XPLORER)**

1. Top cover
2. Screw
3. Instrument panel cover
4. Bolt
5. Lock ring
6. Indictors
7. Enrichment (choke) knob
8. Wiring harness
9. Handlebar
10. Ignition key
11. Pod mounting bracket
12. Key or ignition switch
13. Holders
14. Steering shaft
15. Self-locking nut

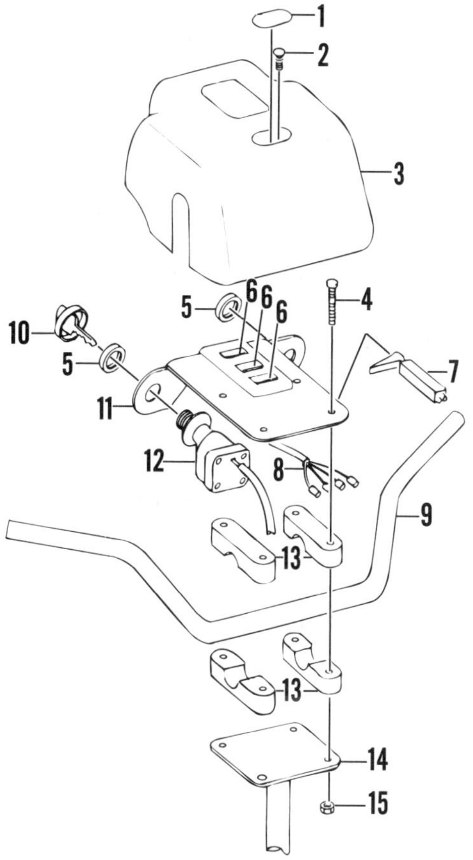

12

3. Alternating from side to side, slowly tighten the bolts securing the control arm to the frame mounting brackets. Tighten the bolts to the torque specification listed in **Table 2**.

4. After tightening the bolts, move the control arm up and down to ensure freedom of movement. The arm must move up and down with no binding. If binding occurs, remove the control arm and correct the problem immediately.

5. Install the front drive axle as described in Chapter Ten.

6. Install the front strut as described in this chapter.

7. Install the front wheel as described in this chapter.

8. Lower the vehicle and check the movement of the front suspension prior to riding it. Push down on the front bumper several times to make sure the control arms are moving up and down correctly.

9. Test drive the ATV slowly to make sure all suspension components are operating correctly.

HANDLEBAR

Removal

Refer to **Figure 37** for Sportsman models and **Figure 38** for Xplorer models.

CAUTION

Cover the front fender and seat with a heavy cloth or tarp to protect them from any brake fluid that may be accidentally spilled. Use soapy water to wash any spilled brake fluid from a painted or plated surface immediately to prevent damaging to the finish. Rinse the area thoroughly with clean water, making sure that both brake fluid and soap are removed.

1A. On Xplorer models, perform the following:

a. Remove the top cover from the instrument panel cover.

b. Remove the two screws securing the instrument panel cover and remove the cover.

1B. On Sportsman models, remove the headlight upper pod (A, **Figure 39**) as described under *High-Beam Headlight (Sportsman Models), Bulb Replacement* in Chapter Eleven.

2. Remove the master cylinder (B, **Figure 39**) from the handlebar as described in Chapter Fourteen. Rest the master cylinder on the front fender. Keep the hydraulic brake reservoir upright to prevent fluid from spilling and air from entering the brake system. Do not detach the brake line from the master cylinder, unless it is going to be removed from the vehicle.

CAUTION
Do not allow the master cylinder to hang by its hose.

3. Remove all ties or bands holding the wires and cables to the handlebar.

4. Remove the screws securing the left switch assembly (C, **Figure 39**), then remove the switch housing from the handlebar. Lay the switch assembly on the front fender.

5. Remove the screws and clamp securing the throttle and right switch assembly (**Figure 40**) to the right side of the handlebar and remove the assembly. Lay the assembly on the front fender. Do not allow the cable to be kinked, crimped or damaged.

6A. On Xplorer models, perform the following:

a. Remove the four bolts and self-locking nuts securing the handlebar upper holder, instrument panel cover mounting bracket, handlebar and lower holder. Discard the self-locking nuts.

b. Remove the handlebar upper holder and the handlebar. Leave the instrument panel cover mounting bracket and lower holder in place on the steering column.

6B. On Sportsman models, perform the following:

a. Remove the four bolts and self-locking nuts securing the handlebar upper holder (A, **Figure 41**), handlebar and lower holder. Discard the self-locking nuts.

b. Remove the handlebar upper holder and the handlebar (B, **Figure 41**). Leave the lower holder and the pod-mounting bracket in place on the steering column.

39

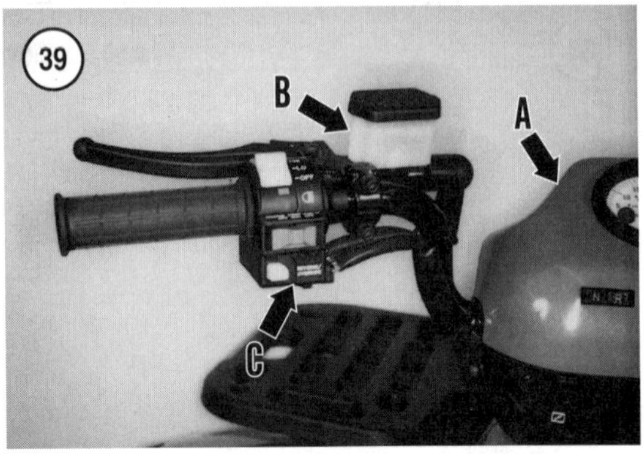

40

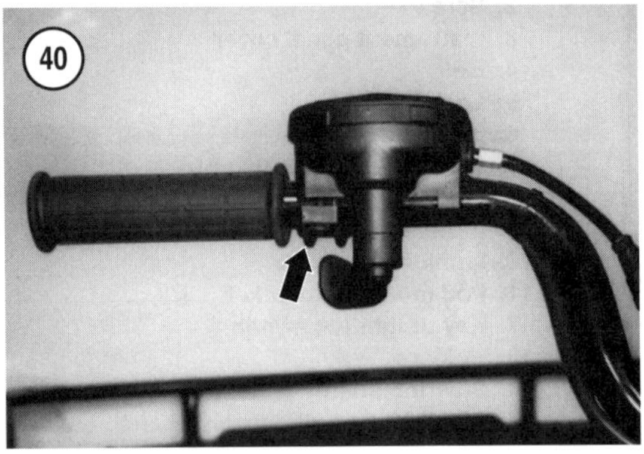

7. To maintain a good grip on the handlebar and to prevent it from slipping, clean the knurled section of the handlebar with a wire brush. It should be kept rough so it will be held securely by the upper and lower holders.

8. Also clean any metal from the upper and lower holders that may have been gouged loose by handlebar slippage.

Installation

1. Align the bolt holes in the lower holder and the pod mounting bracket with the steering column holes.

2A. On Xplorer models, perform the following:

a. Install the handlebar upper holder and instrument panel cover mounting bracket into place

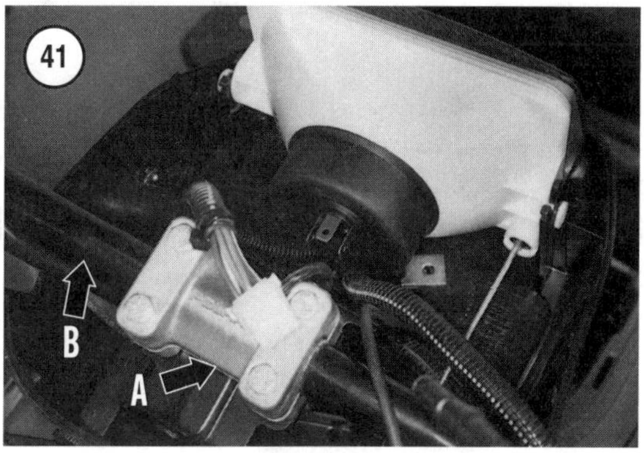

on the lower holder and install the mounting bolts through all four components.

b. Install *new* self-locking nuts and tighten them finger-tight.

2B. On Sportsman models, perform the following:

a. Install the handlebar and upper holder (A, **Figure 41**) into place on the lower holder and install the mounting bolts through all four components.

b. Install *new* self-locking nuts and tighten them finger-tight.

3. Raise the handlebar into position and tighten the forward bolts first and then tighten the rear bolts. Tighten all four bolts to the torque specification listed in **Table 2**.

4. If a new handlebar is being installed, also install new grips. Follow the manufacturer's directions for installing and sealing grips to the handlebar.

5. Position the left switch housing (C, **Figure 39**) onto the handlebar and seat it next to the grip as shown. Tighten the switch screws securely.

6. Position the brake master cylinder (B, **Figure 39**) on the handlebar and install the clamp. Tighten the bolts securely.

7. Position the throttle and right switch assemblies (**Figure 40**) onto the handlebar and secure them with clamp screws. Tighten the screws securely.

8. Check the brake lever, throttle lever and switch positions on both sides of the handlebars while sitting on the seat. Tighten the clamp screws securely when the controls are comfortably positioned.

9. After all assemblies have been installed, test each one to make sure it operates correctly with no binding. Correct any problem at this time.

10A. On Xplorer models, perform the following:

a. Install the instrument panel cover and two screws. Tighten the screws securely.

b. Install the top cover onto the instrument panel cover.

10B. On Sportsman models, remove the headlight upper pod (A, **Figure 39**) as described under *High-Beam Headlight (Sportsman Models), Bulb Replacement* in Chapter Eleven.

11. Secure the housing wiring harness to the handlebar with wire and cable ties, making sure that wires and cables are properly routed with no sharp bends.

TIE RODS

Refer to **Figure 42**.

Removal

The tie rods connect the steering shaft to the steering arm portion of the strut supports. Each tie rod includes an inner and outer end attached to a threaded rod. The individual parts can be replaced separately.

The outer tie rod end (**Figure 43**) can be replaced without detaching the tie rod inner end from the steering shaft. When replacing the inner tie rod end, first remove the complete tie rod from the vehicle so that the inner end and tie rod can be properly assembled.

1. Support the vehicle and remove the front wheel(s) as described in this chapter.

2. Remove the front fender as described in Chapter Fifteen.

3. Before detaching either end of the tie rod, identify the placement of the ends. If improperly installed, the tie rod ends may hit other components causing damage and possible loss of control.

4. To disconnect the tie rod ball joint from the front strut, perform the following:

a. Remove the cotter pin from the castellated nut (**Figure 44**).

CAUTION
Do not use a forked tool to separate the tie rod from the front strut; this will usually damage the rubber boot, even when used carefully.

b. Loosen the castellated nut until it is flush with the end of the threaded stud.

12

(42)

STEERING AND SUSPENSION

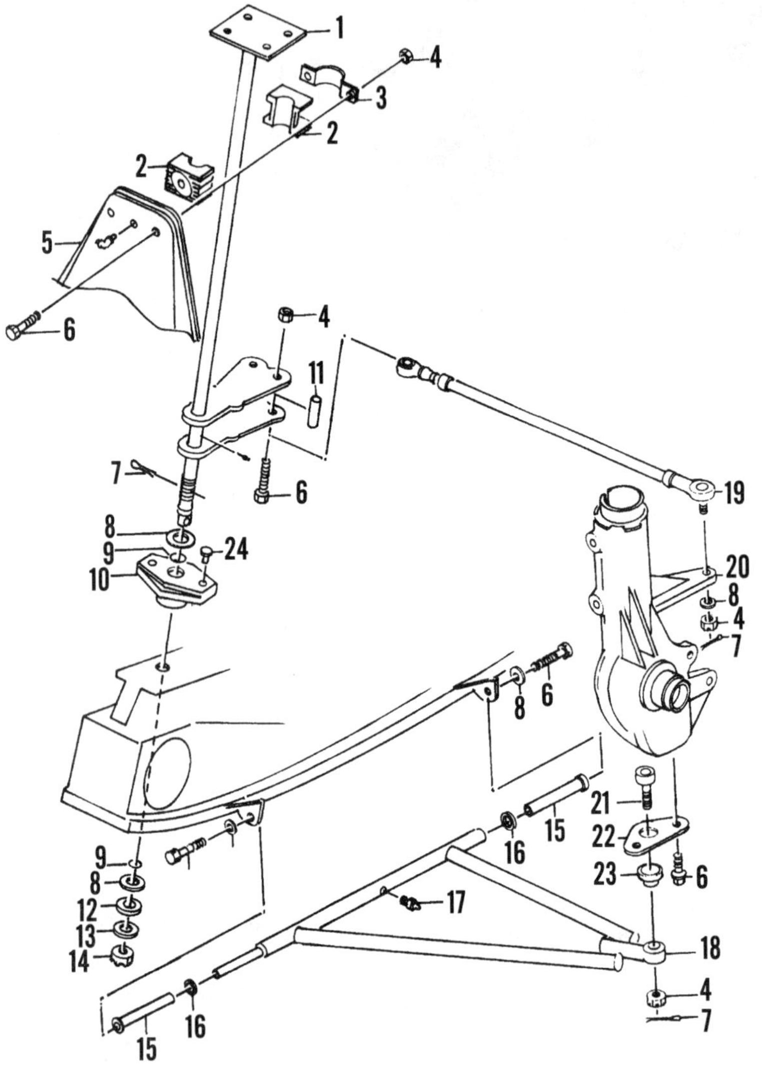

1. Steering shaft
2. Upper bushing blocks
3. Clamp
4. Nut
5. Frame
6. Bolt
7. Cotter pin
8. Washer
9. O-ring
10. Lower bushing block
11. Spacer
12. Thrust bearing
13. Washer
14. Nut
15. Long bushing
16. Flat bushing
17. Grease fitting
18. Control A-arm
19. Tie rod
20. Strut support
21. Ball joint
22. Ball joint mounting bracket
23. Rubber boot
24. Rivet

43

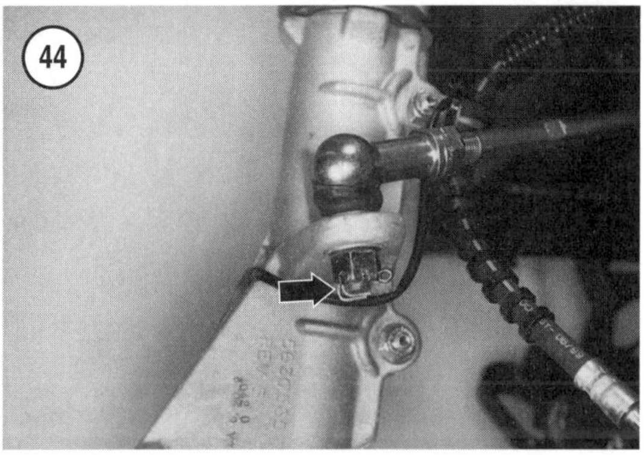
44

45

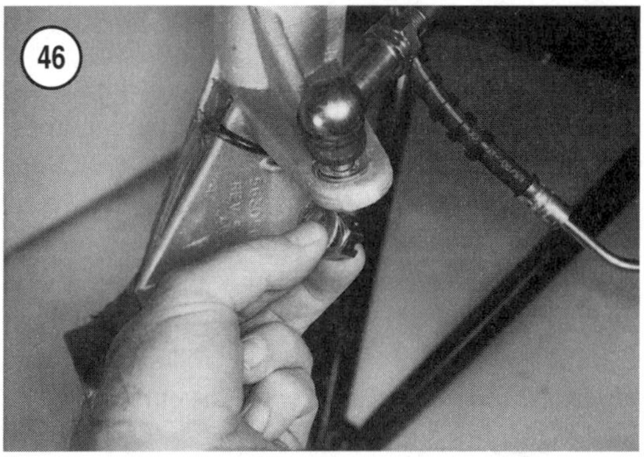
46

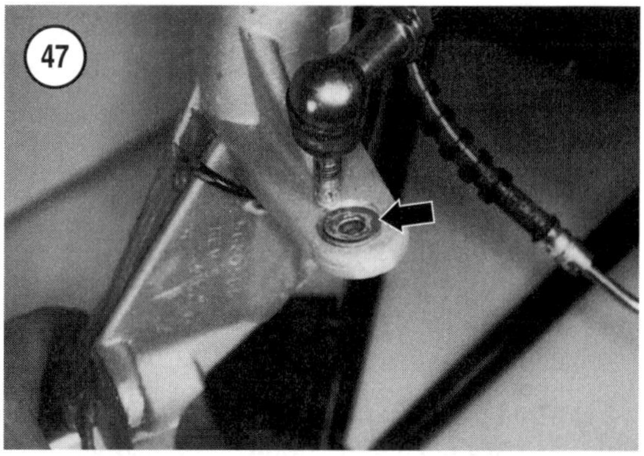
47

CAUTION
Make sure the castellated nut is flush with the end of the stud. If any stud threads are exposed, they may be damaged in the next step. Also, do not use a hard-faced hammer as the castellated nut as well as the stud may be damaged.

c. Tap on the castellated nut with a soft-faced hammer (**Figure 45**) to loosen the tie rod ball joint stud from the front strut.

d. Unscrew and remove the castellated nut and washer (**Figure 46**) from the ball joint stud.

e. Carefully lift the tie rod up and off the steering arm portion of the front strut. Remove the washer (**Figure 47**) located between the two parts.

f. Secure the outer end of the tie rod to the frame with a bungee cord or piece of wire while disconnecting the inner tie rod.

5. If only the outer tie rod end is going to be replaced, it is not necessary to detach the inner end. Refer to *Tie Rod Disassembly/Assembly* in this chapter.

CAUTION
The self-locking nuts used on the inboard end of the tie rods bolts must be discarded every time they are removed. Once removed, they have lost their locking ability and a new nut must be installed.

6A. To disconnect the *left side* inner tie rod end from the steering shaft plate, perform the following:

a. Loosen the self-locking nut (A, **Figure 48**) securing the tie rod to the steering shaft plate.

NOTE
There are two plates at the lower end of the steering shaft and a spacer (B, ***Figure 48****) is located between them. The tie rod mounting bolt goes through the plates.*

b. Hold onto the inboard end of the tie rod, then remove the bolt (C, **Figure 48**) and nut from the tie rod and the two plates. Remove the spacer (B, **Figure 48**) and reinstall it on the bolt along with the nut to avoid misplacing them.

c. Disconnect the inner end of the tie rod (D, **Figure 48**) from the steering shaft plates and remove the tie rod from the vehicle.

6B. To disconnect the *right side* inner tie rod end from the steering shaft plate, perform the following:

a. Loosen the self-locking nut (A, **Figure 49**) securing the tie rod to the steering shaft plate.

b. Hold onto the inboard end of the tie rod, then remove the bolt (B, **Figure 49**) and nut from the tie rod and the two plates.

c. Disconnect the inner end of the tie rod (C, **Figure 49**) from between the steering shaft plates and remove the tie rod from the vehicle.

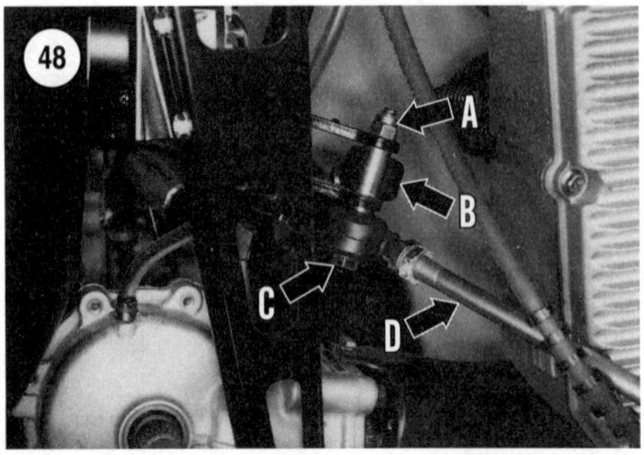

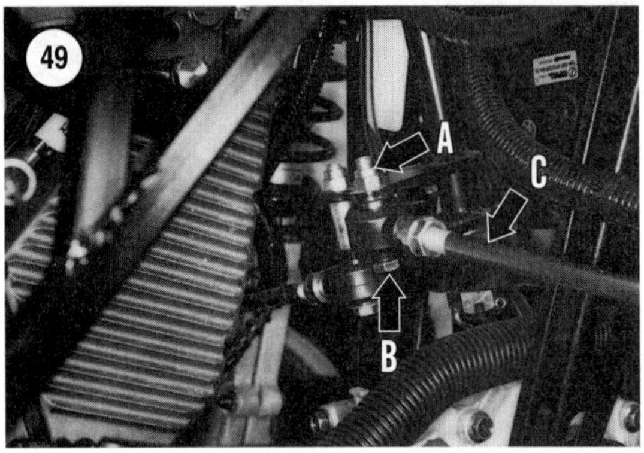

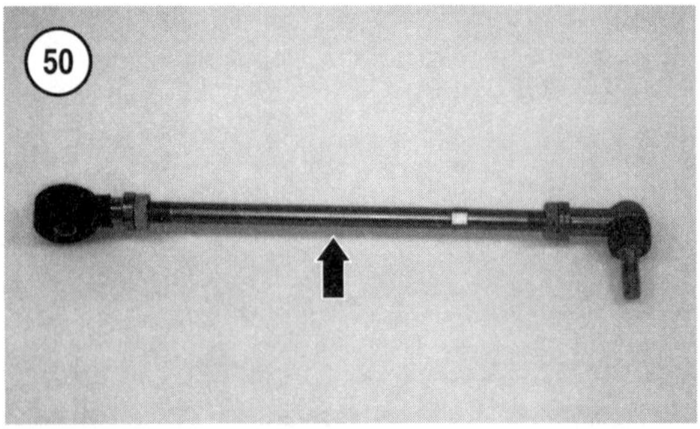

Inspection

NOTE
When cleaning the tie rods, do not immerse the outboard end ball joint in any type of solvent that could contaminate the grease and/or damage the rubber boot.

1. Clean the tie rod and dry it thoroughly.
2. Inspect the tie rod shaft for damage. There should be no creases or bends along the shaft. Check with a straightedge placed against the tie rod shaft (**Figure 50**).
3. Inspect the rubber boot at the tie rod end. If the rubber boot is damaged, dirt and moisture can enter the swivel joint and destroy it. If the boot is damaged in any way, disassemble the tie rod and replace the boot and the tie rod end.
4. Pivot the tie rod end (A, **Figure 51**) back and forth by hand. If the tie rod end moves roughly or with excessive play, replace it.

Disassembly/Assembly

1. Prior to disassembly, lay the tie rod assembly on a piece of large paper. Draw an accurate outline around the tie rod shaft, locknuts and the fitting at each end. This will show the proper relationship of all parts and the distance between the locknuts. Carefully measure the distance between the locknuts and record this on the drawing.
2. The outboard end of the tie rod has left-hand threads. Mark the nut adjacent to the outboard tie rod end to identify it as the outboard end. Mark it with a

51

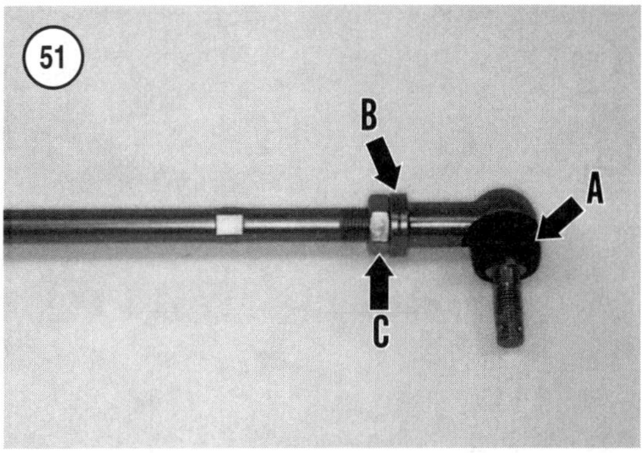

52

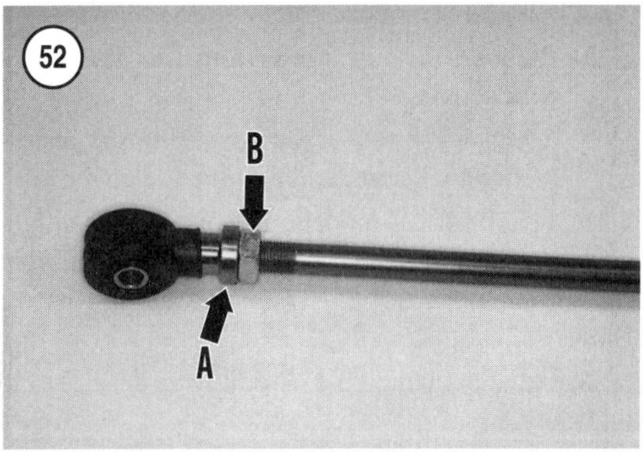

53

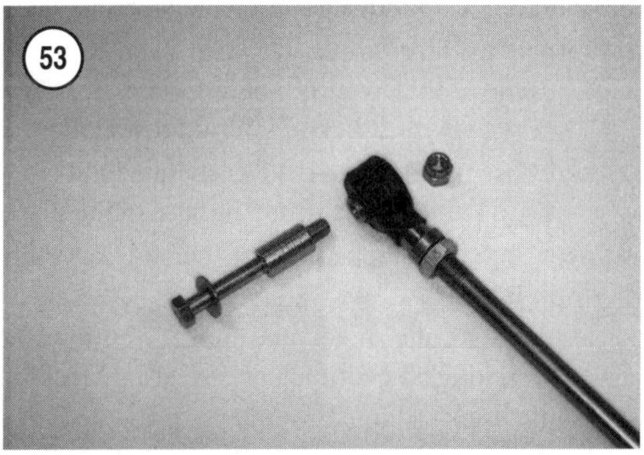

permanent marking pen, centerpunch or file mark. This end has left-hand threads and must be positioned correctly during assembly.

NOTE
The locknut on the outboard tie rod has left-hand threads and is loosened by turning it clockwise.

3. On the outboard end, hold the tie rod end (B, **Figure 51**) with one wrench and loosen the locknut (C, **Figure 51**) with a second wrench.

NOTE
The inboard tie rod locknut has right-hand threads and is loosened by turning it counterclockwise.

4. On the inboard end, hold the tie rod end (A, **Figure 52**) with one wrench and loosen the locknut (B, **Figure 52**) with a second wrench.
5. Loosen the locknut(s), unscrew and remove the damaged tie rod end(s).
6. Thoroughly clean the threaded ends of the shaft and threads in the tie rod end.
7. Thread the locknuts onto the correct end of the tie rod shaft.
8. Thread the fittings onto the correct end of the tie rod shaft. Thread the fittings on approximately the same distance as noted in Step 1. Do not tighten the locknuts until the toe-out is adjusted as described in *Front Wheel Toe-out* in Chapter Three.

Installation

WARNING
It is important to install the tie rods with the ends facing the correct direction so the tie rods and ends will not interfere with any other parts.

1A. Install the *left side* inboard end of the tie rod end (D, **Figure 48**), onto the steering shaft as follows:
  a. Separate the bolt, spacer and nut (**Figure 53**).
  b. Install the inboard end of the tie rod end (D, **Figure 48**), onto the lower surface of the steering shaft.
  c. Correctly position the spacer (B, **Figure 48**) between the two plates on the base of the steering shaft.
  d. Install the bolt (C, **Figure 48**) up from the bottom going through the tie rod fitting, the lower plate, the spacer and the upper plate. Hold the bolt in position and install the *new* self-locking nut (A, **Figure 48**). Tighten the nut finger-tight at this time.

1B. Install the *right side* inner tie rod end onto the steering shaft plate as follows:
  a. Separate the bolt and nut.
  b. Correctly position the tie rod fitting between both steering shaft plates, then install the bolt (B, **Figure 49**) up from the bottom going through the lower plate, the tie rod fitting and the upper plate. Hold the bolt in position and

12

install the *new* self-locking nut (A, **Figure 49**). Tighten the nut finger-tight at this time.

2. Install the outboard end of the tie rod end, equipped with a threaded stud, onto the steering arm portion of the strut support as follows:
   a. Place the washer (**Figure 47**) on top of the steering arm and align the bolt hole.
   b. Carefully insert the tie rod threaded stud down through the upper washer and the steering arm portion of the strut support. Push it down until it is seated.
   c. Install the lower washer and the castellated nut (**Figure 46**) onto the threaded stud.
   d. Tighten the castellated nut to the torque specification listed in **Table 2**.
   e. Install a *new* cotter pin and bend the ends over completely as shown in **Figure 44**. If the cotter pin holes do not align, slightly tighten the nut—do not loosen it to achieve alignment.
3. Tighten the self-locking nut, installed in Step 1 to the torque specification listed in **Table 2**.
4. Install the front fender as described in Chapter Fifteen.
5. Install the front wheels as described in this chapter.
6. Check the front wheel toe-out and adjust as necessary before tightening the locknuts against the tie rod ends. Measure toe-out as described in Chapter Three.

STEERING SHAFT

The steering shaft pivots on a split bushing block at the top and a bushing block at the lower end. Adjustable tie rods connect the steering shaft to the steering arm portion of the front strut.

Removal/Installation

Refer to **Figure 42**.

1. Remove the front fender assembly as described in Chapter Fifteen.
2. Remove the fuel tank as described in Chapter Six.
3. Remove both front wheels as described in this chapter.
4. Remove the inboard ends of both tie rods from the two plates on the base of the steering post. Support the inboard ends of the tie rods to the chassis with bungee cords or wire.

54

5A. On Xplorer models, perform the following:
   a. Remove the top cover from the instrument panel cover.
   b. Remove the two screws securing the instrument panel cover and remove the cover.

5B. On Sportsman models, remove the headlight upper pod as described under *High-Beam Headlight (Sportsman Models), Bulb Replacement* in Chapter Eleven.

6. Remove the handlebar assembly as described in this chapter.
7. Unscrew and remove the grease fitting.
8. Working at the lower end of the steering shaft, perform the following:
   a. Remove the cotter pin and discard it. A new cotter pin must be used during installation.
   b. Loosen then remove the castellated nut (**Figure 54**) and washer from the base of the shaft.
9. Working at the upper end of the steering shaft, perform the following:
   a. Remove the bolts and nuts securing the mounting bracket and upper bearing blocks to the frame section.
   b. Remove the mounting bracket, the upper bearing blocks and the strap at the back side of the rear bearing block.
10. Carefully lift the steering shaft from the frame. Do not snag any electrical wires or hoses during removal.
11. Install the steering shaft by reversing the removal procedure while noting the following:
   a. Tighten the castellated nut securely.
   b. Install a *new* cotter pin and bend the ends over completely as shown in **Figure 55**. If the cotter pin holes do not align, slightly tighten the nut—do not loosen it to achieve alignment.

55

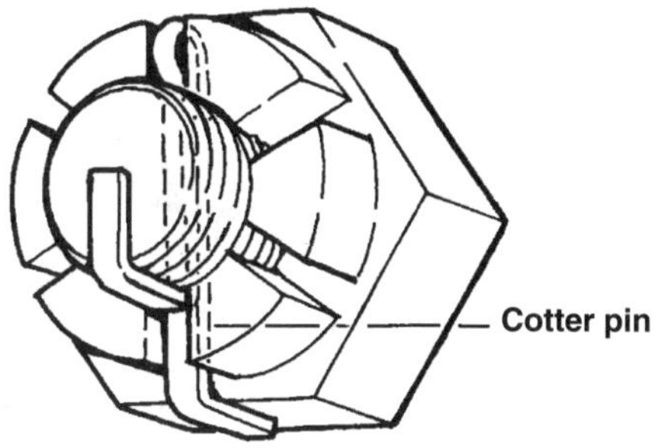

Inspection

1. Wash all parts in solvent and dry thoroughly.
2. Inspect the steering shaft carefully. Check the bushing areas of the shaft for wear. Check the shaft for being bent, especially if the vehicle has been involved in a collision or spill. If the shaft is bent or twisted in any way, it must be replaced. A bent shaft will cause rapid and excessive wear to the bushings and may stress other components in the frame and steering system. Check the shaft between V-blocks.
3. Inspect the tie rod attachment holes in the two plates on the base of the steering shaft. Check the hole(s) for elongation, cracks or wear. Check the two steering shaft plates for bending. Replace the steering shaft if necessary.
4. Inspect the upper bushing blocks for the following:
   a. Worn or damaged bearing block halves.
   b. Bent or damaged bolts or clamps.
5. Inspect the lower steering shaft threads. If severely scored or damaged, replace the steering shaft and the bushing assembly.
6. Inspect the steering shaft washers and bushing assembly. If the bushing is severely worn or damaged, replace the bushing block as described in this chapter. If the O-rings are worn, flattened, cut or swollen, replace both O-rings during re-assembly.

Steering Shaft Lower Bushing Replacement

All models are equipped with an upper bushing and lower bushing. The upper bushing is a split block as shown and the lower bushing block is riveted to the frame.

1. Remove the steering shaft from the frame as described in this chapter.
2. Drill out the rivets attaching the bushing block to the frame, and then remove the bushing block.
3. Clean the frame bushing mounting area thoroughly.
4. Install the new bushing block using new hardened rivets.
5. Complete assembly by reversing the removal procedure. Coat the bushings with grease before assembling, then grease the bushings as described in Chapter Three after assembly.

TIRES AND WHEELS

The vehicle is equipped with tubeless, low-pressure tires designed specifically for off-road use only. Rapid tire wear will occur if riding the vehicle on paved surfaces. Due to their low-pressure requirements, use a hand-operated air pump to inflate instead of an air compressor.

CAUTION
Do not overinflate the tires, as they will be permanently distorted and damaged.

NOTE
Additional inflation pressure in the original equipment tires will not improve the ride or handling characteristics of the vehicle.

Tire Changing

The front and rear tire rims used on all models have a deep built-in ridge (**Figure 56**) to keep the tire bead seated on the rim under severe riding conditions. This feature also tends to keep the tire on the rim during tire removal.

A special tool is required for tire changing on these models. A typical tool is shown in **Figure 57**.

1. Mark the tire with an arrow indicating the direction of forward rotation. Also mark the tire and wheel to indicate its location on the vehicle.
2. Remove the valve stem cap and core and deflate the tire. Do not reinstall the core at this time.
3. Lubricate the tire bead and rim flanges with a liquid dish washing detergent or a rubber lubricant.

12

Press the tire sidewall/bead down to allow the liquid to run into and around the bead area. Also apply lubricant to the area where the bead breaker arm will come in contact with the tire sidewall.

4. Position the wheel in the bead breaker.

5. Slowly work the tire tool, making sure the tool is against the inside of the rim, and break the tire bead away from the rim (**Figure 58**).

6. Use both hands to press down on the tire on each side of the tool and break the rest of the bead free from the rim.

NOTE
If the rest of the tire bead cannot be broken loose, raise the tool, rotate the tire/rim assembly and repeat Steps 4 and 5 until the entire bead is broken loose from the rim.

7. Turn the wheel over and repeat Steps 4-6 to break the bead loose from the opposite side.

8. Remove the tire from the rim using tire irons (**Figure 59**).

9. Clean the rims and tire sealing surfaces.

10. Inspect the tire sealing surface on both sides of the rim (**Figure 60**). If the rim is bent, it may leak air. Repair or replace the rim as required.

11. Inspect the tire for cuts, tears, abrasions or any other defects.

12. To replace the valve stem, perform the following:

a. Support the rim and pull the old valve stem out of the rim. Discard the old valve stem.
b. Clean the valve stem hole in the rim.
c. Lubricate the new valve stem with tire lubricant.
d. Pull the new valve stem into the rim from the inside out, until it snaps into place (**Figure 61**).

13. Apply clean water to the rim flanges, tire beads and on the outer flange of the rim. Make sure the rim flange is clean. Wipe with a lint-free cloth.

CAUTION
Do not coat the tire beads nor the rim with any tire mounting lubricant or a liquid dish washing detergent. These solutions will leave a slippery residue on the tire that can allow the tire to slip on the rim, causing air pressure loss.

56

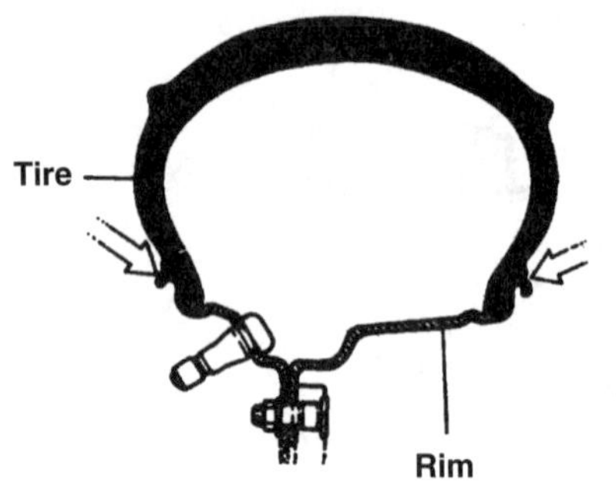

57

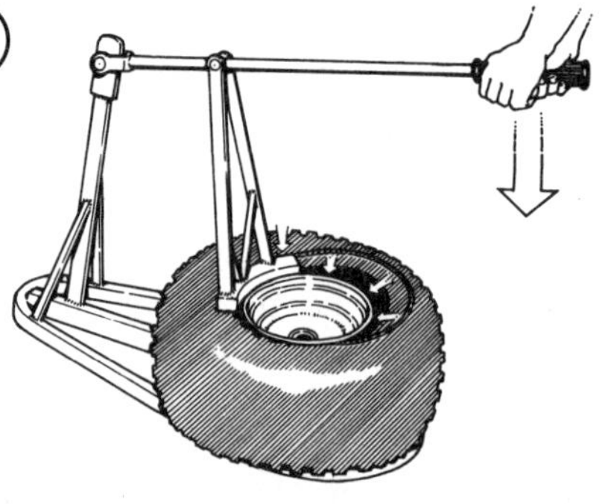

58

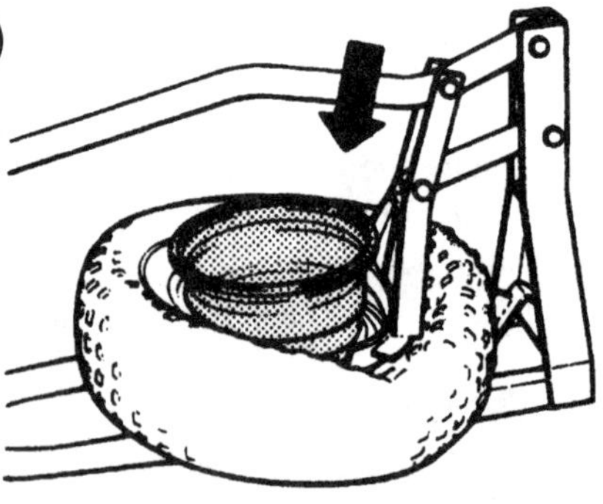

59

TIRE REMOVAL

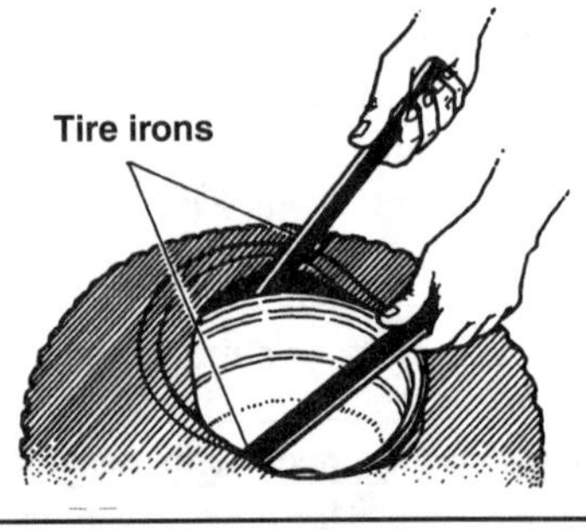

60 RIM INSPECTION

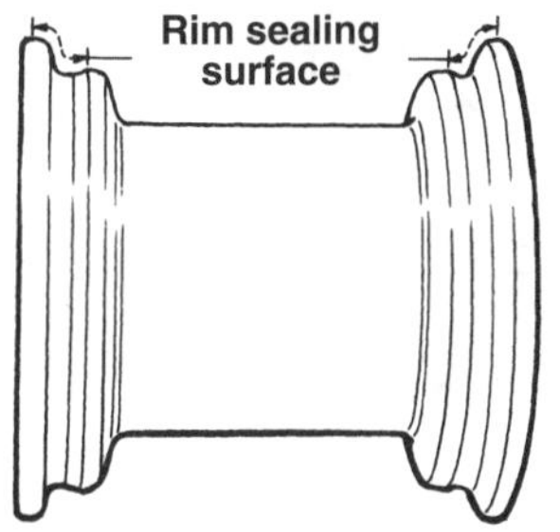

61 VALVE INSTALLATION

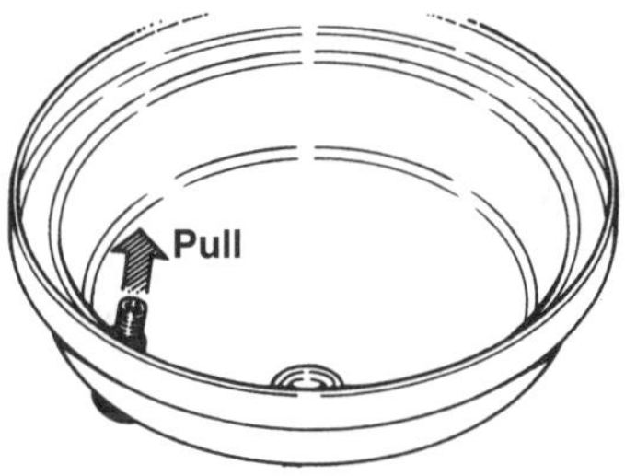

62 TIRE INSTALLATION

63

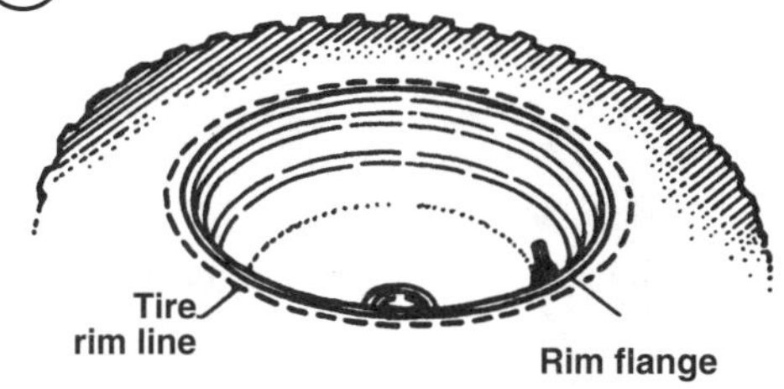

14. Position the rim on the floor with the outside flange up.
15. Position the tire so the directional arrow on the tire points toward the direction of rotation while the vehicle is moving forward.
16. Start the inside bead of the tire onto the outside of the rim.
17. Press the inside bead of the tire onto the rim with both hands (**Figure 62**).
18. Press the outside bead onto the tire in a similar manner.
19. Apply water to both beads and inflate the tire to the pressure value listed in **Table 3**.
20. Deflate the tire and let it sit for approximately one hour.
21. Inflate the tire to the recommended air pressure. Refer to **Table 3**.
22. Check the rim line (**Figure 63**) molded into the tire around the edge of the rim. It must be equally spaced all the way around. If the rim line spacing is not equal, the tire bead is not properly seated. Deflate the tire and unseat the bead completely. Lubricate the bead and re-inflate the tire.
23. Check for air leaks and install the valve cap.

Cold Patch Repair

This is the preferred method to patch a tire. The rubber plug-type of repair is recommended only for an emergency repair, or until the tire can be patched correctly with the cold patch method.

Follow the manufacturer's instructions for the tire repair kit to be used. If there are no instructions, use the following procedure.

1. Remove the tire from the wheel as described in this chapter.
2. Prior to removing the object that punctured the tire, mark the location of the puncture with chalk or crayon on the outside of the tire, then remove the object (**Figure 64**).
3. On the inside of the tire, roughen the area around the hole slightly larger than the patch (**Figure 65**). Use the cap from the tire repair kit, a pocketknife or coarse sandpaper. Do not scrape vigorously, as this will cause additional damage.
4. Clean the area with a nonflammable solvent. Do not use an oil-based solvent, as it will leave a residue and render the patch useless.
5. Apply a small amount of the special cement to the puncture and spread it with a finger.

12

64

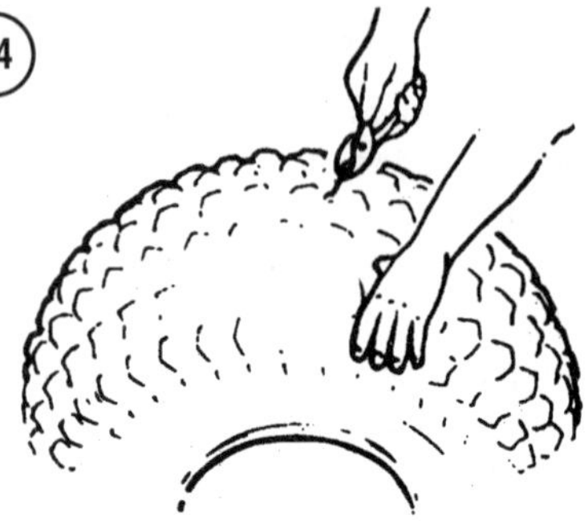

65

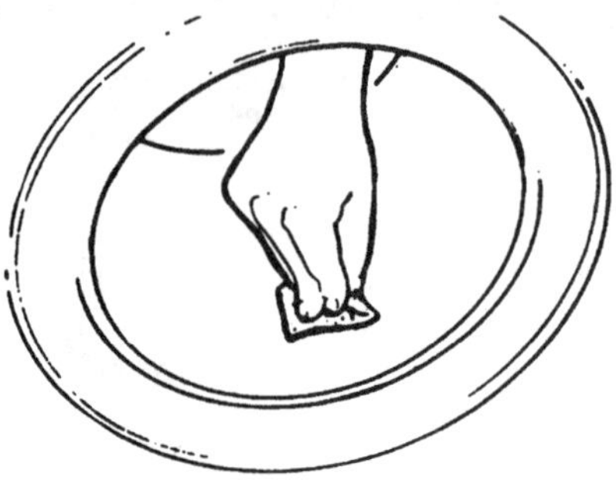

6. Allow the cement to dry until tacky—usually 30 seconds or so is sufficient.
7. Remove the backing from the patch.

CAUTION
Do not touch the newly exposed rubber or the patch will not stick firmly.

8. Center the patch over the hole. Hold the patch firmly in place for about 30 seconds to allow the cement to dry. If available, use a roller to help press the patch into place (**Figure 66**).
9. Dust the area with talcum powder.

66

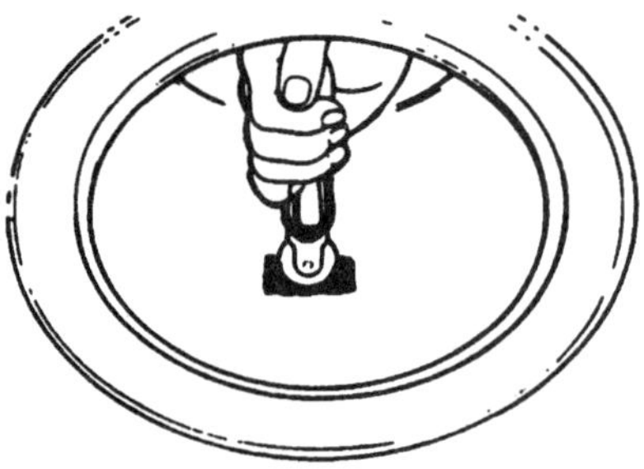

Table 1 FRONT SUSPENSION SPECIFICATIONS

Item	Specification
Independent MacPherson strut front suspension	
Turning radius unloaded	165 cm (65 in.)
Front strut travel	15.87 cm (6.25 in.)

Table 2 FRONT SUSPENSION TORQUE SPECIFICATIONS

Item	N•m	in.-lb.	ft.-lb.
Front wheel lug nuts	20	–	15
Front strut			
Top mounting nut	20	–	15
Strut pinch bolt nuts	20	–	15
Ball joint bracket bolts	11	97	–
Control arm			
Mounting bolts	41	–	30
Ball joint stud nut	34	–	25
Handlebar upper holder bolts	13-17	–	10-13
Tie rod			
Jam nut	16-19	–	12-14
Castellated nut	33	–	24
Inboard end mounting bolt and nut	35-41	–	25-30

Table 3 TIRE INFLATION PRESSURE (COLD)*

Model	kPa	PSI
Front wheels	34.5	5
Rear wheels	34.5	5

*Tire pressure for original equipment tires. After market tires may require different inflation pressure.

NOTE: Refer to the Supplement at the back of this manual for information unique to 2001-on models, including the Sportsman 400.

CHAPTER THIRTEEN

REAR SUSPENSION

This chapter contains repair and replacement procedures for the rear wheel, rear hub and independent rear suspension components. Service to the rear suspension consists of periodically checking bolt tightness, replacing the control arm bushings and servicing the rear spring/shock unit.

Torque specifications are listed in **Table 2**. **Table 1** and **Table 2** are located at the end of this chapter.

NOTE

The majority of the nuts used in the rear suspension are of the self-locking type. These nuts must be replaced every time they are removed, as they have lost their locking ability during removal. If reinstalled, they will not secure the bolt to the correct tightening torque specification.

WARNING

The majority of the procedures in this chapter specify the removal of the rear rack and rear fender. After the rear fender is removed, the rear rack support ends are exposed on each side and present a dangerous protrusion during additional component removal and installation. For protection, wrap several brightly colored shop cloths around each end as shown in ***Figure 1****.*

REAR WHEELS

Removal/Installation

1. Place the vehicle on level ground and set the parking brake. Block the front wheels so the vehicle will not roll in either direction.

2. Shift the transmission into NEUTRAL.

3. Mark the rear tires with an L (left side) or R (right side) so that they will be installed onto the same side of the vehicle from which they were removed. If the tire is to be removed from the rim, also mark the tire

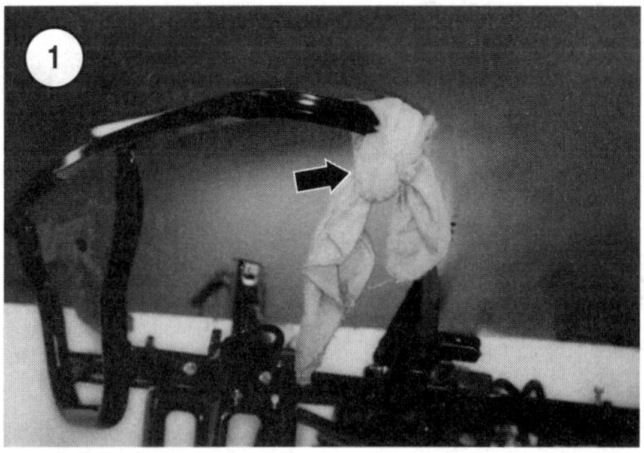

and the wheel with an arrow indicating the direction of rotation when traveling forward.
4. Loosen but do not remove the four lug nuts (**Figure 2**) securing the wheel to the rear hub.
5. Raise the rear of the vehicle with a small hydraulic or scissor jack. Place the jack under the frame with a piece of wood between the jack and the frame.
6. Place block(s) under the frame to support the vehicle securely with the rear wheels off the ground.
7. Remove the four wheel lug nuts, loosened in Step 4, and remove the rear wheel.
8. Clean the lug nuts in solvent and dry thoroughly.
9. Inspect the wheel for cracks, bending or other damage. If damage is severe, replace the wheel as described under *Tires and Wheels* in Chapter Twelve.

NOTE
Install the lug nuts with their shoulder side facing toward the wheel. This is necessary to correctly center the wheel on the rear hub.

10. Install the wheel onto the hub and install the lug nuts (**Figure 2**). Finger-tighten the lug nuts until the wheel is positioned squarely against the rear hub.

WARNING
Always tighten the lug nuts to the correct torque specification or the nuts may work loose.

11. Use a torque wrench and tighten the lug nuts in a crisscross pattern to the torque specification listed in **Table 2**.

NOTE
In Step 12, make sure both rear wheels are off the ground prior to rotating the wheel.

12. After the wheel is installed, rotate it and apply the rear brake several times to make sure that the wheel rotates freely and that the brake is operating correctly.
13. Lower the vehicle to the ground and recheck the torque on the lug nuts.
14. Test ride the vehicle slowly to make sure the rear wheels are installed correctly.

TIRE CHANGING AND TIRE REPAIRS

Refer to Chapter Twelve for tire service.

SHOCK ABSORBER

Removal/Installation

1. Remove the rear fender as described in Chapter Fifteen.

NOTE
It is not necessary to remove the rear wheel, but it does provide additional working room.

2A. Remove the rear wheel(s) as described in this chapter.
2B. Lift the rear of the vehicle off the ground. Block the rear portion of the frame, so that both rear wheels are off the ground and that there is no weight on the rear suspension arms. This will result in no pressure on the shock absorber.
3. Remove the bolt and self-locking nut (**Figure 3**) securing the lower end of the shock absorber to the lower control arm. Discard the self-locking nut.
4. Hold onto the shock absorber and remove the bolt and self-locking nut (A, **Figure 4**) securing the upper end of the shock absorber to the frame.

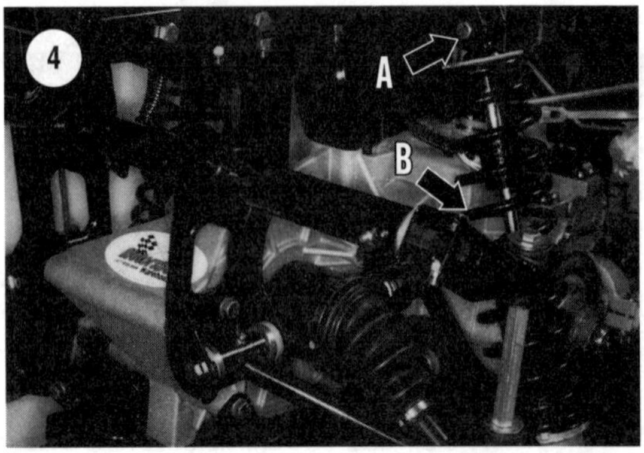

5. Remove the shock absorber (B, **Figure 4**) from the frame.
6. Install by reversing these steps while noting the following:
   a. Clean the shock mounting bolts with solvent and dry thoroughly.
   b. Install *new* nuts. Tighten the mounting bolts and nuts to the torque specification listed in **Table 2**.

Shock Inspection

If an aftermarket shock absorber has been installed, inspect it and service it according to the manufacturer's instructions.

1. Inspect the damper unit (A, **Figure 5**) for oil leakage and make sure the damper rod (B, **Figure 5**) is straight. Also inspect the rod for rust or other damage.
2. Inspect the upper (**Figure 6**) and lower (A, **Figure 7**) rubber pivot bushings for wear or deterioration. If damaged, replace the shock absorber.
3. If necessary, remove and inspect the spring as described in the following procedure.

Spring Removal/Installation

1. Remove the shock absorber as described in this chapter.
2. Measure and record the spring preload position before removing the spring.
3. Rotate the spring preload adjuster (B, **Figure 7**) to the softest setting.
4. Install the shock absorber into a shock absorber spring compressor following the manufacturer's instructions.

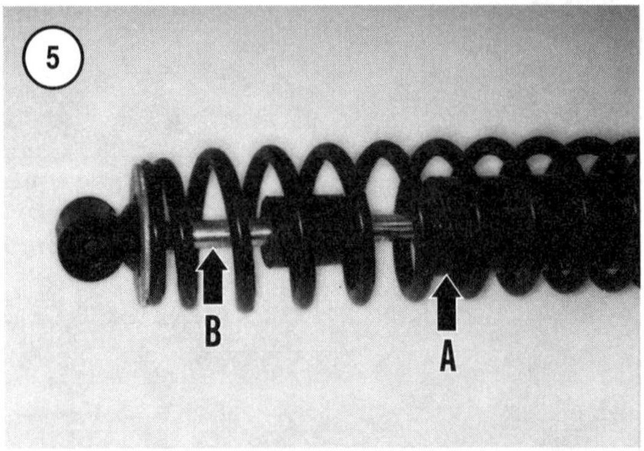

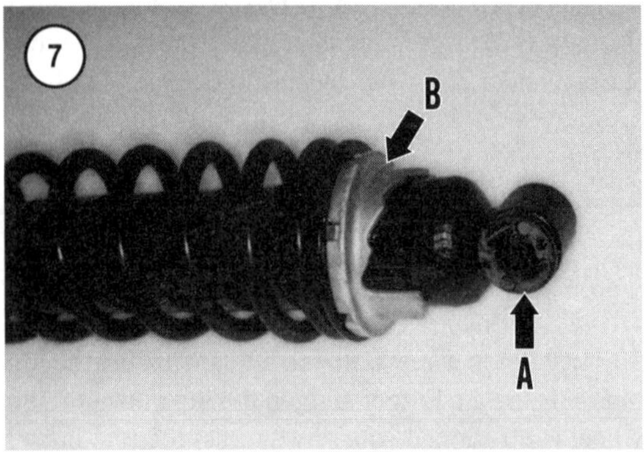

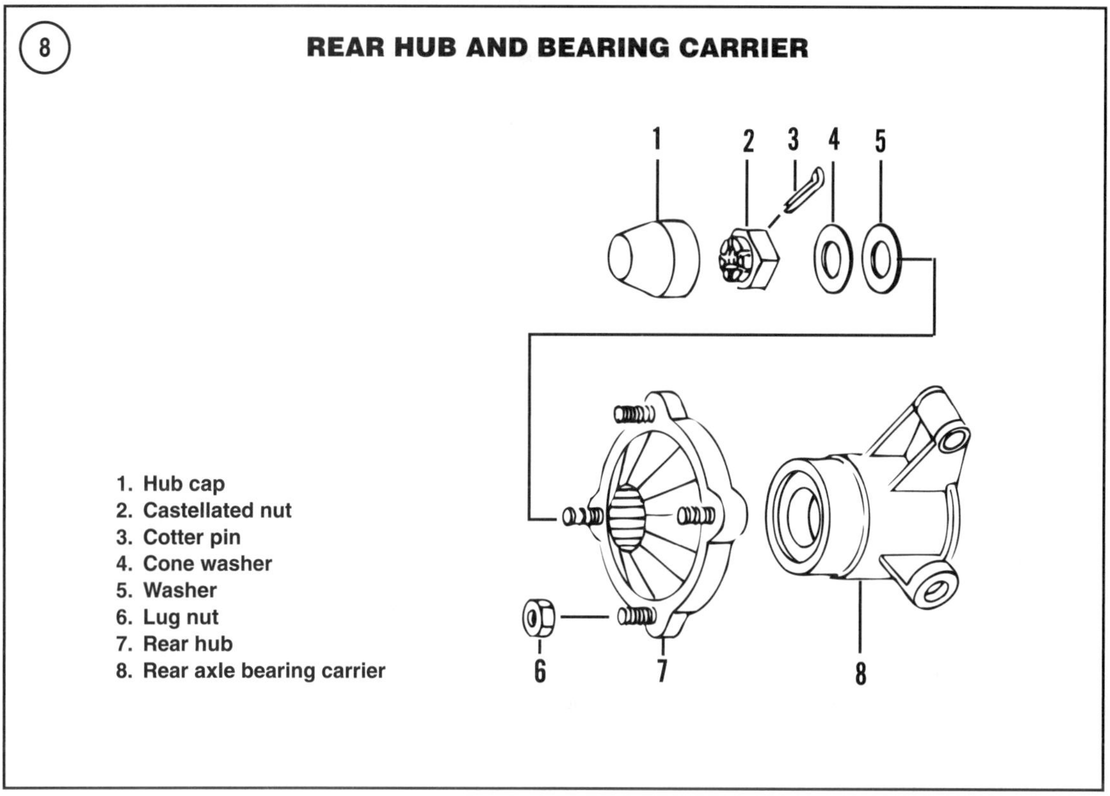

5. Compress the spring and remove the spring retainer from the top of the shock.

6. Reinstall the spring by reversing these steps. Adjust the spring preload to the previous setting.

REAR HUB AND BEARING CARRIER

Removal

Refer to **Figure 8** and **Figure 9**.

1. Park the vehicle on level ground and set the parking brake. Block the front wheels so the vehicle will not roll in either direction.
2. Raise the rear of the vehicle with a small hydraulic or scissor jack. Place the jack under the frame with a piece of wood between the jack and the frame.
3. Place block(s) under the frame to support the vehicle securely with the rear wheels off the ground.
4. Remove the rear wheel(s) as described in this chapter.
5. Remove the hub cap (**Figure 10**).
6. Remove the cotter pin (**Figure 11**) and discard it. A new cotter pin must be installed.
7. Loosen, but do not remove the castellated nut (**Figure 12**) on the rear axle.
8. Remove the castellated axle nut and the conical washers (**Figure 13**) from the axle.

NOTE
It may be necessary to use a wheel puller to remove the rear hub from the end of the rear axle.

9. Remove the rear hub (**Figure 14**) from the rear axle.
10. Remove the bolt (A, **Figure 15**) and self-locking nut (B, **Figure 15**) securing the upper control arm to the rear axle bearing carrier.
11. Remove the bolt and two washers (**Figure 16**) securing the lower control arm to the rear axle bearing carrier hub on both sides.
12. Hold onto the drive axle and withdraw the rear hub (**Figure 17**) from the drive axle.

NOTE
The rear axle is held in place and will not slide out of the transmission.

(9)

REAR SUSPENSION

1. Bolt
2. Washer
3. Stabilizer arm bracket
4. Nut, self-locking
5. Bushing
6. Stabilizer linkage rod
7. Stabilizer support
8. Washer
9. Bushing
10. Mounting bracket
11. Bushing
12. Bushing
13. Upper control arm
14. Frame mounting bracket
15. Grease fitting
16. Rear axle bearing carrier
17. Lower control arm
18. Bushing
19. Bearing carrier bushing
20. Washer
21. Bushing

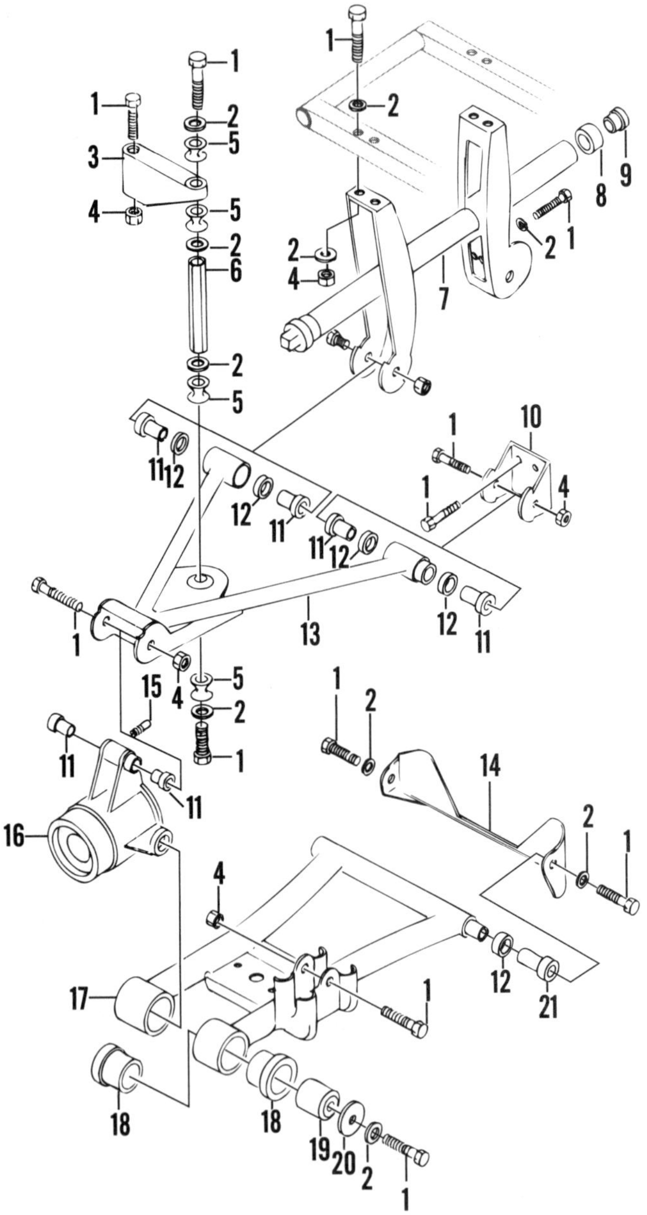

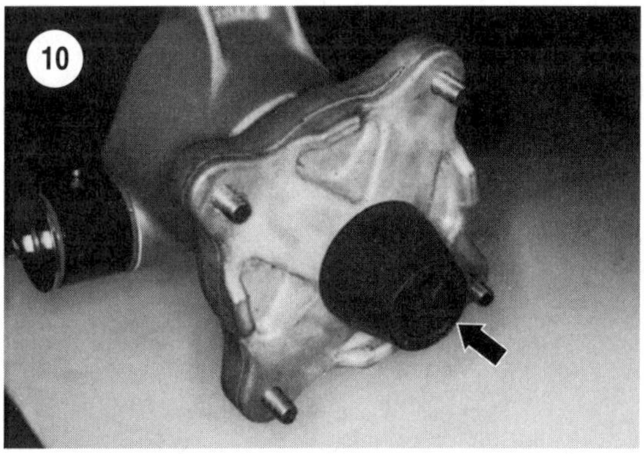
10

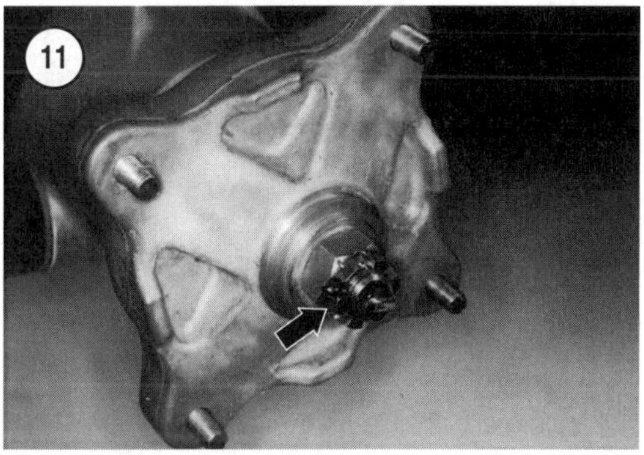
11

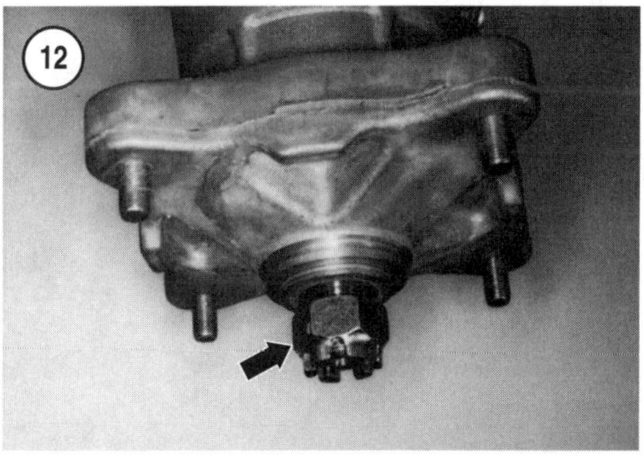
12

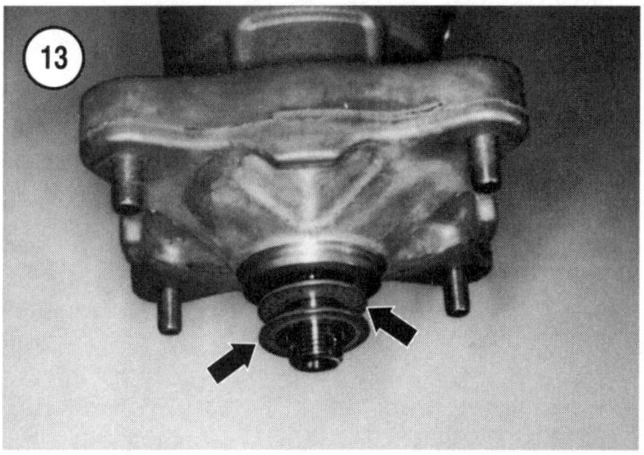
13

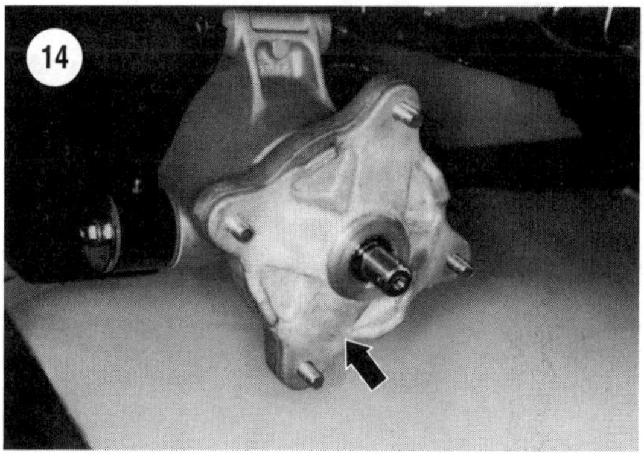
14

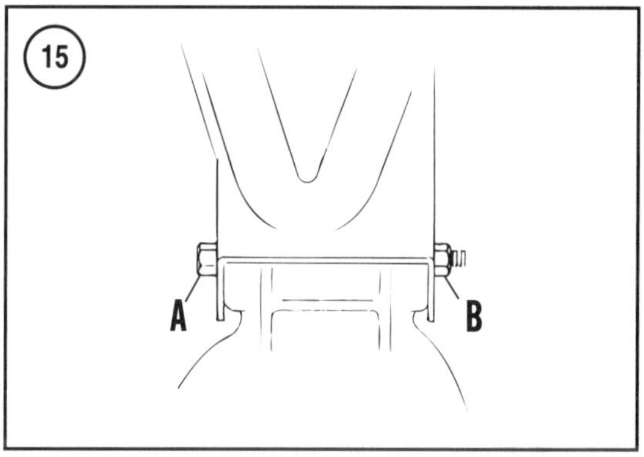
15
A
B

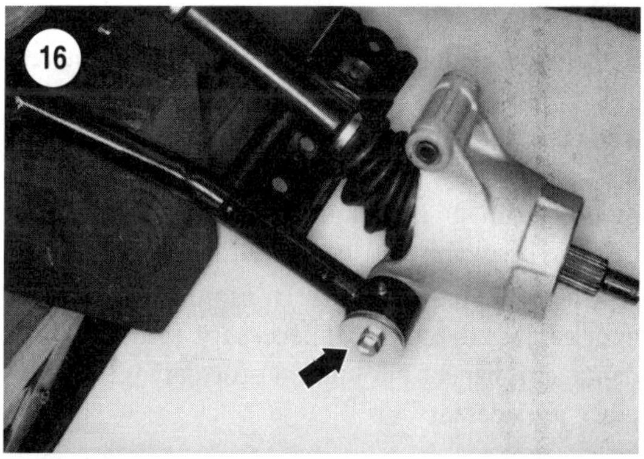
16

17

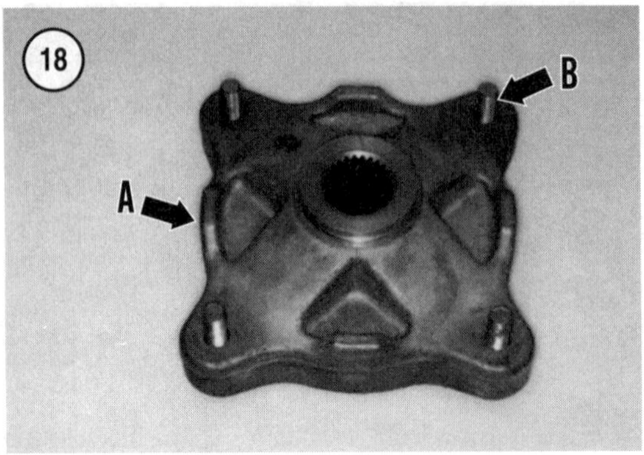

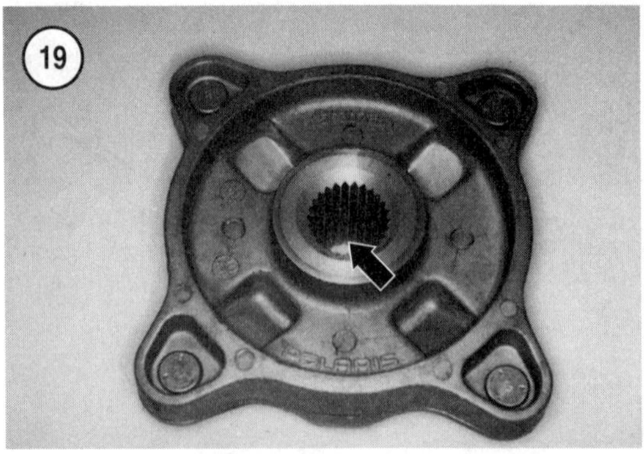

13. Lower the outer end of the drive axle and rest it on the lower control arm.
14. Inspect the rear hub and bearing carrier as described in this chapter.

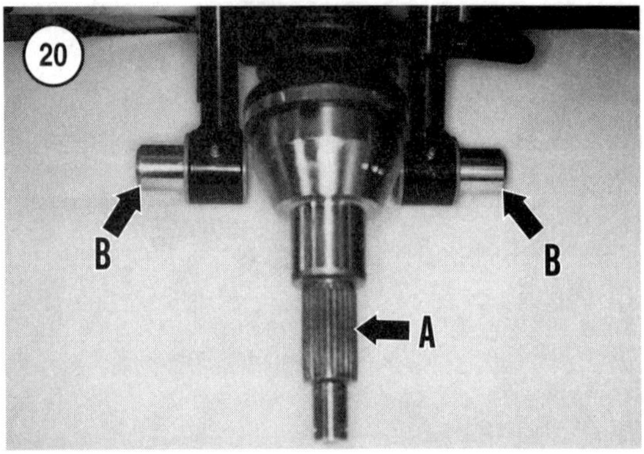

Inspection

Rear hub

1. Clean the rear hub and the end of the rear axle with solvent and dry thoroughly.
2. Inspect the rear hub (A, **Figure 18**) for cracks or other damage. If damage is severe, replace the hub.
3. Inspect the hub splines (**Figure 19**) and the rear axle splines (A, **Figure 20**) for wear or damage. Slide the rear hub onto the rear axle and try to rotate it. It should be a tight fit with no rotational movement. If damage is minor, clean it up with a file. If damage is severe, replace the damaged part(s).
4. Check the lug nut studs (B, **Figure 18**) for damage. Replace the stud(s) if necessary. If the studs are damaged, inspect the lug nuts for damage and replace as necessary.

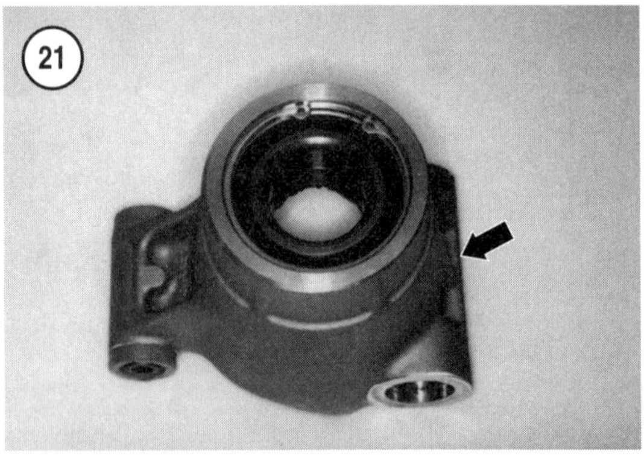

Rear axle bearing carrier

1. Inspect the exterior of the rear axle bearing carrier (**Figure 21**) for cracks or damage. Replace if necessary.
2. Turn the inner race of the bearing (A, **Figure 22**) by hand. Make sure the bearing turns smoothly without excessive play or noise. Replace the bearing if damaged, replace it as described in this chapter.
3. Make sure the circlip (B, **Figure 22**) securing the bearing is secure in the carrier groove.

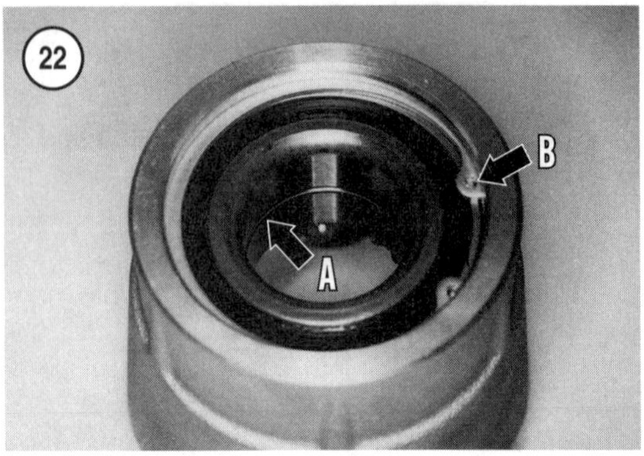

23

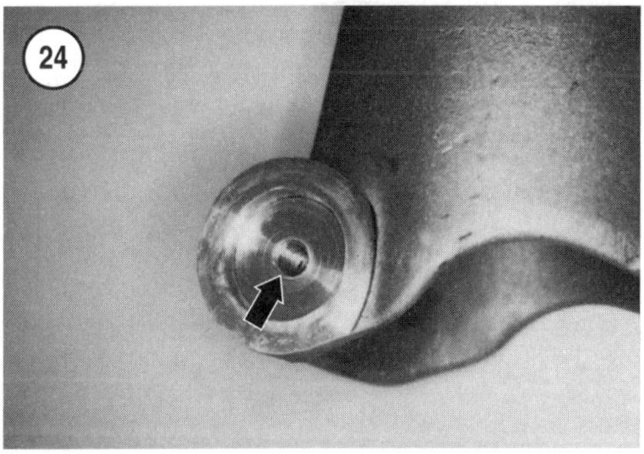
24

25

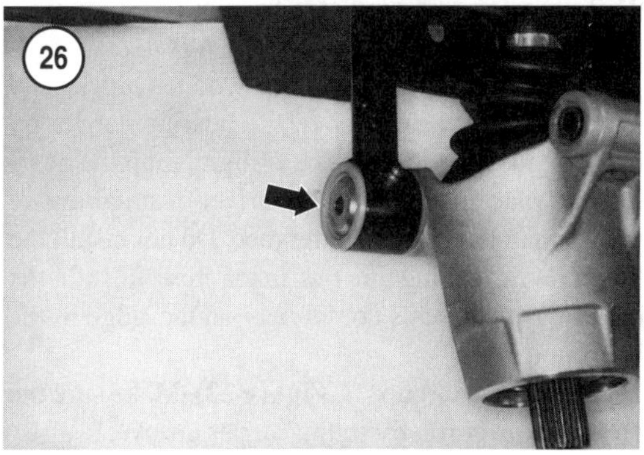
26

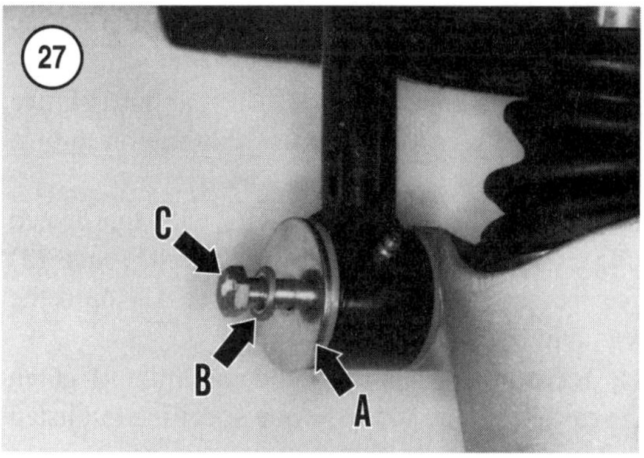

27

4. Check the bushings (**Figure 23**) where the carrier is attached to the upper control arm. Replace the bushings if necessary.
5. Inspect the internal threads (**Figure 24**) for wear or damage where the carrier is attached to the lower control arm. If damage is minimal, clean the threads with a metric tap. If damage is severe, replace the rear axle bearing carrier.
6. Make sure the grease fitting (**Figure 25**) is clear. Remove and clean out if necessary.

Installation

1. Apply a light coat of all-purpose grease to the inner race of the bearing and to the rear axle shaft where the bearing rides.
2. Make sure the inner bushings (B, **Figure 20**) are in place on the lower control arm. Apply a light coat of grease to the outer surfaces of the bushings.
3. Install the rear axle bearing carrier onto the rear axle and push it on until it stops.
4. Install the rear axle bearing carrier onto the lower control arm.
5. Push the bushings in until they bottom (**Figure 26**) against the rear axle bearing carrier and align the bolt holes.
6. Install a large washer (A, **Figure 27**), then a smaller washer (B, **Figure 27**) and bolt (C, **Figure 27**) through the lower control arm and into the rear axle bearing carrier. Repeat for the other side of the lower control arm. Tighten the bolts securely at this time.
7. Move the rear axle bearing carrier up into position on the upper control arm. Insert the bolt from the rear and install a *new* nut. Tighten the nut securely at this time.
8. Make sure the rear axle bearing carrier is correctly seated within both the upper and lower con-

13

trol arms. Tighten the bolts and nut to the torque specification listed in **Table 2**.

9. Align the splines and install the rear hub (**Figure 14**) onto the rear axle. Tap the rear hub on until it bottoms.

10. Position the conical washers with the dished side facing out and install the washers (**Figure 13**) and the castellated axle nut (**Figure 12**) onto the rear axle.

11. Have an assistant apply the rear brake. Tighten the castellated nut to the torque specification listed in **Table 2**.

12. Verify that one pair of openings in the castellated nut is aligned with the cotter pin hole in the rear axle. If not, align opening by tightening the axle nut. Do not loosen the axle nut to align the openings.

WARNING
Always install a new cotter pin.

13. Insert the *new* cotter pin through the openings in the castellated nut and rear axle hole. Bend the end of the cotter pin over completely (**Figure 28**).

14. Install the hub cap (**Figure 10**). Make sure it is seated correctly within the rear wheel.

15. Install the rear wheel(s) as described in this chapter.

Rear Axle Bearing Carrier Bearing Replacement

1. Remove the rear axle bearing carrier as described in this chapter.

2. Remove the circlip (B, **Figure 22**).

3. Turn the bearing carrier over and place it on wooden blocks.

4. Using an appropriate size drift placed in the relief (**Figure 29**), carefully tap on the perimeter of the outer race and remove the bearing from the bearing carrier.

5. Inspect the bearing carrier for burrs, wear or damage.

6. Clean out the bearing receptacle in the carrier.

7. Place the new bearing in a freezer. Chilling it slightly reduces the outer diameter of the bearing while heating the bearing carrier expands the bearing receptacle in the carrier.

8. Heat the bearing carrier to approximately 212° F (100° C) in a shop oven or on a hot plate.

28

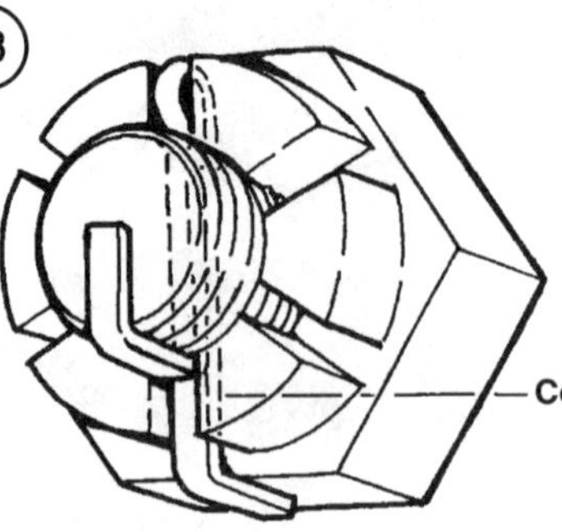

29

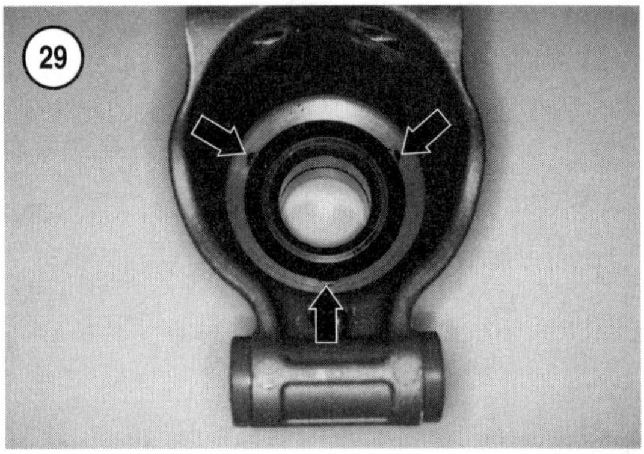

30

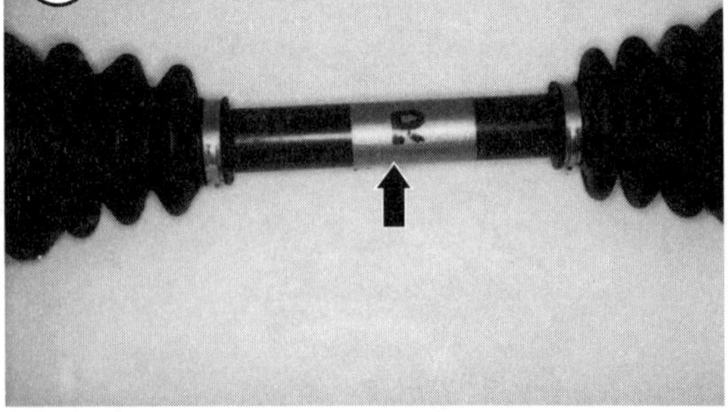

9. Remove the bearing carrier from the shop oven or hot plate with welders gloves—*it is hot.*

10. Place the bearing carrier on wooden blocks and install the new bearing into the bearing carrier by hand, if possible. If necessary, slightly tap the bearing into place using a bearing driver or suitable size socket that matches the outer race. Do not install the bearing by driving on the inner race. Install the bearing until it seats completely on the ridge in the bearing carrier.

11. Install the circlip (B, **Figure 22**). Make sure the circlip seats correctly in the carrier groove.

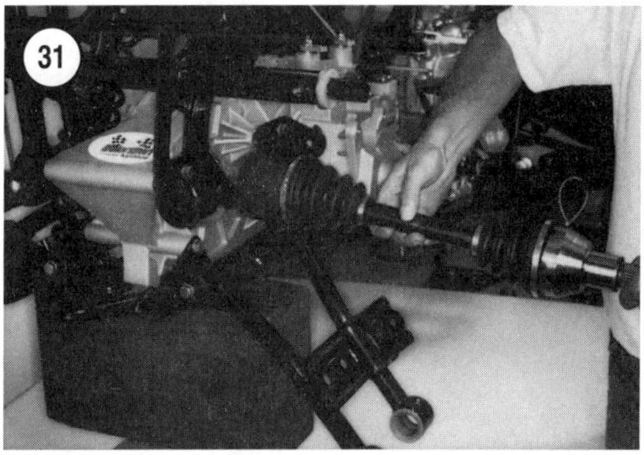

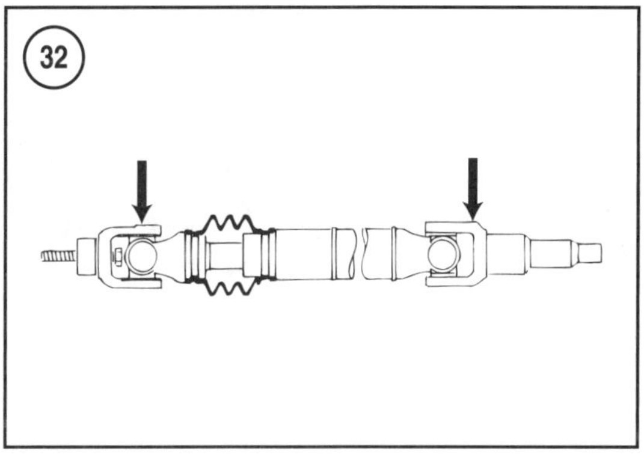

12. Install the rear axle bearing carrier as described in this chapter.

REAR AXLES

Refer to **Figure 9**.

Removal

1. Place the vehicle on a level surface and block the front wheels so the vehicle cannot roll in any direction.
2. Remove the rear hub and the rear axle bearing carrier as described in this chapter.
3. Prior to removing the rear axle(s), mark them with a R (right side) (**Figure 30**) or L (left side) so they will be reinstalled on the same side.
4A. On 1996-1998 models, perform the following:

NOTE
The internal threaded spacer will usually remain with the right side rear axle. It may remain attached to either rear axle during this procedure. Be sure to remove the spacer when removing both rear axles and make sure it is correctly secured to one of the axles during installation.

NOTE
The 9/16 in. bolts are secured to the internal threaded spacer with a threadlocking compound and may be difficult to loosen.

a. Use a 9/16 in. open end wrench and loosen the attachment bolt securing the inner universal joint to the internal threaded spacer located within the transmission output gear.
b. Hold onto the rear axle, slowly pull the rear axle out of the transmission while loosening the bolt.
c. Remove the rear axle from the transmission and frame.

4B. On 1999-on models, perform the following:

a. Hold the rear axle straight out from the transmission (**Figure 31**).
b. Pull sharply outward on the rear axle to dislodge the inner CV joint locking ring from the transmission output gear.
c. Remove the rear axle from the transmission and frame.

5. Repeat for the other rear axle.
6. Inspect the rear axle as described in this chapter.

Inspection

1. Thoroughly clean the exterior of the rear axle(s) in solvent.

NOTE
Rubber boot replacement requires partial disassembly of the rear axle. The rear axle components must be cleaned, repacked and aligned during assembly, therefore refer this service to a Polaris dealership.

CAUTION
*On all models, it is suggested that the rubber boot(s) be replaced by a Polaris dealership. **If** the rear axle is disassembled for boot replacement on 1996-1998 models, it must be assembled correctly. During assembly, the inboard and outboard U-joint yokes **must be aligned** as shown in **Figure 32** to avoid excessive vibration.*

13

2. Inspect the rubber boot(s) (A, **Figure 33**) for hardness, tears or damage. If grease is observed on the outer surface of the boot, it has escaped through a tear or hole. Have the boot(s) replaced by a Polaris dealership.
3. Make sure the rubber boot retaining clamps (**Figure 34**) are secure. Replace if necessary.
4. Check the drive axle for damage (B, **Figure 33**).
5. Inspect the outboard rear spindle splines (A, **Figure 35**) for wear or damage. Minor damaged can be cleaned up with a fine-cut file, but if damage is severe, replace the damaged parts.
6. Inspect the spindle nut threads (B, **Figure 35**) for damage.
7A. In 1996-1998 models, perform the following:
   a. Inspect the outer universal joint for wear or damage.
   b. Inspect the threads on the bolt securing the drive axle to the internal threaded spacer. If damaged, have the bolt replaced by a Polaris dealership.
   c. Inspect the outer splines on the universal joint yoke for wear, where it attaches to the transmission output gear.
   d. Inspect the internal threaded spacer for damage, replace if necessary.
7B. On 1999-on models, perform the following:
   a. Inspect the CV joints for wear or damage.
   b. Inspect the outer splines (**Figure 36**) on the inboard CV joint for wear, where it attaches to the transmission output gear.
   c. Make sure the locking ring (**Figure 37**) is in place and secure on the CV joint splines. Do not remove the locking ring unless it is going to be replaced. Install a new ring if damaged or loose.
8. On 1996-1998 models, thoroughly clean off all threadlocking compound from the internal threaded spacer and rear axle attachment bolts.

Installation

1996-1998 models

NOTE
The internal threaded spacer must be attached to one of the rear axles prior to installation. Attach it to the right side rear axle and install the right side rear axle into the transmission first.

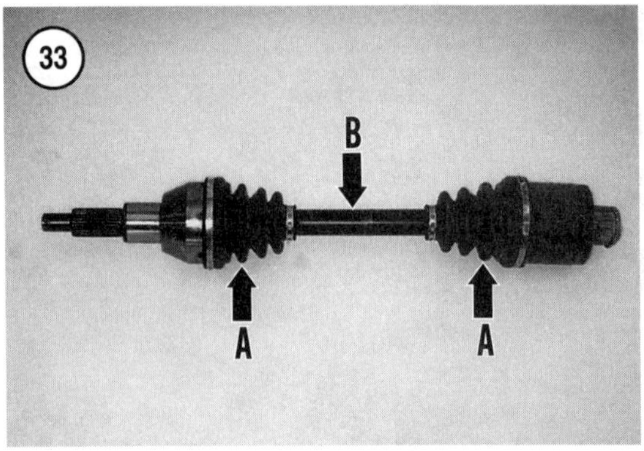

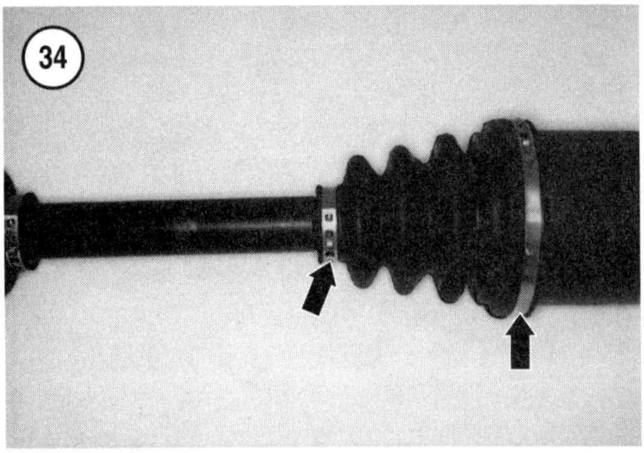

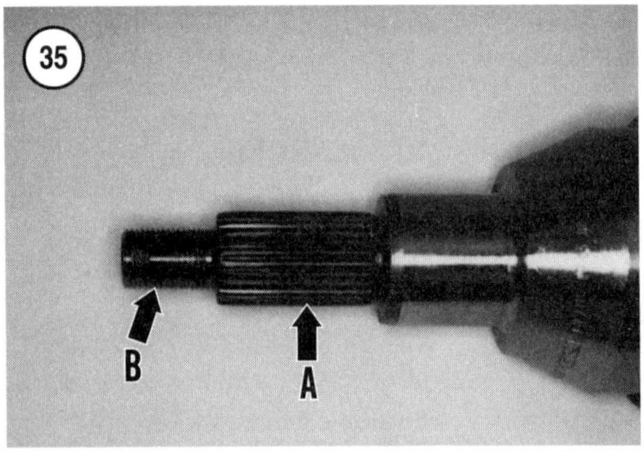

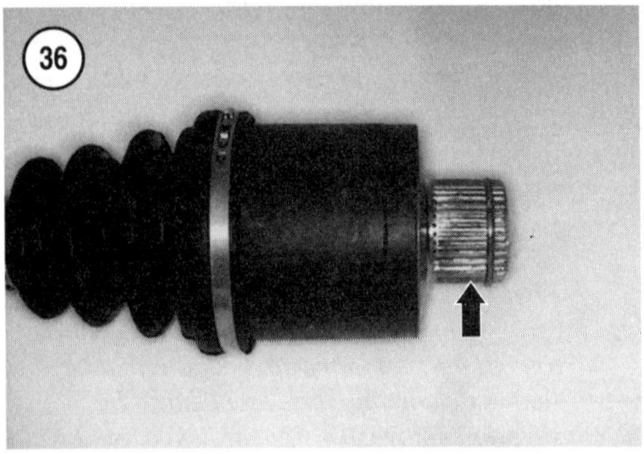

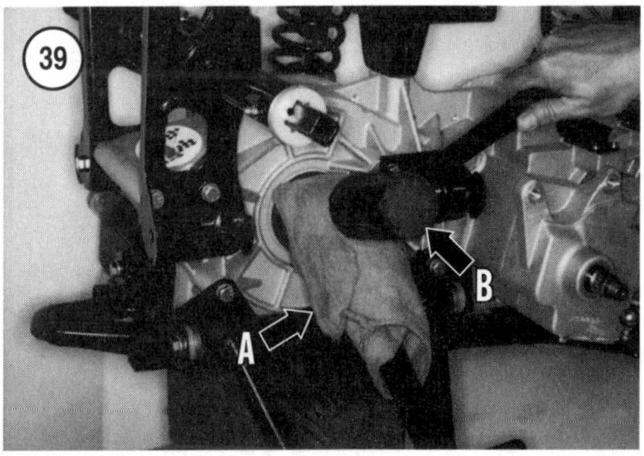

1. Apply ThreeBond TB1360, or equivalent, threadlocking compound to the right side rear axle attachment bolt and install the internal threaded spacer onto the bolt. Secure the spacer and tighten the bolt to the torque specification listed in **Table 2**.

2. Apply antiseize compound to the outer splines of the inboard U-joint.

3. Align the splines and install the right side rear axle into the transmission and secure the outboard end in its normal position.

4. Install the right side rear axle bearing carrier and rear hub as described in this chapter.

5. Apply ThreeBond TB1360, or equivalent, threadlocking compound to the left side rear axle attachment bolt.

6. Apply antiseize compound to the outer splines of the inboard U-joint.

7. Align the splines and partially install the left side rear axle into the transmission until the bolt makes contact with the internal threaded spacer. Hold the rear axle straight out and start threading the bolt into the spacer by hand while slowly pushing the axle into the transmission. Continue to hand tighten the bolt and push the rear axle into place.

8. Secure the rear axle and tighten the bolt to the torque specification listed in **Table 2**.

9. Install the left side rear axle bearing carrier and rear hub as described in this chapter.

10. Rotate the rear axles by hand to make sure they rotate freely with no binding or roughness.

1999-on models

1. Apply antiseize compound to the outer splines of the inboard CV joint of the right side rear axle. Also apply it to the transmission output gear inner splines (**Figure 38**).

CAUTION
*Do **not** tap on the end of the rear axle to install it into the transmission. The balls within the CV joints will be damaged.*

2. Align the splines and install the right side rear axle into the transmission output gear. It may be necessary to tap on the inner CV joint to aid in installation. If necessary, wrap a shop cloth (A, **Figure 39**) around the inner rubber boot. Carefully tap on the cloth and inner CV joint with a rubber mallet (B, **Figure 39**) to force the locking ring into the transmission output gear groove.

3. After the rear axle is installed, pull back on it to make sure it is correctly secured in the transmission (**Figure 31**). If the axle slides out, it was not installed correctly.

4. Install the right side rear axle bearing carrier and rear hub as described in this chapter.

5. Repeat Steps 1-4 for the left side rear axle.

6. Shift the transmission into neutral.

(40)

REAR SUSPENSION

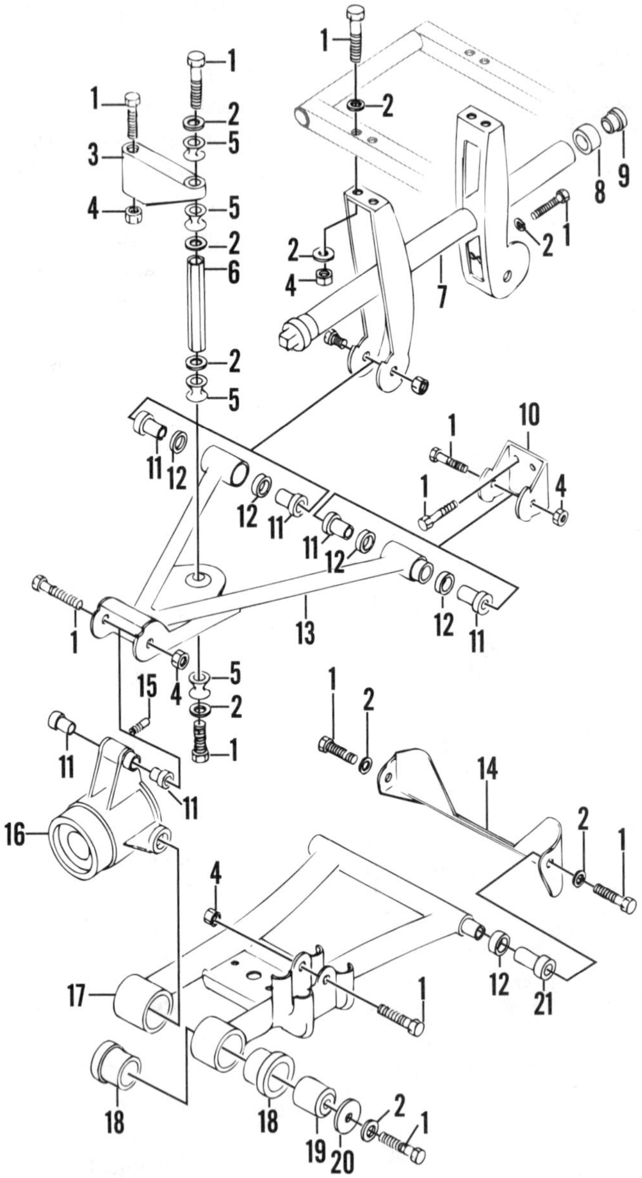

1. Bolt
2. Washer
3. Stabilizer arm bracket
4. Self-locking nut
5. Bushing
6. Stabilizer linkage rod
7. Stabilizer support
8. Washer
9. Bushing
10. Mounting bracket
11. Bushing
12. Bushing
13. Upper control arm
14. Frame mounting bracket
15. Grease fitting
16. Rear axle bearing carrier
17. Lower control arm
18. Bushing
19. Bearing carrier bushing
20. Washer
21. Bushing

41

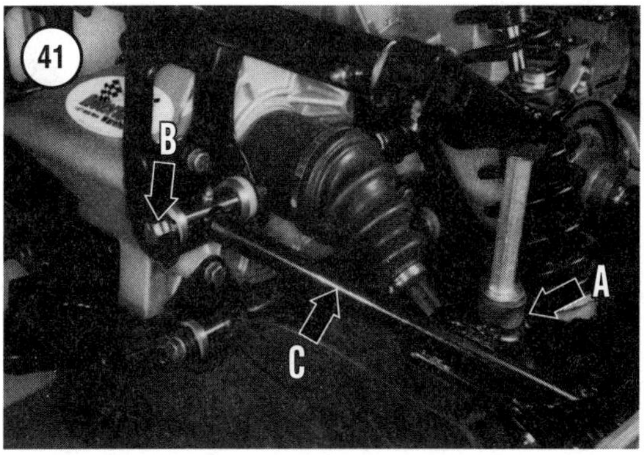

42

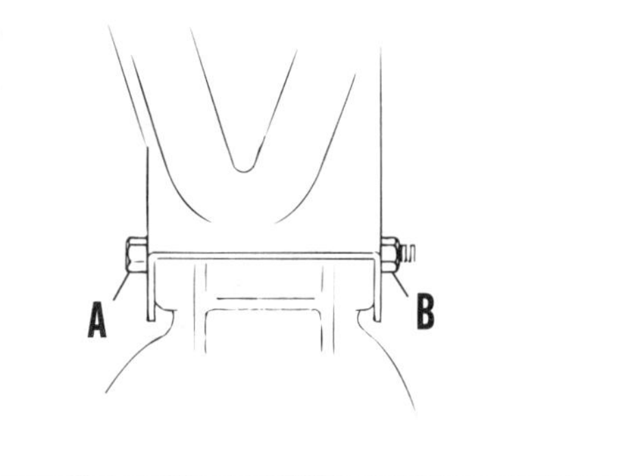

43

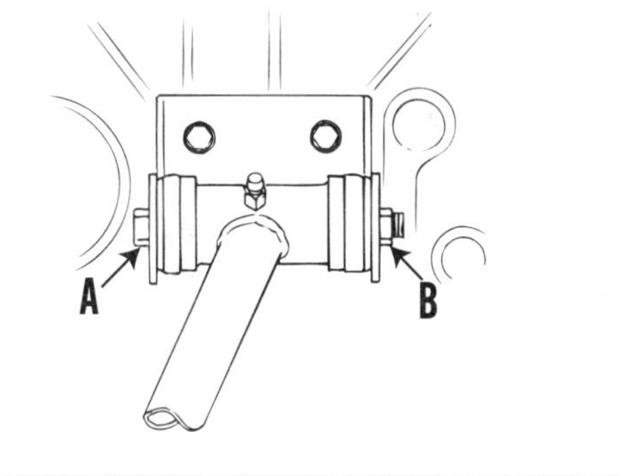

7. Rotate both rear axles by hand to make sure they rotate freely with no binding or roughness.

UPPER CONTROL ARM

Removal/Installation

Refer to **Figure 40**.

1. Remove the rear fender as described in Chapter Fifteen.
2. Remove the rear wheel on the side to be serviced as described in this chapter.
3. Remove the bolt, washer and bushing (A, **Figure 41**) securing the stabilizer linkage rod to the upper control arm. Reinstall the bushing, washer and bolt onto the linkage rod.
4. Remove the bolt (A, **Figure 42**) and self-locking nut (B, **Figure 42**) securing the upper control arm to the rear axle bearing carrier.
5. Remove the bolt (A, **Figure 43**) and self-locking nut (B, **Figure 43**) securing the upper control arm to the mounting bracket on the transmission.
6. Remove the bolt (B, **Figure 41**) and self-locking nut securing the upper control arm to the stabilizer support.
7. Remove the upper control arm (C, **Figure 41**) from the frame.
8. Inspect the upper control arm as described under *Upper and Lower Control Arm Inspection* in this chapter.
9. Install by reversing these removal steps while noting the following:
   a. Grease the upper control arm bushings prior to installation. Make sure the bushings are in place prior to installation.
   b. Install *new* self-locking nuts.
   c. Refer to **Table 2** for torque specifications.
   d. Grease the upper control arm bushing grease fittings as described in Chapter Three.

LOWER CONTROL ARM

Removal/Installation

Refer to **Figure 40**.

1. Remove the rear fender as described in Chapter Fifteen.
2. Remove the rear wheel on the side to be serviced as described in this chapter.
3. On models so equipped, remove the bolts and lower control arm shield.
4. Remove the bolt and self-locking nut (**Figure 44**) securing the shock absorber lower mount to the lower control arm.

NOTE
The following steps are shown with the upper control arm removed to better illustrate the steps.

13

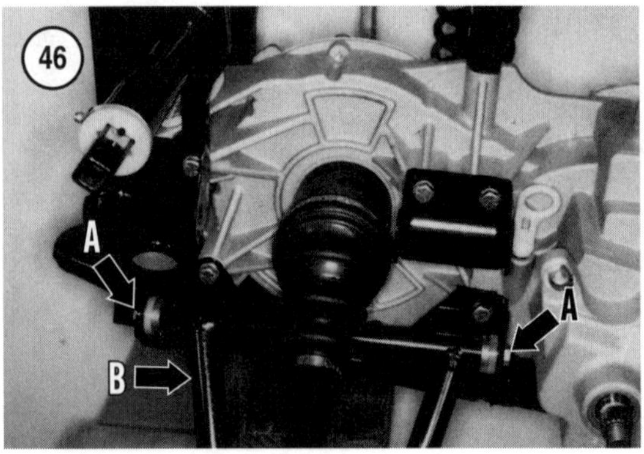

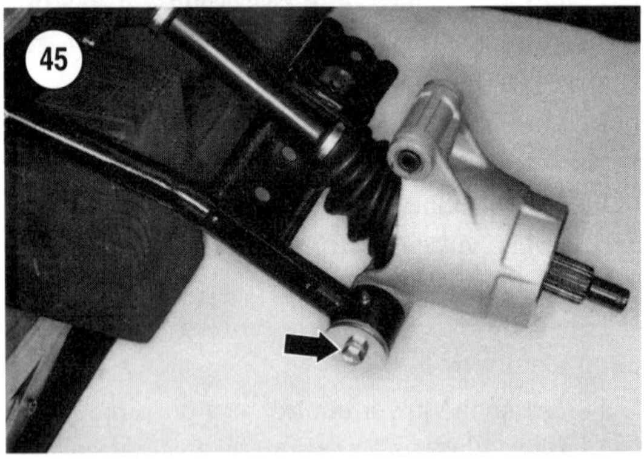

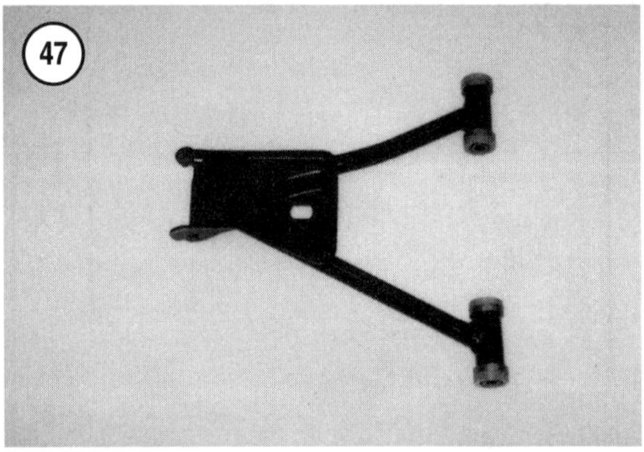

5. Remove the bolt and two washers (**Figure 45**) on each side that secure the lower control arm to the rear axle bearing carrier.

6. Secure the upper control arm and rear axle up to the frame with a bungee cord or rope.

7. Lower the control arm.

8. Remove the bolt and washer (A, **Figure 46**) on each side securing the lower control arm to the mounting bracket on the frame.

9. Remove the lower control arm (B, **Figure 46**) from the frame.

10. Inspect the lower control arm as described under *Upper and Lower Control Arm Inspection* in this chapter.

11. Install by reversing these removal steps while noting the following:

   a. Grease the lower control arm bushings prior to installation. Make sure the bushings are in place prior to installation.
   b. Install *new* self-locking nuts.
   c. Refer to **Table 2** for torque specifications.
   d. Grease the lower control arm bushing grease fittings as described in Chapter Three.

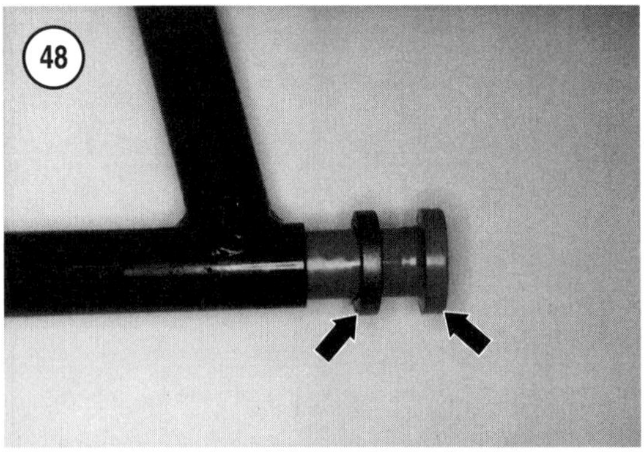

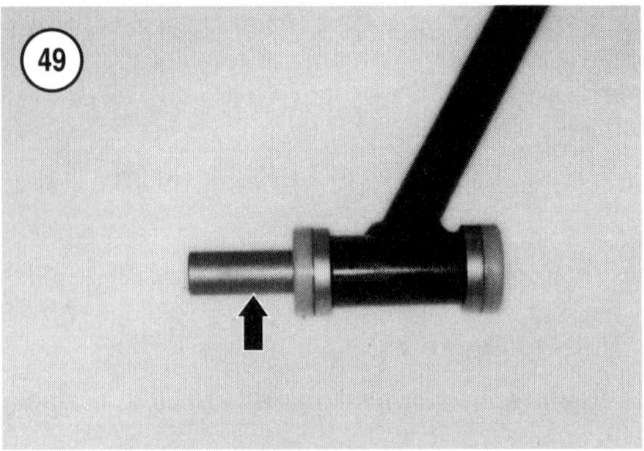

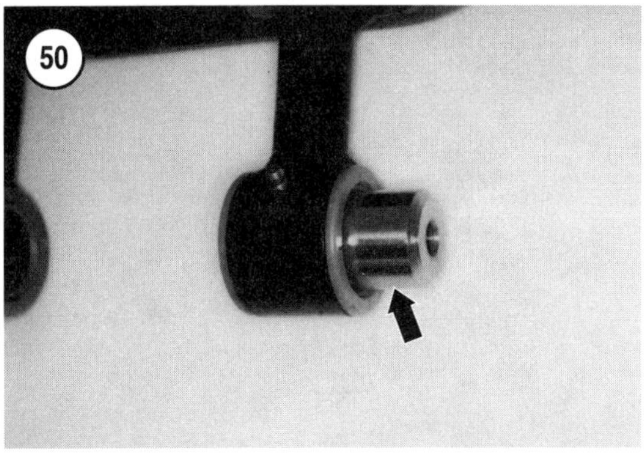

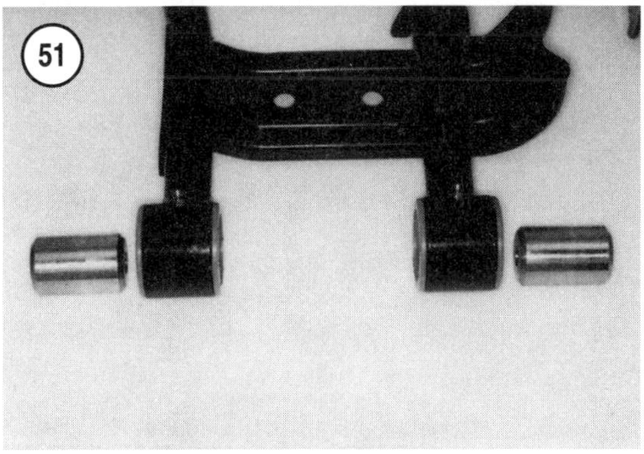

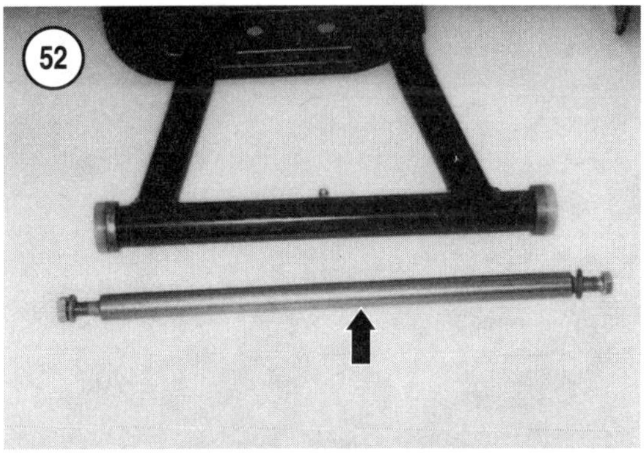

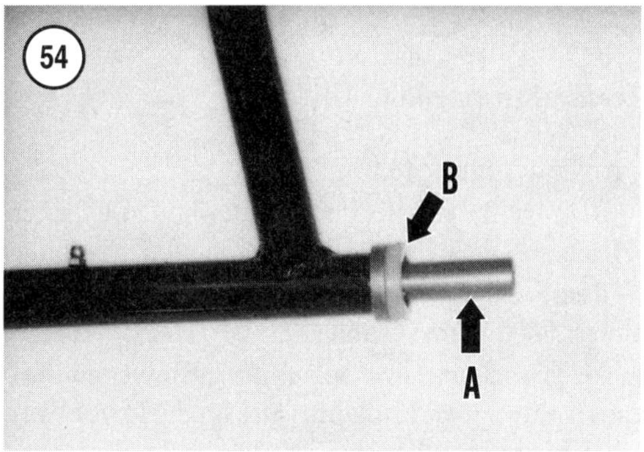

UPPER AND LOWER CONTROL ARM INSPECTION

1. Check the welded sections on the control arms (**Figure 47**) for cracks or fractures.

2. Carefully pry out and remove the pivot bushings from the control arms. Refer to **Figure 48** and **Figure 49**.

3. On the lower control arm, perform the following:

   a. Carefully pry out and remove the bearing carrier bushing (**Figure 50**) from each side (**Figure 51**).

   b. Withdraw the shaft (**Figure 52**) and check for straightness. Replace if bent or corroded.

   c. Inspect the shock absorber mounting bracket (**Figure 53**) for wear or damage. Check the mounting holes for cracks or elongation.

4. Thoroughly clean the pivot bolts, pivot bushings and shaft in solvent and dry with compressed air.

5. Insert the pivot bolt, or shaft (A, **Figure 54**) into each pivot bushing (B, **Figure 54**, typical) and check for a snug fit. The pivot bolts must rotate freely but without any play. There are no specifications for either part; replace both parts if either is worn or damaged.

6. Unscrew the grease fittings. Refer to **Figure 55** and **Figure 56**. Clean out with solvent and blow dry with compressed air. Make sure the fittings are clear. If necessary, clean out with a piece of wire. Install the grease fittings and tighten securely.

7. Check the pivot bolts for straightness and damaged threads.

STABILIZER LINKAGE

Removal/Installation

Refer to **Figure 40**.

1. Remove the rear fender as described in Chapter Fifteen.
2. Remove the rear wheel on the side to be serviced as described in this chapter.
3. Place a suitable size jack under the lower control arm. Apply upward jack pressure on the lower control arm to place the stabilizer linkage and bracket in a neutral position with no strain on the mounting points.
4. Remove the bolt, washer and rubber bushing (A, **Figure 57**) securing the stabilizer linkage rod (B, **Figure 57**) to the upper control arm. Reinstall the rubber bushing, washer and bolt onto the rod.
5. Remove the bolt, washer and rubber bushing (A, **Figure 58**) securing the stabilizer linkage rod to the stabilizer support. Reinstall the bushing, washer and bolt onto the rod.
6. Remove the bolt and self-locking nut (B, **Figure 58**) securing the stabilizer arm bracket to the stabilizer support.
7. Remove the stabilizer arm bracket (C, **Figure 58**) from the stabilizer support bar.
8. Inspect the linkage rod and arm bracket as described in this chapter.
9. Install by reversing these removal steps while noting the following:

CAUTION
*The rubber bushings must be installed correctly onto the linkage rod as shown in the following illustrations. The relief (**Figure 59**) on each side of the rubber bushing must be positioned so it can be compressed with the natural movement of the upper control arm.*

a. Position the rubber bushing and linkage rod as shown in **Figure 60** on the lower control arm.
b. Position the rubber bushings and linkage rod as shown in **Figure 61** on the stabilizer arm bracket.
c. Install a *new* self-locking nut.
d. Refer to **Table 2** for stabilizer arm bracket torque specifications.

55
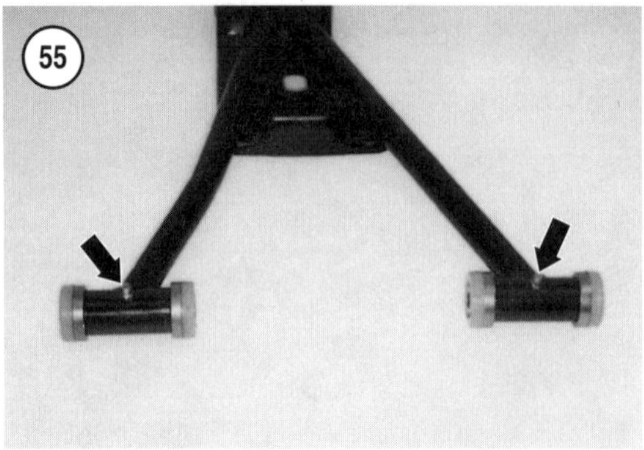

56

57
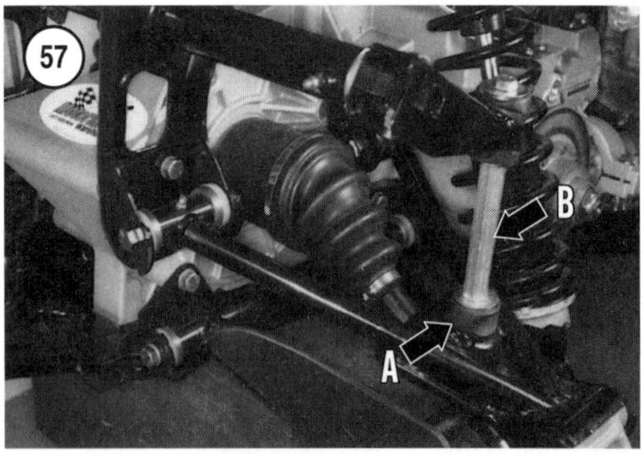

58
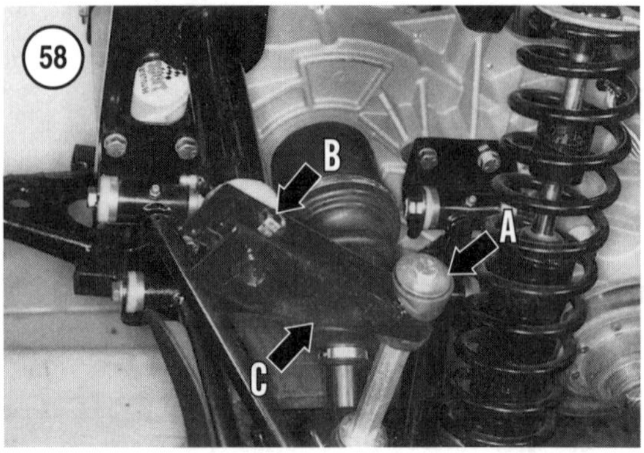

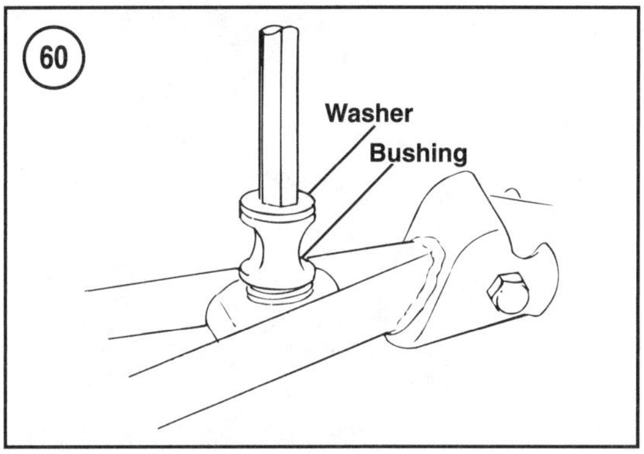

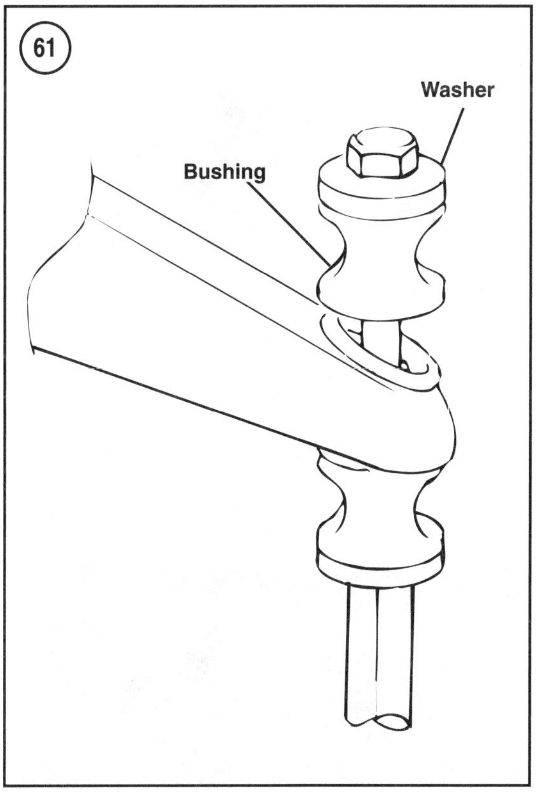

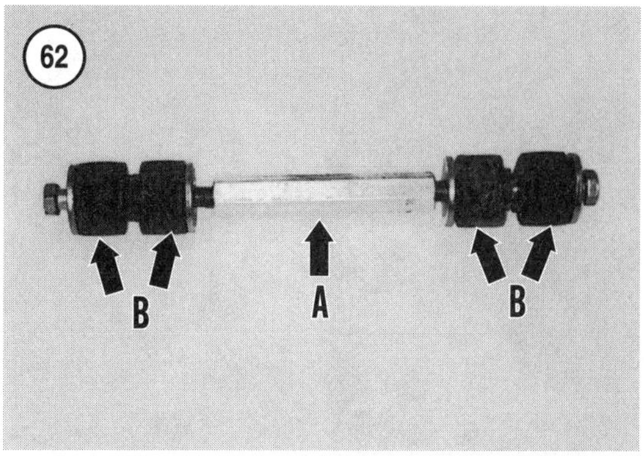

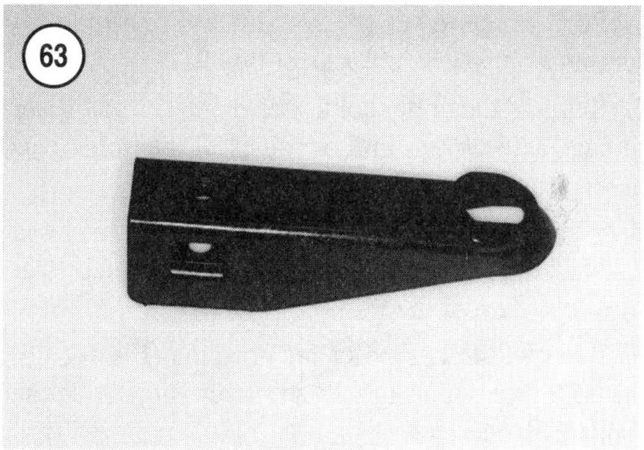

Inspection

1. Inspect the linkage rod (A, **Figure 62**) for wear or damage.
2. Inspect the arm bracket (**Figure 63**) for cracks or other damage.
3. Check the rubber bushings (B, **Figure 62**) for deterioration. Replace all four bushings as a set even if one or two are damaged.

STABILIZER SUPPORT

Removal/Installation

Refer to **Figure 40**.

1. Remove the rear fender as described in Chapter Fifteen.
2. Remove the rear wheel on the side to be serviced as described in this chapter.
3. Remove both shock absorbers as described in this chapter.
4. Place a suitable size jack under the *rear* of the transmission to support it after the stabilizer support is removed.

5. Support the lower control arm and rear axle assemblies on wooden blocks or boxes.

6. Remove the upper control arm and the stabilizer linkage assembly from both sides of the vehicle as described in this chapter.

7. Remove the two bolts (**Figure 64**), washers and self-locking nuts on each side securing the stabilizer support to top of the frame.

8. Remove the two bolts and washers (**Figure 65**) on each side securing the stabilizer support to the transmission.

NOTE
It may be necessary to slightly lower the rear of the transmission to ease stabilizer support removal. If so, raise the transmission back up to the normal position after the support is removed.

9. Pull the stabilizer support straight back and out of the frame (**Figure 66**).

10. Inspect by reversing these removal steps while noting the following:

   a. Install *new* self-locking nuts.
   b. Refer to **Table 2** for stabilizer support torque specifications.

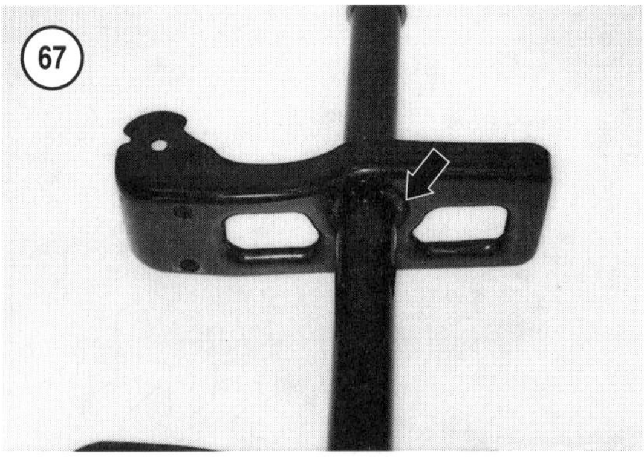

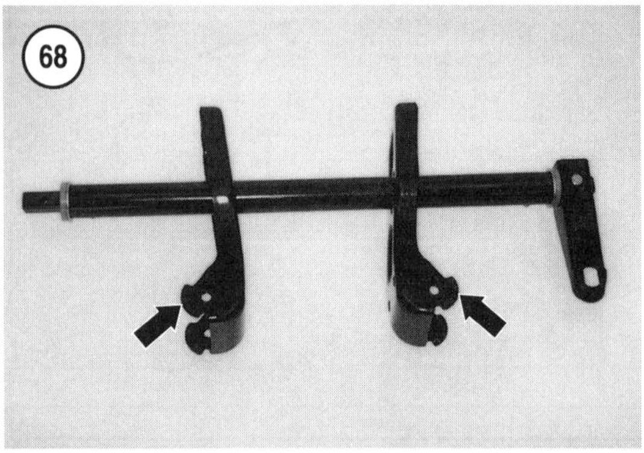

Inspection

1. Check the welded sections (**Figure 67**) on the stabilizer support for cracks.

2. Check the mounting bolt holes (**Figure 68**) for cracks or elongation.

3. Withdraw the stabilizer bar (A, **Figure 69**) from the stabilizer support tube.

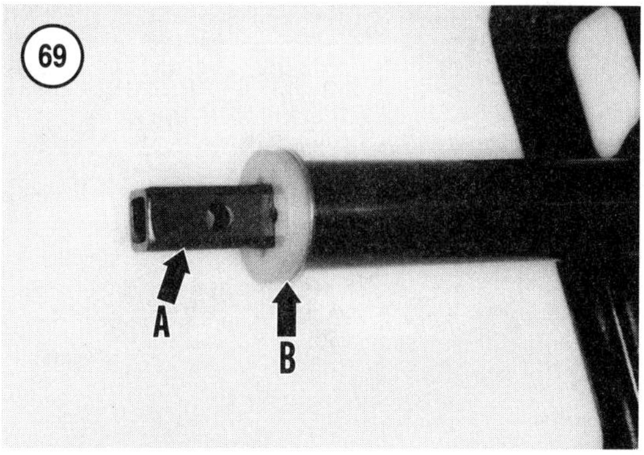

4. Carefully pry out and remove the pivot bushings (B, **Figure 69**) from each end of the stabilizer support.
5. Thoroughly clean the bar and pivot bushings in solvent and dry with compressed air.
6. Check the bushings for wear or deterioration. Replace as a set on each side even though only one set is worn.
7. Check the bar for straightness and the stabilizer arm bracket mounting bolt holes for cracks or elongation.
8. Replace all worn or damaged parts.

Table 1 REAR SUSPENSION SPECIFICATIONS

Item	Specification
Independent progressive rate rear suspension with anti-roll bar and dual shock absorbers	
Rear suspension travel	24 cm (9.5 in.)

Table 2 REAR SUSPENSION TORQUE SPECIFICATIONS

Item	N•m	in.-lb.	ft.-lb.
Rear wheel			
Lug nuts	20	–	15
Hub castellated nut	136	–	100
Shock absorber			
Upper and lower bolt and nut*	41	–	30
Upper control arm			
To transmission bracket bolt and nut*	48	–	35
To rear hub axle bearing carrier bolt and nut*	48	–	35
Lower control arm			
To frame bolt and nut*	41	–	30
To rear hub axle bearing carrier bolt and nut*	41	–	30
Stabilizer support to frame bolt and nut*	24	–	18
Stabilizer arm bracket bolt and nut*	24	–	18
Rear axle attachment bolt-to-internal threaded spacer (1996-1998 models)	48	–	35

* Install new self-locking nuts.

13

NOTE: Refer to the Supplement at the back of this manual for information unique to 2001-on models, including the Sportsman 400.

CHAPTER FOURTEEN

BRAKES

This chapter describes service procedures for the front brakes and the output shaft brake. **Table 1** and **Table 2** are located at the end of this chapter.

DISC BRAKES

There are two types of brake systems used on the various models.

On 1996-1997 models, the front master cylinder controls the front disc brakes and the output shaft brake. The rear pedal controls the output shaft brake via mechanical means.

On 1998-on models, the front master cylinder controls the front disc brake and the dual-hydraulic output shaft brake. The rear master cylinder also controls the dual-hydraulic output shaft brake. The output shaft brake caliper can be controlled by either or both master cylinders.

Brake Service

The disc brake system transmits hydraulic pressure from the master cylinders to the brake calipers. This pressure is transmitted from the caliper(s) to the brake pads, which grip both sides of the brake disc(s) and slow the ATV. As the pads wear, the pistons move out of the caliper bores to automatically compensate for wear. As this occurs, the fluid level in the reservoir goes down. This must be compensated for by occasionally adding fluid.

The proper operation of this system depends on a supply of clean brake fluid (DOT 3) and a clean work environment when any service is being performed. Any tiny particle of debris that enters the system can damage the components and cause poor brake performance.

Brake fluid is hygroscopic (easily absorbs moisture) and moisture in the system will reduce brake performance. It is a good idea to purchase brake fluid in small containers and discard any small quantities that remain. Small quantities of fluid will quickly absorb the moisture in the container. Use only fluid clearly marked DOT 3. If possible, use the same brand of fluid. Do not replace the fluid with DOT 5 (silicone) fluid. It is not possible to remove all of the old fluid and DOT 5 is not compatible with other types. Silicone type fluids used in systems for which they were not designed will cause internal seals to swell and deteriorate. Do not reuse drained fluid and discard old fluid properly.

Proper service also includes carefully performed procedures. Do not use any sharp tools inside the master cylinders or calipers or on the pistons. Any damage to these components could cause a loss in the systems ability to maintain hydraulic pressure. If there is any doubt about having the ability to correctly and safely service the brake system, have a profession technician perform the task.

Consider the following when servicing the brake system:

1. The hydraulic components rarely require disassembly. Make sure it is necessary.
2. Keep the reservoir covers in place to prevent the entry of moisture and debris.
3. Clean parts with an aerosol brake parts cleaner or isopropyl alcohol. Never use petroleum based solvents on internal brake system components. They will cause seals to swell and distort.
4. Do not allow brake fluid to contact plastic, painted or plated parts. It will damage the surface.
5. Dispose of brake fluid properly.
6. If the hydraulic system has been opened (not including the reservoir cover) the system must be bled to remove air from the system. Refer to *Bleeding the System* in this chapter.

WARNING

*Whenever working on the brake system, do **not** inhale brake dust. It may contain asbestos, which can cause lung injury and cancer. Wear a facemask that meets OSHA requirements for trapping asbestos particles, and wash both hands and forearms thoroughly after completing the work.*

WARNING

***NEVER** use compressed air to clean any parts of the brake system as this will release the harmful brake pad dust. Use an aerosol brake cleaner to clean parts when servicing any component still installed on the vehicle.*

FRONT BRAKE PAD REPLACEMENT

There is no recommended interval for changing the brake pads. Pad wear depends greatly on riding conditions. Check the pads for wear prior to each ride or when the brake pads wear close to the edge of the brake disc. Measure the thickness of each brake pad with a vernier caliper or ruler and compare it to the dimensions listed in **Table 1**.

Replace both brake pads in *both calipers* at the same time. Do not disconnect the hydraulic brake hose from the brake caliper for brake pad replacement, disconnect the hose only if the caliper assembly is going to be removed.

Refer to **Figure 1**.

1. Remove the front wheels as described in Chapter Eleven.
2. Unscrew and remove the pad adjust screw (**Figure 2**).

NOTE

*Only one bolt is shown in **Figure 3**, remove both bolts.*

3. Remove both bolts and washers (**Figure 3**) securing the brake caliper mounting and remove the caliper from the brake disc.
4. When repositioning the brake pads in the caliper, the master cylinder brake fluid level will rise as the caliper piston is repositioned. Perform the following:
   a. Clean the top of the master cylinder of all debris.
   b. Place a plastic drop cloth over the front fender and fuel tank.
   c. Remove the top cover, screws, cover (**Figure 4**) and diaphragm from the master cylinder.

WARNING

Brake fluid is poisonous; do not siphon it by mouth.

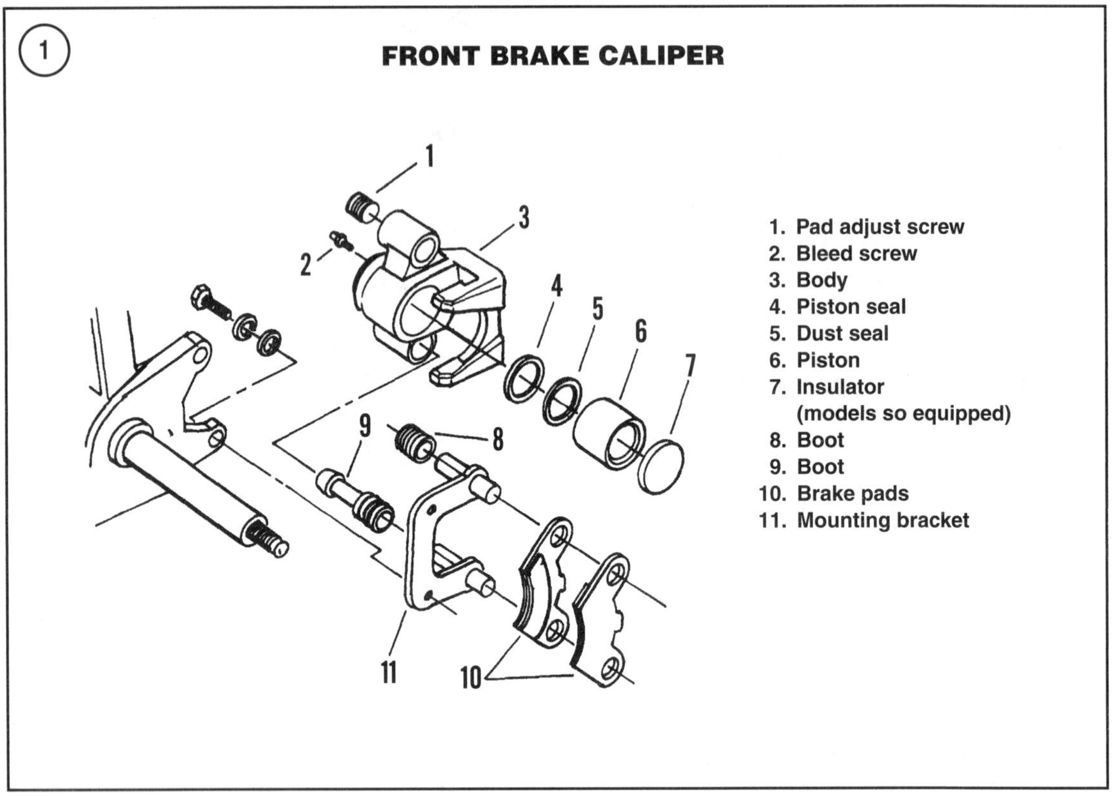

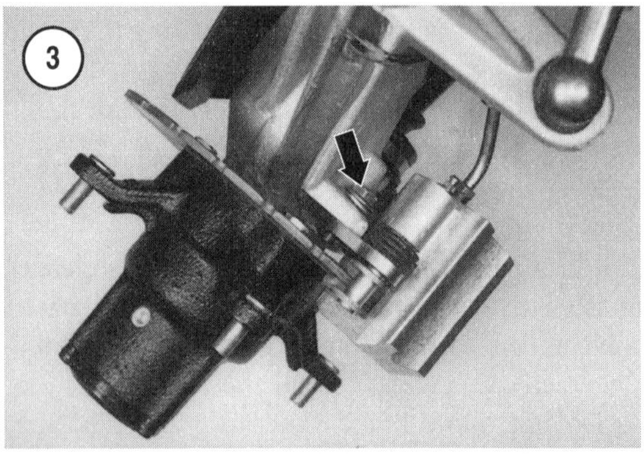

5. Install a large C-clamp onto the caliper and position it directly over the piston (**Figure 5**). Tighten the C-clamp and push the mounting bracket and the brake pads in toward the piston and push the piston back into the caliper cylinder. Constantly check the reservoir and remove fluid, if necessary, prior to it overflowing. Remove the C-clamp.

6. The piston should move freely. If it does not, remove and service the caliper as described in this chapter.

7. Push the mounting bracket all way against the caliper to allow room for brake pad removal.

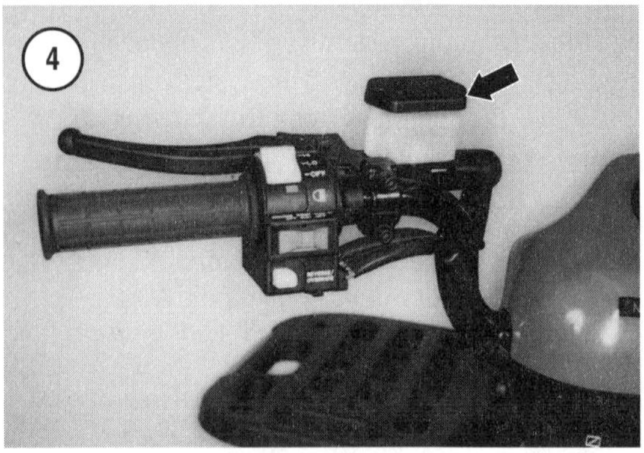

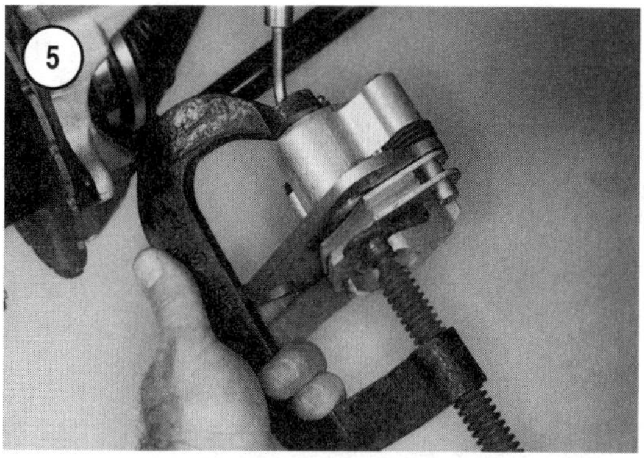

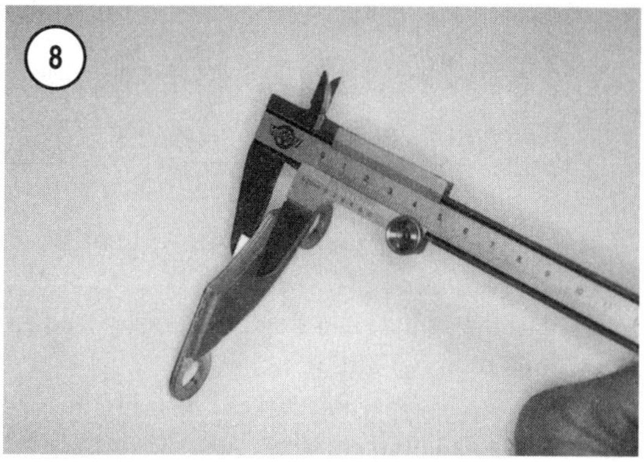

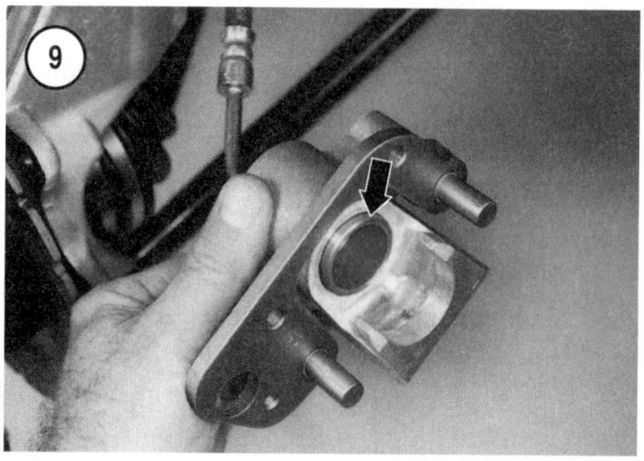

8. Remove both brake pads (**Figure 6**) from the caliper.

9. Inspect the brake pads (**Figure 7**) for uneven wear, damage or grease contamination. Replace the pads as a set, if necessary.

NOTE
Measure the brake pad lining as well as the metal backing plate.

10. Measure the thickness of each brake pad with a ruler or vernier caliper (**Figure 8**). Replace the brake pads if the thickness of either pad is worn to the service limit in **Table 1**.

11. Inspect the brake disc for nicks, corrosion and radial groove damage. If damaged, remove the brake disc as described in this chapter.

12. Check the end of the piston (**Figure 9**) for fluid leakage. If the seal is damaged and/or if there is fluid leakage, overhaul the brake caliper as described in this chapter.

NOTE
When purchasing new pads, check with the dealership to make sure the friction compound of the new pad is compatible with the disc material. Remove any roughness from the backs of the new pads with a fine-cut file.

13. Partially move the mounting bracket away from the caliper body. Move the rubber boots away and apply a light coat of high-temperature grease to the mounting bracket pins (**Figure 10**), then move the mounting bracket back into place.

14. Compress the mounting bracket to make sure the rubber boot and bushing are fully seated.

15. Install the inboard brake pad (**Figure 11**), then the outboard brake pad (**Figure 12**) into the mounting bracket pins.

16. Slowly move the mounting bracket away from the piston to lock the brake pads in place within the caliper (**Figure 13**). Separate the brake pads to allow room for the brake disc.

17. Install the caliper onto the brake disc being careful not to damage the leading edge of the brake pads.

18. Align the mounting bolt holes with the front strut and install the bolts. Tighten the bolts (**Figure 3**) to the torque specification listed in **Table 2**.

NOTE
To control the flow of hydraulic fluid, punch a small hole into the brake fluid container seal next to the edge of the pour spout. This will help eliminate fluid spillage especially while adding fluid to the very small brake reservoir.

WARNING
Use brake fluid clearly marked DOT 3 from a sealed container. Other types may vaporize and cause brake failure. Always use the same brand name; do not intermix as many brands are not compatible. Do not intermix silicone-based (DOT 5) brake fluid, as it can cause brake component damage leading to brake system failure.

19. Refill the master cylinder reservoir to maintain the correct fluid level as indicated on the side of the reservoir. Install the diaphragm and cover and tighten the screws securely.

20. With the wheels still off the ground, spin the wheels and activate the brake lever as many times as it takes to refill the caliper cylinder and correctly locate the brake pads against the disc.

21. Install the pad adjust screw and turn it in (**Figure 2**) until the outboard brake pad contacts the brake disc, then back it out 1/2 turn.

22. Install the front wheels as described in Chapter Twelve.

WARNING
Do not ride the vehicle until it is established that the brakes are operating correctly with full hydraulic advantage. If necessary, bleed the brakes as described in this chapter.

10

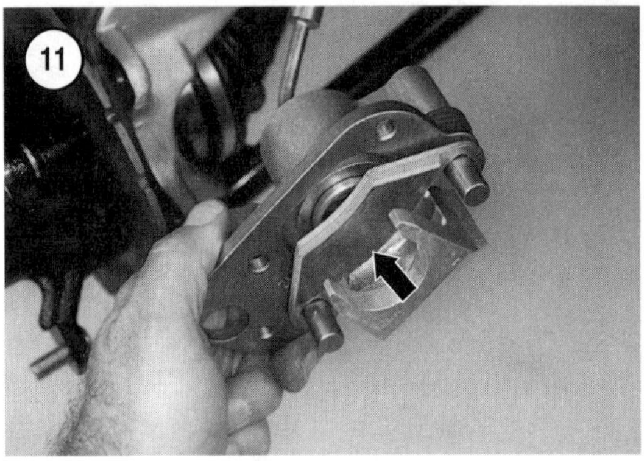
11

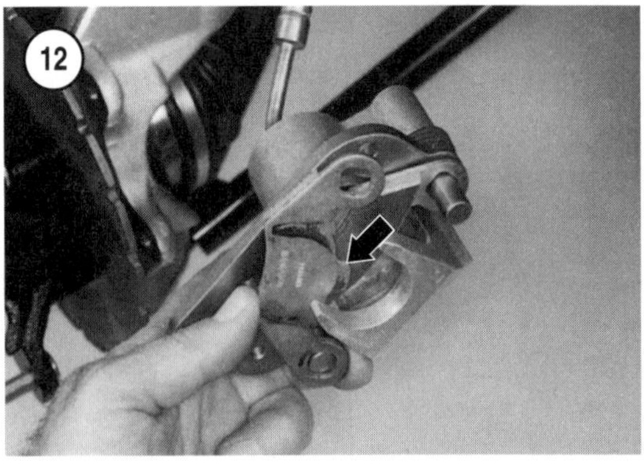
12

NOTE
The following instructions apply to original equipment-type pads only. If using aftermarket brake pads, follow the manufacturer's break-in instructions.

23. Bed the pads in gradually with a burnishing procedure as follows:
   a. Start the vehicle and slowly increase speed up to 30 mph (48 km/h).
   b. *Gradually* apply the brakes and bring the vehicle to a complete stop.

13

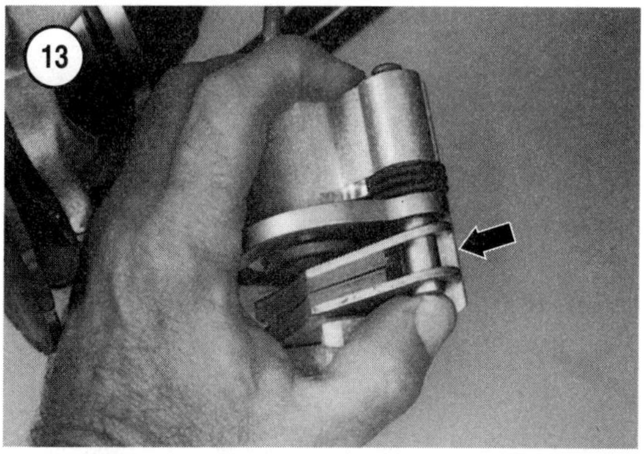

14

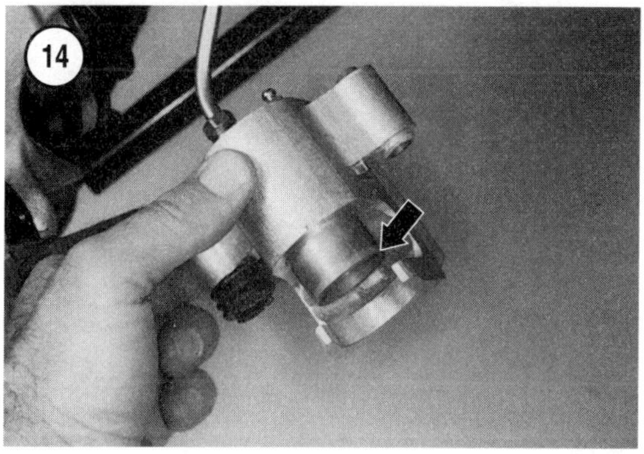

15

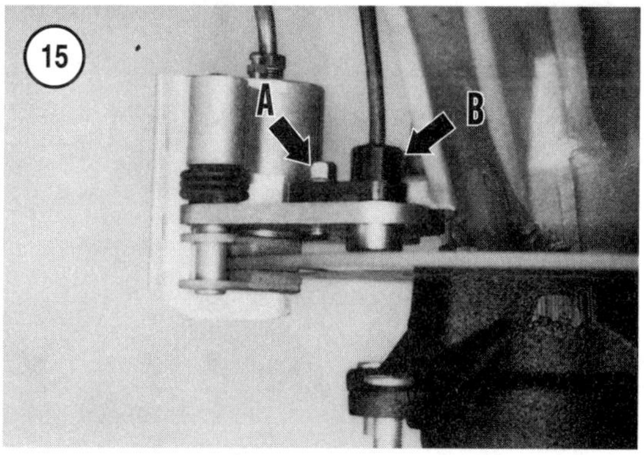

c. Repeat this procedure ten times.
d. For the first 2-3 days of riding, use only light pressure as much as possible. Immediate hard application will glaze the new brake pads and greatly reduce the effectiveness of the brake.

FRONT CALIPER

Removal/Installation

Refer to **Figure 1**.

CAUTION
Do not spill any brake fluid on the front strut assembly and front suspension components. Wash off any spilled brake fluid immediately, as it will destroy the finish. Use soapy water and rinse completely.

NOTE
If the caliper is not going to be disassembled for service, proceed to Step 2.

1. If the caliper assembly is going to be disassembled for service, perform the following:

NOTE
By performing substeps b and c, compressed air may not be necessary for piston removal during caliper disassembly.

a. Remove the brake pads as described in this chapter.
b. Reinstall the caliper assembly and tighten the caliper mounting bolts securely.

CAUTION
Do not allow the piston to travel out far enough to come in contact with the brake disc. If this happens the piston may scratch or gouge the disc during caliper removal.

NOTE
***Figure 14** shows the caliper removed to better illustrate the step.*

c. Slowly apply the brake lever to push the piston part way out of caliper assembly (**Figure 14**) for ease of removal during caliper service.
d. Loosen and remove the brake hose from the caliper.
e. Place the loose end of the brake hose in a reclosable plastic bag to prevent the entry of debris and to prevent any residual brake fluid from dripping out.

2. On 1999-on models, perform the following:
a. Remove the bolt and washer (A, **Figure 15**) securing the speed sensor to the caliper mounting bracket.

b. Remove the speed sensor (B, **Figure 15**) from the bracket and move the sensor out of the way.

NOTE
*Only one bolt is shown in **Figure 3**, remove both bolts.*

3. Remove both bolts and washers (**Figure 3**) securing the brake caliper and remove the caliper from the brake disc.
4. Loosen and remove the brake hose (**Figure 16**) from the rear of the caliper.
5. If necessary, disassemble, inspect and assemble the front caliper as described in this chapter.
6. Install by reversing these removal steps while noting the following:
   a. Install the brake hose and fitting onto the backside of the caliper and tighten the fitting only finger-tight (**Figure 17**).
   b. Carefully install the caliper assembly onto the disc, being careful not to damage the leading edge of the brake pads.
   c. Install the caliper mounting bolts and tighten to the torque specifications listed in **Table 2**.
   d. Tighten the brake hose and fitting (**Figure 18**) securely.
   e. Bleed the brake as described under *Bleeding the System* in this chapter.

WARNING
Make sure the brakes are operating properly before riding the vehicle.

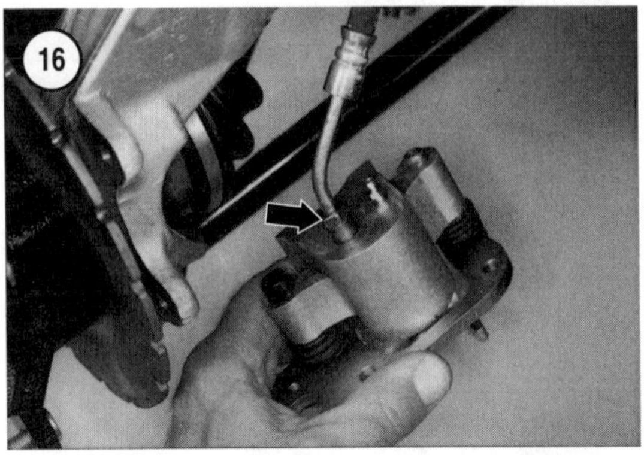
16

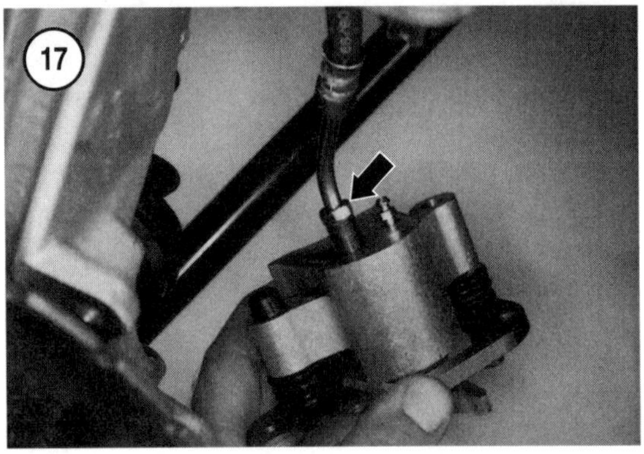
17

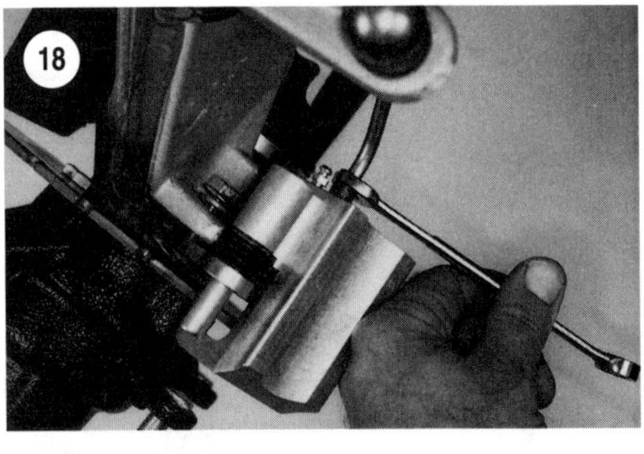
18

Disassembly

Refer to **Figure 1**.
1. Remove the brake pads as described in this chapter.
2. Remove the front caliper as described in this chapter.
3. Remove the mounting bracket from the caliper body.

NOTE
If the piston was partially forced out of the caliper body during removal, Steps 4-6 may not be necessary. If the piston or caliper bore is corroded or very dirty, a small amount of compressed air may be necessary to completely remove the piston from the body bore.

4. Place a piece of softwood or folded shop cloth over the end of the piston and the caliper body.

WARNING
*In the next step, the piston may shoot out of the caliper body. Keep all fingers out of the way. Wear shop gloves and apply air pressure gradually. Do **not** use high-pressure air or place the air hose nozzle directly against the brake hose fitting inlet in the caliper body. Hold the air nozzle away from the inlet, allowing some of the air to escape.*

19

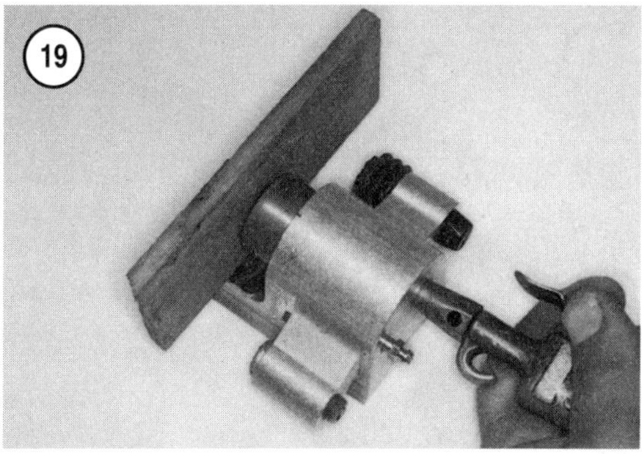

20

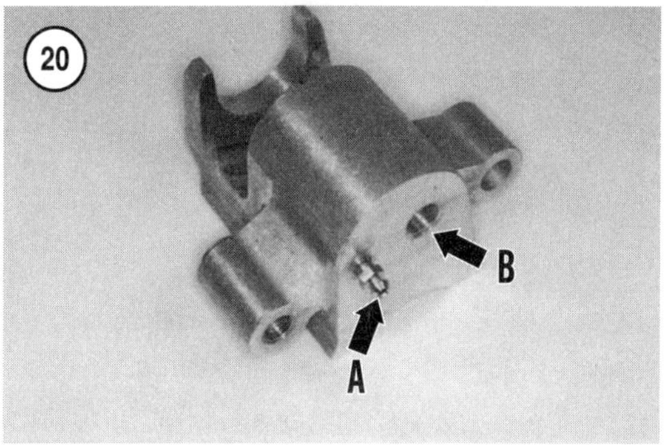

21

5. Apply the air pressure in short spurts to the brake hose inlet fitting (**Figure 19**) and force out the piston. Remove the piston. Use a service station air hose if compressed air is not available.

CAUTION
In the following step, do not use a sharp tool to remove the dust and piston seals from the caliper cylinders. Do not damage the cylinder surface.

6. On models so equipped, remove the insulator from the piston.

7. Remove the dust seal and piston seal from the inside of the cylinder.

8. Unscrew and remove the bleed valve (A, **Figure 20**) from the backside of the caliper.

Inspection

CAUTION
Never use petroleum-based solvents on internal brake system components. Any residual solvent will cause the new seals to swell and distort.

1. Clean the caliper body and piston in denatured alcohol or fresh DOT 3 brake fluid. Wear eye protection and blow dry with compressed air directing the air flow and residual fluid away from you.
2. Use compressed air to make sure the fluid passageway in the base of the piston bore is clear.
3. Inspect the dust and piston seal grooves (A, **Figure 21**) in the caliper body for damage. If damaged or corroded, replace the caliper assembly.
4. Inspect the brake hose inlet fitting threads (B, **Figure 20**) in the backside of the caliper body. If worn or damaged, clean out with a thread tap or replace the caliper assembly.
5. Inspect the bleed screw threaded hole in the caliper body. If worn or damaged, clean out with a thread tap or replace the caliper assembly.
6. Make sure the bleed screw is clean and open. Clean out if necessary with fresh brake fluid. Install the bleed screw and tighten it securely.
7. Inspect the caliper body (B, **Figure 21**) for damage; replace the caliper body if necessary.
8. Inspect the caliper piston bore for cracks, deep scoring or excessive wear. If rusty or corroded, replace the caliper assembly.
9. Check the caliper piston for scratches, scoring or rust. If it is rusty or corroded, replace the piston.
10. Measure the inside diameter of the piston bore. Replace the caliper if the bore diameter exceeds the service limit dimension listed in **Table 1**.
11. Measure the outside diameter of the piston (**Figure 22**) with a micrometer or vernier caliper. Replace the piston if the diameter is less than the service limit dimension listed in **Table 1**.
12. The piston seals help to maintain correct brake pad-to-disc clearance. If the seals are worn or damaged, the brake pads will drag and cause excessive wear and increase brake fluid temperature. Replace

the piston seal and dust seal if the following conditions exist:

a. Brake fluid leaks around the inboard brake pad.
b. Stuck piston seal.
c. There is a large difference in the inner and outer brake pad thickness.

NOTE
Never reuse an old dust or piston seal. Very minor damage or age deterioration can make the seals useless.

13. Inspect the brake pads (**Figure 7**) for uneven wear, damage or grease contamination. If the pad thickness is with specification, clean off the pad surface with an aerosol brake cleaner to remove any surface contamination.

NOTE
When the brake system is operating correctly, the inboard and outboard brake pads should be approximately the same thickness. If there is a large difference in pad wear, the piston seals are faulty and not allowing the piston to return properly. This causes one pad to drag against the disc.

Assembly

NOTE
Use only new DOT 3 brake fluid when brake fluid is called for in the following procedure.

1. Install the bleed valve into the back side of the caliper and tighten securely.
2. Soak the piston seal and dust seal in brake fluid for approximately five minutes.
3. Lightly coat the piston and cylinder bore with fresh DOT 3 brake fluid.
4. Install a new piston seal (A, **Figure 23**) into the groove inside the cylinder bore.
5. Install a new dust seal (B, **Figure 23**) into the outside groove of the cylinder bore.

NOTE
Check that both seals fit squarely into their respective cylinder bore grooves. If a seal is not installed properly, the caliper assembly will leak and braking performance will be reduced.

22

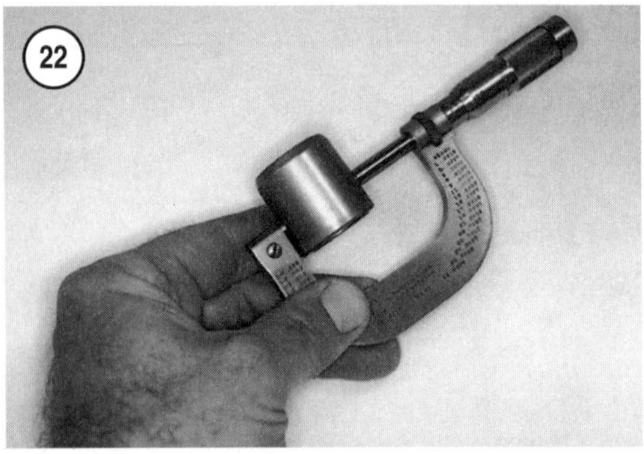

23

24

6. Position the piston with the closed end going in first and install the piston into the cylinder bore (**Figure 24**). On models so equipped, install the insulator onto the piston.
7. If removed, install the boot (**Figure 25**) onto the caliper body.
8. If the mounting bracket was removed, perform the following:

25

26

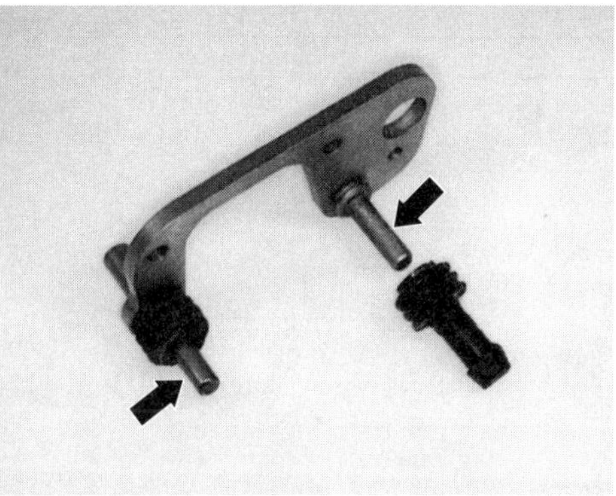

27

a. Apply a thin coat of high-temperature brake grease, or equivalent, to the caliper mounting bracket shafts (**Figure 26**)

b. Slide the mounting bracket (**Figure 27**) into the caliper. Slide the bracket back and forth, without removing it, to distribute the grease and to check the shafts for binding. The bracket must move smoothly; if any binding is noted, remove the bracket and inspect the shafts for damage. Wipe off any excess grease from the outside of the caliper or bracket.

9. Install the brake pads as described in this chapter.
10. Install the brake caliper assembly as described in this chapter.
11. Bleed the brake as described under *Bleeding the System* in this chapter.

OUTPUT SHAFT BRAKE PAD REPLACEMENT (1996-1997 MODELS)

There is no recommended interval for changing the brake pads. Pad wear depends greatly on riding conditions. Measure the thickness of each brake pad with a vernier caliper or ruler and compare to the dimensions listed in **Table 1**. Always replace both pads in the caliper at the same time. Do not disconnect the hydraulic brake hose from the brake caliper for brake pad replacement, disconnect the hose only if the caliper assembly is going to be removed.

Refer to **Figure 28**.

1. Remove the seat as described in Chapter Fifteen.
2. Remove the front and rear fenders as described in Chapter Fifteen.
3. If not removed during rear fender removal, remove the right-side foot well.
4. Disconnect the foot brake lever linkage rod from the caliper.
5. Remove the two bolts, lockwashers and washers securing the brake caliper to the transmission and move the caliper off of the brake disc.
6. When repositioning the brake pads in the caliper, the master cylinder brake fluid level will rise as the caliper piston is repositioned. Perform the following:
   a. Clean the top of the master cylinder of all debris.
   b. Place a plastic drop cloth over the front fender and fuel tank.
   c. Remove the top cover, screws, cover (**Figure 29**) and diaphragm from the master cylinder.

WARNING
Brake fluid is poisonous; do not siphon it by mouth.

7. Push on the backside of the outboard brake pad and push the brake pads in toward the piston. Push the piston back into the caliper cylinder. Constantly check the reservoir and remove fluid, if necessary, prior to it overflowing.

14

(28)

OUTPUT SHAFT BRAKE CALIPER (1996-1997)

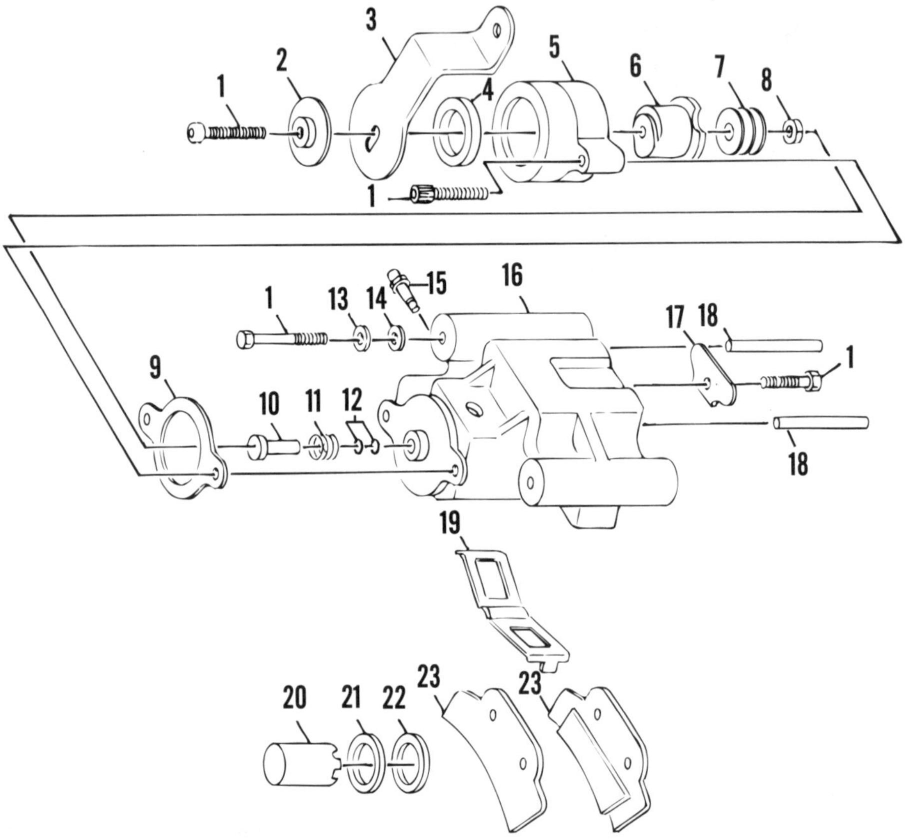

1. Bolt
2. Square cone washer
3. Caliper brake arm
4. Seal
5. Stationary ramp
6. Movable ramp
7. Washers
8. Nut (left-hand threads)
9. Gasket
10. Apply pin
11. Spring
12. O-ring
13. Lockwasher
14. Washer
15. Bleed screw
16. Body
17. Plate
18. Brake pad retaining pin
19. Anti-rattle spring
20. Piston
21. Piston seal
22. Dust seal
23. Brake pads

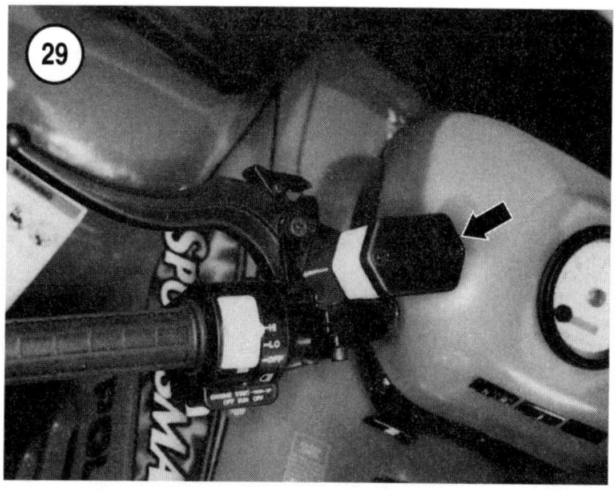

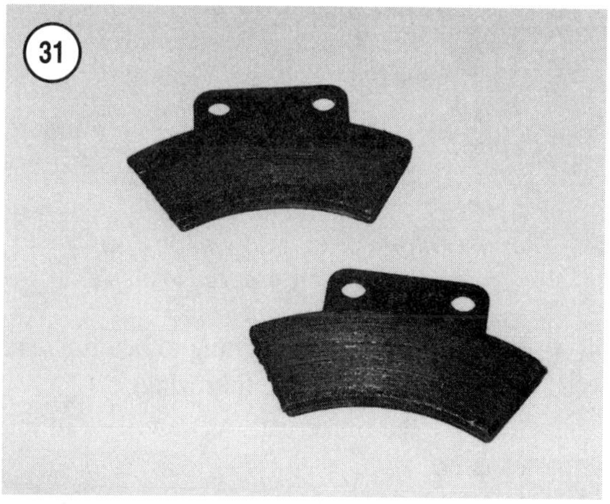

8. The piston should move freely. If it does not, remove and service caliper as described in this chapter.

9. To relieve pressure on the pad retaining pins, press the brake pads down onto the antirattle spring. Use needlenose pliers to remove the pad retaining pins (**Figure 30**) from the caliper.

10. Remove the outboard brake pad then the inboard brake pad.

11. Inspect the brake pads (**Figure 31**) for uneven wear, damage or grease contamination. Replace the pads as a set, if necessary.

NOTE
Measure the brake pad lining as well as the metal backing plate.

12. Measure the thickness of each brake pad with a ruler or vernier caliper. Replace the brake pads if the thickness of either pad is less than the service limit in **Table 1**.

13. Inspect the brake disc for nicks, corrosion and radial groove damage. If damaged remove the brake disc as described in this chapter.

14. Check the end of the piston for fluid leakage. If the seal is damaged and/or if there is fluid leakage, overhaul the brake caliper as described in this chapter.

NOTE
When purchasing new pads, check with the dealership to make sure the friction compound of the new pad is compatible with the disc material. Remove any roughness from the backs of the new pads with a fine-cut file; blow them clean with compressed air.

15. If removed, install the antirattle spring into the caliper body.

16. Install the inboard brake pad, then the outboard brake pad into the caliper body.

17. Press the brake pads down onto the antirattle spring and install the pad retaining pins. Push the pins in until they are completely seated in the caliper.

18. Install the caliper onto the brake disc being careful not to damage the leading edge of the brake pads.

19. Align the mounting bolt holes with the frame and install the bolts, lockwashers and washers. Tighten the bolts to the torque specification listed in **Table 2**.

NOTE
Make sure there is sufficient brake fluid in the master cylinder reservoir prior to performing Step 20. Add brake fluid if necessary.

20. With the rear wheels still off the ground, spin the rear wheels and activate the brake lever as many

times as it takes to refill the caliper cylinder and correctly locate the brake pads against the disc.

NOTE
To control the small flow of hydraulic fluid, punch a small hole into the brake fluid container seal next to the edge of the pour spout. This will help eliminate fluid spills, especially while adding fluid to the very small brake reservoir.

WARNING
Use brake fluid clearly marked DOT 3 from a sealed container. Other types may vaporize and cause brake failure. Always use the same brand name; do not intermix, as many brands are not compatible. Do not intermix silicone-based (DOT 5) brake fluid, as it can cause brake component damage leading to brake system failure.

21. Refill the master cylinder reservoir, if necessary, to maintain the correct fluid level as indicated on the side of the reservoir. Install the diaphragm and cover and tighten the screws securely.
22. Connect the foot brake lever linkage rod onto caliper.
23. Install front and rear fenders and seat as described in Chapter Fifteen.

WARNING
Make sure the brakes are operating correctly with full hydraulic advantage before riding the vehicle. If necessary, bleed the brakes as described in this chapter.

NOTE
The following instructions apply to original equipment-type pads only. If using aftermarket brake pads, follow the manufacturer's break-in instructions.

24. Bed the pads in gradually with a burnishing procedure as follows:
   a. Start the vehicle and slowly increase speed up to 30 mph (48 km/h).
   b. *Gradually* apply the brakes and bring the vehicle to a complete stop.
   c. Repeat this procedure 10 times.

32

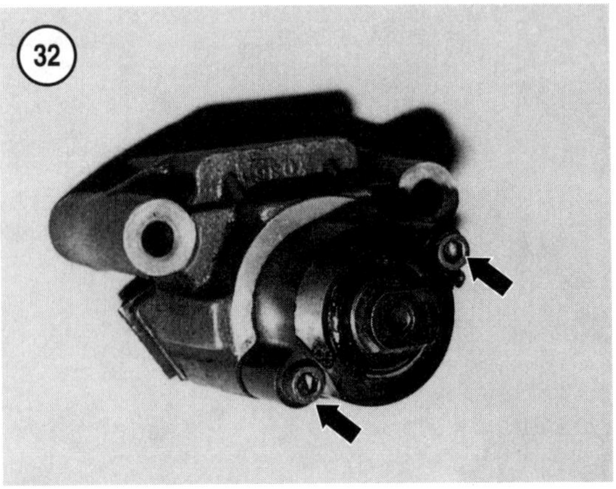

   d. For the first 2-3 days of riding, use only light pressure as much as possible. Immediate hard application will glaze the new friction pads and greatly reduce the effectiveness of the brake.

OUTPUT SHAFT BRAKE CALIPER (1996-1997 MODELS)

Removal/Installation

Refer to **Figure 28**.

CAUTION
Do not spill any brake fluid on the frame. Wash off any spilled brake fluid immediately; it will destroy the finish. Use soapy water and rinse completely.

NOTE
If the caliper is not going to be disassembled for service, proceed to Step 2.

1. If the caliper assembly is going to be disassembled for service, perform the following:
   a. Remove the brake pads as described in this chapter.
   b. Reinstall the caliper assembly and tighten the caliper mounting bolts securely.

CAUTION
Do not allow the piston to travel out far enough to come in contact with the brake disc. If this happens the piston may scratch or gouge the disc during caliper removal.

33

c. Slowly apply the brake lever to push the piston part way out of caliper assembly for ease of removal during caliper service.
d. Loosen and remove the brake hose from the rear of the caliper.
e. Place the loose end of the brake hose in a reclosable plastic bag to prevent the entry of debris and to prevent any residual brake fluid from dripping out.

2. Remove the caliper mounting bolts and remove the output shaft caliper from the transmission.
3. If necessary, disassemble, inspect and assemble the output shaft caliper as described in this chapter.
4. Install by reversing these removal steps while noting the following:
   a. Carefully install the caliper assembly onto the disc, being careful not to damage the leading edge of the brake pads.
   b. Install the caliper mounting bolts and tighten to the torque specifications listed in **Table 2**.
   c. Bleed the brake as described under *Bleeding the System* in this chapter.

WARNING
Make sure the brakes operate properly before riding the vehicle.

Disassembly

Refer to **Figure 28**.

1. Remove the brake pads as described in this chapter.
2. Remove the caliper as described in this chapter.
3. Make an alignment mark on the caliper body and the stationary ramp. To ensure correct alignment during assembly.

NOTE
***Figure 32** shows the caliper brake arm removed to better illustrate the step. It is not necessary to remove the caliper brake arm.*

4. Remove the two screws (**Figure 32**), then remove the stationary ramp assembly. Remove the gasket from the caliper body and discard it.
5. Remove the brake apply pin and spring (**Figure 33**).

NOTE
If the piston was partially forced out of the caliper body during removal, Steps 6-8 may not be necessary. If the piston or caliper bore are corroded or very dirty; a small amount of compressed air may be necessary to completely remove the piston from the body bore.

6. Place a piece of soft wood or folded shop cloth over the end of the piston and the caliper body.

WARNING
*In the next step, the piston may shoot out of the caliper body. Keep all fingers out of the way. Wear gloves and apply air pressure gradually. Do **not** use high-pressure air or place the air hose nozzle directly against the brake hose fitting inlet in the caliper body. Hold the air nozzle away from the inlet, allowing some of the air to escape.*

7. Apply the air pressure in short spurts to the brake hose inlet fitting and force the piston out of the caliper bore.

CAUTION
In the following step, do not use a sharp tool to remove the dust and piston seals from the caliper cylinders. Do not damage the cylinder surface.

8. Remove the dust seal and piston seal (**Figure 34**) from the inside of the cylinder.
9. Remove the O-ring seals (**Figure 35**) from the brake apply pin bore in the caliper body.
10. Unscrew and remove the bleed screw from the backside of the caliper.

Inspection

CAUTION
Never use petroleum-based solvents of any kind on internal brake system components. Any residual solvent will cause the new seals to swell and distort and require replacement.

1. Clean the caliper body and piston in denatured alcohol or fresh DOT 3 brake fluid. Wear eye protection and blow dry with compressed air directing the air flow and residual fluid away from you.
2. Make sure the fluid passageway in the base of the piston bore is clear. Apply compressed air to make sure it is clear.
3. Inspect the dust and piston seal grooves in the caliper body for damage. If they are damaged or corroded, replace the caliper assembly.
4. Inspect the brake hose inlet fitting in the backside of the caliper body. If worn or damaged, clean out with a thread tap or replace the caliper assembly.
5. Inspect the bleed screw threaded hole in the caliper body. If worn or damaged, clean out with a thread tap or replace the caliper assembly.
6. Inspect the bleed screw. Make sure it is clean and open. Apply compressed air to the opening and make sure it is clear. Clean out if necessary with fresh brake fluid. Install the bleed screw and tighten securely.
7. Inspect the pad retaining pins (**Figure 30**) for excessive wear, damage or uneven wear. The pins must be clean and in good condition for proper brake operation.
8. Inspect the caliper body for damage; replace the caliper body if necessary.
9. Inspect the caliper piston bore for cracks, deep scoring, or excessive wear.
10. Check the caliper piston for scratches, scoring or rust.
11. Measure the inside diameter of the piston bore with a snap gauge or vernier caliper. Replace the caliper if the bore diameter is less than the service limit dimension listed in **Table 1**.
12. Measure the outside diameter of the piston with a micrometer or vernier caliper. Replace the piston if the diameter is worn to less than the service limit dimension listed in **Table 1**.
13. The piston seals help to maintain correct brake pad to disc clearance. If the seals are worn or damaged, the brake pads will drag and cause excessive wear and increase brake fluid temperature. Replace the piston seals and dust seals if the following conditions exist:

a. Brake fluid leaks around the inboard brake pad.

b. Piston seal is stuck.

c. There is a large difference in the inner and outer brake pad thickness.

NOTE
Never reuse an old dust or piston seal. Very minor damage or age deterioration can make the seals useless.

14. Inspect the brake pads (**Figure 31**) for uneven wear, damage or grease contamination. If the pad thickness is within specification, clean off the pad surface with an aerosol brake cleaner to remove any surface contamination.

34

35

NOTE
When the brake system is operating correctly, the inboard and outboard brake pads should be approximately the same thickness. If there is a large difference in pad wear, the piston seals are faulty and not allowing the piston to return properly. This causes one pad to drag against the disc.

Assembly

NOTE
Use only new, DOT 3 brake fluid when brake fluid is called for in the following procedure.

1. Install the bleed valve into the backside of the caliper and tighten securely.
2. Apply brake fluid to the new O-ring seals and install them into the brake apply pin bore in the caliper body (**Figure 35**). Make sure they are properly seated in the grooves.
3. Soak the piston seal and dust seal in fresh DOT 3 brake fluid for approximately five minutes.
4. Lightly coat the piston and cylinder bore with brake fluid.
5. Install a new piston seal into the second groove in the cylinder bore.
6. Install a new dust seal into the first groove in the cylinder bore.
7. Turn the caliper so the brake hose fitting threaded hole is facing up. Pour in about 1/4 ounce of brake fluid into the opening and into the piston bore.

NOTE
Check that both seals fit squarely into their respective cylinder bore grooves. If a seal is not installed properly, the caliper assembly will leak and braking performance will be reduced.

8. Position the piston with the closed end going in first and install the piston into the cylinder bore.
9. Apply high-temperature grease to the brake apply pin and install the spring and pin into the body (**Figure 33**).
10. Install a new gasket on the body.
11. Refer to the marks made in Step 3 of *Disassembly*, align the two marks and install the stationary ramp assembly onto the caliper body. Install the two screws (**Figure 32**) and tighten securely.
12. Attach the brake hose to the caliper and securely tighten the fitting with a flare nut wrench.
13. Install the brake pads as described in this chapter.
14. Install the brake caliper assembly as described in this chapter.
15. Bleed the brake as described under *Bleeding the System* in this chapter.

OUTPUT SHAFT BRAKE PAD REPLACEMENT (1998-ON MODELS)

There is no recommended interval for changing the brake pads. Pad wear depends greatly on riding habits and conditions. Measure the thickness of each brake pad with a vernier caliper or ruler and compare to the dimensions listed in **Table 1**.

Always replace both pads in the caliper at the same time. Do not disconnect the hydraulic brake hose from the brake caliper for brake pad replacement, disconnect the hose only if the caliper assembly is going to be removed.

1. Remove the seat as described in Chapter Fifteen.
2. Remove the front and rear fenders as described in Chapter Fifteen.
3. If not removed during rear fender removal, remove the right-side foot well.
4. Remove two bolts, lockwashers and washers (**Figure 36**) securing the brake caliper to the transmission. Carefully remove the caliper up and off of the brake disc.

5. Release the hook portion of the retaining pin (**Figure 37**) from the caliper. Do not open the hook portion any more than necessary, as the pin tension may be lost.
6. Withdraw the retaining pin from the caliper.
7. Remove the inboard and outboard brake pads (**Figure 38**) out through the bottom of the caliper.
8. When repositioning the brake pads in the caliper, the master cylinder brake fluid level will rise as the caliper piston is repositioned. Perform the following:
   a. Clean the top of the front master cylinder to remove all debris.
   b. Place a plastic drop cloth over the front fender and fuel tank, under the master cylinder, to protect them from any accidental brake fluid spills.
   c. Remove the screws securing the top cover (**Figure 29**).
   d. Remove the top cover and diaphragm from the master cylinder.

WARNING
Brake fluid is poisonous; do not siphon it by mouth.

9. Carefully push the pistons back into the caliper cylinders. Constantly check the reservoir to make sure brake fluid does not overflow. Remove fluid, if necessary, prior to it overflowing.
10. The pistons should move freely. If they do not, remove and service the caliper as described in this chapter.
11. Inspect the brake pads (**Figure 39**) for uneven wear, damage or grease contamination. Replace the pads as a set, if necessary.
12. Measure the thickness of each brake pad with a ruler or vernier caliper (**Figure 40**). Replace the brake pads if the thickness of either pad is less than the service limit in **Table 1**.
13. Inspect the brake disc for nicks, corrosion and radial groove damage. If damaged, remove the brake disc as described in this chapter.
14. Check the end of each piston for fluid leakage. If the seals are damaged and/or if there is fluid leakage, overhaul the brake caliper as described in this chapter.

NOTE
When purchasing new pads, check with the dealership to make sure the friction compound of the new pad is compatible with the disc material. Remove any roughness from the backs of the new pads with a fine-cut file.

37

38

39

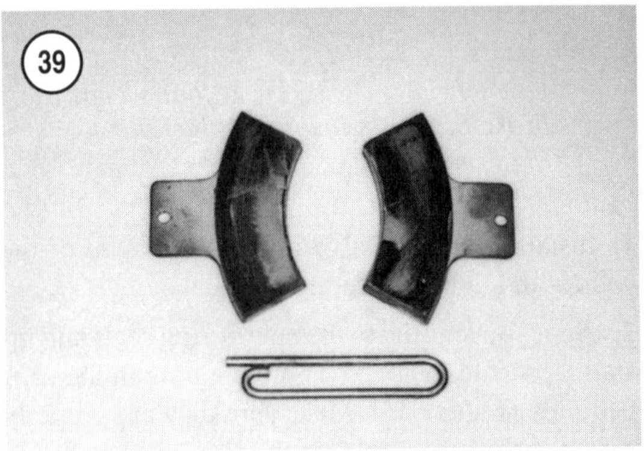

15. Install the inboard brake pad, then the outboard brake pad into the bottom of the caliper (**Figure 41**).

16. Align the brake pad retaining pin holes (A, **Figure 42**) with the holes in the caliper (B, **Figure 42**) and slowly insert the retaining pin through the caliper, outboard brake pad, inboard brake pad and the caliper. Push the retaining pin in until it stops.

40

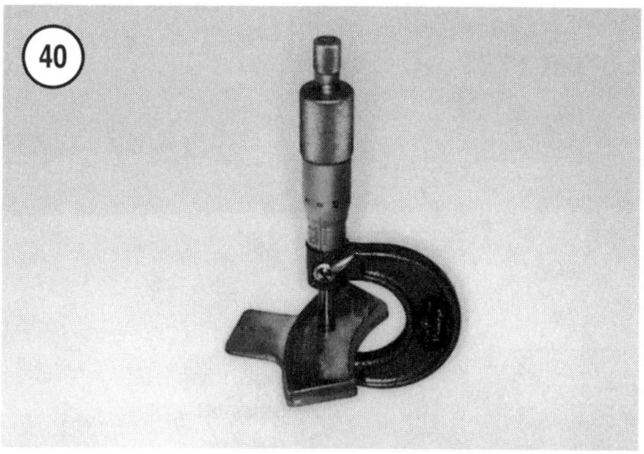

41

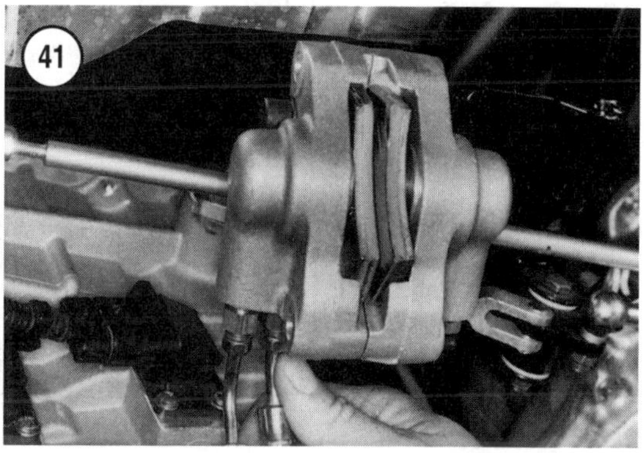

42

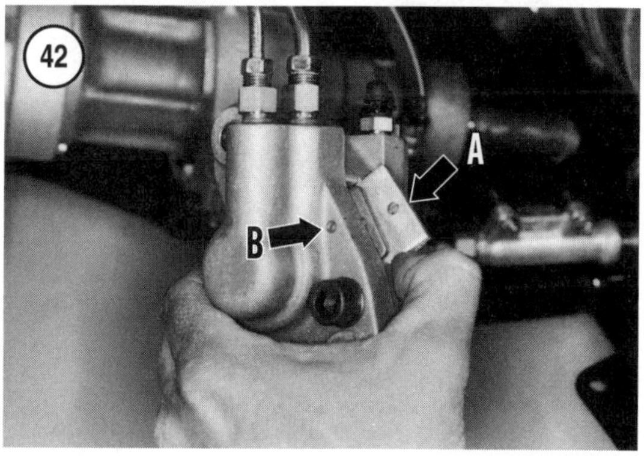

17. Use needlenose pliers to install the hook portion into the caliper hole (**Figure 37**) and make sure it is hooked correctly. Do not open the hook portion any more than necessary as the pin tension may be lost.

NOTE
To control the small flow of hydraulic fluid, punch a small hole into the edge of the brake fluid container seal. This will help eliminate fluid spillage especially while adding fluid to the very small brake reservoir.

18. Install the caliper onto the brake disc. Install the two bolts, lockwashers and washers (**Figure 36**) securing the brake caliper to the transmission. Tighten the bolts to the torque specification listed in **Table 2**.

WARNING
Use brake fluid clearly marked DOT 3 from a sealed container. Other types may vaporize and cause brake failure. Always use the same brand name; do not intermix, as many brands are not compatible. Do not intermix silicone-based (DOT 5) brake fluid, as it can cause brake component damage leading to brake system failure.

19. Refill the master cylinder reservoir, if necessary, to maintain the correct fluid level as indicated on the side of the reservoir. Install the diaphragm and cover and tighten the screws securely.
20. With the wheels still off the ground, spin the right wheel and activate the brake lever as many times as it takes to refill the caliper cylinders and correctly locate the brake pads against the disc.
21. Install the front and rear fenders as described in Chapter Fifteen.
22. Install the seat as described in Chapter Fifteen.

WARNING
Make sure that the brakes are operating correctly with full hydraulic advantage before operating the vehicle.

NOTE
The following instructions apply to original equipment type pads only. If using aftermarket brake pads, follow the manufacturer's break-in instructions.

23. Bed the pads in gradually with a burnishing procedure as follows:
   a. Start the vehicle and slowly increase speed up to 30 mph (48 km/h).
   b. *Gradually* apply the brakes and bring the vehicle to a complete stop.
   c. Repeat this procedure 10 times.
   d. For the first 2-3 days of riding, use only light pressure as much as possible. Immediate hard application will glaze the new friction pads and greatly reduce the effectiveness of the brake.

43

OUTPUT SHAFT CALIPER (1998-ON)

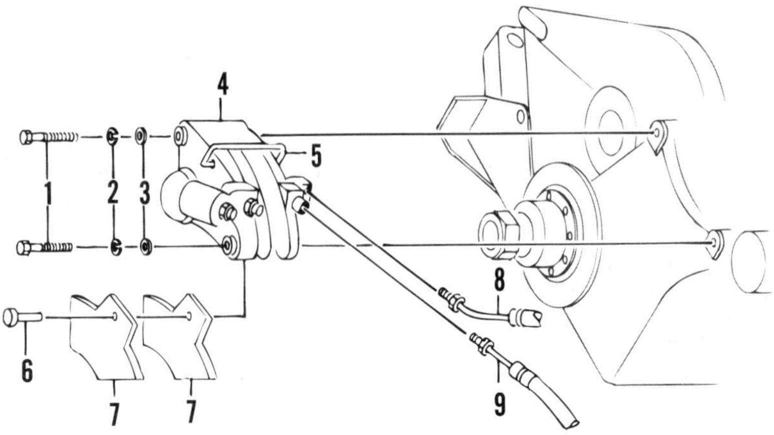

1. Mounting bolt
2. Lockwasher
3. Washer
4. Caliper assembly
5. Clip
6. Retaining pin
7. Brake pads
8. Brake line (rear master cylinder)
9. Brake line (front master cylinder)

OUTPUT SHAFT BRAKE CALIPER (1998-ON MODELS)

Removal

Refer to **Figure 43**.

NOTE
If the caliper is not going to be disassembled for service, proceed to Step 2.

1. If the caliper assembly is going to be disassembled for service, perform the following:
   a. Loosen the Allen bolt on the backside of the caliper (**Figure 44**).
   b. Remove the brake pads as described in this chapter.

CAUTION
Do not allow the pistons to travel out far enough to come in contact with the brake disc. If this happens, the pistons may scratch or gouge the disc during caliper removal.

44

   c. Slowly apply the brake lever to push the pistons part way out of caliper assembly for ease of removal during caliper service.
2. Loosen, then disconnect, both fittings (**Figure 45**) securing the brake hoses to the caliper.
3. Remove the bolts, lockwashers and washers (**Figure 36**) securing the caliper to the transmission. Remove the caliper up and off the brake disc.
4. Disconnect both fittings (**Figure 45**) and brake hoses from the caliper.
5. Place the loose end of the brake hoses in a reclosable plastic bag to prevent the entry of debris

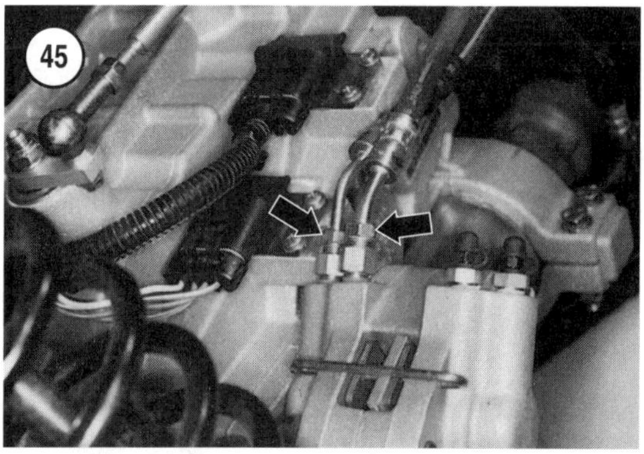

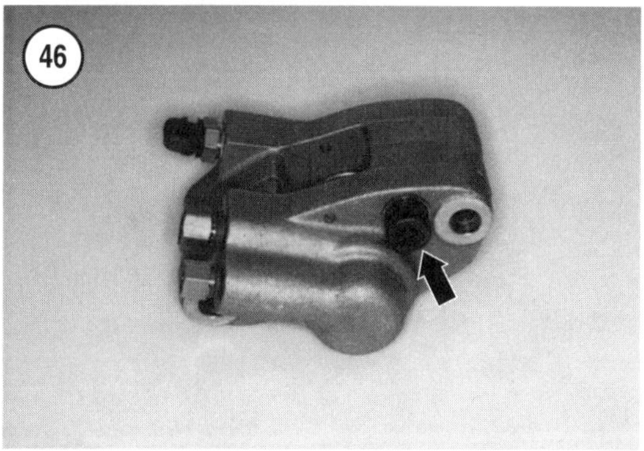

and to prevent any residual brake fluid from dripping out.

6. If necessary, disassemble, inspect and assemble the output shaft caliper as described in this chapter.

Installation

1. Connect both fittings (**Figure 45**) and brake hoses onto the caliper. Do not tighten at this time.
2. If removed, install the brake pads as described in this chapter.
3. Carefully install the caliper assembly onto the disc, being careful not to damage the leading edge of the brake pads.
4. Install the caliper mounting bolts, lockwashers and washers (**Figure 36**) and tighten to the torque specifications listed in **Table 2**
5. Tighten both fittings (**Figure 45**) securing the brake hoses to the caliper securely.
6. If the caliper was disassembled, securely tighten the Allen bolt on the backside of the caliper (**Figure 44**).
7. Bleed the brake as described under *Bleeding the System* in this chapter.

WARNING

Make sure the brakes are operating correctly with full hydraulic advantage before operating the vehicle. If necessary, bleed the brakes as described in this chapter.

Disassembly

NOTE

There are no new or service limit specifications for the caliper assembly. Replacement piston seals, dust seals and piston are available.

1. Remove the caliper as described in this chapter.
2. Remove the Allen bolt (**Figure 46**) securing the caliper halves together.
3. Carefully separate the caliper halves and remove both O-ring seals from the outboard caliper half.

NOTE

If the pistons were partially forced out of the caliper body during removal, Steps 2-4 may not be necessary. If the piston or caliper bores are corroded or very dirty, a small amount of compressed air may be necessary to completely remove the pistons from the body bores.

4. Place a piece of soft wood or folded shop cloth over the end of the piston and the caliper body. Turn this assembly over with the piston facing down.

WARNING

*In the next step, the piston may shoot out of the caliper body. Keep all fingers out of the way. Wear shop gloves and apply air pressure gradually. Do **not** use high-pressure air or place the air hose nozzle directly against the brake hose fitting inlet in the caliper body. Hold the air nozzle away from the inlet, allowing some of the air to escape.*

5. Apply the air pressure in short spurts to the brake hose inlet fitting (**Figure 47**) and force out the piston. Use a service station air hose if compressed air is not available.
6. Withdraw the piston from each caliper half.

CAUTION

In the following step, do not use a sharp tool to remove the piston seal from the caliper cylinders. Do not damage the cylinder surface.

7. Remove the dust seal (A, **Figure 48**) and piston seal (B, **Figure 48**) from the cylinder of each caliper half.
8. Unscrew and remove the bleed valves from the outboard caliper half.

Inspection

CAUTION
Never use petroleum-based solvents of any kind on the internal brake system components. Any residual solvent will cause the new seals to swell and distort and require replacement.

1. Clean the caliper bodies and pistons (**Figure 49**) in denatured alcohol or fresh DOT 3 brake fluid. Wear eye protection and blow dry with compressed air directing the air flow and residual fluid away from you.
2. Make sure the fluid passageways (**Figure 50**) in the base of the piston bore are clear. Apply compressed air to make sure they are clear.
3. Inspect the piston seal and dust seal grooves (**Figure 51**) in each caliper body for damage. If it is damaged or corroded, replace the caliper assembly.
4. Inspect the brake hose inlet threaded holes and fittings (**Figure 52**) in the caliper body. If worn or damaged, clean out with a thread tap or replace the caliper assembly.
5. Inspect the bleed screw inlet fittings in the caliper body. If worn or damaged, clean out with a thread tap or replace the caliper assembly.
6. Inspect the bleed screws and caps. Make sure they are clean and open. Apply compressed air to the openings and make sure they are clear. Clean out if necessary with fresh brake fluid. Install the bleed screws and tighten securely.
7. Inspect both caliper bodies (**Figure 53**) for damage, replace the caliper assembly if necessary.
8. Inspect the caliper piston bores (**Figure 54**) for cracks, deep scoring, or excessive wear.
9. Check the caliper pistons (**Figure 55**) for scratches, scoring or rust.
10. The piston seals help to maintain correct brake pad to disc clearance. If the seals are worn or damaged, the brake pads will drag and cause excessive

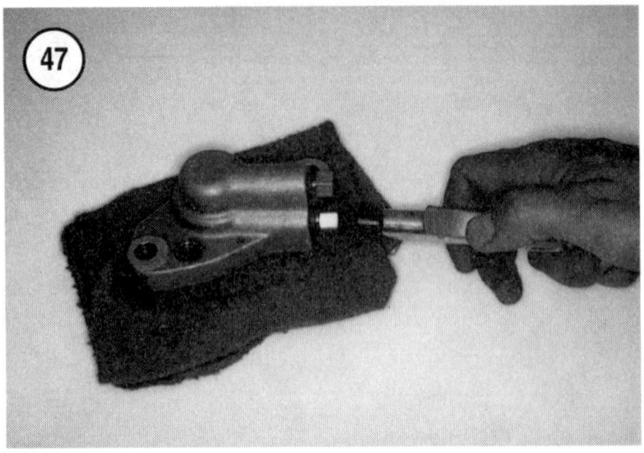

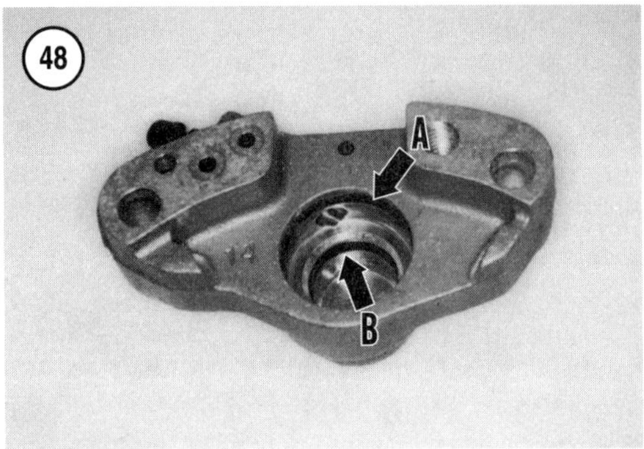

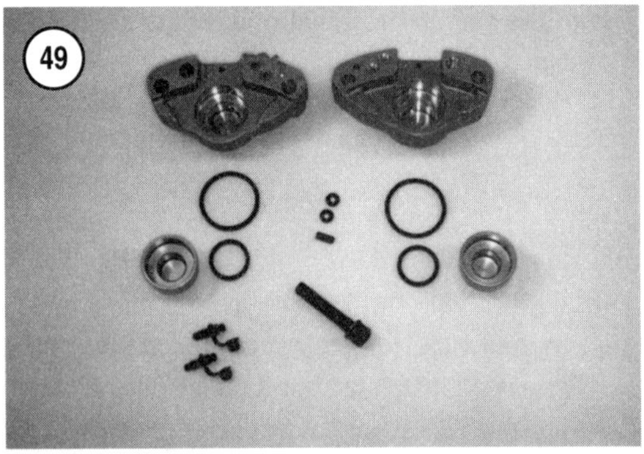

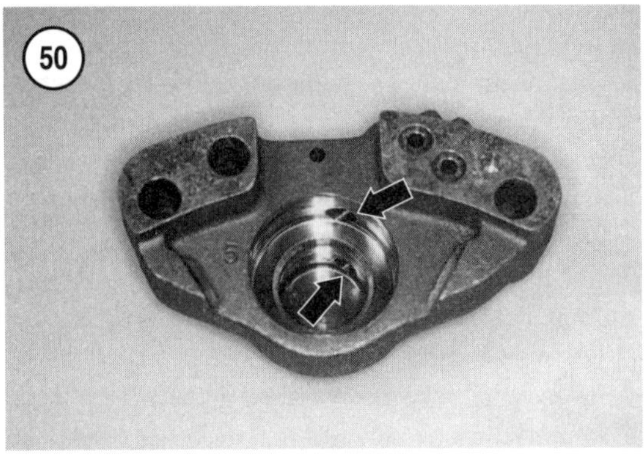

51

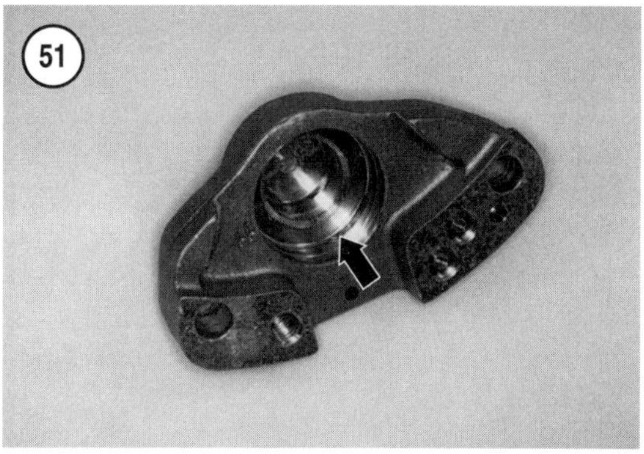

52

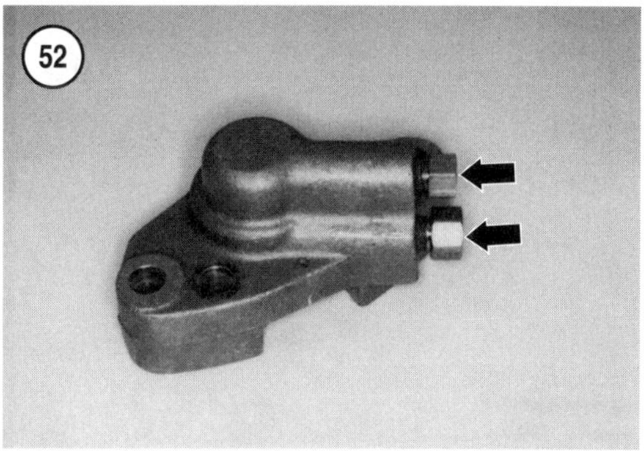

53

54

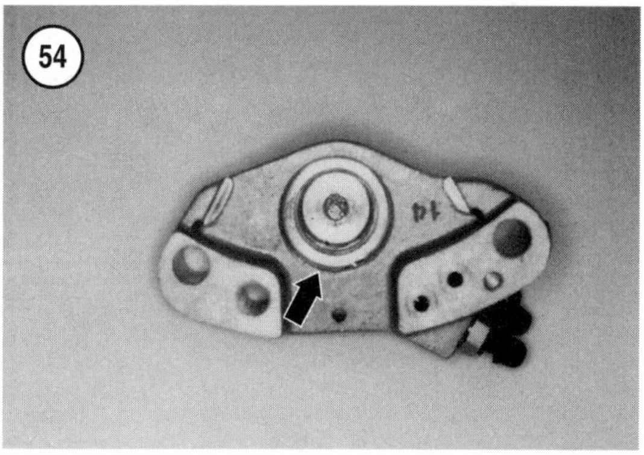

55

wear and increase brake fluid temperature. Replace the piston seals if the following conditions exist:

a. Brake fluid leads around either brake pad.
b. Stuck piston seal(s).
c. There is a large difference in the inner and outer brake pad thickness.

NOTE
Never reuse an old piston seal. Very minor damage or age deterioration can make the seals useless.

11. Inspect the brake pads (**Figure 39**) for uneven wear, damage or grease contamination. If the pad thickness is with specification, clean off the pad surface with an aerosol brake cleaner to remove any surface contamination.

NOTE
When the brake system is operating correctly, the inboard and outboard brake pads should show the same approximately amount of wear. If there is a large difference in pad wear, the piston seals are faulty and not allowing the piston to return properly. This causes one pad to drag against the disc.

Assembly

NOTE
Use only new, DOT 3 brake fluid when brake fluid is called for in the following procedure.

1. Soak the piston seals in brake fluid for approximately five minutes.
2. Lightly coat the pistons and cylinder bores with brake fluid.

3. Install a new piston seal (B, **Figure 48**) into the inner groove in the cylinder bore of each caliper.
4. Install a new dust seal (A, **Figure 48**) into the outer groove in the cylinder bore of each caliper.

NOTE
Check that the seals fit squarely into the cylinder bore groove. If a seal is not installed properly, the caliper assembly will leak and braking performance will be reduced.

5. Position the piston with the smaller closed end going in first (**Figure 56**) and install the piston into the cylinder bore. Push the piston in until it bottoms (**Figure 57**).
6. Repeat for the other piston.
7. Install *new* O-ring seals (**Figure 58**) into the receptacle in the outboard caliper half.
8. If removed, install the locating pin (**Figure 59**). Push it in until it bottoms.
9. Assemble the two caliper halves together (**Figure 60**) and make sure the locating pin and both small O-ring seals are still located correctly.
10. Install the Allen bolt (**Figure 46**) securing the caliper halves together. Finger tighten the bolt at this time. After the caliper has been installed, tighten the Allen bolt to the torque specification listed in **Table 2**.
11. Install the brake caliper assembly as described in this chapter.

FRONT MASTER CYLINDER

Removal/Installation

1. Park the vehicle on level ground and block the wheels so the vehicle cannot roll in either direction.
2. Cover the area under the master cylinder.

CAUTION
If brake fluid should contact any surface, wash the area immediately with soapy water and rinse completely. Brake fluid will damage plastic, painted and plated surfaces.

3. Loosen the clamp bolts (**Figure 61**) securing the master cylinder to the handlebar.
4. Clean the top of the master cylinder of all debris.
5. Remove the screws securing the top cover (A, **Figure 62**).

56

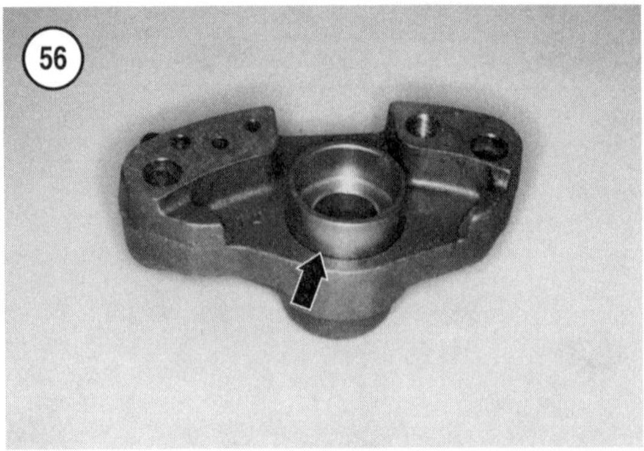

57

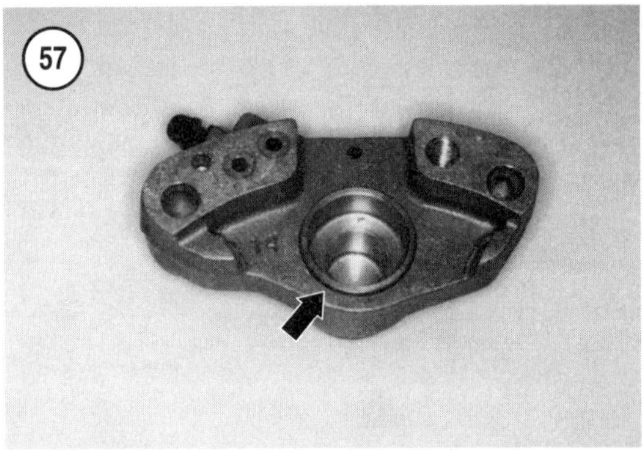

58

59

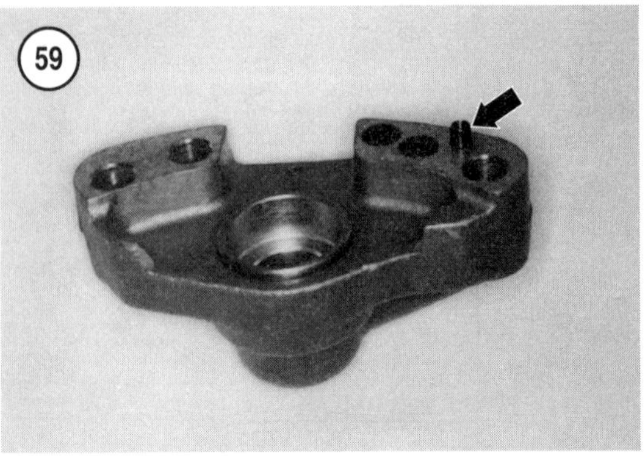

60

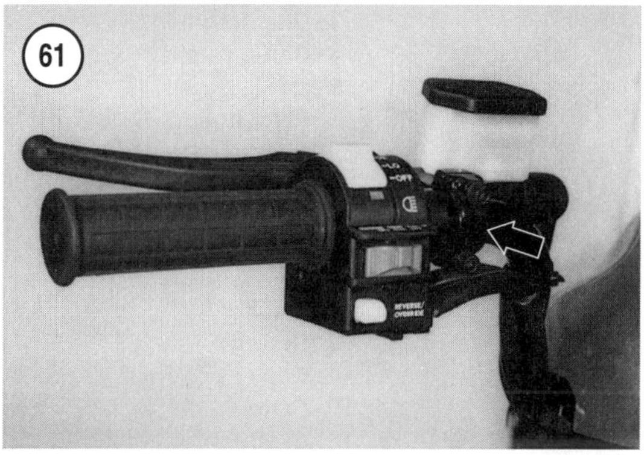
61

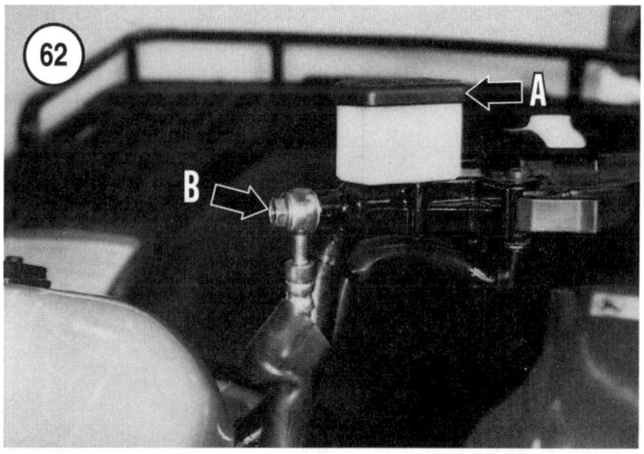

62

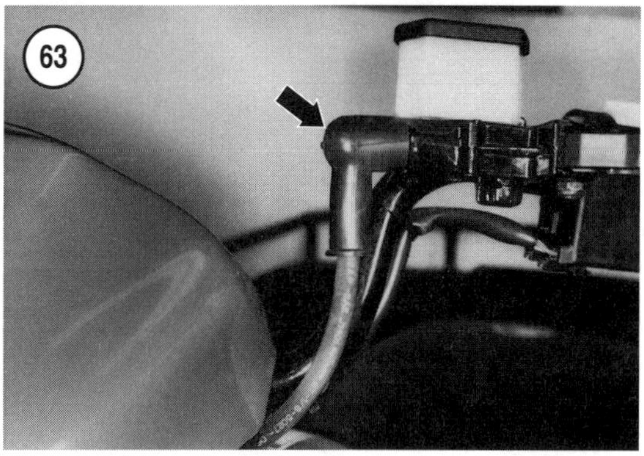
63

6. Remove the top cover and diaphragm from the master cylinder.

7. Use a clean syringe to remove the brake fluid from the reservoir. Discard the brake fluid.

8. Slide the rubber boot (**Figure 63**) off the brake hose fitting.

9. Remove the banjo bolt and sealing washers (B, **Figure 62**) securing the upper brake hose to the master cylinder. Place the loose end of the upper brake hose in a reclosable plastic bag and seal it to prevent contamination and the discharge of brake fluid. Secure the hose to the handlebar in the upright position.

10. Remove the clamp bolts (**Figure 61**) and remove the master cylinder from the handlebar.

11. If the master cylinder is being removed and is not going to be serviced, place it in a reclosable plastic bag and seal it.

12. Install by reversing these removal steps while noting the following:

   a. Move the master cylinder to a position where the brake lever suits the desired riding position, then tighten the clamp bolts.
   b. Attach the brake hose to the master cylinder with the banjo bolt and new sealing washers. Tighten the banjo bolts to the torque specification listed in **Table 2**.
   c. Refill the master cylinder with DOT 3 brake fluid and bleed the brake as described in this chapter.

WARNING

Do not ride the vehicle until the brakes are working properly. Make sure that the brake lever travel is not excessive and that the lever does not feel soft or spongy. If either condition exists, bleed the system again.

Disassembly

Refer to **Figure 64** for 1996-1998 models and to **Figure 65** for 1999-on models.

NOTE

There are no new or service limit specifications for the front master cylinder assembly.

1. Remove the master cylinder as described in this chapter.

64

FRONT MASTER CYLINDER (1996-1998)

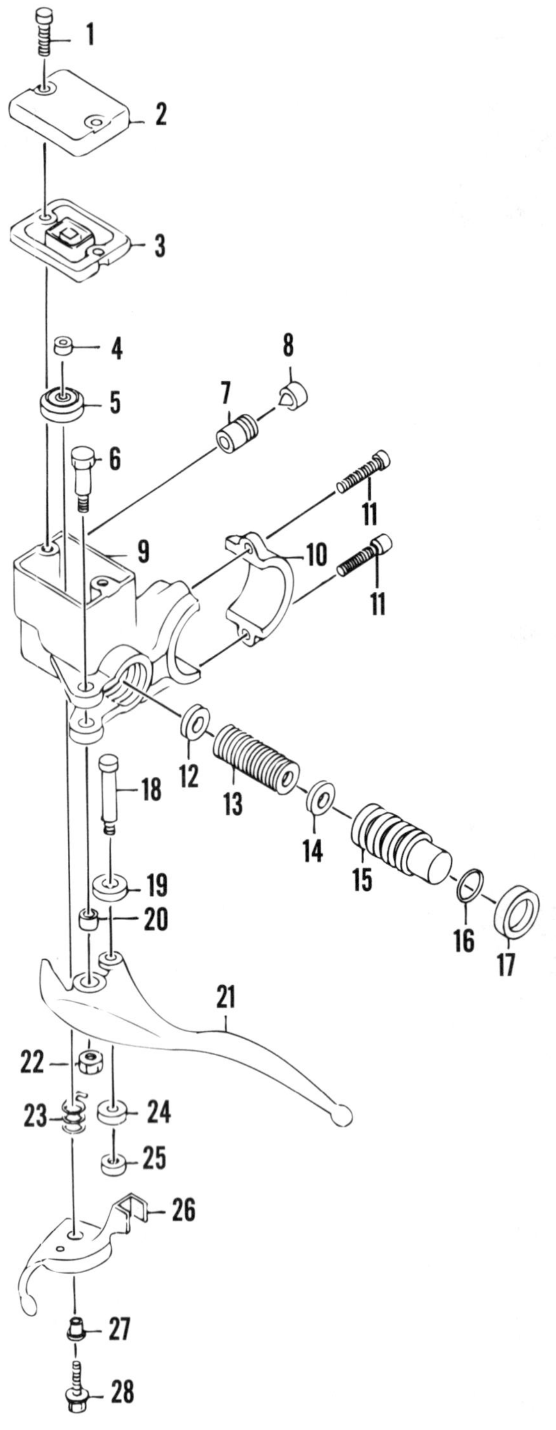

1. Screw
2. Cover
3. Diaphragm
4. Baffle washer
5. Baffle
6. Pivot bolt
7. Sight glass
8. Seal
9. Body
10. Clamp
11. Screw
12. Washer
13. Spring
14. Cup
15. Piston
16. O-ring
17. Dust seal
18. Pivot bolt
19. Washer
20. Bushing
21. Brake lever
22. Nut
23. Spring
24. Roller
25. E-clip
26. Parking brake lever
27. Bushing
28. Bolt

(65)

FRONT MASTER CYLINDER (1999-ON)

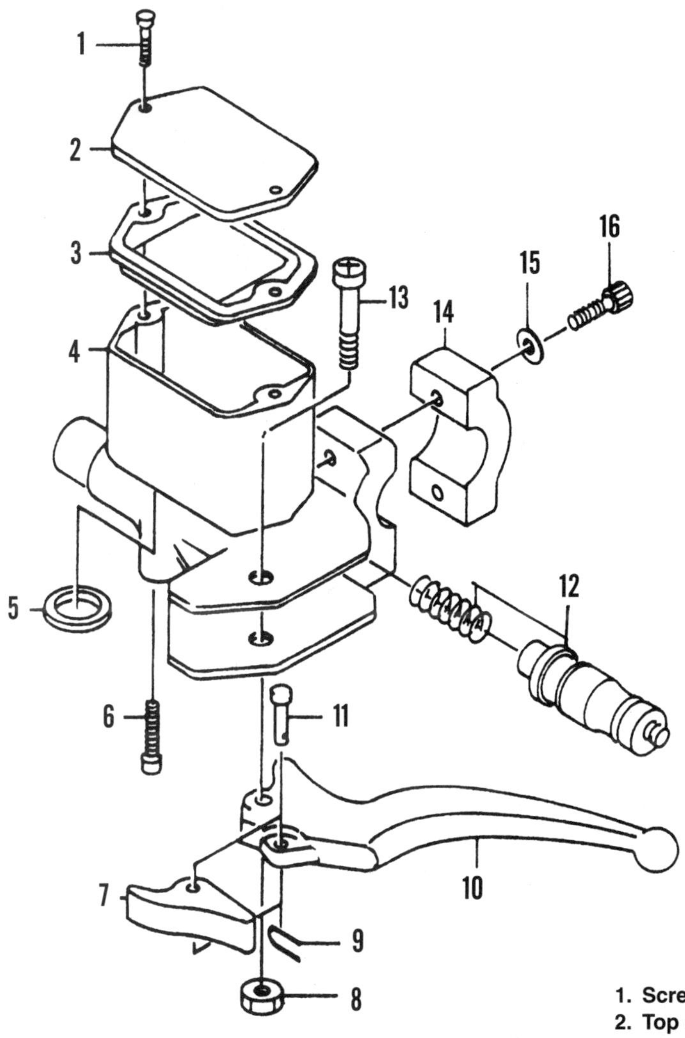

1. Screw
2. Top cover
3. Diaphragm
4. Reservoir
5. Reservoir seal
6. Screw
7. Parking brake lever
8. Nylock nut
9. Spring
10. Brake lever
11. Pivot pin
12. Piston/spring assembly
13. Pivot bolt
14. Clamp
15. Washer
16. Bolt

2. Remove the brake lever pivot bolt (**Figure 66**) and nut securing the brake lever to the master cylinder and remove the brake lever.
3. Remove the screws attaching the master cylinder cover, then remove the cover and diaphragm (**Figure 67**).

NOTE
If there is brake fluid leaking from the piston bore, the piston cup is worn or damaged. Replace the piston assembly during re-assembly.

NOTE
On 1996-1998 models, after the dust seal is removed from the piston bore area, the spring will force the piston out of the bore. Be ready to catch the piston to avoid damage.

4A. On 1996-1998 models, perform the following:
   a. Carefully remove the dust seal from the groove in the piston bore area where the hand lever actuates the piston assembly.
   b. Remove the piston, spring and washer from the master cylinder bore.

4B. On 1999-on models, remove the piston and spring from the master cylinder bore.
5. On 1999-on models, if brake fluid has been leaking from the base of the master cylinder reservoir, perform the following:
   a. Turn the master cylinder over and remove the two screws securing the reservoir to the body.
   b. Remove the reservoir and the reservoir seal.

Inspection

1. Clean all parts in isopropyl alcohol or fresh DOT 3 brake fluid. Inspect the body cylinder bore surface and piston contact surfaces for signs of wear and damage. If less than perfect, replace the master cylinder assembly. The body cannot be replaced separately.
2. Inspect the piston cup for signs of wear and damage.
3. If the reservoir was removed, make sure the compensating and supply ports are clear.
4. Make sure the fluid passage in the bottom of the master cylinder reservoir is clear.
5. Inspect the piston contact surface for signs of wear and damage. If less than perfect, replace the piston assembly.

6. Check the end of the piston for wear caused by the hand lever. If worn, replace the piston assembly.
7. Check the hand lever pivot lugs on the master cylinder body for cracks or elongation. If damaged, replace the master cylinder assembly.
8. Inspect the pivot hole in the hand lever. If worn or elongated, replace the lever.
9. Inspect the threads in the bore for the banjo bolt. If worn or damaged, clean out with a metric thread tap or replace the master cylinder assembly.
10. Check the top cover and diaphragm for damage and deterioration and replace as necessary.
11. Inspect the parking brake lever for ease of movement. Make sure the spring is in place and is working properly.

Assembly

1. Coat the new cups and the new piston assembly in fresh DOT 3 brake fluid. Coat the inside of the cylinder bore with fresh brake fluid.
2. If removed, position the cup with the open end facing toward the spring end of the piston. Install the cup onto the piston.

CAUTION
When installing the piston assembly, do not allow the cups to turn inside out, as they will be damaged and allow brake fluid leakage within the cylinder bore.

3. Position the spring with the tapered end facing the piston.
4A. On 1996-1998 models, perform the following:
   a. Install the washer, spring and piston assembly into the cylinder. Push them in until they bottom in the cylinder.

67

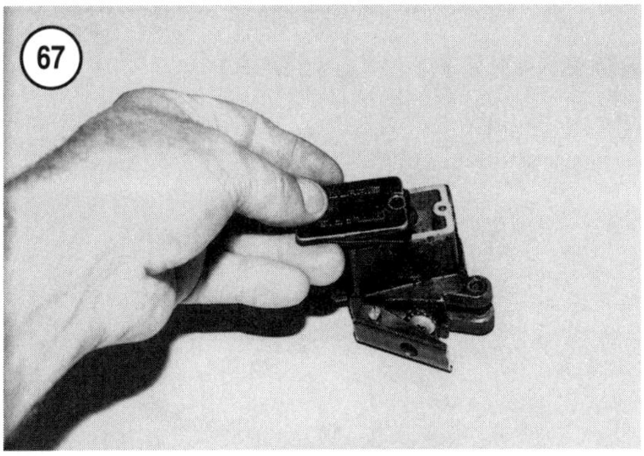

b. Push the piston assembly on, hold it there and install the new dust seal. Make sure the dust seal is correctly seated in the groove. Push on the piston; it should spring back against the dust seal.

4B. On 1999-on models, install the spring and the piston into the master cylinder bore.

5. On 1999-on models, if the reservoir was removed, perform the following:
   a. Make sure the mating surfaces of the body and reservoir are clean.
   b. Install a new reservoir seal and apply fresh brake fluid to the seal.
   c. Correctly position the reservoir onto the body making sure the seal is seating correctly onto both parts.
   d. Hold both parts together and install both mounting screws. Tighten the screws evenly and securely—do not overtighten or the threads will be stripped out of the reservoir.

6. Install the hand lever, bolt and nut. Tighten the bolt and nut securely, then make sure the hand lever operates freely within the master cylinder. There should be no binding.

7. Install the diaphragm, cover and screws. Tighten the screws only finger-tight at this time.

8. Install the master cylinder as described in this chapter.

REAR MASTER CYLINDER

NOTE

The 1996-1997 models are not equipped with a rear master cylinder. The output shaft caliper is either controlled hydraulically by the front master cylinder or mechanically by the rear brake pedal.

Removal/Installation (1998 Models)

Refer to **Figure 68**.

1. Park the vehicle on level ground and block the wheels so the vehicle cannot roll in either direction.
2. Remove the seat as described in Chapter Fifteen.
3. Remove the front and rear fenders as described in Chapter Fifteen.
4. If not removed during rear fender removal, remove the right-side foot well.
5. Cover the area under the rear master cylinder.
6. Remove the cotter pin and clevis pivot pin securing the plunger to the linkage.
7. Disconnect the reservoir hose from the master cylinder.
8. Loosen the reservoir cap and drain the brake fluid into a container.
9. Place the loose end of the reservoir hose in a reclosable plastic bag and seal it to prevent contamination and the discharge of brake fluid. Secure the hose to the frame in the upright position.
10. Remove the bolts and nuts securing the master cylinder to the frame bracket.
11. Partially remove the master cylinder from the frame.
12. Unscrew the brake hose fitting from the master cylinder. Plug the hose fitting on the master cylinder to prevent the dripping of brake fluid.
13. Place the loose end of the brake hose in a reclosable plastic bag and seal it to prevent contamination and the discharge of brake fluid. Secure the hose to the frame in the upright position.
14. Remove the master cylinder from the frame.
15. If necessary, remove the bolt and nut securing the reservoir to the frame mounting bracket. Remove the reservoir and hose from the frame.
16. Install by reversing these removal steps while noting the following:
    a. Install the brake line to the master cylinder and tighten securely.
    b. Tighten the master cylinder mounting bolts securely.
    c. Refill the master cylinder with DOT 3 brake fluid and bleed the brake as described in this chapter.

WARNING

Do not ride the vehicle until the brakes are working properly. Make sure that the brake lever travel is not

(68) **REAR MASTER CYLINDER AND BRAKE PEDAL (1998)**

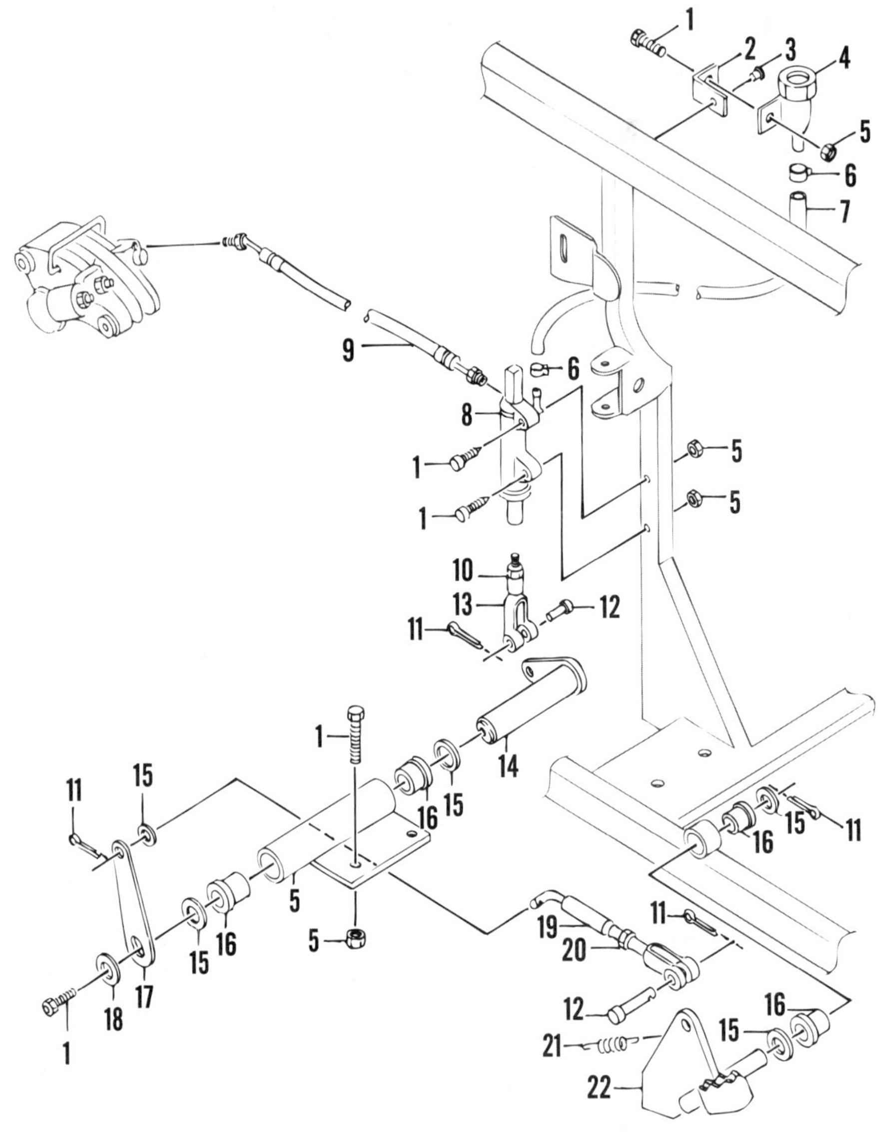

1. Bolt
2. Bracket
3. Plug
4. Reservoir
5. Nut
6. Hose clamp
7. Reservoir hose
8. Master cylinder
9. Brake line
10. Plunger
11. Cotter pin
12. Clevis pivot pin
13. Clevis
14. Linkage
15. Washer
16. Bushing
17. Lever
18. Washer
19. Linkage rod
20. Adjust nut
21. Spring
22. Brake pedal

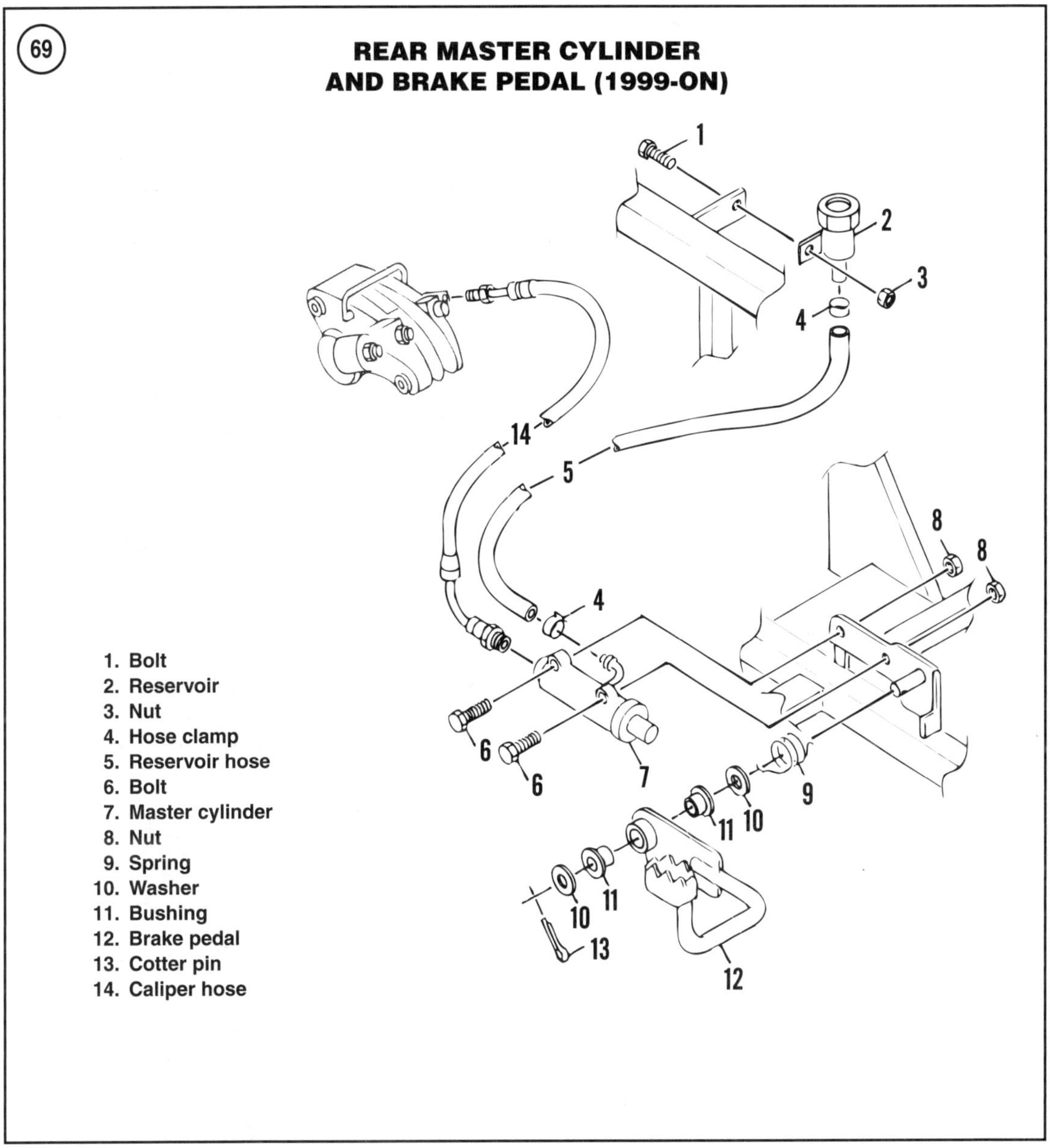

excessive and that the lever does not feel soft or spongy. If either condition exists, bleed the system again.

Removal/Installation (1999-On Models)

Refer to **Figure 69**.

1. Park the vehicle on level ground and block the wheels so the vehicle cannot roll in either direction.
2. Remove the seat as described in Chapter Fifteen.
3. Remove the front and rear fenders as described in Chapter Fifteen.
4. If not removed during rear fender removal, remove the right-side foot well.
5. Cover the area under the rear master cylinder.
6. Disconnect the reservoir hose (**Figure 70**) from the backside of the master cylinder.
7. Loosen the reservoir cap (**Figure 71**) and drain the brake fluid into a container.
8. Place the loose end of the reservoir hose in a reclosable plastic bag and seal it to prevent contami-

nation and the discharge of brake fluid. Secure the hose to the frame in the upright position.

9. Unscrew the brake hose fitting (A, **Figure 72**) from the rear of the master cylinder. Plug the hose fitting on the master cylinder to prevent brake fluid from dripping.

10. Place the loose end of the brake hose in a reclosable plastic bag and close it to prevent contamination and the discharge of brake fluid. Secure the hose to the frame in the upright position.

11. Remove the bolts and nuts securing the master cylinder (B, **Figure 72**) to the frame bracket.

12. Remove the master cylinder from the frame.

13. If necessary, remove the bolt and nut (**Figure 73**) securing the reservoir to the frame. Remove the reservoir and hose from the frame.

14. Install by reversing these removal steps, while noting the following:

   a. Install the brake line to the master cylinder and tighten securely.
   b. Tighten the master cylinder mounting bolts securely.
   c. Refill the master cylinder with DOT 3 brake fluid and bleed the brake as described in this chapter.

WARNING

Do not ride the vehicle until the brakes are working properly. Make sure the brake lever travel is not excessive and that the lever does not feel soft or spongy. If either condition exists, bleed the system again.

Disassembly/Inspection/Assembly

The rear master cylinder is a sealed unit with no replacement parts available.

BRAKE HOSE REPLACEMENT

Refer to **Figure 74**.

Front Master Cylinder Brake Hose

1. Park the vehicle on level ground and block the wheels so the vehicle cannot roll in either direction.

2. Remove the front fender as described in Chapter Fifteen.

3. Cover the area under the master cylinder.

70

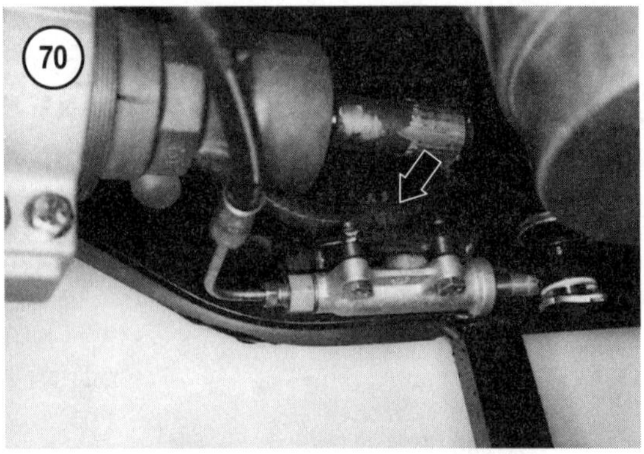

71

72

73

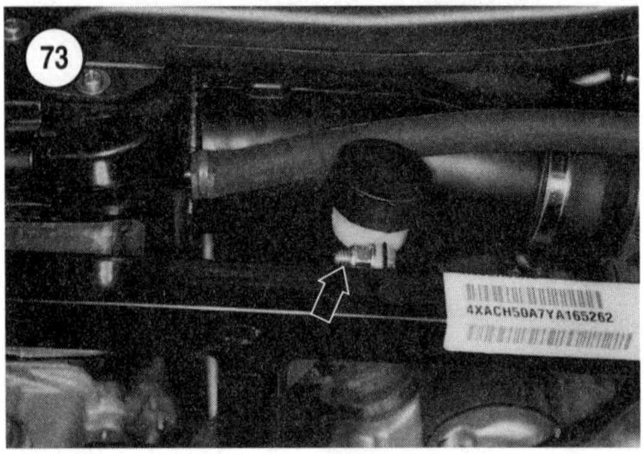

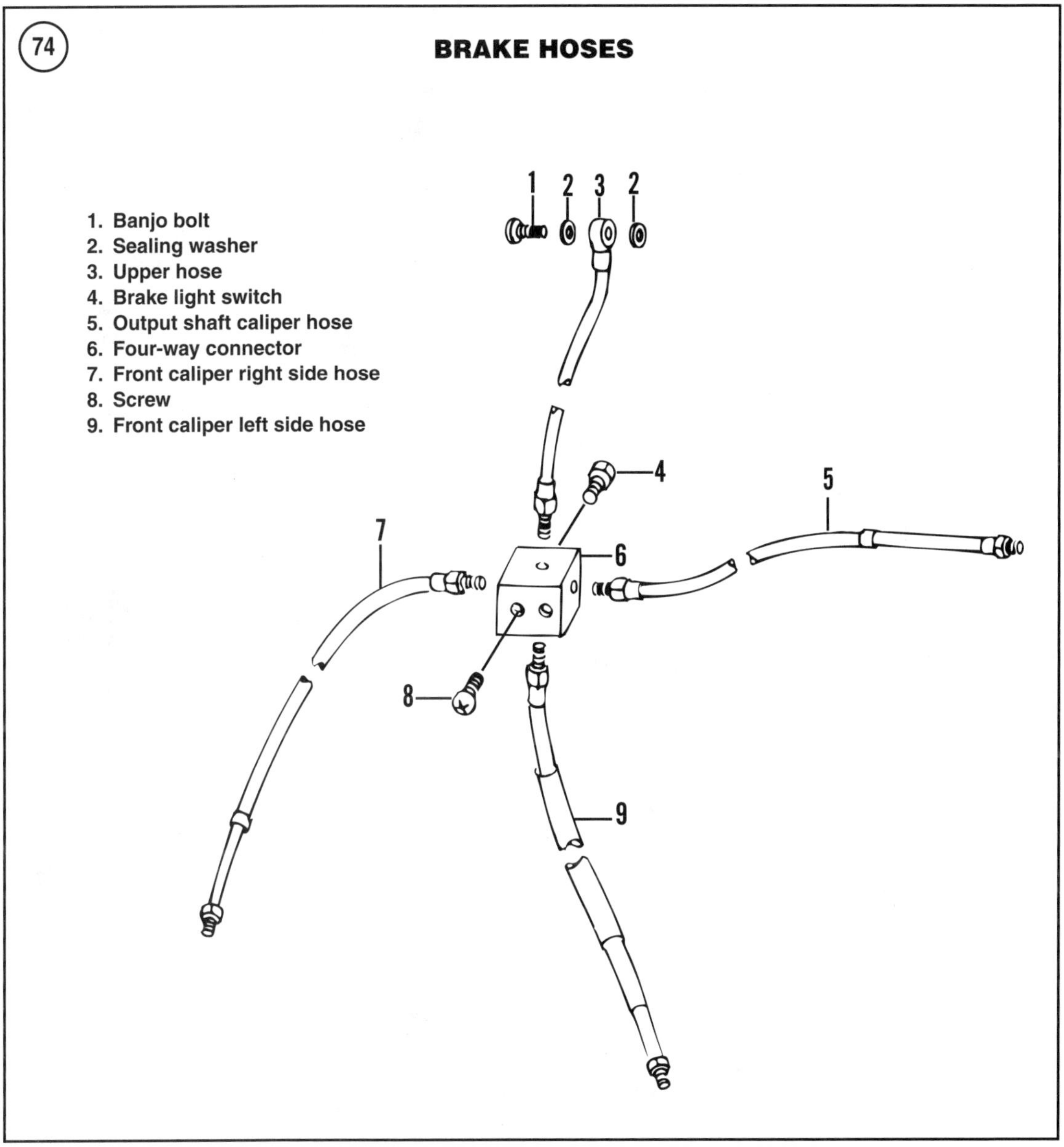

4. Clean the top of the master cylinder of all debris.
5. Remove the screws securing the top cover (A, **Figure 62**).
6. Remove the top cover and diaphragm from the master cylinder.
7. Use a clean syringe to remove the brake fluid from the reservoir. Discard the brake fluid.
8. Slide the rubber boot (**Figure 63**) off the brake hose fitting.
9. Remove the banjo bolt and sealing washers (B, **Figure 62**) securing the upper brake hose to the master cylinder. Place the loose end of the upper brake hose in a reclosable plastic bag and close it to prevent contamination and the discharge of brake fluid. Secure the hose to the handlebar in the upright position.

10. Disconnect the brake hose from the upper fitting on the four-way connector (A, **Figure 75**).

11. Remove any tie wraps securing the brake hose to the chassis.

12. Note the routing of the brake hose through the frame. The brake hose must follow the exact same path when installed to avoid any kinks or damage.

13. Install the new hose in the reverse order of removal while noting the following:
   a. Tighten the brake hose fitting securely.
   b. Attach the brake hose to the master cylinder with the banjo bolt and new sealing washers. Tighten the banjo bolts to the torque specification listed in **Table 2**.
   c. Refill the master cylinder with DOT 3 brake fluid and bleed the brake as described under *Bleeding the System* in this chapter.

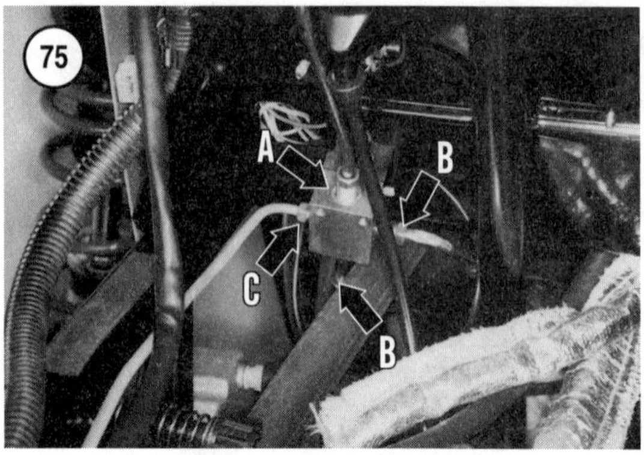

Front Caliper Brake Hoses

1. Remove the front fender as described in Chapter Fifteen.
2. Disconnect the brake hose from the caliper(s) (**Figure 76**).
3. Place the end of the brake hose over a container and let the brake fluid drain out into the container.
4. Disconnect the brake hose fittings from the right side and lower outlets on the four-way connector (B, **Figure 75**).
5. Remove any tie wraps securing the brake hose(s) to the chassis.
6. Note the routing of the brake hose(s) through the frame and suspension components. The brake hose(s) must follow the exact same path when installed to avoid any kinks or damage. Make sure the hose does not come in contact with the suspension and/or wheels.
7. Install new hose(s) in the reverse order of removal while noting the following:
   a. Tighten the brake hose fittings securely.
   b. Refill the front master cylinder reservoir and bleed the front brake system as described under *Bleeding the System* in this chapter.

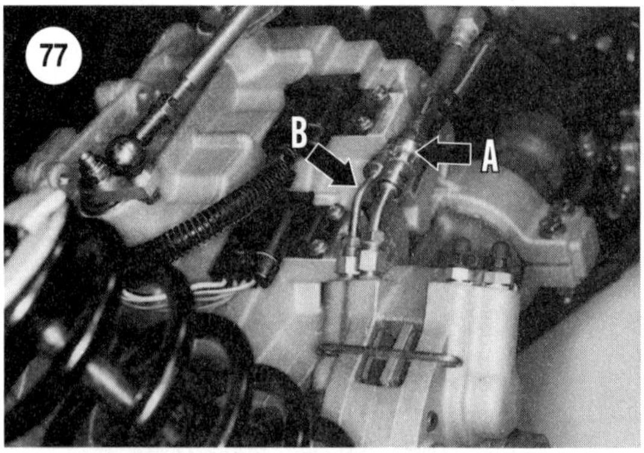

Output Shaft Caliper Brake Hoses

There are two types of brake hose routing on the various models.

On 1996-1997 models there is one brake hose from the four-way fitting to the output shaft caliper.

On 1998-on models there is one brake hose from the four-way fitting to the output shaft caliper and one brake hose from the rear master cylinder to the output shaft caliper.

1. Remove the front and rear fenders as described in Chapter Fifteen.

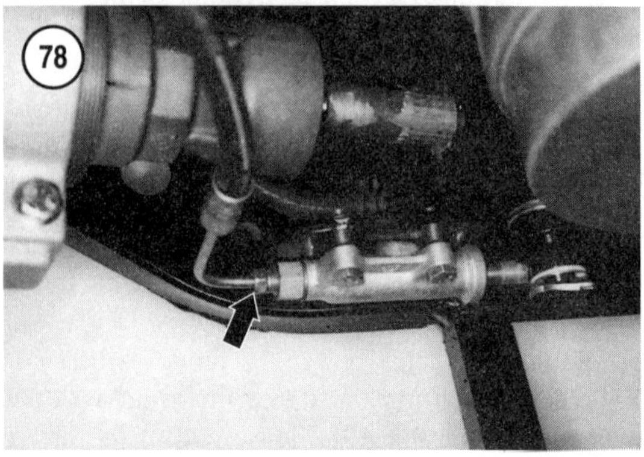

79

REAR BRAKE PEDAL (1996-1997)

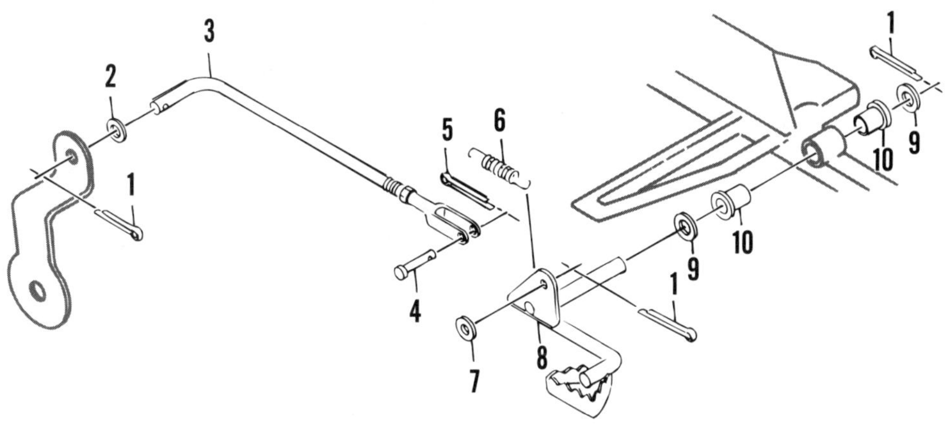

1. Cotter pin
2. Washer
3. Linkage rod
4. Clevis pin
5. Cotter pin
6. Spring
7. Washer
8. Brake pedal
9. Washer
10. Bushing

2. Remove the rear caliper as described in this chapter.

3A. On 1996-1997 models, perform the following:

a. Disconnect the output shaft caliper brake hose fitting from the left side outlet on the four-way connector.
b. Disconnect the brake hose from the output shaft caliper fitting.

3B. On 1998-on models, perform the following:

a. Disconnect the output shaft caliper front brake hose fitting from the left side outlet on the four-way connector (C, **Figure 75**).
b. Disconnect the front brake hose from the output shaft caliper fitting (A, **Figure 77**).
c. Disconnect the rear brake hose fitting from the rear master cylinder fitting **(Figure 78)**.
d. Disconnect the rear brake hose from the output shaft caliper fitting (B, **Figure 77**).

4. Place the end of the brake hoses over a container and let the brake fluid drain out into the container.

5. Remove any tie wraps securing the brake hose(s) to the chassis.

6. Note the routing of the brake hose(s) through the frame. The brake hose(s) must follow the exact same path when installed to avoid any kinks or damage.

7. Install new hose(s) in the reverse order of removal while noting the following:

a. Tighten the brake hose fittings securely.
b. Refill the front and rear master cylinder reservoirs and bleed the front and rear brake system as described under *Bleeding the System* in this chapter.

REAR BRAKE PEDAL

Removal/Installation (1996-1997 Models)

Refer to **Figure 79**.

1. Remove the rear fender and the right-side footwell as described in Chapter Fifteen.
2. Remove the cotter pin and withdraw the clevis pin from linkage rod.
3. Disconnect the linkage rod from the brake pedal.
4. Working under the frame, remove the cotter pin and washer securing the brake pedal to the pivot point of the frame.

5. Withdraw the brake pedal from the frame and reinstall the washer and cotter pin onto the brake pedal to avoid misplacing them.
6. If necessary, remove the bushing from each side of the frame pivot point.
7. To remove the linkage rod, remove the cotter pin and disconnect the linkage rod from the caliper brake arm.
8. Install by reversing these removal steps while noting the following:
   a. Apply grease to all pivot points prior to installation.
   b. Install *new* cotter pins and bend the ends over completely.

Removal/Installation (1998 Models)

Refer to **Figure 68**.

1. Remove the rear fender and the right-side footwell as described in Chapter Fifteen.
2. To remove the brake pedal only, perform the following:
   a. Remove the cotter pin and clevis pin securing the linkage rod to the brake pedal.
   b. Remove the cotter pin and inner washer securing the brake pedal to the pivot point of the frame.
   c. Withdraw the brake pedal and outer washer from the frame and reinstall the inner washer and cotter pin onto the brake pedal to avoid misplacing them.
   d. Inspect the bushings within the pivot point on the frame; replace if worn or damaged.
3. To remove the linkage assembly, perform the following:
   a. Disconnect the linkage rod from the brake pedal as described in Step 2.
   b. Remove the cotter pin and clevis pin securing the linkage to the rear master cylinder clevis.
   c. Remove the two bolts and nuts securing the pivot mounting plate to the frame and remove the assembly.
4. To disassemble the pivot mounting plate and linkage, perform the following:
   a. Remove the linkage assembly as described in Step 3.
   b. Remove the bolt securing the lever to the linkage.

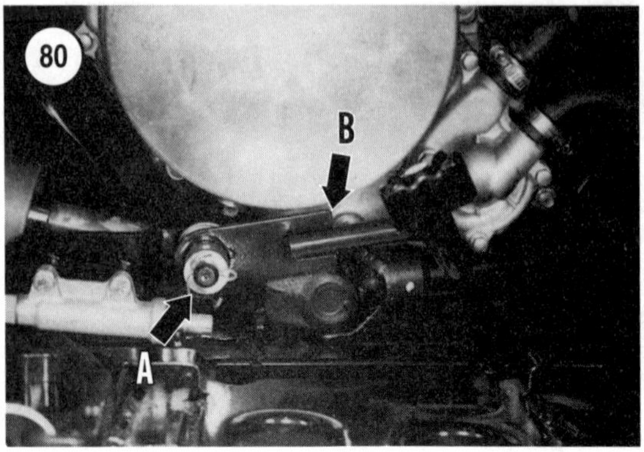

   c. Remove the washer, lever and washer from the linkage.
   d. Withdraw the linkage and washer from the pivot mounting plate.
   e. Inspect the bushings within the pivot mounting plate; replace if worn or damaged.
5. Assemble and install by reversing these disassembly and removal steps while noting the following:
   a. Apply grease to all pivot points prior to installation.
   b. Install *new* cotter pins and bend the ends over completely.

Removal/Installation (1999-On Models)

Refer to **Figure 69**.

1. Remove the rear fender and the right-side footwell as described in Chapter Fifteen.
2. Remove the cotter pin and washer (A, **Figure 80**) securing the rear brake pedal to the frame pivot shaft.
3. Withdraw the brake pedal (B, **Figure 80**) from the frame pivot shaft.
4. Remove the washer and spring from the frame pivot shaft.
5. If necessary, remove the bushing from each side of the brake pedal pivot point.
6. Install by reversing these removal steps while noting the following:
   a. Apply grease to all pivot points prior to installation.
   b. Install a *new* cotter pin and bend the ends over completely.
   c. Attach the spring to the brake pedal and frame.

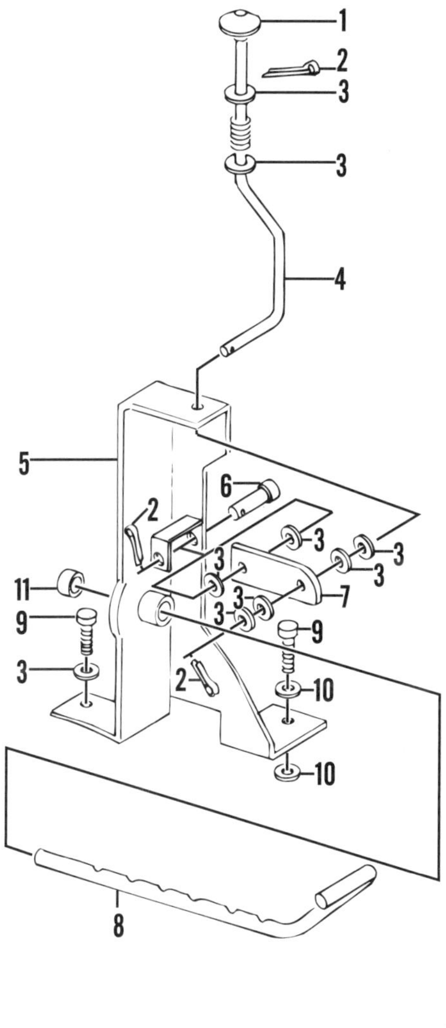

1. Knob
2. Cotter pin
3. Washer
4. Brake lock lever
5. Mounting bracket
6. Clevis pin
7. Brake pawl
8. Ratchet rod
9. Bolt
10. Washer
11. Bushing

REAR BRAKE LEVER (1996-1997 SWEDEN MODELS)

Removal/Installation

Refer to **Figure 81**.

1. Remove the rear fender and the right-side footwell as described in Chapter Fifteen.
2. Remove the cotter pin and clevis pin securing the brake pawl to the mounting bracket.
3. Remove the cotter pin and washers securing the brake lock lever to the brake pawl.
4. Disengage the brake lock lever from the brake pawl along with the two washers.
5. Withdraw the brake lock lever from the mounting plate.
6. Remove the ratchet rod from the mounting plate.
7. Install by reversing these removal steps while noting the following:
   a. Apply grease to all pivot points and sliding surfaces prior to installation.
   b. Install *new* cotter pins and bend the ends over completely.

FOOT BRAKE (1998-ON SWEDEN MODELS)

Removal/Installation

Refer to **Figure 82**.

1. Remove the rear fender and the right-side footwell as described in Chapter Fifteen.
2. Disconnect the spring from the brake pawl and handle. Remove the spring.
3. Remove the cotter pin and clevis pin securing the linkage to the brake pawl.
4. Remove the cotter pin and washers securing the linkage to the brake handle.
5. Remove the nut and large washer securing the brake handle to the bracket.
6. Install by reversing these removal steps while noting the following:
   a. Apply grease to all pivot points prior to installation.
   b. Install *new* cotter pins and bend the ends over completely.

BRAKE DISC

The front brake discs are attached to the front hubs. The rear brake disc is attached to the

82

REAR BRAKE PEDAL (SWEDEN 1998-ON)

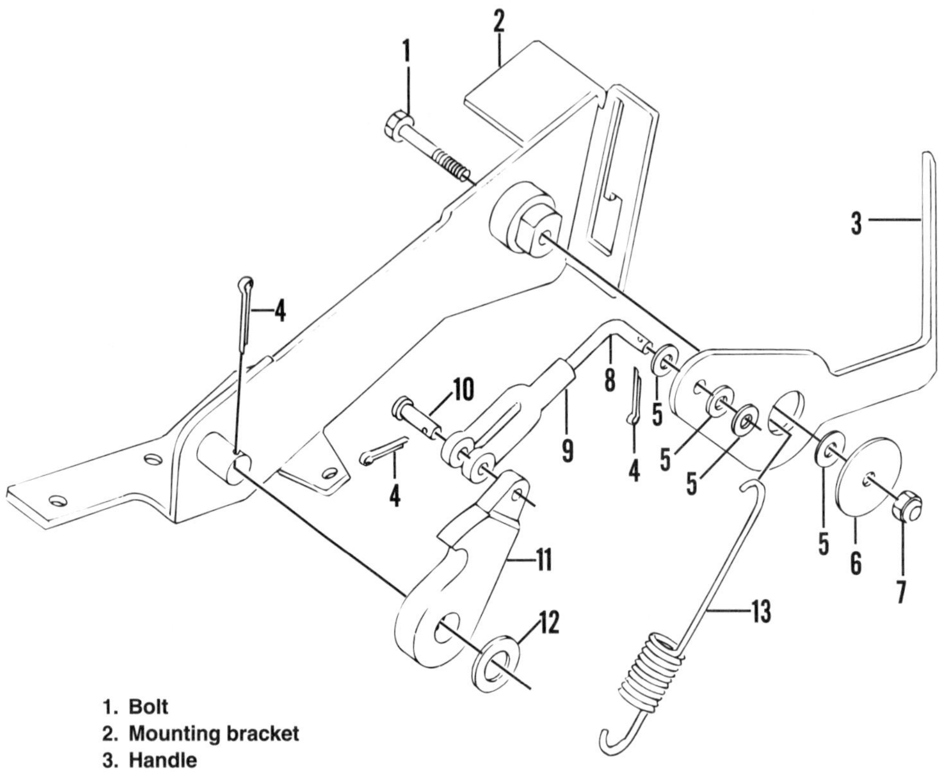

1. Bolt
2. Mounting bracket
3. Handle
4. Cotter pin
5. Washer
6. Large washer
7. Self-locking nut
8. Linkage
9. Clevis
10. Clevis pivot pin
11. Brake pawl
12. Bushing
13. Spring

transmission output shaft on the right side of the transmission.

Inspection

It is not necessary to remove the disc from the wheel to inspect it. Small nicks and marks on the disc (**Figure 83**) are not important, but radial scratches deep enough to snag a fingernail reduce braking effectiveness and increase brake pad wear. If these grooves are evident, and the brake pads are wearing rapidly, replace the disc.

The standard and wear limit specifications are listed in **Table 2**.

When servicing the brake discs, do not have the discs reconditioned (ground) to compensate for any warpage. The discs are thin and grinding only reduces their thickness, causing them to warp quite rapidly. If the disc is warped, the brake pads may be dragging on the disc; this causes the disc to overheat.

Refer to Brakes in Chapter Two for troubleshooting.

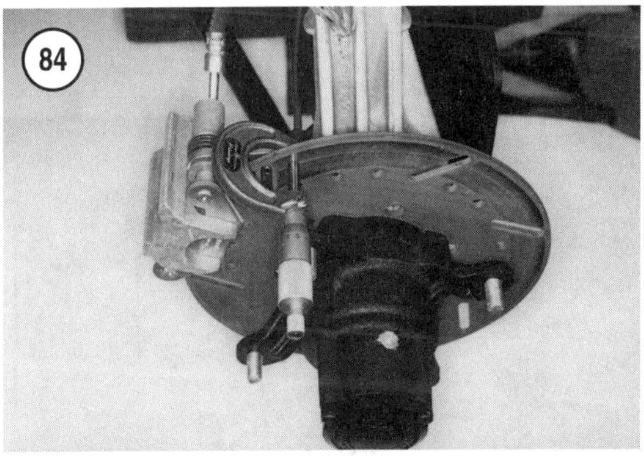

1. Securely support the vehicle with all four wheels off the ground.

2A. For front brake discs, remove the front wheels as described in Chapter Twelve.

2B. For output shaft disc, remove the rear fender and right-side footwell as described in Chapter Fifteen.

3. Measure the thickness around the disc at several locations with a micrometer. Refer to **Figure 84** and **Figure 85**. Replace the disc if the thickness varies at different locations around the disc (**Table 1**).

4. Make sure the disc bolts are tight prior to performing this check. Use a magnetic stand with the dial indicator stem against the brake disc. Turn the hub, transmission output shaft or rear axle and measure the runout. If the runout exceeds the specification in **Table 1**, replace the disc.

5. Clean any rust or corrosion from the disc and wipe the disc clean with an aerosol brake cleaner. Never use petroleum based solvent that may leave an oil residue on the disc. Do not touch the pad surface of the disc after cleaning.

Removal/Installation

1. To remove the front brake disc, perform the following:
   a. Remove the front hub(s) as described in Chapter Ten.
   b. Remove the bolts (**Figure 86**) securing the disc to the wheel hub and remove the disc.
2. To remove the output shaft disc, perform the following:
   a. Remove the rear fender and right-side footwell as described in Chapter Fifteen.
   b. Have an assistant apply the rear brake.
   c. Loosen the nut (A, **Figure 87**) securing the brake disc to the output shaft.
   d. Remove the caliper assembly (B, **Figure 87**) as described in this chapter.
   e. Remove the nut and washer (A, **Figure 88**) then withdraw the brake disc (B, **Figure 88**) from the output shaft splines.
3. On the output shaft disc, inspect the inner splines (**Figure 89**) for wear or damage.
4. Install by reversing the removal steps while noting the following:
   a. On the front brake disc, tighten the disc mounting bolts to the torque listed in **Table 2**.

b. Tighten the output shaft disc nut to the torque listed in **Table 2**.

BLEEDING THE SYSTEM

This procedure is not necessary unless the brakes feel spongy, there has been a leak in the system, a component has been replaced or the brake fluid has been replaced.

If after bleeding the system, air continues to enter the system, check for a leak. Check the brake light switch (A, **Figure 90**) and all of the fittings for tightness, including those at the four-way connector (B, **Figure 90**).

Brake Bleeder Process

This procedure uses a brake bleeder that is available from motorcycle or automotive supply stores.

1. Park the vehicle on level ground and block the wheels so the vehicle cannot roll in either direction.
2. Remove the rear fender and right-side footwell as described in Chapter Fifteen.
3. Remove the dust cap(s) from the bleed valve on the caliper assemblies. Refer to **Figure 91** for the front and **Figure 92** for the rear.
4. Connect the brake bleeder and wrench to the bleed valve on the caliper assembly.

CAUTION
Cover the surrounding areas with a heavy cloth or plastic tarp to protect it from the accidental spilling of brake fluid. Wash any brake fluid off of any plastic, painted or plated surface immediately; it will destroy the finish. Use soapy water and rinse completely.

5A. On the front master cylinder, perform the following:

a. Clean all debris from the top of the master cylinder cover.
b. Remove the screws securing the top cover (**Figure 93**).
c. Remove the top cover and diaphragm from the master cylinder.

5B. On 1998-on rear master cylinders, unscrew the cover (**Figure 94**) and remove the diaphragm from the reservoir.

87

88

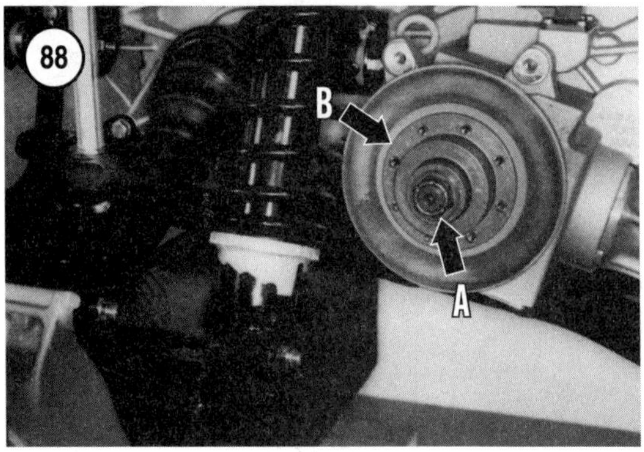

89

90

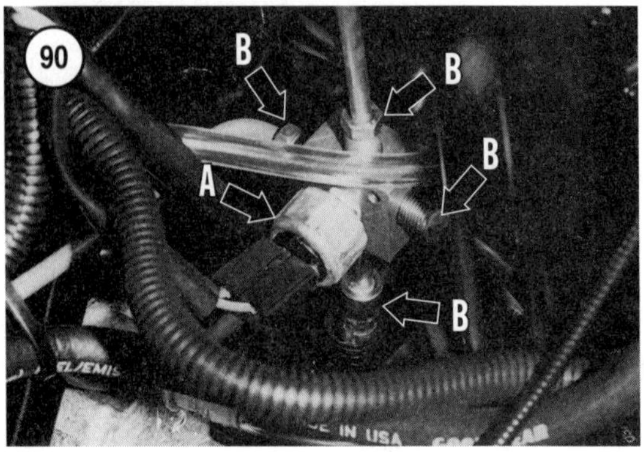

91

92

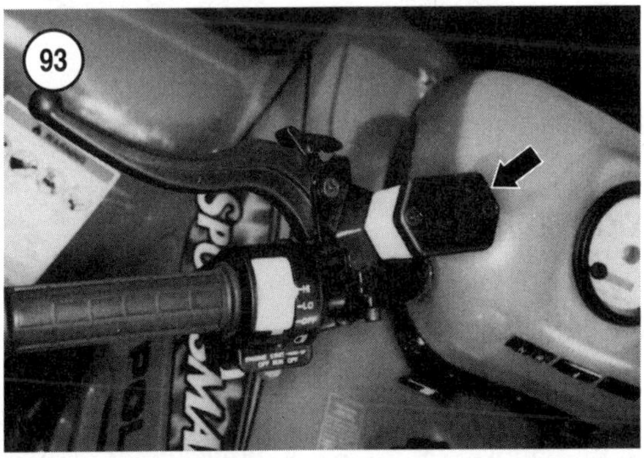

93

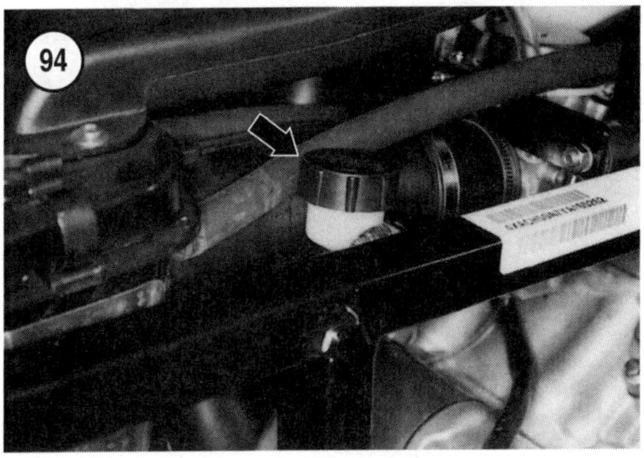

94

6. Fill the reservoirs almost to the top lip; insert the diaphragm and the cover loosely. Leave the cover in place during this procedure to prevent dirt from entering.

WARNING
Use brake fluid from a sealed container marked DOT 3 only (specified for disc brakes). Other types may vaporize and cause brake failure. Do not intermix different brands or types; they may not be compatible.

7. If the front master cylinder was drained, it must be bled before bleeding the entire system. Perform the following:

a. Remove the brake hose from the master cylinder as described in this chapter. Tie the loose end of the hose up to the handlebar or frame.

b. Place several shop cloths under the master cylinder to catch the expelled brake fluid.

c. Hold a thumb over the brake hose hole in the master cylinder and fill the reservoir with DOT 3 brake fluid. Do not remove the thumb.

d. While holding a thumb over the hole, pump the brake lever or pedal several times. Then hold the lever or pedal in the depressed position.

e. Reduce thumb pressure on the brake hose hole. Some brake fluid and air bubbles will leak out. Reapply thumb pressure.

f. Repeat substeps d and e until no air bubbles bleed out of the hole and there is resistance felt at the lever or pedal.

g. Check the reservoir fluid level and top it off if necessary.

h. Reconnect the brake hose onto the master cylinder. Tighten the brake hose fitting to the torque specification listed in **Table 2**.

i. Wash off any spilled brake fluid before continuing.

CAUTION
The bleed screws are made of a relatively soft metal. If they are tight, first loosen the bleed screw with a 6-point socket, then use a 1/4 in. wrench to open and close them.

8. Open the following bleed valves:

a. At the front caliper assembly, open the bleed valve about one-half turn and pump the brake bleeder.
b. At the output shaft caliper assembly, open the bleed valve about one-half turn and pump the brake bleeder.

NOTE
If air is entering the brake bleeder hose from around the bleed valve, apply several layers of Teflon tape to the bleed valve. This should make a good seal between the bleed valve and the brake bleeder hose.

9. As the fluid enters the system and exits into the brake bleeder the level will drop in the reservoir. Maintain the level at about 3/8 in. (9.5 mm) from the top of the reservoir to prevent air from being drawn into the system.
10. Continue to pump the lever on the brake bleeder until the fluid emerging from the hose is completely free of bubbles. At this point, tighten the bleed valve.

NOTE
Do not allow the reservoir to empty during the bleeding operation or more air will enter the system. If this occurs, the entire procedure must be repeated.

11. When the brake fluid is free of bubbles, tighten the bleed valve, remove the brake bleeder tube and install the bleed valve dust cap.
12. If necessary, add fluid to correct the level in the reservoir. It should be to the upper level line.
13. Install the diaphragm and cover and tighten the screws securely.
14. Test the feel of the brake lever. It should be firm and should offer the same resistance each time it is operated. If it feels spongy, it is likely that there is still air in the system and it must be bled again. When all air has been bled from the system and the fluid level is correct in the reservoir, double-check for leaks and tighten all fittings and connections.
15. Install the rear fender and chain guard as described in Chapter Fifteen.

WARNING
Before riding the ATV, make certain that the brake is operating correctly by operating the lever and pedal several times.

16. Test ride the ATV slowly at first to make sure that the brakes are operating properly.

Without a Brake Bleeder

1. Park the vehicle on level ground and block the wheels so the vehicle cannot roll in either direction.
2. Remove the rear fender and right-side footwell as described in Chapter Fifteen.
3. Remove the dust cap(s) from the bleed valve on the caliper assemblies.
4. Connect a length of clear tubing and wrench to the bleed valve on the caliper assembly. Refer to **Figure 91** for the front and **Figure 92** for the rear.
5. Place the other end of the tube into a clean container. Fill the container with enough fresh brake fluid to keep the end submerged. The tube should be long enough so that a loop can be made higher than the bleed valve to prevent air from being drawn into the caliper during bleeding.

CAUTION
Cover the surrounding areas with a heavy cloth or plastic tarp to protect it from the accidental spilling of brake fluid. Wash any brake fluid off of any plastic, painted or plated surface immediately; as it will destroy the finish. Use soapy water and rinse completely.

6A. On the front master cylinder, perform the following:
a. Clean the top of the master cylinder cover of all debris.
b. Remove the screws securing the top cover (**Figure 93**).
c. Remove the top cover and diaphragm from the master cylinder.

6B. On 1998-on rear master cylinder, unscrew the cover (**Figure 94**) and remove the diaphragm from the reservoir.
7. Fill the reservoirs almost to the top lip; insert the diaphragm and the cover loosely. Leave the cover in place during this procedure to prevent dirt entering.

WARNING
Use brake fluid from a sealed contuiner marked DOT 3 only (specified

for disc brakes). Other types may vaporize and cause brake failure. Do not intermix different brands or types; they may not be compatible.

8. If the master cylinder was drained, it must be bled before bleeding the entire system. Perform the following:

a. Remove the brake hose from the master cylinder as described in this chapter. Tie the loose end up to the handlebar or frame.
b. Place several shop cloths under the master cylinder to catch the expelled brake fluid.
c. Hold a thumb over the brake hose hole in the master cylinder and fill the reservoir with DOT 3 brake fluid. Do not remove the thumb.
d. While holding a thumb over the hole, pump the brake lever or pedal several times. Then hold the lever or pedal in the depressed position.
e. Reduce thumb pressure on the brake hose hole. Some brake fluid and air bubbles will leak out. Reapply thumb pressure.
f. Repeat substeps d and e until no air bubbles bleed out of the hole and there is resistance felt at the lever or pedal.
g. Check the reservoir fluid level and top it off if necessary.
h. Reconnect the brake hose onto the master cylinder. Tighten the brake hose fitting to the torque specification listed in **Table 2**.
i. Wash off any spilled brake fluid before continuing.

CAUTION

The bleed screws are made of a relatively soft metal. If they are tight, first loosen the bleed screw with a 6-point socket, then use a 1/4 in. wrench to open and close them.

9. Slowly apply the front brake lever or rear brake pedal as follows:

a. Hold the lever or pedal in the applied position.
b. At the front caliper assembly, open the bleed valve about one-half turn. Allow the lever or pedal to travel to its limit. When this limit is reached, tighten the bleed valve.
c. At the output shaft caliper assembly, open the bleed valve about one-half turn. Allow the lever or pedal to travel to its limit. When this limit is reached, tighten the bleed valve.

10. As the fluid enters the system and exits into the container the level will drop in the reservoir. Maintain the level at about 3/8 in. (9.5 mm) from the top of the reservoir to prevent air from being drawn into the system.

11. Continue to pump the lever or pedal until the fluid emerging from the hose is completely free of bubbles. Hold the lever in or the pedal depressed, tighten the bleed valve and install the dust cap.

NOTE

Do not allow the reservoir to empty during the bleeding operation or more air will enter the system. If this occurs, the entire procedure must be repeated.

12. If necessary, add fluid to correct the level in the reservoir. It should be to the upper level line.

13. Install the diaphragm and cover and tighten the screws securely.

14. Test the feel of the brake lever. It should be firm and offer the same resistance each time it is operated. If it feels spongy, it is likely that there is still air in the system and it must be bled again. When all air has been bled from the system and the fluid level is correct in the reservoir, double-check for leaks and tighten all fittings and connections.

15. On 1998-on models, install the rear fender and chain guard as described in Chapter Fifteen.

14

WARNING

Before riding the ATV, make certain that the brake is operating correctly by operating the lever and pedal several times.

16. Test ride the ATV slowly at first to make sure that the brakes are operating properly.

Table 1 and Table 2 are on the following page.

Table 1 BRAKE SYSTEM SPECIFICATIONS

Item	New mm (in.)	Service limit mm (in.)
Brake pad thickness*		
Front brake and output shaft	7.0 (0.275)	3.81 (0.150)
Front caliper and output shaft caliper (1998-on)		
Piston bore inside diameter	30.252-30.277 (1.191-1.192)	30.30 (1.193)
Piston outside diameter	30.125-30.163 (1.186-1.1875)	30.311 (1.11855)
Output shaft caliper (1996-1997)		
Piston bore inside diameter	25.476-25.502 (1.003-1.004)	25.57 (1.005)
Piston outside diameter	25.324-25.362 (0.9970-0.9985)	25.31 (0.9965)
Brake disc thickness		
Front brake	3.810-4.166 (0.150-0.164)	3.556 (0.140)
Output shaft (all models)	4.496-4.750 (0.177-0.187)	4.242 (0.167)
Brake disc thickness variance	–	0.051 (0.002)
Brake disc runout		
Front brake	–	0.50 (0.020)
Output shaft	–	0.25 (0.010)

* Specification is for lining material and backing plate combined.

Table 2 BRAKE SYSTEM TORQUE SPECIFICATIONS

Item	N•m	in.-lb.	ft.-lb.
Brake line banjo bolts	20	–	15
Front brake disc mounting bolts	25	–	18
Front caliper bolts	25	–	18
Front master cylinder			
Clamp bolt	6	53	–
Cover screws	5	44	–
Output shaft caliper mounting bolts			
1996-1997 models	20	–	15
1998-on models	25	–	18
Output shaft disc mounting bolts	45	–	33

CHAPTER FIFTEEN

BODY

This chapter contains procedures to remove and install the seat, body panels and the bumpers. It is suggested that as soon as the part is removed from the vehicle, all mounting hardware (small brackets, bolts, nuts and washers) be reinstalled so they will not be misplaced.

15

SEAT

Removal/Installation

1. Lift the seat latch at the rear of the seat (**Figure 1**), pull the seat toward the rear and disengage the front tabs from the rear of the fuel tank. Remove the seat.

2. Inspect the front tab (**Figure 2**) for damage. Check the latch mechanism (**Figure 3**) to make sure it operates correctly. Tighten any loose fasteners if necessary.

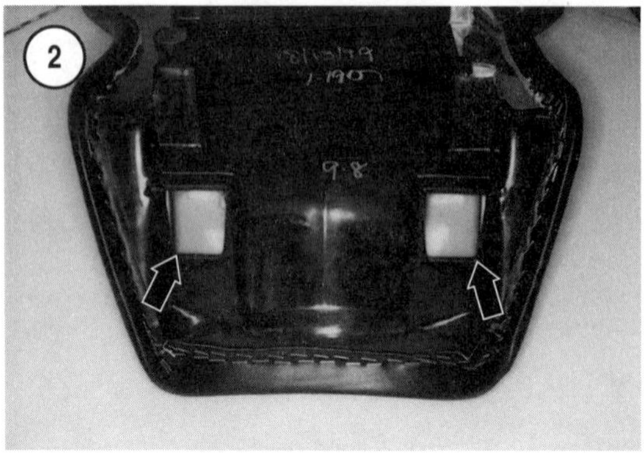

4

FRONT RACK, RAIL AND GRILLE

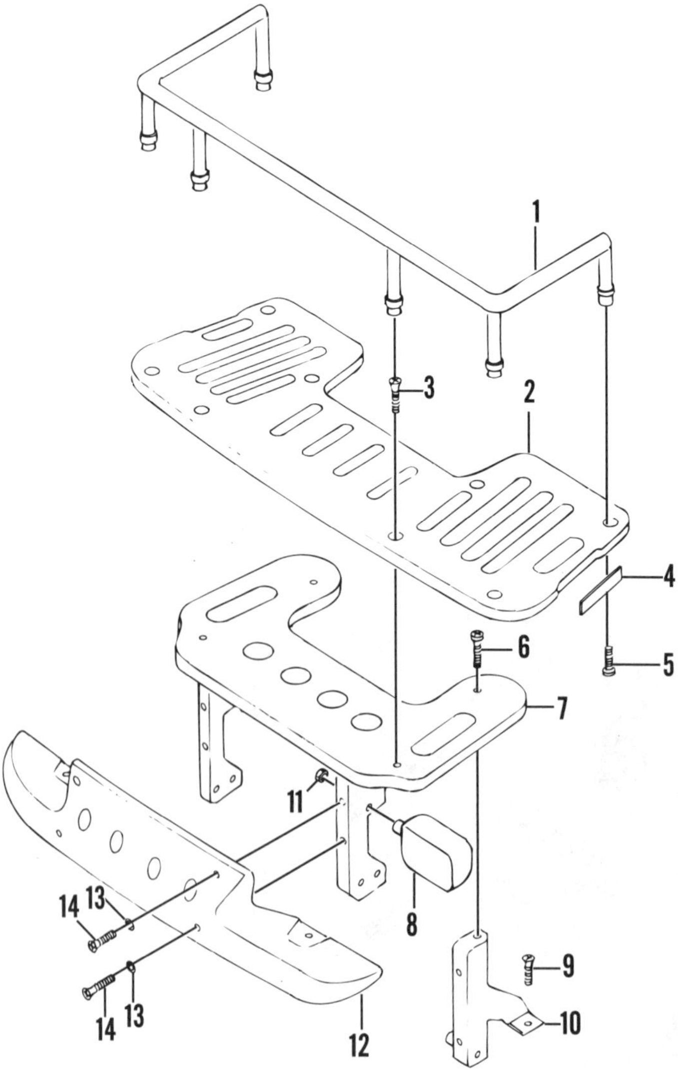

1. Front rack rail
2. Front rack
3. Torx bolt (T-27)
4. Reflex reflector
5. Bolt
6. Bolt
7. Rack mount
8. Low-beam headlight
9. Screw
10. Side support
11. Nut
12. Grille
13. Washer
14. Torx bolt (T-40)

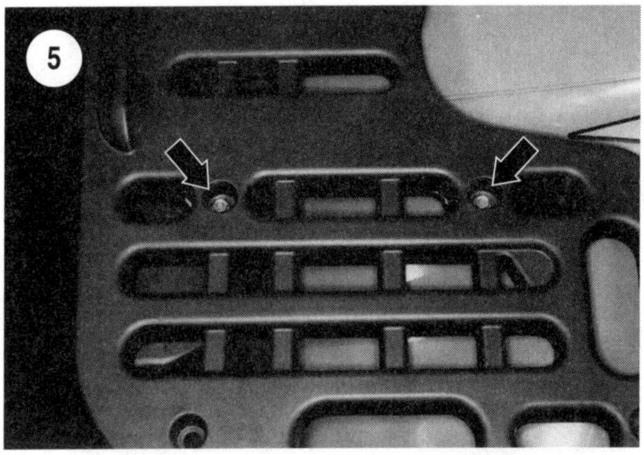

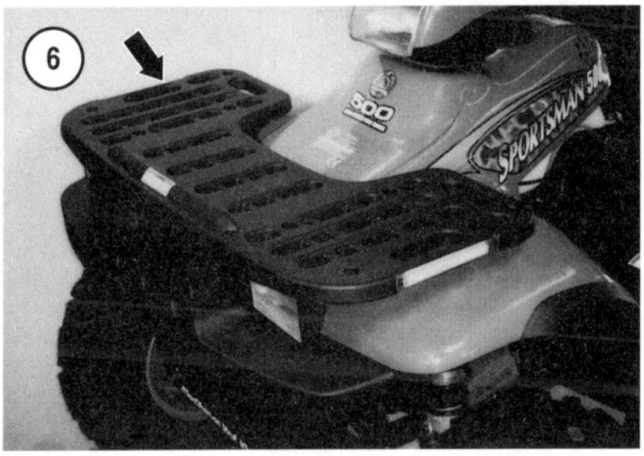

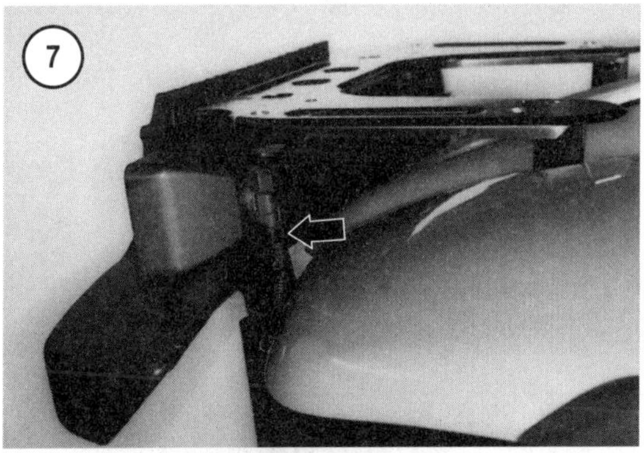

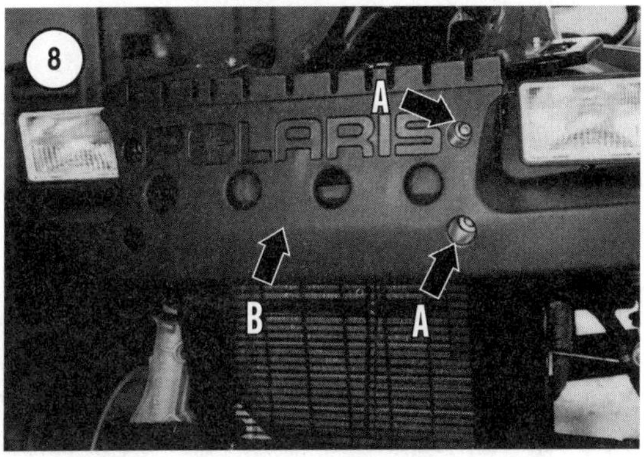

3. To install the seat, engage the front seat tabs with the fuel tank slots. Push the rear of the seat down to lock it in place.
4. Make sure the seat is firmly locked in place.

WARNING
After the seat is installed, pull up on it firmly and move it from side to side to make sure it is securely locked into place. If the seat is not correctly installed, it may slide to one side or the other when riding the vehicle. This could lead to the loss of control and a possible accident.

FRONT RACK AND GRILLE

Removal/Installation

Refer to **Figure 4**.

NOTE
This procedure is shown without the optional front rack rail.

1. Park the vehicle on level ground and set the parking brake.
2. To remove the front rack, perform the following:
   a. Remove the two screws (**Figure 5**) on each side securing the front rack and front rack rail to the rack mount.
   b. Lift the front rack (**Figure 6**) and rail straight up and off the rack mount.

NOTE
The grille can remain attached to the front rack mount or can be removed separately.

3. To remove the grille, perform the following:
   a. Disconnect the electrical connector (**Figure 7**) from each grille-mounted headlight.
   b. Remove the two No. 40 Torx screws and washers (A, **Figure 8**) on each side securing the front grille to the rack mount.
   c. Pull the front grill (B, **Figure 8**) forward and remove it from the rack mount.
4. To remove the rack mount, perform the following:
   a. Remove the bolts (A, **Figure 9**) securing the rack mount to the frame and frame support.

9

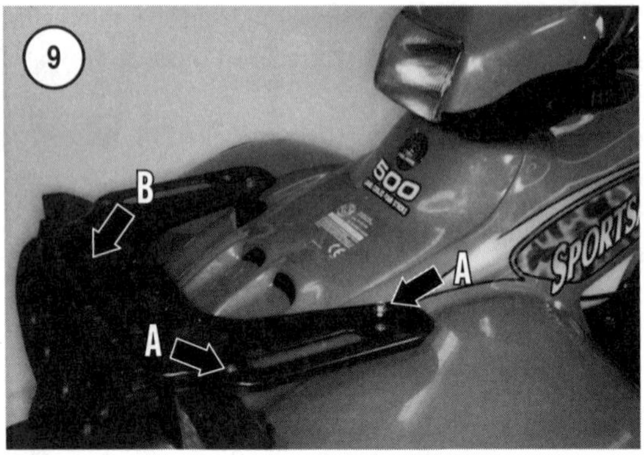

10

11

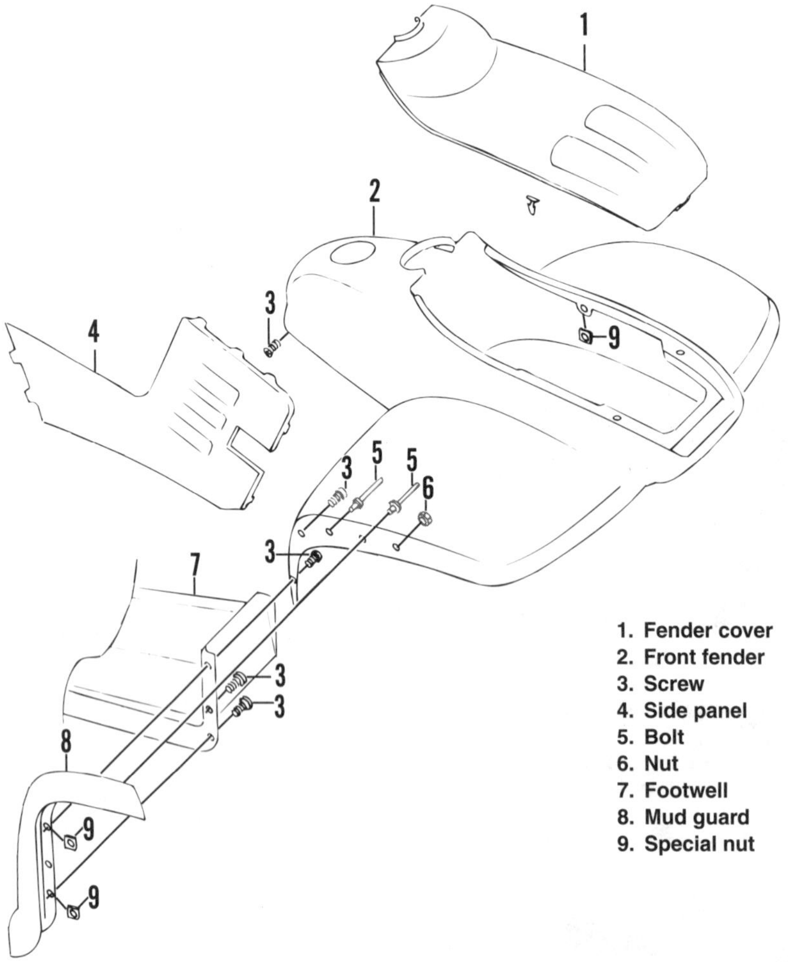

1. Fender cover
2. Front fender
3. Screw
4. Side panel
5. Bolt
6. Nut
7. Footwell
8. Mud guard
9. Special nut

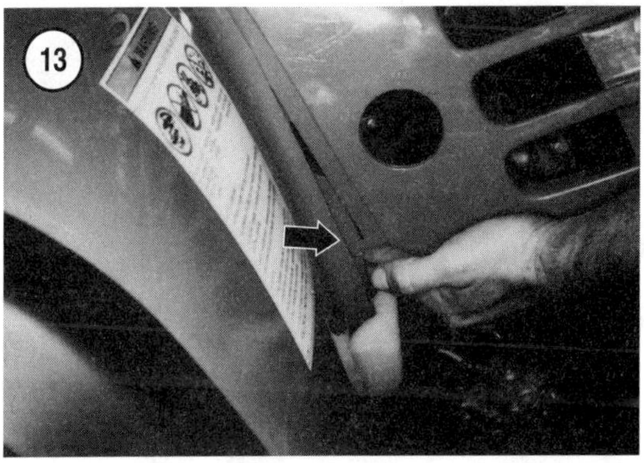

b. Remove the rack mount (B, **Figure 9**) from the frame.

5. To remove the side support, perform the following:

a. Remove the front fender as described in this chapter.

b. Remove the bolts securing the side support (**Figure 10**) and remove the side support.

c. Repeat for the other side if necessary.

6. If necessary, remove the four screws securing the rail to the front rack and remove it.

7. Install by reversing these removal steps. Tighten all mounting screws and bolts securely.

SIDE PANELS

Removal/Installation

Refer to **Figure 11**.

1. Park the vehicle on level ground and set the parking brake.
2. Remove the seat as described in this chapter.

CAUTION
The locking tabs are fragile and will crack or break if they are not disengaged correctly. Do not apply unnecessary stress on the tabs during removal and installation.

3. Grasp the rear portion of the side panel with both hands.
4. Pull the panel forward and straight out and disengage the two rear locking tabs (**Figure 12**) from the rear fender.
5. Pull up on the rear portion and disengage the front upper and lower locking tabs (**Figure 13**) from the front fender.
6. Grasp the rear portion that has just been released and push downward and disengage the top rear three locking tabs (**Figure 14**) from the front fender.
7. Remove the side panel.
8. Repeat for the other side panel.
9. Install by reversing these removal steps.

FRONT FENDER

Removal/Installation

15

Refer to **Figure 11**.

1. Park the vehicle on level ground and set the parking brake.
2. Remove the seat as described in this chapter.
3. Remove the front rack and rack mount assembly (A, **Figure 15**) as described in this chapter.

CAUTION
The locking tabs are fragile and will crack or break if not disengaged correctly. Do not apply undo stress on the tabs during removal and installation.

4. Remove the side panels as previously described in this chapter.
5. Disengage the side and rear locking tabs (**Figure 16**) and remove the front fender cover.
6A. On Xplorer models, perform the following:
   a. Remove the top cover from the instrument panel cover.
   b. Remove the two screws securing the instrument panel cover and remove the cover.
6B. On Sportsman models, perform the following:
   a. Remove the headlight upper pod as described under *High-Beam Headlight (Sportsman Models), Bulb Replacement* in Chapter Eleven.
   b. Remove the screws securing the headlight lower pod to the steering stem mounting bracket. The lower pod must be loose to allow removal of the front fender. It is not necessary to remove the lower pod.
7. Remove the screw on each side securing the front fender to the fuel tank mounting bracket (**Figure 17**).
8. Remove the upper inner bolt, washer and nut (**Figure 18**) securing the fender and mudguard to the footwell. Repeat for the other side.
9. Remove the two lower inner screws (A, **Figure 19**) securing the front fender to the footwell. Repeat for the other side.
10. Working within the front cover area, remove the screw (B, **Figure 15**) on each side securing the front fender to the frame mount.
11. Unscrew and remove fuel fill cap.

NOTE
The following requires the aid of an assistant since it is necessary to work with the front and rear portions of the front fender at the same time.

12. Lift the rear portion of the front fender straight up and off the fuel tank fill neck (**Figure 20**).
13. Lift the front portion of the front fender straight up and off the rack mount side supports (**Figure 21**).

CAUTION
On Sportsman models, it is very easy to scratch the lower headlight pod and front fender in Step 14. Lift the front fender up slowly and follow it path past the handlebar assembly.

15

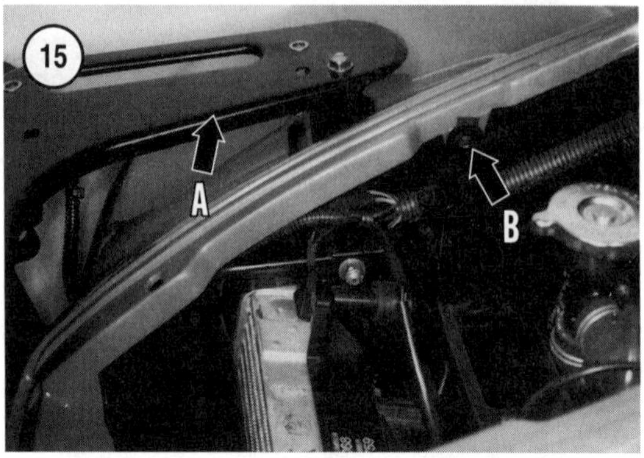

16

17

18

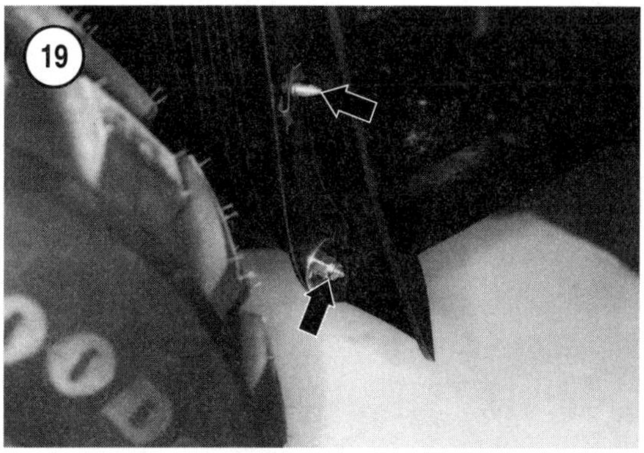

19

20

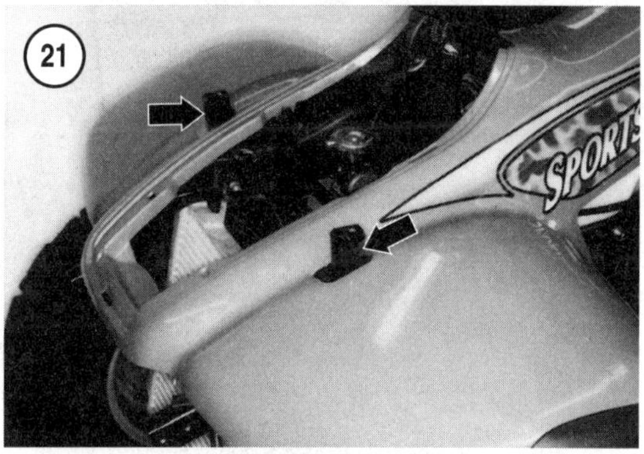

21

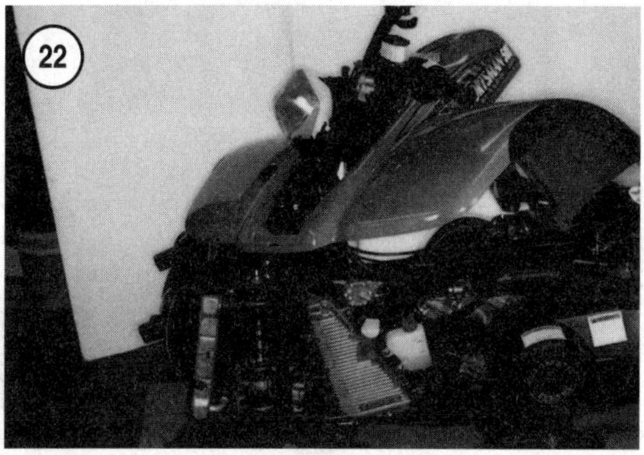

22

14. Carefully rotate the front fender sideways (**Figure 22**) and lift it up to clear the headlight lower pod (Sportsman models) and handlebar assembly. Remove the front fender from the frame.
15. Reinstall the fuel fill cap and tighten securely.
16. Install by reversing these removal steps. Do not overtighten the screws as the plastic fender may fracture at the mounting points.

FRONT BUMPER (MODELS SO EQUIPPED)

Removal/Installation

Refer to **Figure 23**.

1. Park the vehicle on level ground and set the parking brake.
2. Loosen all four bolts on each side securing the front bumper to the radiator guard.
3. Remove the lower three bolts on each side.
4. Have an assistant hold onto the front bumper and remove the two remaining bolts.
5. Remove the front bumper.
6. Install by reversing these removal steps. Tighten the bolts securely.

RADIATOR GUARD

Refer to **Figure 23**.

1. Park the vehicle on level ground and set the parking brake.
2. On models so equipped, remove the front bumper.
3. Remove the front rack and grille as described in this chapter.
4. Disconnect the electrical connectors (A, **Figure 24**) from the voltage regulator/rectifier.
5. Remove the lower bolts (**Figure 25**) securing the lower portion of the radiator guard to the frame.
6. Remove the upper bolt (B, **Figure 24**) on each side securing the upper portion of the radiator guard to the frame.
7. Carefully pull the radiator guard and side shield assembly straight forward and out of the frame.
8. Inspect the radiator guard and side shield assembly (**Figure 26**) for damage. If necessary, remove the retainers and remove the side shield(s) (**Figure 27**) from the side of the radiator guard.
9. Install by reversing these removal steps. Tighten the bolts securely.

23

RADIATOR GUARD AND BUMPER

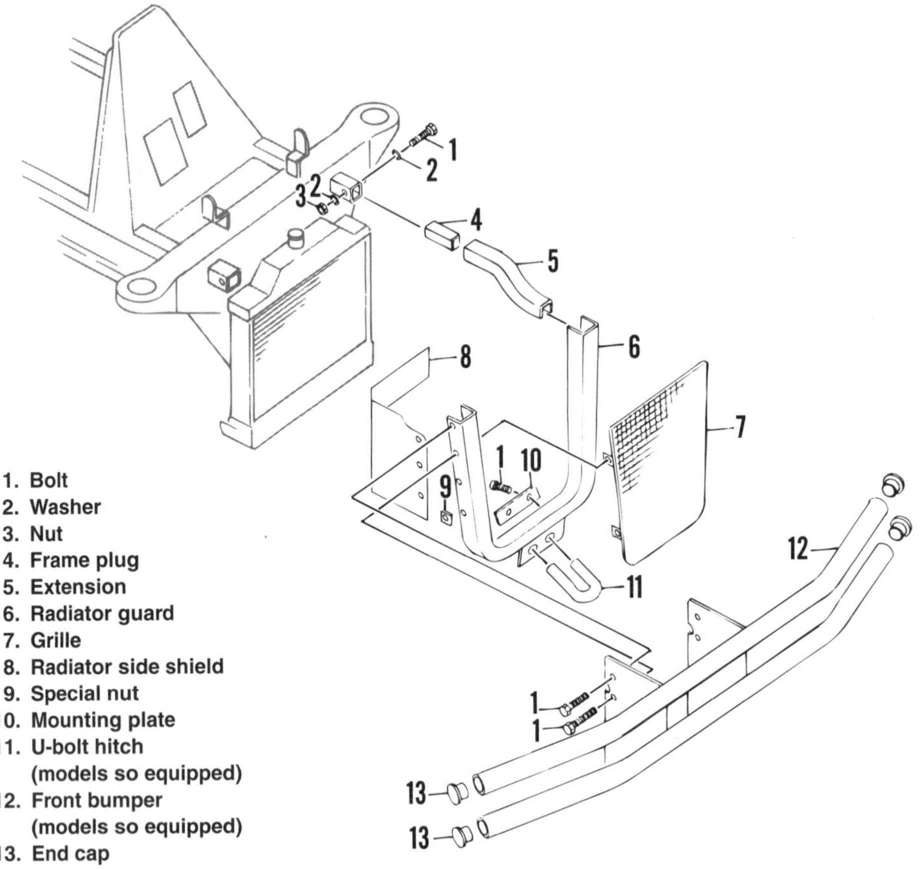

1. Bolt
2. Washer
3. Nut
4. Frame plug
5. Extension
6. Radiator guard
7. Grille
8. Radiator side shield
9. Special nut
10. Mounting plate
11. U-bolt hitch (models so equipped)
12. Front bumper (models so equipped)
13. End cap

24

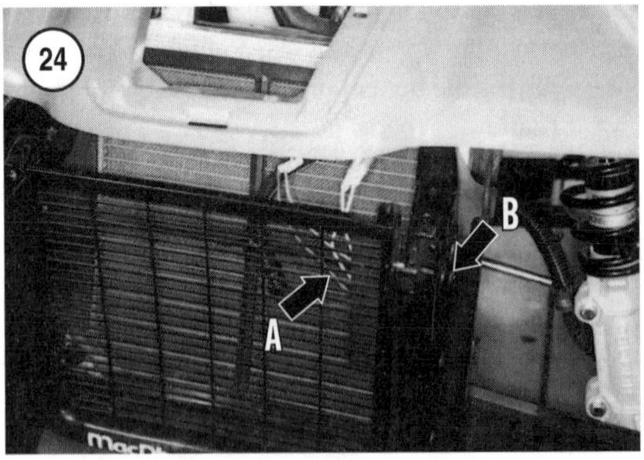

25

26

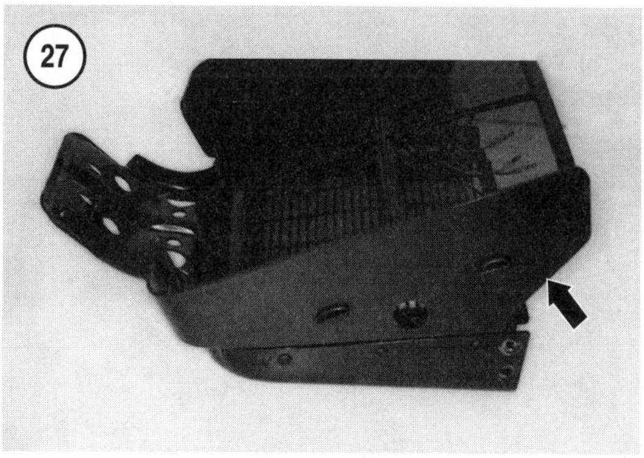

27

28

REAR RACK, RAIL AND BUMPER

1. Rear rack rail
2. Torx bolt (T-27)
3. Rear rack
4. Reflex reflector
5. Rear bumper
   (models so equipped)
6. End cap
7. Screw
8. Rear rack support
9. Nut
10. Self-locking nut
11. Spacer
    (models so equipped)
12. Bracket
13. Bolt
14. Self-locking nut
15. Rack mount
16. Washer
17. Spacer
18. Washer
19. Bolt

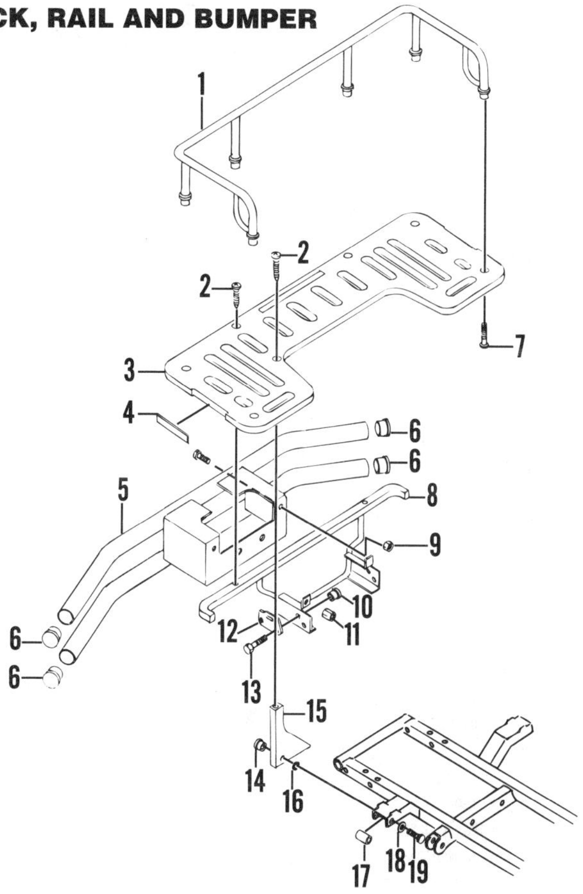

REAR RACK

Removal/Installation

Refer to **Figure 28**.

1. Park the vehicle on level ground and set the parking brake.

2. Remove the seat as described in this chapter.

3. Remove the front bolt (A, **Figure 29**) and rear bolt (B, **Figure 29**) on each side securing the rear rack support.

4. Lift the rear rack straight up and off the rear fender (**Figure 30**).

29

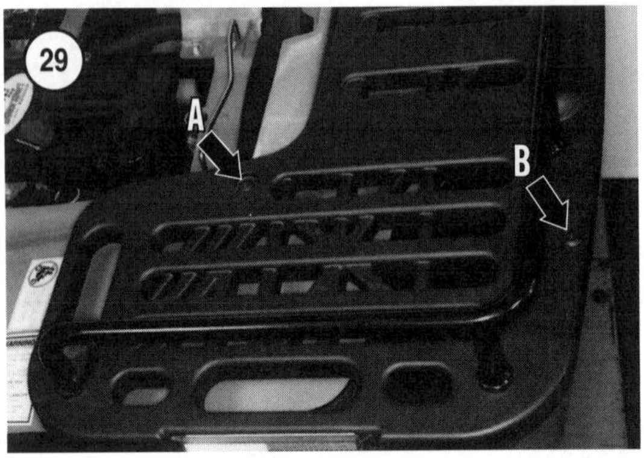

30

31

REAR FENDER

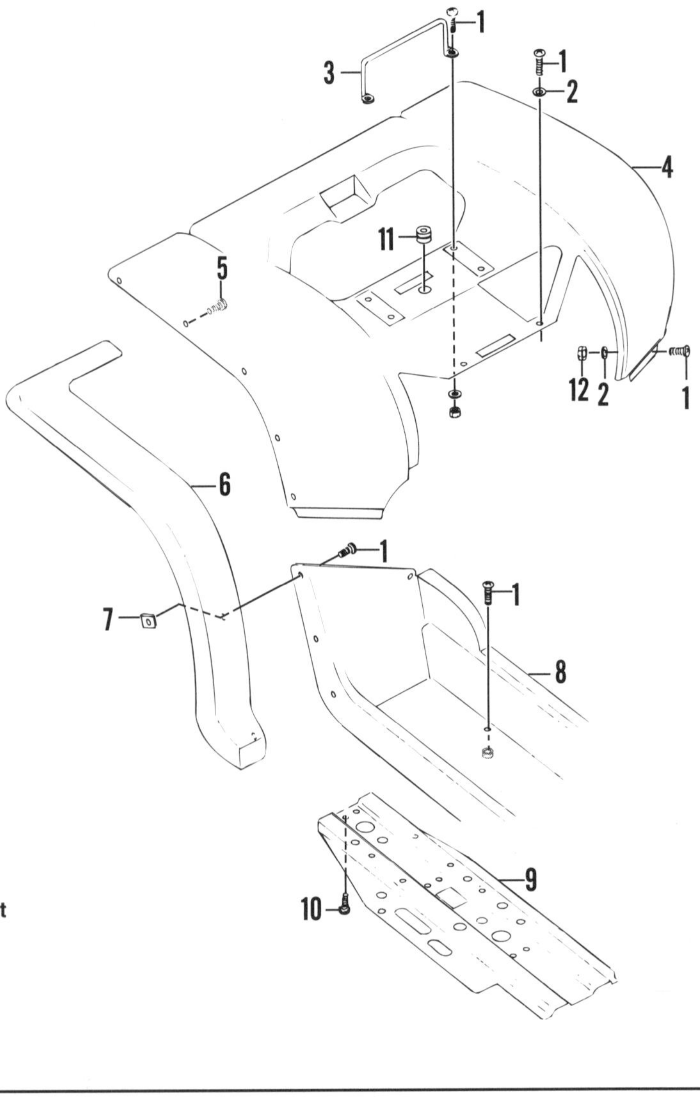

1. Bolt
2. Washer
3. Seat retainer
4. Rear fender
5. Screw
6. Mud guard
7. Special nut
8. Footwell
9. Frame support (part of frame)
10. Bolt
11. Rubber grommet
12. Self-locking nut

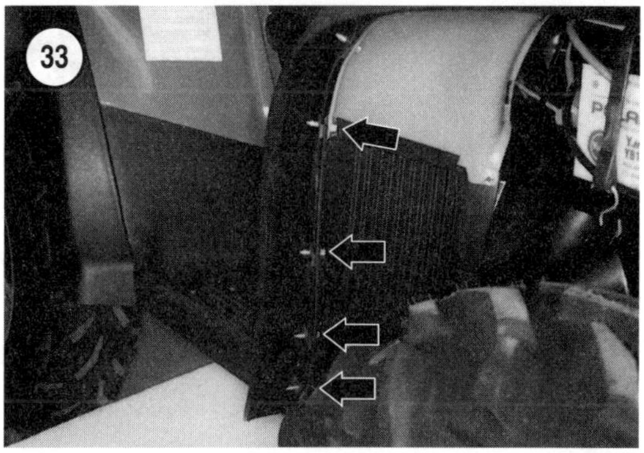

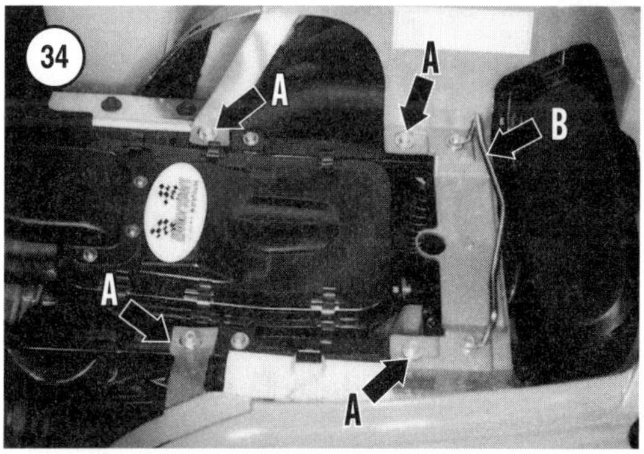

5. If necessary, remove the six screws securing the rail to the rear rack and remove it.
6. If necessary, remove the screws and nuts securing the rear rack support and remove it from the frame.
7. Install by reversing these removal steps. Tighten all mounting screws and bolts securely.

REAR FENDER

Removal/Installation

Refer to **Figure 31**.

1. Park the vehicle on level ground and set the parking brake.
2. Remove the seat and rear rack as described in this chapter.
3. On the left side, perform the following:
   a. Remove the screw, washer and nut (**Figure 32**) securing the rear fender to the footwell.
   b. Remove the four screws (**Figure 33**) securing the mudguard to the footwell.
4. Repeat for the other side.
5. In the area under the seat, remove the four bolts and washers (A, **Figure 34**) securing the rear fender to the frame. Do not remove the two bolts securing the seat stay (B, **Figure 34**). It can remain attached to the fender.
6. Working under the rear fender, disconnect the taillight electrical connector (**Figure 35**).
7. Carefully lift the rear fender straight up and remove it from the frame.
8. Install by reversing these steps. Do not overtighten the bolts as the plastic fender may fracture at the mounting points.

FOOTWELLS

Removal/Installation

Refer to **Figure 11** and **Figure 31**.

1. Remove the screws securing the footwell to both the front and rear fenders and mudguards as described in this chapter.
2. Remove the four screws (**Figure 36**) and self-locking nuts securing the footwell to the frame support.

3. Remove the footwell from the frame. Do not lose the rear spacer (**Figure 37**) located between the rear fender and footwell. Tie wrap it in place.
4. Repeat for the other side if necessary.
5. Install by reversing these removal steps while noting the following:
   a. Tighten the screws securely.
   b. Install new self-locking nuts and tighten securely.

REAR BUMPER (MODELS SO EQUIPPED)

Removal/Installation

1. Park the vehicle on level ground and set the parking brake.
2. Loosen all three bolts and nuts securing the rear bumper to the rear rack support.
3. Have an assistant hold onto the rear bumper and remove the bolts and nuts.
4. Remove the rear bumper.
5. Install by reversing these removal steps. Tighten the bolts securely.

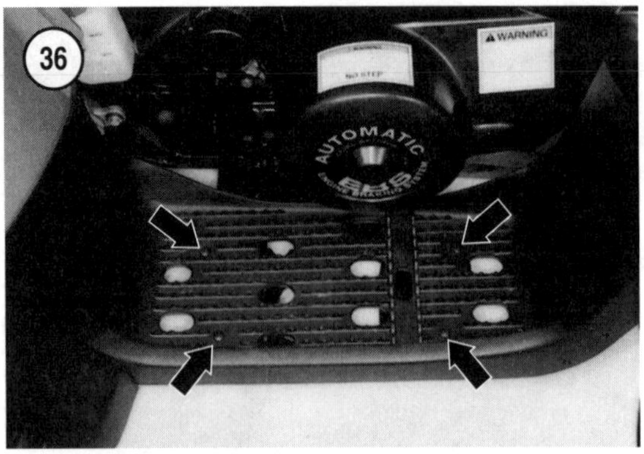

36

37

SUPPLEMENT

2001-2003 SERVICE INFORMATION

This Supplement contains all procedures and specifications unique to the 2001-2003 models, including the Sportsman 400. If a specific procedure is not included in this Supplement, unless otherwise specified, refer to the information in the previous chapters of this manual.

The headings in this Supplement correspond to those in the previous chapters. **Tables 1-8** are located at the end of the Supplement.

CHAPTER ONE

GENERAL INFORMATION

Refer to **Table 1** for model year and numbers. Refer to **Table 2** for general dimensions.

CHAPTER TWO

TROUBLESHOOTING

STARTING THE ENGINE

The engine starting procedure is the same as on prior models with the following exception. The choke is now controlled with a knob (**Figure 1**) instead of a toggle lever as on prior years.

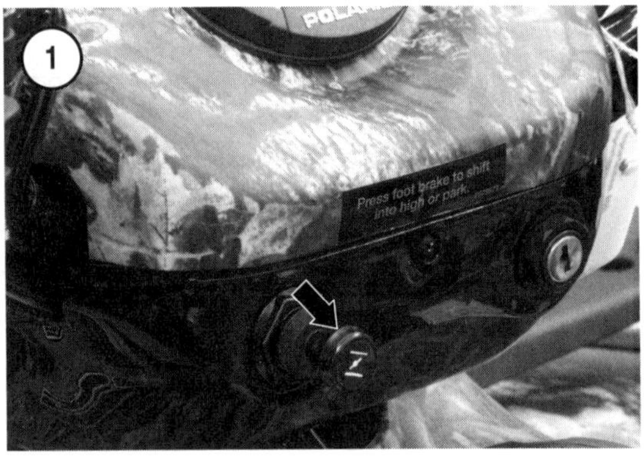

IGNITION SYSTEM

All models are equipped with a transistorized ignition system. The ignition system is the same as on prior models except for the CDI electrical connectors as shown in **Figure 2**. Refer to the wiring diagrams at the end of this manual for the specific model and year being worked on.

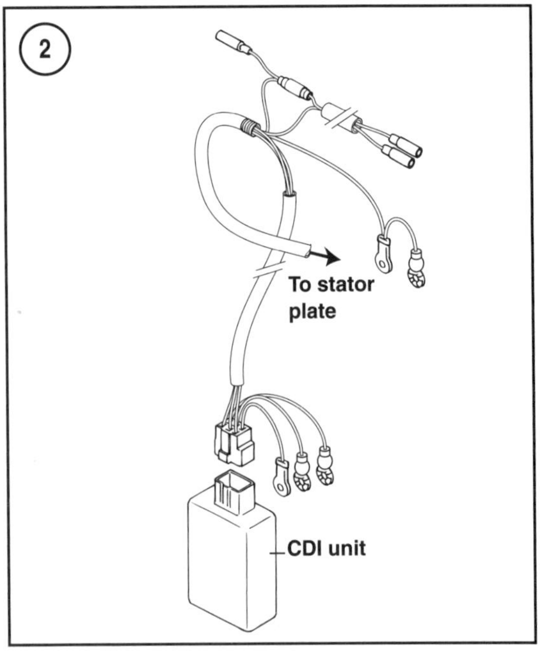

Exciter Coil and Trigger Coil Test

Refer to **Table 3** for test specifications.

1. Locate the electrical cables leading from the engine flywheel CDI stator to the CDI unit. Carefully disconnect the exciter coil and pulse coil connectors from the CDI unit.

2A. On 2001-2002 and early 2003 400cc models, measure the exciter coil resistance using an ohmmeter set at R × 100. Measure resistance between the following terminals on the alternator side of the connectors and check the resistance:

a. Between red and green terminals.

b. Between black/red and green terminals.

2B. On later 2003 400 cc models and all 500 cc models, measure the exciter coil resistance using an ohmmeter set at R × 100. Measure resistance between the following terminals on the alternator side of the connectors and check the resistance:

a. Between red and black/red.

b. Between red terminal and ground.

3. Measure the trigger coil resistance using an ohmmeter set at R × 100. Measure resistance between the white and white/red terminals on the CDI magneto side. Refer to **Table 1** for test specifications.

4. If either the exciter coil and/or pulser coil does not meet any of these specifications, the CDI magneto stator assembly must be replaced. The individual coils cannot be replaced.

5. If the coils test as specified, reconnect the exciter coil and pulse coil connectors onto the CDI unit.

CHAPTER THREE

LUBRICATION, MAINTENANCE AND TUNE-UP

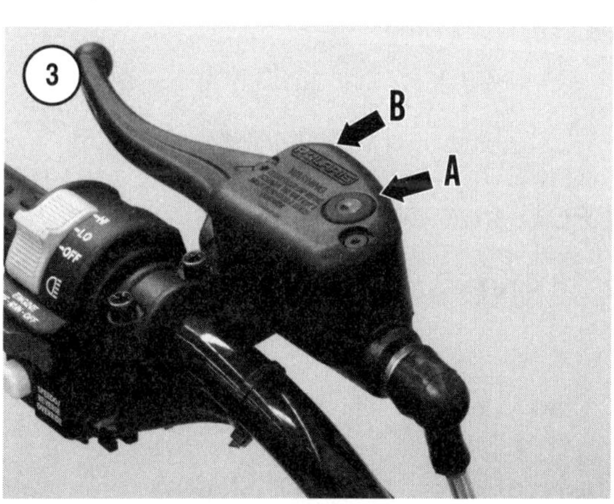

PERIODIC MAINTENANCE

Disc Brake System Inspection (2003 Models)

On 2003 models (400 and 500 cc) the rear brake is located on the right side rear axle. Inspect the brake pads and install new pads if they are worn to the wear limit groove or to the dimension listed in **Table 4**. There is also a new front master cylinder. The front brake calipers on all models are the same.

Front Brake Fluid Level Check and Fill

Maintain the hydraulic fluid level in the reservoir at the maximum level. If it is necessary, add brake fluid to correct the level.

1. Place the vehicle on level ground and set the parking brake.

2. Clean the top surface of the master cylinder reservoir.

3. Look straight down onto the sight glass on master cylinder reservoir cover (A, **Figure 3**). If the fluid level is correct, the sight glass will be dark. If the level is low, the sight glass will have a lightened, clear appearance.

4. If the fluid level is low, perform the following:

   a. Position the handlebar so the front master cylinder is horizontal.

   b. Remove the screws securing the reservoir cover and remove the reservoir cover (B, **Figure 3**).

   c. Refill the master cylinder reservoir, if necessary, to maintain the correct fluid level as indicated on the side of the reservoir.

   d. Install the diaphragm and cover. Tighten the cover screws securely.

Air Filter Element (2003 Models)

The air filter service procedure is the same as on prior models with the following exception. To prevent rattles and air leaks, make sure the air filter is resting on the support in the base of the air filter air box prior to installing the cover.

ENGINE TUNE-UP

Spark Plug Heat Range

Refer to **Table 4** for the spark plug heat range.

Gapping and Installing the Spark Plug

Refer to **Table 4** for the spark plug gap specification.

Carburetor Idle Mixture Adjustment Sportsman 500 Models

The carburetor idle mixture adjustment is the same as on prior models with exception of the pilot air screw setting. Refer to **Table 4** for the air screw specification.

CHAPTER FOUR

ENGINE TOP END

Refer to **Table 5** general engine specifications.

The Sportsman 400 model was introduced in 2001. This vehicle is basically the same as the larger 500 cc model with the major change taken place with the bore and stroke.

1. Sportsman 400:
   a. Displacement: 425 cc.
   b. Bore: 87.9 mm (3.461 in.).
   c. Stroke: 70 mm (2.756 in.).
2. Sportsman 500 and Sportsman 500 HO:
   a. Displacement: 499 cc.
   b. Bore: 92 mm (3.6248 in.).
   c. Stroke: 75 mm (2.955 in.).

Service specifications are listed in **Table 6**.

CYLINDER BLOCK

Inspection (Sportsman 400 Models)

The inspection procedure for the cylinder block is the same as the Sportsman 500 models with the exception of the cylinder bore dimension listed in **Table 6**.

PISTON AND PISTON RINGS

Piston Inspection (400 cc and 500 cc Models)

The inspection procedure for the piston is the same as prior Sportsman 500 models with the exception of the piston outside diameter dimensions listed in **Table 6**.

CHAPTER FIVE

ENGINE LOWER END

ENGINE

Removal/Installation (2002-on Models)

The removal and installation of the engine is the same as on prior models with exception of some minor variations of the engine mounting hardware (**Figure 4**).

After the engine is removed from the frame, inspect all of the rubber mounts for damage and/or deterioration. Replace as necessary.

FLYWHEEL AND STATOR PLATE

Removal/Installation

The flywheel and stator plate service procedures are the same as on prior models except for the CDI electrical connectors as shown in **Figure 2**.

4

ENGINE MOUNTS (2002-ON)

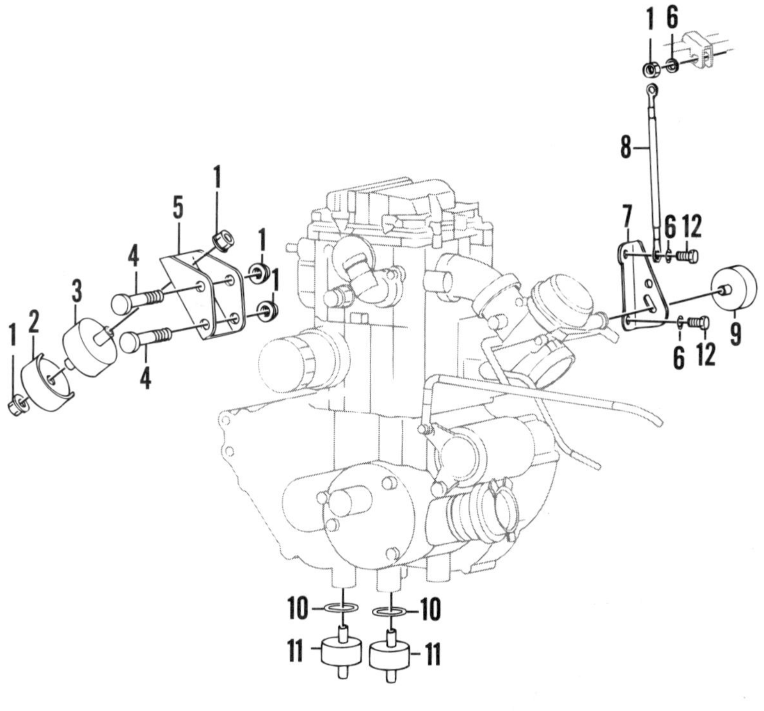

1. Flange locknut
2. Rubber mount bracket
3. Rubber mount
4. Bolt
5. Front mount bracket
6. Lockwasher
7. Top mount bracket
8. Ground strap
9. Rubber mount
10. Washer
11. Rubber mount

CHAPTER SIX

FUEL SYSTEM

CARBURETOR (SPORTSMAN 500 H.O. MODELS)

Removal/Installation

1. Place the vehicle on level ground and set the parking brake.
2. Remove the seat as described in Chapter Fifteen.
3. Remove the front fender as described in Chapter Fifteen.
4. Remove the clamping band, or tie-wrap, and remove the front portion of the PVT air exhaust duct.
5. Remove the air filter air box as described in Chapter Six.
6. Remove the two nuts and washers and two screws securing the carburetor mounting bracket to the frame.
7. Mark all hoses prior to disconnecting them from the carburetor.
8. Disconnect the fuel supply hose from the carburetor: Plug the end of the fuel supply hose.
9. Loosen the front clamp, slide the carburetor back and free it from the intake manifold on the cylinder head.
10. At the throttle cable midline adjuster on the left side, perform the following:
    a. Slide the rubber boots off the adjuster.
    b. Loosen the locknut and loosen the adjuster to allow maximum slack in the cable.
11. Disconnect the throttle cable from the carburetor as follows:
    a. Remove the carburetor side cover mounting screws and remove the side cover and O-ring seal.
    b. Disconnect the cable end from the throttle wheel.
    c. Loosen and remove the throttle cable fitting, then withdraw the throttle cable from the throttle case.
12. Loosen, then remove the starting enrichment valve (choke) cable from the carburetor.
13. Remove the carburetor from the engine and frame.
14. Place a clean lint-free shop cloth or a plug into the intake manifold to keep out debris.
15. Install by reversing these removal steps, while noting the following:
    a. Insert the throttle cable into the throttle case fitting and attach the cable end to the lever.
    b. Tighten the throttle cable fitting securely.
    c. Make sure the O-ring seal is in place on the throttle case prior to installing the cover. Tighten the cover screws securely.
    d. Insert the starting enrichment valve (choke) onto the carburetor and tighten the retainer.
    e. Operate the throttle lever and the starting enrichment (choke) controls several times. Make sure the throttle lever moves smoothly at the carburetor with no binding and that the cable end does not pop out.
    f. Adjust the throttle cable free play as described in Chapter Three.

Disassembly

Refer to **Figure 5**.

1. Remove the screws securing the cover.
2. Remove the cover and the spring.
3. Carefully withdraw the throttle valve/diaphragm assembly. Do not damage the jet needle extending out of the bottom of the throttle valve.
4. To disassemble the throttle valve/diaphragm assembly, perform the following:
    a. Slowly push the jet needle up to dislodge the spring seat.
    b. Remove the spring seat, jet needle, E-ring and spacer.
5. Remove the screws and remove the float bowl and O-ring gasket.
6. Pull straight up and remove the float assembly. Do not lose the needle valve attached to the float tang.
7. Pull straight up and remove the needle valve seat.
8. Unscrew and remove the pilot jet.
9. Unscrew and remove the main jet and the spacer ring.
10. Unscrew and remove the air jet.
11. Do not remove the pilot screw assembly.

(5) **MIKINI CARBURETOR 40 MM**

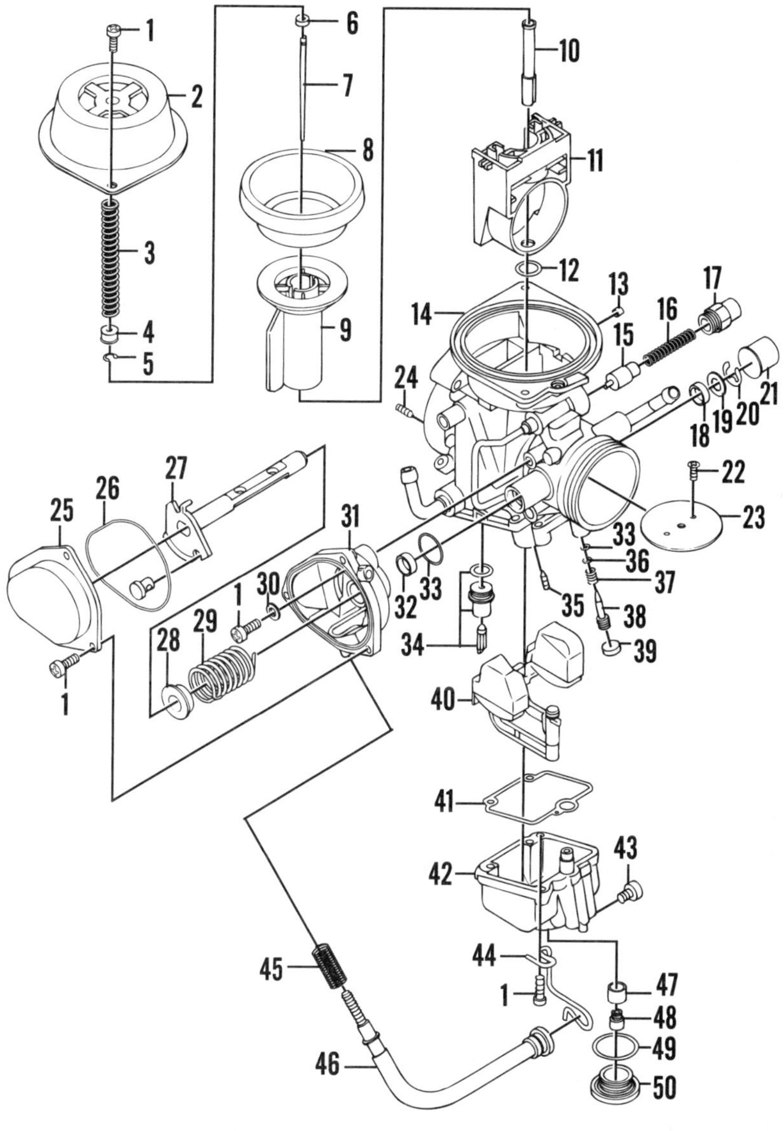

1. Screw
2. Cover
3. Spring
4. Spring seat
5. E-clip
6. Spacer
7. Jet needle
8. Diaphragm
9. Throttle valve
10. Needle jet
11. Jet block assembly
12. O-ring
13. Cap
14. Body
15. Choke plunger
16. Spring
17. Choke plunger guide
18. Collar
19. Washer
20. E-clip
21. Cap
22. Screw
23. Throttle plate
24. Air jet
25. Cover
26. O-ring gasket
27. Throttle shaft
28. Spring seat
29. Spring
30. Lockwasher
31. Case
32. Collar
33. O-ring
34. Needle jet assembly
35. Pilot jet
36. Washer
37. Spring
38. Pilot screw
39. Plug
40. Float assembly
41. O-ring gasket
42. Float bowl
43. Drain screw
44. Clamp
45. Spring
46. Throttle adjuster cable
47. Spacer ring
48. Main jet
49. O-ring gasket
50. Drain plug

16

12. Remove the needle jet from the jet block assembly.
13. If necessary, carefully slide out the jet block assembly from the top of the carburetor.
14. If necessary, unscrew and remove the throttle adjust cable and spring.
15. If necessary, remove the screws and remove the throttle shaft cover and O-ring gasket.

NOTE
Further disassembly is not necessary or recommended. Do not remove the throttle shaft assembly. If these parts are damaged, replace the carburetor assembly as these items are not available separately.

16. Clean and inspect all parts as described under *Cleaning and Inspection* in this supplement.

Assembly

1. If removed, install the remove the throttle adjust cable and spring and tighten securely.
2. If removed, install the jet block assembly with a *new* O-ring on the base. Make sure it is seated correctly.
3. Install the needle jet as follows:
   a. Correctly align the needle jet flat with the flat in the carburetor body.
   b. Insert the needle jet into the top of the carburetor and into the post. Push it in until it bottoms.
   c. After installation check that the needle jet flat is aligned with the flat in the carburetor body.
4. Install the air jet and tighten securely.
5. Install the main jet spacer ring and tighten securely.
6. Install the pilot jet and tighten securely.
7. Make sure the O-ring is in place, then install the needle valve seat. Push it down until it bottoms.
8. Install the needle valve onto the float tang.
9. Install the float assembly while aligning the needle valve with the needle valve seat. Push the float assembly down firmly until it is fully seated.
10. Install the O-ring gasket into the float bowl and install the float bowl. Tighten the screws securely.
11. To assemble the throttle valve/diaphragm assembly, perform the following:
   a. Onto the jet needle install the E-clip.
   b. Install the spacer and the spring seat.
   c. Install the jet needle assembly into the throttle valve/diaphragm assembly.
12. Install the spring into throttle valve/diaphragm assembly to hold the jet needle in place.
13. Install the throttle valve/diaphragm assembly into the carburetor body. Make sure the outer perimeter of the diaphragm is seated correctly in the body groove.
14. Install the cover and the screws and tighten securely.
15. After the cover is in place, insert a finger into the carburetor body venturi and push up on the throttle valve assembly. The assembly must move up and return without any binding. If the throttle valve assembly does not move freely, the spring may be out of position within it and the cover. Correct this problem at this time.

CLEANING AND INSPECTION

CAUTION
The carburetor body is equipped with plastic parts that cannot be removed. Do not dip the carburetor body, O-rings, float assembly, needle valve or diaphragm and vacuum slide assembly in a carburetor cleaner or other harsh solution that can damage these parts. Polaris does not recommend the use of a caustic carburetor cleaning solvent. Instead, clean the carburetor and related parts in a petroleum based solvent, or Simple Green. Then thoroughly rinse in clean hot water.

1. Initially clean all parts in mild petroleum based cleaning solution. Then clean in hot soap and water and rinse with hot water. Thoroughly dry with low pressure compressed air.

CAUTION
*If compressed air is not available, allow the parts to air dry or use a clean lint-free cloth. Do **not** use a paper towel to dry carburetor parts, as small paper particles may plug openings in the carburetor housing or jets.*

2. Allow the carburetor to dry thoroughly before assembly and blow dry with compressed air. Blow out the jets with compressed air.

CAUTION
*Do **not** use wire or drill bits to clean jets as minor gouges in the jet can alter flow rate and upset the air/fuel mixture.*

3. Inspect the float bowl O-ring gasket. Replace the O-ring gasket if it is hard or starting to deteriorate.
4. Make sure the drain screw is in good condition and does not leak; replace the drain screw if necessary.
5. Inspect the O-ring seal on the drain plug. Replace the O-ring if it is hard or starting to deteriorate.
6. Inspect the throttle valve diaphragm for cracks, deterioration or other damage. Check the sides of the throttle valve for excessive wear.
7. Install the throttle valve, into the jet block assembly and move it up and down in the bore. The throttle valve, should move smoothly with no binding or excessive play. If there is excessive play, replace the throttle valve, and/or jet block assembly.
8. Inspect the jet needle tapered end for steps, uneven wear or other damage. Replace if damaged.
9. Check the inlet valve needle seat O-ring seal for hardness or deterioration, replace if necessary.
10. Inspect the inlet valve needle seat for steps, uneven wear or other damage.
11. Insert the inlet valve needle into the seat and slowly move it back and forth and check for smooth operation. If either part is worn or damaged, replace the inlet valve assembly.
12. Inspect the needle valve tapered end for steps, uneven wear or other damage.
13. Inspect all jets. Make sure all holes are open and none of them are either worn or damaged.
14. Inspect the float for deterioration or damage. If the float is suspected of leakage, place it in a container of water and push it down. If the float sinks or if bubbles appear, indicating a leak, replace the float.
15. Inspect the starting enrichment (choke) valve plunger, spring and guide holder for wear or damage.
16. Make sure all openings in the carburetor body are clear. Clean out if they are plugged in any way, then apply low pressure compressed air to all openings.
17. Check the cover for cracks or damage; replace if necessary.
18. Make sure the throttle plate screws are tight.
19. Inspect the carburetor body for internal or external damage. If damaged, replace the carburetor assembly, as the body cannot be replaced separately.
20. Move the throttle lever back and forth from stop-to-stop and check for free movement. The throttle lever should move smoothly and return under spring tension. If it sticks in any position, replace the carburetor housing.

CARBURETOR TESTS AND ADJUSTMENTS

Inlet Valve Seat Inspection

The float valve sealing ability can be checked with a small hand-held pressure pump.

1. Turn the assembled carburetor upside down on the top cover.
2. Attach a small hand-held pressure pump to the fuel inlet fitting.
3. Apply 34.5 kPa (5 psi) of pressure to the inlet fitting.
4. The needle and seat should hold this pressure indefinitely.
5. If the needle and seat do no pass this test, replace both parts.
6. Remove the hand-held pressure pump.

Float Height Adjustment

To maintain a constant fuel level in the carburetor float bowl, the fuel inlet valve is controlled by the float. Because the height of the fuel affects the air/fuel mixture throughout the engine's operating range, make sure the float position is correctly adjusted.

1. Remove the carburetor as described in this chapter.
2. Remove the mounting screws and remove the float bowl and O-ring gasket.
3. Hold the carburetor on its side so the tang in the middle of the float arm is just touching the fuel valve. Use a float level gauge, vernier caliper or small ruler and measure the distance from the carburetor body gasket surface to the float. The correct distance is listed in **Table 7**.
4. If the float height is incorrect, adjust as follows:

a. Carefully bend the tang in the center of the float arm with a small screwdriver to adjust the float level.
b. Recheck the float level as described in Step 3. Repeat until the float level adjustment is correct.

5. Install the O-ring gasket into the float bowl and install the float bowl. Tighten the screws securely.
6. Install the carburetor as described in this chapter.

Jet Needle Adjustment

The position of the jet needle can be adjusted to affect the air/fuel mixture for medium throttle openings.

1. Remove the carburetor as described in this chapter.
2. Remove the screws securing the cover.
3. Remove the cover and the spring.
4. Carefully withdraw the throttle valve/diaphragm assembly.
5. To disassemble the throttle valve/diaphragm assembly, perform the following:
   a. Slowly push the jet needle up to dislodge the spring seat.
   b. Remove the spring seat, jet needle, E-ring and spacer.
6. Remove the E-ring and spacer from the jet needle.
7. Refer to **Table 7** for standard size jet needle and standard E-ring location from the top of the jet needle.

NOTE
Record the clip position prior to removal.

8. Raising the needle (lowering the E-ring) will enrichen the mixture during mid-throttle opening, while lowering the needle (raising the E-ring) will lean the mixture.
9. Install the jet needle, vacuum slide and diaphragm as described in this chapter.

Main Jet Replacement

The size of the main jet affects the air/fuel mixture during wide-open throttle operation. Different size main jets are available and can be installed to change the mixture for operation at high engine speeds.

1. Remove the carburetor as described in this chapter.
2. Unscrew and remove the drain plug and O-ring seal from the float bowl. Unscrew and remove the main jet.
3. Do not remove the spacer ring under the main jet.
4. The size is stamped on the jet. The main jet size listed in **Table 7** is recommended for operation at ambient temperatures of 5-26° C (40-80° F) at altitudes of 0-900 m (0-3000 ft.). A smaller size main jet may be required for optimum performance at higher altitudes and at warmer temperatures. A larger main jet may be used at colder temperatures.
5. Install the main jet and reassemble the carburetor by reversing the disassembly procedure.

CHAPTER EIGHT

CLUTCH/DRIVE BELT SYSTEM

DRIVE BELT

A drain plug (**Figure 6**) is added to the new clutch outer cover. If the vehicle has been ridden through deep water, water may have entered the clutch cover and drive belt area. If necessary, unscrew the drain plug and drain out any water.

After draining, shift the transmission into neutral and rev the engine slightly to expel the moisture.

Install the drain plug and O-ring seal and tighten securely.

6

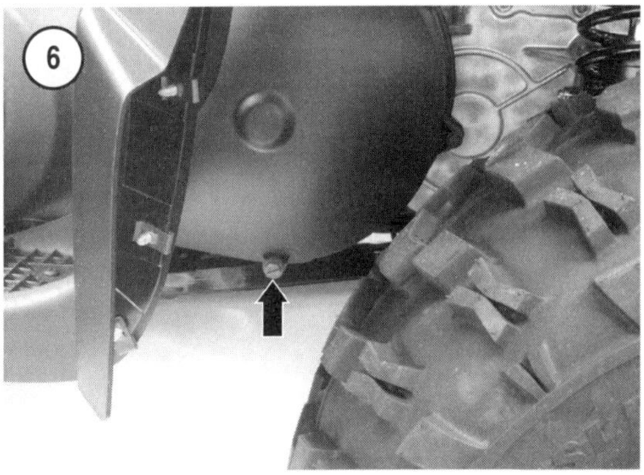

DRIVEN PULLEY (2003 MODELS BUILT AFTER 07/08/02)

Disassembly/Assembly

The driven pulley is basically the same as on prior models except for some of the components within the fixed sheave as shown in **Figure 7**.

The shaft that was an integral part of the fixed sheave is not a separate component. Follow the disassembly and assembly procedures described in Chapter Eight and refer to **Figure 7** while servicing the fixed sheave.

7

DRIVEN PULLEY (2003 MODELS BUILT AFTER 7/08/02)

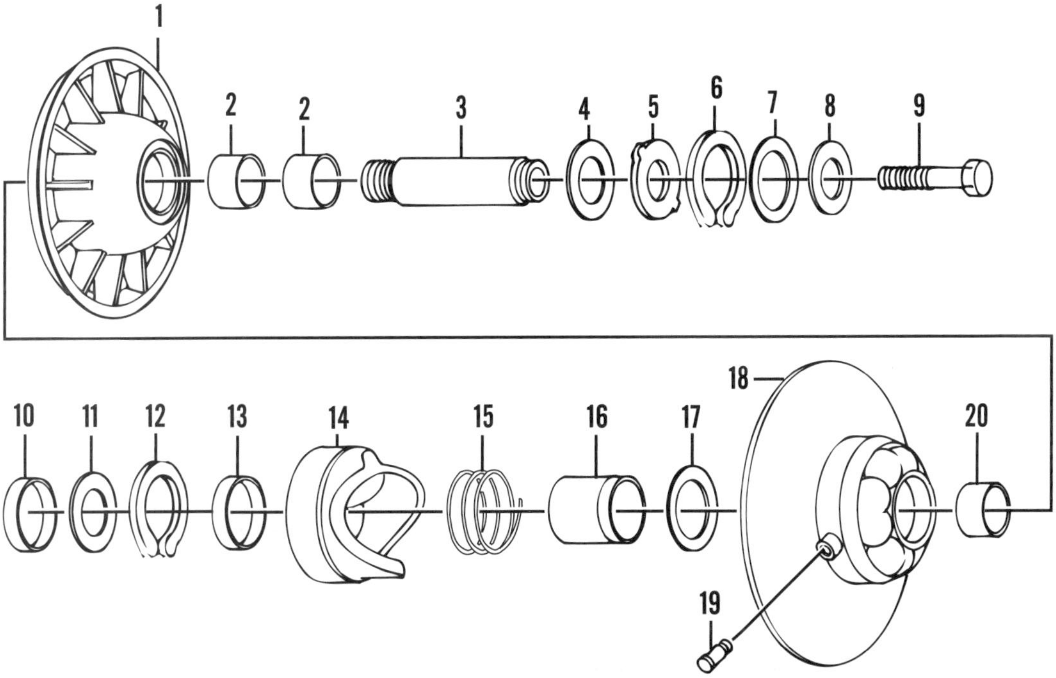

1. Fixed sheave
2. Bearing
3. Shaft
4. Washer
5. Plate
6. Circlip
7. Dome washer
8. Lockwasher
9. Bolt
10. Spacer
11. Washer
12. Circlip
13. Spacer
14. Helix
15. Spring
16. Bearing
17. Washer
18. Movable sheave
19. Pin
20. Bearing

CHAPTER NINE

TRANSMISSION

TRANSMISSION

Removal/Installation (2003 Models)

The removal and installation of the transmission is the same as on prior models with the following exception. The transmission output shaft brake caliper and disc are no longer located on the transmission.

The rear disc brake assembly is now located on the right side rear wheel hub.

CHAPTER ELEVEN

ELECTRICAL SYSTEM

LIGHTING SYSTEM

High-Beam Headlight (2003 Models)

Bulb replacement

The removal and installation of the high-beam headlight bulb is the same as on prior models with the exception of the removal of the headlight upper pod. On these models the upper pod (**Figure 8**) is held in place with three screws; one at each front corner (**Figure 9**) and one at the back (**Figure 10**).

9

8

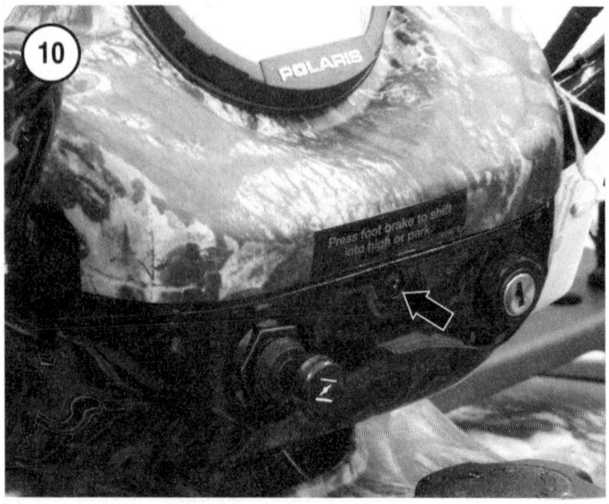
10

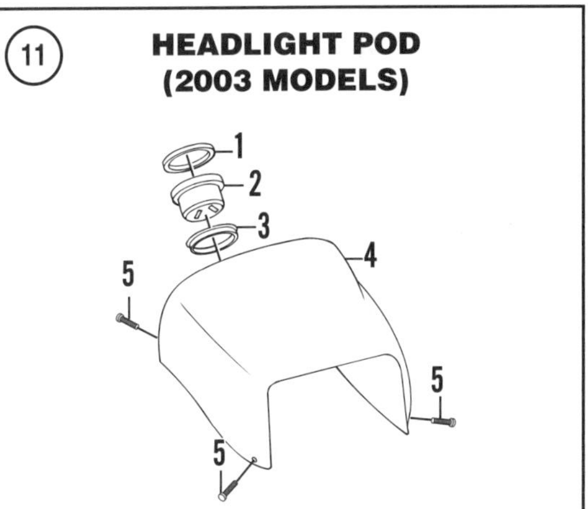

1. Trim bezel
2. Speedometer
3. Rubber mount
4. Headlight pod
5. Screw

ELECTRICAL COMPONENTS

Speedometer (2003 Models) Removal/Installation

1. Remove the three screws (**Figure 11**) securing the headlight upper pod and speedometer (**Figure 12**) to the lower pod.
2. Partially lift up the upper pod and disconnect the two multi-pin electrical connectors from the speedometer.
3. Remove the headlight upper pod and speedometer.
4. Withdraw the speedometer housing out through the front of the headlight upper pod.
5. Install the speedometer into the front of the headlight upper pod. Push it in until it bottoms.
6. Move the headlight upper pod into position and connect the two multi-pin electrical connectors onto the speedometer.
7. Install the three screws securing the headlight upper pod to the lower pod.

CHAPTER TWELVE

FRONT SUSPENSION AND STEERING

STEERING SHAFT (2002-ON MODELS)

The steering shaft (**Figure 13**) pivots on a split bushing block at the top and a bearing at the lower end. Adjustable tie rods connect the steering shaft to the steering arm portion of the front strut.

Removal/Installation

1. Remove the front fender assembly as described in Chapter Fifteen.

2. Remove the fuel tank as described in Chapter Six.

3. Remove both front wheels as described in Chapter Twelve.

4. Remove the inboard ends of both tie rods from the two plates on the base of the steering post. Support the inboard ends of the tie rods to the chassis with Bungee cords or wire.

5. Remove the headlight upper and lower pod as described under *High-Beam Headlight (Sportsman*

(13)

STEERING SHAFT (2002-ON MODELS)

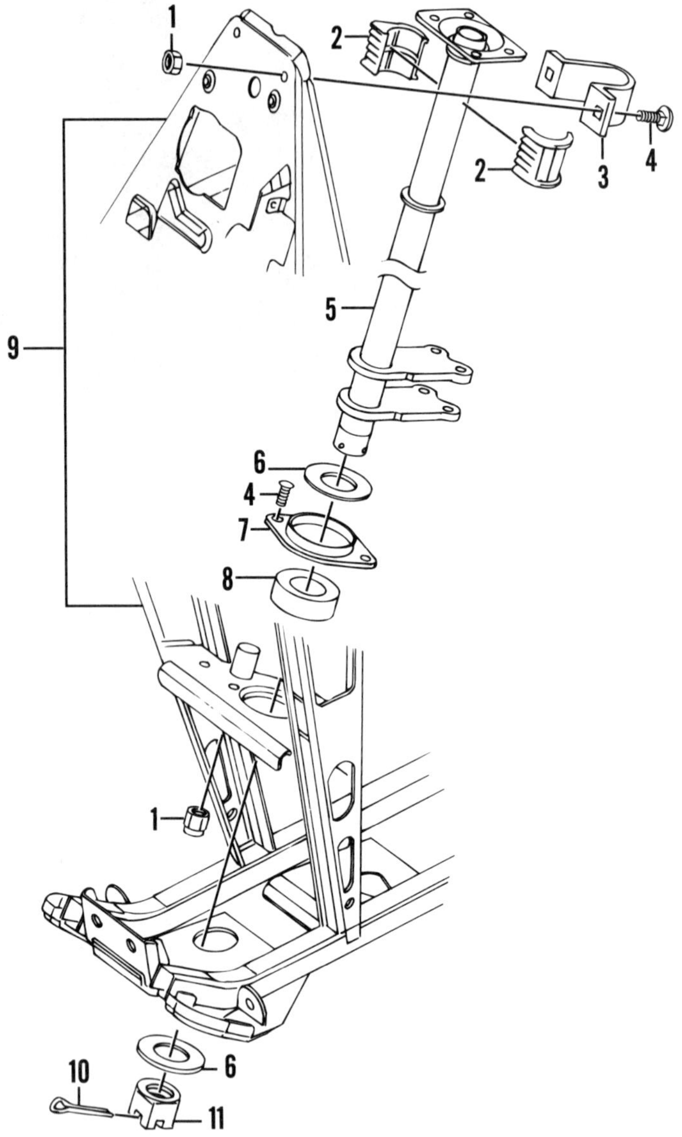

1. Locknut
2. Upper bushing blocks
3. Clamp
4. Bolt
5. Steering shaft
6. Bushing
7. Flange plate
8. Bearing
9. Frame
10. Cotter pin
11. Nut

14

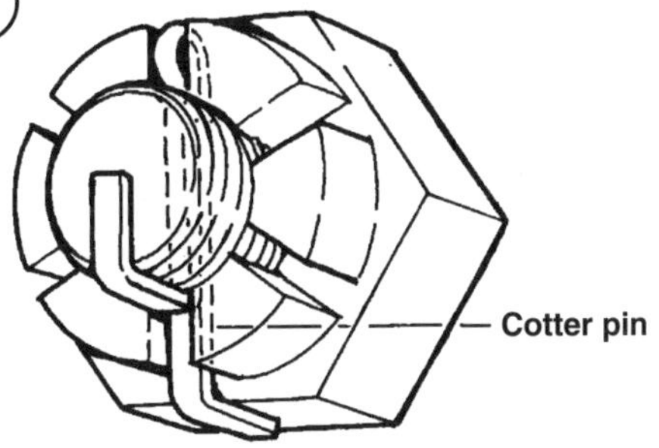

Models), Bulb Replacement in Chapter Eleven and this chapter.

6. Remove the handlebar assembly as described in Chapter Twelve.
7. Unscrew and remove the grease fitting.
8. Working at the lower end of the steering shaft, perform the following:
   a. Remove the cotter pin and discard it.
   b. Loosen then remove the castellated nut and flat bushing from the base of the shaft.
9. Working at the upper end of the steering shaft, perform the following:
   a. Remove the bolts and nuts securing the mounting clamp and upper bushing blocks to the frame section.
   b. Remove the mounting clamp, the upper bushing blocks and the clamp at the backside of the frame.
10. Carefully lift the steering shaft from the frame. Do not snag any electrical wires or hoses during removal.
11. Install the steering shaft by reversing the removal procedure while noting the following:
   a. Tighten the castellated nut securely.
   b. Install a *new* cotter pin and bend the ends over completely as shown in **Figure 14**. If the cotter pin holes do not align, slightly tighten the nut—do not loosen it to achieve alignment.

Lower Bearing Replacement

All models are equipped with the upper bushing blocks and the lower bearing. The upper bushing is a split block and the lower bearing is bolted to the frame.

1. Remove the steering shaft from the frame as described in this chapter.
2. Remove the bolts and nuts securing the flange and bearing to the frame. Remove the flange and bearing.
3. Clean the frame bearing mounting area thoroughly.
4. Install the new bearing and flange. Install the bolts and *new* self-locking nuts. Tighten the nuts securely.
5. Complete assembly by reversing the removal procedure. Coat the bushings with grease before assembling, then grease the bushings as described in Chapter Three again after assembly.

CHAPTER THIRTEEN

REAR SUSPENSION

REAR HUB AND BEARING CARRIER (2003 MODELS)

Removal

Refer to **Figure 15**.

1. Park the vehicle on level ground and set the parking brake. Block the front wheels so the vehicle will not roll in either direction.
2. Raise the rear of the vehicle with a small hydraulic or scissor jack. Place the jack under the frame with a piece of wood between the jack and the frame.
3. Place block(s) under the frame to support the vehicle securely with the rear wheels off the ground.
4. Remove the rear wheel(s) described in Chapter Thirteen.
5. Remove the hub cap (A, **Figure 16**).

15

REAR HUB AND BEARING CARRIER (2003 MODELS)

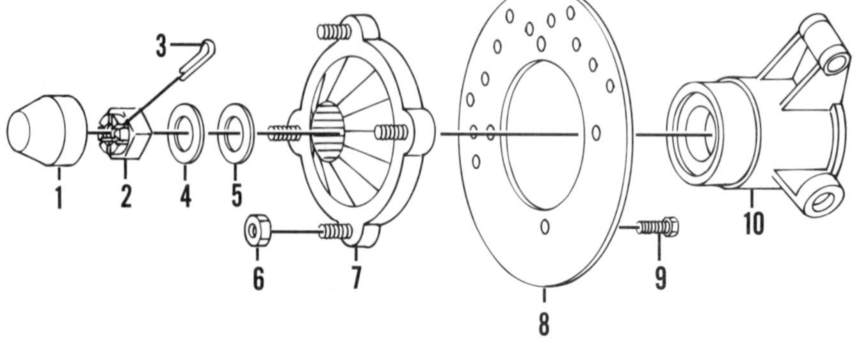

1. Cap
2. Castelated nut
3. Cotter pin
4. Conical washer
5. Conical washer
6. Lug nut
7. Rear hub
8. Brake disc (right side only)
9. Bolt
10. Rear axle bearing carrier

6. On the right side, remove the rear brake caliper (B, **Figure 16**) as described in this supplement.

7. Remove the cotter pin (A, **Figure 17**) and discard it. A new cotter pin must be installed.

8. Loosen and remove the castellated nut (B, **Figure 17**) on the rear axle.

9. Remove both conical washers (**Figure 18**) from the axle.

NOTE

It may be necessary to use a wheel puller to remove the rear hub from the end of the rear axle.

10. Remove the rear hub (**Figure 19**) from the rear axle.

11. Remove the bolt (A, **Figure 20**) and self-locking nut (B) securing the upper control arm to the rear axle bearing carrier. Discard the nut.

12. Remove the bolt and two washers (C, **Figure 20**) securing the lower control arm to the rear axle bearing carrier hub on both sides.

13. Hold onto the drive axle (D, **Figure 20**) and withdraw the rear hub (E) from the drive axle.

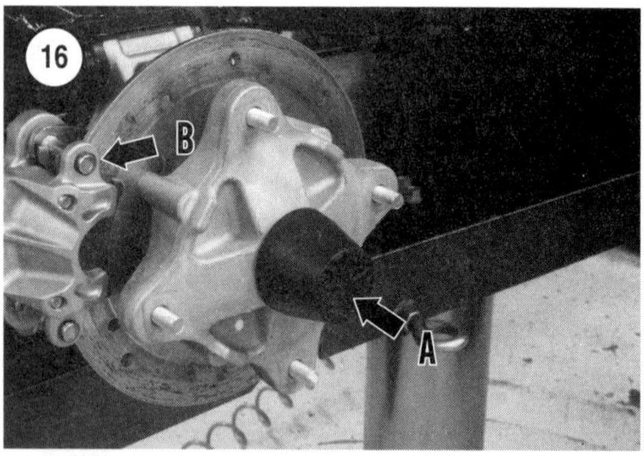

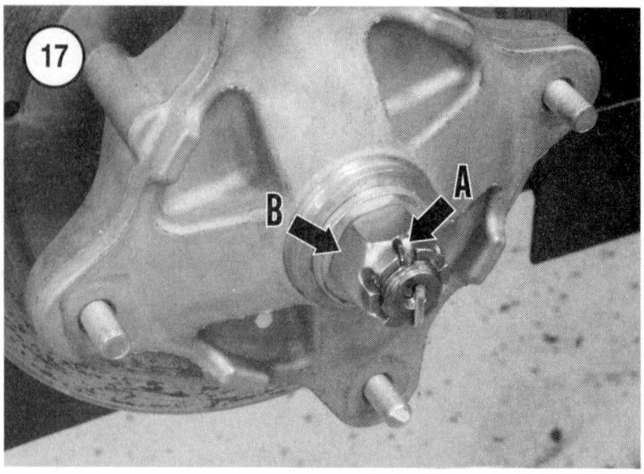

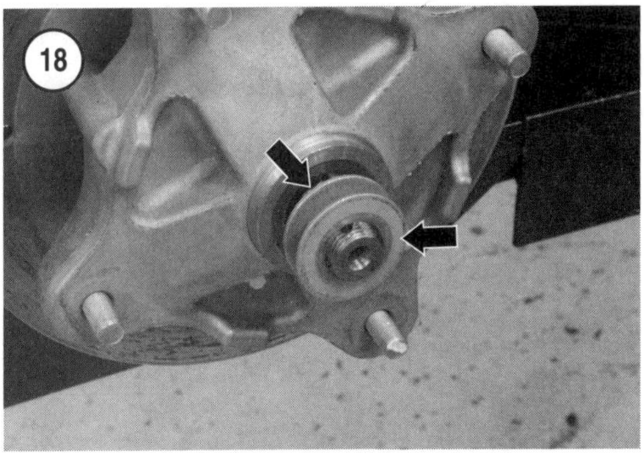
18

19

20

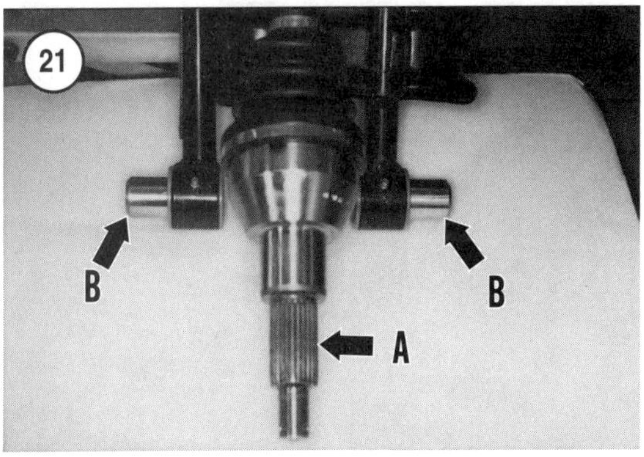

21

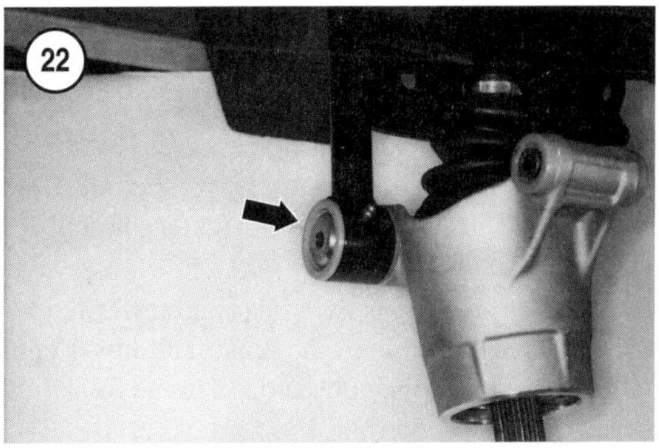
22

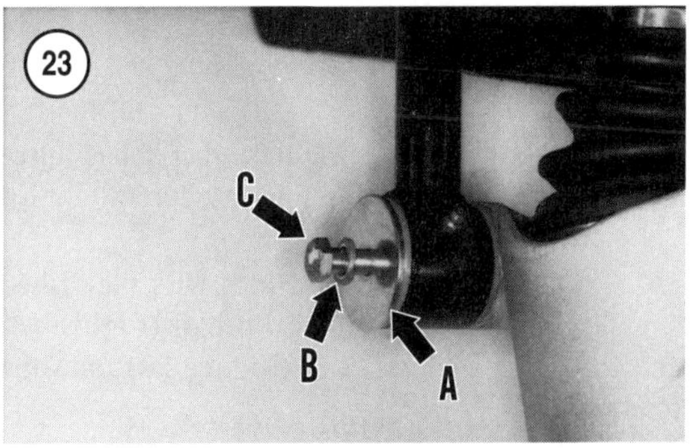

23

NOTE
The rear axle (A, ***Figure 21****) is held in place and will not slide out of the transmission.*

14. Lower the outer end of the drive axle and rest it on the lower control arm.
15. Inspect the rear hub and bearing carrier as described in this chapter.

Installation

1. Apply a light coat of all-purpose grease to the inner race of the bearing and to the rear axle shaft where the bearing rides.
2. Make sure the inner bushings (B, **Figure 21**) are in place on the lower control arm. Apply a light coat of grease to the outer surfaces of the bushings.
3. Install the rear axle bearing carrier onto the rear axle and push it on until it stops.
4. Install rear axle bearing carrier onto the lower control arm.
5. Push the bushings in until they bottom (**Figure 22**) against the rear axle bearing carrier and align the bolt holes.
6. Install a large washer (A, **Figure 23**), then a smaller washer (B) and bolt (C) through the lower

control arm and into the rear axle bearing carrier. Repeat for the other side of the lower control arm. Tighten the bolts securely at this time.

7. Move the rear axle bearing carrier up into position on the upper control arm. Insert the bolt from the rear and install a *new* nut. Tighten the nut securely at this time.

8. Make sure the rear axle bearing carrier is correctly seated within both the upper and lower control arms. Tighten the bolts and nut to the following specifications:

   a. Upper control arm bolt and nut: 48 N•m (35 ft.-lbs.).

   b. Lower control arm bolt and nut: 41 N•m (30 ft.-lbs.).

9. Align the splines and install the rear hub (**Figure 19**) onto the rear axle. Tap the rear hub on until it bottoms.

10. Position both conical washers with the dished side facing out and install the washers (**Figure 18**) and the castellated axle nut (**Figure 24**) onto the rear axle.

11. On the right side, install the rear brake caliper (B, **Figure 16**) as described in this supplement.

12. Have an assistant apply the rear brake. Use a torque wrench and tighten the castellated nut to 136 N•m (100 ft.-lbs.).

13. Verify that one pair of openings in the castellated nut is aligned with the cotter pin hole in the rear axle. If not, align opening by tightening the axle nut. Do not loosen the axle nut to align the openings.

WARNING
Always install a new cotter pin.

14. Insert the *new* cotter pin through the openings in the castellated nut and the rear axle hole. Bend the end of the cotter pin over completely (**Figure 14**).

15. Install the hub cap (A, **Figure 16**). Make sure it is seated correctly within the rear wheel.

16. Install the rear wheel(s) as described in Chapter Thirteen.

Inspection

1. Clean the rear hub and end of rear axle with solvent and dry thoroughly.

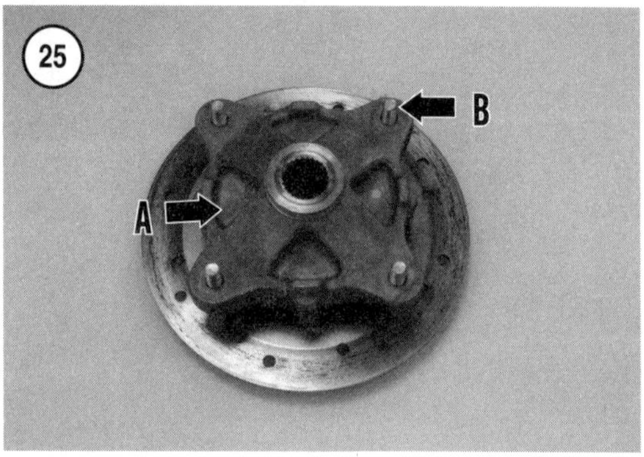

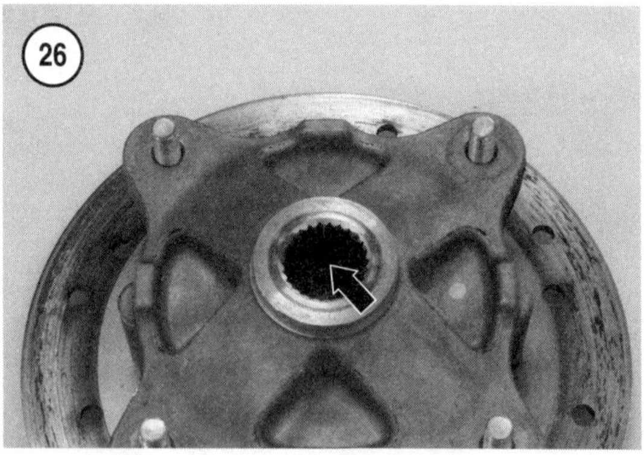

2. Inspect the rear hub (A, **Figure 25**) for cracks or other damage. If damage is severe, replace the hub.

3. Inspect the hub inner splines (**Figure 26**) and the rear axle outer splines (**Figure 27**) for wear or damage. Slide the rear hub onto the rear axle and try to rotate it. It should be a tight-fit with no rotational movement. If damage is minor, clean up with a file. If damage is severe replace the damaged part(s).

4. Check the lug nut threaded studs (B, **Figure 25**) for damage. Replace the stud(s) is necessary. If the studs are damaged, inspect the lug nuts for damage and replace as necessary.

CHAPTER FOURTEEN

BRAKES

Refer to **Table 8** for brake torque specifications.

REAR BRAKE PAD REPLACEMENT (2003 MODELS)

There is no recommended interval for changing the friction pads in the disc brakes. Pad wear depends greatly on riding habits and conditions. The pads should be checked for wear prior to each ride or when the brake pads wear close to the edge of the brake disc.

Always replace both pads in the caliper at the same time. Do not disconnect the hydraulic brake hoses from the brake caliper for brake pad replacement, disconnect the hoses only if the caliper assembly is going to be removed.

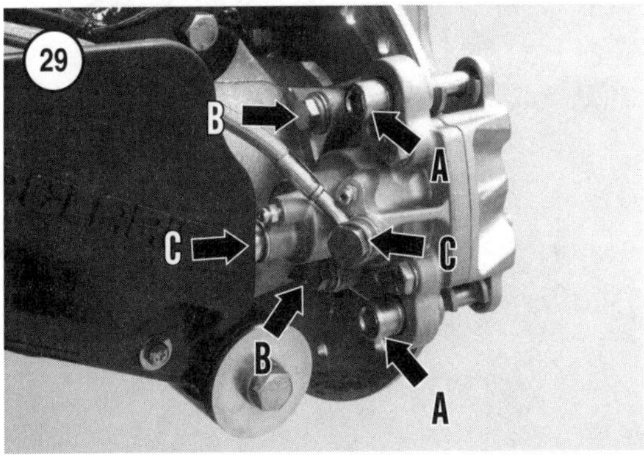

1. Park the vehicle on level ground. Block the front wheels so the vehicle will not roll in either direction.
2. Raise the rear of the vehicle with a small hydraulic or scissor jack. Place the jack under the frame with a piece of wood between the jack and the frame.
3. Place block(s) under the frame to support the vehicle securely with the rear wheels off the ground.
4. Remove the right side rear wheel described in Chapter Thirteen.
5. Remove the small snap ring (**Figure 28**) from both slide pin bolts.
6. Loosen both pad pin bolts (A, **Figure 29**), then remove both hex bolts (B) securing the brake caliper and remove the caliper from the brake disc.
7. When repositioning the brake pads in the caliper, the master cylinder brake fluid level will rise as the caliper piston is repositioned. Perform the following:
   a. Clean the top of the master cylinder of all dirt and foreign matter.
   b. Place a plastic drop cloth over the front fender and fuel tank, under the master cylinder, to

16

30

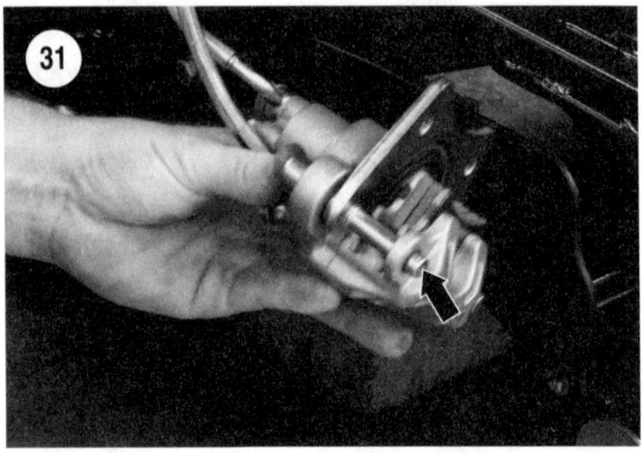
31

protect it from any accidental brake fluid spills.

c. Remove the screws securing the top cover (**Figure 30**).

d. Remove the top cover and diaphragm from the master cylinder.

WARNING
Brake fluid is poisonous. Do not siphon off with the mouth as it may be ingested.

8. Push on the inboard brake pad and push the piston back into the caliper cylinder. Constantly check the reservoir to make sure brake fluid does not overflow. Remove fluid, if necessary, prior to it overflowing.

9. The piston should move freely. If it does not, remove and service the caliper as described in this chapter.

10. Remove both slide pin bolts (**Figure 31**) loosened in Step 6.

11. Remove both brake pads and the bracket from the caliper.

12. Inspect the brake pads (**Figure 32**) for uneven wear, damage or grease contamination. Replace the pads as a set, if necessary.

NOTE
Measure the brake pad lining as well as the metal backing plate. Do not measure only the lining thickness.

13. Measure the thickness of each brake pad with a ruler or vernier caliper. Replace the brake pads if the thickness of either pad is worn to the service limit of 4.6 mm (0.180 in.).

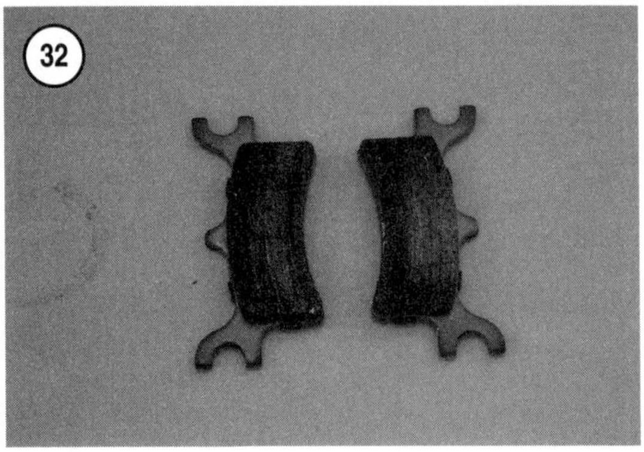
32

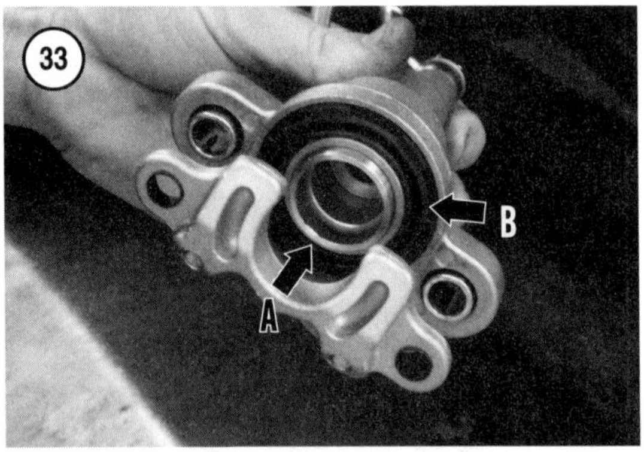

33

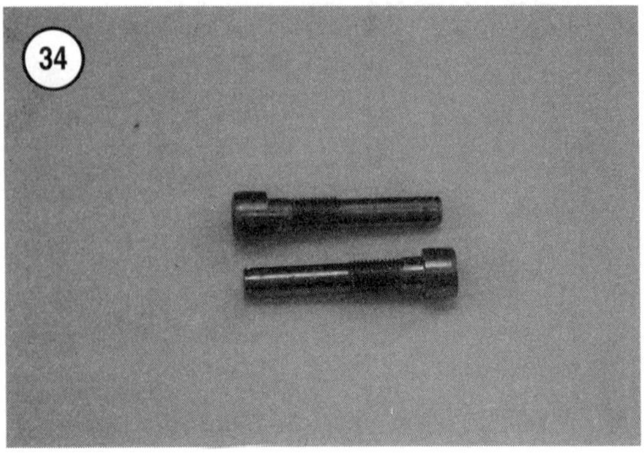
34

35

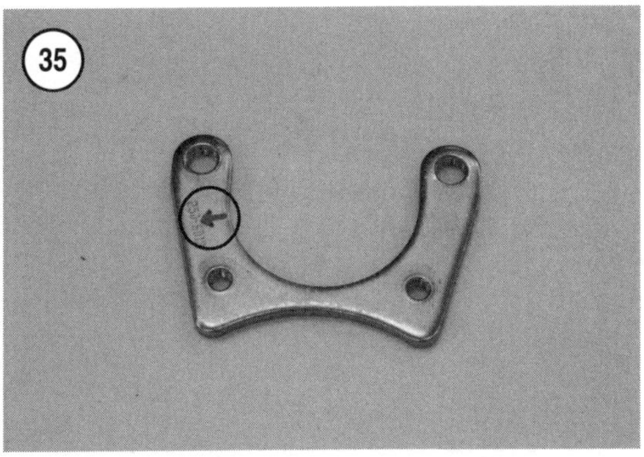

36

37

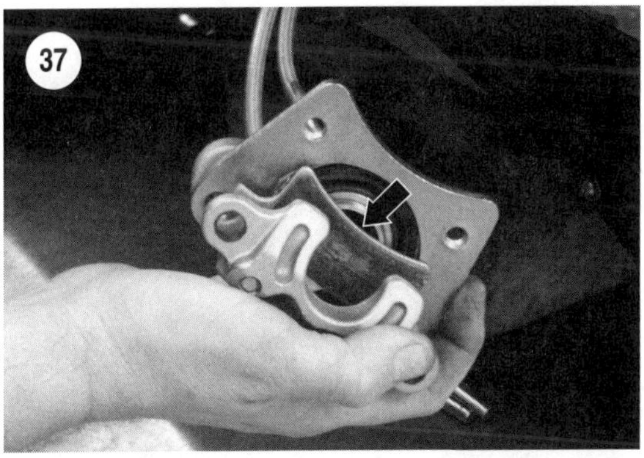

38

14. Inspect the brake disc for nicks, corrosion and radial groove damage. If damaged, remove the brake disc as described in this chapter.
15. Check the end of the piston (A, **Figure 33**) for fluid leakage. If the seal (B, **Figure 33**) is damaged and/or if there is fluid leakage, overhaul the brake caliper as described in this chapter.
16. Inspect the slide pin bolts (**Figure 34**) for wear or thread damage. Replace if necessary.
17. Position the bracket with the manufacturer"s marks (arrow) (**Figure 35**) facing in toward the piston and install the bracket (**Figure 36**).
18. Install the inboard brake pad (**Figure 37**), then the outboard brake pad (**Figure 38**) into the caliper.
19. Correctly position the brake pads and the bracket. Install the slide pin bolts (**Figure 31**) and push them through both brake pads and the bracket, then into the caliper. Tighten the pin bolts securely.
20. Install the caliper onto the brake disc being careful not to damage the leading edge of the brake pads.
21. Install both caliper mounting bolts (B, **Figure 29**) and tighten to 25 N•m (18 ft.-lbs.).
22. Tighten the slide pin bolts (A, **Figure 29**) to 41-48 N•m (30-35 ft.-lbs.).
23. Install the small snap ring (**Figure 28**) onto the end of both slide pin bolts. Make sure they are correctly seated in the slide pin bolt grooves.

WARNING

Use brake fluid clearly marked DOT 3 from a sealed container. Other types may vaporize and cause brake failure. Always use the same brand name; do not intermix as many brands are not compatible. Do not intermix silicone based (DOT 5) brake fluid as it can cause brake component damage leading to brake system failure.

NOTE

To control the flow of hydraulic fluid, punch a small hole into the seal of the DOT 3 brake fluid container next to the edge of the pour spout. This will help eliminate fluid spillage especially while adding fluid to the very small brake reservoir.

24. Refill the master cylinder reservoir to maintain the correct fluid level as indicated on the side of the reservoir. Install the diaphragm and cover and tighten the screws securely.

25. Install the right side rear wheel described in Chapter Thirteen.
26. With the wheels still off the ground, spin the wheels and activate the brake lever as many times as it takes to refill the caliper cylinder and correctly locate the brake pads against the disc.

WARNING
Do not ride the vehicle until it is established that the brakes are operating correctly with full hydraulic advantage. If necessary, bleed the brakes as described in this chapter.

NOTE
The following instructions apply to original equipment type pads only. If using aftermarket brake pads, follow the manufacturer's break-in instructions.

27. Bed the pads in gradually with a burnishing procedure as follows:
   a. Start the vehicle and slowly increase speed up to 30 mph (48 km/h).
   b. *Gradually* apply the brakes and bring the vehicle to a complete stop.
   c. Repeat this procedure ten times.
   d. For the first 2-3 days of riding by using only light pressure as much as possible. Immediate hard application will glaze the new friction pads and greatly reduce the effectiveness of the brake.

REAR CALIPER (2003 MODELS)

Removal

1. Park the vehicle on level ground. Block the front wheels so the vehicle will not roll in either direction.
2. Raise the rear of the vehicle with a small hydraulic or scissor jack. Place the jack under the frame with a piece of wood between the jack and the frame.
3. Place block(s) under the frame to support the vehicle securely with the rear wheels off the ground.
4. Remove the right side rear wheel described in Chapter Thirteen.
5A. If the caliper is not going to be serviced, perform the following:

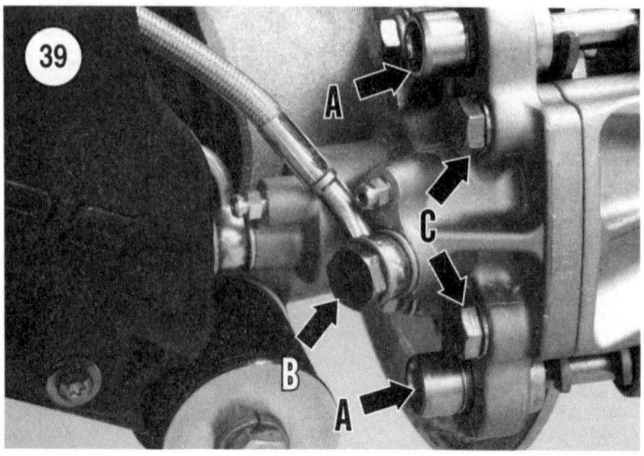

   a. Remove both bolts (A, **Figure 39**) securing the brake caliper and remove the caliper from the brake disc.
   b. If the brake pads are still in place, insert a spacer block between the brake pads to keep them separated.

NOTE
The spacer block prevents the piston from being forced out of the caliper if the brake lever or pedal is accidentally applied while the brake caliper is removed from the brake disc.

5B. If the caliper assembly is going to be disassembled for service, perform the following:
   a. Remove the brake pads as described in this chapter.
   b. Slowly apply the brake lever to push the piston part way out of caliper assembly for ease of removal during caliper service.

CAUTION
The banjo bolt head (B, ***Figure 39****) is very shallow and will easily round off.*

   c. Use only a six-point socket or six-point box wrench and loosen the banjo bolt (B, **Figure 39**) on both metal brake lines. Remove both banjo bolts and sealing washers.
   d. Place the loose end of both brake hoses in a reclosable plastic bag to prevent the entry of debris.

6. If necessary, disassemble, inspect and assemble the rear brake caliper as described in this chapter.

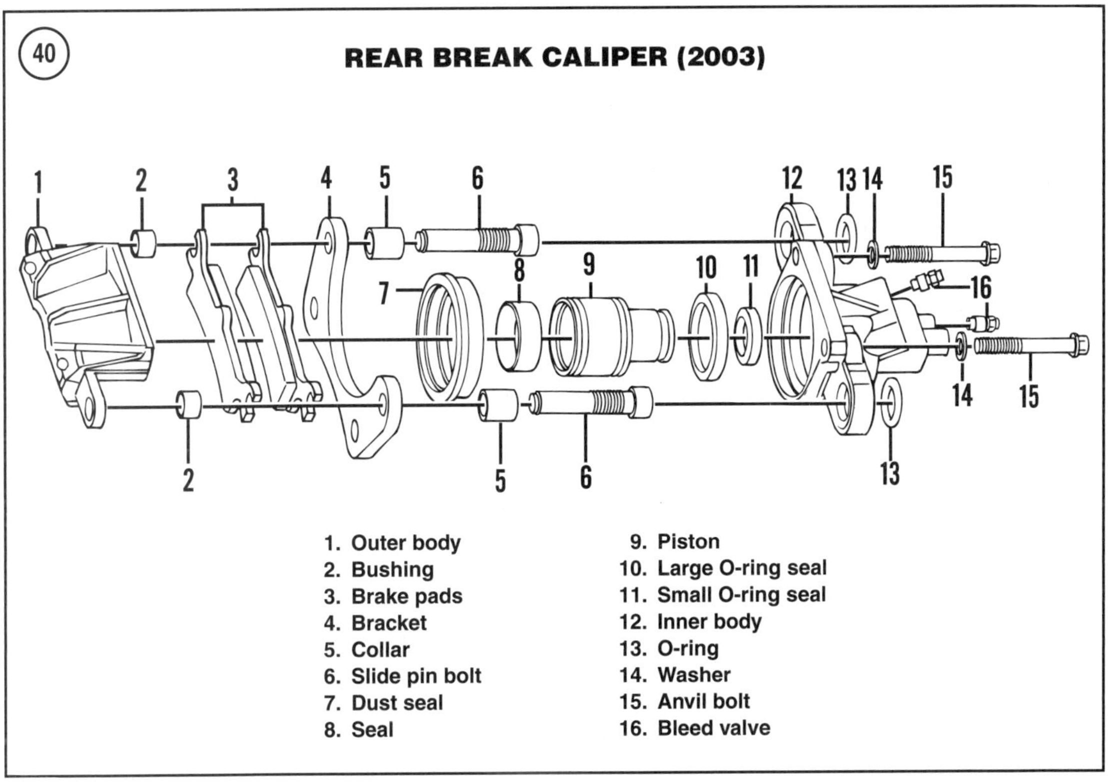

Installation

1A. If the brake caliper was not serviced, perform the following:

a. If installed, remove the spacer block from between the brake pads.
b. Install the caliper onto the brake disc being careful not to damage the leading edge of the brake pads.
c. Install both caliper mounting bolts (A, **Figure 39**) and tighten to 25 N•m (18 ft.-lbs.).

1B. If the caliper was serviced, perform the following:

a. Connect both brake line fittings (B, **Figure 39**) onto the caliper and do not tighten the union bolts at this time.
b. Install the caliper onto the brake disc being careful not to damage the leading edge of the brake pads.
c. Install both caliper mounting bolts (A, **Figure 39**) and tighten to 25 N•m (18 ft.-lbs.).
d. Install new sealing washer on each side of the banjo bolt fittings and tighten the fittings to 21 N•m (15 ft.-lbs.).
e. Bleed the brake as described under *Bleeding the System* in Chapter Fourteen.

WARNING

Do not ride the vehicle until it is established that the brakes are operating correctly with full hydraulic advantage. If necessary, bleed the brakes as described in this chapter.

Disassembly

Refer to **Figure 40**.

NOTE

There are no new or service limit specifications for the caliper assembly. The piston and dust seals can be replaced.

1. Prior to remove the rear caliper, loosen the anvil bolts (C, **Figure 39**) securing the caliper halves together.
2. Remove the caliper, the brake pads and bracket as described in this supplement.

3. Remove the anvil bolts (C, **Figure 39**) securing the caliper halves together.
4. Carefully separate the caliper halves .

NOTE
If the piston was partially forced out of the caliper body during removal, steps 2-4 may not be necessary. If the piston or caliper bore are corroded or very dirty; a small amount of compressed air may be necessary to completely remove the pistons from the body bores.

5. Place a piece of soft wood or folded shop cloth over the end of the piston and the caliper body. Turn this assembly over with the piston facing down.

WARNING
*In the next step, the piston may shoot out of the caliper body like a bullet. Keep all fingers out of the way. Wear shop gloves and apply air pressure gradually. Do **not** use high pressure air or place the air hose nozzle directly against the brake hose fitting inlet in the caliper body. Hold the air nozzle away from the inlet allowing some of the air to escape.*

6. Remove one of the bleed screws.
7. Apply the air pressure in short spurts to the bleed screw opening and force out the piston. Use a service station air hose if compressed air is not available.
8. Withdraw the piston from the caliper half.

CAUTION
In the following step, do not use a sharp tool to remove the piston seal from the caliper cylinders. Do not damage the cylinder surface.

9. Remove the dust seal and piston seal from the piston.
10. Unscrew and remove the remaining bleed valve.

Inspection

CAUTION
Never use petroleum-base solvents of any kind on the brake system's internal components. Any residual solvent remaining within a caliper component will cause the new seals to swell and distort and require replacement.

1. Clean the caliper bodies and piston in denatured alcohol or fresh DOT 3 brake fluid. Wear eye protection and blow dry with compressed air directing the air flow and residual fluid away from you.
2. Make sure the fluid passageways in the base of the piston bore are clear. Apply compressed air to make sure they are clear.
3. Inspect the piston seal and dust seal grooves in the piston for damage. If it is damaged or corroded, replace the piston and seals.
4. Inspect the brake line fitting threaded holes in the caliper body. If worn or damaged, clean out with a thread tap or replace the caliper assembly.
5. Inspect the bleed screw inlet fittings in the caliper body. If worn or damaged, clean out with a thread tap or replace the caliper assembly.
6. Inspect the bleed screws and caps. Make sure they are clean and open. Apply compressed air to the openings and make sure they are clear. Clean out if necessary with fresh brake fluid. Install the bleed screws and tighten securely.
7. Inspect both caliper bodies for damage, replace the caliper assembly if necessary.
8. Inspect the caliper piston bore for cracks, deep scoring, or excessive wear.
9. Check the caliper piston for scratches, scoring or rust.
10. Remove the bushing and O-rings from the inner caliper body. Inspect both bushings for wear or damage and replace as a set if necessary. Replace the O-rings if hardened or starting to deteriorate.
11. The piston seals help to maintain correct brake pad to disc clearance. If the seals are worn or damaged, the brake pads will drag and cause excessive wear and increase brake fluid temperature. Replace the piston seals if the following conditions exist:
   a. Brake fluid leads around either brake pad.
   b. Stuck piston seal(s).
   c. There is a large difference in the inner and outer brake pad thickness.

NOTE
Never reuse an old piston or dust seal. Very minor damage or age deterioration can make the seals useless.

12. Inspect the brake pads for uneven wear, damage or grease contamination. If the pad thickness is

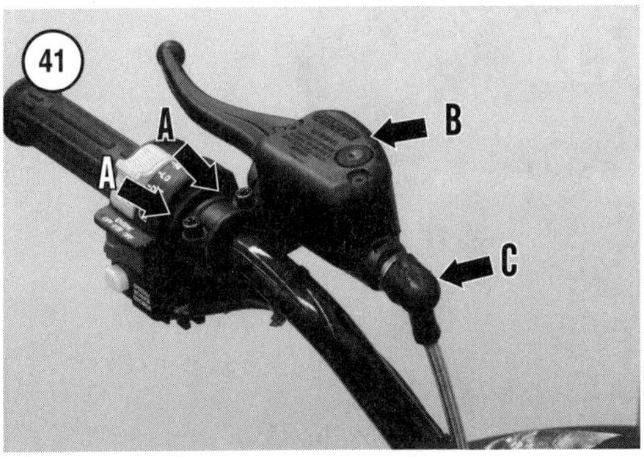

with specification, clean off the pad surface with an aerosol brake cleaner to remove any surface contamination.

NOTE
When the brake system is operating correctly, the inboard and outboard brake pads should show the same approximately amount of wear. If there is a large difference in pad wear, the piston seals are faulty not allowing the piston to return properly, this causes one pad to drag against the disc.

Assembly

NOTE
Use only new, DOT 3 brake fluid when brake fluid is called for in the following procedure.

1. Soak the piston and dust seals in brake fluid for approximately 5 minutes.
2. Lightly coat the piston and cylinder bore with brake fluid.
3. Install a *new* piston seal into the smaller inner groove in the piston.
4. Install a *new* dust seal into the larger outer groove in the piston.

NOTE
Check that both seals fit securely into the piston grooves. If the seals are not installed properly, the caliper assembly will leak and braking performance will be reduced.

5. Position the piston with the smaller closed end going in first and install the piston into the cylinder bore. Push the piston in until bottoms.
6. Install *new* O-rings and the bushings into the inner caliper body.
7. Assemble the two caliper halves together.
8. Install the anvil bolts securing the caliper halves together and tighten securely.
9. Install the bleed valves and tighten securely.
10. Install the bracket, the brake pads and the caliper as described in this chapter.
11. Tighten the anvil bolts (C, **Figure 39**) to 22-25 N•m (16-18 ft.-lbs.).

FRONT MASTER CYLINDER

The internal portion of the 2002-on front master cylinder is not serviceable. Some external components are available in kit form as follows:

1. Master cylinder lever kit: includes the lever, pivot pin and snap ring.
2. Master cylinder cap kit: includes the cap, sight glass, diaphragm and screws.
3. Master cylinder clamp kit: includes the clamp and screws.
4. Mater cylinder parking brake kit: includes the lever and spring.

Portions of the 2001 model are serviceable. Check with the dealership for the availability of replacement parts prior to disassembling the master cylinder.

Removal/Installation

1. Park the vehicle on level ground and block the wheels so the vehicle cannot roll in either direction.
2. Cover the area under the master cylinder to prevent brake fluid from damaging any component that it might contact.
3. Loosen the clamp bolts (A, **Figure 41**) securing the master cylinder to the handlebar.

CAUTION
If brake fluid should contact any surface, wash the area immediately with soapy water and rinse completely. Brake fluid will damage plastic, painted and plated surfaces.

4. Clean the top of the master cylinder of all dirt and foreign matter.

16

5. Remove the screws securing the cover (B, **Figure 41**).

6. Remove the cover and diaphragm from the master cylinder.

7. Use a clean syringe to remove the brake fluid from the reservoir. Discard the brake fluid.

8. Slide the rubber boot (C, **Figure 41**) off the brake hose fitting.

CAUTION
*The banjo bolt head **(Figure 42)** is very shallow and will easily round off.*

9. Use only a six-point socket or six-point box wrench and loosen the banjo bolt (**Figure 42**) on the metal brake line.

10. Remove the banjo bolt and sealing washers (**Figure 42**) securing the upper brake hose to the master cylinder. Place the loose end of the upper brake hose in a reclosable plastic bag and close it to prevent contamination. Secure the hose to the handlebar in the upright position.

11. Remove the clamp bolts (A, **Figure 41**) and remove the master cylinder from the handlebar.

12. If the master cylinder is being removed and is not going to be serviced; place it in a reclosable plastic bag and close it.

13. Install by reversing these removal steps, while noting the following:

   a. Move the master cylinder to a position where the brake lever suits the desired riding position, then tighten the clamp bolts.
   b. Attach the brake hose to the master cylinder with the banjo bolt and new sealing washers. Tighten the banjo bolts to 21 Nm (15 ft.-lbs.).
   c. Refill the master cylinder with DOT 3 brake fluid and bleed the brake as described in this chapter.

WARNING
Do not ride the vehicle until the brakes are working properly. Make sure that the brake lever travel is not excessive and that the lever does not feel soft or spongy. If either condition exists, bleed the system again.

Disassembly (2001 Models Only)

Refer to **Figure 43**.

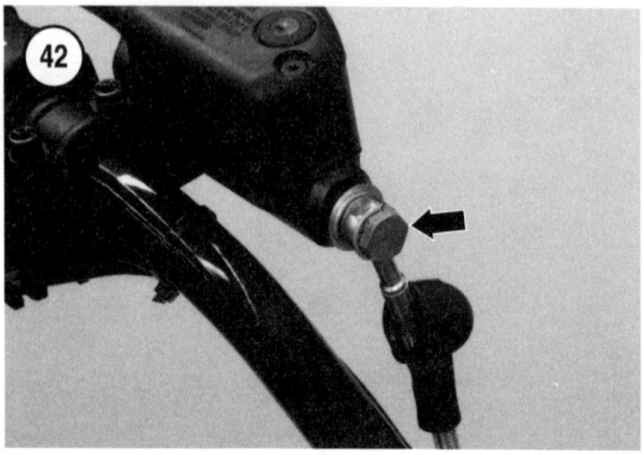

NOTE
There are no new or service limit specifications for the front master cylinder assembly. Check with the dealership for the availability of replacement parts prior to disassembling the master cylinder.

1. Remove the master cylinder as described in this chapter.

2. Remove the snap ring securing the brake lever to the master cylinder. Remove the pivot pin and the brake lever. Do not lose the parking brake spring.

3. Remove the screws attaching the master cylinder top cap, then remove the cap and the diaphragm.

NOTE
If there is brake fluid leaking from the piston bore, the piston cup is worn or damaged. Replace the piston assembly during re-assembly.

NOTE
After the dust seal is removed from the piston bore area, the spring will force the piston out of the bore. Be ready to catch the piston to avoid damage.

4. Carefully remove the dust seal from the groove in the piston bore area where the hand lever actuates the piston assembly.

5. Remove the outer spring, washer, piston and inner spring from the master cylinder bore. Note the direction of the outer spring as it must be installed in the same direction.

Inspection

1. Clean all parts in isopropyl alcohol or fresh DOT 3 brake fluid. Inspect the body cylinder bore surface

43

FRONT MASTER CYLINDER (2001-ON MODELS)

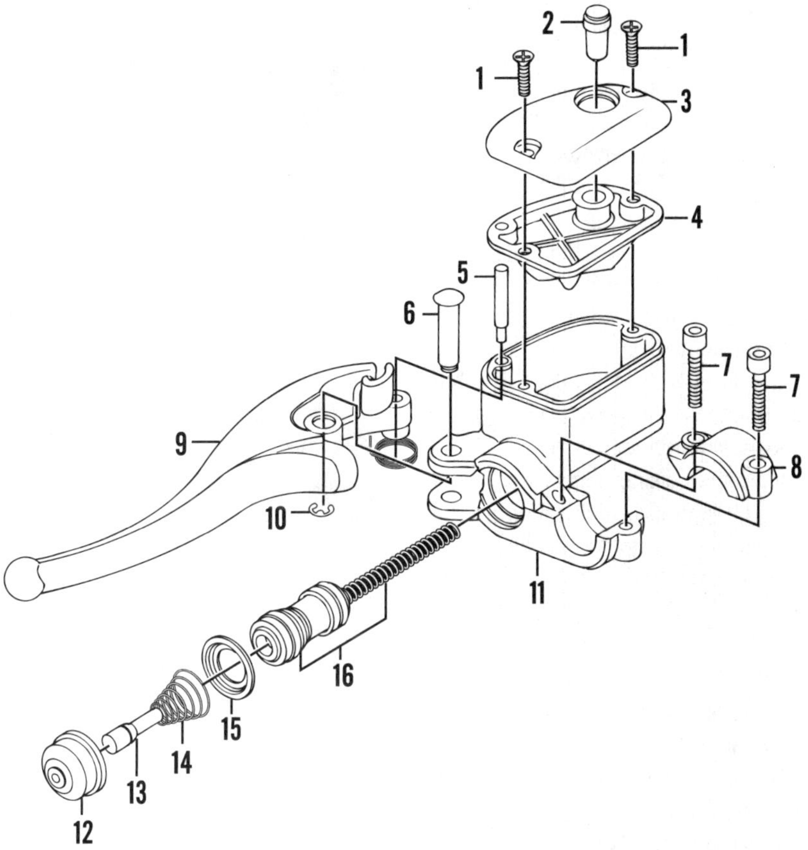

1. Screw
2. Sight glass
3. Cover
4. Diaphragm
5. Pin
6. Lever pivot pin
7. Bolt
8. Clamp
9. Lever
10. E-clip
11. Body*
12. Outer dust seal*
13. Plunger*
14. Spring*
15. Seal*
16. Piston and return spring assembly*

*Item Nos. 12-16 are available as the master cylinder piston assembly on 2001 models only.

and piston contact surfaces for signs of wear and damage. If less than perfect, replace the master cylinder assembly. The body cannot be replaced separately.
2. Inspect the piston cup for signs of wear and damage.
3. Make sure the vent slots in the top cap are clear and unobstructed. Clean out if necessary.
4. Make sure the fluid supply port in the bottom of the master cylinder body is clear.
5. Inspect the piston contact surface for signs of wear and damage.
6. Check the end of the piston for wear caused by the hand lever.
7. Check the hand lever pivot lugs on the master cylinder body for cracks or elongation. If damaged, replace the master cylinder assembly.
8. Inspect the pivot hole in the hand lever. If worn or elongated, replace the lever.
9. Inspect the threads in the bore for the banjo bolt. If worn or damaged, clean out with a metric thread tap or replace the master cylinder assembly.
10. Check the top cap and diaphragm for damage and deterioration and replace as necessary.
11. Inspect the parking brake lever for ease of movement. Make sure the spring is in place and is working properly.

Assembly

1. Coat the new cups and piston assembly in fresh DOT 3 brake fluid. Coat the inside of the cylinder bore with fresh brake fluid.
2. If removed, position the piston cups with the open end facing toward the inner spring end of the piston. Install the cups onto the piston.

CAUTION
When installing the piston assembly, do not allow the cups to turn inside out as they will be damaged and allow brake fluid leakage within the cylinder bore.

3. Install the return spring and the piston into the master cylinder bore.
4. Install the washer and outer spring into the master cylinder bore. Push them in until they bottom in the cylinder bore.
5. Push the piston assembly on, hold it there and install the new dust seal. Make sure the dust seal is correctly seated in the groove. Push on the piston, it should spring back against the dust seal.
6. Install the hand lever, pivot pin and snap ring. Make sure the snap ring is correctly seated in the pivot pin bore. Make sure the hand lever operates freely within the master cylinder. There should be no binding.
7. Install the diaphragm, top cover and screws. Tighten the screws only finger tight at this time.
8. Install the master cylinder as described in this chapter.

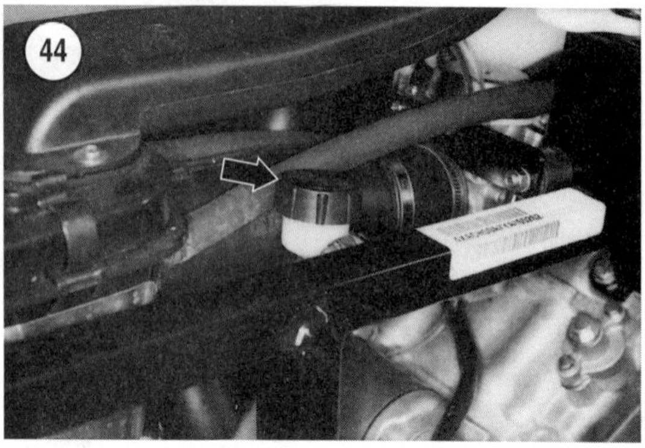

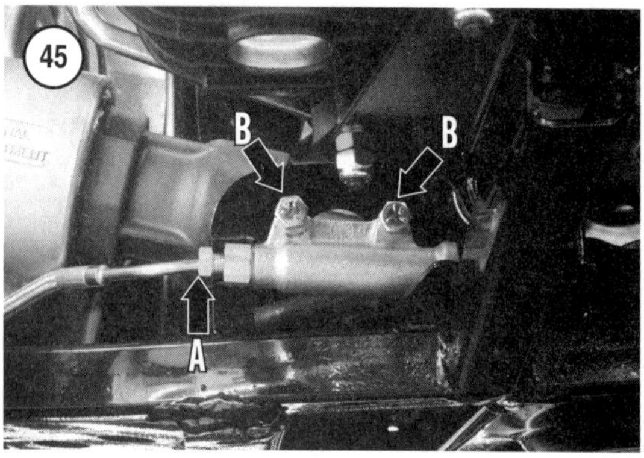

REAR MASTER CYLINDER (2003 MODELS)

Removal/Installation

1. Park the vehicle on level ground and block the wheels so the vehicle cannot roll in either direction.
2. Remove the seat as described in Chapter Fifteen.
3. Remove the front and rear fenders as described in Chapter Fifteen.
4. If not removed during rear fender removal, remove the right side foot well.

46

47

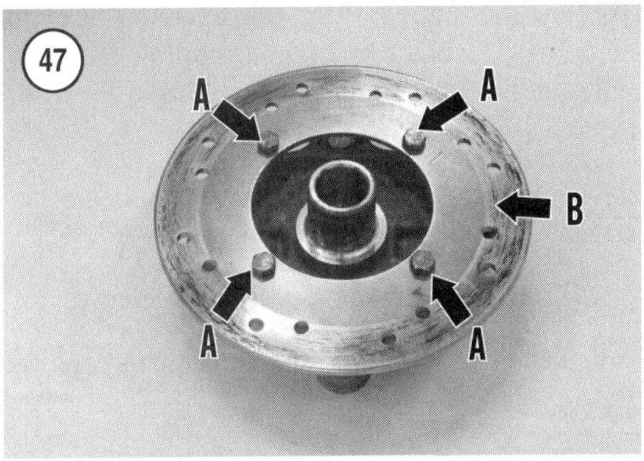

48

5. Cover the area under the rear master cylinder to prevent brake fluid from damaging any component that it might contact.

6. Disconnect the reservoir hose from the backside of the master cylinder.

7. Loosen the reservoir cap (**Figure 44**) and drain the brake fluid into a container.

8. Place the loose end of the reservoir hose in a reclosable plastic bag and close it to prevent contamination and the discharge of brake fluid. Secure the hose to the frame in the upright position.

9. Unscrew the brake hose fitting (A, **Figure 45**) from the rear of the master cylinder. Plug the hose fitting on the master cylinder to prevent the dripping of brake fluid.

10. Place the loose end of the brake hose in a reclosable plastic bag and close it to prevent contamination and the discharge of brake fluid. Secure the hose to the frame in the upright position.

11. Remove the bolts and nuts securing the master cylinder (B, **Figure 45**) to the frame bracket.

12. Remove the master cylinder from the frame.

13. If necessary, remove the bolt and nut (**Figure 46**) securing the reservoir to the frame. Remove the reservoir and hose from the frame.

14. Install by reversing these removal steps, while noting the following:

   a. Install the brake line to the master cylinder and tighten securely.

   b. Tighten the master cylinder mounting bolts securely.

   c. Refill the master cylinder with DOT 3 brake fluid and bleed the brake as described in this chapter.

WARNING

Do not ride the vehicle until the brakes are working properly. Make sure that the brake lever travel is not excessive and that the lever does not feel soft or spongy. If either condition exists, bleed the system again.

REAR BRAKE DISC (2003 MODELS)

Removal/Installation

1. Remove the rear hub as described in this supplement.

2. Remove the bolts (A, **Figure 47**) securing the brake disc to the rear hub.

3. Remove the brake disc (B, **Figure 47**) from rear hub.

4. Install by reversing these removal steps. Tighten the bolts securely.

Inspection

Inspect the rear brake disc thickness (**Figure 48**) as described in Chapter Fourteen. The service specifications are as follows:

a. New: 4.496-4.750 mm (0.177-0.187 in.).
b. Service limit: 4.242 mm (0.167 in.).

BRAKE HOSE REPLACEMENT (2003 MODELS)

Rear Brake Hose

1. Park the vehicle on level ground. Block the front wheels so the vehicle will not roll in either direction.
2. Remove the front and rear fenders as described in Chapter Fifteen.
3. Raise the rear of the vehicle with a small hydraulic or scissor jack. Place the jack under the frame with a piece of wood between the jack and the frame.
4. Place block(s) under the frame to support the vehicle securely with the rear wheels off the ground.
5. Remove the right side rear wheel described in Chapter Thirteen.
6. Use a flare fitting wrench and loosen, then disconnect, the fitting (A, **Figure 45**) securing the metal brake line to the master cylinder.

CAUTION
The banjo bolt head is very shallow and will easily round off.

7. Use only a six-point socket or six-point box wrench and loosen the banjo bolt on both metal brake lines. Remove both banjo bolts and sealing washers.

8. Place the loose end of the brake hoses in a reclosable plastic bag to prevent the entry of foreign matter and prevent any residual brake fluid from dripping out.

9. Use a flare fitting wrench and loosen, then disconnect the brake hose from the four-way connector.

10. Note the routing of the brake hose(s) through the frame. The brake hose(s) must follow the exact same path when installed to avoid any kinks or damage.

11. Install new hose(s) in the reverse order of removal while noting the following:

a. Tighten the brake hose fittings securely.

b. Install *new* sealing washers at the rear master cylinder.

c. Refill the front and rear master cylinder reservoirs and bleed the front and rear brakes system as described under *Bleeding the System* Chapter Fourteen.

Table 1 MODEL YEAR AND NUMBER

Year	Model number
2001	
Sportsman 400	A01CH42AA
Sportsman 400	A01CH42AB
Sportsman 400	A01CH42AC
Sportsman 500 DUSE[1]	A01CH50AD
Sportsman 500 H.O.	A01CH50AA
Sportsman 500 H.O.	A01CH50AB
Sportsman 500 H.O.	A01CH50AE
Sportsman 500 H.O.	A01CH50AF
Sportsman 500 H.O.	A01CH50AJ
2002	
Sportsman 400	A02CH42AA
Worker 400 (International)	A02CH42EB
Sportsman 400 RSE[2]	A02CH42AC
Sportsman 400 DUSE[1]	A02CH42AD
Sportsman 400	A02CH42AE
Sportsman 400 Desert	A02CH42AF

(continued)

Table 1 MODEL YEAR AND NUMBER (continued)

Year	Model number
2002 (continued)	
Sportsman 500 H.O.	A02CH50AA
Worker 500 (International)	A02CH50EB
Sportsman 500 RSE[2]	A02CH50AC
Sportsman 500 DUSE[1]	A02CH50AD
Sportsman 500 H.O.	A02CH50AE
Sportsman 500 H.O. Desert	A02CH50AF
Sportsman 500 H.O. Freedom	A02CH50AL
2003	
Sportsman 400	A03CH42AA, AB, AC, AD, AE, AH, AJ, AU[3]
Sportsman 500 H.O.	A03CH50AA, AB, AC, AD, AE, AH, AJ, AU[3]

1. Sportsman Ducks Unlimited Special Edition (DUSE)
2. Sportsman Remington Special Edition (RSE)
3. Model letters denote different colors and graphics.

Table 2 GENERAL DIMENSIONS

Model	2001-2001Models cm (in.)	2003 Models cm (in.)
400 cc		
Height	116.8 (46)	114 (45)
Length	205.7 (81)	205.7 (81)
Width	114.3 (45)	117 (46)
Wheel base	129.5 (51)	128 (51)
500 cc		
Height	121.9 (48)	114 (45)
Length	205.7 (81)	216 (85)
Width	116.8 (46)	117 (46)
Wheel base	128.5 (50.5)	128 (51)

Table 3 ELECTRICAL SYSTEM SPECIFICATIONS

Item	Specifications
Alternator stator coils	
Sportsman 400 (2001-2002 and early 2003)	
Exciter coils	
Green to red	3.2 ohms
Green to black/red	446 ohms
Trigger coils	
White to white/red	97 ohms
Sportsman 400 (late 2003), 500 and 500 H.O.	
Exciter coils	
Red to black/red	1.9 ohms
Red to ground	Infinity
Trigger coils	
White to white/red	97 ohms

16

Table 4 MAINTENANCE AND TUNE-UP SPECIFICATIONS

Item	Specifications
Disc brake pad thickness wear limit	
2003 Sportsman 500 rear brake	4.6 mm (0.180 in.)
All other models and years	3.81 mm (0.150 in.)
Spark plug	
400 cc	
Heat range	NGK BKR5E
Gap	0.9 mm (0.036 in.)
500 cc	
Heat range	
2001	NGK BKR5E
2002-on	NGK BKR6E
Gap	
2001-on	0.9 mm (0.036 in.)
Carburetor pilot air screw (40 mm)	
2001	2 1/2 turns out
2002-on	2 turns out

Table 5 GENERAL ENGINE SPECIFICATIONS

Item	Specifications
Engine type	Four-stroke, SOHC, single cylinder
Cooling system	Liquid
Bore and stroke	
Sportsman 400	87.9 × 70 mm (3.461 × 2.756 in.)
Sportsman 500 and 500 H.O.	92 × 75 mm (3.6248 × 2.955 in.)
Displacement	
Sportsman 400	425 cc
Sportsman 500 and 500 H.O.	499 cc
Compression ratio	
Sportsman 400	9.2 to 1
Sportsman 500 and 500 H.O.	10 to 1

Table 6 ENGINE TOP END SPECIFICATIONS

Item	New mm (in.)	Service limit mm (in.)
Cylinder block bore		
400 cc	87.900-87.920 (3.4606-3.4614)	–
500 cc	92.00-92.02 (3.6221-3.6228)	–
Taper limit (400 & 500 cc)	–	0.050 (0.0020)
Out of round (400 & 500 cc)	–	0.050 (0.0020)
Piston outer diameter		
400 cc		
Standard	87.875-87.885 (3.459-3.460)	–
0.25 mm oversize	88.125-88.135 (3.469-3.470)	–
0.50 mm oversize	88.375-88.385 (3.479-3.480)	–

Table 7 CARBURETOR SPECIFICATIONS–40 MM

Item	Specification
Model	BST40 Mikuni
Main jet	152.5
Jet needle/E-clip position	
2001	KE-3 (683)
2002-on	6MGH1-94-3
Needle jet	X-6
Throttle valve	120
Pilot air jet	1.3
Pilot screw	
2001	2 1/2 turns out
2002-on	2 turns out
Valve seat size	1.5
Float height	13.7-15.7 mm (0.539-0.618 in.)
Idle speed	1100-1300 rpm

Table 8 REAR SUSPENSION AND BRAKE TORQUE SPECIFICATIONS (2003 MODELS)

Item	N•m	ft.-lb.
Banjo bolts	15	15
Caliper anvil volts	22-25	16-18
Caliper slide pin bolts	41-48	30-35
Control arm bolts and nuts		
Lower	41	30
Upper	48	35
Flare nuts	21	15
Rear caliper mounting bolts	25	18
Rear rub nut	136	100

INDEX

F

O

P

R

S

1996-1997 SPORTSMAN 500
1997 XPLORER 500

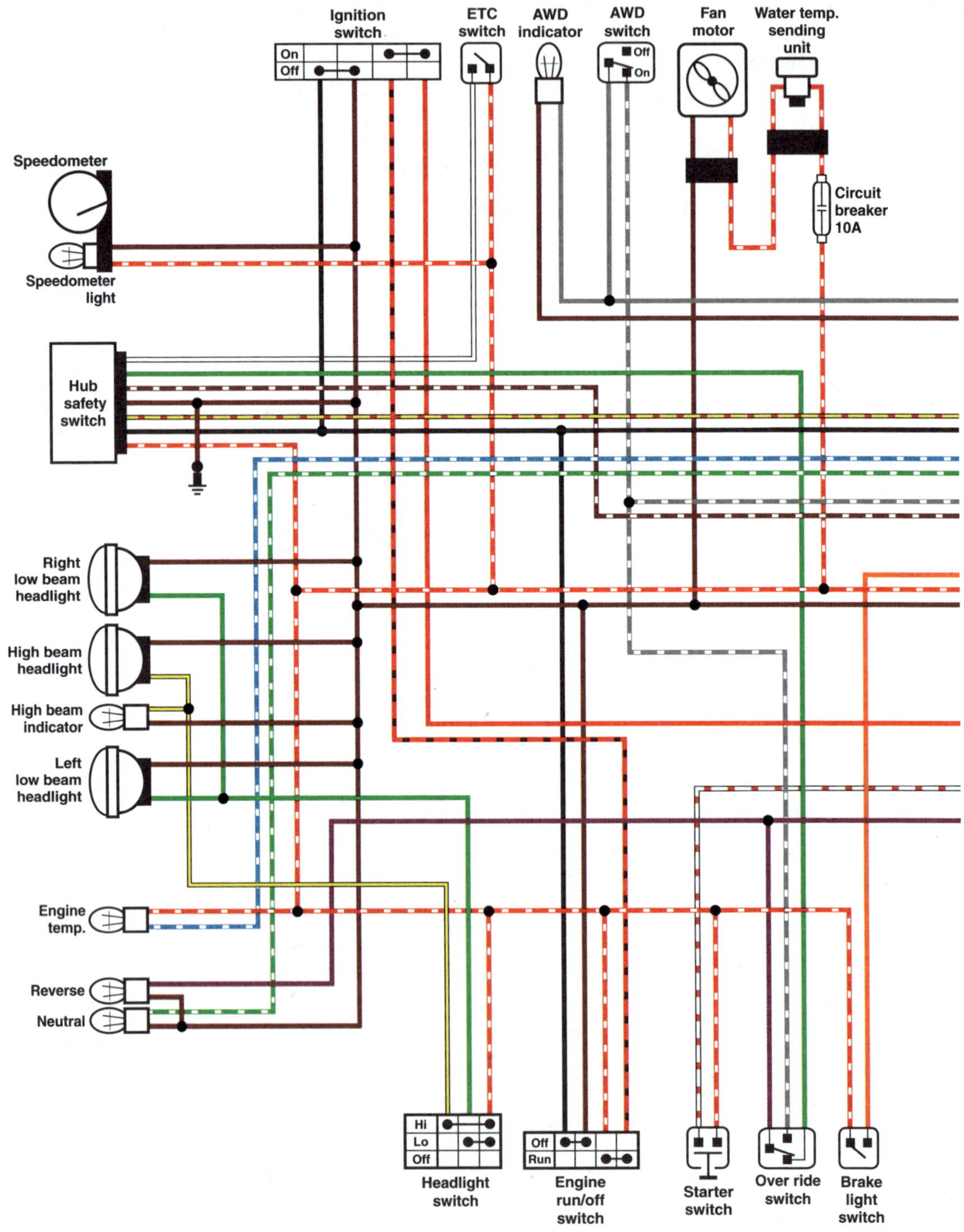

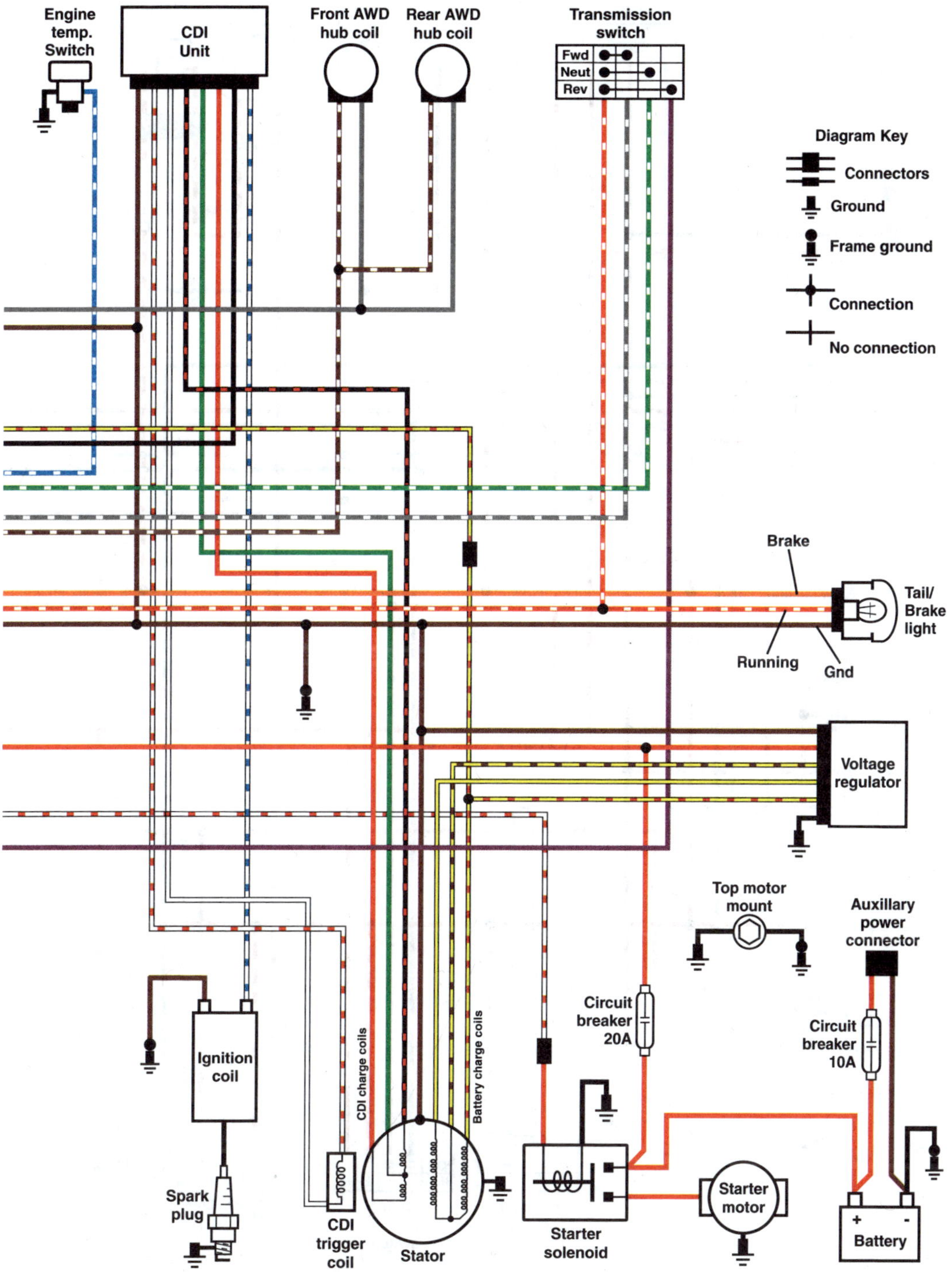
Engine temp. Switch
CDI Unit
Front AWD hub coil
Rear AWD hub coil
Transmission switch
Fwd
Neut
Rev
Diagram Key
Connectors
Ground
Frame ground
Connection
No connection
Brake
Tail/ Brake light
Running
Gnd
Voltage regulator
Top motor mount
Auxillary power connector
Circuit breaker 20A
Circuit breaker 10A
CDI charge coils
Battery charge coils
Ignition coil
Spark plug
CDI trigger coil
Stator
Starter solenoid
Starter motor
Battery
+
-

18

1998 SPORTSMAN 500

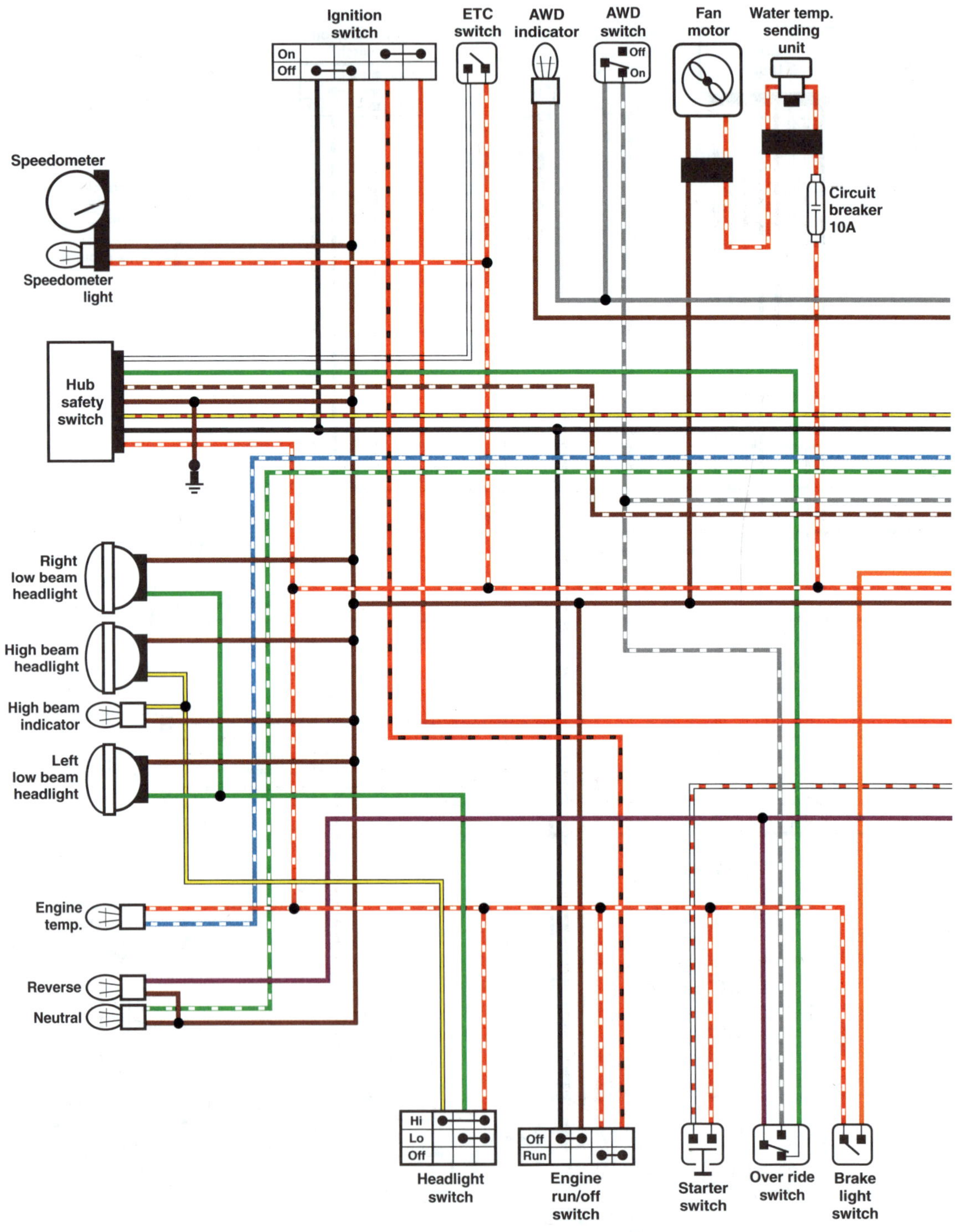

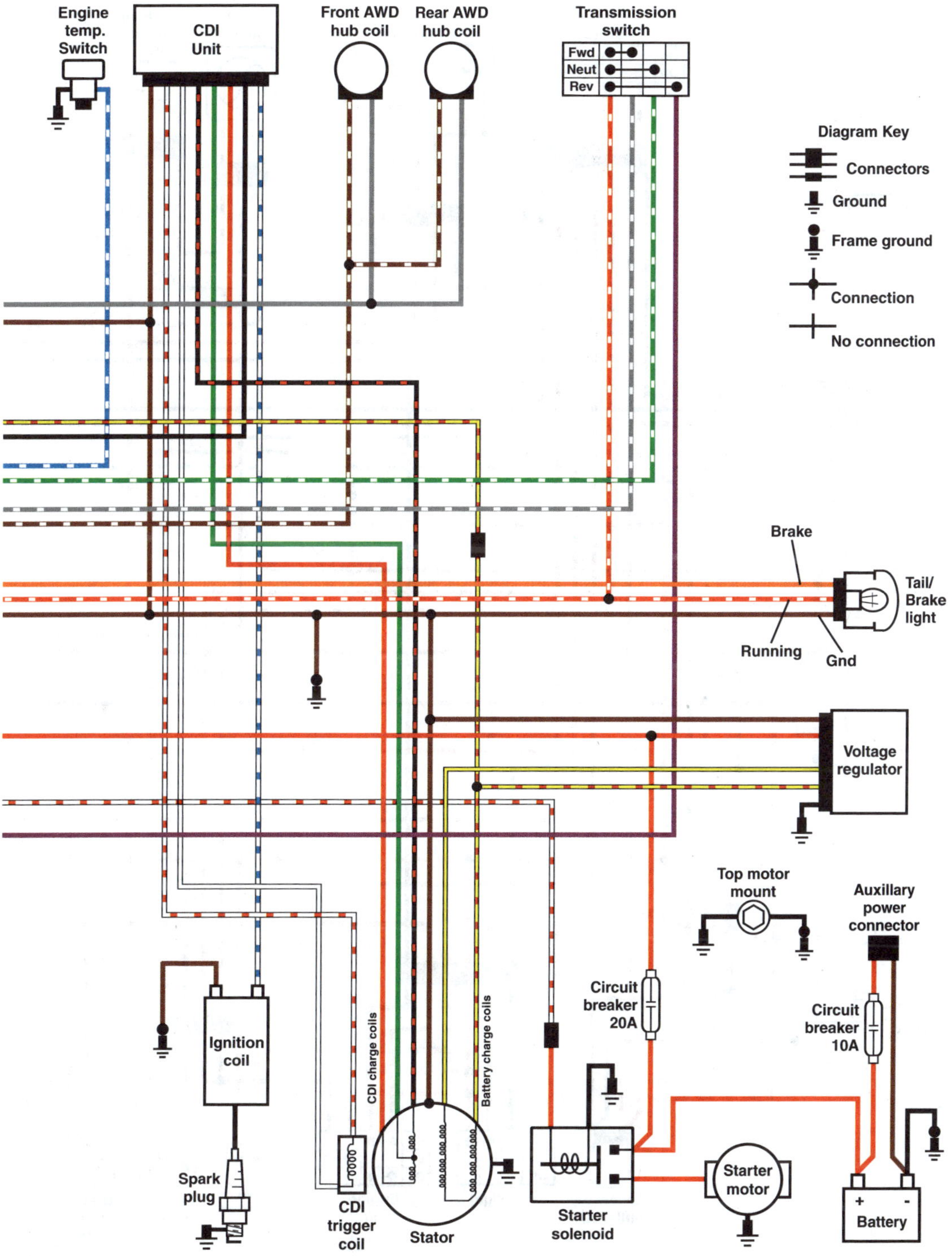
Engine temp. Switch
CDI Unit
Front AWD hub coil
Rear AWD hub coil
Transmission switch
Fwd
Neut
Rev
Diagram Key
Connectors
Ground
Frame ground
Connection
No connection
Brake
Tail/ Brake light
Running
Gnd
Voltage regulator
Top motor mount
Auxillary power connector
Circuit breaker 20A
Circuit breaker 10A
Ignition coil
Spark plug
CDI charge coils
Battery charge coils
CDI trigger coil
Stator
Starter solenoid
Starter motor
+
-
Battery

1999-2000 SPORTSMAN 500 AND WORKER 500 (INTL)

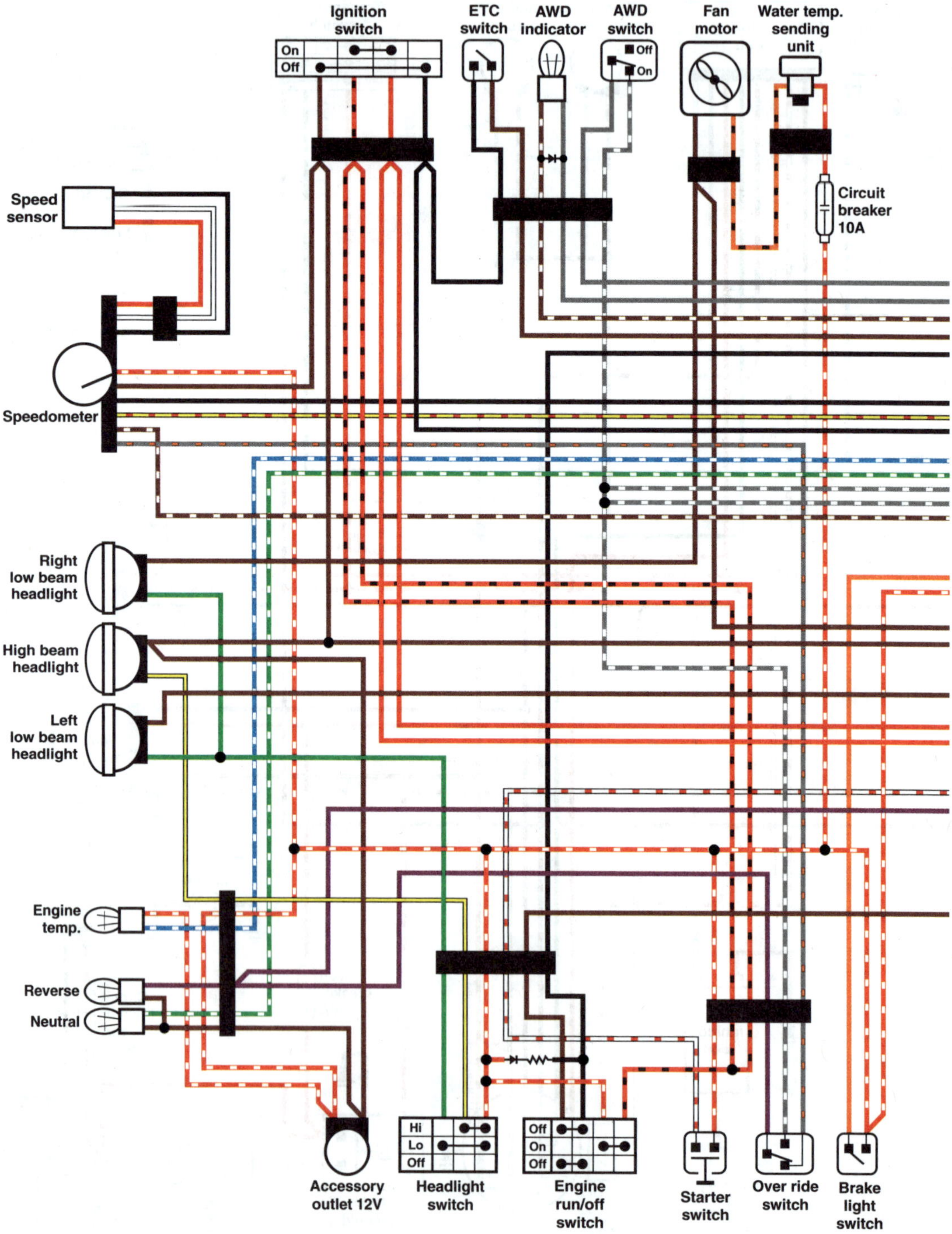

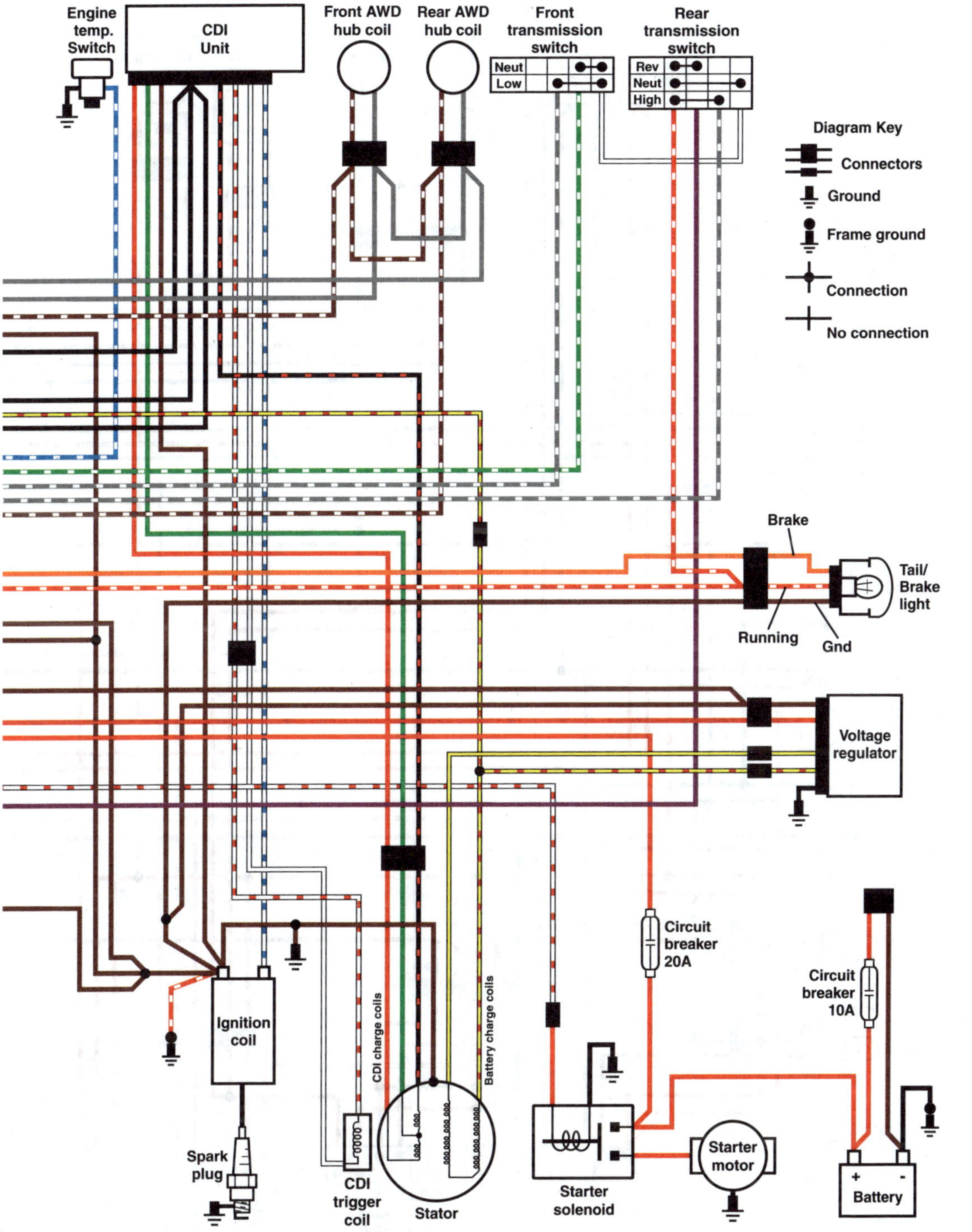
Engine temp. Switch
CDI Unit
Front AWD hub coil
Rear AWD hub coil
Front transmission switch
Neut
Low
Rear transmission switch
Rev
Neut
High
Diagram Key
Connectors
Ground
Frame ground
Connection
No connection
Brake
Tail/ Brake light
Running
Gnd
Voltage regulator
Circuit breaker 20A
Circuit breaker 10A
Ignition coil
Spark plug
CDI charge coils
CDI trigger coil
Stator
Battery charge coils
Starter solenoid
Starter motor
+
-
Battery

18

2001 (EARLY) SPORTSMAN 500

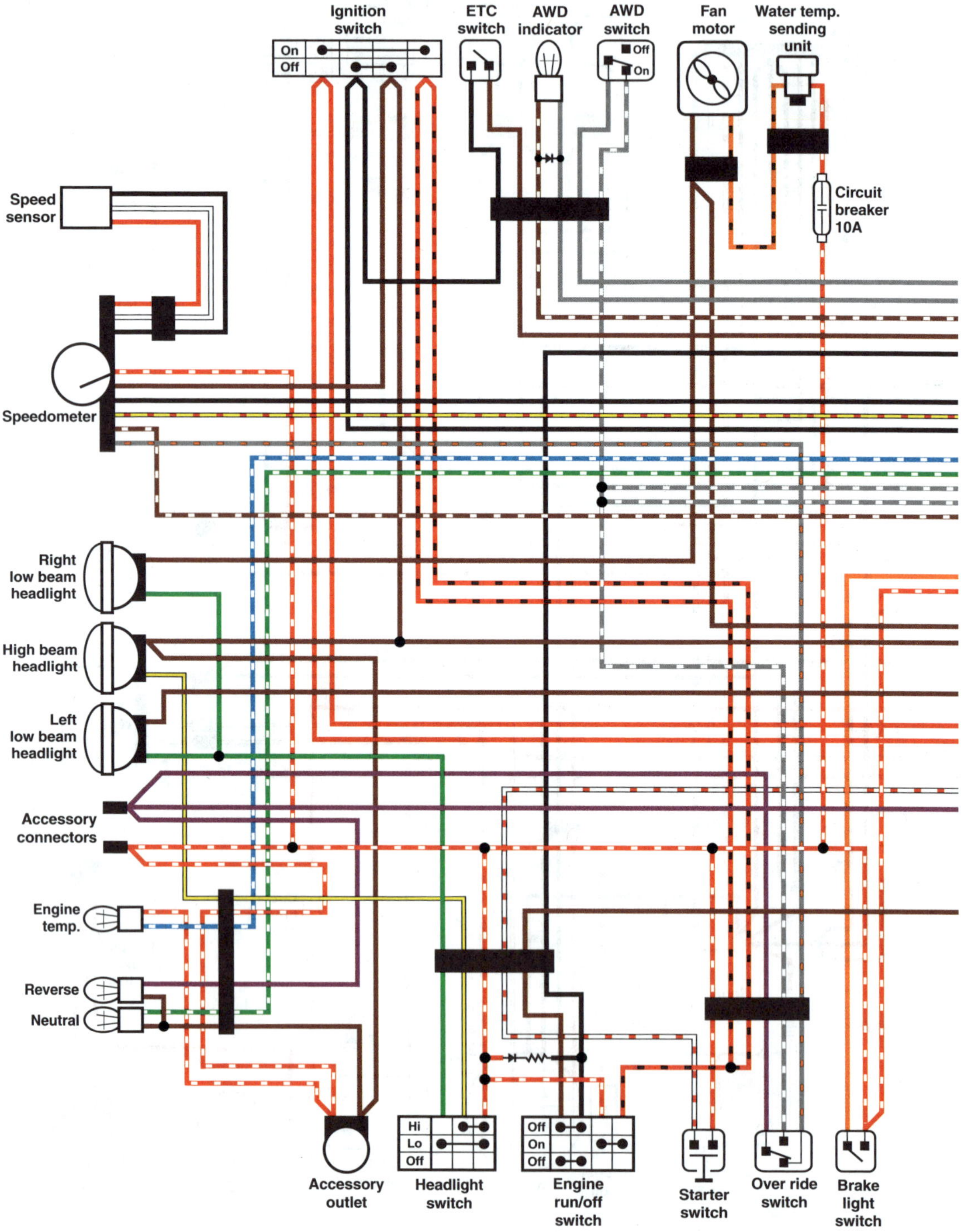

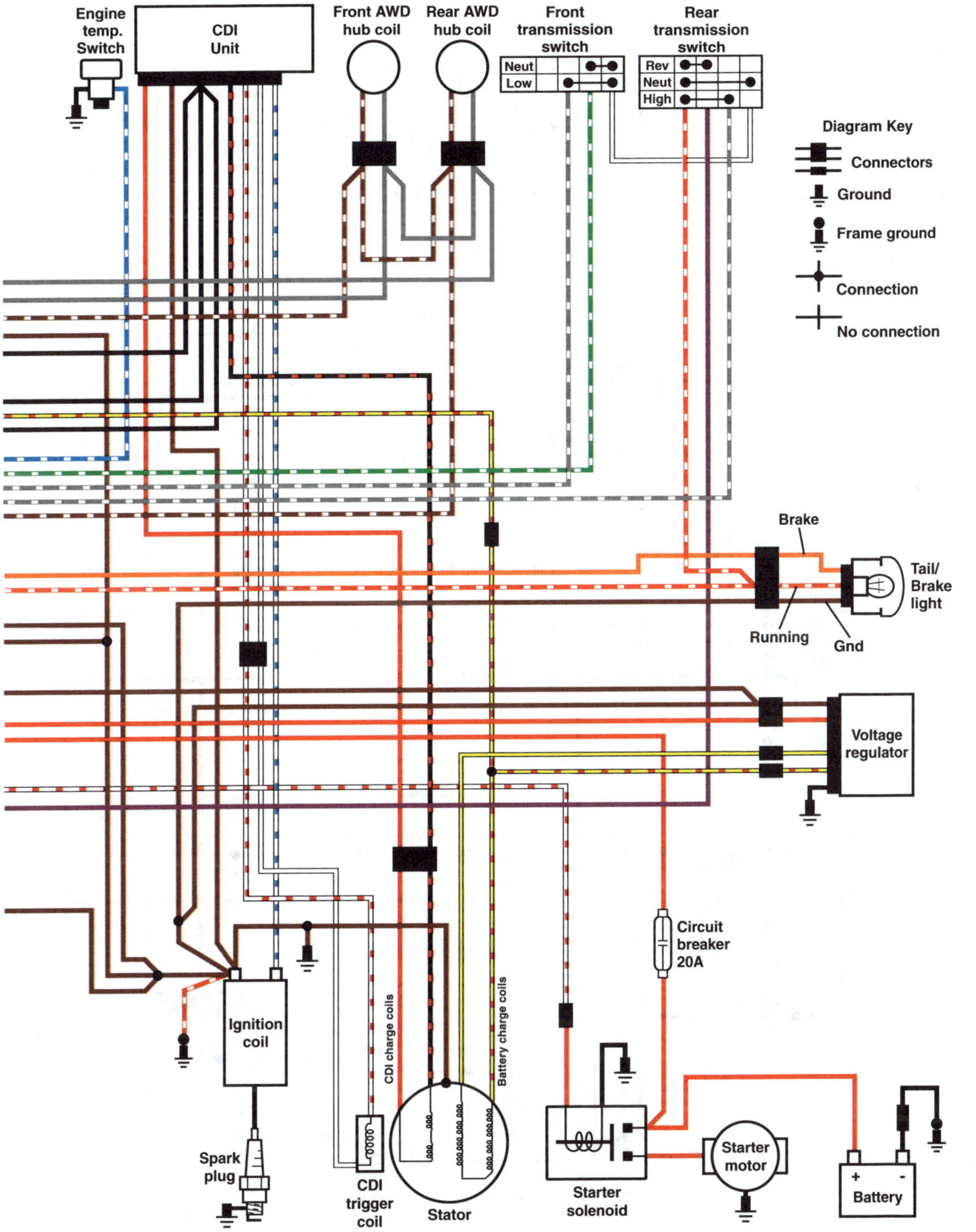
Engine temp. Switch
CDI Unit
Front AWD hub coil
Rear AWD hub coil
Front transmission switch
Neut
Low
Rear transmission switch
Rev
Neut
High
Diagram Key
Connectors
Ground
Frame ground
Connection
No connection
Brake
Tail/ Brake light
Running
Gnd
Voltage regulator
Circuit breaker 20A
CDI charge coils
Battery charge coils
Ignition coil
Spark plug
CDI trigger coil
Stator
Starter solenoid
Starter motor
Battery
+
-

2001 (LATE) SPORTSMAN 500

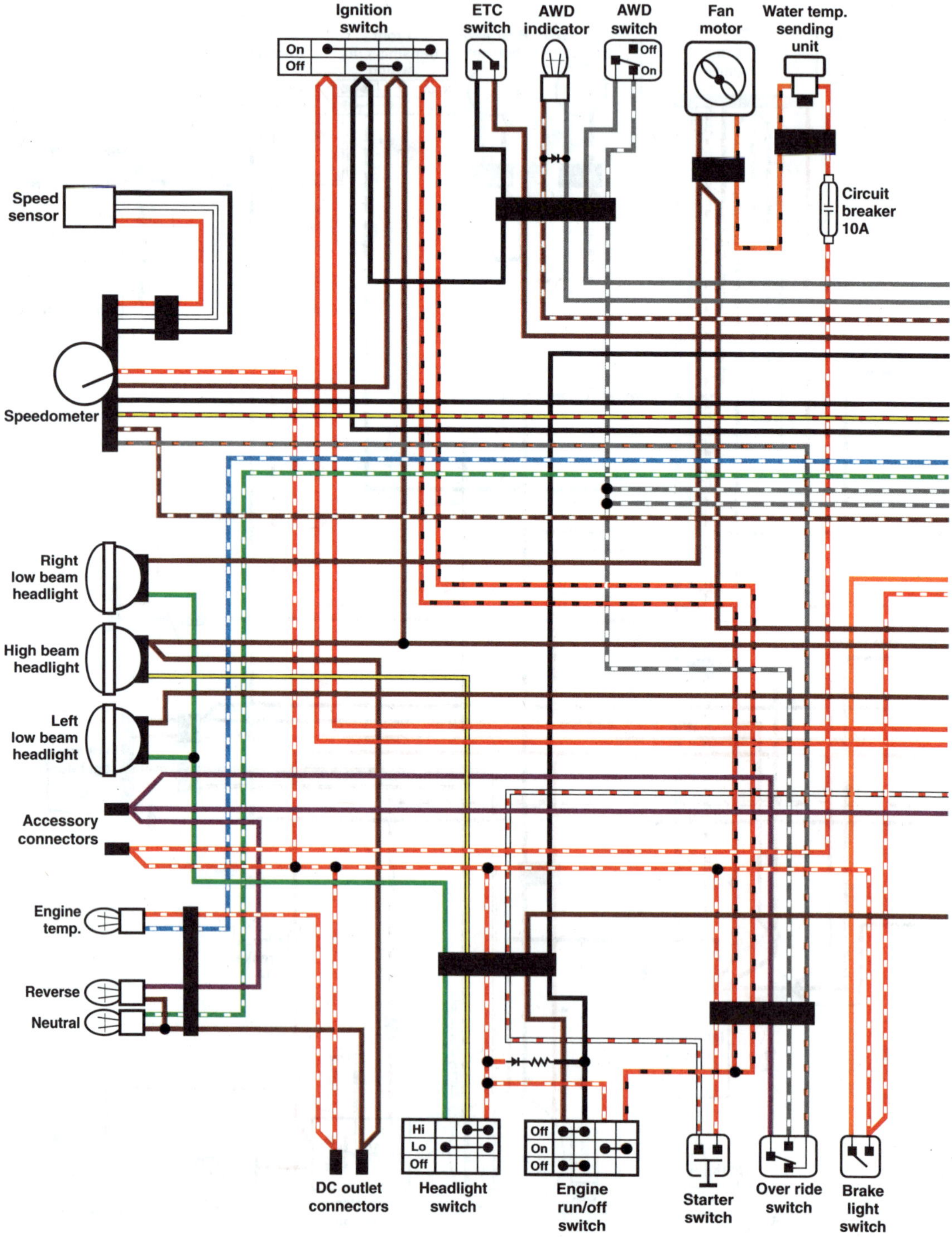

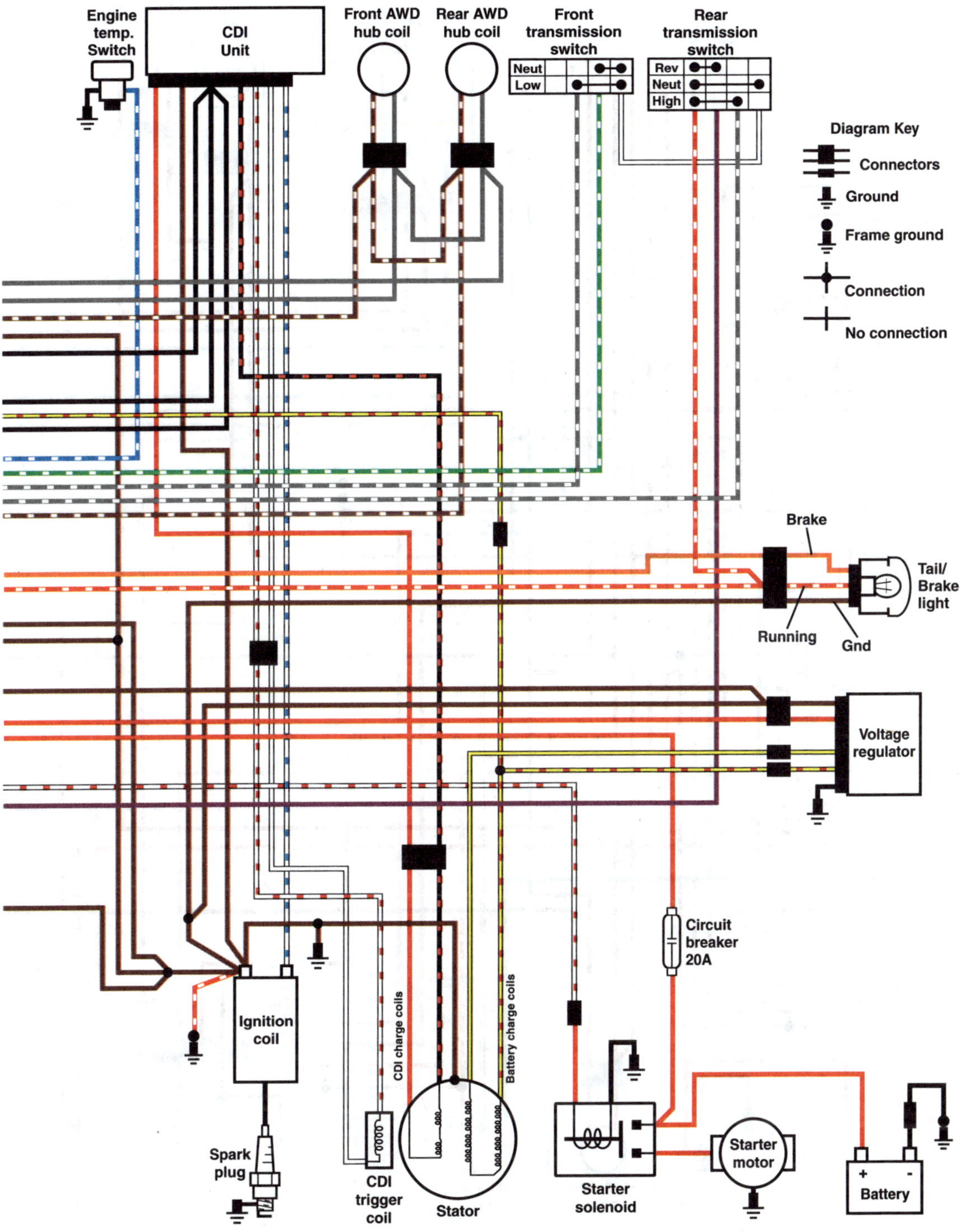
Engine temp. Switch
CDI Unit
Front AWD hub coil
Rear AWD hub coil
Front transmission switch
Neut
Low
Rear transmission switch
Rev
Neut
High
Diagram Key
Connectors
Ground
Frame ground
Connection
No connection
Brake
Tail/ Brake light
Running
Gnd
Voltage regulator
Circuit breaker 20A
Ignition coil
Spark plug
CDI charge coils
CDI trigger coil
Stator
Battery charge coils
Starter solenoid
Starter motor
+
-
Battery

2002 SPORTSMAN 500

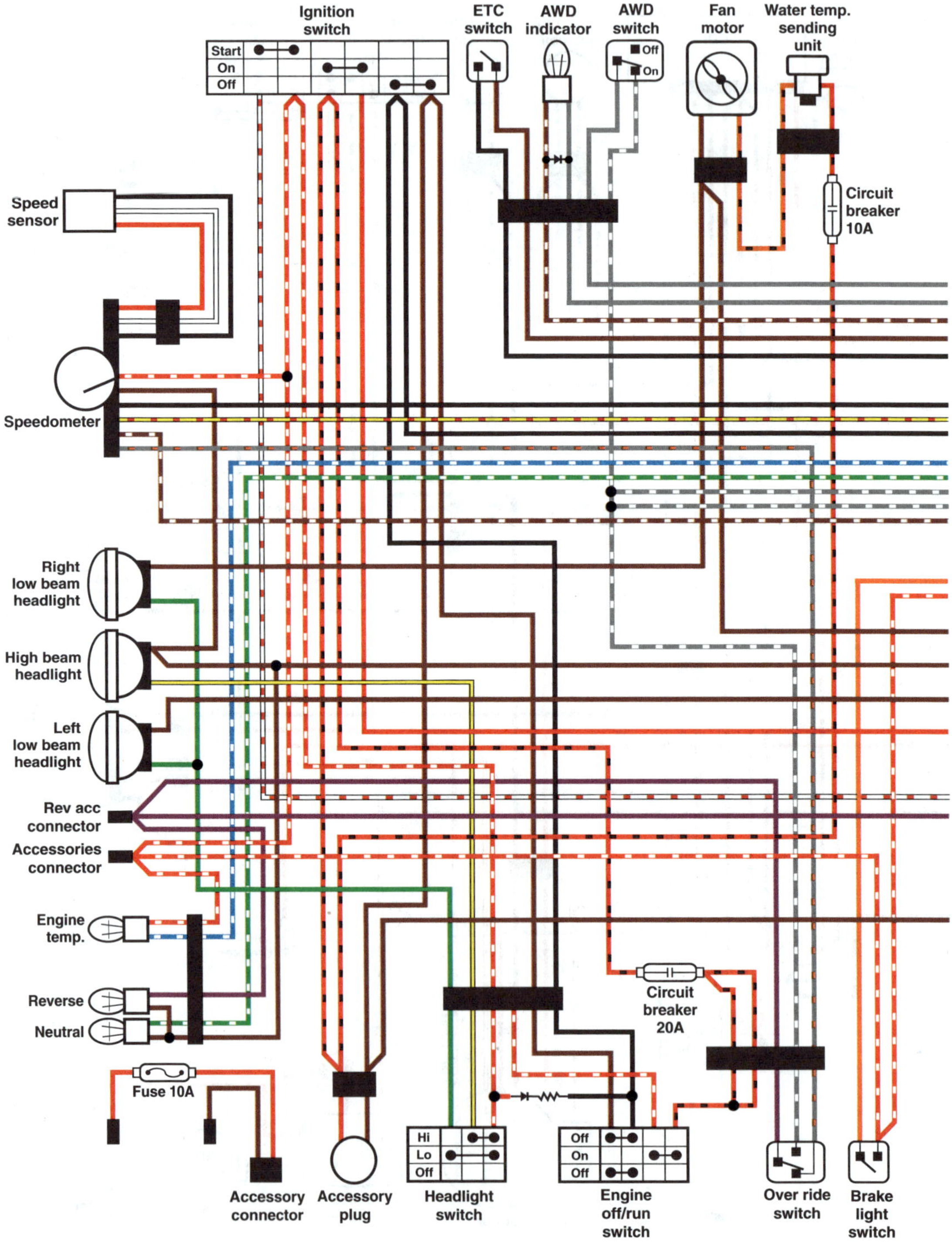

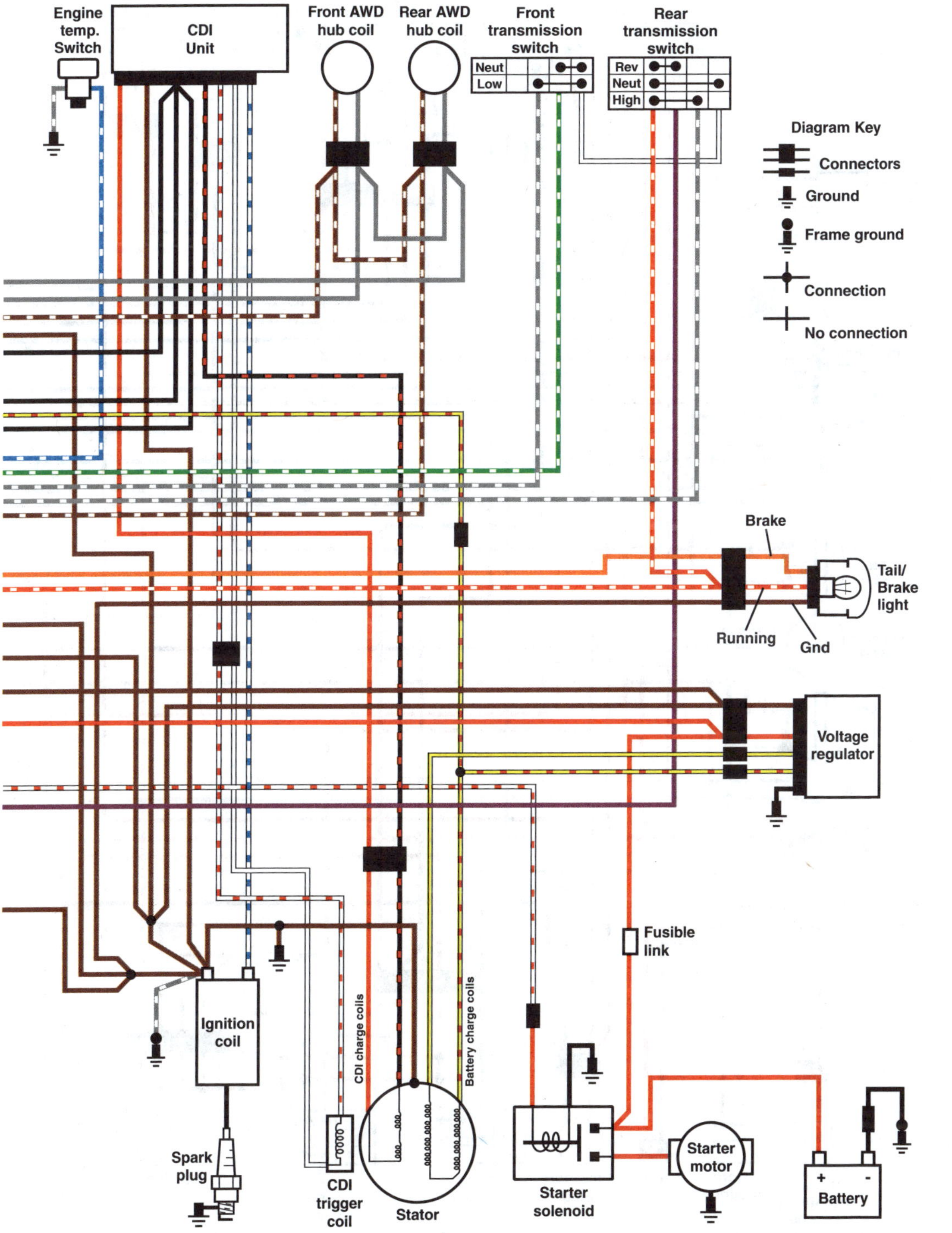
Engine temp. Switch
CDI Unit
Front AWD hub coil
Rear AWD hub coil
Front transmission switch
Neut
Low
Rear transmission switch
Rev
Neut
High
Diagram Key
Connectors
Ground
Frame ground
Connection
No connection
Brake
Tail/ Brake light
Running
Gnd
Voltage regulator
Fusible link
CDI charge coils
Battery charge coils
Ignition coil
Spark plug
CDI trigger coil
Stator
Starter solenoid
Starter motor
+
-
Battery

2003 SPORTSMAN 500

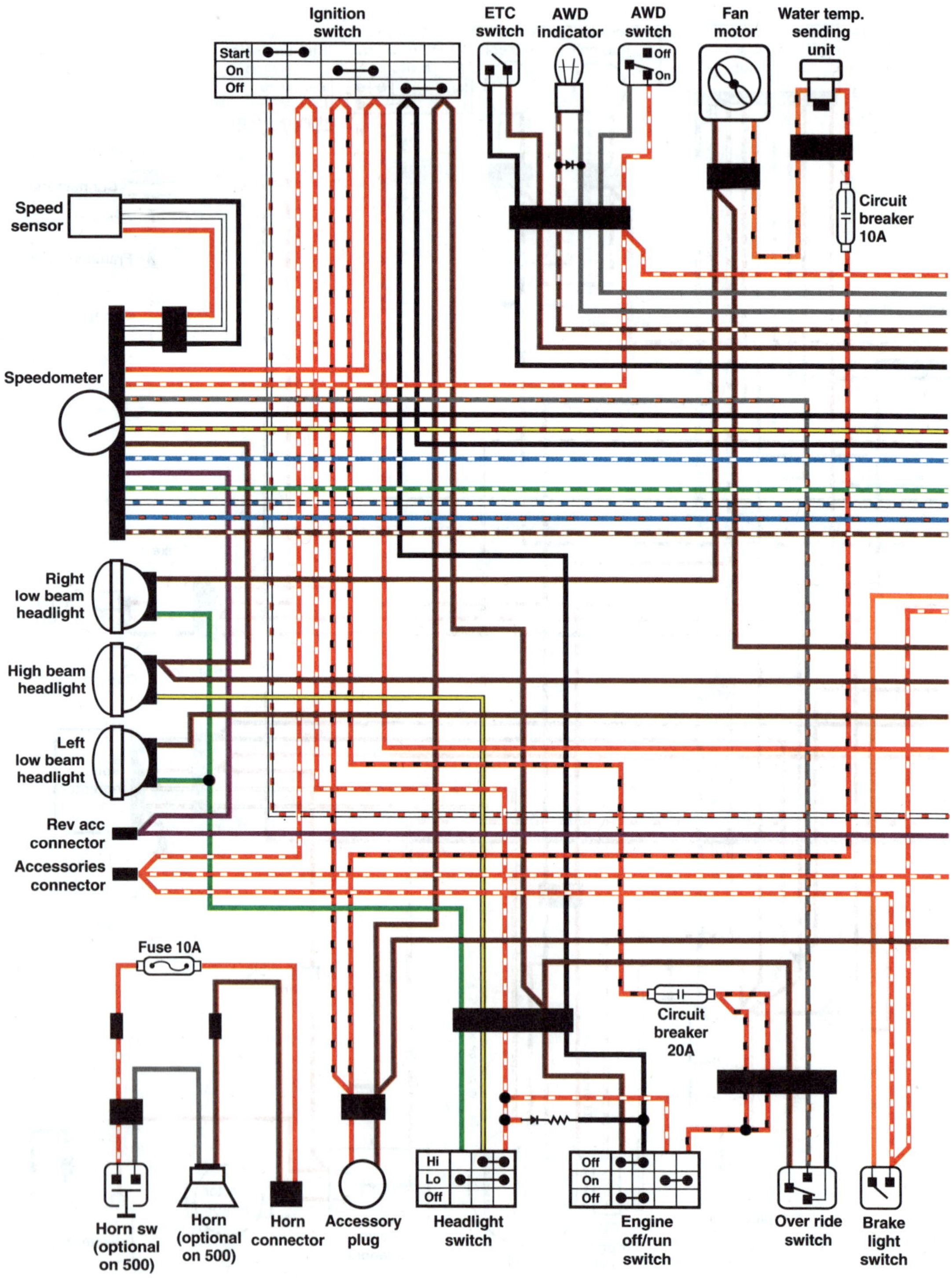

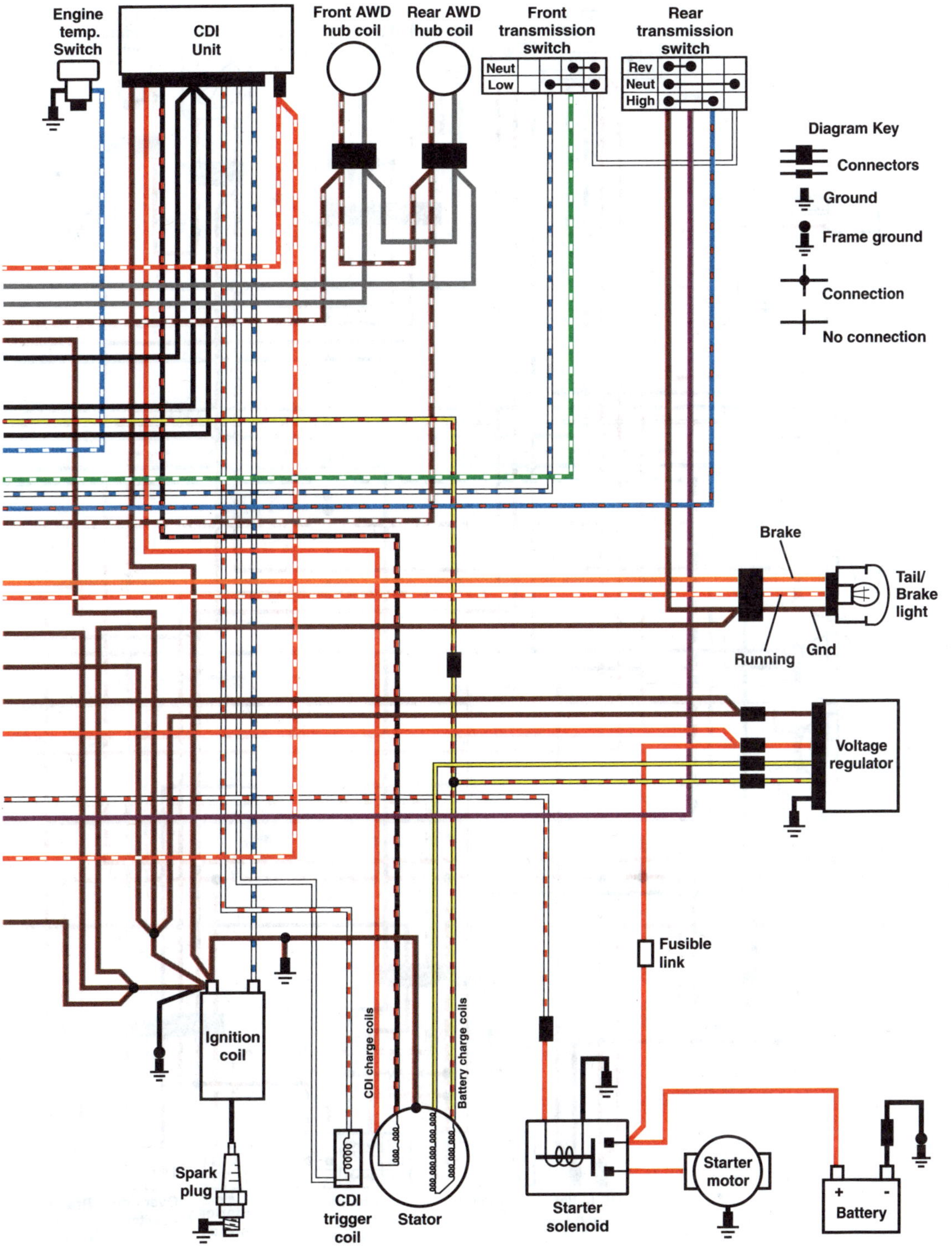
Engine temp. Switch
CDI Unit
Front AWD hub coil
Rear AWD hub coil
Front transmission switch
Neut
Low
Rear transmission switch
Rev
Neut
High
Diagram Key
Connectors
Ground
Frame ground
Connection
No connection
Brake
Tail/ Brake light
Running
Gnd
Voltage regulator
Fusible link
Ignition coil
Spark plug
CDI charge coils
Battery charge coils
CDI trigger coil
Stator
Starter solenoid
Starter motor
Battery
+
-

2001 SPORTSMAN 400

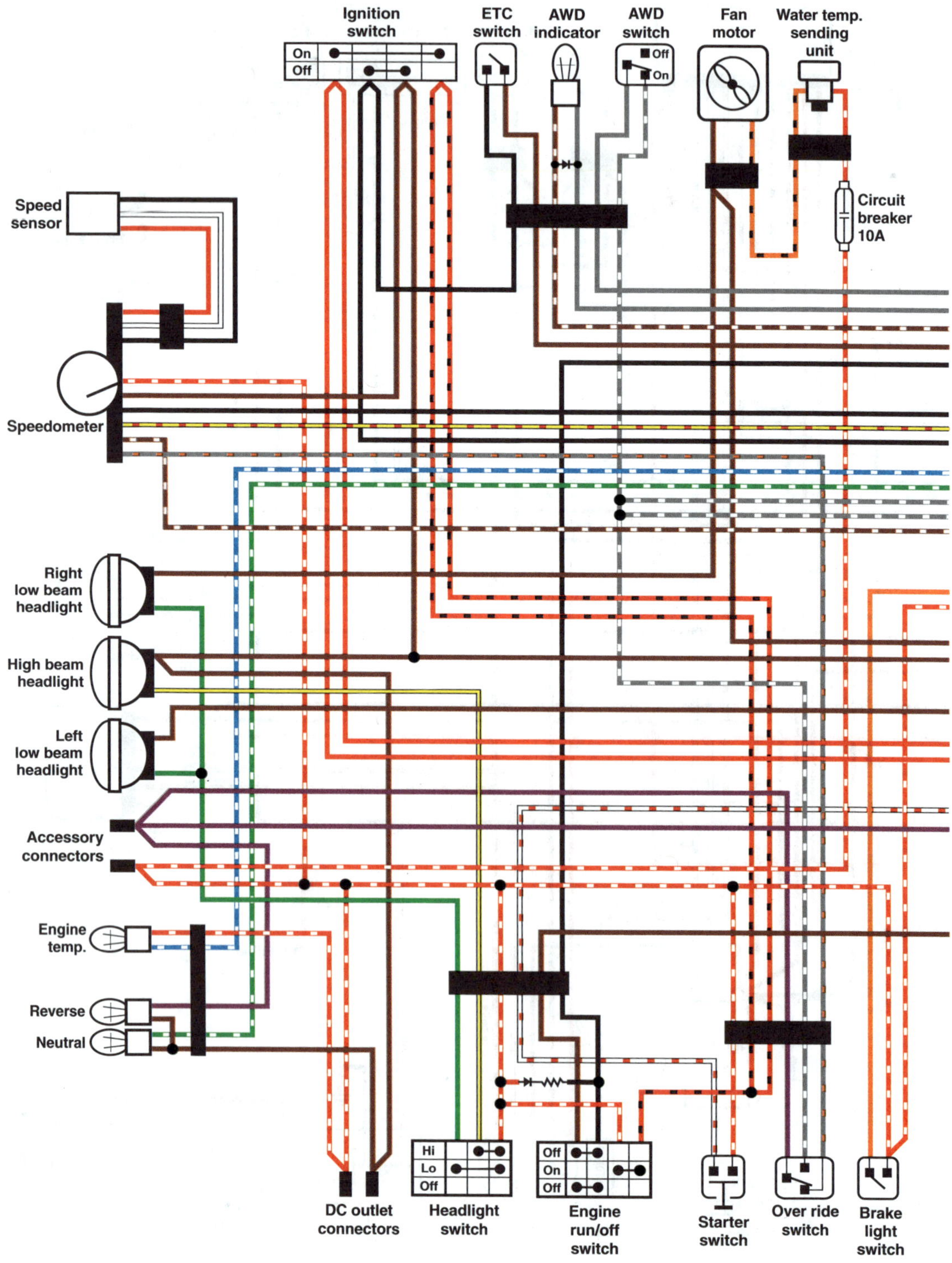

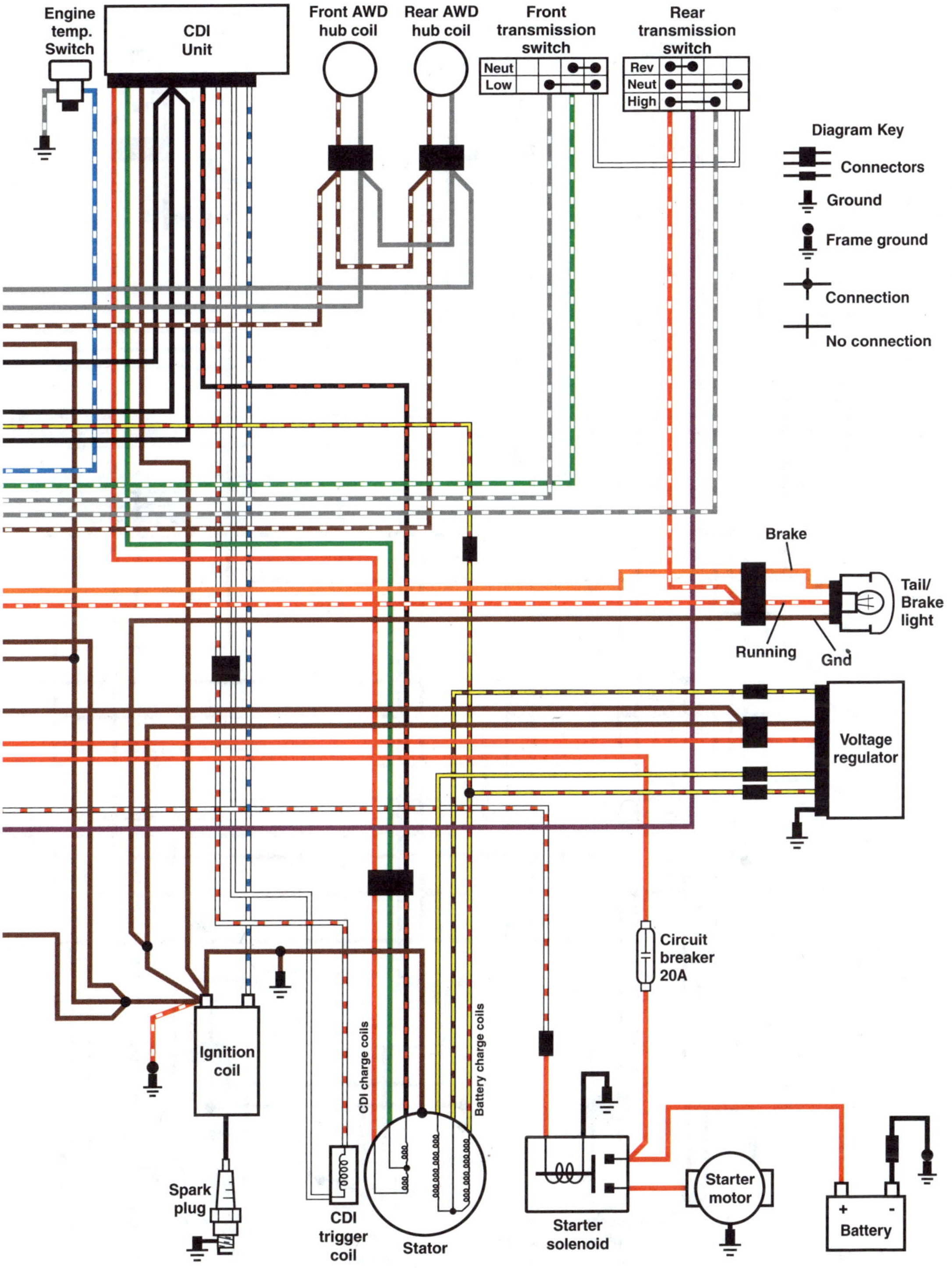
Engine temp. Switch
CDI Unit
Front AWD hub coil
Rear AWD hub coil
Front transmission switch
Neut
Low
Rear transmission switch
Rev
Neut
High
Diagram Key
Connectors
Ground
Frame ground
Connection
No connection
Brake
Tail/ Brake light
Running
Gnd
Voltage regulator
Circuit breaker 20A
Ignition coil
Spark plug
CDI charge coils
Battery charge coils
CDI trigger coil
Stator
Starter solenoid
Starter motor
Battery
+
-

2002 SPORTSMAN 400

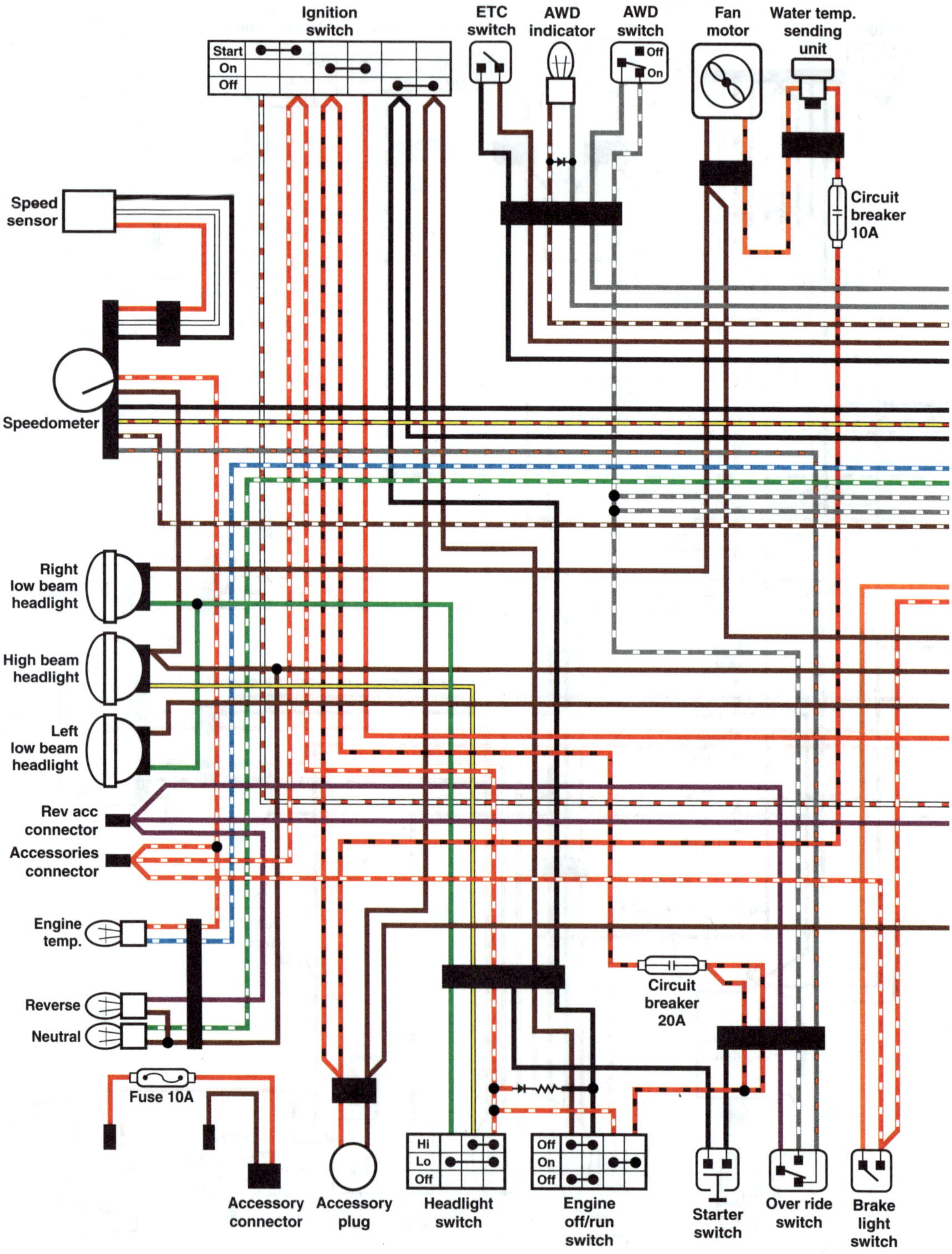

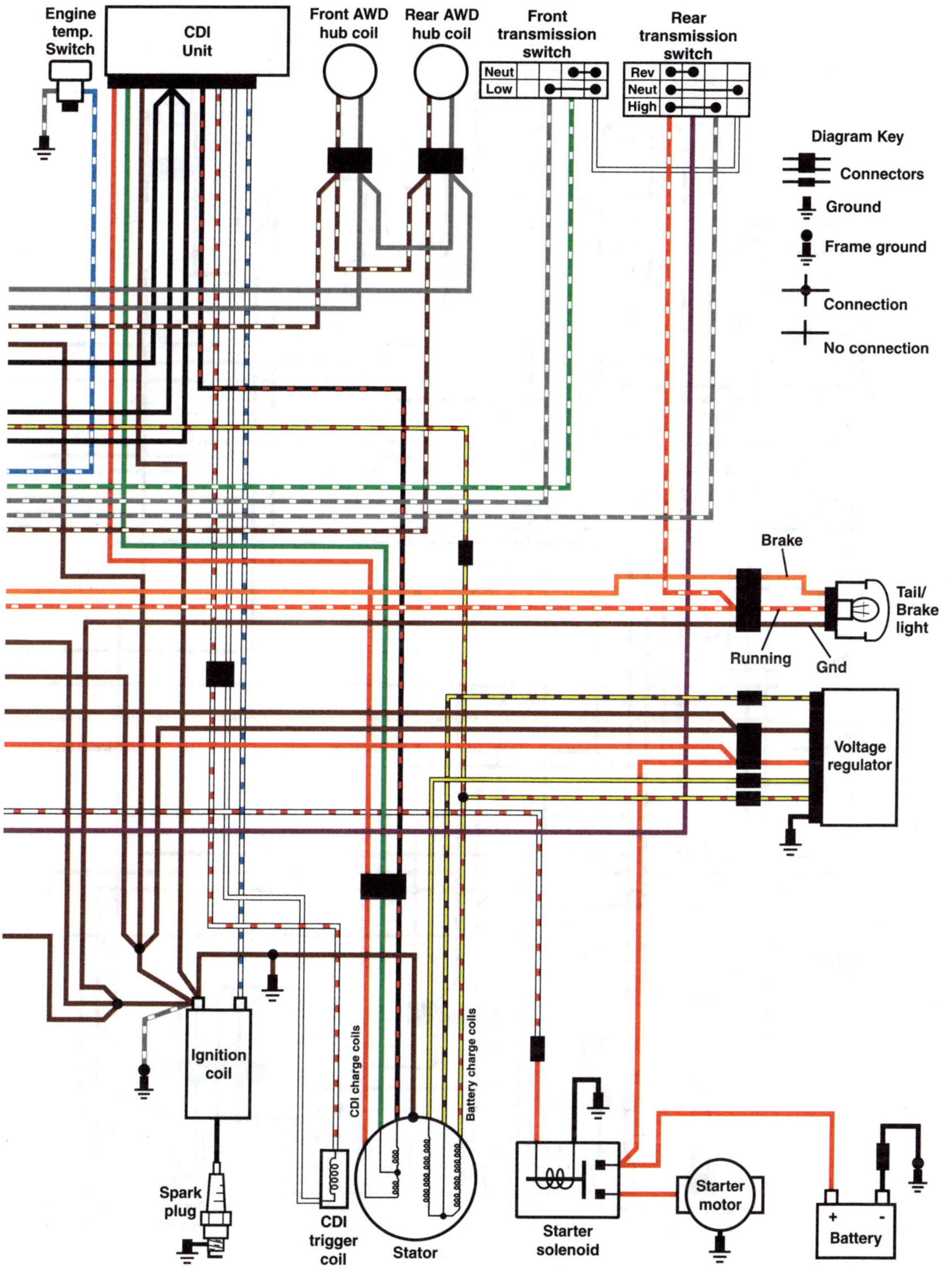
Engine
temp.
Switch
CDI
Unit
Front AWD
hub coil
Rear AWD
hub coil
Front
transmission
switch
Neut
Low
Rear
transmission
switch
Rev
Neut
High
Diagram Key
Connectors
Ground
Frame ground
Connection
No connection
Brake
Tail/
Brake
light
Running
Gnd
Voltage
regulator
Ignition
coil
Spark
plug
CDI charge coils
Battery charge coils
CDI
trigger
coil
Stator
Starter
solenoid
Starter
motor
+
-
Battery

2003 (EARLY) SPORTSMAN 400

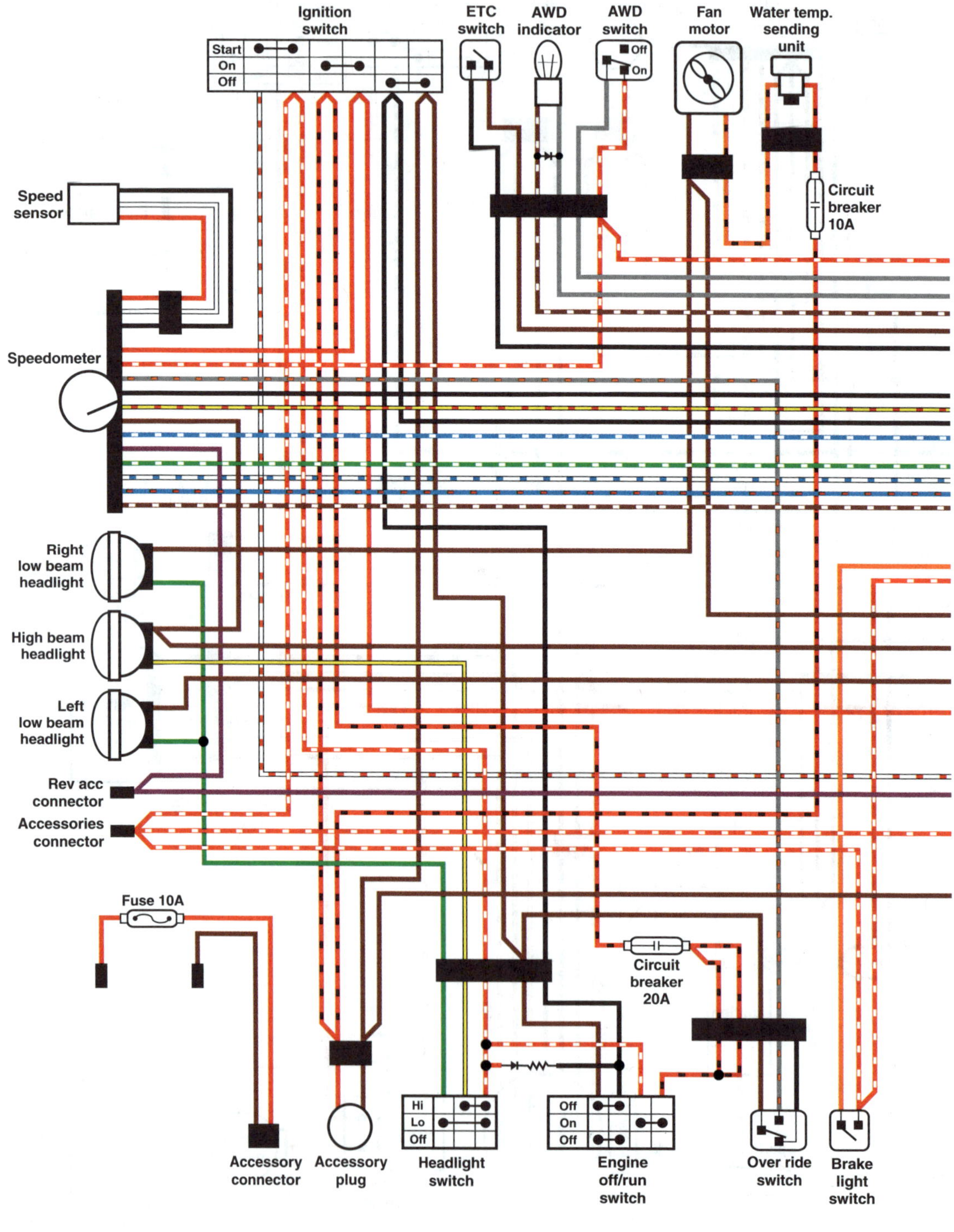

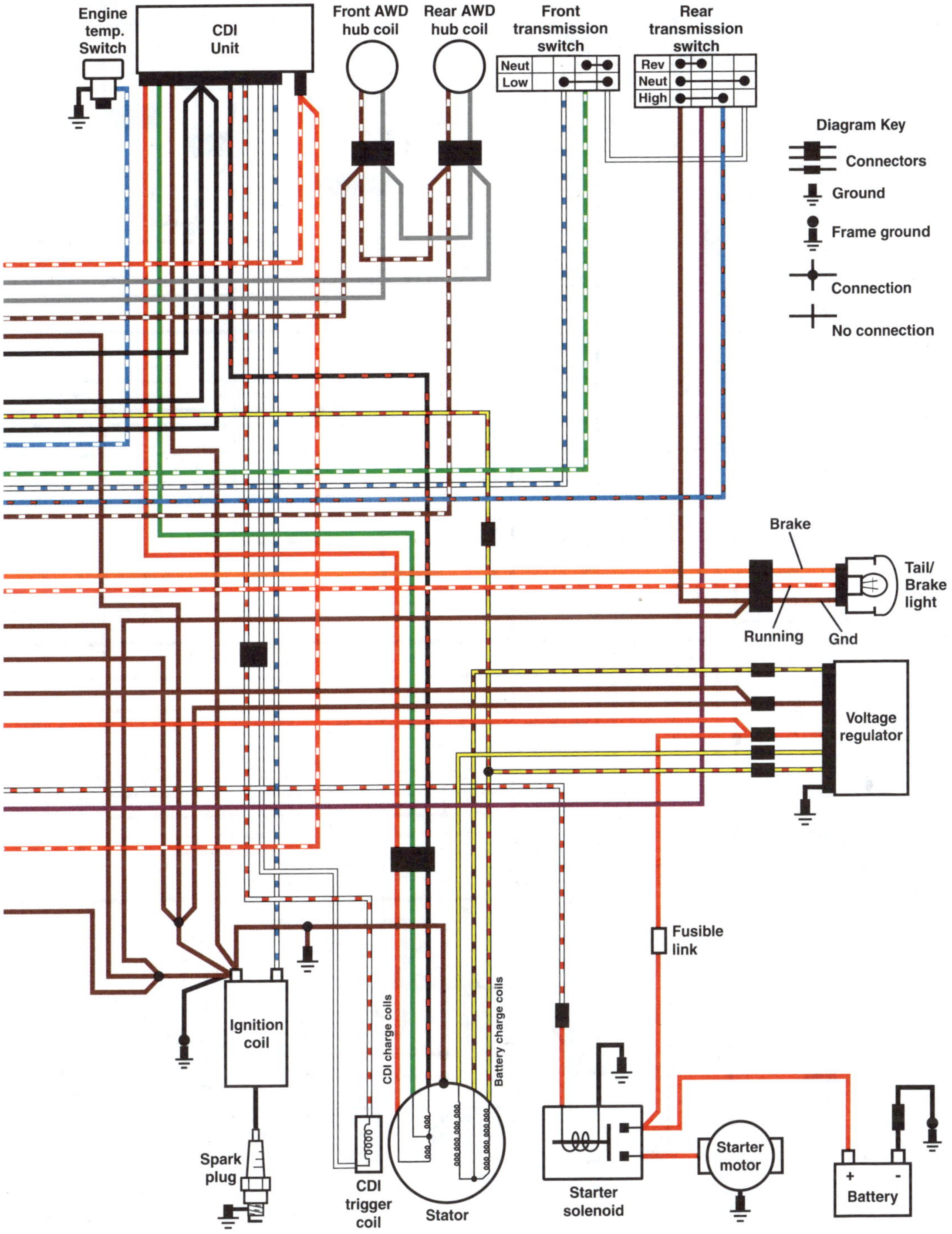
Engine temp. Switch
CDI Unit
Front AWD hub coil
Rear AWD hub coil
Front transmission switch
Neut
Low
Rear transmission switch
Rev
Neut
High
Diagram Key
Connectors
Ground
Frame ground
Connection
No connection
Brake
Tail/ Brake light
Running
Gnd
Voltage regulator
Fusible link
Ignition coil
CDI charge coils
Battery charge coils
Spark plug
CDI trigger coil
Stator
Starter solenoid
Starter motor
Battery

2003 (LATE) SPORTSMAN 400

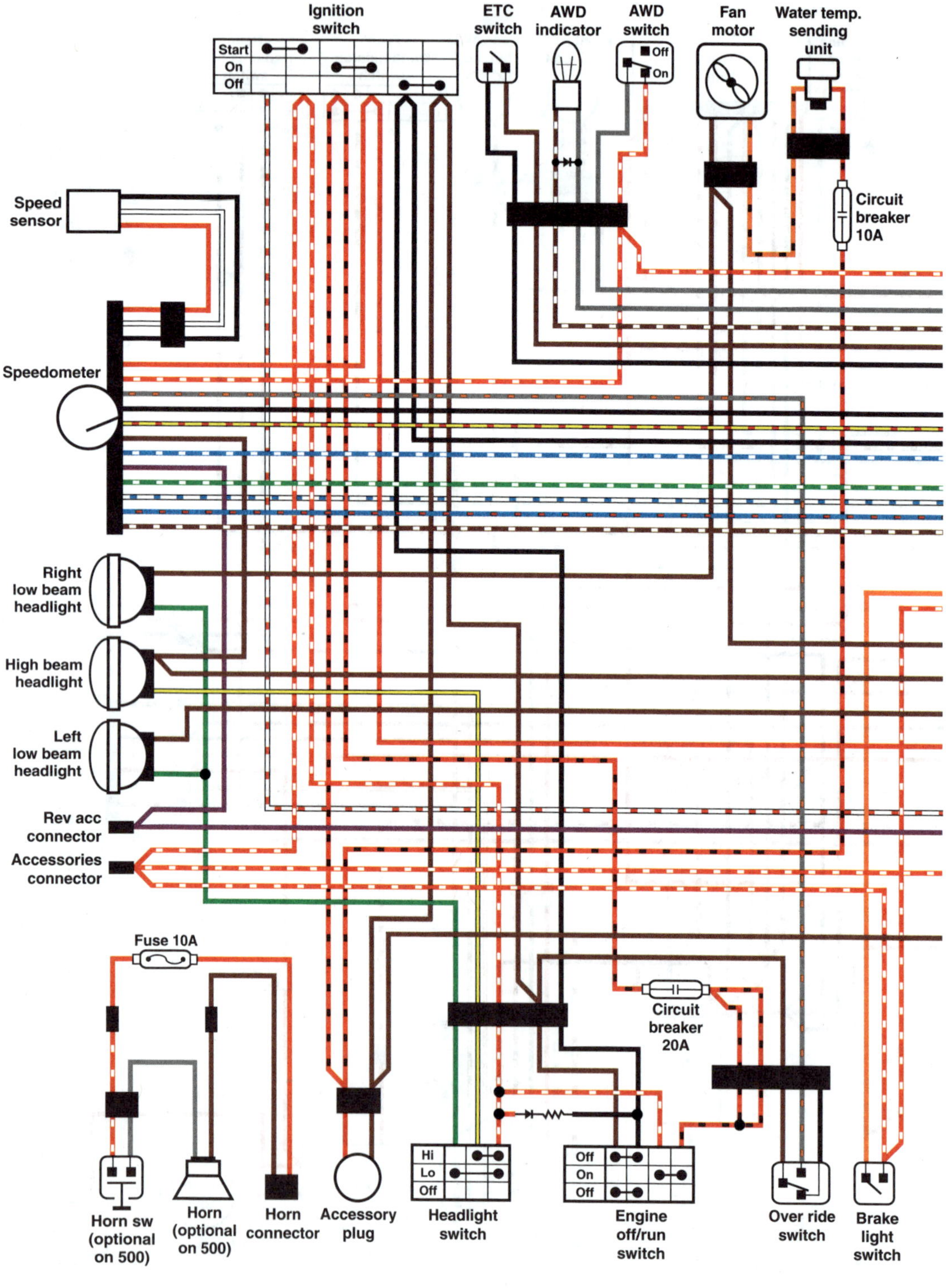

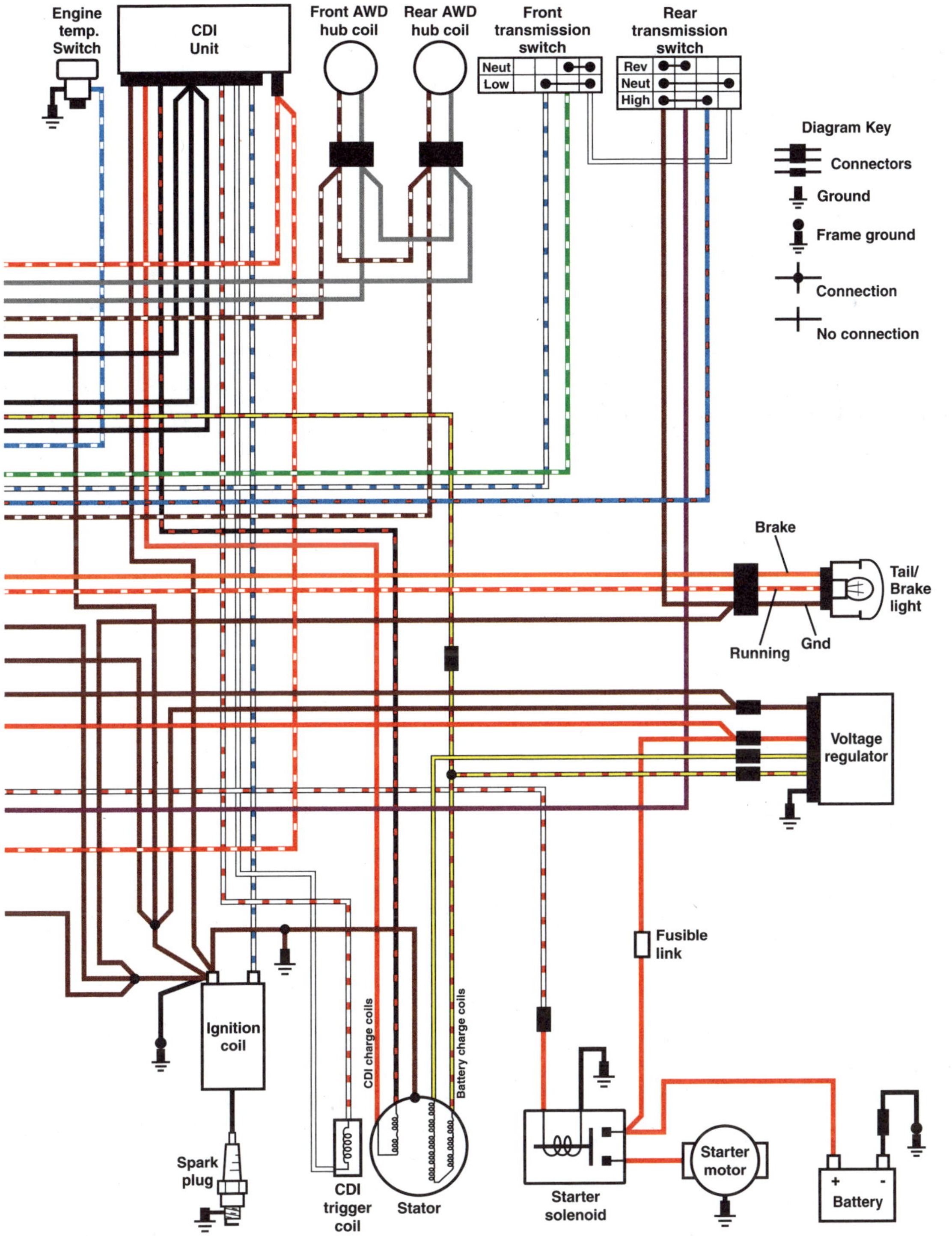
Engine temp. Switch
CDI Unit
Front AWD hub coil
Rear AWD hub coil
Front transmission switch
Neut
Low
Rear transmission switch
Rev
Neut
High
Diagram Key
Connectors
Ground
Frame ground
Connection
No connection
Brake
Tail/ Brake light
Running
Gnd
Voltage regulator
Fusible link
Ignition coil
Spark plug
CDI charge coils
Battery charge coils
CDI trigger coil
Stator
Starter solenoid
Starter motor
+
-
Battery

NOTES

NOTES

NOTES

MAINTENANCE LOG

Date	Hours	Type of Service